Letter of Intent in International Contracting

Ekaterina
Pannebakker

Letter of Intent in International Contracting

intersentia

METRO

Intersentia Ltd
Sheraton House | Castle Park
Cambridge | CB3 0AX | United Kingdom
Tel.: +44 1223 370 170 | Fax: +44 1223 370 169
Email: mail@intersentia.co.uk
www.intersentia.com | www.intersentia.co.uk

Distribution for the UK and Ireland:
NBN International
Airport Business Centre, 10 Thornbury Road
Plymouth, PL6 7 PP
United Kingdom
Tel.: +44 1752 202 301 | Fax: +44 1752 202 331
Email: orders@nbninternational.com

Distribution for Europe and all other countries:
Intersentia Publishing nv
Groenstraat 31
2640 Mortsel
Belgium
Tel.: +32 3 680 15 50 | Fax: +32 3 658 71 21
Email: mail@intersentia.be

Distribution for the USA and Canada:
International Specialized Book Services
920 NE 58th Ave. Suite 300
Portland, OR 97213
USA
Tel.: +1 800 944 6190 (toll free) | Fax: +1 503 280 8832
Email: info@isbs.com

Letter of Intent in International Contracting

ISBN 978-1-78068-449-9
D/2016/7849/176
NUR 727

British Library Cataloguing in Publication Data. A catalogue record for this book is available from the British Library.

ACKNOWLEDGMENTS

This study is a result of a doctoral trajectory, during which many people supported me. Their help is deeply appreciated.

Particular words of gratitude are owed to my promotors: Xandra Kramer for her encouragement and professionalism in supervision and Siewert Lindenbergh for his thoughtful input at the last stage of the research. I am grateful to Ellen Hey and Sanne Taekema for their coaching during the drafting of research proposal. At the last stage of writing, I appreciate the time of the members of the doctoral committee Harriët Schelhaas, Neil Andrews, and Alex Geert Castermans who have kindly agreed to read the typescript, and value the interest of the other committee members Sanne Taekema, Bob Wessels, Rieme-Jan Tjittes and Filip De Ly.

Thanks are also due to Filip De Ly and the *Groupe de Travail Contrats Internationaux* for always having reminded me about the law in practice; from among the Groupe's members, a particular note of gratitude is owed to Denis Philippe for sharing his thoughts about an arbitration clause in a letter of intent.

Part of the research was conducted abroad. The stay at the University of Cambridge (UK) greatly contributed to the study. I respectfully thank Neil Andrews for his kind invitation. The time in Italy at the UNIDROIT was inspiring and fruitful, thanks to the UNIDROIT staff in Rome. It was kind of Anna Veneziano to explain in broad brushstrokes the general structure of the DCFR. It was also a privilege to meet young professionals. I am indebted to Morgane Bona-Pellissier for her help in accessing sources of French law and to Alexandra Logue for a general discussion about the US legal system. A note of acknowledgment is also due to the UK Foundation for International Uniform Law for the financial contribution to the stay in Italy.

My colleagues at Erasmus School of Law have made the research time a pleasant human experience. I am grateful to Laura van Bochove for insights into the Dutch culture and language and for her integrity in the common tasks we still happen to have. Thanks to Alina Ontanu for having loyally shared with me the workplace and good times in Cambridge, to Erlis Themeli, Piotr Wilinski, Marta Kolacz, Denise Korthals Altes Biemans, Steven Stuij, Monique Hazelhorst and fellow PhD candidates for many interesting discussions. Thanks to the former student assistants Sander Rijsterborgh, Ramses de Leeuw, Tom Vleeschhouwer, and the secretariat of the Private law department for technical support.

That Laura van Bochove and Erlis Themeli accepted to stand by me as paranymphs at the ceremony of the doctoral defence is a great favour.

The last words of gratitude are to my mother and my family for their humour and encouragement and to Nelleke Stolwijk for all her practical help, genuine cheer and optimism.

The law is stated at the end of August 2016.

Ekaterina Pannebakker
Rotterdam, autumn 2016

CONTENTS

ABBREVIATIONS

A.	Atlantic Reporter
A.D.	New York Supreme Court Appellate Division Reports
A.L.R.	American Law Reports
AC	Appeal Cases
AC	Law Reports: Appeal Cases
Alaska	Supreme Court of Alaska
ALI	American Law Institute
All ER (Comm)	All England Reports (Commercial Cases)
All ER	All England Law Reports
Ariz.	Supreme Court of Arizona
Ariz.App.	Court of Appeals of Arizona
Ark.	Arkanzas Reports / Supreme Court of Arkansas
B.R.	Bankruptcy Reporter
BLR	Business Law Reports
Bulletin	Bulletin des arrêts des chambres civiles de la Cour de cassation
C.A.1	United States Court of Appeals, First Circuit
C.A.2	United States Court of Appeals, Second Circuit
C.A.3	United States Court of Appeals, Third Circuit
C.A.4	United States Court of Appeals, Fourth Circuit
C.A.5	United States Court of Appeals, Fifth Circuit
C.A.6	United States Court of Appeals, Sixth Circuit
C.A.7	United States Court of Appeals, Seventh Circuit
C.A.8	United States Court of Appeals, Eighth Circuit
C.A.9	United States Court of Appeals, Ninth Circuit
C.A.10	United States Court of Appeal, Tenth Circuit
C.A.11	United States Court of Appeals, Eleventh Circuit
C.A.D.C.	United States Court of Appeals, District of Columbia Circuit
C.C.A.8	Circuit Court of Appeals, Eighth Circuit
CA	Cour d'Appel
Cal. App. 1st Dist.	District Court of Appeal, First District, Division 1, California
Cal.	Supreme Court of California
Cal.Rptr.	California Reporter
Call.App.	California Appeals Court

Cass 1 civ	Cour de cassation, 1re Chambre civile
Cass 2 civ	Cour de cassation, 2e Chambre civile
Cass 3 civ	Cour de cassation, 3e Chambre civile
Cass com	Cour de cassation, Chambre commerciale
Cass mixte	Cour de cassation, Chambre mixte
Cass req	Cour de Cassation, Chambre des requêtes (abolished in 1947)
Cf	Compare
Ch	Law Reports: Chancery Division
CILL	Construction Industry Law Letter
CISG	United Nations Convention on Contracts for the International Sale of Goods
CLC	Commercial Law Cases
Colo.	Supreme Court of Colorado
Con LR	Construction Law Reports
Const LJ	Construction Law Journal
Costs LR	Costs Law Reports
CP Rep	Civil Procedure Reports
D. Mass	United States District Court, District Massachusetts
D. Md.	United States District Court, District Maryland
D. Minn.	United States District Court, District Minnesota
D. Or.	United States District Court, District Oregon
D.C. App.	District of Columbia Court of Appeals
D.C. Cir	United States Court of Appeals, District of Columbia Circuit
D.C.Cal	District Court of Appeal, District California
D.C.S.C.	United States District Court, District South Carolina
DC	Divisional Court
DCFR	Draft Common Frame of Reference
Del.	Supreme Court of Delaware
E.D. Va.	United States District Court, Eastern District Virginia
E.D. Wash.	United States District Court, Eastern District Washington
E.D.N.Y.	United States District Court, Eastern District New York
ECLI	European Case Law Identified
EMLR	Entertainment and Media Law Reports
ER	English Reports
EWCA	Court of Appeal
EWHC Ch	High Court (Chancery Division)
EWHC	High Court
Ex	Court of Exchequer
F. Appx	Federal Appendix
F.Supp.	Federal Supplement
Fed. Cir.	United States Court of Appeals, Federal Circuit
Fla.	Supreme Court of Florida
FSR	Fleet Street Reports
Ga.	Supreme Court of Georgia
Hawaii	Supreme Court of Hawaii

HL	House of Lords
HR	Hoge Raad der Nederlanden
Ill.	Supreme Court of Illinois
Ill.App.	Appellate Court of Illinois
Ind. Ct. App.	Court of Appeals of Indiana
J	Justice
JOR	Tijdschrift Jurisprudentie Onderneming & Recht
JORF	Journal Officiel de la République Française
Kan. App.	Court of Appeals of Kansas
KB	Law Reports: King's Bench Division
KBD	High Court, King's Bench Division
LJ	Lord Justice
Lloyd's Rep Bank	Lloyd's Law Reports Banking
Lloyd's Rep	Lloyd's Law Reports
LR	Law Reports
Mass.	Supreme Judicial Court of Massachusetts
Mass.App.	Appeals Court of Massachusetts
Md. Spec. App.	Court of Special Appeals of Maryland
Me.	Supreme Judicial Court of Maine / Maine
Mich.	Supreme Court of Michigan
Mo. App. W. Dist	Missouri Court of Appeals, Western District
MR	Master of the Rolls
N.D. Cal.	United States District Court, Northern District California
N.D. Ill.	United States District Court, Northern District Illinois
N.D. Tex.	United States District Court, Northern District Texas
N.E.	North Eastern Reporter
N.H.	Supreme Court of New Hampshire
NJ	Nederlandse Jurisprudentie
NJB	Nederlands Juristenblad
NJF	Nederlandse Jurisprudentie Feitenrechtspraak
N.J.Super.A.D	Superior Court of New Jersey, Appellate Division
n.p. in Bulletin	Not published in Bulletin des arrêts de la Cour de cassation
N.W.	North Western Reporter
N.Y.	Court of Appeals of New York
N.Y.	New York Supreme Court
N.Y.A.D.	Supreme Court, Appellate Division, New York
N.Y.S.	New York Supplement
Nev.	Supreme Court of Nevada
NSWLR	New South Wales Law Reports (Australia)
Ohio App.	Court of Appeals of Ohio
OJ	Official Journal of the European Communities
Or.	Supreme Court of Oregon
P & CR	Property, Planning and Compensation Reports
P	Pacific Reporter
Pa.	Supreme Court of Pennsylvania

Pa.	Supreme Court of Pennsylvania
Pa.Super.	Superior Court of Pennsylvania
PECL	Principles of European Contract Law
PO	Patent Office
PRG	Praktijkgids
QB	Law Reports: Queen's Bench Division
QBD	High Court, Queen's Bench Division
Rb.	Rechtbank
RPC	Reports of Patent, Design and Trade Mark Cases
RTR	Road Traffic Reports
RvdW	Rechtspraak van de Week
S.C.	Supreme Court of South Carolina
S.D. Iowa	United States District Court, Southern District of Iowa
S.D.N.Y.	United States District Court, Southern District of New York
S.E.	South Eastern Reporter
SC	United Kingdom Supreme Court
So.	Southern Reporter
SW	South Western Reporter
TCC	Queen's Bench Division (Technology & Construction Court)
Tenn. App.	Court of Appeals of Tennessee
Tex. Civ. App.	Court of Civil Appeals of Texas
Tex.App.	Court of Appeals of Texas
TLR	Times Law Reports
UCC	Uniform Commercial Code (US)
U.S.	United States Reports
UKHL	House of Lords
UKSC	United Kingdom Supreme Court
ULC	National Committee of Commissioners on Uniform States Laws
UNCITRAL	United Nations Commission on International Trade Law
UNIDROIT	International Institute for the Unification of Private Law
UPICC	UNIDROIT Principles of International Commercial Contracts 2010
Va.	Supreme Court of Virginia
W. Va.	Supreme Court of Appeals of West Virginia
W.D. Wis.	United States District Court, W.D. Wisconsin
Wash.	Supreme Court of Washington
Wis.	Supreme Court of Wisconsin
WL	West Law number
WLR	Weekly Law Reports

Chapter 1

INTRODUCTION

1.1. Memorandum of agreement in Texaco v. Pennzoil

In 1984, two US companies – Pennzoil and Getty Oil negotiated a merger. They signed a 'memorandum of agreement'. However, before the transaction was finalized Getty Oil broke off negotiations. The company concluded a merger contract with a third party – Texaco – which offered a higher price for the shares. Pennzoil brought an action against Texaco, declaring that Texaco had tortiously interfered with the transaction in process. To sustain the claim, Pennzoil had to prove that the 'memorandum of agreement' between Pennzoil and Getty Oil was binding and therefore, in respect of this document, Getty Oil had no right to break off negotiations to conclude a contract with third party. According to the court, the memorandum of agreement was binding, representing the prospects of the transaction. At first instance, it was held that Texaco had interfered with the prospects of the transaction; an award of 11 billion US dollars, including damages, interest and punitive damages was granted. On appeal, punitive damages were reduced from three to two billion. Nevertheless this amount remains one of the largest damages awards in US history.

The decision in *Texaco* v. *Pennzoil*[1] gave rise to questions concerning a variety of areas of law. Focusing on the 'memorandum of agreement', why was it qualified as a prospect of a transaction? Can such document preclude the possibility of breaking off negotiations in order to accept a more profitable offer? Is this the case even if the document does not establish that negotiations are exclusive? Could an enforceable provision on exclusivity be included into letter of intent? If such a document binds the parties, what is the nature of the obligations it may contain, as compared to the effects of the final contract? How do these effects relate to freedom of contract? To what extent may the parties agree in advance on recovery in case negotiations fail? Could the parties have kept their negotiations non-binding by explicitly stating this in their 'memorandum of understanding'? Could they have created some binding obligations to structure the deal,

1 729 S.W.2d 768 (Tex.App 1987), applying New York law. The case is a landmark on the theme of letter of intent. Its importance for this topic is discussed inter alia in Draetta 1988; Klein 1988; Loncle/Trochon 1997; Schmidt 2002, at 267 ff.; Fontaine/De Ly 2009, at 41–42.

while remaining free to not conclude the final negotiated contract? In other words, could parties create by consent an arena for conducting parallel negotiations, retain their discretion to accept higher bids and deploy other negotiation tactics, while contractually specifying the scope of their eventual liability?

Three decades after the dispute in *Texaco v. Pennzoil*, memoranda of agreement and similar documents still raise similar questions and can create more financial and legal risks than they prevent. This is especially so in international contracting, given the divergence in the approaches to negotiations across jurisdictions.

1.2. Defining letter of intent

1.2.1. Multitude of interchangeable titles

The use of 'memoranda of understandings', 'letter of intent' and similar documents has attracted the attention of legal scholars and practitioners since the 1970s.[2] The literature of that time defines letter of intent in transactions broadly as any 'pre-contractual written instrument that reflects preliminary agreements or understandings of one or more parties to a future contract'.[3] This broad definition covers a plethora of other documents used in practice as equivalent to letter of intent, but called differently. The main titles referred to in case law and literature include 'memorandum of understandings' 'commitment letter', 'binder', 'agreements in principle', and 'heads of agreement'.[4] The manner of merchants to attribute these names without always implying a precise legal meaning has been even called a 'terminological anarchy'.[5]

1.2.2. From broad definition to qualification

In response to the increasing use of letter of intent in commercial practice, the broad definition advanced in the 1970s has acquired several nuances in subsequent literature. The first step in legal reasoning was the suggestion that the legal effects of each concrete document in a dispute were primarily a matter of interpretation.[6] On the one hand, the term 'letter of intent' remained in use as a common label for any of the documents

2 Fontaine 1977; Pevtchin 1979; Farnsworth 1990b.

3 Lake/Draetta 1994, at 5–6. The formulation refers to the one given in *Garner* v. *Boyd*, 330 F. Supp. 22, 24 (N.D. Tex. 1970): 'letter of intent is customarily employed to reduce to writing a preliminary understanding of the parties'.

4 Farnsworth 1990b, at 22.

5 Fontaine/De Ly 2009, at 30.

6 Schoordijk 1984, at 92–106 (Dutch law); Schut 1986 (Dutch law); Grosheide 1989 (Dutch law); Lutter 1998 (German law); Furmston/Norisada/Poole 1998 and Furmston/Tolhurst 2010 (England and Commonwealth); Lake/Draetta 1994 (US, English, Italian, French, German law); Holger 2000 (German law, US law); Fontaine/De Ly 2009 (comparative perspective). See also Capecchi 2004 (Italian law); Péloquin/Assié 2006 (Canadian law); Domeniconi 2013 (Swiss law). More generally, see ICC 1990; Fontaine 2002.

mentioned above, and this remains the case today. On the other hand, none of these titles provided precise guidance on the legal effects of the documents. Due to the legal uncertainty that may arise in these documents, one commentator has even called letter of intent an 'invention of evil' to discourage its use in practice.[7]

The second step of reasoning was to suggest guidelines to aid interpretation. The functions of letter of intent have been described, along with comparative law reflections and economic analysis of bargaining using precontractual documents.[8] The broad definition of letter of intent mentioned above has been related essentially to existing legal concepts and doctrines.

This has led to the conclusion that any document in question could in many cases be qualified under one of the existing legal concepts.[9] The concepts invoked included the final contract as well as offer and acceptance – the elements of the main doctrine used in most legal systems to assess contract formation. Literature also refers to a conditional contract (that is, a proper contract where the commencement of execution is subject to completion of a condition), a gentlemen's agreement (engagement in honour, but not in law),[10] and to the concept of promise. These findings have undoubtedly facilitated the task of interpreting precontractual documents, but have not eliminated legal uncertainty surrounding the use of letter of intent, especially in the context of international transactions.

1.2.3. Working definition: contractually organized negotiations

More recently, Fontaine and De Ly have suggested a restrictive definition of letter of intent. These authors have contended that only one type of precontractual document falls outside the existing legal categories, and, therefore, warrants further analysis. These are 'specific letters of intent' which represent 'contractual agreements preliminary to the conclusion of the final contract or contracts'.[11] Such documents 'either deal with certain precise aspects of the negotiations or with the progressive formation of the future contract'.[12]

This restrictive definition forms the basis of the working definition adopted for this study. Narrowing down this study to this type of letter of intent is justified by two

7 Klein 1988, at 143 (referring to the expression of S.R. Volk, former senior partner of Shearman & Sterling New York).

8 See Schwartz/Scott 2007.

9 Cordero Moss 2007a; Fontaine/De Ly 2009; Furmston/Tolhurst 2010, chapter 7 'Letters of Intent'; Wessels 2010.

10 On this concept see Rudden 1999 (comparative synthesis); for US law see Bernstein/Zekoll 1998; Allen 2000; for English law see *Rose and Frank Company v. Crompton and Brothers* [1925] AC 445 (HL); for French law, see Oppetit 1979; for Dutch law see Wessels 1984; Grosheide 2004.

11 Fontaine/De Ly 2009, at 37.

12 Ibid.

considerations. Firstly, this study aims to add a new perspective to the view of letter of intent in the existing scholarship, which has already made significant progress in reflecting on this kind of document. Secondly, an extensive description of all the issues involved in the context of contract formation (in domestic law and at international level) would not aid further understanding of letter of intent. This is due to the fact that, as will be explained below, letter of intent should be seen not only as an object of interpretation, but as a distinct pattern of business self-regulation at the level of the 'living' and developing international *lex mercatoria*.

1.3. Problems posed by issuing letter of intent and this study's hypothesis

To understand the issues raised by letter of intent, it is worth taking a glimpse into the different levels of rule-making.

1.3.1. Note on levels of rule-making

Rules are created at various levels, national law and international regulation being the main levels of rule-making. The national law of a country consists of rules regarded as law in a particular jurisdiction.[13] International regulation includes primarily 'hard law' – binding rules created by bilateral and multilateral agreement between States. These are international conventions, treaties and specific EU regulation. Furthermore, an important part of international regulation consists of 'soft law' instruments. Soft law has no binding effect. However, it possesses high persuasive authority due to the reputation and experience of its drafters.[14] Soft law is the result of the work of renowned academics; since the second half of the twentieth century they have restated the best known and broadly accepted international principles and rules. Furthermore, international regulation includes business self-regulation – the constantly evolving and developing rule-making within the transnational *lex mercatoria*.[15] These rules do not emanate from States, but are created by the business community.

As will be explained further, by identifying the problems raised by the practice of using letter of intent at each of these levels, the following hypothesis may be formulated. Arguably, letter of intent represents a pattern that emerges at the level of business self-regulation and stems from the attempts by private parties to frame the dynamics of complex negotiations and mitigate the financial risks involved by the use of private regulation.

1.3.2. National level: contract formation and precontractual liability

At the level of national regulation, the question as to whether a written document entails any contractual obligation is in most countries addressed primarily by the doctrine of offer

13 Tamanaha 2000, at 313 following the view of Teubner. See Teubner 1997.
14 Veneziano 2013. Further on international soft law, see Chapter 8.
15 On *lex mercatoria* and relevant literature see Section 2.1.

and acceptance.[16] This doctrine has been developed based on the formation of simple 'discrete' contracts with 'neither context nor continuity'.[17] However, modern transactions have become increasingly sophisticated and complicated. Mergers and acquisitions of companies, large-scale construction and development contracts, sales of hi-tech machinery, and joint research agreements in the innovative domains are good illustrations of these transactions. These may involve numerous stakeholders, exchanges of information and know-how, and a number of other issues to be solved before the transaction is 'closed'.[18] The potential profits of such contracts are high and the contracts have a 'lasting effect' on both parties.[19] As a consequence, only detailed negotiations offer the possibility of working out all the details necessary to reach the possible future agreement. The precontractual period – the time between the start of negotiations and the conclusion of the contract – may last several weeks or even several years. During this time, negotiators may begin shaping the future contract. They may also exchange information without the aim of binding themselves to any concrete commitments. Negotiators may wish to streamline the entire process of reaching the final contract by taking on some commitments, without being bound by the final contract. They may wish to make clear that no final contract is formed, but create some binding obligations which are limited to the period of negotiations. It is worth noting as well, that the parties' goals and considerations may change during the course of negotiations. Finally, it is unsurprising that statements and conduct are used as bargaining tactics. In contrast with the static offer and acceptance doctrine, all the issues mentioned are dynamic.

National regulation also sets limits on the manner of bargaining in the course of negotiations.[20] This is done primarily through non-contractual regulation, but approaches differ considerably across jurisdictions. In the civil law traditions, these rules are generally referred to as 'precontractual liability' – a set of rules that imposes positive duties in negotiations based on contract law, non-contractual regulation or both. By contrast, common law tradition adopted a very guarded approach to the limitations of precontractual bargaining. The law generally is not meant to interfere with freedom of bargaining. Limits are set not by imposition of general contract law duties, but through specific 'piecemeal solutions'[21] developed mainly outside contract law.

The rules on precontractual liability have been frequently referred to as vague by national commentators, while letter of intent has been called a 'safe harbour' developed by the parties to concretize the obligations and remedies.[22]

16 A fundamental comparative analysis has been undertaken under the direction of Schlesinger. See also Section 2.3.1.
17 Brownsword 2013, at 119.
18 Fontaine 2013.
19 Shapiro/Posner 2006, at 140.
20 Giliker 2002; Fontaine 2002; Cartwright/Hesselink 2008; Beale 2010, at 371–426; Van Erp 2011; Von Hein 2012. See also Kessler/Fine 1964; Farnsworth 1987; Von Mehren 1991; Hondius 1991; Zimmermann/Whittaker 2000; Hondius 2004; Couret/Dondero 2012.
21 *Interfoto Picture Library Limited* v. *Stiletto Visual Programmes Limited* [1989] QB 433 (EWCA) 439 (Lord Bingham).
22 Van Bijnen 2005, at 155.

In this way, the use of letter of intent is closely related to the topic of precontractual liability. The precise question it raises is whether letter of intent has an impact on the general regime of negotiations, including the relevant remedies. In other words, the question is to what extent may the default rules may be modified by private regulation?[23]

1.3.3. *International level: hypothesis on privatization of negotiations in business self-regulation*

The divergence in approaches to the general regime of negotiations across jurisdictions, namely the increasing influence of the theories underpinning precontractual liability, has led to legal uncertainty in international transactions. Some decades ago, a distinguished commentator described the experience of US companies negotiating contracts in countries with a civil law tradition as follows: 'Given the fact that the notion of pre-contractual liability does not exist in common law, some American companies have been very surprised to see damages claims petitioned against them and their liability involved because the law that had already been chosen – or could be determined through obvious clues – [established] the principle of this liability, which they ignored'.[24]

In the contemporary international context, business parties appear to be more aware of the difference between negotiation regimes than they were some decades ago. Against the background of their divergence, letter of intent may be regarded, *ex hipothesi*, as a flexible tool to clarify the parties' duties and obligations even at the stage of negotiations by 'privatizing'[25] the regulation of negotiations. It is hypothesized that this practice may be regarded as a non-codified trade usage: 'a pattern of repetitive behaviour among merchants' which has to some degree acquired normative force and is 'observed as a legally binding obligation, not for mere courtesy, convenience or expediency'.[26]

Turning to uniform and harmonized rules, it should be noted that the most relevant set of hard law rules – the United Nations Convention on Contracts for the International Sale of Goods (CISG)[27] – does not explicitly address the precontractual stage, and it is debated whether negotiations of contract fall within the Convention's scope.[28] The UNIDROIT Principles of International Commercial Contracts (UPICC)[29] and the Principles of European Contract Law (PECL)[30] – both dedicated primarily to contract

23 To contrast: the theme of precontractual liability relates to the question of whether and under what conditions one may be held liable during negotiations, and primarily for breaking off negotiations.

24 Lalive 1983, at 44–45. The English translation of the quote is taken from Couret/Dondero 2012, at 350.

25 For the concept of 'privatization' of rules in commercial practice see Nottage 2012, at 160; Cafaggi 2011a, Cafaggi 2011b.

26 Goode 1997, at 8. See also Goode/Kronke/McKendrick 2015, para 1.63 ff, para 4.48, noting the role of comparative law in establishing trade usage.

27 United Nations Convention on Contracts for the International Sale of Goods (Vienna, 1980).

28 See on modern debate Fogt 2014; on CISG see also Chapter 8.

29 UNIDROIT Principles of International Commercial Contracts 2010, available at www.unilex.info.

30 Lando/Beale 2000; Lando 2003.

law – contain specific provisions relating to negotiations of contract.[31] The Draft Common Frame of Reference (DCFR)[32] which includes in its scope non-contractual relations contains specific rules on negotiations in its part dedicated to contract law.[33] However, the soft law instruments offer no straightforward approach to the business practice of using letter of intent. Their application to contractually organized negotiations requires further interpretation. The hypothesis advanced above may arguably serve as a guidance for further development of the international approach to contractually organized negotiations 'in an effort in favour of ... a single body able to provide an authoritative interpretation of uniform law instruments'.[34]

As illustrated more generally, issuing letter of intent in international transactions precipitates unsecured financial interests, unwanted obligations, and liability. This warrants further research on the specifics of the contractual organization of negotiations and its legal effects.

1.4. Research question

This research will address the following question. To what extent can the law, particularly international regulation, accommodate the practice of contractually organising or 'privatising' negotiations made through a letter of intent?

This study aims to add a new dimension to the understanding of private regulation of negotiations through formulating a harmonized international approach. Harmonization is understood in this research broadly, comprising not only unification of law through international conventions,[35] but also harmonization through non-binding principles, restatements of law and convergence of business practices.[36]

The research is addressed to legal practitioners and scholars. A better understanding of private regulation of negotiations may contribute to academic knowledge on international trade usages. In practice, it may also enhance legal certainty and financial security of the parties at the beginning of an international business relationship. As stated by Goode, '[b]usinessmen ... attach great importance to flexibility, to a legal environment which enables them to develop new commercial instruments, new business practices, confident in the knowledge that they will be upheld by the courts as producing their desired legal effects...'.[37]

31 Articles 2.1.15, 2.1.16, 1.8 UPICC; Articles 2:301, 2:302 PECL.
32 Von Bar/Clive 2010.
33 Book II, Chapter 3 DCFR.
34 Basedow 2003, at 49.
35 See on terminology Boele-Woelki 2010, at 34–35, noting that *unification* supposes that 'the same solution applies everywhere... if a difficulty concerning a given relationship to arise', while *harmonization* aims to reconcile different approaches in various systems and thus does not require relying on one rule applicable to all.
36 De Ly 2012.
37 Goode/McKendrick 2010, at 1348.

The main research question may be divided into three sub-questions.

- First, what is the nature of a letter of intent?
- Second, what are the similarities in and the differences between the national approaches of the selected jurisdictions to the legal effect and remedial consequences of the contractual organization of negotiations? How can the converging and diverging tendencies be explained?
- Third, how can the existing international approach to contract negotiations formulated in international instruments (e.g., the UPICC, PECL, and DCFR) be interpreted and developed in light of the answers to the previous questions?

Before elaborating on the methods chosen to answer these questions, the focus and the scope of the research need to be specified.

1.5. Focus and scope

This study focuses on contractually organized negotiations – the business practice reflected in the working definition of letter of intent provided above. The following main situations will be addressed.

1. Cases where the parties purport to keep negotiations non-binding and free from any regulation, contractual and non-contractual.
2. Cases where the parties endorse an obligation to conduct negotiations in a specific way, for example require *bona fides* with or without specifying the content of this duty.
3. Cases where parties purport to create stand-alone obligations confined to the process of negotiations and limited in time to the contract formation. For example, exclusivity, confidentiality obligations, provisions on distribution of costs during negotiations and in case of their failure, limitation of liability (both contractual and non-contractual), and dispute resolution.
4. Remedies available in case of breach of the obligations set out above.

The focus specified above implies the main limitation of the scope of the research to international commercial contracts. Some other limitations are called for by the context of using letter of intent and also by practical considerations.

First, this study's concern is essentially with *commercial* contracts, because letter of intent is primarily used in the context of commercial transactions. The term 'commercial' covers transactions between private parties made in the course of their business and in order to obtain profit.[38] The research addresses general contract law, as opposed to specific contracts. The submissions are primarily valid for international sales contracts.

[38] The definition is based on Farnsworth 2006, at 905–906. Farnsworth notes, though, that a distinction between 'civil' and 'commercial' contracts is not shared by all developed legal systems.

The specificities of corporate transactions, contractual joint ventures, franchising contracts, licence agreements are touched upon to a lesser extent but are generally covered by this research. By contrast, contracts where the parties are regarded as socially and economically weak (consumer contracts, insurance, and employment contracts), public-private partnerships and tenders fall outside the scope of the research, because special regulation is often applicable to these contracts, both at the national and international levels.

Second, the research is particularly interested in *international* contracts, given the aim of the study to enhance legal certainty in international contracting. The term 'international' is understood broadly as a transaction involving interests of international trade.[39]

Third, it is worth noting that questions of applicable law and competent forum form an important component of the reflection on international transactions. However, this study will not touch upon private international law aspects of the privatization of negotiations as such. Private international law is, as Lipstein has put it, 'a technique and not a system of substantive rules'.[40] It raises a separate set of questions and would make the study excessively broad. Nonetheless, identifying the applicable law and competent forum requires the characterization of a claim. To the extent the findings of this study might help in characterizing the claim, the research may be relevant for private international law purposes.[41]

Fourth, a particular note is warranted on the concept of *contract*. Contract is one of the core matters of the law of obligations and at the same time, perhaps one of the most difficult concepts to define.[42] This study regards as contracts the agreements, promises and other acts perceived as contracts in each legal system.[43] It also takes into account definitional considerations underpinning soft law instruments and re-calls different contract law theories.[44] This research uses the terms contract, agreement, and promise interchangeably.

39 No unanimously accepted criterion of 'internationality' of contract exists in the literature. International instruments rely on various criteria, usually specific to the purpose and scope of each instrument. For instance, the CISG relies on the criterion of places of business required to be in different states (Article 1(1) CISG). Other international instruments rely on the criteria of the parties' place of habitual residence, incorporation, the place or conclusion or execution of the contract. See for an overview Kessedjian 2013, at 12–19.

40 Lipstein 1981, at 2.

41 On some private international law aspects of letter of intent see Deelen 1984; Lutter 1998, at 145 ff.; Rigaux 1990; Holger 2000, at 243 ff.; case C-334/00 *Fonderie Officine Meccaniche Tacconi SpA* v. *Heinrich Wagner Sinto Maschinenfabrik GmbH (HWS)* [2002] ECR I-07357; Jobard-Bachellier 1995; Wessels/Van Wechem 2003, at 31–43; Volders 2009; Benedict 2013; Hage-Chahine 2012.

42 Hogg 2013.

43 Binding power of contract relies on different considerations in different legal systems and legal philosophical currents. It is possible to name, in particular, promissory theories of contract, will-based theories, reliance-based theories, and others. See for an overview Von Mehren 2008; Morgan 2013. See also Gordley/Von Mehren 2006, at 63.

44 See Section 2.3.2.

The study draws a distinction between the concept of *final contract,* on the one hand, and *'dynamics' of negotiations,* on the other hand. The *final contract* or, using the US terminology *ultimate agreement* is the negotiated deal and the end result of the entire transaction. The *precontractual period* or the *'dynamics' of negotiations* is the exchange occurring in the course of negotiations, on the other hand. As a starting point, it is convenient to submit that negotiations cover all relations that occur before the final contract comes into existence. This period broadly corresponds to the time when parties may be subject to precontractual liability or other regulation applicable to the process of negotiations.[45] This distinction will be addressed in more detail in Chapter 2, which advances the concept of dynamics of negotiations.

Fifth, as noted above the issues raised by the practice of using letter of intent at the national level relate to the doctrine of *offer and acceptance.*[46] In considering the extent to which this research requires the offer and acceptance doctrine to be addressed, several points should be taken into account. This doctrine is frequently used as guidance on the interpretation of letter of intent. However, for this purpose, this study may rely upon the existing findings. For instance, Lake and Draetta have undertaken a comparative research. They have considered letter of intent (in the broad meaning) from the perspective of offer and acceptance and contract law doctrines related to preliminary agreements in common law and civil law jurisdictions.[47] Furmston and Tolhurst have addressed letter of intent from the broader perspective of the practice of contract formation. Their study covers English law along with the developments in a number of other common law countries.[48] Fontaine and De Ly have offered an illustrative overview of various examples of documents called letter of intent in international contracting practice.[49]

The mainstream method of addressing letter of intent is the use of existing legal categories. This is especially the case in the courts' reasoning, primarily because the pleadings are predominantly based on arguing that the final contract is formed. Alternatively, claims may be based on engaging precontractual liability in the civil law traditions and on advancing an argument to apply tort law. These arguments may involve at a certain point a discussion as to whether the final contract was formed. According to the literature, the debate is increasingly shifting from a focus on offer and acceptance towards a reflection upon other mechanisms of contract formation.[50] For this reason, a detailed description of the offer and acceptance rules would not be productive in answering the research question in this study. The research will consider the doctrine of offer and acceptance limitedly, *in abstracto* and only when its discussion is not dissociable from the argument being advanced. More concretely, a note on offer and acceptance will be needed to contrast its statics with the dynamics of negotiations.

45 On the refined definition see Section 2.5.
46 See Section 1.3.
47 Lake/Draetta 1994 (addressing contract law in France, Italy, Germany, US, and England).
48 Autralia, New Zealand, Canada, Singapore, and US. See Furmston/Tolhurst 2010.
49 Fontaine/De Ly 2009, chapter 1 'Letters of Intent'.
50 Von Mehren 1991, at 54–55; Schwenzer/Mohs 2006, at 246; Fogt 2014.

Sixth, on a more general note, this study adopts the perspective of contract formation. This approach follows the choice made by the international soft law instruments. They perceive negotiations as an issue inherent to the formation of contract, as specific provisions on negotiations have been included into soft law on contract. At the same time, at the national level, a large part of regulation applicable to negotiations is non-contractual. Nevertheless, all the fields relevant at the national level will be discussed, because these may help in accommodating letter of intent within the provision of soft law instruments.

While contract formation is the main perspective of this research, it will not discuss vitiated consent,[51] because the remedial consequences of defects in consent relate to the final contract, essentially its nullity. However, this study is primarily interested in negotiations that fail before the final contract comes into existence. For the same reason, the study will not address the relevance of letter of intent to the interpretation of the final contract concluded by the parties.

Lastly, this research does not aim to draw conclusions in the field of international business negotiations.[52] The interdisciplinary argument from the literature on negotiations will have the limited function of highlighting modern trade practices and will be used only as a vehicle for drawing together business contracting practice and the legal analysis.

1.6. Methodology

1.6.1. Comparative functional method in three steps

This research aims to contribute to the development of law and knowledge on trade usages. The most appropriate tools for this purpose are offered by the comparative functional method for the following reasons.[53] Comparative law analysis is frequently used for formulating submissions valid at the international level.[54] Furthermore, the diverging approaches to the regulation of negotiations in different legal systems demand to be addressed from a comparative perspective.

Comparative functional method prescribes starting with the formulation of a problem to be solved; this is usually a socio-economic question. Once the problem is formulated, the solutions adopted in different jurisdictions should be described. Thereafter, the differences and similarities should be drawn together. Their comparison enables

51 Defects of contractual consent resulting from undue influence, duress, mistake and unconscionability.

52 The field of negotiation studies is sketched in Weiss 2006. See also Chapter 2 of this study.

53 Comparative law scholarship is extensive. For an overview, including critiques see Michaels 2006, at 339 ff.; Riles 2001. See also seminal David/Brierley 1968; Reitz 1998; Zweigert/Kötz 1998; Legrand 1999; Sacco 2000–2001; Markesinins/Fedtke 2009; Glenn 2014.

54 On this use and the main objections, see Berger 2010, at 71–76.

conclusions to be drawn on the questions for which the comparative analysis was undertaken, that is, to suggest the answer to the identified socio-economic problem. This study follows these three steps, which will be elaborated in more detail below.

1.6.2. *The first step: interdisciplinary argument to identify parameters for comparison*

The first step in reasoning will consist in identifying the content of letter of intent. This 'concept building'[55] will be based on the existing knowledge on letter of intent in the legal scholarship. At the same time, it will be necessary to draw attention to the business practice of creating letter of intent. As noted by Örücü, the first stage of comparative law analysis 'is dependent on the availability of data'.[56] '[D]ata can best be obtained by employing social science methodology'.[57] Within this research, the inquiry into the content of letter of intent requires, besides legal scholarship, information on the practice of negotiations.

More concretely, it requires the gathering of two sets of information. Firstly, close attention should be paid to the negotiation process. The relevant information can be found in the developing field of study focusing on negotiations, referred to in this research as 'negotiation studies'. No empirical research into the practice of business negotiations has been conducted within this study. It has relied on the outcome of negotiation studies, which in their turn largely rely on social science methodology. The present research assumes that negotiations studies reflect empirical reality.[58] Chapter 2 will discuss in what way the insights offered by negotiation studies may provide arguments for legal analysis of letter of intent.

Secondly, the content of letter of intent is formed by the obligations that parties include in their texts in practice. A readily available source of information on this is offered by the published case law. In fact, case law may be considered in different ways. On the one hand, it may be regarded as an illustration of an existing general principle or a source of emerging principle. On the other hand, case law may be regarded as a text in itself. For instance, case law contains numerous quotes of texts of letters of intent which have given rise to disputes.

The texts of letter of intent published as part of case law will be collected. They may provide information on the most salient issues in negotiations. Chapter 2 will develop the manner of selecting these issues. Thereafter, the provisions of letter of intent relating to issues relevant for the dynamics of negotiations will be selected. This way of systematic collection and analysis of case law, along with 'recording consistent features … brings

55 Örücü 2012, at 565.
56 Ibid.
57 Ibid.
58 See also Section 2.1, in particular footnote 95.

the rigor of social science to our understanding of case law, creating a distinctively legal form of empiricism'.[59] Using this source will enable the collection of examples of the obligations frequently included into letter of intent.[60] These obligations will in turn form the main parameters for the comparative observations.[61]

1.6.3. The second step: comparison, selected jurisdictions

In the second step in the analysis, this study will describe the approaches to letter of intent in the law[62] of four selected jurisdictions: England and Wales, the US, France and the Netherlands and will discuss four international instruments: the CISG, UPICC, PECL and DCFR.

Several considerations underlie this restrictive choice of jurisdictions and international instruments, which deserves some further explanation. The selection seeks primarily to reflect the divergence in the legal regimes concerning negotiations and precontractual liability. From this perspective, the jurisdiction of England and Wales warrants attention, because this common law tradition only admits that a pre-contractual document may trigger contractual obligations in a restricted way. The English legal system is also important as a frequently chosen legal regime and jurisdiction in international transactions.[63]

Furthermore, English and Dutch law respectively have been referred to as two 'extreme' approaches to precontractual liability.[64] Therefore, Dutch law is worth discussing to reflect this opposition. Dutch law provides an example of a civil law tradition initially close to French law, but which turned towards a Germanic approach with the reforms of the Dutch Civil code in the 1990s.

French law has been chosen to present a civil law tradition *par excellence*. In 2016, the French law of obligations has been reformed. Some of the (relative) innovations introduced by the reform[65] codify the regime of negotiations which has been developed in the case law and which is directly relevant for the research question addressed in this book.

59 Hall/Wright 2008, at 64.

60 The ambition of the collection is not to provide quantitative analysis. It is confined to collecting illustrations, being a methodologically qualitative search for pertinent representative illustrations. Further remarks on the collection and provenance of the examples are made in Section 7.2.

61 As recalled by Markesinis and Fedtke, the functional method has been criticized for basing its conclusions on the choice of parameters. The scholars note that there is 'no reason why a researcher or an author cannot set out his own parameters and then work within them' as long as the context in which the parameters are analysed is not disregarded. See Markesinis/Fedtke 2009, at 37.

62 The analysis regards as law the rules considered as law in each jurisdiction. See Tamanaha 2000, at 313; see also Siems 2014, at 18.

63 See inter alia Cuniberti 2014; Kramer 2014, para 2 and 3.

64 Cartwright/Hesselink 2008, at 461.

65 Pannebakker 2016.

The comparison also includes the US. This jurisdiction is relevant because of the high impact on world trade of the US economy. It also adds a transatlantic perspective that reaches beyond regulation in the European Union. Furthermore, the United States has a sophisticated legal system, with abundant case law and detailed regulation of a number of issues. Another important reason for addressing the US is that the modern approach to negotiations in business is arguably influenced or at least informed by the US literature on negotiations.[66]

All the selected jurisdictions are Western legal systems; this general choice has been made for the following reason. Western legal systems are the most comparable, but more importantly, these jurisdictions have sophisticated and well-developed rules applicable to negotiations. Rules developed in these jurisdictions frequently serve as examples for law-makers in many countries of the world. From a practical perspective, the law and scholarship are available and easily accessible. Furthermore, these countries have an important impact on international trade. One may object to this submission and note that whilst it is a strong arguments in favour of including the US, international trade is increasingly dominated by Asian and Latin American countries. Countries' trade impact also varies across the economic sectors. However, in many non-Western countries, the regulation of negotiations is a relatively recent development or is based on the approach of one of the Western models. As a consequence, analysis of these jurisdictions, insightful though it may be, would have offered only limited information on the research question of this study.

Along with the selected jurisdictions, this book will discuss major international instruments. The CISG deserves attention as the most prominent uniform law on international sales contracts. This instruments' attitude to negotiations keeps on generating debates.[67] All the soft law instruments that will be analysed – the UPICC, PECL and DCFR – include provisions on negotiations within the rules on contract formation. As noted above, the international harmonization of law instruments regard negotiations as an issue of contract law. The Chapter will also refer to some rules on dispute resolution harmonized at the international level, namely, the Convention on the Recognition and Enforcement of Foreign Arbitral Awards (New York, 1958) and the EU Regulations Brussels I-bis,[68] Rome I[69] and Rome II.[70] It should be noted that the Proposal for a regulation on a Common European Sales Law[71] has been also studied, but will not

66 See Chapter 2.

67 See recently Torsello 2014.

68 Regulation (EU) No 1215/2012 of the European Parliament and of the Council of 12 December 2012 On Jurisdiction and the Recognition and Enforcement of Judgments in Civil and Commercial Matters (Recast).

69 Regulation (EC) No 593/2008 of the European Parliament and of the Council of 17 June 2008 On the Law Applicable to Contractual Obligations.

70 Regulation (EC) No 864/2007 of the European Parliament and of the Council of 11 July 2007 On The Law Applicable to Non-Contractual Obligations.

71 European Commission, Proposal for a Regulation of the European Parliament and of the Council on a Common European Sales Law, 11 October 2011, COM(2011) 635.

be reported due to the withdrawal of this project.[72] The approaches to letter of intent in these jurisdictions and international instruments will be described consecutively, because this provides context to the parameters for comparison in a sufficiently nuanced and logical manner.

Furthermore, comparative functional method departs from the presumption that all the jurisdictions arrive at the same solution, even if different means are sometimes used. The renowned comparative law scholars Zweigert and Kötz have formulated this expectation as follows: '[a]s a general rule developed nations answer the needs of legal business in the same or in a very similar way. Indeed it almost amounts to *praesumptio similitudinis*, a presumption that the practical results are similar'.[73] In this way, comparative law analysis allows us to uncover *functional* equivalents, as opposed to *formal* equivalents. In the light of this presumption, it may be recalled that the search for general functional similarities in the field of precontractual liability has already been undertaken. Comparative studies have contended that no common core of rules on precontractual liability is in place, at least in the EU legal systems. Moreover, different jurisdictions come to diverging solutions.[74] As a consequence, this research does not expect to find complete formal and functional equivalents in this field. However, even in the absence of formal and functional equivalents, a possibility exists, in principle, that similar effects can be achieved by private *contractual* regulation.[75] It is the latter possibility that this study explores as the potential premise for a harmonized international approach.

1.6.4. The third step: towards a harmonized approach

The third step in the comparative law analysis consists in the explanation of the reasons for the similarities and differences uncovered and drawing conclusions within the remit of the research. As noted above, this study aims to formulate an approach to letter of intent (e.g. contractually organized negotiations) within the interpretation of the existing soft law instruments. Sometimes, a further stage that precedes the conclusions is identified by comparative scholars: the stage of evaluation. By evaluation they understand the choice of a 'better law' – the law that offers the most appropriate solution to the socio-economic problem under discussion.[76] However, it appears appropriate to refrain from identifying a 'better law' for the following reason. Arguably, no sound international approach to the field of negotiations of contract may be based on choosing a 'better law'. This was proven at the diplomatic conference for the adoption of the CISG, where lively debates on the best approach led to the exclusion of this question from the scope of the

72 Annex 2, Commission Work Programme 2015, Strasbourg, 16.12.2014 COM(2014) 910, http://ec.europa.eu/atwork/pdf/cwp_2015_withdrawals_en.pdf. The Commission's Work Programme for 2015 mentions the new goal to issue a '[m]odified proposal in order to fully unleash the potential of ecommerce in the Digital Single Market'. The content of this falls outside the scope of the present study.

73 Zweigert/Kötz 1998, at 40.

74 Cartwright/Hesselink 2008, at 449 ff.; Van Erp 2011. See also Giliker 2002.

75 Gilson 2001; Siems 2014, at 233–234.

76 Michaels 2006, at 373.

Conventions scope. The search for a compromise based on a 'common core'[77] or common denominator in the field of precontractual liability has also turned out to be difficult, because the countries' solutions diverge considerably. As noted above, the possibility of coming to a common core through contractual regulation or 'privatization' of the existing rules might be a pathway to an international approach.

For that matter, instead of searching for a better law, some convergence in solutions that may be reached by contract – private regulation – will be sought. More concretely, the study will suggest interpretation of the international soft law instruments addressed in the light of comparative law findings. A possible critique to this approach would emphasize that national laws are not the main way of interpreting soft law instruments.[78] However, identification of similarities and differences in the national laws is an important premise for eventual unification or harmonization of law.[79] Uniform rules based on comparative law are said to have a high level of legitimacy for those concerned by the rules.[80] Furthermore, drafters of international soft law instruments are informed by comparative law. Therefore, formulating a uniform and coherent interpretation of soft law instruments informed by comparative law findings appears to be the most valuable addition to the existing scholarship.

In drawing its conclusions, this research will rely primarily on classical legal hermeneutics: analysis of legal scholarship and discussion of the internal coherence and logic of a given legal framework.

1.7. Sources and translation

To answer the research question, this study will rely on a number of primary and secondary sources. Primary sources will be used to describe the law in the selected jurisdictions. For the jurisdictions of England and Wales and the US, case law will form the primary source,[81] because it is the main method of law-making on the discussed topics in common law traditions. In discussing Dutch and French law, the codified systems of law, primary attention will be paid to statutory regulation. However, case law will also receive close attention in civil law traditions, because the approach to letter of intent in civil law countries has been for a large part developed in case law.[82] Furthermore, databases on international instruments including CISG, UPICC, and case law referring

77 The term 'common core' was first used by Schlesinger. See Schlesinger 1968. It has been later upheld by a large scale project including studies of many aspects of European private law. See www.common-core.org.

78 Michaels 2015, at 78.

79 See Hondius 2011, at 5.

80 Micklitz 2007.

81 Primary sources for England and Wales are available in the database Westlaw UK, and for the United States – in the database Westlaw International.

82 Primary sources for France include the open access database www.legifrance.gouv.fr and the subscription databases Dalloz, LexisNexis, Lamyline, Lextenso. Primary sources for the Netherlands include the open access database www.rechtspraak.nl and the subscription database Kluwer Navigator.

thereto, will be used.[83] Secondary sources – scholarly writings and commentaries – will help to interpret the relevant legal regulation, illuminate its context, and follow its genesis.

While the book is written in English, not all the used sources are in this language. This calls for a brief note on translation. The research will refer to the existing official or other published translations where these are available. For instance, the Dutch Civil code has been translated into English.[84] A number of French statutes are also available in a translated version.[85] Most of the other quotations have been translated by the author of this study. Generally, this research attempts to stay terminologically close to the concepts adopted in the UPICC, as it is one of the best known and authoritative soft law instruments.

1.8. Outline of the study

Chapter 2 will address the practice of negotiations and the content of letter of intent. It will focus on two questions. First, what is the content of letter of intent? Second, how can the provisions reflecting the dynamics of negotiations be identified? Answering both questions requires attention to be drawn to the practice of negotiations. Chapter 2 will inquire how the laymen's approach of the contracting parties to negotiations through strategies and tactics can be conceptualized in legal terms, e.g. to suggest a manner to address contractual negotiations as a dynamic process.

Chapters 3, 4, 5, and 6 will be dedicated to the national approaches to the effect of letter of intent and the related remedies in the selected legal systems: the Netherlands, France, England and Wales, and the United States.

The regulation of negotiations in Dutch law has been compared to an 'invisible magnetic field'[86] based on the requirement of reasonableness and fairness. Chapter 3 will expand upon the possibilities for the parties to limit or waive this 'magnetic field' in Dutch law through the regulation of negotiations by letter of intent.

83 These sources are the *Translex* database on various sources of *lex mercatoria* containing excerpts from arbitral awards, www.trans-lex.org; database *Unilex* on CISG and UPICC, www.unilex.info; PACE database on CISG at www.cisg.law.pace.edu.

84 Warendorf/Thomas/Curry-Sumner 2013.

85 English translations are available at www.legifrance.gouv.fr. The last amendment to the French Civil code was made by a bill that is not yet translated. See *Ordonnance no 2016-131 du 10 février 2016 Portant Réforme du Droit des Contrats, du Régime Général et de la Preuve des Obligations* JORF 0035 of 11 February 2016. See also draft *Ordonnance* for the Reform of the Law of contract, the General Regime of Obligations, and Proof of Obligations (draft Ordonnance), www.justice.gouv.fr/publication/j21_projet_ord_reforme_contrats_2015.pdf. See also the English translation of the draft *Ordonnance* by J. Cartwright, B. Fauvarque-Cosson and S. Whittaker, www.textes.justice.gouv.fr/art_pix/Draft-Ordonnance-for-the-Reform-of-the-Civil-Codepdf.pdf.

86 Nieuwenhuis 2010, at 289.

The reform of the French law of obligations of 16 February 2016 has completed the *Code Civil* with the regulation of contractual negotiations under the umbrella of precontractual good faith. This was described as 'particularly rigorous ethics of negotiations'.[87] Chapter 4 will identify the possibilities for and limitations to the private regulation of negotiations in the French context.

English law regards negotiations as a genuinely adversarial process[88] with a limited role for contract law, while non-contractual regulation is primarily relevant. Chapter 5 will discuss to what extent parties may contractually organize negotiations against this background of English law.

US law addresses negotiations in terms of risk and bargain.[89] The mainstream US approach heavily accentuates the search for the final contract based on a test of the parties' intentions. However, some state laws take a more nuanced view. Chapter 6 will describe the approach to letter of intent adopted by the case law of the US states and in the harmonized rules at the federal level.

Chapter 7 will discuss the provisions frequently included in letters of intent. It will provide illustrations of such provisions that may be found in the published case law. Each provision will then be discussed from a comparative perspective. In this way Chapter 7 will draw together the national approaches to letter of intent and offers a practical reference on the content of letter of intent. Furthermore, the Chapter will identify and explain the main converging and diverging tendencies.

Chapter 8 will discuss the CISG and the rules on negotiations formulated in international soft law – the UPICC, PECL, and DCFR. It will prepare the concluding reflection on the main question of this study – the question as to how the existing international rules should be interpreted to apply to the practice of letter of intent.

The concluding Chapter 9 will suggest a harmonized approach to letter of intent by recommending the interpretation of the existing soft law instruments.

87 Mazeaud 2001, at 640.
88 *Walford* v. *Miles* [1992] 2 AC 128 (HL).
89 Farnsworth 2004, at 190.

Chapter 2

DYNAMICS OF NEGOTIATIONS AND THE CONTENT OF LETTER OF INTENT

2.1. Introduction

As noted in the Introduction, this study hypothesizes that letter of intent is a distinct pattern in business practice that may amount to a commercial usage: 'a pattern of repetitive behaviour among merchants... observed from a sense of legally binding obligations, not for mere courtesy, convenience or expediency'.[90] But what is the content of this pattern?

This Chapter will focus on the content of letter of intent, provide an insight into the letter of intent and its role in practice and thereby frame further research. The Chapter will answer the following questions. What kind of issues form the content of letter of intent generally? Though the provisions differ in each document, can some general pattern be identified? How can the provisions which reflect the dynamics of negotiations be identified? The Chapter will draw attention to the practice of negotiations[91] and identify the patterns of issues relevant in the course of negotiations. These issues will form the parameters for the comparative observations made at a later stage (in Chapter 7).

The modern trend towards forming contracts in negotiations has been mapped by negotiation studies.[92] A growing body of research conducted over the past thirty years[93] provides information on the way in which parties negotiate contracts in practice, and the methods used to organize, influence, and manage the negotiation process. Alongside this theoretical understanding, negotiation studies have resulted in practical advice to negotiators on conducting negotiations with the aim of reaching a (profitable) agreement.

90 Goode 1997, at 8. See also Goode/Kronke/McKendrick 2015, para 1.63 ff., 4.48 ff.

91 This Chapter is partly based on Pannebakker 2013.

92 Negotiations studies represent an interdisciplinary field that uses the methods of social psychology, economics and management science. See Druckman 2011, at 142. See also Dupont 1990, at 289; Weiss 2006.

93 From the considerable literature, see Dupont 1990; Lax/Sebenius 2006; Weiss 2006; Dupont 2006; Mnookin 2010; Lempereur/Colson 2010; Maude 2014; Lewicki/Barry/Saunders 2015 with further references.

In this way, negotiation studies have streamlined a conscientious approach on the part of dealmakers to the strategies and tactics of their negotiations in a complex deal. The knowledge on negotiations has increasingly acquired practical relevance for dealmakers who can obtain sophisticated, practice-oriented advice on the way to negotiate deals with the best possible outcome.[94] For example, setting the target of gaining a 'win-win' result in negotiations was a fresh and innovative idea in business education, whereas currently, it is almost a routine part of negotiation techniques which is learned by the majority of operational personnel.

Insights from negotiation studies have shed light, in particular, on the manner in which commercial parties conduct negotiations in practice and the issues relevant in negotiating a transaction. Therefore, it may be suggested that negotiation studies can be taken into account in legal analysis, namely, to provide arguments for the legal analysis of letter of intent. This submission is based on two assumptions: first, that contract law is closely connected with the realities it regulates, and second, that the knowledge of negotiations reported in negotiation studies reflects the empirical reality of negotiations.[95]

Considering the rules and patterns created by commercial parties as a basis for legal analysis as suggested above subscribes to the idea of legal pluralism. One of its early proponents, Romano,[96] suggested that legal rules can emanate not only from states, but can also be created by various communities, including the international business community. Translated in terms of law, this self-regulation represents a part of the *lex mercatoria,* – the 'living' and developing transnational business self-regulation.[97] The use of the term 'transnational', and not international or cross-border, for this purpose indicates the relative independence of this self-regulation from any state rules. How can self-regulation be identified? As Horn formulates it:[98]

> [t]he truly crucial question comes when we find such de facto similarities and must ask whether the clauses, rules or patterns have some normative effects beyond the individual

94 See inter alia Fisher/Ury/Patton 2012. See also practically orientated projects of the Program on Negotiation (PON) at Harvard Law School, www.pon.harvard.edu/about; 'Clingendael' Netherlands Institute of International Relations, www.clingendael.nl; ESSEC IRÉNÉ (*Institut de Recherche et de l'Enseignement sur la Négociation*), http://irene.essec.edu/.

95 On interdisciplinary studies in private law, see generally with further references van Boom/Giesen/Verheij 2008; Van Boom/Giesen/Verheij 2013. See also Van Klink/Taekema 2011. The degree to which this Chapter's argument is interdisciplinary corresponds to the borrowing of arguments from another discipline, on the scale advanced by van Klink and Taekema.

96 The theory formulated by the Italian theorist Santi Romano in 1918. See Romano 2002 (reedited text dated 1945). On the subsequent fundamental development of the concept *lex mercatoria* see Berger 2010, at 1–13; see also inter alia Goldman 1983 (one of the first to argue that *lex mercatoria* is a separate legal order, independent of national orders); Schmitthoff 1987 (describing the practices of international trade and underlining their importance for trade).

97 Considerable literature exists on *lex mercatoria.* See inter alia seminal Kahn 1961; Goldman 1986; Lord Justice Mustill 1987; Berman/Dasser 1990; De Ly 1992; Berger 2010; Dalhuisen 2013; Loquin 2013.

98 Horn 1972, at 514, quotation translated by Berger in Berger 2010, at 60 (footnote 62). In the last sentence, I have replaced the word 'practice' by 'usage' to avoid tautology.

contract in which they are expressly included or referred to. Here, we return to our problem, whether international practice might have created international commercial usage or even customary law.

To identify the issues relevant for the parties in complex negotiations, this Chapter will first describe the approach to the process of contract negotiations in negotiation studies (Section 2.1). Thereafter, it will recall the critique of the static character of the legal assessment of contract formation given in legal scholarship (Section 2.2). This critique seen in the light of negotiation studies will allow suggestions to be made as to the manner of identifying the obligations by which parties frame the dynamics of negotiations in the texts of letter of intent (Section 2.3). Concluding remarks will explain how arguments from negotiation studies may be used to address letter of intent (Section 2.4).

2.2. Negotiations

Negotiation studies address the process of negotiations in terms of strategies and tactics (2.2.1) and distinguish two different parts of negotiations: the substantive and the dynamic constituents (2.2.2).

2.2.1. Strategies and tactics

The term 'negotiations' means an interaction of two or more actors faced simultaneously with divergences and interdependences who voluntarily look for a mutually acceptable solution that allows them to create, maintain or develop a relationship.[99] Negotiations are analysed as an activity whereby participants with diverging interests search for agreement despite a difference in their points of view. This search for agreement is analysed in terms of strategy, 'the overall plan to accomplish one's goal in a negotiation', and tactics, the 'short-term, adaptive moves designed to enact or pursue broad (or higher-level) strategies'.[100]

Depending on the strategy and tactics used by the parties, most researchers distinguish two main types of negotiations: the 'integrative' and the 'distributive' type.[101] This distinction is widely accepted despite the absence of unanimity in approaches to negotiations.[102] Integrative negotiations are characterized as a search for agreement

99 'See Dupont 1990, at 11: [L]a négociation est une activité qui met face à face deux ou plusieurs acteurs qui, confrontés à la fois à des divergences et à des interdépendances, choisissent (ou trouvent opportun) de rechercher volontairement une solution mutuellement acceptable qui leur permet de créer, maintenir ou développer (ne fût-ce que temporairement) une relation'. For an overview of other definitions of negotiations, see Kaplan 2010, at 13–43.

100 Lewicki/Barry/Saunders 2015, at 116.

101 Lewicki/Barry/Saunders 2015, at 110–111. Walton/McKersie 1991, at 4–5. Walton and McKersie have used the terms 'integrative' and 'distributive' 'bargaining' which correspond to a large extent to the 'cooperative' and 'conflict' negotiation and to the 'integrative' and 'distributive' 'dimension' of negotiations respectively in the terms subsequently used by other authors. See Dupont 2006, at 32–33.

102 For an overview of the approaches to negotiation, see Dupont 2006, at 99–112.

between non-conflicting parties, while distributive negotiations are pertinent for an interaction between parties with conflicting interests.

More concretely, in *integrative* negotiations, the interests of the parties are complementary or not conflicting; negotiations are driven by the parties' common goal.[103] One party is willing to believe that the other's interests are valid, while both parties make it explicit by their behaviour and act accordingly.[104] For example, making promises is listed amongst the tactics of integrative negotiations.[105] Furthermore, the integrative approach is often characterized by negotiating over a long period of time because the tactics of integrative negotiation are said to be more successful when the parties have some time between the negotiation itself and the supposed start of implementation of the outcome of this negotiation (for example, the time between the start of negotiations and the start of the execution of a contract). Generally, the tactics of integrative negotiations presume a certain level of cooperation between the parties and an extended exchange of information about the priorities and preferences of each party. In this context, negotiation studies refer to various written documents in which parties engage to frame negotiations. These documents, also called (in the terminology used by negotiation studies) 'presettlement settlements'[106] are characterized by negotiation studies as follows. 'These settlements result in a firm, legally binding written agreement between the parties (it is more than a gentlemen's agreement)'.[107] At the same time, negotiation studies admit that such documents 'may simply establish a framework within which the more comprehensive agreement can be defined and delineated'.[108] This characterization supposes that the documents are created: 'in advance of the parties undertaking full-scale negotiations, but the parties intend that the agreement will be replaced by a more clearly delineated long-term agreement that is to be negotiated'.[109]

By contrast, in *distributive* negotiations the interests of the negotiating parties are usually conflicting. The tactics of distributive negotiation are to a certain extent aggressive. An example of a distributive tactic is public disclosure. Making public information about the development of negotiations makes third parties immediately aware of a possible future agreement. This tactic may have the effect of putting the other party under pressure to conclude an agreement that has been publicly announced.[110]

A combination of integrative and distributive negotiation is also possible. However, it has been argued that this combination would represent only a change in the cooperative

103 Lewicki/Barry/Saunders 2015, 110–111.
104 Lewicki/Barry/Saunders 2015, at 101–102.
105 Schelling 2006.
106 Lewicki/Barry/Saunders 2015, at 102 referring to the term advanced by Gillespie and Bazerman in 1998.
107 Ibid.
108 Ibid.
109 Ibid.
110 Lewicki/Barry/Saunders 2015, at 60, 316, 347 ff.

and distributive episodes of the entire process of negotiation, while these would still be characterized as only one type.[111] The decisive characteristic allowing a classification of concrete negotiations as one or the other type is the intention of the parties regarding the outcome of negotiations.[112] If the initial intention of the parties is coming to an agreement 'because of the situation',[113] or because of the person with whom a negotiation is conducted,[114] then even if the negotiation becomes distributive, it would be easy to go back to the integrative approach after a distributive period. For example, the entire negotiation process may be characterized as integrative if parties face an issue that cannot be resolved during an initially integrative negotiation, then turn to an expert or a mediator or an internally contractually appointed dispute board (and this might be a distributive period) and thereafter come back to the discussion and thus, come back to the integrative approach.[115]

2.2.2. Substantive and dynamic constituents

The analysis of negotiations in terms of strategies and tactics answers the question as to *how* the parties come to an agreement, allowing a general characteristic to be given to the process of negotiations. Alongside this characteristic of the negotiation process, negotiation studies have identified the patterns of issues which are negotiated. These issues answer the question as to *what* is negotiated. The next Section will be dedicated to the elaboration of this characteristic of negotiations.

According to negotiation studies, negotiations are characterized by two different constituents: the substantive constituent that is directly related to the content of contracts (rights and obligations of the parties under the final agreement being negotiated) and the dynamic constituent related only to the management of the negotiations.

In order to sketch the substantive constituent, negotiation studies emphasize that negotiations always arise in connection with a product, a service, or a concrete change of the current situation desired by the parties.[116] The parameters of this service, product or change of a situation are the end result of these negotiations. These parameters represent the *substantive* constituent of negotiations (also called their technical, objective or economic constituent).[117] This constituent embraces, therefore, all the issues related to the end result of negotiations, including the questions of price, quality, deadlines for a service or milestones of a project, payment conditions, guarantees and other characteristics of the product or service. These issues usually represent the content of the future eventual contract.

111 Dupont 2011, at 48.
112 Dupont 2011, at 48. 'Intention' is not a normative concept in negotiation studies.
113 Dupont 2011, at 48.
114 Ibid.
115 Ibid.
116 Dupont 1990, at 215.
117 Ibid.

Simultaneously to the substantive constituent, negotiations include the second constituent, that is, the *dynamic* constituent (also called 'relational' constituent).[118] It embraces the processes separated from the core and content of the future contract. The dynamic constituent includes, for instance, planning, timing and structuring of the negotiations, as well as the distribution of tasks if necessary during the negotiations. These issues are not the same as the issues included in the eventual final contract. However, the issues forming the dynamic constituent are relevant for the management of the negotiation process within the context of a business deal.

Negotiation studies detail the content of these issues and their relevance for the management of negotiations. The usual flow of negotiations includes the stages of gathering information and the subsequent use of this information in bidding. Bidding is defined as 'the process of making moves from one's initial, ideal position to the actual outcome'.[119] These are followed by 'closing the deal' and implementing the agreement.[120] The *timing and structuring of negotiations* are named as important elements in managing the closing of the deal. These include the questions of 'What is the time period of the negotiation? If negotiators expect long, protracted deliberations, they might want to negotiate the time and duration of the sessions. When do we start? For how long do we meet? When do we need to end?... What will happen if we deadlock?'[121] Furthermore, the *formalization of the development* of negotiations: 'How will we keep track of what is agreed to?'[122] This is done, for instance, through intermediary documents, such as time schedules, letters, protocols, memoranda and other similar documents. These become particularly relevant since '[i]n large scale negotiations, process and outcome are intertwined and recurring, not single iterations'.[123] Furthermore, negotiation studies suggest that if an agreement is complex, it would most probably be 'reviewed by experts and specialists – attorneys, financial analysts, accountants, engineers, and so on'.[124] Implicitly confirming the distinction between the substantive and the dynamic constituent of negotiations, it is usually important for negotiators that 'discussions about these dynamic issues should occur *before* the major substantive issues are raised' in order to allow time for the proper working out of the details of the final contract. The dynamic constituent represents, therefore, the 'environment' of the transaction and the field where the negotiations are managed by the parties by using strategies, tactics, timing and structuring of the negotiation process.

2.3. Statics in contract formation

Returning to legal analysis from negotiation studies, it may be noted that legal analysis draws no explicit distinction between the constituents of negotiations. Nonetheless, this

118 Ibid.
119 Lewicki/Barry/Saunders 2015, at 122.
120 Ibid.
121 Lewicki/Barry/Saunders 2015, at 141.
122 Ibid.
123 Weiss 2006, at 307; Shapiro/Posner 2006.
124 Lewicki/Barry/Saunders 2015, at 142.

distinction is implicitly made by scholars who have criticized the statics in the analysis of contract formation. These critiques are primarily focused on the doctrine of offer and acceptance. A note on this doctrine (2.3.1) will facilitate the discussion of its static character (2.3.2).

2.3.1. *Note on offer and acceptance*

The doctrine of offer and acceptance has received significant scholarly attention. For this reason, it does not need not a great deal of elaboration. It will be addressed in a condensed way, *in abstracto*. However, a note on offer and acceptance is necessary to contrast its statics with the dynamics of negotiations.

The rules of offer and acceptance form the basis of the rules on contract formation in most legal systems.[125] It has proved to be a viable and flexible tool to assess contract formation. Since the nineteenth century when this doctrine was formulated,[126] it has been adapted to the changes in contracting practices, for example, the conclusion of contracts online.[127] This doctrine is also part of the soft law harmonized at international and European level, including the United Nations Convention on Contracts for the International Sale of Goods (CISG),[128] UNIDROIT Principles of International Commercial Contracts 2010 (UPICC),[129] the Principles of European Contract Law (PECL)[130] and the Draft Common Frame of Reference (DCFR).[131]

The core of this doctrine is as follows. The rules of offer and acceptance draw the line between 'what is and what is not a contract'[132] and delimit the contract from any other relationship. In order to form a contract an offeror has to make a proposal – an offer – to perform an act (or to abstain from acting) to the offeree, and the offeree has to accept this offer.[133] The moment of contract formation is the precise time at which an offer established by an offeror with a sufficient level of certainty and completeness is accepted by an offeree. These rules are designed to answer the questions as to whether a contract is formed and at which moment it is formed. Furthermore, this doctrine designates the method of assessing the conditions on which a contract is formed. This is done by defining the acts that qualify as offer, acceptance, and the sending and receipt of each of these.

125 See inter alia with further references Schlesinger 1968a, at 74; Zweigert/Kötz 1998, at 356 ff.; Blanchard 2008 (on international contracts); comparative observations to Section II. – 4:201 DCFR; Beale 2010, at 241–317; Furmston/Tolhurst 2010; Harvey/Schillig 2010; Ferrari 2012; Illmer 2012.

126 See for the civil law countries: Pothier 1806; for the common law countries: *Payne* v. *Cave* (1789) 100 ER 502 (Court of King's Bench). For the historical roots in Roman law, see Zimmermann 1996, at 560 ff.

127 Nolan 2010, at 61; Furmston/Tolhurst 2010, at 160 and 159 ff.

128 United Nations Convention on Contracts for the International Sale of Goods (Vienna, 1980). Articles 14–24 CISG.

129 Article 2.1.1 UPICC and generally Chapter 2 Section 1 UPICC. See also Articles 14–24 CISG.

130 Chapter 2 Section 2 PECL.

131 Chapter 2 Section 2 DCFR.

132 Smith 2004, at 168.

133 Farnsworth 2006, at 915 ff.; Schlesinger 1968a, at 1 ff.

Stated in this way, these rules are common to most legal systems at national level. These rules also form the doctrine of offer and acceptance within the theory of contract law. However, the detailed and more concrete content of the offer and acceptance rules varies in different legal systems.[134] For instance, different national approaches resolve in different ways the questions of what qualifies as an offer, whether or not an offer can be revoked before its acceptance and what qualifies as acceptance.[135] Seen from a comparative perspective, these differences limit the possibilities of analysing this doctrine *in abstracto*. To put it differently, any apparent further similarity between the concepts within this doctrine is a 'booby-trap',[136] because, in many respects, their similarity is only on the surface, whereas a closer examination reveals divergences.

A general discussion of the doctrine of offer and acceptance is therefore possible only if one moves away from concrete legal systems[137] to look at the rules of contract formation accepted generally in most legal systems. The UPICC are an appropriate reference[138] for this purpose for a number of reasons. They represent a modern restatement[139] of national approaches in different countries with a world-wide territorial scope,[140] and they are formulated as a harmonized instrument as a result of considerable research and debate.[141] Furthermore, the UPICC are used not only as an academic reference and a source of inspiration for legislators in various countries,[142] but also as a persuasive authority for international arbitrators, national courts and drafters of international contracts[143] as a choice of a neutral non-state or transnational law.[144]

The rules on offer and acceptance in the UPICC rely on the core of the doctrine described above, but are broader. According to the UPICC, 'A contract may be concluded either by the acceptance of an offer or by conduct of the parties that is sufficient to show

134 For example, the exact point in time when the offer is considered to be accepted is based on different principles, namely the principles of 'information', 'reception', 'expedition' and 'declaration'. See for an overview Ferrari 2012, at 625 ff.

135 Von Mehren 1991, at 54.

136 Schlesinger 1968a, at 56.

137 This transnational approach, 'without differentiating between common law and civil law' systems is possible from the point of view of contract law theory. See Smith 2004, at viii-ix.

138 See also Chapter 2, Section 2 PECL and Book II Chapter 4 DCFR adopting the approach resembling that of the UPICC.

139 On this concept, see Jansen 2010, at 92 ff.

140 Bonell/Peleggi 2009.

141 Vogenauer, 'Introduction', in Vogenauer 2015, at 9 ff. Further on the UPICC, see Chapter 8 of this study.

142 Lake 2011, at 696 ff.

143 See for some empirical evidence Lake 2011, at 702. See generally inter alia Michaels 'Preamble I' in Vogenauer 2015, at 81–90; Berger 2010, at 202; Vogenauer 2014; Bonell 2006.

144 The question as to whether parties can validly choose *lex mercatoria* generally, and the UPICC particularly, as the law applicable to their international contract has been the subject of academic debate. For an overview of the debate, see Lando 2000. It is currently undisputed that a choice for UNIDROIT as applicable law is valid, if the dispute is subject to arbitration. See Bortolotti 2014.

agreement'.[145] The reliance on the 'traditional mechanism'[146] of offer and acceptance as the main tool of analysis of contract formation is underlined by the drafters of the UPICC in the official comments.[147] The UPICC include all three main elements of offer and acceptance doctrine (the offer, the acceptance and the moment of their meeting). Additionally, other behaviour (or 'conduct') demonstrating an agreement of the parties may qualify as formation of a contract. The main rule on contract formation extends therefore to cases that are more complicated than a simple acceptance of an offer. These are situations where a meeting of parties' wills is in place, but the analysis of their meeting through offer and acceptance might be excessively fictional, for instance, formation of a multiparty contract,[148] formation of contract by conduct, formation of contract by simultaneous execution, and contracts formed in negotiations.[149]

The UPICC approach is primarily motivated by the 'special needs of international commerce'[150] and by the idea of freedom of contract. Furthermore, the commentators characterize the UPICC as 'modern and innovative'[151] and state that the classical mechanism of offer and acceptance 'does not necessarily have to apply in the world of international commercial contracts'.[152] The Articles of Chapter 2 (Formation and authority of agents) of the UPICC are designed primarily for the 'traditional mechanism' of offer and acceptance, while Articles 2.1.12–2.1.18 provide the possibility of forming a contract by conduct.

The offer is defined in the UPICC as 'a proposal for concluding a contract';[153] the offer should be 'sufficiently definite and indicate the intention of the offeror to be bound in case of acceptance'.[154] The acceptance is defined as an availing of this opportunity: 'a statement made by or other conduct of the offeree indicating assent to an offer is an acceptance'.[155]

To summarize, in a relationship which can lead to the formation of a contract, either (1) an offer, an acceptance, and a moment of their meeting can be identified or (2) other behaviour (conduct) of parties indicating the end of the negotiation and the beginning of a contractual relationship should be in place. If the parties are involved in complex

145 Article 2.1.1 UPICC.
146 Vogenauer, 'Introduction', in Vogenauer 2015, at 19.
147 Official Comments to Article 2.1.1 UPICC.
148 See Furmston/Tolhurst 2010, at 12, invoking the *ratio* of the English case *Clarke* v. *Dunraven* [1897] AC 59 (HL).
149 See also Siems 2004. Discussing contracts formed by conduct, Siems refers to contracts open to more than one party, face-to-face contracts, joint signature contracts, contracts formed by conduct and contracts formed by written declaration, calling them 'unevenly formed contracts'.
150 Vogenauer, 'Introduction', in Vogenauer 2015, at 18.
151 Vogenauer, 'Introduction', in Vogenauer 2015, at 19.
152 Ibid.
153 Article 2.1.2 UPICC.
154 Ibid.
155 Article 2.1.6(1) UPICC.

negotiations, it becomes difficult to apply these elements to letter of intent whereby the parties attempt to create contractual obligations even at the stage of negotiations.

2.3.2. Existing critique of statics in the analysis of contract formation

The doctrine of offer and acceptance has been criticized in legal theory for failing to take into account the dynamics of the process whereby the contract may be negotiated and come into existence. Such critique can be traced back to the contract theories of the period 1970–1980 and has been advanced in the contemporary scholarship.

One of first extensive comparative studies of this doctrine made in the early 1970s[156] has already contended that the offer and acceptance rules do not easily apply to an analysis of negotiations in complex transactions. This major study notes that 'the businessmen who originally conduct the negotiations, often will consciously refrain from ever making a binding offer, realizing as they do that a large deal tends to be complex'.[157] This observation goes on to describe the further development of the transaction: '[a]fter a number of drafts have been exchanged and discussed, the lawyers may finally come up with a draft which meets the approval of all of them, and of their clients. It is only then that the parties will proceed to the actual formation of the contract, and often this will be done by way of a formal "closing"'.[158]

In the terms used by Atiyah,[159] the doctrine of offer and acceptance still perceives complex transactions as simple dealings. It therefore fails to take into account the process whereby parties shape their agreements. As a consequence, if a contract is formed in negotiations, the courts often 'reason backwards',[160] declaring that a contract exists, and then look for 'something that resembles offer and acceptance'.[161] This critique of the offer and acceptance rules emphasizes their static character. It stresses also that this doctrine fails to take into account the dynamics of negotiations and futurity in the assessment of contract formation. Within the context of formation of a complex agreement, the notion of futurity corresponds to the planning of relationships and their adaptation to changing circumstances.

The futurity of the process whereby parties come to agreements has also been emphasized by the US scholar Macneil. He called the back and forth of opinions and progressive development of the parties' relationship in the course of the contract formation a

156 Schlesinger 1968. See also Rodière 1976.
157 Schlesinger 1968, at 1584–86.
158 Schlesinger 1968, 1584–86.
159 This type of critique has been advanced in the scholarship referred to as the 'contract-as-tort' theory. It emphasizes the growing role of tort law in relations traditionally classified within the law of obligations as belonging to the domain of contract law. See Atiyah 1979; Gilmore 1995.
160 Atiyah/Smith 2005, at 41.
161 Smith 2004, at 176.

'relational' aspect of contract.[162] Macneil has argued that contract law should have different (varying) rules depending on the degree to which the relational aspect is present in a contract. To enable this, he suggested using a framework of 'norms' for analysing contract.[163] Another US scholar, Feinman, has pointed also to the need for contract law to accommodate modern transactions by providing a 'framework for parties who engage in business planning'.[164] This framework would allow parties 'to create relations, to determine their content, to avoid them altogether'.[165]

It is to be noted, however, that Macneil's and Feinman's theories have attracted criticism themselves. Macneil's views have been perhaps most criticized for not having proposed rules that would be predictable and certain enough to replace the doctrines currently used.[166] As Macneil himself has contended, concluding on a resonance that the relational contract theory created in legal thought: 'We are all relationists now, but not when it comes to law'.[167]

Yet, the critiques of the vision of contract formation as static, in opposition to the dynamics of negotiating a deal, have acquired considerable influence. Furthermore, the claim that contract law should take account of the process whereby parties come to an agreement remains valid.

More recent scholarship has also pointed to the need for the law to accommodate transaction planning and the progressive development of deals. For instance, Farnsworth has drawn a distinction between the 'ultimate agreement' (that is, the negotiated final contract) and the 'preliminary regime' emerging, according to Farnsworth, in the US case law. The preliminary regime corresponds to various agreements on the development of negotiations. Farnsworth has also noted the growing general attention given to precontractual negotiations and preliminary agreements in twentieth century contract law. He indicated this field as a theme for further research and eventual development.[168]

A British scholar, Brownsword, in his general reflection, has also touched upon the statics in the legal analysis, but went beyond the discussion of the offer and acceptance rules. Brownsword has argued in favour of a more sophisticated theory of consent in English

162 Macneil elaborated a theory called 'relational' theory of contract. It embraces both the formation and the execution of contracts. For a selection of works by Macneil see Campbell 2001.

163 These norms are 'role integrity'; 'reciprocity'; 'implementation and planning'; 'effectuation of consent'; 'flexibility'; 'contractual solidarity'; 'restitution, reliance and expectation interests'; 'creation and restraint of power'; 'propriety of means'; 'harmonisation with the social matrix' and the 'relational' norms 'preservation of the relation' and 'harmonisation of relational conflict'. Campbell 2001, at 125.

164 This type of critique is sometimes referred to as 'neo-classical' contract theory, primarily relevant to US law. See Feinman 1990, at 1285 ff.

165 Feinman 1990, at 1288. See also Eisenberg 2000, at 1813; Hart 2009.

166 See for an overview of the critique (including Collins, Eisenberg, Posner) Vincent-Jones 2001. See also Mitchell 2009, at 21–22; Braucher/Kidwell/Whitford 2013.

167 Macneil 2001, at 383–384.

168 Farnsworth 1990a at 210–213.

law. He submitted that legal analysis should develop the theory of 'double-banked'[169] consent, whereby '[f]irst, the parties must consent to the terms of the auxiliary agreement; and then they must consent to the terms of the main contract'.[170] He suggested that 'to avoid an infinite regress running back from an auxiliary agreement to cover the main contract, and a pre-auxiliary agreement to cover the auxiliary agreement, and so on, there needs to be a jurisprudence that delineates what constitutes a valid (authorising) auxiliary agreement'.[171] In his reflection, Brownsword has also indicated the main problematic threads raised by his suggestion. Though his elaboration is relatively detailed,[172] it is not sufficiently extensive to be used as a matter of general contract theory. It also focuses primarily on English law. According to Brownsword, the search for the possibility of accommodating the double-banked consent is also a matter for further research.[173]

The submissions discussed so far have been made by British and American scholars and are valid primarily in relation to the US and English legal systems. As to the civil law traditions, the relational contract theorists have not gone unheard,[174] but have had only limited resonance. This appears to be primarily due to the fact that civil law traditions have developed the concept of preliminary agreement (*avant-contrat, voorovereenkomst*).[175] These preliminary agreements are perceived as proper contracts concluded before the final negotiated contract. Such agreements are based on the distinction between the final contract and the process of negotiations. To a certain extent, the possibility of creating a preliminary agreement diminishes the need for offer and acceptance to take into account the process of negotiations. The latter falls within the scope of a preliminary agreement. It is worth noting that the theory of preliminary agreements was developed not as a critique of the offer and acceptance rules, but as an independent tool based on freedom of contract.

Another avenue of legal thought has explored the idea that contract law in its entirety has only limited relevance for contracting practice. In particular, attempts have been made to evaluate the importance of the informal relationship during the formation of a contract. For instance, it has been claimed that informal relationships are more important in business than contractual ones.[176] Scholars supporting this idea have argued that a variety of motives other than law regulate the negotiations, formation and execution of contracts. As a consequence, parties can become interdependent because of various

169 Brownsword 2006, at 300.
170 Brownsword 2006, at 299.
171 Brownsword 2006, at 298.
172 Brownsword 2006, at 298–317.
173 Brownsword 2006, at 298–318.
174 See inter alia with further references Boismain 2005; Courdier-Cuisinier 2006. No extensive discussion of relational contract theory could be found in Dutch scholarship.
175 For a comparative synthesis of critical remarks in continental scholarship, see Fontaine 2002.
176 This view is often referred to as 'Wisconsin school of law and sociology'. See Macaulay 1963 and a follow-up article Macaulay 1985. For further empirical research on the process of business transactions, see Beale/Dugdale 1975; 1982; Korobkin 2002 (noting that the considerations of Macaulay have been only limitedly reproduced); Lewis 1982.

informal, non-contractual attachments. According to this view, these attachments, informal practices and understandings may represent an integral part of contractual negotiations and of the contract as well. Other researchers, in opposing the importance of the informal relationship in the formation of contracts, have argued that contract law plays an important role regulating *ex ante* the way parties shape long-term relationships.[177]

On a general note: all the abovementioned authors make a distinction between the final contract and a preliminary regime. The latter covers contractual obligations which are confined to framing and organizing negotiations. They also note the existence of mechanisms used in practice but not covered by legal analysis, and suggest that legal reasoning needs the tools to analyse these.

2.4. Identifying the dynamics

The reasoning will now turn to a discussion of the role of insights on negotiations in negotiation studies to identify the content of letter of intent. To do so, it will consider the existing critique of the static character of offer and acceptance in the light of negotiation studies (2.4.1) and suggested drawing a distinction between the substance of the final contract and the dynamics of negotiations (2.4.2). Thereafter, further use of distinction in this study will be discussed (2.4.3).

2.4.1. *The critique of the offer and acceptance rules in the light of negotiation studies*

The previous Section expanded upon the critique of the static character of the offer and acceptance rules. This critique may be reformulated in the light of negotiation studies. Based on this, it may be suggested that the distinction between the substantive and dynamic constituents of negotiations play a role in legal analysis.

As discussed earlier, the issues pertaining to the substance and content of the future contract represent the substantive constituent of negotiations. If one relates the critiques of the doctrine of offer and acceptance to the distinction between the two constituents of negotiations, this doctrine seems to be designed to assess only the substantive constituent of negotiations. By contrast, various precontractual documents appear to relate only to the dynamic constituent of negotiations, because they represent an environment in which the transaction is made. Precontractual documents do not always contain obligations that are to form part of the future contract. These may be confined to the provisions on the management of negotiations and other issues within the dynamic constituent of the negotiations.[178]

177 Arrighetti/Bachmann/Deakin 1997. The finding of these authors differentiates, however, between countries (Germany, Great Britain, and Italy).

178 Such distinction echoes the Roman law opposition sometimes made by civilian scholars between the *essentialia negotii* and *accidentalia negotii*. The former are the issues relating first and foremost to the

Therefore, identifying which constituent a concrete document or any conduct in the contract formation refers, may be used as a criterion for deciding whether this represents an element forming a contract.

It is worth noting that the two constituents may overlap in the negotiations. For instance, if the process of negotiations is documented, various precontractual documents can be created. These documents can be related to the dynamic constituent only (including the issues related only to the management of negotiations). Alternatively, the documents can combine issues from both the substantive and dynamic constituents (and thus include both the issues concerning the management of negotiations and the agreed conditions of a future contract).

If no distinction between the two constituents is made, the elements of the doctrine of offer and acceptance are easily confused with other issues arising at the precontractual stage. This confusion appears to be one of the main difficulties in the interpretation of precontractual documents and identification of their legal effects. This also appears to be one of the important reasons for the uncertainty surrounding the practice of creation of letter of intent.

2.4.2. Criterion for distinguishing between statics and dynamics

Therefore, it may be suggested that to identify the obligations related primarily to the dynamics of negotiations, the content of a concrete document should be divided into two constituents. Two overlapping constituents should be separated; thereafter, the dynamic constituent should be searched for in the document. If the constituent to which a document belongs is identified, it becomes easier to define whether a concrete provision relates to the formation of the final contract or to the organization of the negotiations. Those provisions not covered by the offer and acceptance rules may be regarded as the dynamics of negotiations. These provisions are to be discussed further in this study as the primary content that parties purport to privatize at the negotiations stage.

The arguments to support this submission can be drawn from consideration of the following example. An arbitration award by the ICC Paris International Court of Arbitration applying the UPICC[179] illustrates first, the situation where the substantive and the dynamic constituents overlap and second, the method adopted to draw a distinction. In this case, a 'Memorandum of Understanding' had been signed by parties during their negotiations. The document contained various precontractual

substance of the final contract, while the latter are 'special arrangements of the parties which did not determine the nature of the contract'. See Zimmermann 1996, at 234. However, both elements in this distinction are associated with the final contract and not with the negotiation process.

179 ICC Paris International Court of Arbitration Award 8331 (1996) 10 *Bulletin de la Cour Internationale d'Arbitrage de la CCI* (1999), www.trans-lex.org/208331/mark_932000. On this arbitral award see also Fontaine/De Ly 2009, at 38–39.

understandings. On the one hand, it included obligations related to the sale by one party of vehicles and spare parts to the other party. On the other hand, the document described the parties' understandings regarding their negotiations, future cooperation and organization of the after-sale services. When a dispute arose, one of the main issues that the arbitral tribunal had to address was the legal status of the Memorandum of Understanding. Based on the analysis of this document, the arbitrators decided that it included two types of conditions. The conditions of the first type represented 'specific conditions ... that are the result of parties' agreements and should therefore be considered as final between them unless they are amended by subsequent contracts approved by the parties'. By contrast, the second type of condition represented a 'general description of the parties' intention to enter into certain agreements'. The second type of condition was held not to be binding on the substance, but to represent an obligation on the parties to use their 'best efforts' to implement the general agreements into specific terms, on the basis of the Article 5.1.4 UPICC.

The reasoning in this arbitral award implicitly confirms the difference between the substantive and dynamic constituents of the process of contract formation. The award does not directly refer to this difference as a criterion for the delimitation between the two types of conditions in the Memorandum of Understanding in question. Its conditions are classified into contractual on the one hand, and other conditions on the other hand. However, an explicit reference to why the issues are classified in this way would strengthen the reasons for the decision as follows. The argument in the award is based on the arbitrators' understanding of the text of the document. They analysed the formulation of each condition and decided on this basis whether it represented a condition of a contract (a binding 'final obligation'). The analysis of the text led to an assessment by the arbitral tribunal of the context of negotiations and the entire relationship between the parties. Nonetheless, the award does not specify the concrete way in which this analysis was made. By contrast, the flow of the argument in this award can be understood through the distinction between the substantive and dynamic constituents of negotiations. The arbitrators' general line of reasoning corresponds to the distinction between these two constituents. The award mentions firstly the conditions related to the substance of the contract and corresponded to the substantive constituent. The conditions that were considered to be contractual were conditions that could have been assessed through the doctrine of offer and acceptance. Secondly, the award mentions other conditions related to understandings of the parties that did not represent contractual obligations. These conditions might be classified as corresponding to the dynamic constituent because these were forward-looking understandings between the parties to shape their eventual deals. A reference to this distinction, therefore, could have illuminated the motivation behind the decision in this award because it would make explicit the course of the argument used in the text analysis.

Hence, the distinction between two types of obligations related to two different constituents of negotiations exists in a legal assessment, albeit implicitly, as appears from the example of the ICC Paris award provided above.

2.5. Conclusion

Chapter 1 advanced the hypothesis that letter of intent represents a pattern in transnational business self-regulation. The view of contractual negotiations adopted in negotiation studies supports this hypothesis for the following reasons. Negotiations have relatively stable patterns and are not a chaotic process. While informal interaction appears to be relevant (the mere existence of the dynamic constituent of negotiations confirms the relevance of informal relations), the structuring of negotiations in letter of intent is clearly a formalization of the salient elements of the negotiation process.

In this way, the definition of letter of intent[180] can be concretized by stating that letter of intent contains contractually organized *dynamics* of negotiations. The content of letter of intent is formed primarily by the provisions framing the dynamics of negotiations.

The contours of these dynamics are charted by the description of tactics and strategies used in negotiations. For example, naming public disclosure as one of the aggressive tactics used in negotiations illustrates that the issue of confidentiality may become particularly relevant during contractual negotiations. Using these provisions of letter of intent, negotiating parties set the limits on the possible tactics of negotiations, clarify the issues relevant primarily to the negotiation process, and contain the risks involved in the management of complex transactions.

Furthermore, the distinction between the statics of negotiations and dynamics implies that further inquiry into the dynamics of negotiations in this study should not include the rules of offer and acceptance.[181] As contended above, legal analysis is well equipped to ascertain the statics in contractual negotiations through the rules of offer and acceptance. By contrast, it is less prepared to ascertain the dynamics of negotiations.

In the same vein as the need to develop a framework of 'a double-banked consent',[182] and the distinction between the final contract and preliminary regimes,[183] expressed within the critiques of statics in contract formation, the following may be suggested. The provisions framing the dynamics of negotiations in letter of intent should be addressed as stand-alone and *severable* (separable)[184] from the final contract and from other provisions of the same document. Negotiations may be approached as a dynamic process only if each concrete issue or act within the negotiations is addressed separately from the other issues in negotiation and from the substance of the final contract. For instance, in the ICC Paris award above, the negotiation process had to be deconstructed into separate conditions. It could not be seen as an entire process because its separate parts played

180 Section 1.2.3.

181 Compare: Lake/Draetta 1994 (these authors include the offer and acceptance rules in their analysis).

182 Brownsword 2006, at 300.

183 Farnsworth 1987.

184 These two terms are used in interchangeable manner. In the current literature, the term is used primarily for dispute resolution clauses.

different roles in the parties' relationship. Following the interpretation of these obligations as being separate, they were interpreted as having different legal effects. Consequently, if a precontractual document combines issues referring to both constituents of negotiations, every negotiated obligation should be isolated – severed – from the other issues addressed in the document and analysed separately. This approach will be adopted further in this study.

Having said that, letter of intent may, indeed, represent a trade usage, because it reflects a stable pattern of issues related to the dynamics of negotiations; the content of these issues still needs to be concretized. While negotiation studies shed light on the scope of issues that form the dynamics of negotiations, they do not provide information on concrete clauses whereby the parties privatize their negotiations. To find these clauses, a collection of the texts of letter of intent has been undertaken within this study. The collection includes texts of letter of intent quoted in the published case law in each selected jurisdiction.[185] This Chapter has formulated a criterion of distinction between the two constituents of negotiations. This criterion has been applied to identify the relevant provisions. The results of this identification are reported in Chapter 7 where these extracted provisions will form the parameters for comparison and each provision will be discussed from a comparative perspective.

185 On the method see Sections 1.6 and 7.2.

Chapter 3

DUTCH LAW

3.1. Introduction

Dutch law regards the process of contract negotiations as a relationship regulated by law. In the Netherlands, the idea that a party may be bound by law during contractual negotiations goes back to the work of Telders.[186] At the beginning of the twentieth century, this scholar examined situations where an offer could not be revoked and the reasons for this irrevocability. He invoked inter alia the concepts that would frequently be echoed in the subsequent case law and scholarship – those of detrimental reliance and expectation that a contract will be formed. Dutch literature has also acknowledged the cognate French and German doctrines contemporary with the work of Telders.[187] But Dutch law has followed its own path of development. The German concept of fault in conclusion of contract (*culpa in contrahendo*) attributed to Von Ihering[188] has remained foreign to Dutch law, as has the French doctrine.[189]

The modern Dutch approach to negotiations relies upon three pillars: an overarching duty of reasonableness and fairness[190] (the Dutch concept of *bona fides*) that is, strictly speaking an issue of tort law,[191] the framework of preliminary agreements, and the general tort law. This Chapter will examine these fields of regulation in order to answer the following question. To what extent may parties modify or waive these rules by organizing their negotiations contractually and what are the consequences of this 'privatization' for liability in Dutch law?

186 Telders 1937.

187 For an overview of the evolution and influences, see Van Dunné 1990, at 71; De Kluiver 1992 at 188 ff.

188 See Von Ihering 1861. This German scholar advanced the concept of *culpa in contrahendo* (fault in conclusion of a contract) referring to contractual liability.

189 De Kluiver 1992, at 188 ff. and 281.

190 Articles 6:2(2), 6:248(2) Dutch Civil code.

191 This basis flows from three cases called in literature Effectenlease: HR 5 June 2009, ECLI:NL:HR:2009:BH2811, *NJ* 2012, 183 Levob/Bolle; HR 5 June 2009, ECLI:NL:HR:2009:BH2815, *NJ* 2012, 182 De Treek/Dexia; HR 5 June 2009, ECLI:NL:HR:2009:BH2822, *NJ* 2012, 184 Stichting Gedupeerden Spaarconstructie/Aegon. See Van Boom/Lindenbergh 2009.

The first pillar of regulation is based on the overarching duty of reasonableness and fairness. As the Dutch Civil code (*Burgerlijk Wetboek*) contains no specific provisions on the process of negotiations, this duty has served as a vehicle for the development of the concept of liability for breaking off negotiations. The *Hoge Raad der Nederlanden* – the highest judicial authority in the Netherlands – has progressively shaped it by interpreting the general law of obligations. The *Hoge Raad* has formulated a set of factors to be weighed in order to decide whether breaking off negotiations is acceptable from the point of view of reasonableness and fairness. Based on these factors, withdrawal from negotiations may be regarded as unacceptable (*onaanvaardbaar*). This may lead to liability of the withdrawing party, and the remedies may go as far as a court order to negotiate further. The regulation of negotiations in Dutch law has even been compared to an invisible magnetic field[192] where parties may inadvertently lose the possibility of avoiding obligations. The second possible outcome of the application of these factors is that a withdrawal from negotiations will be deemed acceptable from the point of view of reasonableness and fairness and, therefore, lawful. According to the literature, this is the most frequent outcome; the *Hoge Raad* has also emphasized the exceptional and severe character of liability for breaking off negotiations.[193]

The second pillar of regulation is formed by the framework of the preliminary agreement (*voorovereenkomst, voorbereidende overeenkomst* and other). Dutch case law and scholarship acknowledge different types of preliminary agreements. Early reflections on these go back to the beginning of the twentieth century.[194] However, no unanimously accepted classification has been developed, and the analysis remains highly fact specific. As a matter of fact, Dutch case law draws a distinction between the preliminary agreement, on the one hand, and the final contract (*hoofdovereenkomst*), on the other.[195] Dutch scholars seem to agree that a preliminary agreement may contain stand-alone obligations, binding only during negotiations and irrespectively of the success or failure of the formation of the eventual agreement.[196]

Finally, the third pillar of the general tort law completes the regulation of negotiations. In the context of contract formation, the main situation where tort law is relevant is related to the tortious use of business sensitive information exchanged in negotiations.

To address the possibilities of contractually modifying or waiving the regulation outlined above, this Chapter will proceed as follows. It will start with a brief explanation of the approach to the sources of Dutch law and terminology (Section 3.2). Thereafter, it will address the restrictions on freedom of negotiations implied by the development of liability for breaking off negotiations in Dutch law (Section 3.3), discuss the framework of preliminary agreements (Section 3.4), and touch upon the application of tort law

192 Nieuwenhuis 2010, at 289.
193 HR 12 August 2005, ECLI:NL:HR:2005:AT7337, *NJ* 2005, 467 CBB/JPO.
194 Goudeket 1906.
195 Hijma 2013, at 68; Asser/Hartkamp and Sieburgh 2014, para 93.
196 Blei Weissmann 2013, §1.16.

(Section 3.5). A note will also be made on the doctrine of unjust enrichment (Section 3.6). Having addressed the elements of the framework, the Chapter will provide more details on the clauses with which parties frequently regulate the dynamics of negotiations (Section 3.7). Finally, the Chapter will describe the available remedies, conditions and nature of liability (section 3.8), and provide concluding remarks (section 3.9).

3.2. Sources of Dutch law and terminology

3.2.1. Dutch Civil code, case law, and scholarship

This Chapter will rely on the provisions of the Dutch Civil code (*Burgerlijk Wetboek*) – the main source of the law of obligations in the Netherlands. The legal system of this country belongs to the civil law tradition and relies primarily on codified law. The general part of the law of obligations is provided in Book 6 of the Dutch Civil code. This text has been in force since 1992; it is the result of the reform of the Dutch private law that took place some decades ago to renew the former civil code which had been in force since 1838. Prior to this, the French *Code Napoléon* was directly applicable in the Netherlands.

Despite the importance of the Dutch Civil code as a general source of the law of obligations, it has limited relevance to the regulation of negotiations. During the last reform of the law of obligations, the Dutch legislator consciously decided not to include a draft provision on liability for breaking off negotiations in the Dutch Civil code. Instead, the rules applicable to negotiations are essentially to be found in the case law of the Dutch courts interpreting and detailing codified law.

Therefore case law has considerable relevance for understanding the Dutch approach to contractual negotiations. Strictly speaking, case law is not a source of law in the Netherlands. Nevertheless, it forms an inherent part of the regulation of many issues. The case law of the highest judicial authority – the *Hoge Raad* – plays a major role within the existing body of case law. Its informal precedents, sometimes referred to as standard cases (*standaardarresten*), contribute to the interpretation of law, concretize its application (especially in relation to open norms), and fill the gaps in regulation. The *Hoge Raad* often reasons in terms of criteria or factors that should be taken into account in the application of a legal rule to concrete factual situations.[197] Case law of the *Hoge Raad* only rarely contradicts statutory law,[198] though the *Hoge Raad* may set aside statutory provisions in exceptional cases based on the limiting function of reasonableness and fairness.[199] The standard cases are often referred to as a source of authority both by scholars and courts, although critiques are not infrequent. As to the style of writing, the

197 Asser/Hartkamp and Sieburgh 2014, para 391–435.

198 One of the rare exceptions is a 1972 case where the *Hoge Raad* stated that two old articles of the Commercial Code no longer had the force of law. See Hartkamp 2011, at 27 referring to HR 3 March 1972, ECLI:NL:HR:1972:AB3597, *NJ* 1972, 339 Maring.

199 By way of example, see HR 28 April 2000, ECLI:NL:HR:2000:AA5634, *NJ* 2000, 431 Asbest-arrest.

Hoge Raad usually avoids extensive citing of the documents and evidence in the case. Case law is easily accessible: important cases decided by the *Hoge Raad* and lower courts are published and available online.[200]

Finally, the works of scholars are inherent to understanding Dutch law. This source of knowledge has a secondary authority compared to statutes and case law, but will not be disregarded in this Chapter. Literature will be referred to for explanation, interpretation of case law, and highlighting scholarly opinions.

3.2.2. Translation of terms

Most of the examined sources are in Dutch so it appears appropriate to clarify the main choices made in translating Dutch terms into English. The translation of key concepts is based firstly on the Dutch texts translated into English, for instance, the Dutch Civil code,[201] and secondly on the existing comparative literature.[202] The translated terms which are frequently used include reasonableness and fairness (*redelijkheid en billijkheid*)[203] and justified interests (*gerechtvaardigde belangen*).[204] The Chapter also refers to the concept of the reasonable belief that the negotiated contract will be concluded (*gerechtvaardigd vertrouwen dat de overeenkomst tot stand zou komen*).[205] In scholarship, this term has also been translated as justified detrimental reliance on the imminent conclusion of the negotiated contract.[206] Finally, the terms unacceptable[207] and inadmissible[208] translate the Dutch terms *onaanvaardbaar, ongeoorloofd*. The term *voorovereenkomst* has been translated as pre-contract or contract to negotiate, and *rompovereenkomst* is referred to as a trunk contract.[209]

3.3. Negotiations as an invisible magnetic field

Freedom of contract is the starting point in the regulation of negotiations in Dutch law.[210] Although it is not directly established by the Dutch Civil code, a number of its provision provide freedom of contract indirectly.[211] Dutch scholarship refers in this regard to the positive and negative aspects of the freedom of contract. On the positive

200 The most accessible open source is www.rechtspraak.nl. All important cases are published, although the site publishes only around 1 per cent of the total existing cases.
201 The main reference is Warendorf/Thomas/Curry-Sumner 2013.
202 The main reference is Cartwright/Hesselink 2008, especially at 46–50.
203 Warendorf/Thomas/Curry-Sumner 2013, inter alia at 719.
204 Cartwright/Hesselink 2008, at 47.
205 Ibid.
206 Cartwright/Hesselink 2008, at 50.
207 Warendorf/Thomas/Curry-Sumner 2013, at 665, see translation of Article 6:109 Dutch Civil code.
208 Cartwright/Hesselink 2008, at 48. These authors also use 'no longer allowed' and 'unlawful'.
209 Grosheide 2004.
210 See inter alia HR 12 August 2005, ECLI:NL:HR:2005:AT7337, *NJ* 2005, 467 CBB/JPO.
211 Asser/Hartkamp and Sieburgh 6-III 2014, para 41; para 50 points to Articles 1:121, 6:248 (1), and 3:40 Dutch Civil code.

side is the possibility to choose the party with whom to contract, to decide to enter into a contract, and to define its content. The negative side includes the possibility to freely withdraw from negotiations without incurring liability.[212]

However, the principle has a number of limitations; these are to be found both in the Dutch Civil code and in case law. In essence, these limitations come down to the following. Each party negotiating a contract must take into account the other party's justified interests. This implies that each party is free to break off negotiations, *unless* this would be inadmissible/not allowed because the other party has justified detrimental reliance on the imminent conclusion of the negotiated contract or because of other circumstances of the case.

The impact of these limitations on the parties' legal relationship has been compared to an invisible magnetic field:[213] the further the negotiations advance, the closer the scrutiny used by the courts to ascertain the parties' conduct. At the same time, the way in which the required advancement of negotiations is established remains a complex issue for the courts and scholars. As guidance on this, the *Hoge Raad* has developed a set of factors to measure the advancement of negotiations and to define whether breaking off negotiations is acceptable from the point of view of reasonableness and fairness. This Section will elaborate further on freedom of negotiations, the content of these restrictions, and the application of the factors named by the *Hoge Raad*.

3.3.1. Freedom of negotiations

Freedom of negotiations flows from the fundamental principle of freedom of contract in Dutch law. The *Hoge Raad* has emphasized the primary role of freedom of contract in the regulation of the negotiation process by stating that liability for breaking off negotiations is a severe measure to be applied exceptionally (*een strenge en tot terughoudendheid nopende maatstaf*).[214] According to the literature, this emphasis implies a high threshold for restricting the freedom to break off negotiations. Furthermore, if such liability is admitted, the court must thoroughly set out the motivation for its decision.[215]

3.3.2. Limitations of freedom of negotiations and factors to balance

Limitations to the principle of freedom of negotiations in Dutch law have developed in a somewhat eclectic way. This development has followed a path from an almost absolute freedom of negotiations towards restrictions that were broadly interpreted. Subsequently,

212 HR 23 October 1987, ECLI:NL:HR:1987:AD0018, *NJ* 1988, 1017 VSH/Shell; HR 12 August 2005, ECLI:NL:HR:2005:AT7337, *NJ* 2005, 467 CBB/JPO. See inter alia Hijma 2013, §14; Blei Weissmann 2013, §1.31 with further references.

213 Nieuwenhuis 2010, at 289.

214 HR 12 August 2005, ECLI:NL:HR:2005:AT7337, *NJ* 2005, 467 CBB/JPO.

215 Blei Weissmann 2013, §1.43.

the emphasis has returned to the freedom of negotiations and the exceptional character of any limitations.

More concretely, until 1957, the only regulation of contractual negotiations was a general unwritten duty of care in tort.[216] A shift in the approach has been marked by the case Baris/Riezenkamp (1957).[217] By stating that negotiations are subject to the general duty of *bona fides*, the *Hoge Raad* has opened the gates to a broad interpretation of the practical implications of this duty.

The broadest interpretation was made in the case Plas/Valburg (1982).[218] In this case, the *Hoge Raad* analysed negotiations as a process in three stages, progressively limiting the freedom to walk away from the transaction.[219] This approach was immediately criticized for its linear character and the vague criteria used to distinguish the stages. More recent commentators still regard this critique as valid.[220] Significantly, the Plas/Valburg approach has also led to suggestions that negotiating parties may and should avoid legal uncertainty by creating preliminary agreements, because these would possibly represent private law 'safe harbours'[221] clarifying the parties' positions in negotiations.

The Dutch legislator has been sensitive to these critiques. It demonstrated a reserved approach to a proposal to regulate the process of negotiations in the Dutch Civil code[222] at the time of the reform of the Dutch law of obligations in the 1990s. It was found that

216 Article 1401 Old Dutch Civil code.

217 HR 15 November 1957, ECLI:NL:HR:1957:AG2023, NJ 1958, 67 Baris/Riezenkamp.

218 HR 18 June 1982, ECLI:NL:HR:1982:AG4405, *NJ* 1983, 723 Plas/Valburg.

219 According to Plas/Valburg, during the first stage, freedom of negotiations is not limited by any legal regulation and each party may withdraw from negotiations without liability. At the second stage, the restrictions of good faith may start to play a role. Breaking negotiations off may be regarded as inadmissible and, as a consequence, a party breaking off negotiations may be held liable (the *Hoge Raad* has not concretized the scope of liability). Finally, the third stage is reached when parties are justified in expecting that a contract would imminently result from the negotiations. Good faith implies that breaking off at the third stage is unlawful (*onaanvaardbaar*). This may have two consequences. Either the breaking party is liable for the damage, including loss of profit (*gederfde winst*), or the court may order the parties to negotiate further 'in a constructive manner' (*op constructieve wijze*) to finalize negotiations.

220 See summarizing critiques: Hartlief 2005; Tjittes 2006, at 140. The three-stage approach has been criticized for its linear character. According to Plas/Valburg, the negotiation process only becomes increasingly binding with time, whereas twists and returns to previous negotiating positions are possible in practice. The later critique has also resulted in a view that parties can be easily held liable during the negotiations, leading to legal uncertainty.

221 Van Bijnen 2005, at 155 ff.

222 Article 6.5.2.8a *Ontwerp Nieuw BW.* See Reehuis/Slob 1991 1441–1443: The negotiating parties must take into account each other's justified interests in the conduct of negotiations. Each of them is free to break off negotiations, unless this would be unlawful on the basis of the justified expectation of the other party that a contract will be imminently formed or on the basis of the other circumstances of the case.
Onderhandelende partijen zijn verplicht hun gedrag mede door elkaars gerechtvaardigde belangen te laten bepalen. Ieder van hen is vrij de onderhandelingen af te breken, tenzij dit op grond van het

the time was not ripe for such express regulation. Moreover, due to the vagueness of the case law developments, the inclusion in the Dutch Civil code of an express provision on liability for breaking off negotiations was considered undesirable.[223]

In addition, the *Hoge Raad* has also limited the impact of the Plas/Valburg approach in the cases VSH/Shell,[224] CBB/JPO[225] and subsequent cases. Instead of approaching negotiations as a process in stages (as in Plas/Valburg), the case law has identified several factors that need to be taken into account to establish whether it is appropriate to limit freedom of negotiations.

3.3.2.1. Reasonableness and fairness

The main requirement in the conduct of negotiations in Dutch law is the duty of reasonableness and fairness.[226] The *Hoge Raad* stated in the case Baris/Riezenkamp (1957) that negotiations of a contract create a '*special legal relationship regulated by good faith*' ('*bijzondere door goede trouw beheerste rechtsverhouding*').[227] According to the *Hoge Raad*, this implies that the negotiating parties must take into account each other's *justified interests* starting from the first interaction.[228] On a terminological note, it is worth recalling that the reform of the Dutch law of obligations has replaced 'good faith' with the term 'reasonableness and fairness' (*redelijkheid en billijkheid*).[229] The requirement is formulated as an open norm and is applicable to all obligations as an overarching duty. It has a fundamental character in Dutch law; its application is a mandatory legal provision that may not be waived by the parties' agreement.[230]

Dutch law sets objective standards of reasonableness and fairness. This means compliance with the norm is not confined to the subjective attitude or state of mind of a party. The party's conduct should be assessed objectively by reference to the attitude that a similar party would have in similar circumstances.[231]

Reasonableness and fairness transcends the law of obligations through its three functions. Firstly, the open norm on reasonableness and fairness may be a source of positive obligations – both under a contract and extra-contractually – this is the supplementing

gerechtvaardigd vertrouwen van de wederpartij in het tot stand komen van een overeenkomst of in verband met de andere omstandigheden van het geval onaanvaardbaar zou zijn.

223 Reehuis/Slob 1991, at 1443, 1444–1448.

224 HR 23 October 1987, ECLI:NL:HR:1987:AD0018, *NJ* 1988, 1017 VSH/Shell.

225 HR 12 August 2005, ECLI:NL:HR:2005:AT7337, *NJ* 2005, 467 CBB/JPO.

226 Articles 6:2(2), 6:248(2) Dutch Civil code.

227 HR 15 November 1957, ECLI:NL:HR:1957:AG2023, NJ 1958, 67 Baris/Riezenkamp.

228 Blei Weissmann 2013, §1.32.1 and 1.28. Compare inter alia De Kluiver 1994, at 50–52 (noting that negotiations do not always imply a legal relationship).

229 Articles 6:2 and 6:248 Dutch Civil code.

230 Hijma/Olthof 2014, para 300; Hesselink 1999.

231 Hartkamp 2011, at 49.

(or the gap filling) function of this norm.[232] Secondly, it has a limiting function and precludes any conduct incompatible with the requirements of reasonableness and fairness making that conduct inadmissible/unacceptable (*onaanvaardbaar*). Any right may be exercised only to the extent that its exercise does not become inadmissible from the perspective of reasonableness and fairness. Thirdly, reasonableness and fairness is a basis for interpretation. In all the three functions, the content of reasonableness and fairness has been developed by the jurisprudence of the *Hoge Raad* and to a certain extent by lower courts.[233] The duty of reasonableness and fairness has served as a basis for the development of further limitations to freedom of negotiations.

3.3.2.2. Expectation of the imminent conclusion of the negotiated contract

According to the *Hoge Raad*, breaking off negotiations is unacceptable from the point of view of reasonableness and fairness if *the party who claims recovery* of damage *expected that negotiations would imminently result in conclusion of the contract.*[234] This statement has two elements. Firstly, it is not the expectations of both parties that are relevant. The only relevant expectation is that of the party claiming to have suffered detriment from the other party's withdrawal from the negotiations. Second, not every kind of expectation is relevant. The expectation should be related to the formation of *the* negotiated contract (by contrast with the expectation of *a* contract referred to in the abandoned approach of the Plas/Valburg case). In this way, the future transaction should be either clearly defined or easily definable at the moment of the failure of negotiations.[235] As was explained in the case ABB/Staat,[236] the length of negotiations does not automatically result in an increase of expectation. The advancement of negotiations in substance – not in time – is relevant for the assessment of reliance and expectation.

To assess the extent of expectation in concrete cases, the *Hoge Raad* has suggested addressing the following factors: firstly, the extent of the parties' *agreement about the manner in which to deal with points that remain to be negotiated*;[237] secondly, the extent of the parties' *agreement on the substantive points of the eventual final contract.*

The following examples illustrate the application of these factors. Absence of reliance (according to the court) is illustrated by the case Shell/Van Esta Tjallingii.[238] The parties negotiated a lease contract, and the negotiations failed. At the moment when negotiations failed, the parties still needed to negotiate three important conditions of the future lease,

232 Hartkamp 2011, at 50.
233 Hartkamp 2011, at 47.
234 HR 23 October 1987, ECLI:NL:HR:1987:AD0018, *NJ* 1988, 1017 VSH/Shell. Notably, the factors assess not the reliance that negotiations *have* already resulted in a concluded contract, but the expectation that they *would* result in the future. See Tjittes 2006, at 140.
235 Tjittes 2006, at 140.
236 HR 4 October 1996, ECLI:NL:HR:1996:ZC2158, *NJ* 1997, 65 ABB/Staat.
237 HR 1 June 2012, ECLI:NL:HR:2012:BV1748, *NJ* 2012/471 Almere/Weermekers.
238 HR 16 June 1995, ECLI:NL:HR:1995:ZC1760, *NJ* 1995, 705 Shell/Van Esta Tjallingii.

including the yearly price indexation. The way to establish these conditions was neither defined nor negotiated.[239] In this situation, no reliance could arise according to the *Hoge Raad*. In another case, parties negotiated a project for the construction of a World Trade Centre in Nice, France. The parties signed a partnership agreement (*convention de partenariat*) sketching in a general manner the project of the future construction and the way in which to conclude the construction contract. One party broke off negotiations. The other party claimed recovery of damage under liability for breaking off negotiations. The court had to analyse the circumstances in which negotiations were broken off. The analysis included the assessment of the binding power of the partnership agreement and its practical impact. The court concluded that no substantive points were agreed in relation to furthering the project at the moment of failure of negotiations. Consequently, no justified reliance was created by the preliminary agreement at hand.[240] In another example, parties negotiated the acquisition of a company. The company operated a brasserie at rented premises. When the negotiations were broken off, the parties had not yet reached agreement on the amount to be paid in rent for the premises, nor had they defined the date of the company acquisition. These two circumstances were decisive in the court's conclusion that no reliance on the imminent conclusion of the contract could have been created at that time.[241]

Note that the presence of *documents purporting to organize negotiations contractually* has been regarded as a fact contributing to the creation of reliance that the negotiated contract will imminently be formed. For instance, in Greenib Car/Van Dam the *Hoge Raad* took into account a detailed letter of intent purporting to describe the manner in which further negotiations would be conducted.[242] In another case, parties entered into an agreement to prepare the future eventual acquisition of a company. This agreement established three preparatory phases preceding the final contract. In the first phase, the owner of one party had to work as an employee for the other party for a maximum of one year. During this period, the parties had to decide whether they were willing to go forward with the acquisition. During the course of the first phase, the negotiations broke off. According to the court, no reliance could arise during this phase, because the very essence of the splitting into phases established by the preliminary agreement consisted in securing the possibility to break off negotiations, at least during the first phase.[243]

The case Greenib Car/Van Dam[244] cites another factor that may be relevant for the creation of reliance: the *conduct of the party breaking off negotiations in his relations with third parties as if the contract has been concluded*. In this case, Greenib and Van Dam negotiated a contract under which Van Dam would become a dealer of the cars sold by

239 Ibid.
240 HR 27 April 2007, ECLI:NL:HR:2007:BA2509, *NJB* 2007, 1069.
241 Rb. Noord-Holland 4 June 2014, ECLI:NL:RBNHO:2014:7141, nº 2730042 / CV EXPL 14–897.
242 HR 1 March 2013, ECLI:NL:HR:2013:BY6755, *NJ* 2013/142 Greenib Car/Van Dam.
243 Hof Amsterdam 30 August 2007, ECLI:NL:GHAMS:2007:BC6965, *NJF* 2008, 121 referred to as a standard case, despite not being decided by the *Hoge Raad*.
244 HR 1 March 2013, ECLI:NL:HR:2013:BY6755, *NJ* 2013/142 Greenib Car/Van Dam.

Greenib. The negotiations were accompanied by signing a letter of intent. Though the document was detailed, it was not the final negotiated contract. Nevertheless, Greenib introduced Van Dam as its dealer to third parties. This was noted by the court as susceptible to generating reliance by Van Dam that the contract would be formed imminently.

Further detail on the assessment of reliance has been given by the case CBB/JPO.[245] The *Hoge Raad* has stated that even if one party expects the negotiated contract to be imminently formed, negotiations may be broken off without liability. This is because, according to the *Hoge Raad, the measure and manner in which the party breaking off negotiations has contributed to the creation* of this expectation should also be taken into account when imposing liability. In this way, the provenance of and grounds for reliance may play a role in establishing liability. Reliance caused by facts external to the party breaking off negotiations may not lead to liability. By contrast, *inducing* reliance during negotiations may have legal consequences for the inducing party, if this party subsequently withdraws from negotiations.

3.3.2.3. Justified interest of the party breaking off negotiations

In the case De Ruiterij/MBO (1996),[246] the *Hoge Raad* stated that the *justified interests (gerechtvaardigde belangen) of the party breaking off negotiations* should also be taken into account when deciding on liability. According to the *Hoge Raad*, breaking off negotiations may become lawful (and thus not entail liability) if it is justified by the interest of the party breaking off negotiations. For instance, the fact that it is impractical or very difficult for a party to continue negotiations may justify withdrawal from negotiations without liability.[247] Withdrawal may also be justified if the other negotiating party has an inflexible and unreasonable attitude.[248]

According to the *Hoge Raad, changes in circumstances* may affect the parties' justifiable interests during the negotiations.[249] The justified interest of the party breaking off negotiations should be assessed at the moment of breaking off. In this way, the criterion enables changes in the parties' positions and attitudes to be taken into account. In this light, unexpected circumstances may play an important a role. Notably, the *Hoge Raad* does not mean drastic changes in the parties' positions. The literature underlines the difference between this approach and the provision on *force majeure* of Article 6:258 Dutch Civil code.[250] For example, in the case De Ruiterij/MBO, a general worsening of the economic situation in the hotels market was regarded by the *Hoge Raad* as a

245 HR 12 August 2005, ECLI:NL:HR:2005:AT7337, *NJ* 2005, 467 CBB/JPO (where the *Hoge Raad* stressed that liability for breaking off negotiations is a severe measure to be applied exceptionally).

246 HR 14 June 1996, ECLI:NL:HR:1996:ZC2105, *NJ* 1997, 481 De Ruiterij/MBO.

247 De Kluiver 1992, at 239; Hesselink 1992.

248 HR 26 February 1993, ECLI:NL:HR:1993:ZC0890, *NJ* 1993, 289 AFF/Mc Donald's.

249 De Kluiver 1992, at 239.

250 Tjittes 2006, at 141.

circumstance that may considerably change the justified interest of the party breaking off negotiations.[251] By contrast, changes in the internal policy of the party breaking off negotiations are not regarded as a good reason to break off negotiations.[252]

3.4. Contract to negotiate

The process of negotiations and formation of a contract may be regulated by binding contractual obligations.[253] The possibility to create such obligations is provided primarily by the principle of freedom of contract. Next to this, Dutch law acknowledges the framework of various types of contracts to negotiate (or *pacta in contrahendo*).[254] According to the academic literature, this framework allows the creation of stand-alone obligations which bind the parties contractually, but which are independent of the final contract. These obligations may be limited to the regulation of the process of negotiation and bind the parties irrespectively of success or failure in concluding the final contract.[255]

This Section aims to show how the conceptual framework of contracts to negotiate in Dutch law enables contractual organization of the negotiation process. In essence, contractual framing of negotiations influences the nature of eventual liability. In the presence of a contract to negotiate, liability is in most cases based on the breach of a contractual obligation.[256]

3.4.1. Gradual formation of contract

Dutch law is said to enable the gradual formation of a contract:[257] the growth of contractual consensus can be found not only in the exchange of offer and acceptance, but also in exchanges lacking a straightforward sequence of offer and acceptance.[258] This reaching of a consensus may be qualified either as a concluded final contract or as the coming about of *some* contractual obligations.

Practically, the possibility of finding some contractual obligations leads to three ways to interpret the facts. First, the court may find that a final contract is formed. Second, the court may conclude that the parties have reached sufficient agreement on several points to be bound by a trunk contract (*rompovereenkomst*).[259] The literature defines trunk contract as

251 HR 14 June 1996, ECLI:NL:HR:1996:ZC2105, *NJ* 1997, 481 De Ruiterij/MBO.

252 Hof 's-Gravenhage 16 October 2002, ECLI:NL:GHSGR:2002:AJ3708, *PRG* 2003, 6076.

253 Asser/Hartkamp and Sieburgh 6-III 2014, para 201; Hijma 2013, at 78; Hartkamp 2005 para 361a section IV. See also Snijders 2015.

254 Hartkamp 2011, at 62.

255 Van den Berg 1990, para 387 ff.; De Kluiver 1992, at 103 ff.; Van Dunné 2004, at 237–239; Van Bijnen 2005, at 338–339; Wessels 2010; Blei Weissmann 2013, §1.13.

256 Blei Weissmann 2013, §1.35.1–2 and 1.34.1–6.

257 Hartkamp 2011, para 63 ff.; Van Dunné 2004, at 232 ff.

258 Blei Weissmann 2013, §1.7; Asser/Hartkamp and Sieburgh 2014, para 189.

259 The English translation of the term follows Grosheide 2004.

a contract based on the partial meeting of minds.[260] The missing terms of the trunk contract may be implied by the court or should be further defined by the parties. This option is close to finding a final contract. The third option provides the main point for consideration in this Section. The court can find that the parties have reached some agreement regarding merely the process of negotiations and in this way a preliminary agreement has come about.[261] A preliminary agreement may contain obligations binding the parties during the negotiations irrespectively of the success or failure of the formation of the final contract. The choice of interpretation is to a large extent decided on a case-by-case basis by the court.

These three interpretations show that the framework of contract law is broader than the rules applicable solely to preliminary agreements (as contrasted with the final contract). The literature usually addresses these rules alongside the offer and acceptance doctrine.[262]

Furthermore, no clear-cut or unanimously accepted rule enables a distinction between the types of preliminary agreements included in the third option. This Section will focus on the criteria applied to define the type of preliminary agreement in place. These criteria have essentially been developed in the case law. They are applied not only to ascertain the final contract, but also to search for a preliminary agreement and in order to differentiate between various types of preliminary agreements.

3.4.2. *Types of contracts to negotiate*

Dutch scholars and case law draw a distinction between the main contract – the final contract (*hoofdovereenkomst*) – on the one hand, and the agreements leading to its formation – preliminary agreements – on the other. However, no unanimously accepted classification of the types of preliminary agreements exists. The following terms are frequently used: agreements to conclude a contract (*afspraken tot het sluiten van een overeenkomst*), agreements helping in conclusion of a contract (*hulpovereenkomst*),[263] preparatory agreements (*voorbereidingsovereenkomst*).[264] All of these cover only the process of formation, and prepare the path for the eventual final contract. This provision regulates the formal validity of preliminary agreements. It states that the validity of a preliminary agreement is subject to the same requirements of form as are established for the final contract.[265] Next to this, the term agreements about the process (*procedurele*

260 Blei Weissmann 2013, §2.6. See also Schoordijk 1984, at 40–51, 92–102, 106; De Kluiver 1992, at 110–114; Van Bijnen 2005, at 335–345; Smits 2003, para 26; Van Dunné 2004, at 235 ff. and 260–264; Hartkamp 2005, para 361a; Wessels 2010, para 1.4.2; Asser/Hartkamp and Sieburgh 6-III 2014, para 92, 94, 96–97; 190–206; 283–287.

261 De Kluiver 1992, at 103 ff.; Blei Weissmann 2013, §1.34; Asser/Hartkamp and Sieburgh 6-III 2014, para 92.

262 See for instance Blei Weissmann 2013; Asser/Hartkamp and Sieburgh 2014, para 106.

263 Asser/Hartkamp and Sieburgh 2014, para 92. See also De Kluiver 1992, at 103 ff.; Blei Weissmann 2013, §1.34.

264 Schut 1986, at 9 and 73, Schoordijk 1999, at 7; Blei Weissmann 2013, §1.19.

265 This provision has solved the question of the formal validity of the preliminary agreement that raised several debates in the literature.

afspraken) has been used. This term emphasizes the document's focus on the process of negotiations in contrast to the substance of the final contract.[266] Furthermore, the terms letter of intent and memorandum of understanding are also well known in the Dutch literature, case law, and practice.[267] The term agreement on the intention (*intentieovereenkomst*) is also used. It underlines the contractual nature of the document.[268]

As noted earlier, the rules applicable to preliminary agreements have been developed primarily in case law. The only term mentioned in the Dutch Civil code is the term pre-contract (*voorovereenkomst*).[269] Article 6:226 of the Dutch Civil code referring to this term indirectly confirms the existence of the framework of contracts to negotiate.

3.4.3. Criteria of distinction

How is the distinction made in Dutch law between the final contract and preliminary agreement and between different types of preliminary agreements? The criteria for this distinction have been formulated by the *Hoge Raad* in the case Polak/Zwolsman.[270] It names a number of issues to be addressed in order to establish whether parties have reached agreement sufficient to be bound by a contract. These are formulated primarily to assess the formation of the final contract. However, the *Hoge Raad* has stated in a later case, Groeneveld/Hadegro,[271] that the same test should be applied to assess whether parties have come to a preliminary agreement, because according to the *Hoge Raad*, agreement on some points in negotiations can lead to the formation of the final contract, but can also lead to the formation of a preliminary agreement.

In the light of the Polak/Zwolsman criteria, trunk contracts are more easily found in negotiations where the parties have reached agreement on the most important – essential – points of the final contract. However, the question as to which points are regarded as essential has not received a clear-cut answer. For example, agreement on price is not regarded as an essential condition of a contract generally, but agreement on the price may be crucial for the formation of sales contract.[272]

According to Dutch scholars and courts, distilling the essential terms is especially difficult in the context of complex transactions.[273] On the one hand, the Dutch Civil

266 Van Dunné 2004, at 237–238; Smits 2006, at 50.

267 Wessels 2010 with further references.

268 See for example HR 1 June 2012, ECLI:NL:HR:2012:BV1748, *NJ* 2012/471 Almere/Weermekers.

269 Article 6:226 Dutch Civil code. See also Asser/Hartkamp and Sieburgh 2014, para 92.

270 HR 14 June 1968, ECLI:NL:HR:1968:AC3608, *NJ* 1968, 331 Polak/Zwolsman.

271 HR 17 December 1999, ECLI:NL:HR:1999:AA3883, *NJ* 2000, 184 Groeneveld/Hadegro.

272 Article 7:4 Dutch Civil code; Blei Weissmann 2013, §2.32.1; Asser/Hartkamp and Sieburgh 6-III 2014, para 95–97.

273 De Kluiver 1992, at 2–7 and 10–11; Van Dunné 2004, at 237–239; Van Bijnen 2005, at 336–337; Ruygvoorn 2009, at 34–35; Wessels 2010, at 20; Blei Weissmann 2013, §2.4; Asser/Hartkamp and Sieburgh 6-III 2014, para 96.

code presumes that no contract is entirely complete. In this way, parties do not have to reach agreement on all the elements of the contract for the final contract to be formed, because the law can supply the rules on the points not detailed by the parties.[274] On the other hand, the greater the complexity of the transaction, the more difficult is the application of the Dutch Civil code to flesh out the rules for a concrete situation.

The main criterion is the following: the *intentions* (*bedoelingen*) of the parties, as these can be defined on the basis of the points agreed; the issues that still have to be agreed; and the plans to negotiate further. In Groeneveld/Hadegro, the *Hoge Raad* stated that the interpretation of the parties' intentions should include the assessment of the parties' *conduct* and the *justified reliance on the imminent formation of the contract*. Furthermore, *customs* and *habits* characteristic to the relevant sector should also be taken into account. *Other circumstances of the case* are also relevant.[275] This points to an assessment of the entire context of the case. Generally, the parties' interactions are interpreted on the basis of their intentions, law and reasonableness and fairness.[276] In practice, the courts' reasoning remains highly facts specific. The interpretation of written documents is guided by another standard case – Haviltex.[277] In that case, the *Hoge Raad* explained that the interpretation of the language used by the parties cannot simply follow the literal meaning of the text. Instead, the meaning should be interpreted in the context of all the circumstances of the case. The meaning that the parties would reasonably attribute to the text within all the circumstances of the case should guide the interpretation. This approach balances the search for the parties' subjective understanding of the document with the objective criteria of reference.[278] According to the *Hoge Raad*, the higher the sophistication of the contracting parties, the lower the relevance of the Haviltex guidelines. More concretely, their relevance decreases according to the extent to which the document at hand is made by professional parties involved in commercial contracting. There, the direct literal interpretation of the language can constitute the primary factor.[279]

3.5. Tort law: misuse of information received in negotiations

The field of tort law comes into play directly when conduct during negotiations (by contrast to breaking off) is qualified as tort. The discussion of such conduct is to be found in Dutch scholarship,[280] while case law offers few concrete examples of such conduct.

274 Article 6:248(1) Dutch Civil code. Further basis for this approach in the Dutch Civil code is provided by Articles 7:4, 7:405(2), 7:601(2), 6:248(1). This basis is discussed in HR 6 June 1997, ECLI:NL:HR:1997:AG7242, *NJ* 1998, 723 AZG/Het Noorden.

275 HR 17 December 1999, ECLI:NL:HR:1999:AA3883, NJ 2000, 184 Groeneveld/Hadegro.

276 See also Article 6:248 Dutch Civil code; HR 26 September 2003, ECLI:NL:HR:2003:AF9414, *NJ* 2004, 460 Regiopolitie Gelderland-Zuid/Hovax.

277 HR 13 March 1981, ECLI:NL:HR:1981:AG4158, *NJ* 1981, 635 Ermes c.s./Haviltex.

278 Asser/Hartkamp and Sieburgh 2014, para 372.

279 HR 5 April 2013, ECLI:NL:HR:2013:BY8101, *NJ* 2013, 214 Lundiform/Mexx (the case related to the interpretation of an 'entire agreement clause').

280 Van Schilfgaarde 1983; Castermans 1994; Nieuwenhuis 2010.

The current case law approach can be found in one line of cases, all of which emanate from lower courts and fail to have the persuasive authority of the *Hoge Raad*'s case law.[281] These cases deal with the misuse of information obtained in negotiations. On the facts of the most recent case in this line,[282] during the preparations for the finals of the 2000 UEFA European Football Championship, Feijenoord stadium negotiated a project with Varel, a producer of security equipment, to install video surveillance. In the course of negotiations, Varel made a detailed offer with the characteristics of the system required to satisfy Feijenoord's needs, including the recommendations of the police. The offer specifically mentioned that its content was confidential. The negotiations failed, and shortly after the failure of negotiations, the stadium passed on the content of the offer to Siemens, Varel's competitor in the market for video surveillance systems. According to Feijenoord, this was done to avoid restarting the entire project from the beginning. Siemens took note of the competitor's offer and made a competitive proposal to Feijenoord. The stadium concluded a contract with Siemens. Varel sued Feijenoord claiming damages for breaking off negotiations contrary to the requirement of reasonableness and fairness.

The case involved the issues of confidentiality and reasonableness and fairness, as well as liability for breaking off negotiations. However, the court's reasoning contains no mention of the limitations to the freedom of negotiations, nor of factors to test whether breaking off negotiations was unacceptable from the point of view of reasonableness and fairness. An express statement in the offer that it was of a confidential nature was not qualified as a contractual obligation of confidentiality. Instead, the court qualified as tortious the manner in which the Varel offer was set aside. It granted recovery of the positive contractual interest (*positief contractsbelang*), i.e. the amount of profit that Varel would have gained from the contract with the stadium, as calculated by Varel.[283] As has been noted above, this case merely illustrates the potential application of general tort law to misconduct in negotiations, while it is not possible to regard this application as developed in Dutch law.

3.6. The limited role of unjust enrichment

According to the *Hoge Raad*, the doctrine of unjust enrichment does not apply to negotiations and formation of contract.[284] This position has been criticized by the majority of Dutch scholars. Specifically, they have argued that the doctrine of unjust enrichment (*ongerechtvaardigde verrijking*) represents a possible basis for a claim of restitution of

281 Hof 's-Gravenhage 16 October 2002, ECLI:NL:GHSGR:2002:AJ3708, *PRG* 2003, 6076; Hof 's-Gravenhage 29 January 2003, ECLI:NL:GHSGR:2003:AO1837, *PRG* 2004, 6139; Hof 's-Gravenhage 28 January 2004, ECLI:NL:GHSGR:2004:AO7536, *PRG* 2004, 6182.

282 Hof 's-Gravenhage 28 January 2004, ECLI:NL:GHSGR:2004:AO7536, *PRG* 2004, 6182; Blei Weissmann §1.18.2.

283 In the two other cases, recovery of a positive contractual interest was not admitted.

284 HR 18 April 1969, ECLI:NL:HR:1969:AC4925, *NJ* 1969, 336 Katwijk/Westdijk. Subsequent case law demonstrates no change in the *Hoge Raad*'s position.

benefit transferred during negotiations. For instance, scholars note that the position of the *Hoge Raad* was voiced before the reform of the Dutch Civil code. They submit that under current Dutch law, unjust enrichment provides an appropriate basis to claim performance made in anticipation of a contract. Articles 6:203 and 6:212 of the Dutch Civil code are referred to as a basis for this claim.[285] This field of law is said to offer, along with tort law, an appropriate way to recover the damage, if the rules on contract or on the liability for breaking off negotiations offer no adequate recovery. This theoretical possibility is also underlined by the fact that the claim under the doctrine of unjust enrichment in Dutch law is not subsidiary to claims in tort or contract.[286] The *Hoge Raad* approach may evolve in this direction in the future, but no changes have taken place so far.

3.7. Dynamics of negotiations addressed in case law

The framework of preliminary agreements enables the parties to create stand-alone obligations which are binding *before* the formation of the final contract and *irrespectively* of the success or failure of the negotiations.[287] This Section will elaborate on such obligations discussed in the Dutch case law and literature.

Prior to this, an important peculiarity of the Dutch law is worth noting, because it is relevant for any attempt to regulate negotiations contractually. In the Dutch legal system, contractual regulation of negotiations is always subject to the test of reasonableness and fairness. As a consequence, the court may qualify a preliminary arrangement, some of its provisions, or the mere conduct of one or both parties as contrary to reasonableness and fairness. The court may then declare obligations contained in the preliminary agreement invalid, and mandatory rules on the liability for breaking off negotiations would be applicable instead.[288] As will be explained below, the reasonableness and fairness test has been especially relevant in cases concerning the parties' attempts to contractually postpone the moment at which the final contract should be regarded as formed, to explicitly qualify negotiations as non-binding, and to limit liability for breaking off negotiations or to establish the distribution of costs in the event that negotiations are broken off.

3.7.1. Agreement to negotiate

The *Hoge Raad* has confirmed the possibility of creating a binding obligation to negotiate before the final contract is formed. This was clearly admitted in the case Huurdersvereniging Koot BV/ Handelsonderneming Koot BV.[289]

285 Blei Weissmann 2013, §1.101 and ff.; Asser/Hartkamp and Sieburgh 6-III 2014, para 201; Hijma 2012, at 73; Ruygvoorn 2009, at 116; De Kluiver 1992, 275; Smits 2003, at 48–49; Van Dunné 2004, at 285; Hartkamp 2005, nr. 361a; Hartlief 2005.

286 Hartkamp 2011, at 244.

287 Blei Weissmann 2013, §1.13 and 1.34.6.1.

288 Blei Weissmann 2013, §1.51.

289 HR 11 March 1983, ECLI:NL:HR:1983:AG4551, *NJ* 1983, 585 Huurdersvereniging Koot BV/ Handelsonderneming Koot BV; see also Asser/Hartkamp and Sieburgh 6-III 2014, para 195; Blei

According to the *Hoge Raad*, the content of the obligation to negotiate is defined primarily based on the interpretation of the preliminary agreement at hand.[290] If the preliminary agreement specifies the parties' conduct, the court should follow the elaboration made by the parties. In the same way, if a remedy of specific performance is awarded, the content of the order to negotiate should also primarily rely on the parties' own planned shaping of the final contract. By contrast, if the preliminary agreement is silent on this, the content of this obligation comes down to the general duty of reasonableness and fairness: parties must negotiate in a constructive manner (*op constructieve wijze*) to finalize negotiations.

Dutch case law characterizes the obligation to negotiate as an obligation to use all possible and available means (*inspanningsverplichting*): an obligation to negotiate under Dutch law is not an undertaking to reach the result (*resultaatsverplichting*), e.g. to conclude the final contract.[291]

Scholars have also discussed the situation where, in the presence of an obligation to negotiate, negotiations fail and a third party is somehow involved in the failure of negotiations (either it is involved in parallel negotiations, or makes a better offer with or without being aware of the on-going negotiations). According to the literature, if the party that breaks off negotiations conducts parallel negotiations with a third party at the moment of breaking off negotiations, a court may order this party to make the same offer as the one negotiated with the third party, provided that negotiations were broken off in breach of the obligation to negotiate.[292] De Kluiver speaks about an obligation to give 'the last chance' to come to an agreement before negotiations are broken off.[293] The inherent difficulty in this lies in establishing what chance should be regarded as the last one in the context of breaking off negotiations. Furthermore, this suggestion appears to give rise to other questions. These relate to the position of the third party. One may consider a situation in which the last chance is given: an offer with the same content. The other party (to negotiations that are about to be broken off) agrees. The offeror cannot conclude a contract with the third party. In this case, it is unclear whether the third party may also sue for breaking off negotiations. It is unclear whether it matters which negotiations started earlier. These questions are so far left unanswered in the academic literature, but point to a very relative operability of the eventual obligation to give a 'last chance'.

Weissmann 2013, §1.63.4.1.1; see also HR 27 May 2011, ECLI:NL:HR:2011:BP8707, *RvdW* 2011/686 Hemubo Betontechniek B.V./VVE Flatgebouw Strandhotel Zandvoort.

290 HR 29 October 2010, ECLI:NL:HR:2010:BN5612, *NJB* 2010, 2051 Heijmans c.s./DLO; HR 27 May 2011, ECLI:NL:HR:2011:BP8707, *RvdW* 2011/686 Hemubo Betontechniek B.V./VVE Flatgebouw Strandhotel Zandvoort; HR 1 June 2012, ECLI:NL:HR:2012:BV1748, *NJ* 2012/471 Almere/Weermekers.

291 HR 4 October 1996, ECLI:NL:HR:1996:ZC2158, *NJ* 1997, 65 ABB/Staat.

292 Blei Weissmann 2013, §1.73.1. See also De Kluiver 1992, at 117–124; Van Dunné 2004, at 255.

293 De Kluiver 1992, at 117–124.

3.7.2. *Agreement to negotiate in good faith*

It will not come as a surprise that a contractual obligation to negotiate in good faith is binding under Dutch law. The content of this obligation refers to the limitations imposed by reasonableness and fairness discussed earlier (in Section 3.3 and the previous Section on agreement to negotiate). From this perspective, this obligation mainly reiterates the requirement to comply with the requirements of reasonableness and fairness.

The difference that a contractual obligation can make to the general requirement to conduct negotiations in good faith can lie in the detail of the content of the obligation. Such a clause may provide concretization and guidance on what is expected from the parties. In this way, it may guide the court on its interpretation of the facts of the case. Furthermore, due to a contractualized duty of good faith the regime under which liability is imposed may shift to contractual.[294]

3.7.3. *Provision on the non-binding character of negotiations*

3.7.3.1. Subject to contract provisions

A tentative submission has been made in the literature that a provision expressly placing negotiations outside the final contract may be enforceable under Dutch law. In practice, this provision is often formulated as stating that negotiations are 'subject to contract'.[295] This means that negotiations are non-binding until the final contract is concluded or until it is concluded in a specific form. At the same time, scholars have pointed to a number of limitations on the possibility of making negotiations non-binding until the final contract comes about in an express manner.

The submission on the validity of a 'subject to contract' clause in Dutch law is based on both the reasoning of the *Hoge Raad* and the lower courts. The case Van Engen/Mirror Group[296] offers an example where such a clause has been upheld by the *Hoge Raad* in the way it was drafted, e.g. keeping negotiations non-binding. In this case, a Dutch company, Van Engen, and an English company, Mirror, negotiated a project relating to the possible production of a new newspaper. The parties signed a letter of intent. This document expressly stated that the parties' negotiations would become binding only when and if the final contract was signed. Moreover, the decision on the conclusion of the final contract depended on the results of a feasibility study. The letter of intent drafted in English stated as follows: 'All matters will be dealt with expressly in a binding agreement to be signed by all parties after the result of the feasibility study have become known'. Mirror broke off

294 Blei Weissmann 2013, §1.34.1–6 and 1.35.1–2.

295 Van Hooijdonk/Tjittes 2009, at 71 ff.; Wessels 2010, para 3.2–3.3. On these clauses see also De Kluiver 1992, at 15–24 ff.; De Kluiver/Schwarz 1998, at 103–108; Van Bijnen 2005, at 335–343; Van Dunné 2007, at 276 ff.; Ruygvoorn 2009, at 157–241; Wessels 2009a, at 260–262.

296 HR 24 November 1995, ECLI:NL:HR:1995:ZC1890, *NJ* 1996, 162 Van Engen/Mirror Group.

negotiations. Van Engen claimed recovery of damage resulting from the breaking off of negotiations by Mirror. When the *Hoge Raad* had to decide on the issue, it drew attention to the provision of the letter of intent quoted above. According to the *Hoge Raad*, this clause clearly pointed to the possibility reserved by Mirror to withdraw from negotiations. It confirmed that Mirror could lawfully break off negotiations without liability.

According to Wessels, the case Van Engen/Mirror Group indirectly confirms that an express provision on the non-binding character of negotiations excludes the application of the rules on liability for breaking off negotiations.[297]

In another case, a court upheld as enforceable a provision in a preliminary agreement precluding the formation of the final contract.[298] In that case, parties negotiated the purchase of twenty-five aeroplanes. They signed a letter of intent on some modalities of the further negotiations and some details of the future purchase. However, the negotiations failed, and one party claimed that the purchase agreement was formed. The court drew attention to the text of the letter of intent. Firstly, it noted that the parties had clearly drawn a distinction between the 'definitive contract' and the letter of intent. Secondly, the court took into account the complexity of the transaction. According to the court, the nature of the purchase contract is that the final contract could, in principle, come into existence even without negotiations, or, as it could happen in that case, without further negotiations being necessary. However, important details of the transaction at hand were clearly lacking. For instance, the parties had not yet negotiated the terms of the maintenance and repairs of the planes, the guarantee customarily accompanying such purchase. The preliminary agreement did not mention the outcome of negotiations on the training of the pilots, cabin staff and ground staff, while these conditions are customarily inherent to such a transaction.[299]

Similar logic was followed in another case involving negotiations concerning the sale of shares in the company which owned a historical steam ship 'SS Rotterdam'. The negotiating parties signed a preliminary document called 'Process Letter Project SS Rotterdam'. This document emphasized the parties' right to withdraw from negotiations at any time at no cost to either party'.[300] Subsequently, the negotiations were broken off. The potential buyer succeeded in his request for a court injunction on the sale of shares to third parties. In this dispute, a concrete third party was identified, as it was clear on the facts of the case which company the owner of the ship appeared to be willing to sell the ship to. However, the injunction was not upheld on appeal, because of the reservation made in the 'Process Letter Project SS Rotterdam' and the right to withdraw from negotiations flowing from the reservation. The conclusion was that the parties were only in an early stage of negotiations.[301]

297 Wessels 2010, at 43; in the same sense see Van Hooijdonk/Tjittes 2009, at 71 ff.

298 Rb. Midden-Nederland 2 October 2013, ECLI:NL:RBMNE:2013:3861, *NJF* 2013/494.

299 Ibid, at 4.4 and 4.5.

300 Hof Den Haag 7 May 2013, ECLI:NL:GHDHA:2013:BZ9634, *NJF* 2013/241, para 3.

301 Hof Den Haag 7 May 2013, ECLI:NL:GHDHA:2013:BZ9634, *NJF* 2013/241.

It is worth noting at the same time that provisions expressly mentioning the non-binding nature of negotiations should be seen in the light of the requirement of reasonableness and fairness.[302] This sets the limits on the extent to which the parties may keep negotiations at the negotiations stage and thereby prevent their relationship from being deemed to be the final contract. Wessels has noted, for example, that a provision purporting to have such effect would be disregarded if it is entered into by a party with the sole aim of preventing negotiations with a third party.[303]

Furthermore, a court may find it appropriate to make a broader interpretation of the entire context of negotiations. As a result, it may decide that parties have waived the reservation by their conduct subsequent to the creation of a reservation in a preliminary agreement. In this way, the non-binding character of negotiations can be overruled by the parties' conduct subsequent to the moment when the parties qualified their exchanges as non-binding.[304]

3.7.3.2. Honourable pledge

Dutch law acknowledges the concept of gentleman's agreement, whereby parties attempt to keep the relationships (mentioned in the gentleman's agreement) binding in honour, but not in law.[305] Academic literature has advanced the view that it creates only a so-called 'natural' obligation[306] that the courts would not enforce if it is not performed. However, Dutch courts do not always enable parties to keep their relationships outside the law.[307] They may requalify the provisions containing an 'honourable pledge' relying on the same manner of assessment as that set out above in relation to provisions 'subject to contract'.

3.7.4. Coming about of the final contract within the discretion of one of the parties

Dutch law allows the parties to leave the formation of the final contract, as well as the withdrawal from negotiations, at the discretion of one party.[308] However, the exercise of this power is limited by a general provision of the Dutch Civil code. It states: '[i]f reasonableness and fairness so require, the condition is deemed to be fulfilled in the event that the party who had an interest in its non-fulfilment has prevented its fulfilment'.[309] This means that a court in a given situation will address all the

302 Wessels 2010, at 44.
303 Ibid.
304 De Kluiver 1992, at 16; Van Bijnen 2005, at 340–343; Blei Weissmann 2013, §2.47.4 with further references.
305 See Wessels 1984; Dirix 1986, at 2119 ff.; Grosheide 1998.
306 Hijma/Olthof 2014, para 19–302.
307 Den Tonkelaar 2009.
308 Wessels 2010, at 48.
309 Article 6:23(1) Dutch Civil Code.

circumstances at hand. It will decide whether the discretionary power was exercised in the manner admissible within the requirements of reasonableness and fairness.[310]

An agreement that the formation of the final contract is 'subject to board approval' is frequently made in preliminary agreements drafted in English.[311] In the Dutch legal system, such provisions are, in principle, binding and prevent the conclusion of the final contract until such approval is given.[312] The exercise of this approval is also tested by the courts in the light of the requirement of reasonableness and fairness.[313]

Furthermore, Dutch scholars have noted that the foreign inspiration for this clause raises the question of interpretation of the term 'board' under Dutch law.[314] The question is namely whether the concept corresponds to the executive (operational) direction or to the non-executive organ and no consistent interpretation has been made in case law.[315]

3.7.5. Exclusivity

Dutch courts have upheld as binding provisions to exclusively negotiate a transaction.[316] Exclusivity is one of the clear examples of a possible stand-alone obligation, independent from the actual formation of the final contract. Exclusivity may be upheld as a binding obligation even if the other provisions of the preliminary agreement are regarded as non-binding.[317]

It is worth noting that no overarching duty of exclusivity of negotiations is established by Dutch law. Positive freedom of contract implies that parties are free to negotiate the same potential contract with several potential contracting parties.

According to case law, contractual exclusivity of negotiations should be limited in time; a limitation in time can also be implied by the court.[318] For instance, in Stuyvers/Eugster,[319] an exclusivity provision was regarded as irrelevant when after four months of negotiations, parties had not made any progress in coming to an agreement. In Hemubo Betontechniek B.V./VVE Flatgebouw Strandhotel Zandvoort,[320] the court decided that

[310] Van Hooijdonk/Tjittes 2008.
[311] See on this type of clauses Wessels 2010 para 3.4; De Kluiver 1992, at 19 ff.
[312] See for a recent example Hof Amsterdam 26 April 2011, ECLI:NL:GHAMS:2011:BQ5836, LJN BQ5836.
[313] Article 6:248(2) Dutch Civil code. See for example Rb. Arnhem 03 June 2009 ECLI:NL:RBARN:2009:BI9155, LJN BI9155.
[314] Wessels 2010, para 3.4.
[315] Wessels 2010, para 3.4 discussing the case Rb. 's-Gravenhage 1 April 2009, ECLI:NL:RBSGR:2009:BI8533, *JOR* 2009, 183.
[316] De Kluiver 1992, para 113; Wessels 2009a, at 255–258; Blei Weissmann 2013, §1.17; Wessels 2010, at 35.
[317] Wessels 2010, para 2.3.
[318] HR 15 May 1981, ECLI:NL:HR:1981:AG4190 *NJ* 1982, 85 Stuyvers/Eugster; De Kluiver 1992, at 107.
[319] HR 15 May 1981, ECLI:NL:HR:1981:AG4190 *NJ* 1982, 85 Stuyvers/Eugster.
[320] HR 27 May 2011, ECLI:NL:HR:2011:BP8707, *RvdW* 2011/686 Hemubo Betontechniek B.V./VVE Flatgebouw Strandhotel Zandvoort.

the period of exclusivity was ended when all options for further negotiations had been exhausted.

Furthermore, an obligation of exclusivity carries with it an obligation to negotiate (in contrast to an obligation to negotiate which does not imply exclusivity of negotiations).[321] The obligation to negotiate implied by exclusivity of negotiations ends with the end of the exclusivity period. For example, in Hemubo Betontechniek B.V./VVE Flatgebouw Strandhotel Zandvoort,[322] VVE and Hemubo concluded a preliminary agreement including an obligation to conduct exclusive negotiations regarding renovation works to be conducted by Hemubo. After several exchanges, VVE broke off negotiations. Hemubo submitted a claim for liability for breaking off negotiations. The court decided that VVE had made sufficient efforts to come to an agreement, but these had not been fruitful. As a consequence, at the end of the exclusively period, the parties were not bound by an obligation to negotiate and could withdraw from negotiations without liability.

3.7.6. *Confidentiality*

Another type of provision upheld as binding is the obligation on confidentiality of negotiations. This is aimed at establishing non-disclosure of the content of negotiations to third parties, or keeping secret the mere fact that negotiations are taking place.[323] Such an obligation may be upheld as binding even in an otherwise non-binding document.[324]

Dutch law establishes no overarching general duty of non-disclosure of information exchanged in negotiations.[325] Neither the duty to negotiate in good faith nor a contractual obligation to negotiate automatically implies confidentiality of negotiations.[326] Against this background, an obligation of confidentiality in one of the preliminary agreements may serve as a 'safe harbour'[327] to prevent disclosure and use of sensitive information exchanged in negotiations.

The interaction between the absence of confidentiality as a general rule and a contractual non-disclosure at the stage of negotiations is well illustrated by the following case. Parties negotiated a possible cooperation arrangement under a trade name D'Expert, but the

321 For a recent example, see Rb. Den Haag 11 March 2015, ECLI:NL:RBDHA:2015:2751, nº C-09-467930 - HA ZA 14-710. A nuanced view is offered in the literature. Van Dunné suggests, for example, that an obligation to negotiate carries an obligation to negotiate exclusively. See Van Dunné 2004, at 237. Blei Weissmann notes that exclusive negotiations can be expected from the parties when negotiations have reached a stage very close to the formation of the final contract. See Blei Weissmann 2013, §1.68.1.

322 HR 27 May 2011, ECLI:NL:HR:2011:BP8707, RvdW 2011/686 Hemubo Betontechniek B.V./VVE Flatgebouw Strandhotel Zandvoort.

323 Blei Weissmann 2013, §1.18; De Kluiver 1992, at 111–112; Wessels 2009a, at 255–258.

324 Wessels 2010, para 2.2.

325 Blei Weissmann 2013, §1.96.

326 With the exception of fiduciary and other special relations that are generally excluded from the scope of this study.

327 Van Bijnen 2005, at 155 ff.

negotiations failed. Shortly after the failure of negotiations, independently from each other the parties established companies with the name D'Expert. One of the parties claimed recovery of damage claiming that the use of the name discussed in negotiations went against reasonableness and fairness. The court decided that each party was free to use the information and ideas exchanged during the negotiations, including the use of such information for its own profit, but only *if parties have not expressly agreed on confidentiality.*[328] The court noted that the law imposes no general restriction on such use, as long as the innovative ideas are not protected by intellectual property rights.[329] This general statement may find its limitation in tort law. Specifically, misuse of information obtained and generated in negotiations may be sanctioned in tort. This is especially the case where negotiations were started only with the aim of obtaining business-sensitive information.

The question whether the obligation of confidentiality implies an obligation to negotiate (in the same manner as the agreement to negotiate discussed in Section 3.7.1 above) has not been answered in Dutch case law.

3.7.7. *Provisions on costs incurred in negotiations and liability*

To what extent may parties agree in advance on recovery in case negotiations fail?[330] Such anticipation is common in Dutch contracting practice. For example, the model teaming agreement in the construction sector (*Bouwteamovereenkomst*)[331] contains a clause on the distribution of costs in case negotiations for the formation of a construction contract fail.

This question relates to two main issues: the distribution of risks implied by the freedom of negotiations and liability. Firstly, freedom of negotiations implies that each party bears its own costs in negotiations.[332] The type of provision under discussion attempts to re-distribute the risks in contrast to this starting point. To what extent may parties contractually re-distribute risks in negotiations? In principle, parties may re-distribute costs in negotiations.[333]

328 HR 24 December 1999, ECLI:NL:HR:1999:ZC3064, *NJ* 2000, 185, emphasis added.

329 Ibid.

330 Blei Weissmann 2013, §1.14; HR 27 May 2011, ECLI:NL:HR:2011:BP8707, *RvdW* 2011/686 Hemubo Betontechniek B.V./VVE Flatgebouw Strandhotel Zandvoort. See also HR 14 June 1996, ECLI:NL:HR:1996:ZC2105, *NJ* 1997, 481 De Ruiterij/MBO; HR 4 October 1996, ECLI:NL:HR:1996:ZC2158, *NJ* 1997, 65 ABB/Staat.

331 Created in 1992 by the Dutch association of companies in the construction and infrastructure sector *'Bouwend Nederland' Vereniging met volledige rechtsbevoegdheid: Bouwend Nederland, vereniging van bedrijven in de sectoren bouw en infrastructuur.*

332 See for example HR 27 May 2011, ECLI:NL:HR:2011:BP8707, *RvdW* 2011/686 Hemubo Betontechniek B.V./VVE Flatgebouw Strandhotel Zandvoort; Blei Weissmann 2013, §1.83 with further references; Asser/Hartkamp and Sieburgh 2010, para 193.

333 Blei Weissmann 2013, §1.14.1; Van den Berg 1990, para 402; De Kluiver 1992, at 245–247; Van Bijnen 2005, at 343–345; Smits 2003, at 50; Wessels 2009a, at 245–255; Hijma 2013, at 78.

Secondly, unlawful breaking off of negotiations leads to liability. Such a clause may play a role in establishing the measure of liability. To what extent may the parties contractually set the amount of damages recoverable as liability for breaking off negotiations? In principle, most of the Dutch Civil code's provisions on the obligation to compensate loss contain rules from which parties may consensually derogate.[334] Exceptions are Article 6:109(1) on the discretion of a court to reduce a legal obligation to pay damages if this would lead to clearly unacceptable results and 6:96(4) on reasonable costs incurred in obtaining extra-judicial payment.[335] Furthermore, Article 3:40 Dutch Civil code forbids the creation of contractual obligations which are against public order and morality. In this way, liability for intentional harm cannot be limited or excluded. Furthermore, a party may be deprived of the right to rely on a right arising out of an obligation that is unacceptable according to the principles of reasonableness and fairness.[336]

In the context of disputes involving failure of negotiations, the *Hoge Raad* has specified that a provision on the distribution of costs incurred in negotiations created by a preliminary agreement does not prevent the court from granting a higher amount under the heading of liability for breaking off negotiations. The court may disregard such a provision if the requirements of reasonableness and fairness so dictate in the circumstances of the case.[337]

It is also possible for the court to refuse to enforce a provision in the way it is drafted, but takes into account the interpretation of the facts of the case. This approach has been adopted in an important case on preliminary agreements: in Hemubo Betontechniek B.V./VVE Flatgebouw Strandhotel Zandvoort, the *Hoge Raad* emphasized that if the parties agree on specific obligations, these should prevail and form the basis for liability. In the absence of specific contractual regulation, the recovery of costs wasted in negotiations is based on reasonableness and fairness.[338]

3.7.8. Break-up fees

Break-up fees represent compensation to be paid where a party decides not to go forward with the negotiated transaction. Dutch scholarship sometimes refers to these as 'break fees' and 'inducement fees' and has discussed them in the context of merger and

334 Section 10 Book 6 Dutch Civil code. Exceptions are Article 6:109(1) on the discretion of a court to reduce a legal obligation to pay damages if this would lead to clearly unacceptable results and 6:96(4) on reasonable costs incurred in obtaining extra-judicial payment.

335 Article 6:94 Dutch Civil code on the possibility to reduce contractual penalties can be also relevant in this context.

336 Lindenbergh 2014, at 35.

337 De Kluiver/Schwarz 1998; HR 14 June 1996, ECLI:NL:HR:1996:ZC2105, *NJ* 1997, 481 De Ruiterij/MBO. See on this Van Bijnen 2005, at 343–345.

338 HR 27 May 2011, ECLI:NL:HR:2011:BP8707, *RvdW* 2011/686 Hemubo Betontechniek B.V./VVE Flatgebouw Strandhotel Zandvoort. See also Lindenbergh 2014, at 34.

acquisition transactions.[339] In principle, parties may take on an obligation to pay break-up fees if the final contract is not formed. However, to the extent that such a provision attempts to re-distribute costs incurred in negotiations and contractualize the rules on liability, the comments made in the Section above are also relevant to clauses on break-up fees.

Furthermore, in Dutch law a provision on break-up fees can be regarded as penalty clause[340] – in Dutch law a fixed amount of damage recovery and/or an incentive to fulfil an obligation.[341] Article 6:91 Dutch Civil code defines this as 'any clause which provides that an obligor, should he fail in the performance of his obligation, must pay a sum of money or perform another obligation'. Courts have a relatively broad discretionary power in relation to such provisions and may reduce the amount of compensation to be paid by their own motion.[342]

The amount of compensation may be reduced by the court if the payment of a break-up fee would lead to a result unacceptable from the perspective of reasonableness and fairness (within the limiting function of this open norm).[343] More concretely, according to the *Hoge Raad*, the amount of payment should be proportional to the goal of the negotiated transaction. For example, if the only aim of fixing a high amount of compensation is to prevent the acceptance of bids from third parties, the break-up fee has been upheld as binding if this represents an adequate and proportional reaction to the opposed merger (taking into account all the circumstances of the case at hand).[344]

3.7.9. *Dispute resolution*

3.7.9.1. Choice of law

It should be noted as background that in the EU, a uniform instrument regulates the law applicable to cross-border *contractual* relationships: the Rome I Regulation (Rome I).[345] Another uniform instrument – Rome II Regulation (Rome II)[346] – provides the rules on the law applicable to cross-border *non-contractual* relationships. Article 1(2)(i) Rome I expressly excludes obligations related to the mere formation of contract from its scope.

339 See inter alia Van Engelen 2010; Ofner 2003.

340 Van Engelen 2010, at 182.

341 For an international and comparative perspective, Schelhaas 2004.

342 Article 6:94 Dutch Civil code.

343 HR 27 Aril 2007, ECLI:NL:HR:2007:AZ6638, *NJ* 2007, 262.

344 HR 18 April 2003, ECLI:NL:HR:2003:AF2161, *NJ* 2003, 286 RNA/Westfield. See also Article 2:7 Dutch Civil code: a company may even disregard the break-up fees provision if the application of this clause would contradict the goals for which the legal entity has been created.

345 Regulation (EC) No 593/2008 of the European Parliament and of the Council of 17 June 2008 on the Law Applicable to Contractual Obligations (Rome I).

346 Regulation (EC) No 864/2007 of the European Parliament and of the Council of 11 July 2007 on the Law Applicable to Non-contractual Obligations (Rome II).

Rome II is therefore relevant. According to the main relevant rule of Article 12 Rome II, the law applicable to precontractual obligations is the law of the contract which would come about if the negotiations had not failed.[347]

Against this background, the question arises as to whether an obligation submitting negotiations to a chosen law created by a preliminary agreement is a contractual obligation in itself. This would make the Rome I Regulation applicable directly. Although the application of Rome II would perhaps often lead to the same result, the question relates to the mere possibility of negotiations being governed by one choice of law, while the final contract would be governed by another choice of law. This question can be asked hypothetically, for example, in a situation resembling the one in the case Van Engen/ Mirror Group,[348] where an English and a Dutch party eventually regarded their negotiations as being subject to English law (because the letter of intent was drafted in English and used formulations typical of contracting under English law). However, the final contract between the two publishing houses on the production of a quality newspaper in the Netherlands would not necessarily be submitted to the law of England and Wales.

This question would be answered in the affirmative if asked of a Dutch court.[349] Choice of law, even if it is made in a preliminary agreement and before the final contract is formed, has been regarded in the Dutch literature as a stand-alone obligation within the negotiation process.[350] In a recent case, the Rechtbank Amsterdam upheld as binding a choice of law clause made in a letter of intent on the basis of Article 3 Rome I Regulation. The parties chose German law in the letter of intent (the breach of which caused the dispute), and the court applied German law to solve the dispute.[351]

3.7.9.2. Choice of court

Similarly to the choice of law, the choice of court is also regulated in the EU by uniform rules. These are provided by the Brussels I-bis Regulation (Brussels I-bis).[352] Article 25(5) of Brussels I-bis establishes the principle of severability of choice of court agreements. Based on this principle, the validity of the choice of court obligation should be assessed independently of the validity of the document in which the obligation is contained. This provision separates – severs – the questions of validity of the mere preliminary document

347 Article 12 Rome II provides also rules to define applicable law if the law that would have been applied to the negotiated contract cannot be identified. See also Asser/Kramer and Verhagen 10-III 2015, para 1199–1203.

348 HR 24 November 1995, ECLI:NL:HR:1995:ZC1890, *NJ* 1996, 162 Van Engen/Mirror Group.

349 On this question see also Wessels 2009a. Asser/Kramer and Verhagen 10-III 2015, para 952.

350 Blei Weissmann 2013, §1.23.

351 Hof Amsterdam 26 April 2011, ECLI:NL:GHAMS:2011:BQ5836, LJN BQ5836.

352 Regulation (EU) No 1215/2012 of the European Parliament and of the Council of 12 December 2012 on Jurisdiction and the Recognition and Enforcement of Judgments in Civil and Commercial Matters (Recast) (Brussels I-bis).

and the validity of a stand-alone choice of court clause. The provision is recent, it has been introduced in the most recent recast of the Regulation. Article 25(5) states as follows:[353]

> An agreement conferring jurisdiction which forms part of a contract shall be treated as an agreement independent of the other terms of the contract. The validity of the agreement conferring jurisdiction cannot be contested solely on the ground that the contract is not valid.

This provision raises the question whether a choice of court made in a preliminary agreement may qualify as a choice in contract for the purpose of Article 25(5) of Brussels I-bis. This question should be answered in the affirmative in the light of the existing scholarship[354] and case law, though the Dutch cases are not numerous. The decision of the Rechtbank Amsterdam can be given as an example. The case involved a dispute between a Dutch and a German party and related to breaking off negotiations. The court based its competence on the express choice of court made in a preliminary agreement (a Memorandum of Understanding).[355]

Another uniform instrument relevant for this purpose is the Hague Convention on Choice of Court Agreements.[356] The EU is party to this Convention. The aim of the instrument is to have international coverage broader than that of the EU. This Convention also establishes the principle of severability of a choice of court provision in Article 3(d). In this way, an obligation on choice of court which is agreed in a preliminary agreement may arguably be regarded as valid under this Convention.

3.7.9.3. Arbitration

Dutch literature confirms that disputes which may arise during the formation of contract may be submitted to arbitration by a preliminary agreement (thus before the formation of the final contract).[357] The Netherlands are also a member of the New York Convention.[358] This international instrument establishes uniform rules for international arbitration. It includes inter alia the principle of severability of the arbitration agreement.[359] By virtue of this principle, the validity of the arbitration agreement is severed from the document in which it is contained.[360]

353 Article 25(5) Brussels I-bis.
354 See inter alia Wessels/Van Wechem 2011, at 63 ff.
355 Rb. Amsterdam 5 March 2013, ECLI:NL:RBAMS:2013:CA2529, LJN CA2529.
356 Convention on Choice of Court Agreements (The Hague, 2005).
357 Tjittes 2006, at 145; Wessels 2010, at 53.
358 Convention on the Recognition and Enforcement of Foreign Arbitral Awards (New York, 1958).
359 Born 2014, at 913 ff.
360 See Article II and Article V(1)(a) of the Convention on the Recognition and Enforcement of Foreign Arbitral Awards (New York, 1958). While the New York Convention does not directly establish severability of an arbitration agreement, it indirectly assumes it. See Born 2014, at 354 ff.

Not many relevant arbitral awards are published to confirm the statement above. The following published arbitral award of the Netherlands Arbitration Institute (NAI) can be given as an example. There, a clause of the 'Heads of Agreement' submitted precontractual disputes to arbitration by NAI and was enforced.[361] The case concerned negotiations on a project of joint activities between several publishing houses. The negotiating parties established 'Heads of Agreement'. This document created an obligation to negotiate in good faith using all possible means to come to the result in which the joint activity would be exercised. The document also established the conditions under which negotiations could be broken off without liability. The negotiations failed, and a NAI arbitral tribunal was seized with a claim for unlawful breaking off of negotiations. The arbitral tribunal recognized its competence on the basis of the choice of arbitration made in the 'Heads of Agreement'.[362]

3.8. Liability and remedies

This Section will address the remedies available in Dutch law for breaking off negotiations and breach of contractually organized negotiations and discuss the interaction between causes of action. Thereafter, it will sketch the conditions and the nature of liability that may be engaged for misconduct in negotiations.

3.8.1. Remedies

The main remedy for unlawfully breaking off negotiations and for breach of an obligation of preliminary agreements is recovery of damage. Another available remedy is an *order to negotiate* made by injunction issued by the court. This amounts to specific performance – one of the remedies available under Article 3:296 Dutch Civil code, namely specific performance of an obligation to negotiate. An order to negotiate does not preclude a *subsequent* claim for damage if the order does not lead to successful results.[363]

3.8.1.1. Recovery of damage

Dutch law allows recovery of any foreseeable damage caused by unlawfully breaking off negotiations or by a breach of an obligation of a preliminary agreement. The right to recover damage is established by Section 6.1.10 Dutch Civil code. It covers the *consequences* of both the liability based on tort and on contract, whereas the *conditions* for liability in tort and in contract differ.

Dutch law draws a distinction between the so-called negative and positive contract interest.[364] In the context of negotiations of a contract, recovery of the *negative interest*

361 NAI Arbitral Award, 5 September 2000 nr. 22, 2000 *Tijdschrift voor Arbitrage* 107.

362 Ibid.

363 Asser/Hartkamp and Sieburgh 2014, para 198.

364 Asser/Hartkamp and Sieburgh 2010, para 198–199; Lindenbergh 2014, at 66–67.

(*negatief contractsbelang*) consists firstly, in compensation of costs actually incurred in relation to negotiations. Not all such costs qualify as a negative contractual interest. The concept covers only the recovery of costs (incurred in the course of negotiating the contract) that could have been reflected – discounted – in the price of the failed contract. Secondly, recovery of the negative contract interest may also include loss of chance to conclude a contract with a third party.[365]

Recovery of the *positive interest* (*positief contractsbelang*) aims to restore the party to the situation it would have been in if the final contract, negotiations of which failed, had been concluded. This covers not only the costs incurred in relation to negotiations (to the extent these can be discounted in the failed final contract), but also the loss of potential profits from the failed final contract.[366]

The *Hoge Raad* does not limit the loss recoverable under the heading of liability for breaking off negotiations to the negative interest. The possibility of recovering a positive interest has been emphasized in Plas/Valburg,[367] but remains an exceptional measure of liability. As noted earlier, the *Hoge Raad* has developed a number of factors, all of which should be fulfilled in order to establish liability. The recovery remains the subject of academic debate.[368] Furthermore, according to the literature, damages for breaking off negotiations are awarded fairly infrequently, and recovery of positive interests is admitted even less frequently.[369]

3.8.1.2. Order to negotiate

Another type of remedy available in Dutch law is an order to negotiate. If breaking off negotiations is regarded as unacceptable, a court injunction may be issued to order the parties to continue negotiations.[370] The parties should make constructive attempts to reach agreement, but the conclusion of the final contract is not required.[371] This remedy represents specific performance of the obligation to negotiate.[372] An order to negotiate may be accompanied by the measures to secure compliance: by a judicial penalty (*dwangsom*) or by mandatory appointment of a mediator.[373] As has been noted earlier, the obligation to negotiate contained in the court order to negotiate should be limited in time.[374]

365 Asser/Hartkamp and Sieburgh 2014, para 198.
366 HR 23 October 1987, ECLI:NL:HR:1987:AD0018, *NJ* 1988, 1017 VSH/Shell. See also De Kluiver 1992, at 310 (tracing back the history of concepts to Von Ihering and their reception in Dutch law).
367 HR 18 June 1982, ECLI:NL:HR:1982:AG4405, *NJ* 1983, 723 Plas/Valburg.
368 See inter alia Hartlief 2005; Ruygvoorn 2009, at 118–122.
369 Asser/Hartkamp and Sieburgh 2014, para 197; Tjittes 2006.
370 The legal basis for this remedy is Article 3:296 Dutch Civil code.
371 De Boer 2011, at 107; Hartlief 2005, at 1027.
372 Article 3:296 Dutch Civil code.
373 See De Boer 2011, at 119.
374 Blei Weissmann 2013, §1.62.

The *Hoge Raad* recognized the possibility of issuing an order to negotiate in Huurdersvereniging Koot/Handelsonderneming A.F.M. Koot,[375] recently confirmed in Almere/Weernekers.[376] The remedy is underpinned by the requirement of reasonableness and fairness and by the approach established by CBB/JPO.[377]

An order to negotiate usually contains a prescription to continue negotiations. It requires the parties to have a reasonable, real, and open exchange and to provide each other with sufficient time to react. It may also prohibit negotiation of the same transaction with third parties.[378] According to some scholars, an order to negotiate always precludes negotiations with third parties.[379] However, this view is not unanimously shared. According to De Kluiver, an obligation to negotiate implies only the requirement to inform the other party about any parallel negotiations.[380]

A particularly efficient and frequently used way of obtaining specific performance of an obligation to negotiate is the use of a procedure to claim a provisional measure (*kort geding*) available in Dutch law. This procedure enables a party to speedily obtain an injunction (within some days or weeks). A court using this procedure ascertains the facts of the case in a more concise manner than in the normal procedure.[381]

Issuing an order to negotiate is subject to a number of limits primarily related to the added value of this measure in the context of failed negotiations. The criterion of other circumstances of the case and in particular unexpected circumstances (touched upon earlier) plays a role in deciding whether an order to negotiate has practical value.[382] For instance, a court order should not be granted if further negotiations are meaningless because of the worsening of the parties' relations.[383] Furthermore, on a more technical note, an order to negotiate might not make sense if the contract that is being negotiated may be unilaterally withdrawn.[384] In this case, a party breaking off negotiations might agree to conclude the final contract, but use its right to terminate shortly after conclusion.

Other limits on imposing an order to negotiate are related to its practicality. Issuing an order to negotiate might be impractical if a contract with a third party has been concluded

375 HR 11 March 1983, ECLI:NL:HR:1983:AG4551, *NJ* 1983, 585 Huurdersvereniging Koot/ Handelsonderneming A.F.M. Koot.

376 HR 1 June 2012, ECLI:NL:HR:2012:BV1748, *NJ* 2012/471 Almere/Weermekers.

377 HR 12 August 2005, ECLI:NL:HR:2005:AT7337, *NJ* 2005, 467 CBB/JPO.

378 HR 1 June 2012, ECLI:NL:HR:2012:BV1748, *NJ* 2012/471 Almere/Weermekers; De Boer 2011, at 120.

379 Blei Weissmann 2013, §1.68.1; Asser/Hartkamp and Sieburgh 6-III 2010, para 196.

380 De Kluiver 1992, at 120.

381 For a thorough comparative analysis of the Dutch *kort geding* see Kramer 2001.

382 Blei Weissmann 2013, §1.48.4.3 with further references.

383 HR 27 May 2011, ECLI:NL:HR:2011:BP8707, *RvdW* 2011/686 Hemubo Betontechniek B.V./VVE Flatgebouw Strandhotel Zandvoort; Compare Blei Weissmann 2013, §1.71.4.1 (referring to authors who submit that if a party does not want to negotiate further it does not mean that this will lead to a failure of negotiations and even of mediation).

384 Blei Weissmann 2013, §1.71.1.2.

after the failure of negotiations. Does the conclusion of a contract with a third party preclude the possibility of issuing an order to negotiate in Dutch law? Authors have referred to an example of failed negotiations relating to an item that is sold to a third party, and diverging opinions have been expressed in the literature.[385] One view is that the fact of sale renders an order to negotiate inappropriate due to impracticality. The only remedy possible would be the recovery of damage caused by conclusion of the contract with a third party. Van den Berg holds another view, albeit limited to the context of construction contracts. He submits that an order to negotiate is available in combination with an order to return the parties to the position they would have been in had the contract with the third party not been concluded. This implies a rescission of the contract with a third party (*ongedaanmaken van de overeenkomst*).[386]

3.8.2. *Interaction of causes of action*

One obligation may be based on several grounds or one set of facts may give rise to several causes of action.[387] Dutch law enables causes of action to be combined.[388] For example, if a claim may be established in both tort and contract, these may be combined and recovery under both heads may be granted. If cumulating leads to an unacceptable result (from the point of view of reasonableness and fairness) the claimant should choose the head of liability. If the result would still lead to unacceptable results, the claim may be established under only one head of liability.[389]

3.8.3. *Liability for breaking off negotiations: a liability in tort? The debate and its relevance*

As noted earlier, the framework of rules applicable to the process of negotiations in Dutch law is formed by different fields of law: liability for breaking off negotiations, contract and general tort law. If a contractually binding obligation is created during negotiations, the liability for its breach is contractual.[390] In this way, a preliminary agreement either leads to a shift of liability to contractual or adds a contractual cause of action to other actions eventually available.

It is worth noting that the nature of precontractual liability in Dutch law was subject to debate. In case law, liability has sometimes been based on tort, sometimes on *bona fides* (or reasonableness and fairness) or on both of these, and most decisions refer to

385 Blei Weissmann 2013, §1.73.3.1.1 with further references.

386 Asser/Van den Berg 7-VI 2013, para 277.

387 See generally Brunner 1984.

388 Lindenbergh 2014, at 31–32. See with details and nuances Castermans 2012.

389 Ibid.

390 See HR 15 May 1987, ECLI:NL:HR:1987:AC4156, *NJ* 1988, 164 Van Huffel/Van den Hoek where the HR said that the question of whether a preliminary agreement has been created had a consequence for deciding whether liability for breaking off negotiations could be imposed. On this, see Blei Weissmann 2013, §1.40.5.

reasonableness and fairness.[391] Nor are Dutch scholars unanimous as to the nature of liability. Some authors have argued that liability for breaking off negotiations is based on the breach of the contractual duty of good faith.[392] A nuanced view is offered by other authors who have submitted that liability in decisions of the *Hoge Raad* is based on reasonableness and fairness, but construed as liability in tort.[393] According to these authors, the more stringent standards of tort law are also the most appropriate to ensure freedom of negotiations. Another view has been advanced that both contractual reasonableness and fairness and tort form the basis of liability at the same time.[394]

The practical outcome of this debate comes down to the following. Firstly, it relates to the conditions of liability that should be fulfilled and proven to engage liability (the conditions of liability in contract and tort are contrasted in the next Section 3.8.4). Secondly, the literature has also referred to the relevance of the nature of liability in international cases. It is relevant to the characterization of the claim for the application of private international law rules.[395] For the EU, the question of characterization has been arguably solved in the current uniform instruments (see the Section on dispute resolution above).

3.8.4. Conditions of liability in contract and tort

The Dutch Civil code provides a single regime for *consequences* of an obligation to recover damage (this obligation is created either by a breach of a contract or by a breach of a duty in tort).[396] By contrast, the *conditions* for establishing liability in contract and tort are different. This means the answer to the questions of under what conditions and which person can be held liable differs depending on the nature of liability.[397] Contractual liability can be engaged if the following conditions are fulfilled: (1) breach of a contractual obligation,[398] (2) damage,[399] (3) causal link between the breach and the damage.[400] (4) Finally, the breach should be attributable to the party which has allegedly breached the obligation.[401]

391 See on the role of reasonableness and fairness Asser/Hartkamp and Sieburgh 2014, para 191.

392 Asser/Hartkamp and Sieburgh 2014, para 205; Schoordijk 1984, at 61 ff.

393 Drion 1967, para 20; De Kluiver 1992, at 253 ff.; Ruygvoorn 2009, at 270 ff., 290 ff.

394 Smits 2003, at 26. The Hoge Raad appears to have taken a distinct view in the Effectenlease cases, where liability was shaped as tortious (HR 5 June 2009, ECLI:NL:HR:2009:BH2811, *NJ* 2012, 183 Levob/Bolle; HR 5 June 2009, ECLI:NL:HR:2009:BH2815, *NJ* 2012, 182 De Treek/Dexia; HR 5 June 2009, ECLI:NL:HR:2009:BH2822, *NJ* 2012, 184 Stichting Gedupeerden Spaarconstructie/Aegon. See Van Boom/Lindenbergh 2009). However, the Effectenlease cases deal with liability for a failure to inform the consumer. Therefore, these cases provide no direct guidance for the liability discussed in this study.

395 Wessels 2009a; Wessels 2009b.

396 Section 10 Book 6 Dutch Civil code.

397 Lindenbergh 2014, at 30.

398 Article 6:74 Dutch Civil code.

399 Article 6:95 Dutch Civil code.

400 Article 6:98 Dutch Civil code.

401 Article 6:75 Dutch Civil code: '*tenzij niet toerekenbaar*'.

Liability in tort can be engaged if the following conditions are fulfilled: (1) conduct that represents a breach of duty of care in tort,[402] (2) that can be attributed to the person who committed it,[403] and (3) leads to damage.[404] (4) There should be a causal link between the tortious fact and the damage.[405] (5) Finally, the criterion of relativity of liability should be respected. In essence, relativity means that not everyone has a right to recover damages under all circumstances. Only those persons whom the law aims to protect by establishing tort liability may claim damages.[406]

3.9. Conclusion

This Chapter started by quoting the comparison made by a Dutch scholar of the regulation of negotiations in Dutch law to an invisible magnetic field.[407] To conclude on the description of this regulation, some general remarks can be made regarding the possibilities of escaping this magnetic field and diminishing or strengthening its attraction.

As has been explained, the legal framework relevant for answering the main question of this Chapter has three components. It consists firstly, of liability for breaking off negotiations and secondly, of the framework of preliminary agreements (*voorovereenkomst*, *hupovereenkomst* and other). A very limited role is played by the law of tort and the doctrine of unjust enrichment, while development of their application may not be excluded (especially if this follows developments in other countries, for example in the United States).

A complete escape from the magnetic field of the regulation is clearly not possible, because of the existence and the functioning of the open norm of reasonableness and fairness (*bona fides*). This overarching requirement applies to any type of obligation in Dutch law, be it contractual or tortious. The application of this norm to the process of contract formation seems to follow an inductive logic: a collection of the factual applications of good faith fills it with content. However, it does not provide an exhaustive description of the content which might be given to reasonableness and fairness. As a consequence, each obligation that purports to regulate the dynamics of negotiations might be tested having regard to reasonableness and fairness. If it appears from this test that if the provision leads to results which are inadmissible from the point of view of reasonableness and fairness, the provision is not binding. Reasonableness and fairness is a mandatory norm and may not be waived by the parties. Nevertheless, it appears that the parties may steer the application of this open norm towards a concrete situation. That is, the parties may detail the concrete requirements for each party in a preliminary

402 Article 6:162 (2) Dutch Civil code.
403 Article 6:162(3) Dutch Civil code.
404 Article 6:95 ff. Dutch Civil code.
405 Article 6:98 Dutch Civil code.
406 Article 6:163 Dutch Civil code.
407 Nieuwenhuis 2010, at 289.

document. No contractual deviation can be made for wilful misconduct; this is evident from limitations on contractual fixing of liability and from the sanction in tort of misuse of information and know-how obtained in negotiations.

Furthermore, two points are worth noting regarding remedies. Firstly, the damage recoverable as a measure of liability for breaking off negotiations is not limited. This has been expressly stated by the *Hoge Raad* and followed in case law. Both negative and the positive contract interests may be recovered (the terms positive and negative contract interest are used in the legal system of the Netherlands to refer to reliance interest and expectation interest).[408] Dutch scholars have criticized the absence of limitations. For instance, Cartwright and Hesselink have submitted that Dutch law is not in line with many other Western legal systems where recovery of damages is limited, and the limitation is generally set on reliance interest.[409] It can be noted that the absence of limitation is to a certain extent counterbalanced by the fact that liability for breaking off negotiations is an exceptional measure. Scholars have submitted that the practical impact of the absence of limitation is also softened by the fairly infrequent admission of liability for breaking off negotiations in the cases and the even smaller number of instances of recovery of a positive contract interest.[410] Furthermore, cases where recovery has been allowed of both negative and positive contract interests can still be found in case law. Contractual obligations purporting to limit the damages recoverable or to establish the distribution of costs in negotiations and fix break-up fees are carefully considered by the Dutch courts. These provisions might influence the court's reasoning. This is especially true for the interpretation of the text of preliminary agreements drafted by sophisticated commercial partners. However, these obligations are always subject to the test of reasonableness and fairness. As a consequence, these provisions may be disregarded by the court and still lead to recovery of unlimited damage.

The second point to note is that under Dutch law, an order to negotiate may be issued by a court as a remedy for breaking off negotiations, unless there are reasons for not issuing this order. This is a remedy of specific performance of either the overarching duty of reasonableness and fairness or a contractual obligation to negotiate (or to negotiate in good faith). Dutch scholars have been generally reserved as to the appropriateness of an order to negotiate as a remedy for breaking off negotiations. The main reason for this has been the limited impact the court can have on the actual conduct of negotiations by the parties. De Boer notes, for instance, that case law provides examples of some guidance by the court, the latter being limited to references to the conditions accepted on a given market and prices.[411] Van Boom, Van Dam-Lely and Lindenbergh doubt also the beneficial impact of introducing a mediator into negotiations in an order to negotiate further.[412] In the light of one of the functions assigned to the courts – that of reconciliation

408 For establishing a parallel in terms, see De Kluiver 1992, at 310.
409 Cartwright/Hesselink 2009, at 468.
410 Tjittes 2006, at 223.
411 De Boer 2011, at 121 and 126.
412 Van Boom/Van Dam-Lely/Lindenbergh 2011, at 6.

in case of disputes – as debatable as it may be, the positive role of the court should perhaps not be underestimated.

Some parts of the framework appear to offer more possibilities for the parties to shape the dynamics of negotiations. It is to be noted that the liability for breaking off negotiations in Dutch law is focused on the cases where breaking off negotiations is regarded as unlawful. The rules of conduct imposed by the parties flow indirectly from this. At the same time, Dutch law arguably enables the creation of stand-alone obligations that are valid irrespective of success in forming the final contract. In this way, with some reservations discussed in this Chapter, exclusivity of negotiations, confidentiality, as well as dispute resolution may be contractualized or 'privatized' by such stand-alone obligations. Contractual attempts to keep negotiations non-binding until the formation of the final contract have also been upheld as valid. However, the literature stresses that these clauses would not always stand the test of reasonableness and fairness. Nor can they escape the possibility of a broad interpretation by the court of the entire context of negotiations where the court may still find that a final contract is formed.

Chapter 4

FRENCH LAW

4.1. Introduction

French law addresses precontractual negotiations as a relationship that may be regulated by law. The idea of legal duties imposed on the parties once they enter into negotiation is rooted in the views of Saleilles,[413] who came up with a concept of *responsabilité précontractuelle* (precontractual liability) in 1907. In a manner innovative for his time, Saleilles suggested that the mere process of negotiations inevitably binds negotiating parties together by practical, social, and moral links. He advocated that breaking these ties should be qualified as a tort[414] and lead to precontractual liability.

Subsequently, legal regulation of the precontractual period has attracted considerable attention in the French literature.[415] The interest has been further revived with the drafting of the PECL and DCFR and the projects of reforming the French law of obligations.[416]

Since the nineteenth century, precontractual liability has become a usual concept in French law. However, it was scarcely incorporated in legal texts, the main source of French law.[417] This concept was not incorporated into the *Code civil*. The regulation of precontractual relations was based on general principles of the law of obligations and the 'praetorian'[418] judge-made rules. Since the adoption of the Napoleonic Code two centuries ago, French courts have come some distance in interpreting its provisions in the context of practical changes. Over the years of application and interpretation of the

413 Saleilles 1907, building on a study of an Italian scholar Faggella. See Faggella 1906.

414 Saleilles refers to tort in contrast to von Ihering. This German scholar advanced a concept *culpa in contrahendo* (fault in conclusion of a contract) referring to contractual liability. See Von Ihering 1861.

415 See inter alia with further references Congrès des Notaires de France 1964; Mousseron/Guibal/Mainguy 2001; De Coninck 2002; Deshayes 2008; Fages 2012, Part 1 '*Négociations*'.

416 These are two scholarly projects 'Avant-projet Catala' (Catala 2005) and 'Avant-projet Terré' (Terré 2009) as well as the project of the French Ministry of Justice. These projects contain separated sections on formation of contract and preliminary agreements. For an overview, see Mazeaud 2009.

417 Drago 2008.

418 Mousseron/Guibal/Mainguy 2001, at 240–241.

Code civil, judges have developed standards of conduct to be respected by the parties during negotiations. These standards have been referred to as 'particularly rigorous ethics of negotiations'.[419] The sanction for their breach is a liability in tort.

French case law or, to use the exact term, *jurisprudence*[420] has not confined the legal regulation of negotiations to precontractual liability in tort. In French law, parties may organize negotiations contractually. During the last few decades, French judges and scholars have become receptive to the practice of creating various precontractual documents.[421] Drawing on the general provisions of contract law, they have recognized a plethora of *avant-contrats*, including the project of contract, agreement in principle, pre-emption agreement, promise to contract and others.[422] The validity of these documents is underpinned by the distinction made in French scholarship and case law between the future contract and the process of negotiations towards this contract. It is the process of negotiations that is privatized by contractual obligations. These preliminary agreements prepare for the creation of a contract in the future and may bind parties with contractual obligations before the negotiated contract is concluded.

An important step in this development has been taken in 2016 by the reform of the French law of obligations: the *Ordonnance* for the reform of the law of contract, the general regime of obligations, and proof of obligations (the *Ordonnance*).[423] The *Ordonnance* is deemed to enter into force on 1 October 2016, and its provisions will apply to all relations taking place after this date. The *Ordonnance* modernizes French law, and the regulation of contractual negotiations; specifically Articles 1112, 1112–1, 1112–2, 1123 and 1124 of the *Ordonnance*, areas are amongst those parts subject to modernization.[424] The *Ordonnance* establishes the general regime of negotiations codifying the main case law developments on precontractual liability. Furthermore, it defines two types of *avant-contrat*: the pre-emption agreement (Article 1123) and the unilateral promise (Article 1124).

[419] Mazeaud 2001, at 640.

[420] See Section 4.2.1.

[421] See Congrès des Notaires de France 1964; Mousseron/Guibal/Mainguy 2001; Deshayes 2008; Fages 2012, Part I 'Négociations'.

[422] The translation of these terms follows the translation by J. Cartwright and S. Whittaker of *P. Catala, Avant-Projet de Réforme du Droit des Obligations et de la Prescription*, Paris: Documentation Française, 2006. See www.justice.gouv.fr/art_pix/rapportcatatla0905-anglais.pdf (English version); www.justice.gouv.fr/art_pix/RAPPORTCATALASEPTEMBRE2005.pdf (original in French).

[423] *Ordonnance no 2016–131 du 10 février 2016 portant réforme du droit des contrats, du régime général et de la preuve des obligations*, JORF 0035, 11 January 2016. See also *draft Ordonnance for the reform of the law of contract, the general regime of obligations, and proof of obligations* (draft *Ordonnance*), www.justice.gouv.fr/publication/j21_projet_ord_reforme_contrats_2015.pdf. The English translation of the main concepts follows the official translation of the draft *Ordonnance* by J. Cartwright, B. Fauvarque-Cosson and S. Whittaker, www.textes.justice.gouv.fr/art_pix/Draft-Ordonnance-for-the-Reform-of-the-Civil-Codepdf.pdf.

[424] Fauvarque-Cosson 2015; Fauvarque-Cosson 2014, at 62. See also Stijns/Jansen 2016; Schulze/Wicker/Mäsch/Mazeaud 2015; Latina/Chantepie 2015; Stoffel-Munck 2015.

Given this background, this Chapter will address the way in which parties may contractualize the dynamics of their negotiations[425] by creating precontractual documents such as letter of intent. Various areas of regulation in the French legal system and their interaction will be discussed. The Chapter will begin with a note on the sources of French law and translation of the frequently used terms (Section 4.2). Thereafter, it will address the 'ethics of negotiations' – duties imposed by law on the parties in every negotiation, irrespectively of the existence of any precontractual document (Section 4.3). The next parts will be dedicated to various preliminary agreements admitted by French law. Particular attention will be paid to the question as to whether parties can 'contract out' of the duties discussed earlier by creating a precontractual document, for instance, a letter of intent (Section 4.4). The Chapter will also explore the role of the French doctrine of unjust enrichment for restitutions related to the precontractual period, namely, for preparatory work or other investment made before formation of a contract (Section 4.5). Finally, remedies and liability will be discussed (Section 4.6) and some concluding remarks provided (Section 4.7).

4.2. Sources of French law and terminology

The 'praetorian' legal basis of precontractual liability and precontractual agreements calls for a short preliminary remark on the relevant sources of French law (4.2.1) and translation (4.2.2).

4.2.1. Code civil, *reform of 2016, case law and scholarship*

The main source of general rules of law of obligations is the French Civil code – *Code civil*.[426] Some parts of commercial activity, for example, rules on competition and antitrust, are also regulated by the Commercial code. Despite this, the *Code civil* applies to relations between businesses if no specific regulation is established by the Commercial code. In this way, the general part of the legal obligations of the *Code civil* remains relevant for commercial transactions.

As noted in the introduction, the *Code civil* has been recently reformed by the *Ordonnance*.[427] It amends many articles of the *Code civil*. According to Article 9 of the *Ordonnance*, the

425 For the definition of dynamics of negotiations see Chapter 2.

426 Book III, Titles III, IV, and IV bis. Several fundamental principles, for instance freedom of contract, are established by the French Constitution. See Terré/Simler/Lequette 2015, para 24. *Code civil* was adopted in 1804, the time when various customary laws existing on the French territory and Roman law were melted down to form one written code. For the historical and doctrinal sources of the French *Code civil*, see Halpérin 2004, at 46–49 and 56–59; Cornu 2004, at 710 ff.

427 *Ordonnance* is, in principle, an act issued by the executive power within the French separation of powers. On reforming the *Code civil* by an *Ordonnance*, see *Objectifs de la Reforme*, in *Rapport au Président de la République relatif à l'ordonnance no 2016-131 du 10 février 2016 portant réforme du droit des contrats, du régime général et de la preuve des obligations*, JORF 0035, 11 January 2016. See also *Exposé des motifs in the Projet de loi du 27 novembre 2013 relatif à la modernisation et à la simplification du droit et des procédures dans les domaines de la justice et des affaires intérieures*, www.senat.fr/leg/pjl13-175.pdf.

new provisions will enter into force on 1 October 2016; contracts concluded before this date will be subject to the old provisions of the *Code civil*. This Chapter will take into account the provisions of the *Ordonnance*; it will still refer to the 'old' general provisions of the *Code civil*, accompanied, where available by the 'new' article number or content.[428]

This Chapter will also rely on French case law. Within the French system, court decisions, strictly speaking, do not constitute sources of law.[429] It is nevertheless widely accepted that the *Code civil* has always been interpreted and influenced by French judges who have adapted and continue to adapt its application to modern developments.[430] The most important role in this process is played by the decisions of the *Cour de cassation*, the highest judicial authority in civil and commercial matters, ensuring uniformity of interpretation and application of law in France.[431] Although distinct lines of cases can be frequently observed, the *Cour de cassation* itself is not bound by its previous decisions and may depart from these at any time. An important change of approach is called a 'turn in judgment' (*revirement de jurisprudence*). Lower courts usually follow the interpretation of legal norms made by the *Cour de cassation*.[432]

Case law as well as legal provisions are also discussed by legal scholars. Their opinions have a considerable authority in the French system and are often (but not always) taken into account by the courts. Case law is available in electronic databases.[433] These sources deserve particular attention in order to understand the French approach to contractualizing the dynamics of negotiations. The reason is that firstly, until the adoption of the *Ordonnance*, legislative provisions relating to the precontractual period have been scarce. Secondly, case law will inevitably still play an important role in the interpretation of the *Ordonnance*, to the extent that this text codifies the existing judge-made law.

4.2.2. *Translation of terms*

Some light should be shed on the choices made in the translation of terms, as most of the sources used in this Chapter are drafted in French. The study will rely on the official and academic translations of the *Code civil* and other statutes when these are available.[434] The

428 The synoptical table of the articles' correspondence is helpful in this regard. See François 2016.

429 See Article 5 *Code civil*. It prohibits courts from taking decisions attempting to create legal rules (*arrêt de règlement*). On the status of the French case law (*jurisprudence*) in comparative perspective, see Steiner 2010, at 86–92.

430 This development occurs despite the fact that judges do not have legislative competence within the French system of separation of powers.

431 Article L411-2 Code of the Judicial Organization.

432 Stein, at 93. The decisions taken by the *Cour de Cassation*'s *Chambre mixte* or in *Assemblée plénière* carry the most weight, because the highest judicial authority is gathered in full for the most controversial questions of law.

433 Open access database www.legifrance.gouv.fr and subscription databases Dalloz, LexisNexis, Lamyline, Lextenso.

434 For instance, the text of the *Code civil* quoted here and further in this study is a translation in English by G. Rouhette and A. Rouhette-Berton published at the official site of French legislation (last

Ordonnance is not yet translated into English, but an official translation of the draft *Ordonnance*[435] contains the main concepts discussed in this Chapter. Furthermore, translations will be taken from the existing comparative literature which has discussed several important concepts.[436] These include the concept of *avant-contrat* which is either left in French or translated as 'preliminary agreement' to keep the text consistent with other Chapters. The terms designating various preliminary agreements are also based on the existing translations.[437] The concept of *délit* is translated as tort. Two other frequently used expressions are legitimate expectation (*croyance legitime*) and breaking off negotiations in a rude and abrupt manner. The doctrine of unjust enrichment (*enrichissement sans cause*) is named in accordance with other parts of the study, though within the French system a more accurate translation would probably be unjustified enrichment.

A particular note should be made on the term 'letter of intent'. The *Code civil* contains a provision on 'letter of intent' (*lettre d'intention*).[438] Article 2322 defines it as a personal guarantee issued to secure that a debtor executes an obligation he owes to a beneficiary.[439] This definition has been introduced into the *Code civil* in order to clarify the use of such documents in French banking practice. Usually, a document whereby a parent company undertakes to guarantee the financial obligations of its subsidiary to the subsidiary's creditor (for example, a bank or a supplier) is called a caution. Issuing a caution requires an approval of the parent company's executive organs. However, in practice, such guarantee was frequently provided by a document called 'letter of intent'. The question as to whether a simple letter (often called 'letter of intent') could be qualified as a caution gave raise to disputes.[440] To resolve the debate, it was decided to define letter of intent as a caution in the *Code civil*.

This definition does not correspond to the use of the term letter of intent in international commercial practice.[441] The *Code civil*'s '*lettre d'intention*' coexists with the term 'letter

amendment translated: Act No. 2013-404 of 17 May 2013). See https://www.legifrance.gouv.fr/Traductions/en-English/Legifrance-translations.

435 Translation by J. Cartwright, B. Fauvarque-Cosson and S. Whittaker www.textes.justice.gouv.fr/art_pix/Draft-Ordonnance-for-the-Reform-of-the-Civil-Codepdf.pdf.

436 De Coninck 2001; Giliker 2002; Fontaine/De Ly 2009; Giliker 2002; Cartwright/Hesselink 2008.

437 The translation of other terms not included in the draft *Ordonnance* follows the translation by J. Cartwright and S. Whittaker of *P. Catala, Avant-Projet de Réforme du Droit des Obligations et de la Prescription*, Paris: Documentation Française, 2006, www.justice.gouv.fr/art_pix/rapportcatatla0905-anglais.pdf (English version); www.justice.gouv.fr/art_pix/RAPPORTCATALASEPTEMBRE2005.pdf (original in French).

438 Article 2322 *Code civil*: '*La lettre d'intention est l'engagement de faire ou de ne pas faire ayant pour objet le soutien apporté à un débiteur dans l'exécution de son obligation envers son créancier*'. This Article has been inserted into the *Code civil* by a statute in 2006. See *Ordonnance* no 2006-346 du 23 mars 2006 relative aux sûretés, JORF 4475, 24 March 2006.

439 Article 2322 *Code civil*.

440 See inter alia Barré 1995; Pomart 2008.

441 Fages 2011b, paras 115.13-115.19. See also Barré 1995; Bac 2005 (advancing arguments against the insertion of the definition *letter of intent* into the *Code civil*); Jambort 2007 (noting that the terms *lettre de confort* or *lettre de patronage* would be more appropriate for Article 1156 of the *Code civil* in order to

of intent' in international commercial transactions. These became *faux amis* in translation – concepts with similar names, but different meanings in two or more languages. From a legal perspective, these concepts are arguably sufficiently different not to influence each other's interpretation.[442] As a consequence, Article 2322 *Code civil* will not be addressed. It falls outside the scope of this study, due to the focus of this research on international practice.

4.3. Negotiations as particularly rigorous ethics

The starting point for the regulation of precontractual negotiations in French law is the freedom of negotiations (4.3.1). At the same time, a closer look at its application reveals that French judges have increasingly limited the scope of this principle over the last century.[443] Case law has progressively developed specific standards of behaviour that parties should respect during negotiations.[444] These standards have been legally framed as precontractual duties sanctioned by liability in tort. The *Ordonnance* reflects this in the requirement of good faith (4.3.2). All the duties described are interrelated and are often invoked together. As these are distilled from a large number of cases which are often fact specific, the boundaries between these duties are subtle. Their scope may be further concretized by looking at specific cases of their breach (4.3.2).

4.3.1. Freedom of negotiations

Freedom of contract is a constitutional principle in French law.[445] It is underpinned by the theory of autonomy of will and rooted in the nineteenth century Enlightenment philosophy, both of which had an impact on the drafting of the French civil code.[446] Freedom of contract is also one of the fundamental principles of the French law of obligations, implying, in particular, freedom of commerce (*liberté d'entreprendre*). It implies also several rights (or freedoms) related to the precontractual stage: the freedom to enter into negotiations, conclude contracts, withdraw from negotiations, and conduct simultaneous (also called parallel) negotiations with several potential contracting parties. Generally, one party is not obliged to inform his counterpart in negotiations about conducting parallel negotiations.[447]

match the vocabulary of international commerce); Pomart 2008; Simler 2008; Albiges/Dumont-Lefrand 2011, at 188–212.

442 Dondero 2011; Simler 2008.

443 Mazeaud 2001; Mousseron/Guibal/Mainguy 2001, at 13, 37.

444 Mazeaud 2001, at 640; Régis 2013, at 9.

445 See Preamble of the French Constitution of October 4, 1958, www.assemblee-nationale.fr/english; Article 4 *Déclaration des Droits de l'Homme et du Citoyen de 1789*. See also Pérès 2010; Terré/Simler/Lequette 2013, para 24; Albarian 2010a, at 253; Duffy 2006. Freedom of contract is included in all the projects of reform of the French law of obligations as a fundamental principle. See Mazeaud 2009, para 6–8.

446 Arnaud 1969, at 197 ff.; Terré/Simler/Lequette 2013, para 24 ff.

447 Cass com 12 May 2004 N° 00–15618 Bulletin 2004 n° 94.

Freedom of negotiations is recalled and codified in the *Ordonnance*. Its Article 1112 starts by emphasizing freedom of negotiation, providing namely that the commencement, continuation and breaking-off of negotiations may be exercised freely. Firstly, parties are free to enter into precontractual negotiations or refuse to do so; no one can be compelled to commence negotiations.[448] Secondly, once negotiations begin, neither party is obliged to conclude a contract. A judge may not order the parties to bring negotiations to an end (that is, to conclude a contract) if the parties remain in disagreement.[449] In this way, freedom of contract precludes the possibility for judges to order specific performance (execution of an obligation in nature) as a sanction at the precontractual stage, thereby limiting judicial interference in parties' precontractual negotiations. Thirdly, each party has a right to withdraw from negotiations. The *Cour de cassation* refers in its decisions to the 'exercise of right to withdraw from negotiations'.[450] The courts regard this as a use of the freedom of commerce (*liberté d'entreprendre*), including a free choice of contracting partners.[451] Fourthly, in principle, freedom of contract enables parties to conduct parallel negotiations with several potential contractors and finalize only the negotiations he finds the most appropriate.[452]

4.3.2. *Good faith and related duties*

4.3.2.1. Bonne foi as umbrella for precontractual duties

Article 1112 of the *Ordonnance* counterbalances the freedom of negotiations with the requirement to negotiate in good faith. In French law, this is a generalized concept for an honest or even cooperative attitude in a relationship regulated by law.[453] Under the umbrella of the requirement of good faith, the *Ordonnance* introduces the 'ethics of negotiations' developed in case law.

The genesis of their content and liability for breach is based on two articles of the *Code civil*. First, Article 1382 *Code civil* – the general provision on tort – underpinned the concept of precontractual liability, shaped as liability in tort (for *faute*).[454] Second, Article 1134 *Code civil* on the requirement of good faith in the execution of conventions

448 Ghestin 2007a, para 13; Fages 2011a, para 105–29.

449 Cass 2 civ 13 January 2005 N° 03-15828 n.p. in Bulletin.

450 See inter alia from numerous examples Cass 3 civ 28 June 2006 N° 04-20040 Bulletin 2006 n° 164, referring to a 'right of a unilateral withdrawal from precontractual negotiations'; Cass 2 civ 4 March 2004 N° 02-14022 n.p. in Bulletin; Cass 2 civ 10 October 2002 N° 01-03079 n.p. in Bulletin; Le Tourneau 2014, para 838.

451 Cass 2 civ 5 January 1994 N° 92-13856 n.p. in Bulletin.

452 Fages 2011a; Le Tourneau 2014, para 825 ff.; Cass com 26 November 2003 N° 00-10243; N° 00-10949 Bulletin 2003 n° 186 Manoukian.

453 A considerable body of literature discusses the concept of good faith in French law. See *inter* alia with further references Zimmermann/Whittaker 2000, at 32 ff.

454 Ghestin 2007a; Ghestin 2007b.

(e.g. contracts)[455] became the basis of the 'ethics of negotiations'.[456] The *Code civil* established a duty of good faith only for the execution of contracts, but not for their formation.[457] However, the *Cour de cassation* has a long history of broad interpretation of this provision. It has progressively extended the scope of the duty of good faith to the precontractual phase.[458] Legal scholarship in France was generally supportive of this approach.[459] As noted in the academic literature, the extension of the contractual duty of good faith to cover the precontractual phase falls generally under the tendency of 'moralisation of the contemporary contract law'[460] in France.

The requirement of precontractual good faith in Article 1112 of the *Ordonnance* is an open norm. At the same time, considerable case law provides a solid background and guidelines for its practical interpretation. The main 'ethics of negotiations' which counterbalance the freedom of negotiation include loyalty (sanction of conduct with an intention to harm),[461] consistency of conduct (requirement on each party to conduct negotiations in a manner consistent with his own previous behaviour and precluding 'fraudulent gambits'),[462] and transparency (requiring parties to exchange information crucial to the decision on the negotiated contract).[463]

4.3.2.2. Loyalty

According to French case law, parties to negotiations should be 'loyal' to each other. The *Cour de cassation* has stated that 'loyalty has to regulate relations between parties not only in contract, but also during the precontractual period'.[464] In essence, negotiating in a loyal manner means not causing harm to the other party by conduct during negotiations, nor by the manner of withdrawal from negotiations.[465] Certain decisions of the *Cour de cassation* refer in this respect to the general principle of French law forbidding 'abuse of right' (*abus de droit*). This refers to situations in which a right is exercised to the detriment of the other parties, or with an intention to harm, or in an unusual and abnormal way.[466]

455 Article 1134 paragraph 3 *Code civil* (referring to 'convention'). See Article 1103 *Ordonnance* (using the term 'contract' instead of 'convention').

456 Mazeaud 2001, at 640.

457 The draft of the French civil code (*Code civil de l'an VIII*) stated that 'conventions have to be made and executed in good faith', but this redaction has not been adopted. See Terré/Simler/Lequette 2013, para 43.

458 See for an overview of the approach of the *Cour de cassation* Larroumet 1998, para 239; Fages 2011a; Jarrosson 2006, at 197–198; Mazeaud 2001, at 638.

459 Previous projects of reform have also included the duty of good faith in the formation of conventions. See for a synthetic note on the projects see Mazeaud 2009.

460 Mazeaud 2009, para 15.

461 Cass 1 civ 14 June 2000 N° 98–17494 n.p. in Bulletin; see also CA Versailles 10 September 2009 N° 08/04982 JurisData unavailable (*'obligation de rectitude et loyauté'*).

462 Cass com 3 October 1978 N° 77–10915 Bulletin 1978 n° 208.

463 See inter alia Cass 3 civ 18 February 2004 N° 02–17523 n.p. in Bulletin.

464 Cass 1 civ 14 June 2000 N° 98–17494 n.p. in Bulletin; see also *'obligation de rectitude et loyauté'* CA Versailles 10 September 2009 N° 08/04982 JurisData unavailable.

465 Mazeaud 2001.

466 Guinchard/Debard 2013, at 5.

The *Cour de cassation* requires parties not to exercise the rights implied by the freedom of contract, for example the 'right to withdraw from negotiations', in an 'abrupt' way.[467] Conduct contrary to good faith, conduct in 'bad faith', for example, encouraging the other party to negotiations to make considerable investment in order to prepare for the potential deal, are also considered to be contrary to the duty of loyalty. In addition, the courts regard as abusive the use of aggressive techniques in negotiations.[468] This is based on the requirement of subjective good faith mentioned earlier. According to the French courts, a technique – a manoeuvre in negotiations – observed objectively but not corresponding to the party's subjective attitude is a sign of a lack of loyalty.

It is worth noting in this regard that interpretation in French law takes into account the subjective will of the parties.[469] Instead of the formalist approach of Roman law relying primarily on the respect of formalities (*stipulatio*)[470] to regard a contract as formed, the *Code civil* expresses an attachment to the philosophy of autonomy of will typical of the eighteenth and nineteenth century Enlightenment philosophy.[471] The main origin of the formation of a contract is the internal subjective will of the parties, by contrast with its external manifestations and with formalities generally. This does not mean that the subjective will should not be outwardly expressed. For example, accepting a proposition that is offered, but not exteriorizing it does not amount to consent. But an external manifestation of will, be it written or oral, is secondary to the subjective and internal will itself.

This theoretical background of subjective will theory in French law implies that judges look for what the 'common intention of the contracting parties was, rather than pay attention to the literal meaning of the terms'.[472] This explains the relevance of the subjective attitude in the assessment of the parties' conduct in negotiations.

4.3.2.3. Consistent behaviour

Another duty related to the requirement of subjective good faith is consistent behaviour (*coherence*). This prescribes firstly, that one should behave consistently with one's own previous behaviour, and secondly, that actions taken in negotiations do not contradict the parties' subjective attitudes.

The duty of consistent behaviour is illustrated by the way French courts sanction negotiations started 'without an intention to contract', with an 'intention to harm', with the aim of precluding or impeding negotiations with a third party, or with the sole aim of obtaining

467 On further elaboration of the term 'abrupt', see Section 4.3.3.1.

468 Ghestin 2007a, especially footnote 2.

469 Barnes 2008; Arnaud 1969, at 200.

470 Roman law did not protect acts made without respect for formalities. Such acts could not give rise to a cause of action or a liability following the early Roman law principle *ex nudo pacto inter cives Romanos actio non nascitur.*

471 Arnaud 1969, at 197 ff.; Terré/Simler/Lequette 2013, para 7–8.

472 Article 1156 *Code civil* (amended by Article 1188 *Ordonnance*).

commercially sensitive or confidential information.[473] Consistent behaviour is also illustrated by the sanctioning of withdrawal from negotiations in an abrupt way. Furthermore, French judges have found that conducting negotiations with the use of 'fraudulent gambits' (*manœuvres frauduleuses*) is contrary to the duty of coherence. 'Fraudulent gambits' may consist, for example, in providing false information during negotiations. More generally, the *Cour de cassation* has found breach of the duty of consistent behaviour when a party's conduct was in opposition to reliance he had induced in negotiations.

Finally, it is worth noting that the duty of consistent behaviour is closely related to the regulation of vitiation of contractual consent (*vices du consentement*),[474] but is narrower. Whereas vitiated consent affects the validity of a concluded contract, the duty of consistent behaviour discussed above concerns only the precontractual period, and its breach represents a fault in tort.

4.3.2.4. Transparency

French courts have also referred to the duty of transparency. This requires parties to negotiations to provide each other with information. The approach to transparency in negotiations is currently reflected in Article 1112–1 *Ordonnance* which arguably follows the development of this duty in the French case law.

The requirement of transparency in the conduct of negotiations has been shaped as part of a more general obligation to provide information. The latter is established both legally and by judicial practice within a broader context of control of vitiated consent.[475] The difference between the general obligation to provide information and the regulation of negotiations lies in the nature of liability. Whereas the breach of good faith may constitute fault in negotiations and leads to liability in tort, breach of the information provisions leads primarily to invalidity of the concluded contract (due to vitiation of consent).

It should be noted firstly that the *Code civil* established no obligation to provide information in precontractual or contractual relations.[476] Historically, following the idea of the drafters of the *Code civil*, parties had to be cautious and had to inform themselves about the negotiated deal in accordance with the expression 'a buyer should be curious' (from a Latin expression *emptor debet esse curiosus*).[477] This expression reflected the nineteenth century spirit of freedom of contract underpinning the *Code civil*. The obligation to inform has been developed by French courts subsequently, during the last decades of the twentieth century primarily in relation to consumer contracts.[478]

[473] Cass com 3 October 1978 N° 77–10915 Bulletin 1978 nº 208.
[474] Articles 1109–1122 *Code civil* (amended by Articles 1188 ff. *Ordonnance*).
[475] For the broader literature on the obligation of information see inter alia with further references Fabre-Magnan 1992.
[476] See for an elaboration of duty by the French case law Fabre-Magnan 1992.
[477] Terré/Simler/Lequette 2013, para 259.
[478] Currently imposed by Article L. 111–1 Consumer code; Burgard 2011.

Imposing this obligation to inform was aimed at remedying salient imbalances between the parties in terms of access to information and bargaining power. These developments have also touched contracts between commercial parties, albeit to a limited extent.

On the one hand, it remains true that professional parties[479] have no obligation to extensively inform each other about an ordinary product – a product familiar to both parties. It is presumed that a professional contracting within the field of its competencies is familiar with the characteristics of the negotiated product.[480] On the other hand, by contrast with an ordinary product, an obligation to inform exists when the buyer lacks competencies to properly assess the product's characteristics. In fact, in order to define whether an obligation to inform exists, French judges balance the parties' respective competencies based on the established facts of the case.[481] The *Cour de cassation* has stated that when a product is newly developed, the buyer does not have sufficient competencies to fully assess its properties.[482] This approach is generally relevant to contracts for the development or manufacture of innovative products. At the same time, a potential buyer has a reciprocal obligation to explain what its expectations from a product are if the product is developed at the buyer's demand.[483]

The scope of the duty of transparency and information at the precontractual stage is relatively limited. At the same time, it is not underestimated by the French courts when negotiations involve two parties with a considerable difference in competencies regarding the subject of their negotiations.

4.3.2.5. Confidentiality

The *Ordonnance* specifically addresses confidentiality in negotiations. According to Article 1112-2 *Ordonnance*, the party using confidential information obtained in the course of negotiations without permission incurs liability. This provision does not

479 The definition of 'professional' is made by the *Cour de cassation* on a case-by-case basis by assessing competencies of a particular party regarding the particular good or service. Most of the times it corresponds to the term commercial party used in this study.

480 For illustration, see Cass 1 civ 30 November 2004 N° 01-14314 n.p. in Bulletin. In this case, a company sold a substance for a plant's treatment to a professional grower of prunes. The buyer treated fifty hectares of gardens with the substance. A month after the treatment, the fruits fell from the trees and became unfit for consumption. The buyer claimed damages, alleging that the seller had not complied with its obligation of information about the substance's properties. The *Cour de cassation* stated that a professional grower could have informed itself about the properties of the substance in question. No liability of the seller was therefore engaged.

481 For example Cass 1 civ 20 June 1995 N° 93-15948 Bulletin 1995 n° 277. The *Cour de cassation* imposed on a seller of vessels an obligation of information in negotiations about sale of a boat engine, contending that the buyer – a professional in fishing – was not sufficiently competent in boat engines. See also Cass com 19 February 2002 N° 99-13100 n.p. in Bulletin.

482 Cass 3 civ 18 February 2004 N° 02-17523 n.p. in Bulletin.

483 See for illustration Cass com 8 July 2003 N° 01-10495 unpublished, where a client was held partially liable because he had not defined properly his needs and expectations of the future product. The buyer failed to let the producer know that the metallic hooks to be produced were required for use in the mining industry.

mention the possibility of implying a duty of confidentiality. Neither does it go into detail as to what information is to be regarded as confidential. Does the provision cover all information? Should the secret character of information be explicitly mentioned on its disclosure?

According to the French case law and scholarship, each party should observe the confidentiality of information obtained in the course of negotiations. It is certain that not only information protected by the rights of intellectual property should be kept confidential. This approach has been formulated by the *Cour de cassation*[484] in a dispute where a party obtained information on a technological process during the course of negotiations. The process was developed by the other party, but was not yet patented. According to the *Cour de cassation*, the judges did not need to verify whether the process was patented or in the public domain to establish the unfair competition (*concurrence déloyale*). The fact that the information was obtained during negotiations and used without permission was said to be sufficient for establishing fault. This reasoning is based on the more general protection of a commercial secret (*secret des affaires*) in French law.[485]

4.3.3. *Breach of the duty as fault in tort*

In French law, a breach of precontractual duties can constitute a fault in tort. The *Cour de cassation* has qualified a number of types of conduct in this way. According to the academic literature,[486]the variety of approaches taken in case law bears witness to the fragmentation and disparity of the legal grounds on which judges base the 'ethics of negotiations'. Some decisions invoke, for instance, the parties' failure to comply with a precontractual duty, whereas others refer to the theory of abuse of right. Several decisions mention neither precontractual duties, nor the concept of abuse of right. Instead, the *Cour de cassation* simply qualifies a particular behaviour as a fault in the same way as any other tortious conduct, and does not emphasize the precontractual character of the fault.[487] Despite the variety of doctrinal references used by the *Cour de cassation* to motivate its decisions, two categories of fault can be distinguished on a pragmatic basis: fault related to withdrawal from negotiations and fault in conducting negotiations.

4.3.3.1. Fault related to withdrawal from negotiations

In discussing fault related to withdrawal from negotiations, it should be noted in the first place that in French law, parties have a right to withdraw from negotiations as implied by

484 Cass com 3 October 1978 N° 77–10915 Bulletin 1978 n° 208.

485 See with further references Py/Garinot 2015.

486 Fages 2011c, para 117.21.

487 Despite its limited practical relevance, the precise reference for qualifying a particular conduct as fault has been also the subject of debate. Opinions remain divided between references to good faith, loyalty, and prohibition of abuse of right.

freedom of contract. Following this principle, the mere *fact* of withdrawing from negotiations does not amount to a fault. It is the *manner* in which the right to resume negotiations right is exercised that is controlled by the French judges.[488] They take into account several factors, including the degree of advancement of negotiations, the extent to which the withdrawal was belated, the aggrieved party's legitimate expectation (*croyance légitime*), the abruptness of withdrawal, and the reasons for withdrawal.[489]

The degree of advancement and elaboration of negotiations is an important factor in the assessment of fault committed in the course of negotiations. As noted by Mazeaud, freedom of contract diminishes with the progression of negotiations.[490] Breaking off advanced negotiations is frequently a sign of the negotiator's fault.[491] The *Cour de cassation* explains the concept of advanced and elaborate negotiations as follows. The main reference is the duration of negotiations. Their advancement and elaboration is primarily associated by the *Cour de cassation* with the increase in their length.[492] The longer parties negotiate, the higher the probability that negotiations have reached an advanced stage according to the French case law. This approach echoes the ideas of Salleilles, who argued that progression of negotiations binds parties together, and that these ties should not remain unobserved by law.[493]

Some decisions of the *Cour de cassation* contrast with the usual approach. In some cases the highest judicial authority has qualified relatively brief negotiations as advanced. To reach this conclusion it referred to their substance, but not length.[494] For example, clarity on the substance of negotiations accompanied by the payment of 10% of the negotiated price allowed the court to qualify negotiations as very advanced.[495] Generally, however, French courts exclude fault more readily at the beginning of negotiations than when negotiations have lasted for some time, for instance some months or years.[496]

Another factor taken into account is the moment of withdrawal. The courts assess, in particular, whether the withdrawal from negotiations was belated. The *Cour de cassation* has elaborated on this factor in an important case *Manoukian*.[497] In spring 1997, a design company, Alain Manoukian, entered into negotiations with X and Y, both shareholders

488 Mazeaud 2001.

489 See generally Fages 2011c.

490 Mazeaud 2001, at 644.

491 Cass com 20 March 1972 N° 70-14154 Bulletin 1972 n° 93; Cass com 22 April 1997 N° 94-18953 n.p. in Bulletin; Cass com 18 January 2011 N° 09-14617 n.p. in Bulletin.

492 Fages 2011c, para 117-30.

493 Salleilles 1907.

494 A possibility of this way to assess negotiations has been also suggested by French scholars. See Fages 2011c, para 117-30.

495 Cass com 22 April 1997 N° 94-18953 n.p. in Bulletin. See also an example of 'short but advanced negotiaitons' in Cass 1 civ 6 January 1998 N° 95-19199 Bulletin 1998 n° 7.

496 Laithier 2010.

497 Cass com 26 November 2003 N° 00-10243; N° 00-10949 Bulletin 2003 n° 186 Manoukian. See in the same sense Cass com 13 October 2009 N° 08-16634 n.p. in Bulletin.

of the company Stuck, regarding the sale of Stuck's shares. The negotiations proceeded until November 1997, but on November 24, Alain Manoukian learned that on November 10, X had consented to sell the shares in Stuck to a third party, the company Les Complices. Alain Manoukian made a claim against X for a fault in negotiations. It claimed damage resulting from a late communication by X of his decision to conclude a contract with a third party. The *Cour de cassation* found that X's was at fault. It stated in more generally as follows. A party to negotiations commits a tort if he informs the other party about the decision not to contract only after having concluded a contract on the same matter with a third party.

Furthermore, the assessment of precontractual fault often includes an inquiry into the aggrieved party's legitimate expectation of a positive outcome of negotiations (*croyance légitime*). The positive outcome is the conclusion of the negotiated contract. Legitimate expectation is an overarching indicator of precontractual fault, often invoked to reinforce one or several other criteria or colouring the judges' reasoning implicitly.[498] Ghestin calls it 'Ariadne's thread' in the judicial control of the parties' conduct in precontractual negotiations.[499] The usual approach in case law is clearly based on the idea that parties' legitimate expectation in the success of the deal increases with the advancement of negotiations. A withdrawal from negotiations becomes thus decreasingly permissible. French courts tend also to examine the role of the other party in the creation of the legitimate expectations, but this is not explicit in all the decisions.

Next to this, the abruptness of breaking off negotiations plays a role in establishing a precontractual fault. This criterion is often invoked in combination with other factors. The meaning of 'abrupt' has been explained by the *Cour de cassation* in several decisions. A withdrawal was considered to be rude and abrupt in the following situations.

- Negotiations lasted more than one year and included a feasibility study of a project's perspectives. One of the parties, however, refused three final proposals without explaining the reasons and terminated negotiations. This withdrawal was regarded by the court as rude and abrupt.[500]
- Four-year long negotiations of a complex contract included a feasibility study. However, the breaking off of negotiations was not caused by the outcome of the feasibility study. As a consequence, the *Cour de cassation* qualified this withdrawal as abrupt.[501]
- Negotiations were broken off by a letter sent on the day on which signature of the final agreed version of the contract was scheduled.[502] In the same way, terminating

498 Cass com 15 October 2002 N° 00–13738 n.p. in Bulletin; see also Cass com 7 January 1997 N° 94–21561 n.p. in Bulletin; Fages 2011c, para 117–33. See also Muir-Watt 2003.

499 Ghestin 2007a, para 24.

500 Cass com 7 January 1997 N° 94–21561 n.p. in Bulletin.

501 Cass com 7 April 1998 N° 95–20361 n.p. in Bulletin.

502 CA Versailles 10 September 2009 N° 08/04982 JurisData unavailable.

'short but advanced' negotiations the day before the expected signing of a promise to contract was regarded as abrupt.[503]

- A party terminated negotiations based on his conviction that the other party was not interested in concluding the contract. However, the notification about the withdrawal contained neither the reasons for this conviction, nor a precise time for the other party to confirm his willingness to contract. The *Cour de cassation* regarded this conduct as 'brutal and abrupt'.[504]
- A withdrawal from negotiations made with an intention to harm the other party was also found to be abrupt.[505]

Finally, French courts sometimes ascertain whether the withdrawing party had 'legitimate reasons' to break off negotiations. The expression 'legitimate reasons' is contradictory, because the freedom of contract implies the right to withdraw, while the courts control only the way this right is exercised. As a matter of fact, the courts inquire on a case-by-case basis whether any reason objectively justifying the withdrawal is in place and, more importantly, whether the reason corresponds to the objectively assessed circumstances of the case. Within this assessment, serious and objective reasons to break off negotiations are referred to as 'legitimate reasons'. Their absence may constitute a fault.[506] For instance, 'internal considerations of the group of companies' are usually not regarded as a 'legitimate reason' (thus not sufficiently serious and objective) for withdrawing from negotiations.[507] By contrast, when a party is considered to have 'legitimate reasons' to withdraw from negotiations, he may break off even advanced negotiations, and do so even in an abrupt way.[508]

One of the most frequently accepted 'legitimate reasons' to withdraw from negotiations without fault are 'good economic' reasons. The most frequently invoked 'good economic reasons' are these.

- Unilateral withdrawal from negotiations was regarded as legitimate, when one party stopped negotiations because the other party's equipment did not comply with the project's requirements.[509]
- A persisting disagreement between the parties that precludes positive outcome of negotiations can also justify a withdrawal.[510]

503 Cass 1 civ 6 January 1998 N° 95–19199 Bulletin 1998 nº 7.
504 Cass com 22 April 1997 N° 94–18953 n.p. in Bulletin.
505 Cass 3 civ 3 October 1972 N° 71–12993 Bulletin 1972 nº 491.
506 Fages 2011c, para 117–39.
507 Cass com 7 April 1998 N° 95–20361 n.p. in Bulletin.
508 Laithier 2010.
509 Cass com 7 March 2006 N° 04–17177 n.p. in Bulletin. In this case, in negotiations for a contract for outsourcing of production of a sauce, the equipment of the potential contractor was unfit for making the standard packaging of the sauces, whereas the requirements of the machines was communicated at the beginning of negotiations.
510 CA Paris 23 September 2009 N° 07/06702 JurisData 2009–012376; Cass 2 civ 5 January 1994 N° 92–13856 n.p. in Bulletin ('*divergences persistentes quant à une éventuelle formalisation d'un accord*').

- If one party to negotiations provides no documents that may confirm the information he provided during negotiations, the other party has good economic reason to break off negotiations. For example, in one case, parties negotiated a distribution contract. One party claimed the 'expansion of his sales network' in the discussions, but failed to confirm this in any documents. Several requests for such documents remained unsatisfied, and the counterparty broke off negotiations. The *Cour de cassation* found that negotiations were broken off for a 'good economic reason'.[511] In another case, parties negotiated a sales contract. Its execution involved several subsidiaries of one of the parties. At the same time, this party could not attest to the good financial situation of the subsidiaries. After several requests, the counterparty broke off negotiations. The court of first instance (approved later by the *Cour de cassation*) emphasized that the withdrawing party had faced financial difficulties previously. As a consequence, its caution about the solvency of its potential partners constituted a 'good economic reason' to stop negotiations.[512]
- Unsatisfactory results of a financial or legal audit can also constitute a 'good economic reason for withdrawal'. In one case, positive results of an audit was a condition of an acquisition of part of the capital of one of the parties to negotiations. According to the judges, breaking off negotiations on the basis of the audit's unsatisfactory results did not represent a fault.[513]
- An offer made by a third party with more profitable financial conditions – a higher bid – forms a 'good economical reason' for withdrawal from precontractual negotiations, provided the discussions about a lower price offer were one of the main topics of negotiations.[514] In this way breaking off to choose a higher bid was regarded as legitimate, in a case where the counterparty to negotiations was aware of parallel negotiations conducted with third parties and thus of the on-going competition.[515]
- A party has 'good economic reasons' to break off negotiations where he has made several offers, all of which are rejected. In one case, several offers were made during eight months of negotiations.[516]
- The *Cour de cassation* has also found a withdrawal to be justified in the following case. The party in charge of drafting the final version of the contract unexpectedly reflected his own position in the document instead of understandings reached in negotiations. In a 2002 case, parties negotiated a share purchase contract. During the entire period of negotiations, parties remained in disagreement about future control over the company. When an agreement on this issue was reached, one of the parties created a 'definitive version of a contract for signature'. However, instead of the

[511] Cass com 5 May 2009 N° 08–10474 n.p. in Bulletin.

[512] Cass 1 civ 11 February 2010 N° 08–20315. See also Cass com 20 November 2007 N° 06–20332 n.p. in Bulletin (a party withdrew from negotiations because his consultants (a law firm) had found 'unfavorable information' about the other party's financial situation); CA Paris, du 13 September 2007 N° 06/14150 JurisData 2007–344405 (a withdrawal was regarded as justified because a negotiating party has not provided relevant financial information as required by Article L. 141–1 Commercial code).

[513] Cass com 20 November 2007 N° 06–20332 n.p. in Bulletin.

[514] Cass com 26 March 2008 N° 07–11026 n.p. in Bulletin.

[515] CA Paris 12 March 2009 N° 07/07588 JurisData 2009–379005.

[516] Cass 2 civ 4 March 2004 N° 02–14022 n.p. in Bulletin.

agreements reached earlier in negotiations, the text contained the drafters' initial objective at the start of negotiations.[517]

- Negotiations may be terminated if a project for a future product remained at the stage of an imprecise draft. The *Cour de cassation* decided accordingly, disregarding several steps made in the development of a new product by one of the parties. Moreover, the fact that negotiations were broken off in an 'abrupt manner' was disregarded as well.[518]
- Finally, if one of the parties fails to obtain funding necessary for a proper execution of the future contract, the other also has 'good economic reasons' to withdraw from negotiations.[519]

Some scholars argue that by controlling the reasons for withdrawal, French courts have imposed an obligation to show a reason for the decision to break off negotiations.[520]

4.3.3.2. Fault in conducting negotiations

In addition to fault related to withdrawal from negotiations, fault may also reside in parties' *conduct* during negotiations. The following examples illustrate conduct regarded as contrary to good faith, loyalty or transparency.

- Starting negotiations without intention to contract. This is based on the duty of consistent behaviour discussed earlier.
- Continuing negotiations when a decision not to contract has already been taken.[521]
- Any conduct in negotiations with an intention to harm.[522]
- Encouraging the other party to make investment at the precontractual stage, creating an impression and a firm belief that a contract will be concluded.[523] This factor is closely connected to the protection of 'legitimate expectations' addressed earlier.

4.4. Avant-contrat

Precontractual duties envisaged in the previous Section are imposed in all negotiations. If parties do not create any documents preparing a future contract, but simply negotiate, the 'ethics of negotiations' are the only legal regulation of their negotiations. In the French system, the approach changes, however, if parties organize negotiations contractually

517 CA Amiens 26 May 2009 N° 07/00842 JurisData 2009–379094 (un *accord de principe* is concluded, but parties are in persistent disagreement); CA Caen 6 January 2009 N° 07/02486 JurisData 2009–006640; CA Paris 2 July 2008 N° 06/06898 JurisData 2008–368548.

518 Cass com 16 February 2010 N° 09–12097 n.p. in Bulletin.

519 Cass 1 civ 9 January 2007 N° 05–14365 Bulletin 2007 n° 13.

520 Fages 2011c, para 117–39.

521 Cass com 26 November 2003 N° 00–10243; N° 00–10949 Bulletin 2003 n° 186 Manoukian; Cass com 13 October 2009 N° 08–16634 n.p. in Bulletin.

522 Cass 3 civ 3 October 1972 N° 71–12993 Bulletin 1972 n° 491.

523 Cass com 15 October 2002 N° 00–13738 n.p. in Bulletin.

In the French legal system, parties may submit the regulation of precontractual negotiations (or a part of this regulation) to the regime of contract law. French case law recognizes several types of agreements to negotiate (*accords de pourparlers*) and preliminary agreements (*avant-contrats*).[524] These preliminary agreements prepare for the creation of a contract in the future and may bind parties with contractual obligations before the negotiated contract is concluded. A possibility to enter into such agreement flows in French law from the principles of freedom of contract. The progressive recognition of *avant-contrat* in case law relied on the interpretation of the general law of obligations.

Once created, such a document adds a contractual cause of action to the tortious action for fault in negotiations (discussed earlier). In this way, a fault in negotiations leads to liability in tort; a breach of a contractual obligation of the *avant-contrat* leads to contractual liability.[525] A breach of 'ethics of negotiations' remains sanctioned by tort as long as it is not a breach of an agreement to negotiate or a preliminary agreement. For this type of misconduct in negotiations, a contractual cause of action is open to the aggrieved party.[526] In this way, French law enables parties to validly privatize the legal regulation of their precontractual negotiations by complementing, reinforcing or excluding certain precontractual duties (within the limits accepted in case law).

From the plethora of instruments used in practice and discussed in the literature, the *Ordonnance* defines two: the pre-emption agreement (Article 1123) and the unilateral promise (Article 1124).

French scholars have generally welcomed the inclusion in the draft *Ordonnance* of the provisions on two preliminary agreements, because these give a legal basis to the instruments frequently used in practice.[527] As noted earlier, the *Code civil* is silent on the framework of *avant-contrat*. Given the fact that codified law is the primary source of law in France, the provisions on unilateral promise and pre-emption agreement acknowledge the development of law that has *de facto* already taken place.

The provisions have been welcomed primarily for ensuring the enforceability of these preliminary agreements and clarifying the remedies for their breach. This clarification will decrease uncertainty in disputes as to whether *avant-contrats* can have legal effects before the formation of the final contract. Furthermore, fewer doubts will arise as to the measure of liability, while some fifty years ago, such doubts were very sound.[528]

524 See inter alia with further references Congrès des Notaires de France 1964; Mousseron/Guibal/Mainguy 2001; De Coninck 2002; Deshayes 2008; Fages 2012.

525 Terré/Simler/Lequette 2013, para 870 ff. Re-qualification of letter of intent into offer and acceptance is not addressed in detail in this study. See for the French law with further references Laude 1992.

526 CA Versailles 10 September 2009 N° 05/01862 JurisData 2009-012284.

527 Fages 2015; Fages 2014; Mainguy 2014.

528 Congrès des Notaires de France 1964; Schmidt-Szalewski 2000.

However, the positive attitude of French scholars is nuanced. The provision of definitions of preliminary agreements has been criticized for encasing living and developing trade usages related to *avant-contrat* in 'rigid legal moulds'.[529] This critique might explain why the *Ordonnance* does not include an entire inventory of the preliminary agreements frequently used in practice, but is limited to the two most salient ones.[530]

This Section will elaborate on the extent to which parties may actually privatize their negotiations by *avant-contrat*. It will address firstly, two types of agreement to negotiate acknowledged in case law and academic literature (4.4.1). Thereafter, preliminary agreements included in the *Ordonnance* will be discussed (4.4.2).[531]

4.4.1. Agreements to negotiate

4.4.1.1. Project of contract

The project of contract (*projet de contrat*) is worth mentioning first for the following reason. French case law considers it to be the first step in framing negotiations, despite the fact it implies no obligations for the parties.[532] The project of contract represents a draft of the final contract. It is supposed to include all the provisions of the future contract. The project of contract would represent a final contract if it were to witness also a manifestation of the parties' will to conclude a contract, but this is not the aim of this document. The project of contract is said to be established at the very beginning of negotiations when parties have not yet taken a decision to contract, nor manifested their will to do this.

The academic literature and case law refer to two main situations where project of contract is used. Firstly, parties draft a project of contract simply as a starting point of negotiations. This can be done for practical reasons. For example, if negotiations require several stakeholders to be informed. Secondly, project of contract is created to fulfil an obligation of information imposed by law for negotiations of certain contracts. For instance, the Insurance code[533] requires the insurer to provide the insured party with a 'project of contract and its addenda or with an information notice that accurately describes guaranties… and the obligations of the insured'.[534] These documents are not binding on the parties.[535] The Commercial code states that each party authorizing 'an exclusive or almost exclusive' use of its commercial name, mark or sign must provide the other party with a document containing truthful information that enables the latter to

529 Fages 2014; Mainguy 2014.

530 According to S. Bernheim-Desvaux, not including other *avant-contrats* in the draft *Ordonnance* is indeed a voluntary omission. See Bernheim-Desvaux 2015, at 9.

531 This subsection is partly based on Pannebakker 2016.

532 Le Tourneau 2014, para 867; Rozès 1996.

533 Article L 112-2 Insurance code.

534 Ibid.

535 Ibid.

make an informed consent.[536] 'This document, as well *as a project of contract* has to be provided twenty days before the signing of a contract at the latest'.[537] In this way, project of contract may be regarded as a form of private organization of negotiations. However, this document does not imply any obligations for the parties and has merely an informative function.

4.4.1.2. Agreement in principle

Agreement in principle creates a contractually binding obligation to negotiate. Failure to respect an agreement in principle may be sanctioned by contractual liability, because the obligation to negotiate which it implies is contractually binding and enforceable.[538] It reinforces the 'ethics of negotiations' by obliging parties to start negotiations regarding a particular subject or continue negotiations already started in good faith, in a loyal manner.[539] According to French scholars, agreement in principle corresponds to the situation where parties have not yet negotiated essential or other conditions of the future contract.

The scope of the obligation to negotiate implied by the agreement in principle is limited to the mere process of negotiations. More concretely, parties only have to insure negotiations take place, but are not obliged to conclude the final contract. French courts and scholars regard the obligation to negotiate as an 'obligation of means' (*obligation de moyens).*[540] Under this type of obligation, the debtor is required to use all available means for reaching the result expected by the other party. By contrast, the debtor is not required to reach a particular result. In order to prove a debtor's liability for a violation of an 'obligation of means', the creditor must show that not all available means were used. This is opposed to the 'obligation of result' (*obligation de résultat*).[541] The latter type of obligation requires the debtor to reach a concrete result.

Accordingly, under an agreement in principle, parties must not 'sabotage' the process of negotiations. They have to examine documents and proposals of the other party. This is regarded as the means in the sense of the obligation of means. Negotiations do not necessarily have to lead to formation of a contract (formation of contract being the result).

536 This information includes company's experience, perspectives of the market in question, potential clients, the duration, conditions of extention and stopping the contract and the extent of exclusivity. See Article L330–3 Commercial code.

537 Article L330–3 Commercial code.

538 Rozès 1996; Rozès 1998.

539 Schmidt-Szalewski 2000.

540 Terré/Simler/Lequette 2013, para 577–580.

541 Ibid.

4.4.2. *Preliminary agreements in the Ordonnance*

4.4.2.1. Pre-emption agreement

Article 1123 of the *Ordonnance* introduces the concept of pre-emption agreement (*pacte de préférence*). It is 'a contract by which a party undertakes that, in the event that he decides to enter into a contract, he will make the first proposal for that contract to the beneficiary of the pre-emption agreement'.[542] The pre-emption agreement represents a contract in itself. It imposes two obligations. Firstly, it imposes an obligation to negotiate in the same way as agreement in principle (discussed above). Furthermore, the pre-emption agreement creates a contractual limitation on the freedom of one of the parties to choose a future contractor (whereas conducting parallel negotiations remain possible in principle).

Pre-emption can be established, for example, in the following terms:[543]

> The signing parties grant each other a right of mutual pre-emption in case of transfer of their shares ... if they would plan to cede the named shares. This pre-emption right is agreed for the period of Five years starting as of today.

The new rules on pre-emption agreements are primarily case law based. As appears from the case law, a pre-emption agreement can prepare a wide range of contracts.[544] For example, company transactions, establishing preference in buying shares or parts in capital,[545] franchise and partnership agreements,[546] tenancy contracts, and contracts between an author and a publisher for pre-emption in the publication of future works. In some types of transactions, however, the validity of a pre-emption agreement is limited by rules applying to specific types of contracts. For instance, the Intellectual property code limits the scope of pre-emption rights that may be granted by an author to a publisher. It states that an obligation granting a right of preference to a publisher for the publication of his future works is valid.[547] However, a '[t]otal transfer of future works

542 Article 1123 *Ordonnance*.

543 Cass com 15 December 2009 N° 08–21037 Bulletin 2009 n° 173.

544 Fages 2011d, para 120.22. An obligation of pre-emption can be established by a separate agreement, or, alternatively be included into another contract or into company statutes (in case of corporate transactions). This section will focus in the first place on the obligation of pre-emption as such and its effects, whereas the relation between a pre-emption agreement and the future contract will not be discussed.

545 Ginestet 2006. See for example Cass com 12 May 1992 N° 90–11764 n.p. in Bulletin: 'The signing parties undertake to offer the shares held by associated physical persons that would like to sell these in priority to MPA on normal conditions defined in annex for each signing company'.

546 Van De Wynckele-Bazela 2004. See for example Cass 1 civ 6 June 2001 N° 98–20673 Bulletin 2001 n° 166: 'I confirm my agreement to give you priority to take on contracts that we execute together in case of discontinuing operations'.

547 Article L132–4 Intellectual property code.

shall be null and void,'[548] and a pre-emption may be established only for five works of each type (specified) created during five years after the signature of the first publishing contract.[549]

The definition of pre-emption agreement in the *Ordonnance* does not specify whether pre-emption is supposed to be limited in time. In light of the case law, it may be said that the right can be given for a definite or indefinite term.[550] The period of pre-emption is not a condition of enforceability of the pre-emption agreement (with the exception of contracts for publishing mentioned earlier, where the period of pre-emption is limited by the Intellectual property code).[551] The possibility not to agree the period of pre-emption is not regarded as a discretionary condition (*potestative*, e.g. conditions that may be modified unilaterally by one party, are generally unenforceable under French law).[552]

An important peculiarity of a pre-emption agreement is the possibility to establish contractual obligations which are clearly distinct, separate, and independent from the future contract it anticipates. Even though the obligation of pre-emption grants priority to the beneficiary in the debtor's choice of parties to a future contract, neither party gives consent to conclude the future contract. Following this logic, courts have never recognized that a pre-emption agreement has formed a future contract. French judges have furthermore refused to imply terms of the future contract into parties' relations regulated only by a pre-emption agreement.[553]

Article 1123 of the *Ordonnance* defines the consequences of breach of the pre-emption agreement. These complete the effects of the newly codified concept of pre-emption agreement. Consequences of breach will be discussed in the Section on remedies below in this Chapter. At this stage, the following can be noted. The new rules on the pre-emption agreement reflect the solutions suggested in academic debate. The main debate on pre-emption agreements related to the nullity of a contract concluded in breach of the pre-emption agreement. The discussions have been primarily related to the practicality of the remedy,[554] to the interests of third parties, and more generally to the extent to which an *avant-contrat* may have effects for third parties aware of its existence.[555] The availability of this remedy was rather emphatically confirmed by the *Cour de cassation* in 2006,[556] and the *Ordonnance* follows this approach.

548 Article L131-1 Intellectual property code.
549 Article L132-4 Intellectual property code.
550 Cass 3 civ 15 January 2003 N° 01-03700 Bulletin 2003 n° 9.
551 Article L 132-4 Intellectual property code.
552 Cass 3 civ 15 January 2003 N° 01-03700 Bulletin 2003 n° 9.
553 Fages 2011d, para 120.7 notes that the opinions are divided in the scholarship as to whether a pre-emption agreement is an autonomous contract or just a type of unilateral promise subject to a condition.
554 For an overview of the debate see Laithier/Mazeaud 2012.
555 Schmidt-Szalewski 2000; Mestre 1998; Desideri 1997.
556 Cass mix 26 May 2006 N° 03-19376 Bulletin 2006 n° 4.

4.4.2.2. Unilateral promise

Article 1124 of the *Ordonnance* defines the unilateral promise (*promesse unliatérale* as 'a contract by which one party, the promisor, gives another, the beneficiary, a right, for a certain time, to have the option to conclude a contract whose essential elements are determined, and for the formation of which only the consent of the beneficiary is missing'.[557]

The definition contains several elements. First, the unilateral promise represents a contract in itself. Second, the option right that may be provided is supposed to be limited in time. Following the existing case law, the promise will lapse at the expiry of this period.[558] Third, the beneficiary's right relates to a contract, the negotiations for which have already set out the essential elements of the future agreement. Fourth, only the consent of the beneficiary to the final contract is absent, whereas the promisor's consent to the final contract is in place during the period for which the option right is given. The last element is related to the revocability of the unilateral promise. Even if the promise is revoked during the specified period, the contract will still be formed. Furthermore, Article 1124 defines the consequences of breach of a unilateral promise. These will be discussed in Section 4.7.2 below.

The definition of the unilateral promise is primarily case law based. It also reflects the choices made as a result of scholarly debates. One of the main debates related to the revocability of a unilateral promise. The *Ordonnance* takes a position in this relatively long-standing debate between the *Cour de cassation* and French scholars. The reason for the debate is the following. The unilateral promise subjects the formation of the future contract to the unilateral expression of the beneficiary's will. While the promisor has an obligation to maintain his consent to form the contract, it is for the beneficiary to decide to form the contract.[559] The beneficiary can take up one of the two options. It can express its will to buy and thereby form a contract. Alternatively, the beneficiary can give up its position as beneficiary in favour of freedom of contract. This brings the parties back to the same position as before concluding a promise to contract.

Since 1993, the *Cour de cassation* has found that the promise may be revoked, and this revocation would lead to the situation where the final contract is not formed for the lack of consent of one of the parties.[560] According to the *Cour de cassation*, the only possible recovery was reparation in damages. This position was underpinned essentially by the

557 Article 1124 *Ordonnance*.

558 Cass 3 civ 24 March 1993 N° 91–14080 n.p. in Bulletin; Cass 3 civ 8 October 2003 N° 02–11953 Bulletin 2003 n° 176. Earlier case law admitted the creation of a unilateral promise for an undetermined period. Such documents were treated in the same way as contracts for an indefinite term. See Cass 3 civ 17 July 1997 N° 95–19222 Bulletin 1997 n° 173.

559 Le Tourneau 2014, para 877.

560 Cass 2 civ 15 December 1993 N° 91–10199 Bulletin 1993 n° 174. See also Fabre-Magnan 2012 (approving the position of the *Cour de cassation*).

principle of freedom of contract. By contrast, several commentators have noted that the debtor should have no right to revoke his promise for the entire duration of the promise. According to them, this is the only solution that may logically flow from conceptualizing the unilateral promise as a contract. More concretely, if a unilateral promise is regarded as a contract concluded for a definite term, it should be taken into account that such contracts may not be unilaterally withdrawn.[561] The *Ordonnance* adopts the point of view advocated by many French scholars.

4.4.3. *Interim agreement*

Interim agreement (*accord provisoire*) is sometimes included into the category of *avant-contrat*.[562] This type of agreement to agree prepares the conclusion of a contract in the future by contractually fixing certain obligations relevant only for the period of negotiations.[563] These obligations are therefore regarded as 'interim' in comparison with the obligations to be included in the negotiated agreement. These are often obligations of confidentiality, exclusivity, mediation and arbitration, as well as obligations defining the place and time of negotiations, distribution of costs made during negotiations as well as contractual arrangements as a consequence of failed negotiations.

In fact, these agreements are proper contracts, and their validity and breach are regulated by the rules on contractual liability. These rules are applicable notwithstanding success or failure of negotiations, that is, whether or not an interim agreement is followed by the future agreement envisaged.[564]

4.5. Limited role of unjust enrichment

The final point to be mentioned in the discussion of the regulation of precontractual negotiations in French law is the doctrine of unjust enrichment (*enrichissement sans cause*). As has been noted earlier, entering into negotiations is a business risk, because negotiations may fail. However, in practice, parties frequently undertake preparatory works and bear costs in anticipation of a contract. Sometimes a party may benefit from other party's acts or investments made during negotiations.

In French law, next to causes of action in tort and in contract, a cause of action in unjust enrichment is available. This action is based on the principle of equity 'forbidding enrichment at the expense of other'[565] and can remedy possible imbalances created by

561 Wicker 2012; Mainguy 2011 (both disagreeing with the position of the *Cour de cassation*).

562 Fages 2011b, para 115–43 ff.

563 It should be noted, however, that if the judges establish that a partial or interim agreement contains the parties' agreement on all essential conditions of the future contract, the court will with a high probability also find the future contract concluded. See Laude 1992, particularly at 444–446.

564 Fages 2011b, para 115–52.

565 Cass req 15 June 1892 Recueil Sirey 1893, I, 28 Boudier, re-published in Terré/Lequette 1994, at 631.

transfer of benefit without legal grounds This Section will briefly explain the essence of the French doctrine of unjustified enrichment, conditions for liability, and provide an illustration of the application of these rules to benefits received during precontractual negotiations (using the example of a case decided by the *Cour de cassation*).

In the French system, an action for unjustified enrichment is *subsidiary* to claims in tort and contract. It can be admitted only if no cause of action is available.[566] For instance, if a party has a cause of action in tort, the amount of these costs should be claimed as a part of damages in tort.[567] If an obligation in negotiations is contractually organized, contractual liability prevails (both over liability in tort and in unjustified enrichment).[568]

The French doctrine of unjust enrichment is based on the concept of quasi-contract (*quasi-contrat*)[569] and on a judge-made cause of action established in the nineteenth century.[570] The *Cour de cassation* granted this in the *Boudier* case (1892).[571] The concept of quasi-contract stands in French law for obligations emanating neither from tort, nor from contract. These are 'purely voluntary acts of man, from which there results some undertaking towards a third party, and sometimes a reciprocal undertaking of both parties'.[572] As a matter of fact, the term quasi-contract erroneously refers to the word 'contract', because the obligations it entails are obligations in tort. Unjustified enrichment (*actio de in rem verso*) is one of the causes of actions entailed by quasi-contracts. This cause of action has been established by the *Cour de cassation* in the case *Boudier* (1892). It stated that 'the action *de in rem verso* based on the principle of equity that forbids to enrich at the expense of other' has to be allowed in 'all the cases of increase of wealth of a person at the expense of this of the other person occurred without a legitimate reason'.[573]

Several requirements should be observed in order to sustain a claim in unjustified enrichment. Firstly, there should be transfer of wealth from one party to another. The resulting increase of one party's wealth must cause a detriment to the party whose wealth has decreased. Importantly, a link of causality should be established between the enrichment and decrease of wealth.[574] Furthermore, the transfer should have already

566 It is to be noted that an action in unjustified enrichment will be refused if other causes of action are not available either as a result of lapse of time or because of the existence of a court judgment on the same matter. See Terré/Simler/Lequette 2013, para 1065.

567 Mestre/Fages 2005.

568 Pin/Devin 2011. Mestre and Fages note that the subsidiary character of unjustified enrichment should however not enable a party to obtain under the heading of unjustified enrichment more than he could have obtained claiming in contract or in tort. See Mestre/Fages 2005. See on this cause of action Terré/Simler/Lequette 2013, para 1026.

569 Pin/Devin 2011.

570 Malaurie/Aynès/Stoffel-Munck 2015, para 1056.

571 Cass req 15 June 1892 Recueil Sirey 1893, I, 28 Boudier, re-published in Terré/Lequette 1994, at 631.

572 Article 1371 *Code civil* and the corresponding Article 1300 *Ordonnance*. See on this cause of action Terré/Simler/Lequette 2013, para 1026.

573 Cass req 15 June 1892 Recueil Sirey 1893, I, 28 Boudier, re-published in Terré/Lequette 1994, at 631.

574 Terré/Simler/Lequette 2013, para 1067.

occurred at the time of action.[575] Secondly, the transfer of wealth should be made in the absence of a legal reason (for instance, in the absence of contractual obligations). Thirdly, the enrichment of one party should not result from the other party's intentional fault. For example, the enrichment should not be provoked or induced by the party who claims its reimbursement.[576] It follows from the case law of the *Cour de cassation* that simple negligence or absence of caution on the part of the party claiming recovery does not prevent the award of a claim for unjustified enrichment.[577]

Two examples of cases handled by the *Cour de cassation* illustrate the application of principles of unjustified enrichment to precontractual negotiations. Firstly, the *Cour de cassation* confirmed that the principles of unjustified enrichment apply to claims for expenditure incurred for improvement of another's property made in anticipation of a contract, negotiations for which failed.[578] Infotonic Girod and Giraudy, negotiated a possible sale of bill boards for displaying advertising which were installed in the city. The companies could not come to an agreement; the negotiations failed. Six years later, Infotonic Girod learned that for the six years following the failure of negotiations, Giraudy had been using the bill boards it has never bought. Infotonic Girod claimed unjustified enrichment against Giraudy, claiming the amount of benefit Giraudy received from the exploitation of the bill boards. Giraudy insisted in his pleadings that the owner of the bill boards was negligent, because the owner did not undertake any action to prevent their use for six years. The *Cour de cassation* solved the case as follows. It explicitly noted that that Article 1371 of the *Code civil* on quasi-contract and, in particular, the doctrine on unjustified enrichment, apply to the situations where, despite a failure of negotiations, one of the parties incurs costs as if a contract had been concluded or enjoys benefits as if a contract had been concluded. As stated by Mestre and Fages, in this way the *Cour de cassation* pointed to liability for unjustified enrichment as a 'means to restore the balance' between parties' gains.[579] The *Cour de cassation* had to consider the fact that the owner of the bill boards had not undertaken any action to prevent their use. The judges confirmed that imprudence or negligence of the party suffering a detriment because of the other's enrichment does not preclude his right to claim unjustified enrichment. In this case, the aggrieved party's negligence was also found to be irrelevant to the amount of damages awarded.

Secondly, the *Cour de cassation* has confirmed the application of the doctrine of unjust enrichment to situations where one party makes investments during negotiations in anticipation of a contract in another recent case.[580] A consumer goods manufacturer, Calvin Klein Jeanswear Europe (CK), entered into negotiations with Harold Saint

575 Ibid.

576 See generally Aubert 2004.

577 Cass 1 civ 15 December 1998 N° 96-20625 Bulletin 1998 n° 363; Cass 1 civ 13 July 2004 N° 01-03608 Bulletin 2004 n° 208.

578 Cass 1 civ 13 July 2004 N° 01-03608 Bulletin 2004 n° 208.

579 Mestre/Fages 2005.

580 Cass com 9 July 2013 N° 12-17434 n.p. in Bulletin.

Germain (Harold). Harold owed a location convenient for a shop. The negotiations concerned a possible opening of a shop at Harold's location selling goods produced by CK and called 'Calvin Klein Jeans'. In anticipation of a contract, CK invested in fittings and furniture for the future shop. However, negotiations failed after one year, and Harold opened another shop in the same year at the same location. CK made a claim in tort against Harold's, asking for reimbursement in damages caused by this withdrawal. In particular, CK claimed reimbursement for the costs of fitting out and furniture of the future shop. CK submitted that Harold had benefitted from this investment, because it opened the shop in the same year at the same location. Based on the facts of the case, the court of appeal re-qualified on its own motion the legal basis of CK's claim, changing it from tort to quasi-contract. The *Cour de cassation* approved this re-qualification, confirming the application of the principles of unjustified enrichment to such situations.[581]

In practice, cases involving the application of this doctrine to precontractual restitutions are infrequent in the French courts. This can partly be explained by the subsidiary character of this cause of action. Furthermore, the doctrine of unjustified enrichment in French law has not yet attained a high level of sophistication, despite its long history. Another reason is the subsidiary character of the unjust enrichment doctrine.

4.6. Dynamics of negotiations addressed in case law

Several matters relating to the dynamics of negotiations addressed in case law fall within the scope of the framework of *avant-contrat*. Alongside the provisions of *avant-contrat* addressed earlier, the following provisions can be noted: clauses on the non-binding character of negotiations (4.6.1), obligation to negotiate or negotiate in good faith (4.6.2), exclusivity of negotiations (4.6.3), confidentiality (4.6.4), and provisions on dispute resolution (4.6.5).

4.6.1. Provision on the non-binding character of negotiations

French law provides little or no possibility to keep contractual regulations outside the sphere of regulation by law. Until relatively recently, the *Cour de Cassation* used to admit that a 'gentleman's agreement' or honourable pledge (*engagement d'honneur*) enables the parties to 'contract out' of the legal regime.[582] It was regarded only as moral obligations that may not be enforced by a court.

This approach has evolved.[583] In commercial relations, a contrary tendency can be observed: modern case law considers a gentleman's agreement as creating an enforceable

581 In this case, the lower court failed to point to unjustified enrichment as the precise type of quasi-contract applicable.

582 Terré/Simler/Lequette 2013, para 56.

583 Relations in private sphere, for example, family relationship are still susceptible to be framed by honourable pledge that will not be enforced by a court. Terré/Simler/Lequette 2013, para 55.

obligation.[584] For instance, the *Cour de cassation* has found an enforceable obligation in an honourable pledge in which one company commited not to copy products marketed by another company.[585] In a similar way, an obligation formulated initially as a moral obligation to contribute to the statutory capital of an insolvent company was enforced as a legally binding obligation.[586]

4.6.2. *Obligation to negotiate*

Parties may in particular create an *obligation to negotiate* with a contractual nature, reinforcing in this way the requirements of the 'ethics of negotiations' to negotiate in good faith, in a loyal and transparent manner. This obligation is established by both the agreement in principle and the pre-emption agreement. The scope of the obligation to negotiate is in all cases limited to the mere process of negotiations, e.g. an obligation to use all possible means to reach a result.

4.6.3. *Exclusivity*

The *Ordonnance* does not address exclusivity of negotiations; according to the existing case law, parties may validly limit the possibility of conducting parallel negotiations by agreeing on exclusivity of negotiations.[587] The *Cour de cassation* has noted that an *avant-contrat* may contain an enforceable provision on exclusivity of negotiations.[588] It was noted at the same time that such an agreement does not preclude the possibility of engaging tortious liability for breach of requirements concerning the conduct of or breaking off negotiations developed under the umbrella of good faith.

A limited form of exclusivity is also provided by the pre-emption agreement. This does not limit the possibility to conduct parallel negotiations, but imposes limits on the debtor's choice of the first potential counterparty.

Furthermore, French case law recognizes so-called *sincerity* clauses (*clauses de sincérité*) included in precontractual documents.[589] These oblige a party to negotiations to inform the other one about the existence of any parallel negotiations with third parties on the same subject. This obligation can be undertaken by one party as a unilateral engagement or by all parties to negotiations. Whereas a sincerity clause does not limit parallel negotiations as such, it reinforces the obligation to provide information within the duty of transparency in negotiations.[590]

584 See Oppetit 1979; Beignier 1995.
585 Cass com 23 January 2007 N° 05-13189 Bulletin 2007 n° 12.
586 Cass com 18 January 2011 N° 09-69831 Bulletin 2011 n° 3.
587 Cass com 26 November 2003 N° 00-10243; N° 00-10949 Bulletin 2003 n° 186 Manoukian. See *Attendu* 5. See also CA Versailles 5 March 1992 N° 6893/90 JurisData 1992-040895; Le Tourneau 2014, para 892.
588 Cass com 8 October 2013 N° 12-18252 n.p. in Bulletin.
589 Fages 2011b, para 115-61.
590 See Section 4.3.2.4.

4.6.4. *Confidentiality*

In the French case law, confidentiality of negotiations established by an *avant-contat* has been upheld as enforceable.[591] For example, in a case decided by the *Cour d'Appel de Paris*, a letter of intent contained a confidentiality clause. An injunction was granted to prevent misuse of information.[592] In another case, a promise relating to the acquisition of company contained a clause about the confidential nature of negotiations. Despite this clause, representatives of the potential buyer visited the target companies. In the words used by the claimant and the court, this caused, 'a real panic' in the target companies' personnel. The *Cour d'Appel de Lyon* enforced the confidentiality clause.[593]

4.6.5. *Dispute resolution*

The enforceability of dispute resolution clauses inserted into precontractual documents received little attention in the French case law and literature.[594] Scarce discussions relating to the choice of law and choice of court might be due to the following. Le Tourneau notes, however, that a mediation clause may be enforceable as a separate *avant-contrat*.[595] As explained above, French law recognizes the contractual nature of documents established by the parties in preparation of the future contract. Consequently, the contractually binding force of a dispute resolution clause submitting disputes arising in negotiations to arbitration or mediation is therefore not often disputed in practice. The notes made in Chapter 3 on uniform European regulation in the field of choice of law and choice of court hold true for the French system.[596]

As to arbitration, the French regulation of arbitration[597] clearly establishes the principle of severability (separability) of an arbitration clause.[598] This means that the validity of an arbitration clause is independent of the validity of the document in which it is included. In this way, an arbitration clause is not automatically void if there is a reason for invalidity of the document in which it is included. The scope of these reasons is broad and includes all cases of invalidity existing under the French law (*inexistence, nullité, caducité, résolution* and *résiliation*). These cases of invalidity also include situations where parties

591 Fages 2011b, para 115-64; Le Tourneau 2013, para 888.

592 CA Paris 15 October 2013 N° 13/00807 JurisData unavailable.

593 CA Lyon 29 June 2010 N° 09/03313 JurisData unavailable.

594 See however recently Muller/Riske 2013.

595 Le Tourneau 2013, para 892.

596 See Section 3.7.9.

597 *Decret nº 2011-48 du 13 janvier 2011 portant réforme de l'arbitrage*, JORF 0011, 14 January 2011. The French system establishes different regimes for national and international arbitration. In view of the focus of this study, provisions on international arbitration are primarily relevant for this section. See Title II of the named Decree, and Article 1506 extending some provisions on national arbitration to international disputes if parties have not agreed otherwise. See also Jarrosson/Pellerin 2011; Gaillard/De Lapasse 2011.

598 Article 1147 *Decret nº 2011-48 du 13 janvier 2011 portant réforme de l'arbitrage*, JORF 0011, 14 January 2011.

dispute the very existence of the contract.[599] Therefore, an arbitration clause included in one of the documents established at the precontractual stage will be valid, provided it fulfils the conditions for its validity. French law requires, for instance, it should be international (to involve international trade instead of being confined to the French market),[600] must define the procedural rules applicable to arbitration (these may be designated directly or by reference).[601] At the same time, an arbitration clause (or agreement) does not have to fulfil any requirements of form[602]

The *Cour de cassation* has confirmed this approach in at least one case: two companies negotiated a contract and created a *protocole d'accord* which included an arbitration clause. The document was qualified as unenforceable in the first and second instances. The *Cour de cassation* disagreed. It noted that the arbitral tribunal selected by the *protocole d'accord* was competent to decide on the eventual enforceability of this document.[603]

In an ICC arbitral award,[604] the arbitral tribunal faced a dispute following the breaking off of merger negotiations. An arbitration clause was included in this case in a *protocole d'accord*. One of the defendants' arguments against the competence of the arbitral tribunal was a reference to the fact that the liability in question was not of a contractual, but a tortious, nature. Nevertheless, the arbitral tribunal found itself competent to hear the dispute.

4.6.6. *Distribution of costs*

French courts have enforced provisions that distribute costs in negotiations between the parties and solve the question of reparation in case negotiations fail (contractual arrangement of liability).[605] In the context of company transactions, such clauses are sometimes referred to as 'break-up fees'.

In principle, according to French case law, no damages for costs incurred in negotiations can be granted if parties agree to bear own costs in negotiations.[606] French courts have admitted the possibility of contractual regulation of damages caused by a breach of a bi-lateral promise to sell. They upheld the validity of a provision obliging the promisor to pay a certain amount of money to the beneficiary in case of breach of the promise to sell.

599 Carducci 2012 with further references.
600 Cass 1 civ 26 January 2011 N° 09-10198 Bulletin 2011 n° 15.
601 Aricle 1508 *Decret n° 2011-48 du 13 janvier 2011 portant réforme de l'arbitrage*, JORF 0011, 14 January 2011.
602 Article 1507 *Decret n° 2011-48 du 13 janvier 2011 portant réforme de l'arbitrage*, JORF 0011, 14 January 2011.
603 Cass 1 civ 28 November 2006 N° 05-10464 n.p. in Bulletin.
604 ICC Award 6519, Clunet 1991, at 1065 ff., www.trans-lex.org/206519.
605 Mazeaud 2004.
606 CA Paris 8 December 2009 N° 08/21540 JurisData 2009-380605.

Such provisions are referred as *clauses de dédit*.[607] According to the *Cour de cassation*, this amount may not be subject to review by the court if the clause is aimed at providing the possibility to compensate for the breaking off of negotiations, and to enable the break-off.[608]

By contrast, if the clause appears to attempt to force parties to enter into the final contract, it can be qualified as a penalty clause. The court may modify the amount of recovery if it is manifestly excessive or insufficient.[609]

4.7. Liability and remedies

4.7.1. Precontractual liability in tort

According to the French case law, the judicial control of the way parties conduct and exercise the freedom to break off negotiations requires a fault to be established. The fault may entail liability in tort, provided that all the conditions of tort liability are fulfilled.

The nature of liability that may arise in the course of negotiations is also characterized in the *Ordonnance*. The draft *Ordonnance* did this in a straightforward manner. It stated that the breach of the requirement of good faith and the unauthorized use of confidential information attract extra-contractual liability[610] that is, liability in tort.[611] The *Ordonnance* adopts the same approach, but the characterization of liability is implicit. The provisions limiting possible recovery refer to liability for fault committed in negotiations,[612] and this is a reference to liability in tort.

4.7.1.1. Damages

If all the conditions of tortious liability are fulfilled (e.g. fault, damage, and the causal link are established), the aggrieved party is entitled to recovery of damage. The case law of the *Cour de cassation* has long since limited the scope of the recoverable damages to the loss actually sustained in negotiations (*perte subie*). By contrast, the loss of chance to conclude the negotiated contract or loss of gain that could have resulted therefrom cannot be recovered.[613] French law therefore makes a distinction between the loss sustained in negotiation and the eventual bargain that could have been made.

607 Fages 2011e, para 125.54.

608 See Cass 3 civ 5 December 1984 N° 83-11788 Bulletin 1984 n° 207; Cass 3 civ 5 December 1984 N° 83-12895 Bulletin 1984 n° 208.

609 Article 1152 para 2. See Article 1231-5 *Ordonnance*.

610 See Articles 1111 and 1112 draft *Ordonnance*.

611 Articles 1240 ff. *Ordonnance*.

612 Article 1112 *Ordonnance*.

613 See Article 1112 *Ordonnance*. See earlier inter alia with further references Laithier 2010; Ghestin 2007b; Deshayes 2004; De Coninck 2002.

4.7.1.1.1. Sustained loss (perte subie)

Sustained loss is the damage already suffered by the aggrieved party at the moment of the claim. French law distinguishes three types of sustained loss. The first type is *material loss*, awarded the most frequently. This is the amount of costs invested in conducting negotiations or assessing a potential deal. The judges refer to the following costs: costs of preliminary studies, for example feasibility studies and marketing research;[614] costs of adaptation of immovable property in view of its future use;[615] fees paid to external consultants, for example, fees paid to a law firm;[616] and travel costs.[617]

The second type of loss is *harm to the reputation* (*atteinte à la réputation*). French scholars contend that failed negotiations can also cause this kind of damage.[618] However, the courts refrain from awarding this in most cases,[619] or award an amount that is rather symbolic for a company.[620]

Thirdly, the *Cour de cassation* allows recovery of damage that a party may incur as a result of *unfair competition* (*concurrence déloyale*). At the precontractual stage, unfair competition can result for instance from the misuse by a party to failed negotiations of commercially sensitive information which was shared by the other party in negotiations (for example, know-how, trade secrets and similar commercial information). If the misuse consists in taking advantage of such information or using it for his own profit, this will be considered as a fault in tort and the aggrieved party can recover for the damage caused.[621]

4.7.1.1.2. Loss of bargain

According to modern French case law, recovery of the loss of chance of being awarded a contract where negotiations have failed is not admitted. This is followed by the *Ordonnance* which places an explicit limit on recovery for fault in negotiations in

614 Cass com 22 April 1997 N° n.p. in Bulletin; Cass com 1 March 2011 N° 10–12268 n.p. in Bulletin; Cass 2 civ 10 October 2002 N° 01–03079 n.p. in Bulletin; CA Paris 10 March 2000 N° unavailable JurisData 2000–136163; CA Rennes 29 April 1992 N° 04953/91 JurisData 1992–051318 (costs of marketing and management invested in negotiations that lasted two years).

615 Cass com 26 November 2003 N° 00–10243; N° 00–10949 Bulletin 2003 n° 186 Manoukian; Cass com 12 October 1993 N° 91–19456 n.p. in Bulletin.

616 Cass com 13 October 2009 N° 08–16634 n.p. in Bulletin.

617 Cass com 20 March 1972 N° 70–14154 Bulletin 1972 n° 93; Ghestin 2007b, para 3.

618 Fages 2011c, para 117–45; Ghestin 2007b.

619 CA Saint-Denis de la Réunion 26 February 2014 N° 14/43, 12/01331 JurisData 2014–007275; CA Paris 8 December 2009 N° 08/21540 JurisData 2009–380605 (note, however, that in this case a letter of intent contained a provision on the distribution of costs).

620 CA Paris 11 September 2013 N° 11/13785 JurisData 2013–019310 (the amount of 5000 Euro has been awarded for damages to reputation caused by breaking off negotiations); CA Paris 12 March 2008 N° 06/04526 JurisData 2008–357913 (15000 Euros were granted for damage to the company's image); CA Paris 16 February 2001 N° 1999/08172 JurisData 2001–161480.

621 See for example Cass com 3 October 1978 N° 77–10915 Bulletin 1978 n° 208 (use of information on a patent provided in negotiations). Compare however Cass com 7 February 1995 N° 93–14569 n.p. in Bulletin.

Article 1112: it is not possible to recover loss of profits which were expected from the negotiated but non-concluded contract.

The approach of the *Ordonnance* summarizes the settled French case law. Faced with disparities in the approaches adopted by the courts, the *Cour de cassation* has explicitly stated in the *Manoukian* case[622] that a party aggrieved as a result of a precontractual fault was not entitled to recover the amount of money it could potentially have earned if the negotiated contract had been concluded. The *Cour de cassation* explained that 'in the absence of firm and final agreement', the loss of chance of being awarded a contract cannot be recovered, because 'a fault committed in the exercise of a right of unilateral withdrawal from pre-contractual negotiations is not the cause of damage consisting in the loss of chance to make a profit possibly expected from conclusion of a contract'.[623] According to the *Cour de cassation*, the fact of breaking off negotiations as such does not automatically lead to liability. In order to hold a party liable, a fault in tort and the elements of tort liability should also be in place. Furthermore, expectations raised in negotiations are protected by French law to a lesser extent than expectations arising from an existing contract. This approach has been strictly followed by the *Cour de cassation* in its later decisions.[624]

Having said this, it is to be noted that Article 1112 of the *Ordonnance* covers only liability for acting contrary to the requirement of good faith. By contrast, no limit is placed on recovery where liability arises for the unauthorized use of confidential information obtained in the course of negotiations (Article 1112–2 *Ordonnance*). Future case law may follow different paths. One possibility is that the limit in Article 1112 can be interpreted broadly and extended to the liability of Article 1112–2. However, this option eventually goes against the intention of the drafters of the *Ordonnance*, who separated the provisions on *bona fides* and treatment of confidential information. Alternatively, the interpretation may follow a different path and allow recovery of benefits obtained as a result of the misuse of confidential information. However, such liability is perhaps a too far-reaching solution for French law.

By contrast, the *loss of chance to conclude a contract with a third party* can probably be recovered. This recovery relates to the fact that negotiations may impede the exploration of other potential contract opportunities. Doubts regarding the possibility of this recovery are not resolved by the *Ordonnance*.

According to the current case law, this is the only type of loss of bargain that may be recovered for a precontractual fault.[625] The threshold is high for proving the existence of this chance,[626]

622 Cass com 26 November 2003 N° 00–10243; N° 00–10949 Bulletin 2003 nº 186 Manoukian.

623 Ibid.

624 Cass 3 civ 28 June 2006 N° 04–20040 Bulletin 2006 nº 164; Cass 3 civ 7 January 2009 N° 07–20783 Bulletin 2009 nº 5; Cass 3 civ 3 June 2009 N° 08–16813 n.p. in Bulletin; Cass com 18 September 2012 N° 11–19629 Bulletin 2012 nº 163; Cass 3 civ 19 September 2012 N° 11–10532 n.p. in Bulletin.

625 Cass com 7 April 1998 N° 95–20361 n.p. in Bulletin.

626 Ibid.

because the current case law requires this chance to be real and serious.[627] However, if the threshold is reached, French courts have been willing to award, for instance, the loss caused by the fact of being 'locked out' of the market during negotiations. For example, in a 1998 case, a company patented its invention – a method of packaging medicaments. Subsequently it negotiated the use of this patent for four years with one potential partner and without the possibility of negotiating with third parties. However, negotiations failed. The patent owner claimed damages, including the loss of bargain it might have had should it have been able to sell the patent rights to a third party (after the failure of negotiations, the patent owner capitalized the costs of patent as pure loss). Deciding on this case, the *Cour de cassation* expressly confirmed the right of the patent owner to recover the loss of chance of concluding a contract with a third party.[628] A similar decision has also been taken in a case where failed negotiations 'made it impossible for a seller to find another investor'.[629]

Despite the existence of these lines of cases, the reasoning of the *Cour de cassation* in *Manoukian* has cast doubts on the possibility of recovering a loss of chance to conclude a contract with a third party. French scholars have expressed the view that the *Manoukian* approach precluded the recovery of any loss of chance, including the loss of chance to conclude a contract with a third party.[630] The *Ordonnance* leaves this question open. The possibility of such recovery is therefore open to doubt until further decisions of the *Cour de cassation*.

4.7.1.1.3. Note on specific performance

Finally, specific performance or execution in nature (*exécution en nature*) of a precontractual duty cannot be used to enforce precontractual duties under the heading of liability in tort. French courts do not order parties to conclude the contract they have negotiated. This approach is adopted because within the French system, precontractual fault in tort relates only to the negotiation process, but not to the negotiated contract.[631]

4.7.1.2. Decrease of recovery for taking risks

The amount of damages awarded for precontractual fault can also be influenced by the conduct of the aggrieved party. Establishing the extent to which the aggrieved party's conduct is taken into account in the French system, the *Cour de cassation* has noted on several occasions that entering into negotiations entails taking a business risk regarding their outcome. Parties are therefore expected to be cautious about spending money related to negotiations, especially when faced with encouragements to invest.[632] If the

627 CA Rennes 29 April 1992 N° 04953/91 JurisData 1992–051318.
628 Cass com 7 April 1998 N° 95–20361 n.p. in Bulletin.
629 CA Lyon 4 March 1994 N° 93/06401 JurisData 1994–043277.
630 Mazeaud 2006, at 2963 ff.
631 De Coninck 2002.
632 See for example Cass com 15 October 2002 N° 00–13738 n.p. in Bulletin; Cass com 13 October 2009 N° 08–16634 n.p. in Bulletin.

aggrieved party acts without due caution, judges may decrease the amount of damages awarded. This reduction follows the general principles of tort liability (*principe indemnitaire*).[633] The rules on contract liability provide for the same approach.

The application of this approach is well illustrated by a decision of the *Cour de cassation* delivered in 2002.[634] In 1990, when the political situation in the Persian Gulf carried increased risks of pollution of water by hydrocarbons, Total, a multinational oil company, entered into negotiations with a company Saitec. Saitec offered to Total three products it had invented for the urgent treatment of water pollution by hydrocarbons caused by accidents in the sea. During the period of 1991 to 1993, Saitec made considerable investments to increase its stocks of these products following active *encouragements* from Total. However, in 1994, when the risks in the Persian Gulf decreased, Total withdrew from negotiations, whereas Saitec had to commence reorganization proceedings, as its financial health had rapidly worsened, allegedly due to its overstocking of products allocated for Total.

Saitec subsequently claimed against Total for the damage this had caused. In this case, Total was found liable, but only for half of the claimed amount. The *Cour d'Appel de Poitiers*, deciding on the merits, decreased the amount of damages awarded based on two observations. On the one hand, the court established that Total encouraged Saitec for two years to increase its production of the products in question, making promises of future cooperation. Total then withdew from negotiations, basing its decision on a change in its internal commercial policy (Total had transferred the risks related to pollution to its suppliers in most contracts). This reason was considered to be inappropriate ('absence of legitimate reasons for withdrawal') and the withdrawal was regarded as abrupt.

It was noted also that Saitec was not cautious when it proceeded on important investments, thereby risking financial difficulties in case of a failure of negotiations with Total. The *Cour de cassation* confirmed the reasoning of the *Cour d'Appel de Poitiers*. This case illustrates therefore that liability may be shared by a reckless party who suffers damage from a fault of another party in negotiations.

4.7.1.3. Conditions of liability in tort

The legal grounds for precontractual liability in tort are provided by the general provisions on liability in tort (Articles 1382[635] and 1383[636] of the *Code civil* (Articles 1240 and 1241 after the entry into force of the *Ordonnance*). Precontractual fault as such is not

633 Articles 1382, 1383 *Code civil*. See the corresponding Articles 1240 and 1241 *Ordonnance*.

634 Cass com 15 October 2002 N° 00-13738 n.p. in Bulletin.

635 Article 1382 *Code civil*: 'Any act whatever of man, which causes damage to another, obliges the one by whose fault it occurred, to compensate it'. After the entry into force of the *Ordonnance*, this provision comes in Article 1240.

636 Article 1383 *Code civil*: 'Everyone is liable for the damage he causes not only by his intentional act, but also by his negligent conduct or by his imprudence'. After the entry into force of the *Ordonnance*, this provision comes in Article 1241.

sufficient for establishing tortious liability; the aggrieved party must also prove that the fault caused damage. The *Code civil* lays down three conditions for this liability: fault, damage, and a link of causality between these two. Fulfilment of all the three conditions is necessary and sufficient to hold a party to negotiations liable for a precontractual fault. Furthermore, precontractual fault is not presumed; the burden of proof of the fault, incurred damage, and link of causality falls on the aggrieved party.[637]

The intention of the party committing a fault is irrelevant by virtue of Article 1383 of the *Code civil*. Liability can be imposed not only for a fault committed with an intention to harm (a qualified fault), but also for a fault committed by negligence ('*légèreté blâmable*'), unqualified fault on the basis of Article 1383.[638] An intention to harm does therefore not form a necessary condition for liability.

4.7.2. *Contractual liability: remedies for breach of avant-contrat*

Breach of an obligation created by an *avant-contrat* or other contractual organization of negotiations leads to contractual liability.

4.7.2.1. Breach of an obligation to negotiate

French courts limit the remedies for breach of an obligation to negotiate to recovery of damages. In principle, the limitations applicable to recovery are shaped in the same way as those which apply to liability in tort. Notably, the sharing of liability for taking risks is not possible in a case of contractual organization.

Besides this, judges do not order specific performance (*execution in nature*) of this obligation (it would consist in ordering parties to negotiate). The unavailability of the remedy of specific performance is based on the general approach to negotiations in French case law. According to the courts, execution in nature represents 'forced' negotiations. According to them, it would not lead to the expected result of the agreement in principle that is, formation of the final contract.[639]

4.7.2.2. Breach of pre-emption agreement

Article 1123 of the *Ordonnance* defines the consequences of breach of a pre-emption agreement. If a contract is concluded with third party who knows about the existence of the pre-emption, the beneficiary of the pre-emption right may claim damages, and in addition to this, has a right to make two further claims. Firstly, the beneficiary may make a claim for nullity of the contract which has been concluded between the debtor and the

637 Fages 2011c, para 117–9.

638 The *Cour de cassation* has expressly stated this in the case Cass 3 civ 3 October 1972 N° 71-12993 Bulletin 1972 n° 491.

639 Schmidt-Szalewski 2000; Rozès 1998.

third party. If nullity is declared, the debtor and the third party are returned to the positions they were in before the conclusion of the contract. Secondly, the beneficiary may require that he be substituted for the third party in the contract concluded between the debtor and third party. In this way, the claimant may enter into the contract in the place of the third party.

The two latter remedies can be granted only if the third party was aware of both the existence of the pre-emption agreement and of the beneficiary's intention to exercise the pre-emption right.[640] These remedies require the court to address the role of the third party (or parties) in the breach of the pre-emption agreement. Furthermore, such claims may have important consequences for third parties. Article 1123 solves most of the practical issues revealed by case law and literature. As a general rule, contracts in French law may have effects for those third parties who are aware of their existence (*opposabilité du contrat aux tiers*).[641]

As Article 1123 relates directly to these third party effects, it also contains a mechanism for a third party to prevent the claim in nullity. It states as follows: 'A third party may give written notice to the beneficiary requiring him to confirm within a fixed period which has to be reasonable the existence of a pre-emption agreement and his intention to exercise the pre-emption right'.[642] In this way, a party who is aware of any parallel negotiations may, in principle, ensure that these are merely negotiations, and no consent for the final contract is given (by a pre-emption agreement). It is worth noting in this regard that parties to advanced negotiations may have a duty to inform their counterpart of any parallel negotiations. This duty has been implied by French courts under the umbrella of good faith in negotiations. Furthermore, parties may also agree on a contractual obligation of sincerity (*clause de sincerité*) covering the period of negotiations.[643]

Still, how practical is the exercise of this right to confirm the existence of the pre-emption? Article 1123 aims to streamline the parties' approach in practice by prescribing the content of the notice. It goes on to state: 'Such a written notice must state that if he does not reply, the beneficiary of the pre-emption agreement will no longer have the right to claim either to be substituted in any contract concluded with the third party, or nullity of the contract'.[644] The question as to whether the absence of reply effectively leads to an inability to claim nullity remains open.

640 See Article 1123 *Ordonnance*.

641 See Articles 1199 ff. *Ordonnance*. See also inter alia Ghestin/Viney 2008, para 202 and 207–3; Savaux 2012.

642 Article 1123 *Ordonnance*. Cf Article 1125 draft *Ordonnance*: 'Where a third party believes that there may be a pre-emption agreement, he may give written notice to the beneficiary within a reasonable period requiring him to confirm it'.

643 Fages 2011b, para 115–61.

644 Article 1123 *Ordonnance*.

4.7.2.3. Breach of unilateral promise

Article 1124 sets out the consequences of a breach of a unilateral promise. It leads to nullity of the contract concluded with a third party, provided that the third party knew of the existence of the promise. Nullity must be declared by the court unless the parties mutually agree to it. Generally, the parties to a contract which has been declared a nullity are returned to the positions they were in before the conclusion of the contract.

4.7.2.4. Conditions of contractual liability

According to the *Code civil*, failure to perform a contractual obligation leads to liability.[645] Three conditions should be fulfilled to establish contractual liability: failure to perform an obligation, damage, and a link of causality between the two.

According to the *Cour de cassation*, establishing the existence of a contractual obligation and its breach are not sufficient for imposing contractual liability. It is also necessary to establish that a party has incurred damage; 'no damage, no reimbursement'.[646] The damage to be reimbursed should be foreseen or foreseeable on the basis of this obligation. Furthermore, liability of the defendant is presumed,[647] and the defendant bears the burden of proof of execution of the obligation in question.

4.7.3. Interaction of causes of action

The framework of *avant-contrat* allows the negotiating parties to influence, by creating a preliminary agreement, and to contractually frame the measure and the scope of their potential liability. At the same time, this is subject to the limitations placed on the possibility to modify or waive ('privatize') concrete rules.

In particular, the provisions on tort are regarded in French law as part of *ordre public*. These may not be changed or disclaimed by the parties. In this way liability for tortious breach of the duty of good faith in negotiations and the duties referred above as 'ethics of negotiations' remains a relatively independent basis for liability.[648] Even in the presence of *avant-contrat*, part of the relationship can still remain within the regulation of tort law. In fact, only conduct directly in breach of a contractual obligation (in a preliminary document) gives rise to a contractual claim.

By contrast, relations that may be framed by contract may be to a large extent modified or concretized by contractual provisions. In this field, according to the *Code civil*, the court may reduce the stipulated damages if their amount is manifestly excessive or

645 Article 1142 *Code civil*. The *Ordonnance* develops this provision in Articles 1217 ff. *Ordonnance*.
646 Terré/Simler/Lequette 2013, para 561.
647 Terré/Simler/Lequette 2013, para 871.
648 For a recent example see Cass 1 civ 15 May 2015 N° 14–14517 n.p. in Bulletin.

derisory.[649] At the same time, in French law, liability for an intentional fault in breach of a contractual obligation (*faute intentionnelle*) may not be waived or modified by the parties.[650]

In cases that do not amount to intentional fault, if the actual misconduct may be qualified both as breach of *avant-contrat* and fault in negotiations, the contractual cause of action prevails over both liability in tort and unjustified enrichment.[651] The hierarchy of the causes of actions flows from the French principle under which different causes of action cannot be combined, and a party has a limited freedom to choose the cause of action for the claim (*non-cumul de responsabilité*).[652]

4.8. Conclusion

Some time ago, Mazeaud contended that liability arising during the precontractual period remained a 'grey' area of legal uncertainty for the parties with a large margin of evaluation left for the courts.[653] Despite a considerable body of literature on the subject, this remains a fair characterization of the French approach. The *Ordonnance* of 2016 may bring further legal certainty and eventually further flexibility in the French approach. As has been shown, it provides answers to several questions that arose earlier regarding precontractual liability in French law and negotiations organized by *avant-contrat*. For instance, it codifies the requirement of precontractual good faith, places a limit on (some types of) precontractual liability, and clarifies the regime of two types of *avant-contrats*: the pre-emption agreement and unilateral promise. To a large extent, the *Ordonnance* codifies the solutions developed in case law. Yet it may leave some questions unanswered, and the solutions will still depend on further development of the judge-made law.

Two peculiarities of the French regime applicable to contractual organization of negotiations may be emphasized. On the one hand, the courts' approach reveals a certain level of pragmatism. In the assessment of the parties' subjective will, courts refer to objectively ascertainable conduct; the concept of legitimate reasons for breaking off negotiations refers de facto to the balancing of the parties' commercial interests in the bargaining process. Furthermore, French law has been particularly receptive to the practice of contractually organizing negotiations, as reflected by the text of the *Ordonnance*. On the other hand, the courts' reasoning involves several concepts with moral connotations. This amounts to the moralization of law reflected in the rules applicable to contractual of negotiations.

649 Article 1231-5 *Ordonnance*.

650 *Faute lourde* and *faute intentionnelle* are regarded in the same way for this purpose. See Terré/Simler/Lequette, 2013, para 613 ff.

651 Mestre/Fages 2005; Pin/Devin 2011.

652 Terré/Simler/Lequette 2013, para 875 ff.

653 Mazeaud 2008.

As a result of this, the interdependence of contractual liability and liability in tort in relation to contractual negotiations remain relatively complex. While the contracting parties appear to have the freedom to place their relationship into the contract law arena (by creating an *avant-contrat*), the choice of causes of actions, and as a consequence, the parties' influence on the remedy, in case of dispute are limited. More concretely, it appears to be not possible to entirely exclude or considerably limit the application of the precontractual duties in tort by creating contractually binding obligations before the formation of the final contract.

Chapter 5

ENGLISH LAW

5.1. Introduction

English law assumes that negotiations represent a genuinely adversarial process.[654] The freedom *from* being bound by the final contract before the negotiations are finalized is a cornerstone of contract law. This 'negative' side of freedom of contract also implies that contract law imposes no general duties on the parties' behaviour during the course of negotiations. No specific intermediary regime of contractual negotiations has been developed. The so-called 'bare agreements to agree'[655] that is, promises about the manner of negotiating, are not enforceable, the domain of contract and non-contractual regulation being rather sharply divided.[656]

Nevertheless, contractual negotiations are not a period of 'no law'. As Lord Justice Bingham has famously stated, discussing contractual negotiations from a broader perspective of private law, 'English law ... has developed piecemeal solutions in response to demonstrated problems of unfairness'.[657] In the same vein, Lord Justice Mummery has contended that English law addresses 'particular problems of unacceptable conduct occurring in the course of negotiations without unduly hampering the ability of the parties to negotiate their own bargains without the intervention of the courts'.[658] Andrews has compared the English law solutions applicable to negotiations to a 'Swiss army knife'.[659] The available tools include not only contract law doctrines ascertaining the enforceability of contractual promises, but also the law of restitution or unjust enrichment, the duty of confidence developed in equity, and torts of deceit and negligent misrepresentation; the doctrine of estoppel may play a role in this regulation as well.

654 *Walford* v. *Miles* [1992] 2 AC 128 (HL).

655 Ibid 138 (Lord Ackner).

656 This distinction has been most prominently discussed by Atiyah. See Atiyah 1979; see also *Chitty on Contracts* 2015, para 1-026 – 1-039.

657 *Interfoto Picture Library Limited* v. *Stiletto Visual Programmes Limited* [1989] QB 433 (EWCA) 439 (Lord Bingham).

658 *Cobbe* v. *Yeoman's Row Management Ltd* [2006] EWCA Civ 1139, [2006] 1 WLR 2964 [4] (Lord Mummery).

659 Andrews 2015, para 2.02.

This multifaceted framework of regulation provides several solutions applicable to the practice of issuing letter of intent. The solutions are more nuanced than it might appear at first sight, when one's attention is primarily drawn to the unenforceability of 'bare agreements to negotiate'.[660] English law has developed two exceptions to this unenforceability: temporary agreement on exclusive negotiations and undertakings to use best efforts to obtain an export licence or a planning permission. To be treated as exceptions, these should fulfil the criteria of certainty and consideration. These requirements are deeply rooted in the requirements as to the enforceability of a contractual promise. Furthermore, English courts have developed a detailed approach to various provisions whereby the parties may negate contractual intent. The approach to such clauses was developed using another doctrine relevant for contract formation – the assessment of intention to create legal relations.

This Chapter will describe the multifaceted regime of regulation of negotiations in English law to answer the following question. To what extent may parties arrange negotiations contractually and what are the consequences of this contractualization for liability in English law?

The Chapter will firstly briefly address the sources of English law and this study's approach to the sources (Section 5.2). Thereafter, it will address the implications of the assumption that negotiations are a genuinely adversarial process. This assumption leads to the unenforceability of bare agreements to agree; the exceptions to this unenforceability will also be addressed. Attention will be also paid to the debate in academic literature regarding the possible content of *bona fides* in contractual negotiations (Section 5.3). The focus will then shift to the description of the effects of the provisions that negate contractual intent. These include the honourable pledge clause, the formulation that negotiations are 'subject to contract', and attempts to divide letter of intent into binding and non-binding parts (Section 5.4). Thereafter, the Chapter will describe the non-contractual doctrines that may be applied to remedy unacceptable behaviour in the course of negotiations (Section 5.5). Finally, remedies and liability will be discussed (Section 5.6) and concluding remarks will be provided (Section 5.7).

5.2. Sources of English law

The jurisdiction of England and Wales belongs to the common law tradition.[661] Contract law, tort law, and the law of restitution and unjust enrichment are developed primarily in case law. The development and decisions of the law is based on the doctrine of *stare decisis*.[662] By virtue of this doctrine, disputes are resolved in accordance with previous precedents on similar legal questions. If a solution formulated in the existing precedent

660 *Walford* v. *Miles* [1992] 2 AC 128 (HL).
661 Glenn 2014, at 236 ff.
662 Cross/Harris 1991, at 97 ff.

does not apply in the case at hand, the court 'distinguishes' it from the existing precedents. Distinguishing is an important technique within the development of law. English judges are required to provide the reasons for distinguishing and at all times explain the rationale of the adopted approach. At the same time, the entire text of the precedent does not constitute the law. The law is contained in the *ratio decidendi* in the holding - the main part of the judges' reasoning that forms the authority for the adopted solution of the dispute. Other considerations of the judges, called *obiter dicta*, as well as concurring opinions, have only persuasive authority. The parties' pleadings are not binding, though these are usually extensively quoted in the texts of the decisions.

Within the doctrine of *stare decisis*, lower courts are bound by the precedents of the courts further up in the hierarchy. Accordingly, all the courts are bound by the case law of the Supreme Court of the United Kingdom (before the reform of 2009, the House of Lords).[663] The Supreme Court is not bound by its own precedents. It may develop the law and change the approach adopted in its earlier precedents. As noted in the literature, the Supreme Court uses this power in moderation: the Supreme Court 'since it has taken freedom to review its own decisions, will do so cautiously'.[664] The Court of Appeal is bound by its own decisions. The decisions on the Court of Appeal bind the High Courts, County Courts, and special courts.

Along with the case law, English law is to be found in statutes. For instance, in the field of contract law, important regulation is included in the Contracts (Rights of Third Parties) Act 1999, the Misrepresentation Act 1967, and the Sale of Goods Act 1979. Whereas English scholars observe an increase in regulation by statutes frequently due to the need to implement the law of the European Union, the law of contract and the law of tort are rooted in case law and remain essentially to be developed by the courts. This is also the case of the law of restitution and unjust enrichment.

Furthermore, the distinction between the common law and equity in English law should be mentioned. The use of the term 'common law' can lead to confusion, because it is used in the English literature at least in two senses. Firstly, it designates legal systems that rely on judge-made law, including England and Wales, Commonwealth countries and the United States.[665] Common law in this sense is in contrast with the codified law of the civil law traditions.[666] But at the same time, only in English law, 'common law' is in contrast with 'equity'. The concept of equity goes back to the history of English law-making: historically, some courts used to base their decisions on equity. This distinction is less relevant in modern law, since the Judicature Acts 1873 and 1875 allowed courts to

663 The highest judicial authority was reformed in 2009. Since this time, the twelve Law Lords have become Justices of the Supreme Court. They remain members of the British House of Lords, but may not vote, the approach marking the separation of competences between the judiciary and the parliament.

664 *Cassell & Co. Ltd.* v. *Broome and Another* [1972] AC 1027 (HL) 1054.

665 Glenn 2014, at 236 ff.

666 Glenn 2014, at 133–165.

decide the same case both in common law and in equity. Nevertheless, the distinction is still pertinent for understanding the sources of law and remedies.[667]

This study will rely on case law as primary authority, but also refer to academic writing. Legal scholarship has less significance and authority in England and Wales than in the civil law traditions. However, scholarly comments provide information on the genesis of the existing lines of cases and shed light on the existing debates and prospects.

Finally, a reservation on the scope of the material addressed should be made. English law is one of the most developed legal systems in the world; English concepts and doctrines are complex and elaborate. Therefore, it appears appropriate to address the relevant concepts and rules with limited detail but attempt to embed their discussion in the context of the approach to provisions contractualizing negotiations. This choice is made to ensure the coherence of the description of the approach to negotiations and to keep the description within the limited space available in this study.

5.3. Negotiations as adversarial process

English law provides a broad scope of freedom of negotiations (5.3.1). In essence, agreements about the negotiation process are unenforceable (5.3.2) with the exception of temporary 'lock-out' agreements (5.3.3) and a contractual obligation to use best endeavours or best efforts to obtain an export licence or planning permission (5.3.4). The broad scope of freedom of negotiations means that the negotiation period is not subject to any general contract law duties (5.3.4). This is as consistently confirmed in case law as it is debated in the literature. The academic debate therefore deserves to be highlighted in some detail (5.3.5).

5.3.1. Freedom of negotiations

English law relies on the assumption that contractual negotiations are a genuinely adversarial process.[668] It supposes that a party to negotiations aspires to make its own bargain and to pursue its self-interest.[669] This assumption was summarized in *Walford* v. *Miles* – the leading case on negotiations of contract decided by the House of Lords in 1992 as follows:[670]

> Each party to the negotiations is entitled to pursue his (or her) own interest... To advance that interest he must be entitled, if he thinks it appropriate, to threaten to withdraw from further negotiations or to withdraw in fact, in the hope that the opposite party may seek to reopen the negotiations by offering him improved terms.

667 Andrews 2015, para 1.25.

668 *Walford* v. *Miles* [1992] 2 AC 128 (HL) 137 (Lord Ackner). For recent example see *Shaker* v. *Vistajet Group Holding SA* [2012] EWHC 1329 (Comm), [2012] 2 All ER (Comm) 1010, especially [7].

669 *Walford v. Miles* [1992] 2 AC 128 (HL).

670 Ibid 138 (Lord Ackner).

This assumption flows from the principle of freedom of contract – a 'general principle of English law that parties are free to contract as they may see fit'.[671] In the words of Lord Diplock, 'parties to a contract are free to determine for themselves what primary obligations they will accept'.[672] The broad principle of freedom of contract in English law is a matter of policy, and this is especially the case in commercial contracts. 'Legal policy favours the furtherance of international trade. Commercial men must be given the utmost liberty of contracting'.[673]

The broad freedom of contract also implies freedom of negotiations, including the right to withdraw from negotiations at any moment. At any stage of negotiations, parties may walk away from a transaction without contractual liability.[674] Furthermore, freedom of negotiations implies that in English law an obligation to negotiate undertaken in the process of contract formation is not legally enforceable. More broadly, English contract law imposes no general contract law duties upon negotiations. The latter two points will be now discussed in more details.

5.3.2. Unenforceability of agreement to agree and similar

5.3.2.1. Walford v. Miles

An agreement establishing a positive obligation to start, pursue or finalize negotiations, so that a contract is formed, is not enforceable under English law for three main reasons. First, English courts hold 'agreements to agree' (or 'agreements to negotiate') to be void, because they lack consideration.[675] In English law, consideration is a requirement of the formation of a contractual obligation. Consideration represents a form of bargain – a counterpart received in exchange for an obligation. This counterpart should be provided in order to make an obligation enforceable in law, or, to be more precise, to make a promise enforceable in law.[676]

It should be noted that English law distinguishes between the concepts of 'contract', 'promise' and 'agreement'. Contract is understood either as a promise supported by consideration (or made in the form of a deed) or as an agreement supported by an intention to create legal relations, or as a consequence of reliance by one party on

671 *Suisse Atlantique Société d'Armement Maritime S.A.* v. *N.V. Rotterdamsche Kolen Centrale* [1967] 1 AC 361 (HL) 398 (Lord Reid).

672 *Photo Production Ltd* v. *Securicor Transport Ltd* [1980] AC 827 (HL) 848 (Lord Diplock).

673 *Homburg Houtimport BV* v. *Agrosin Private Ltd (The Starsin)* [2003] UKHL 12, [2004] 1 AC 715 [57] (Lord Steyn).

674 This, except for making a misrepresentation and except for breaching a duty to disclose certain information in fiduciary contracts. A fiduciary relationship supposes trust in the parties' relationship. For example, the following relations imply fiduciary duties in commercial context: lawyer to client, bailee to bailor, stockbroker to client, joint venturer to joint venture.

675 *Walford* v. *Miles* [1992] 2 AC 128 (HL).

676 *Chitty on Contracts* 2015, para 4–004.

another.[677] A simple promise is not enforceable. In order to be enforceable in law, a promise should be supported by consideration. '*Chitty on Contracts* defines consideration as something of value, 'either some detriment to the promisee (in that he may give value) or some benefit to the promisor (in that he may receive value)'.[678] For example, payment for a good by a buyer represents consideration in a sales contract. The payment represents a detriment for the buyer and a benefit for the seller of a good. Notably, in a transaction consisting of several acts, and especially in a complex transaction, consideration is required for each promise, thus not for the entire contract or the entire transaction. 'What the law is concerned with is the consideration *for a promise* – not the consideration *for a contract*'.[679] The doctrine of consideration addresses each obligation within a complex transaction separately. Consideration need not be of 'adequate value'. Because of this, consideration has been referred to as a requirement which is rather technical, and this technical character has attracted criticism of this doctrine.[680] In spite of this, consideration remains one of the main doctrines in assessing the existence of a contractual obligation in English law.

Second, agreements to agree lack certainty. Lord Denning MR discussed the lack of certainty of 'agreements to agree' in *Courtney & Fairbairn Ltd* v. *Tolaini Brothers*.[681] He stressed that it is impossible for a judge to define their legal content, and, as a consequence the impossibility of enforcing such provisions:[682]

> If the law does not recognise a contract to enter into a contract (when there is a fundamental term yet to be agreed) it seems to me it cannot recognise a contract to negotiate. The reason is because it is too uncertain to have any binding force. No court could estimate the damages because no one can tell whether the negotiations would be successful or would fall through: or if successful, what the result would be. It seems to me that a contract to negotiate, like a contract to enter into a contract, it is not a contract known to the law.

This reserved approach to any judicial interference into the parties' freedom of negotiations has been subsequently followed in English case law.[683] Currently, the highest authority on 'agreements to negotiate' is the position of House of Lords expressed by Lord Ackner in *Walford* v. *Miles*. 'The reason why an agreement to negotiate, like an

677 McKendrick, 'Contract: In General', in Burrows 2015, para 1.31. On competing theories of contract in English law, see *Chitty on Contracts* 2015, para 1–014 ff.
678 *Chitty on Contracts* 2015, para 4–004 with further English case law from which this definition is deducted.
679 *Chitty on Contracts* 2015, para 4–004.
680 Cartwright 2009b.
681 *Courtney & Fairbairn Ltd.* v. *Tolaini Brothers (Hotels) Ltd* [1975] 1 WLR 297 (EWCA).
682 Ibid 301 (Lord Denning MR).
683 See inter alia *Scandinavian Trading Tanker Co AB* v. *Flota Petrolera Ecuatoriana (The Scaptrade)* [1981] 2 Lloyd's Rep 425 (QBD); *Barbudev* v. *Eurocom Cable Management Bulgaria EOOD* [2012] EWCA Civ 548, [2012] 2 All ER (Comm) 963 [43]-[46]; *Walford* v. *Miles* [1992] 2 AC 128 (HL).

agreement to agree, is unenforceable, is simply because it lacks the necessary certainty'.[684] The House of Lords unanimously agreed.

Third, an agreement that obliges parties to negotiate in order to reach agreement is contrary to the adversarial position of parties in negotiations which is a normative standard in English law. It has been emphasized by Lord Ackner in *Walford* v. *Miles* as follows:[685]

> [W]hile negotiations are in existence either party is entitled to withdraw from those negotiations, at any time and for any reason. There can be thus no obligation to continue to negotiate until there is a 'proper reason' to withdraw. Accordingly a bare agreement to negotiate has no legal content.

5.3.2.2. Best efforts, reasonable endeavours and equivalents

In *Little* v. *Courage Ltd*[686] the Court of Appeal discussed obligations similar in substance to 'agreements to negotiate', but formulated in different terms, more specifically: obligations to 'act reasonably in putting forward the necessary documents for agreement',[687] to 'take all reasonable steps to reach agreement', and to 'use its best endeavours to reach agreement' are not binding in law. The Court of Appeal concluded that the latter are unenforceable in the same way as 'agreements to negotiate'.

Another statement of the Court of Appeal relates 'agreements to agree' to the adversarial position of parties in negotiations. In *Phillips Petroleum Co UK Ltd* v. *Enron*,[688] the Court of Appeal stated that an obligation to 'use reasonable endeavours to agree' could not be a reason for a party to refuse to reach agreement on the grounds of its own commercial self-interest.

A recent confirmation of this approach to obligations to negotiate has been provided in *Multiplex Constructions* v. *Cleveland Bridge*.[689] A dispute in that case concerned construction works at Wembley Stadium. The main contractor reached several preliminary agreements with a steelworks subcontractor regarding fabrication, delivery and erection of a steel bowl and an arch for the stadium. In the course of negotiations, the parties signed 'heads of agreement' and amended these by a 'supplemental agreement'. Later on, the parties disagreed on the valuation of the works performed by the subcontractor. In a dispute resulting from this disagreement, the High Court had to decide on a number of issues, including the validity of a claim for damages for a failure

684 [1992] 2 AC 128 138 (Lord Ackner).
685 Ibid.
686 [1995] CLC 164 (EWCA).
687 Ibid 169 (Lord Millett).
688 *Phillips Petroleum Co (UK) Ltd* v. *Enron (Europe) Ltd* [1997] CLC 329 (EWCA).
689 *Multiplex Constructions (UK) Limited* v. *Cleveland Bridge UK Limited, Cleveland Bridge Dorman Long Engineering Limited* [2006] EWHC 1341 (TCC), 107 Con LR 1 [635]-[637] (Jackson J).

to negotiate (formulated in the claim as a failure to negotiate 'in good faith'). The claim was related to the question of validity of an obligation in the 'heads of agreement' stating as follows:[690]

> The parties shall use reasonable endeavours to agree to re-programme the completion of the subcontract works and to agree a fixed lump sum and/or reimbursable subcontract sum for the completion of subcontract works...and to enter into a further supplemental agreement, recording the agreement contemplated by this clause 7 [of the heads of agreement].

The High Court declared this provision unenforceable. It has explained that was no more than a 'statement of aspirations', which was 'too uncertain to impose a contractual obligation and as such it [was] unenforceable'.[691] The claim for damages for failure to negotiate 'in good faith' was also dismissed.

Looking at the broader picture of the functioning of an 'agreement to negotiate' within the entire document in which it is included, the following should be mentioned. If an 'agreement to negotiate' is included in a document that is otherwise enforceable, the invalidity of the 'agreement to negotiate' does not affect this document. Only the 'agreement to negotiate' is void, whereas the other provisions of this document may remain valid.[692]

5.3.2.3. Agreement to negotiate in good faith

Provisions requiring parties to negotiate a contract in 'good faith' are not valid in English law. This approach has been formulated in *Walford* v. *Miles*.[693] The dictum of Lord Ackner in this regard in *Walford* v. *Miles* is straightforward:[694]

> [T]he concept of a duty to carry on negotiations in good faith is inherently repugnant to the adversarial position of the parties when involved in negotiations... A duty to negotiate in good faith is as unworkable in practice as it is inherently inconsistent with the position of a negotiating party. It is here that the uncertainty lies.

The House of Lords stated in this case that an agreement to negotiate in good faith is void, because it is contrary to the adversarial position of the parties in negotiations and lacks certainty (i.e. lacks sufficient content to guide the court in enforcing the obligation).[695] Furthermore, according to the House of Lords, the unenforceability of an

690 Ibid [633].
691 Ibid [636] (Jackson J).
692 See Peel 2010, at 42 ff. Peel discusses the limitations of the *Walford* v. *Miles* approach and submits that '[w]here there is, otherwise, a binding an enforceable contract, that will not be affected by any further agreement to negotiate, but the agreement to negotiate itself remains unenforceable'.
693 [1992] 2 AC 128 (HL).
694 [1992] 2 AC 128 (HL) 138 (Lord Ackner).
695 Ibid.

agreement to negotiate in good faith flows from the absence of general standard of good faith in English law.

5.3.3. *Exception to unenforceability: lock-out agreement*

While the unenforceability of the agreements on the manner to conduct negotiations is the rule, there are also some exceptions. Some agreements relating to negotiations have been held enforceable in English law.[696] The first exception to be discussed is a clause on exclusivity of negotiations.

5.3.3.1. Lock-out agreement

In English law, 'exclusivity' clauses are usually called 'lock-out' agreements. The term indicates that a party accepts being 'locked out' from negotiating the same transactions with third parties for a certain period of time. He undertakes not to negotiate with third parties. It is worth noting that a 'lock-out' agreement does not create an obligation to negotiate. As stated by Lord Ackner, 'B by agreeing not to negotiate for this fixed period with a third party, locks himself out of such negotiations. He has in no legal sense locked himself *into* negotiations with A'.[697]

5.3.3.2. Requirements of consideration and specified time

The validity of a 'lock-out' provision in a precontractual document is subject to two conditions. Firstly, parties must agree on it for consideration[698] (that is, in exchange of a counterpart). As stated by Lord Ackner, '[t]here is clearly no reason in the English contract law why A, for good consideration, should not achieve an enforceable agreement whereby B' especially if 'expenditure of not inconsiderable time and money' are necessary to properly contemplate the deal.[699]

Secondly, the time for which parties agree not to negotiate with third parties must be specified. This confers sufficient certainty to be enforceable by a court, should a dispute arise.[700] Specifying the time of 'exclusivity' therefore makes a 'lock-out' agreement different from the 'bare agreement to negotiate' which is void, following *Walford* v. *Miles*.

For example, these requirements have been applied in *Pitt* v. *PHH Asset Management Ltd*[701] to a lock-out agreement during negotiations about a sale of land. The parties

696 Andrews 2016, Part II 'Negotiations and competitive bidding'.
697 *Walford* v. *Miles* [1992] 2 AC 128 (HL) 139 (Lord Ackner).
698 Ibid 138 (Lord Ackner).
699 Ibid 139–140 (Lord Ackner).
700 Ibid 139–140 (Lord Ackner). According to some commentators the *Walford* v. *Miles* approach to agreements to negotiate is followed as a matter of policy, rather than because of lack of certainty or clarity about the way to enforce it. See Mills/Loveridge 2011, at 537. See also Peel 2010, especially at 41 ff.
701 [1994] 1 WLR 327 (EWCA). *Cf. Tye* v. *House and Jenning* (1998) 76 P & CR 188 (EWHC).

entered into a 'lock-out' agreement. It specified that parties would exchange contracts regarding the sale within 14 days, and during this time the seller would 'not consider any further offers for the property'.[702] The claimant made steps to exchange contracts within 14 days. Nevertheless, the property was sold a third party who offered a higher price. The Court of Appeal contended primarily that there was consideration for the 14 days' exclusivity.[703] Thereafter, the Court of Appeal enforced the 'lock-out' agreement and ordered a reassessment of the damages for its breach. Notably, according to the Court of Appeal, it was irrelevant that the 'lock-out' agreement was reached during negotiations for a contract that was never concluded. Lord Gibson stated that 'one has to look at what was agreed to see whether or not there was something that was capable of subsisting as a binding contract independently of the continuing negotiations for the sale of the land'.[704] The disputed exclusivity provision was enforced as a separate obligation (or a separate agreement), independent of the assessment of the validity of the negotiated contract itself.

5.3.3.3. Reasonable period of exclusivity implied

Another case illustrates the approach to the period of exclusivity in a commercial case, where a letter of intent was given a strict meaning. In *JSD Corporation PTE Ltd* v. *Al Waha Capital PJSC, Second Waha Lease Ltd*,[705] the High Court implied the period of exclusivity. It found that it was implied that parties agreed to negotiate exclusively for a 'reasonable time' until the end of the period covered by the letter of intent itself. In this case, the parties negotiated the sale of an aircraft. They accompanied the progress of their negotiations with a letter of intent. According to one of the conditions of this letter of intent, one of the parties paid to the other $1 million as a deposit for the future purchase of the aircraft. In exchange for the deposit, the aircraft should have been removed from advertising. Furthermore, the seller was to refrain from negotiating the sale of the aircraft to any third parties. The parties reflected this in the following provision in the letter of intent. The letter of intent specified expressly that this was binding:[706]

> This Clause 5 is legally binding
>
> ...
>
> On execution of this Letter and receipt of the First Deposit by the Seller, Seller shall remove the Aircraft from the market and shall not offer it to any other party for sale or lease until the

702 *Pitt* v. *PHH Asset Management Ltd* [1994] 1 WLR 327 (EWCA) 330.

703 See for the facts of case Ibid 331 ff. According to the Court of Appeal, consideration was provided, since the plaintiff was 'ready', 'willing' and 'able' to exchange contracts, a promise to exchange contracts within a limited time had 'some value for the defendant'; the plaintiff promised not to seize a court with injunction on the actions of the third party (the third party in question was also willing to buy this cottage).

704 Ibid 331.

705 *JSD Corporation PTE Ltd* v. *Al Waha Capital PJSC, Second Waha Lease Ltd* [2009] EWHC 583 (Ch), 2009 WL 648840.

706 Ibid [82].

> transaction is terminated after Seller giving notice to Purchaser of a default under the terms of this Letter or, after its signature, of the Sale and Purchase Agreement.

Subsequently, the seller omitted to remove the aircraft from its advertising, and the negotiations broke down. The potential buyer brought an action against the seller of the aircraft. He declared that the provision in the letter of intent was a valid 'lock-out' agreement, and that seller was in default for failing to remove the aircraft from advertising. The potential buyer requested the potential seller to refund the deposit and asked the court for a freezing injunction on the aircraft, located in an airfield in Essex.

The High Court contended that the dispute was 'essentially ... over the meaning and effect' of the letter of intent. It noted, furthermore, that the parties had clearly designated those obligations that should be considered as contractually binding, and those that should remain non-binding. The High Court upheld this distinction, because it was clearly made by two independent commercial parties with equal positions in negotiations.[707] The High Court found, furthermore, that the parties had agreed on an 'exclusivity' clause (one of the provisions expressly mentioned as 'binding'):[708]

> It is in effect a lock in agreement whereby the parties have locked themselves in to an agreement of exclusivity to attempt to negotiate a sale of Aircraft 345. In my view it has contractual effect as regards clauses expressly made legally binding. Under its terms JSD has to make payments and observe confidentiality. Waha for its part has to observe confidentiality and more importantly not advertise the aircraft for sale and not accept an offer.

According to the High Court, it was irrelevant that no exact duration of exclusivity was expressly agreed in letter of intent. A reasonable time for termination was implied: '[a]s there is no provision for termination apart from default, the duration of the letter of intent in my opinion is for a reasonable time whereupon either party if a reasonable time has elapsed can terminate the same on reasonable notice'.[709]

5.3.3.4. Right of first negotiation

In *Lambert* v. *HTV Cymru (Wales) Limited*,[710] the court allowed a form of exclusivity agreement that is, an agreement on a 'right of first negotiation'. The dispute in this case involved an author and copyright owner of cartoon characters, on the one side, and a television broadcaster with its parent company, on the other. The author granted the television broadcaster an exclusive licence for the use of the copyright in question. Later, with a view to making a film, they also signed a document called 'heads of agreement'

707 *JSD Corporation PTE Ltd* v. *Al Waha Capital PJSC, Second Waha Lease Ltd* [2009] EWHC 583 (Ch), 2009 WL 648840 [9].
708 Ibid [32].
709 Ibid [33].
710 [1998] EMLR 629 (EWCA).

whereby the author undertook to assign its existing and future copyright in the film in exchange for payment and royalties. The Clause 9 of the 'heads of agreement' contained 'a right of first negotiation':[711]

> The Purchaser [the television broadcaster] shall further use all reasonable endeavours to obtain a right of first negotiation from any assignee of the Purchaser for the Author to draw or write "conceptual" children's books in connection with the Film on terms to be negotiated in good faith...

Subsequently, a dispute arose. The disputed matters included the enforceability of this clause. According to the Court of Appeal, the clause was clear and certain enough to give rise to a binding agreement. In the words of Lord Morritt:[712]

> In this case the obligation is not limited to 'rights' which must be unenforceable. First, a 'right of first negotiation' includes some element of lock-out (exclusivity). Second, there are rights which might be described as 'rights of first negotiation' in Butterworth's *Encyclopedia of Forms & Precedents*... The negotiation may or may not succeed, but that is no reason for excusing the contracting party from making any effort at all... For my part, therefore, I would conclude that the concept expressed in the latter part of clause 9 is sufficiently certain to enable the obligation to use all reasonable endeavours to achieve it to be a contractually enforceable obligation.

The Court of Appeal went on to state that a breach of this clause may entitle a party to claim at least nominal damages as a remedy.[713] It should be emphasized, however, that such a right does not imply any obligation to reach agreement in this 'first negotiation'.[714]

5.3.4. *Exception to unenforceability: best endeavours to obtain an export license or a planning permission*

Along with 'lock-out' agreements, another undertaking during negotiations has been distinguished from 'bare agreements to negotiate'. If parties agree within negotiations to use 'best endeavours' or 'reasonable endeavours' to obtain a *planning permission* or *an export licence*, this obligation is valid. The English approach has evolved in two stages. As has been mentioned, the *Walford* v. *Miles* decision states that 'bare agreements to agree' and 'agreements to negotiate in good faith' lack legal content. After *Walford* v. *Miles*, case law considered all obligations relating to precontractual negotiations to be equivalent to 'bare' agreements to negotiate and therefore unenforceable.[715] In *Little* v. *Courage Ltd*,[716]

711 Ibid 633.
712 Ibid 638.
713 Ibid 638–639.
714 *Chitty on Contracts* 2015, para 2–146.
715 For an overview and discussion, see Peel 2010. Peel also notes that it was not entirely clear what Lord Ackner meant by 'bare' agreements to negotiate, and whether he meant agreements ancillary to a contract that already exists.
716 [1995] CLC 164 (EWCA).

best endeavours to obtain a planning permission or an export licence were distinguished from the agreements called 'bare' agreements to negotiate in *Walford* v. *Miles*. Lord Millett has stated as follows:[717]

> An undertaking to use one's best endeavours to obtain planning permission or an export licence is sufficiently certain and is capable of being enforced: an undertaking to use one's best endeavours to agree, however, is no different from an undertaking to agree, to try to agree, or to negotiate with a view to reaching agreement; all are equally uncertain and incapable of giving rise to an enforceable legal obligation.

Furthermore, English case law has also introduced nuances of meaning, whereby the obligation to use 'best endeavours' is stronger than the obligation to use 'reasonable endeavours'. This difference has been described in *Rhodia International Holdings Ltd & Anor* v. *Huntsman International LLC*:[718]

> An obligation to use 'reasonable endeavours' was less stringent than an obligation to use 'best endeavours'. There might be a number of reasonable courses which could be taken in a given situation to achieve a particular aim. An obligation to use reasonable endeavours to achieve the aim probably only required a party to take one reasonable course, not all of them, whereas an obligation to use best endeavours probably required a party to take all the reasonable courses he could.

It is worth noting, finally, that the content of these obligations does not undermine the adversarial position of parties in negotiations which is assumed in English law. As Vos J noted in *CPC Group Ltd* v. *Qatari Diar Real Estate Investment Co*, 'the obligation to use "all reasonable endeavours" does not always require the obligor to sacrifice his commercial interests', nor does it require the obligor to 'ignore or forego its commercial interests'.[719]

5.3.5. No general contract law duties and academic debate

As noted earlier, English contract law imposes no general positive duties on the parties' behaviour in the course of negotiations.[720] This means parties may implement strategies and tactics of negotiations without a high risk of being held liable. For instance, they may freely engage in parallel negotiations. Negotiating parties are not subject to a general

717 Ibid 170 (Lord Millett).

718 [2007] EWHC 292 (Comm), [2007] 1 CLC 59 60.

719 [2010] EWHC 1535 (Ch), [2010] CILL 2908 [252] and [253] (Vos J). In this case, however, the parties had expressly mentioned that 'all reasonable but commercially prudent endeavours' will be applied. This made it easier to reserve a place for commercial interests in execution of this obligation.

720 *Courtney & Fairbairn Ltd.* v. *Tolaini Brothers (Hotels) Ltd* [1975] 1 WLR 297 (EWCA) 301 (Lord Denning MR); *Walford* v. *Miles* [1992] 2 AC 128 (HL).

duty to disclose information,[721] nor to the duty of confidentiality with regards to information exchanged in the course of negotiations.

In the light of an absence of general duties, it is worth noting that during the last decades, the relevance of *bona fides* in negotiations has generated some debate in the English literature.[722] English scholars have noted the increasing reference to the duty of *bona fides* made in the civil law systems and international soft law instruments.[723] This has generated a discussion about the role *bona fides* may have in negotiations under English law. The discussions should be touched upon in view of their relevance for the topic and relative prominence in the literature. However, *bona fides* in negotiations is as frequently discussed in modern scholarship as it is consistently rejected in case law and classical treatises.[724] Therefore, the debate has primarily an academic character.

5.3.5.1. Critiques of the assumption on the adversarial position of parties in negotiations

The assumption that parties to negotiations are always adversarial has not escaped criticism of the English scholars. For instance, Mills and Loveridge[725] have discussed the argument made by Lord Ackner in *Walford* v. *Miles* on the unenforceability of 'bare agreement to agree'. One of their arguments is based on the earlier findings of academics who made an in-depth analysis of different contexts in which contracting takes place.[726] It was contended that cooperation is often more successful and fruitful, both in negotiating transactions and execution of contracts. Against this background, it was argued that 'static market individualism' has evident shortcomings whenever contracting is not adversarial. As a result, 'remedial focus is on violation of the letter rather than the spirit of the deal'.[727] Based on this, Mills and Loveridge have submitted that the classical assumption on the adversarial position of parties in negotiations is excessively simplistic. A flexible legal system would, on the contrary, enable parties to limit freedom of negotiations and take into account that parties sometimes contract cooperatively. Therefore, if parties agreed to negotiate in good faith, they steer the courts' reasoning towards taking into account the cooperative context of the deal. According to

721 As long as this does not constitute misrepresentation causing invalidity of the contract due to vitiated consent. Misrepresentation is a separate topic and falls outside the scope of this study.

722 On 'good faith' in negotiations and English law see with further references Peel 2010; Zimmermann/Whittaker 2000 (Chapter 1, part on England and Wales); Brownsword 1997; Furmston/Tolhurst 2010, at 367 ff.; Beatson/Friedmann 1995; Steyn 1997; Campbell 2014; *Chitty on Contracts* 2015, para 1–039 with further references.

723 International instruments are discussed in Chapter 8.

724 See *Chitty on Contracts* 2015, para 1–039.
Mills/Loveridge 2011, Peel 2010, *Petromec Inc* v. *Petroleo Brasileiro SA Petrobras (No.3)* [2005] EWCA Civ 891, [2006] 1 Lloyd's Rep 121 [119] (Lord Longmore *obiter dictum*); Neill 1992; Steyn 1997; Brownsword 1997.

725 Mills/Loveridge 2011.

726 Arrighetti/Bachmann/Deakin 1997; Brownsword 1997.

727 Brownsword 1997, at 263.

Brownsword, parties may do so for different reasons, generally referred to as 'a matter of enlightened self-interest'.[728] Hoskins has argued that an agreement to agree might be considered enforceable if the intention to create legal relations is in place. Hoskins submits that such intent can be explicitly declared, fulfilling the requirement of certainty by detailed regulation of negotiations.[729]

5.3.5.2. Reflections on possible content of bona fides in negotiations

Supposing that an agreement to negotiate in good faith could be enforceable gave rise to further questions on the possible content of the parties' obligations. English literature contains a discussion on the possible content of *bona fides* in negotiations. Within the discussion on the possible content of an 'agreement to negotiate in good faith', Peel investigated the possible meaning of 'good faith' in this context. Coming back to the statement in *Walford* v. *Miles*[730] that agreements to agree are completely without substance. Peel submits that these may have legal content. This author draws a parallel between the approaches to contractual negotiations and performance. Peel compares agreements to negotiate in good faith to an obligation conferring one party with a discretionary power in the performance of a contract (e.g. contractual power to decide unilaterally on the way to execute a contractual obligation). He examines the requirements that courts have imposed on parties that exercised such discretionary powers under contracts.

Peel submits that the notion of 'good faith' may possibly have the same content as the *minimum* requirements imposed on the exercise of a discretionary power in contract. The English courts have exercised control for instance on whether a contractual discretionary power was exercised 'dishonestly, for an improper purpose, capriciously or arbitrarily', and 'in a way that no reasonable lender, acting reasonably, would do'.[731] The English courts were prepared to grant contractual sanctions for conduct contrary to these requirements. In *Lymington Marina Ltd* v. *MacNamara*, the Court of Appeal implied a term preventing the exercise of discretionary power for reasons that are 'wholly unreasonable', 'in bad faith or capriciously' and 'arbitrary'.[732] The view of Peel does not suggest imposing a general duty of good faith. He stresses that the parties might adhere to a 'standard of good faith *consistent with the negotiating process* in which they have discretion over the formation of contract'.[733]

728 Brownsword 1997, at 29. See more generally Brownsword 1997, at 29–37; Brownsword 2013.

729 Hoskins 2014. See also Trakman/Sharma 2014.

730 [1992] 2 AC 128 (HL).

731 *Paragon Finance Plc* v. *Nash* [2001] EWCA Civ 1466, [2002] 1 WLR 685 [32] (Lord Dyson). See also Hooley 2013, at 66. Hooley addresses the growing body of case law where courts control the exercise of discretionary power under a contract. He concludes that the requirements imposed by courts (within the execution of contract) 'boil down to a requirement of "good faith", in the sense that the party exercising the discretion must do so honestly, and that this can be tested by asking whether the decision is one that no reasonable person acting reasonably could have reached in the circumstances'.

732 [2007] EWCA Civ 151, [2007] 2 All ER (Comm) 825 [37], [42]-[44].

733 Peel 2010, at 56.

Furthermore, *bona fides* in negotiations was discussed in the context of an obligation to negotiate where such a term was included in an existing contract. In *Petromec Inc* v. *Petroleo Brasileiro SA Petrobras (No.3)*[734] one party undertook to execute a technical upgrade of an oil production platform. Parties agreed that 'reasonable costs' should be paid for this upgrade. They also agreed that one party would 'negotiate in good faith with [the other party] the extra costs referred' thereto.[735] In that case, Longmore LJ first noted that a simple agreement to negotiate is void, but contended that that this does not lead to the invalidity of other eventual obligations contained in the same document. However, this clause was not relevant to the dispute in that case and the Court of Appeal did not have to pronounce on the enforceability of this obligation. In the *obiter dictum*, Lord Longmore stated that 'it would be a strong thing to declare unenforceable a clause into which parties have deliberately and expressly entered'.[736]

On a general note, Furmston and Tolhurst have noted that English law is rather familiar with the concept of *bona fides* in the context of contract performance, what cannot be said about contractual negotiations.[737] But even included into a contract, an obligation to use 'best endeavours' or 'all reasonable endeavours', or 'best efforts' to reach consensus on a separate term of contract (not precontractual) can only be valid if clear criteria or machinery for agreement are specified by the parties. These would allow the court to imply or construe this obligation. Otherwise the agreement will be judged to be too uncertain and consequently void.[738] For example, in *Phillips Petroleum Co (UK) Ltd* v. *Enron (Europe) Ltd*[739] an agreement to use 'best endeavours' to agree on a commissioning date were held to be unenforceable.

On a more radical note, Berg[740] elaborates a number of general standards to be complied with by the parties conducting negotiations. His view perhaps goes the furthest from the current approach of the English courts and even scholarly views.

5.3.5.3. Judicial standards of 'reasonableness' of refusal to mediate

Another area of the discussion regarding validity of agreements to agree is also worth mentioning. The English courts have been prepared to sanction 'unreasonable' refusal to mediate. In cases where parties agree to resolve and mitigate a conflict or controversy arising in negotiations through mediation, the English courts have developed standards to determine the 'unreasonableness' of a refusal to mediate. These standards are also discussed by Mills and Loveridge.

734 [2005] EWCA Civ 891, [2006] 1 Lloyd's Rep 121.
735 Ibid [86].
736 Ibid [121].
737 Furmston/Tolhurst 2010, para 12.11.
738 *Phillips Petroleum Co (UK) Ltd* v. *Enron (Europe) Ltd* [1997] CLC 329 (EWCA).
739 [1997] CLC 329 (EWCA).
740 Berg 2003.

The authors establish equivalence between negotiation and mediation.[741] They refer to the following statement in *Aird & Anr* v. *Prime Meridian Limited*: 'It is well-known and uncontentious in this case that mediation takes the form of assisted "without prejudice" negotiation…'[742] and to recent developments in English law regarding mediation. In light of these considerations the authors argue that the lack of certainty emphazised by *Walford* v. *Miles* is, in principle, 'not insurmountable'.[743]

Some guidance as to the factors to be considered by the court in deciding whether a refusal to agree to mediation is unreasonable has been provided by Lord Dyson in *Halsey* v. *Milton Keynes General NHS Trust*. These factors include 'the nature of the dispute', 'the merits of the case', 'the extent to which other settlement methods have been attempted. Furthermore, the courts may assess 'whether the costs of the ADR would be disproportionately high', 'whether any delay in setting up and attending the ADR would have been prejudicial', 'whether the ADR had a reasonable prospect of success'.[744] Therefore, English courts have an inventory of tools to assess when a refusal to proceed with negotiation goes against the settled law. This means, according to Mills and Loveridge, that if English courts find it appropriate, there is sufficient development of law for a court to sanction (and remedy) conduct that is 'unreasonable' in certain cases of negotiations, in particular when parties agreed to resolve their disputes by mediation which is an assisted form of negotiations.

It is to be noted that these standards relate only to the decision not to mediate, but not to the conduct during mediation itself. This is due to the confidential and privileged character of mediation.[745] The courts can assess parties' conduct during mediation only if all the parties have waived the privilege on their communication during mediation.[746] If parties do not waive this privilege, the courts may not control the way parties mediate.[747] In this regard, Andrews has noted that mediation has usually a privileged – confidential – character. As a consequence, the opportunity for the courts to control the parties' conduct would not frequently arise.[748]

As to the remedy for an 'unreasonable' refusal to mediate, English courts have decreased the amount of costs awarded. In *Halsey* v. *Milton Keynes General NHS Trust*, the Court of Appeal derogated (by way of exception) from the procedural rule according to which the losing party bears the costs of litigation.[749] The Court of Appeal distributed the costs

741 See Mills/Loveridge 2011, at 542, stating that there is 'nothing special' in negotiations and discarding the arguments that state to the contrary.

742 [2006] EWCA Civ 1866 [2007] CP Rep 18 [5] (Lord May).

743 Mills/Loveridge 2011, at 533.

744 [2004] EWCA Civ 576, [2004] 4 All ER 920 [16] ff. (Lord Dyson).

745 Andrews 2015, para 4.22.

746 *Carleton (Earl of Malmesbury)* v. *Strutt & Parker (A Partnership)* [2008] EWHC 424 (QB), [2008] 5 Costs LR 736.

747 *Halsey* v. *Milton Keynes General NHS Trust* [2004] EWCA Civ 576, [2004] 4 All ER 920.

748 Andrews 2015, para 4.23.

749 [2004] EWCA Civ 576, [2004] 4 All ER 920.

differently, taking into account an 'unreasonable' failure to mediate. In the same way, in *Carleton (Earl of Malmesbury)* v. *Strutt & Parker (A Partnership)* only 68 per cent of the claimed damages were awarded. This decrease in the amount of the award reflected the costs wasted due to an 'unreasonable' failure to engage in mediation.[750]

5.4. Contract law framework: contractual intent and its negation

As discussed earlier, ascertaining the unenforceability of agreement to agree (following *Walford* v. *Miles*[751]) and its exceptions relies primarily on the doctrines of certainty and consideration. A number of other provisions relevant to the dynamics of negotiations are assessed primarily using another doctrine – the doctrine of intent to create legal relations. More specifically, English law provides the parties with a possibility to delimit (by private contractual regulation) the domain of non-binding and adversarial negotiations from the domain of contract law. Parties may define whether their relations should be interpreted as non-binding negotiations or as a contractual promise enforceable in law. The provisions to be discussed in this regard are the honourable pledge (5.4.1) and the 'subject to contract' provision (5.4.2), dividing letter of intent into binding and non-binding parts (5.4.3).

5.4.1. *Honourable pledge*

English law allows parties to 'contract out of the legal regime'[752] of contract law. To do so, parties may explicitly qualify their agreement as an 'honourable pledge' or 'gentlemen's agreement'. The principle is established in *Rose and Frank Company* v. *Crompton and Brothers*.[753] The dispute arose in this case out of a breach of a document signed by an American seller and its English sales agent. The document contained the following clause:[754]

> This arrangement is not entered into, nor is this memorandum written, as a formal or legal agreement, and shall not be subject to legal jurisdiction in the Law Courts either of the United States or England, but it is only a definite expression and record of the purpose and intention of the three parties concerned, to which they each honourably pledge themselves, with the fullest confidence – based on past business with each other – that it will be carried through by each of the three parties with mutual loyalty and friendly co-operation. This is hereinafter referred to as the 'honourable pledge' clause.

As explained by the House of Lords, such a clause correlates with the interpretation of intent to create legal relations. According to English law, an obligation becomes contractually binding only if it is established that parties have an intention to create legal

750 [2008] EWHC 424 (QB), [2008] 5 Costs LR 736 [88].
751 [1992] 2 AC 128 (HL).
752 Andrews 2015, para 6.05.
753 [1925] AC 445 (HL).
754 Ibid 445–446.

relations.[755] In commercial contracts, the existence of an intention to create legal relations is presumed; and this is a rebuttable presumption.[756] The burden of proof that there was no intention to create legal relationship is 'on the party who asserts that no legal effect is intended, and the onus is a heavy one'.[757] This party can rebut the presumption by proving that either one or both parties were not willing to assume any legal obligations.

Explicit denial of intention to create legal relations renders the understandings reached by the parties non-binding in law and unenforceable in court. The House of Lords gave effect to the 'honourable pledge' and has confirmed it as non-binding in law. As noted in a later decision *Edwards* v. *Skyways Ltd*, intention to create legal relations is to be denied 'by using clear words'.[758]

Furthermore, whether there was an intention to create legal relations is not based on the parties' subjective state of mind. 'The judicial task is not to discover the actual intentions of each party; it is to decide what each was reasonably entitled to conclude from the attitude of the other'.[759] A reasonable person in a position of the parties also takes on the parties' experience and common knowledge, though these might be in turn to a certain extent subjective.[760] In commercial cases, the abstract person referred to is also a reasonable businessmen[761] or 'honest men', as Lord Steyn has put it.[762] The language of the statements is also to be interpreted in a reasonable manner. This manner of interpretation is however not reduced to their literal meaning, but includes also a common sense interpretation and taking into account the context of the transaction.

5.4.2. Negotiations 'subject to contract'

If parties expressly deny their intention to create legal relations, formation of a contract is precluded. One of the types of 'agreement to negotiate' is an agreement stating that the entire negotiation is 'subject to contract'. The legal qualification of this statement in English law depends on the parties' intention, the entire content of the document, and the parties' conduct.[763]

755 *Carlill* v. *Carbolic Smoke Ball* Co [1893] 1 QB 256 (EWCA); Furmston/Tolhurst 2010; Andrews 2015, para 6.01 ff., see also para 6.19 – 6.22; generally see *Chitty on Contracts* 2015, para 2–167 ff.

756 *Edwards* v. *Skyways Ltd* [1964] 1 WLR 349 (QBD) 355; *Esso Petroleum Co. Ltd.* v. *Customs and Excise Commissioners* [1976] 1 WLR 1 (HL).

757 [1964] 1 WLR 349 (QBD); *Chitty on Contracts* 2015, para 1–168, 1–169.

758 *Edwards* v. *Skyways Ltd* [1964] 1 WLR 349 (QBD) 355 (Megaw J): 'Where the subject-matter of the agreement is not domestic or social, but is related to business affairs, the parties may, by using clear words, show that their intention is to make the transaction binding in honour only, and not in law; and the courts will give effect to the expressed intention'.

759 *Attorney General of Belize* v. *Belize Telecom Ltd* [2009] UKPC 10 [2009], 1 WLR 1988 [16] (Lord Hoffmann).

760 McLauchlan 2005, at 484.

761 See *Fiona Trust and Holding Corporation* v. *Privalov* [2007] UKHL 40, [2007] 4 All ER 951.

762 Steyn 1997.

763 *Chitty on Contracts* 2015, para 2–125.

Three lines of cases illustrate the approach to the 'subject to contract' stipulation. In the first line of cases, a stipulation 'subject to contract' corresponds objectively to a situation in which *some matters still need to be negotiated* before a final contract is formed. In the second, the parties stipulate that a *formal document* should be signed after the actual formation of a contract. In the third, exceptional line of cases, parties *tacitly waive* the 'subject contract' stipulation, because their conduct shows that their negotiations are no longer non-binding. These lines of cases will now be addressed in more detail.

5.4.2.1. 'Subject to contract': further matters to be negotiated

If a document mentions that negotiations are 'subject to contract', that precludes formation of contractual obligations by this document. The reason is that the stipulation 'subject to contract' correlates with the doctrine of intention to create legal a relationship. According to this doctrine, parties should intend to create a legal relationship in order to be contractually bound by an obligation (and their intent is presumed in commercial transactions).

At the same time, as has been mentioned, courts do not consider 'subject to contract' in isolation from the rest of the negotiations. An objective assessment of parties' conduct also matters in defining the effect of a stipulation of 'subject to contract'. If parties are still in negotiations, especially if they have not agreed on essential terms of the transaction, there is agreement incomplete,[764] or further agreement is a 'term of the bargain',[765] their precontractual documents made 'subject to contract' remain not binding.[766]

Furthermore, it is not only an express statement of 'subject to contract' that matters. The court can also imply that parties are at the stage of negotiations only. In other words, courts can imply 'subject to contract' in an objective assessment of the parties' conduct, for example, when a legal assessment of the transaction is needed before it may be finalized. The approach of the law to this implication has been summarized in *Benourad* v. *Compass Group Plc:*[767]

> [T]he more complicated the subject matter the more likely the parties are to want to enshrine their contract in some written document to be prepared by their solicitors. This enables them to review all the terms before being committed to any of them. The commonest way of

764 See for example, *Harvey* v. *Pratt* [1965] 1 WLR 1025 (EWCA) – a lease agreement that failed to mention the start of lease; Day's Will Trusts [1962] 1 W.L.R. 1419; see also *Chitty on Contracts* 2015, para 2–119 ff.

765 *Von Hatzfeldt Wildenburg* v. *Alexander* [1912] 1 Ch 284 (EWHC) 285.

766 From numerous decisions, see: *Winn* v. *Bull* (1877) 7 Ch 29 (EWHC); *Chillingworth* v. *Esche* [1924] 1 Ch 97 (EWCA); *Regalian Properties Plc* v. *London Docklands Development Corp* [1995] 1 WLR 212 (EWHC Ch) (promissory estoppel has been not allowed); *British Steel Corp* v. *Cleveland Bridge & Engineering Co Ltd* [1984] 1 All ER 504 (QBD); *Manatee Towing Co Ltd* v. *Oceanbulk Maritime SA (The Bay Ridge)* [1999] 2 All ER (Comm) 306 (QBD); *Emcor Drake & Scull Ltd* v. *Sir Robert McAlpine Ltd* [2004] EWCA Civ 1733, 98 Con LR 1; *Haden Young Ltd* v. *Laing O'Rourke Midlands Ltd* [2008] EWHC 1016 (TCC).

767 [2010] EWHC 1882, 2010 WL 2937470 (QB) [106] (Beatson J).

> achieving this ability is to stipulate that the negotiations are 'subject to contract'. In such a case there is no binding contract until the formal written agreement has been duly executed.

The reasoning also notes that negotiations may also be regarded as being 'subject to contract' in the absence of an express stipulation to this effect. In this case, the status of negotiations is a matter of contractual construction.[768]

No contractual remedies are available for claims arising out of this kind of negotiations which are 'subject to contract' (though, remedies may be available under an extra-contractual claim, as in the case *British Steel Corp* v. *Cleveland Bridge & Engineering Co Ltd*[769] which will be discussed in Section 5.5.3 below.

5.4.2.2. 'Subject to contract': formal contract to be signed or essential term to be agreed

A statement of 'subject to contract' can be interpreted to the effect that a formal contract should be signed after the actual formation of a contract. This is often the case in transactions involving parties' consultants, in particular, legal counsel. In these cases, if changes can still be introduced in the contract, English courts have stated that documents established in negotiations were not binding. For example, in *Winn* v. *Bull*, parties negotiated a contract for the 'lease of a house for a certain term at a certain rent'. One party agreed in writing to take a lease 'subject to the preparation and approval of a formal contract'.[770] However, the parties did not enter into any subsequent 'formal' contract. The High Court held that the parties had not reached any agreement that could be upheld as binding in law and enforced by the court. Jessel MR gave the reason for the decision as follows:[771]

> If two persons agree in writing that up to a certain point the terms shall be the terms of the contract, but that the minor terms shall be submitted to a solicitor, and shall be such as are approved of by him, then there is no contract, because all the terms have not been settled.

The same rationale has been applied in several subsequent cases.[772] By contrast, if the parties describe additional approval as a formality (or 'solemn record'[773]), whereas

768 Ibid. The reasoning at [106] goes on as follows: 'But it is not necessary that there should have been an express stipulation that the negotiations are to be 'subject to contract'... Where there is no such stipulation, this ... is a question of construction'.

769 [1984] 1 All ER 504 (QBD).

770 *Winn* v. *Bull* (1877) 7 Ch 29 (EWHC) 29.

771 Ibid 30 (Jessel MR).

772 See *Rossdale* v. *Denny* [1921] 1 Ch 57 (EWCA) ('subject to a formal contract to embody such reasonable provisions as my solicitors may approve'); *Chillingworth* v. *Esche* [1924] 1 Ch 97 (EWCA) 97 ('subject to a proper contract to be prepared by the vendor's solicitors'); see also generally Furmston/Tolhurst 2010, 219 ff.

773 *Chitty on Contracts* 2015, para 2–123.

negotiations on the essential terms are already completed, the courts may disregard the stipulation 'subject to contract'. For instance, a stipulation that an additional action should be performed by the parties' solicitors does not prevent formation of a contract. This principle has been laid out by the House of Lords in *Rossiter* v. *Miller*.[774] The approach in this case has been subsequently followed in number of decisions.[775] In *Rossiter* v. *Miller*, the parties negotiated a contract for the sale of land and agreed on several conditions for their future agreement. One party informed the other that it had instructed its solicitors to forward the final contract to the other party. When a dispute arose, one of the parties claimed that no contract had been formed. The House of Lords decided, however, that the formation of a contract was complete. 'Everything essential to the completion of it appears on the written documents – the parties, the premises, the conditions, and the price'.[776] The reference to forwarding the written contract stipulated, according to the court, the 'mode of proceeding',[777] but not the formation itself.

5.4.2.3. Implied waiver of 'subject to contract' clause

The law on the stipulation 'subject to contract' has been recently developed by the Supreme Court in *RTS Flexible Systems Ltd* v. *Molkerei Alois Müller GmbH & Co KG*.[778] In that case, the Supreme Court held that the parties had impliedly waived the 'subject to contract' contingency by their conduct. Their letter of intent expressed to be 'subject to contract' was held to be fully contractually binding.

The Supreme Court's reasoning in *RTS Flexible Systems Ltd* v. *Molkerei Alois Müller GmbH & Co KG* relies on the background of previous developments in the approach of the English courts approach which is worth mentioning first. This background was summarized in *Mamidoil-Jetoil Greek Petroleum Co SA* v. *Okta Crude Oil Refinery AD (No.1)*.[779] The Court of Appeal reasoned as follows. If the parties mention at the precontractual stage, that one of the 'essential' terms remains 'to be agreed', this can prevent formation of a contract, because there will remain a fatal uncertainty on 'essential' terms of the future contract. Similarly, if the parties have simply not agreed on an 'essential' term of the final contract, no final contract would come into existence, because such an agreement does not fulfil the requirement of certainty. However, there

774 (1878) 3 AC 1124 (HL).

775 *Filby* v. *Hounsell* [1896] 2 Ch. 737 (EWHC Ch); *Branca* v. *Cobarro* [1947] KB 854 (CA); *ER Ives Investment Ltd* v. *High* [1967] 2 QB 379 (EWCA); *Damon Compania Naviera SA* v. *Hapag-Lloyd International SA (The Blankenstein)* [1985] 1 WLR 435 (EWCA); *Clipper Maritime Ltd* v. *Shirlstar Container Transport Ltd (The Anemone)* [1987] 1 Lloyd's Rep 546 (QBD); *Malcolm* v. *Chancellor, Masters and Scholars of the University of Oxford (t/a Oxford University Press)* [1994] EMLR 17 (EWCA); *Ateni Maritime Corp* v. *Great Marine Ltd (The Great Marine) (No.2)* [1990] 2 Lloyd's Rep 250 (QBD); *Jayaar Impex Ltd* v. *Toaken Group Ltd (t/a Hicks Brothers)* [1996] 2 Lloyd's Rep 437 (QBD).

776 *Rossiter* v. *Miller* (1878) 3 AC 1124 (HL) 1148 (Lord O'Hagan).

777 Ibid 1124.

778 [2010] UKSC 14, [2010] 1 WLR 753.

779 [2001] EWCA Civ 406, [2001] 2 All ER (Comm) 193 [69] (Lord Rix).

might be situations in commercial contracts where parties assume they have entered into a legally binding agreement and conduct themselves accordingly. In these situations, the parties' conduct diminishes the relevance of the 'subject to contract' statement. For instance, if the parties begin executing a transaction, the courts can consider the possibility of upholding the agreement made, rather than denying its legal validity. Rix LJ has noted that this kind of situation arises in particular when parties to negotiations want or need to settle some issues at a later stage of their transaction. According to Rix LJ, one of the signs pointing to the will of parties to settle future issues is an insertion of an arbitration clause into the precontractual agreement. Lord Rix reviewed the development of the law in *Mamidoil-Jetoil Greek Petroleum Co SA* v. *Okta Crude Oil Refinery AD (No.1)* in the following terms:[780]

> In my judgment the following principles relevant to the present case can be deduced from these authorities, but this is intended to be in no way an exhaustive list:
>
> i) Each case must be decided on its own facts and on the construction of its own agreement. Subject to that,
> ii) Where no contract exists, the use of an expression such as "to be agreed" in relation to an essential term is likely to prevent any contract coming into existence, on the ground of uncertainty. This may be summed up by the principle that "you cannot agree to agree".
> iii) Similarly, where no contract exists, the absence of agreement on essential terms of the agreement may prevent any contract coming into existence, again on the ground of uncertainty.
> iv) However, particularly in commercial dealings between parties who are familiar with the trade in question, and particularly where the parties have acted in the belief that they had a binding contract, the courts are willing to imply terms, where that is possible, to enable the contract to be carried out.
> v) Where a contract has once come into existence, even the expression "to be agreed" in relation to future executory obligations is not necessarily fatal to its continued existence.
> vi) Particularly in the case of contracts for future performance over a period, where the parties may desire or need to leave matters to be adjusted in the working out of their contract, the courts will assist the parties to do so, so as to preserve rather than destroy bargains, on the basis that what can be made certain is itself certain. *Certum est quod certum reddi potest.*
> vii) This is particularly the case where one party has either already had the advantage of some performance which reflects the parties' agreement on a long term relationship, or has had to make an investment premised on that agreement.
> viii) For these purposes, an express stipulation for a reasonable or fair measure or price will be a sufficient criterion for the courts to act on. But even in the absence of express language, the courts are prepared to imply an obligation in terms of what is reasonable.
> ix) Such implications are reflected but not exhausted by the statutory provision for the implication of a reasonable price now to be found in section 8(2) of the Sale of Goods Act

780 Ibid.

1979 (and, in the case of services, in section 15(1) of the Supply of Goods and Services Act 1982).

x) The presence of an arbitration clause may assist the courts to hold a contract to be sufficiently certain or to be capable of being rendered so, presumably as indicating a commercial and contractual mechanism, which can be operated with the assistance of experts in the field, by which the parties, in the absence of agreement, may resolve their dispute.

This summary by Rix LJ has prompted the question of the meaning of the concept 'essential' term. To clarify the matter, *RTS Flexible Systems Ltd* v. *Molkerei Alois Müller GmbH & Co KG*[781] refers to the statement made by Lloyd LJ in *Pagnan SpA* v. *Feed Products Ltd*:[782]

> It is sometimes said that the parties must agree on the essential terms and it is only matters of detail which can be left over. This may be misleading, since the word 'essential' in that context is ambiguous. If by 'essential' one means a term without which the contract cannot be enforced then the statement is true: the law cannot enforce an incomplete contract. If by 'essential' one means a term which the parties have agreed to be essential for the formation of a binding contract, then the statement is tautologous. If by 'essential' one means only a term which the Court regards as important as opposed to a term which the Court regards as less important or a matter of detail, the statement is untrue. It is for the parties to decide whether they wish to be bound and if so, by what terms, whether important or unimportant.

He went on to state on the reference of the essential term in negotiations:[783]

> Of course the more important the term is the less likely it is that the parties will have left it for future decision. But there is no legal obstacle which stands in the way of the parties agreeing to be bound now while deferring important matters to be agreed later. It happens every day when parties enter into so- called 'heads of agreement'.

The statement in *Pagnan SpA* v. *Feed Products Ltd* provides guidance on the definition of the concept essential term. It assumes that parties agree in the first place in terms of time on the matters that are essential to the final contract, whereas the issues less important for the final contract are left for further negotiations. This statement echoes the approach of earlier decisions, for example, in *Rossiter* v. *Miller* (1878), where Lord Blackburn said:[784]

> So long as they are only in negotiation either party may retract; and though the parties may have agreed on all the cardinal points of the intended contract, yet, if some particulars

781 [2010] UKSC 14, [2010] 1 WLR 753.

782 [1987] 2 Lloyd's Rep. 601 (EWCA) 619 (Lord Lloyd; O'Connor LJ and Stocker LJ agreed).

783 Ibid.

784 *Rossiter* v. *Miller* (1878) 3 AC 1124 (HL) 1151 (Lord O'Hagan).

> essential to the agreement still remain to be settled afterwards, there is no contract. The parties, in such a case, are still only in negotiation. But the mere fact that the parties have expressly stipulated that there shall afterwards be a formal agreement prepared, embodying the terms, which shall be signed by the parties does not, by itself, show that they continue merely in negotiation. It is a matter to be taken into account in construing the evidence and determining whether the parties have really come to a final agreement or not. But as soon as the fact is established of the final mutual assent of the parties so that those who draw up the formal agreement have not the power to vary the terms already settled, I think the contract is completed.

This is, however, only broad guidance. The meaning of the term 'essential' in complex transactions is defined by English courts using an individual assessment of the circumstances of each case. For instance, the approach of the Supreme Court in *RTS Flexible Systems Ltd* v. *Molkerei Alois Müller GmbH & Co KG*[785] was to establish first whether parties indeed intended to negotiate with a 'subject to contract' reservation. Thereafter, the Supreme Court assessed every term as it was negotiated and fixed in writing in a letter of intent and other written exchanges. It then decided whether it constituted an essential term for the parties on the facts of the case.

The facts of that case were the following. The parties entered into negotiations about a complex project of supply and installation by RTS of automated packaging machinery for Müller's dairy products. They signed a letter of intent 'subject to contract'. The letter of intent contained the price to be paid for the project, a request to commence works and stated that the contract terms of the further agreement should be based on 'MF/1' model form of contract standard terms.[786] A considerable part of the project was executed, and 70 per cent of the agreed price was paid. This happened before the end of negotiations and the signing of an agreement other than the letter of intent. Subsequently, RTS claimed payment of the remaining 30 per cent of the price in court. Müller replied by a counterclaim, asking for damages for defective performance.

The question before the court was whether a contract had been concluded, and if so, on what terms. Three different hypotheses were envisaged in turn by the Queen's Bench Division of the High Court (Technology and Construction Court), the Court of Appeal and the Supreme Court. Firstly, if no contract was concluded, the admissible claim is a claim for payment for the executed works on a *quantum meruit* basis. Secondly, if a simple contract only on the terms of the letter of intent was concluded, there might be liability under this contract (this liability was not limited by the parties) in a letter of intent. Thirdly, if a contract on MF/1 model form's terms was concluded, the 'liquidated

785 [2010] UKSC 14, [2010] 1 WLR 753.

786 Ibid [6]. MF/1 is one of the model forms of contract. See *Institution of Mechanical Engineers, IMechE, Institution of Engineering and Technology, IET, MF/1 (rev 6): Model Form Contract for the Design, Supply and Installation of Electrical, Electronic and Mechanical plant: Including Special Conditions for the Ancillary Development of Software* (London: Institution of Engineering and Technology, 2014).

damages' provision in MF/1 imposing a limit on the supplier's liability would be applicable.

The Technology and Construction Court held at first instance that the parties had concluded a contract on the terms expressed only in the letter of intent, without a reference to the MF/1 model form.[787] This decision was reversed on appeal. The Court of Appeal held that no contract was concluded. Thereafter, the Supreme Court held that the letter of intent represented a binding agreement that incorporated the MF/1 terms and supported this decision as follows. It has emphasized the importance of analysing the facts of the case. To do so, the Supreme Court applied the 'objective principle' (see Section 5.4.4.1 below on the objective principle):[788]

> The general principles are not in doubt. Whether there is a binding contract between the parties and, if so, upon what terms depends upon what they have agreed. It depends not upon their subjective state of mind, but upon a consideration of what was communicated between them by words or conduct, and whether that leads objectively to a conclusion that they intended to create legal relations and had agreed upon all the terms which they regarded or the law requires as essential for the formation of legally binding relations. Even if certain terms of economic or other significance to the parties have not been finalised, an objective appraisal of their words and conduct may lead to the conclusion that they did not intend agreement of such terms to be a precondition to a concluded and legally binding agreement.

The Supreme Court also contended that on the facts of the case, the parties had finalized negotiations on the substance of the agreement, meaning all its essential terms, and the letter of intent reflected the results of their negotiations, including 'the whole agreed contract price'.[789] and the reference to the MF/1 terms. It was emphasized by the Supreme Court that: 'all the terms which the parties treated as essential were agreed and the parties were performing the contract without a formal contract being signed or exchanged, whereas there parties were still negotiating terms which they regarded as essential'.[790]

Furthermore, at the time of the dispute, the parties had completed most of the agreements under the negotiated contract, including execution on both sides (performance of the project and payment of 70 per cent of the project). The Supreme Court noted in this regard that 'it does not seem … to make commercial sense to hold that the parties were agreeing to the works being carried out without any relevant contract terms'.[791] In applying the 'objective principle' the Supreme Court referred to a 'reasonable honest

787 *RTS Flexible Systems Ltd* v. *Molkerei Alois Muller GmbH & Co KG* [2008] EWHC 1087 (TCC), 2008 WL 2148115. See also [2009] EWCA Civ 26, [2009] 2 All ER (Comm) 542.

788 *RTS Flexible Systems Ltd* v. *Molkerei Alois Müller GmbH & Co KG* [2010] UKSC 14, [2010] 1 WLR 753 [45] (Lord Clarke delivering the judgment of the court).

789 Ibid [6].

790 Ibid [87].

791 Ibid [62].

businessman in the position of either RTS or Müller'.[792] Lord Clarke went on to state: '[W]e do not think that the reasonable honest businessman in the position of either RTS or Müller would have concluded as at 25 August that there was no contract between them or that there was a contract on some but not all of the terms that had been agreed'.[793] The parties proceeded with working on the terms of MF/1 incorporated into the letter of intent. According to the Supreme Court, the parties had therefore impliedly waived the 'subject to contract' bar. 'The clear inference is that the parties had agreed to waive the subject to contract clause, viz clause 48. Any other conclusion makes no commercial sense.'[794] After concluding that there was a tacit waiver of the 'subject to contract' bar, the Supreme Court granted to both parties a contractual cause of action. Consequently, not only could payment for the executed works be claimed, but also the contractual counterclaims, and contractual liability for the defects of performance were allowed. *RTS Flexible Systems Ltd* v. *Molkerei Alois Müller GmbH & Co KG* remains an exceptional decision, because its approach is closely related to the specific circumstances of the case.

5.4.3. *Divide into binding and non-binding provisions*

In *JSD Corporation PTE Ltd* v. *Al Waha Capital PJSC, Second Waha Lease Ltd*,[795] the High Court upheld the express distinction between binding and non-binding provisions made by the parties in a letter of intent they signed. In this case, the court took into account that the letter of intent was signed between two independent commercial parties, and that it established clearly the way the parties wanted the deal to progress. The High Court decided therefore that the letter of intent should be given a 'strict meaning' by enforcing what was meant to be enforceable, and not enforcing what was meant by the parties as unenforceable. The document was said to have 'contractual effect as regards clauses expressly made legally binding. Under its terms JSD has to make payments and observe confidentiality'.[796]

5.4.4. *Relevant matters of interpretation*

5.4.4.1. Objective principle

The way freedom of contract counterbalances the judicial interference into parties' arrangements has been characterized as follows: '[t]he court has no power to improve upon the instrument which it is called upon to construe, whether it be a contract, a statute or articles of association. It cannot introduce terms to make it fairer or more

792 Ibid.
793 Ibid [87].
794 Ibid [86].
795 [2009] EWHC 583 (Ch), 2009 WL 648840.
796 Ibid [32] (Smith J).

reasonable. It is concerned only to discover what the instrument means'.[797] The meaning of the analysed terms and the entire transaction is ascertained 'objectively':[798]

> [T]hat meaning is not necessarily or always what the authors or parties to the document would have intended. It is the meaning which the instrument would convey to a reasonable person having all the background knowledge which would reasonably be available to the audience to whom the instrument is addressed.

This *objective principle* is a fundamental principle of interpretation in English contract law.[799] It is applied every time to interpret the parties' conduct and statements. According to this principle, the 'judicial task is not to discover the actual intentions of each party; it is to decide what each was reasonably entitled to conclude from the attitude of the other'.[800] The application of the 'objective principle' consists in relating a conduct or a statement to an understanding that a reasonable person in a position of the party would have (the 'objective test'). As stated by Lord Hoffmann:[801]

> Interpretation is the ascertainment of the meaning which the document would convey to a reasonable person having all the background knowledge which would reasonably have been available to the parties in the situation in which they were at the time of the contract.

A reasonable person in a position of the parties takes on the parties' experience and common knowledge (though these might be in turn to a certain extent subjective).[802] In commercial cases, the hypothetical persons referred to are also a reasonable businessmen[803] or 'honest men', as Lord Steyn has put it.[804] The language of the statements is also to be interpreted in a reasonable manner. This manner of interpretation does not however reduce statements to their literal meaning, but includes a common sense interpretation and takes into account the context of the transaction.

The subjective state of mind and subjective intention of a party is irrelevant for the objective assessment. The 'objective principle', protects a party to which a conduct or a statement is addressed from being surprised by the other party's subjective understanding of its own conduct or statement. For example, if one party states A, but subjectively means B, the other party does not have to guess what B meant;[805] it is sufficient to rely on

797 *Attorney General of Belize* v. *Belize Telecom Ltd* [2009] UKPC 10 [2009], 1 WLR 1988 [16] (Lord Hoffmann).
798 Ibid.
799 *Smith v. Hughes (1870–71) LR 6 QB 597 (Court of Queen's Bench)* 607 (Blackburn J); Andrews 2015, para 1.10. See also Beever 2009; *Chitty on Contracts* 2015, para 2–002.
800 *McCutcheon* v. *David MacBrayne Ltd* [1964] 1 WLR 125 (HL) 128 (Lord Reid).
801 *Investors Compensation Scheme Ltd* v. *West Bromwich Building Society (No.1)* [1998] 1 WLR 896 (HL) 912 (Lord Hoffmann).
802 McLauchlan 2005, at 484.
803 See for example *Fiona Trust and Holding Corporation* v. *Privalov* [2007] UKHL 40, [2007] 4 All ER 951.
804 Steyn 1997.
805 Andrews 2015, para 1.22. See *Paal Wilson & Co A/S* v. *Partenreederei Hannah Blumenthal (The Hannah Blumenthal)* [1983] 1 AC 854 (HL).

an understanding that a reasonable person in the same situation would have. Without this protection, a 'serious inconvenience would be caused by allowing a party to rely on his "real intention"'.[806] It would also be practically difficult for a court to determine what a party subjectively intended by conduct or a statement.[807]

Furthermore, when ascertaining the meaning of contractual provisions, English law makes a distinction between *express* and *implied* terms. Express terms are those stated by parties in their written document, primarily contracts. Their meaning can be *construed* by the court.[808] Construction is a 'process by which a court determines the meaning and legal effect of a contract'.[809] At the same time, if parties have not expressly stated all the terms of a particular type of transaction, a court may *imply* a term into the transaction.

5.4.4.2. Ordinary meaning

In accordance with the objective principle mentioned earlier, the English courts rely primarily on the plain and ordinary meaning of the parties' statements.[810] This is not to say the context is not relevant, but the literal and primarily linguistic interpretation is given priority above the teleological or contextual interpretation. This is especially true for interpretation in the context of commercial transactions. As Lord Diplock stated, 'if detailed semantic and syntactical analysis of words in a commercial contract is going to lead to a conclusion that flouts business commonsense, it must be made to yield to business commonsense'.[811]

5.4.4.3. Implied terms

An English court may *imply* into a transaction a term that is not expressly stated by the parties, if this term constitutes an integral part of a transaction.[812] Implication is made frequently. Andrews notes: 'implied terms... are more common than express terms. Every day, millions of transactions are entered into without writing and without a single spoken word'.[813] He explains further that 'against this silent background, the law fleshes out these transactions by implying terms'.[814]

806 Treitel 2007, para 1-002.
807 Ibid.
808 See inter alia McMeel 2011.
809 *Chitty on Contracts* 2015, para 13-041.
810 *Mannai Investment Co Ltd* v. *Eagle Star Life Assurance Co Ltd* [1997] AC 749 (HL); *Rennie* v. *Westbury Homes (Holdings) Ltd* [2007] EWHC 164 (Ch), [2007] 2 P & CR 12.
811 *Antaios Compania Naviera SA v. Salen Rederierna AB (The Antaios)* [1985] AC 191 (HL) 201 (Lord Diplock). See also with further references *Chitty on Contracts* 2015, para 13-059.
812 Andrews 2015, at 13.01 ff.; Peden 2001, Phang 1998, Steyn 1997.
813 Andrews 2015, para 13.02.
814 Ibid.

Implication is, however, subject to several boundaries, especially in commercial transactions. The House of Lords has held generally, that terms cannot be implied if they would contradict terms clearly expressed by the parties. As stated by Lord Hoffmann, 'the proposed implied term must spell out what the contract actually means:[815]

> [j]udges ... have no right to make contracts for the parties. Their province is to interpret contracts. But language is imperfect and there may be, as it were, obvious interstices in what is expressed which have to be filled up.

English law recognizes three different types of implication of terms. Terms can be implied firstly, in law, secondly, in fact, or thirdly, based on an existing custom or usage. Firstly, when the courts imply a term *in law*, they apply minimal rules for the operation of a standard legal relationship. One of the most common examples is the implication of a 'reasonable' price in sales contracts. Courts may imply the price if parties to a contract have not agreed the price and consider price not to be an essential term that should be negotiated before a contract can be considered formed.[816] In the words of Lord Steyn, terms implied in law are 'incidents impliedly annexed to particular forms of contracts... Such standardized implied terms operate as general default rules'.[817] Terms are implied in law on the basis of statutes[818] containing rules inherent to certain types of transactions or based on judicial precedent. In the latter case, courts are guided by policy considerations. They take into consideration not only the 'necessity' of implying a term 'in order to give business efficacy to the transaction'. This requirement has been established in *Liverpool City Council* v. *Irwin*.[819] They also take into account what is 'reasonable' in transactions of a certain type.[820] In this way, higher courts add a term implied judicially to the terms implied by virtue of a statute.[821] An example of a term implied judicially is the obligation of confidentiality in arbitration.[822]

Secondly, terms implied *in fact* have been characterized by Lord Wright in *Luxor (Eastbourne) Ltd* v. *Cooper* as follows. He starts by noting that the 'presumption is against the adding to contracts of terms which the parties have not expressed'.[823] The starting point is that parties include into their agreement all the matters they find important. But Lord Wright goes on to state that sometimes the court needs to imply a term to give

815 *Luxor (Eastbourne)* Ltd v. *Cooper* [1941] AC 108 (HL) 137–138 (Lord Wright).

816 Sale of Goods Act 1979 (section 8) and Supply of Goods and Services Act 1982 (section 15(1)). Furmston and Tolhurst note that this type of implication is not common for transactions relating to the sale of land. See Furmston/Tolhurst 2010, at 362 (footnote 35).

817 Steyn 1997, at 433, 442.

818 For example, Sale of Goods Act 1979.

819 [1977] AC 239 (HL).

820 See, for instance, *Crossley* v. *Faithful & Gould Holdings Ltd* [2004] EWCA Civ 293, [2004] 4 All ER 447 (employment).

821 *Luxor (Eastbourne)* Ltd v. *Cooper* [1941] AC 108 (HL) 137 (Lord Wright); *Lister* v. *Romford Ice and Cold Storage Co Ltd* [1957] AC 555 (HL) (contract of employment).

822 *Michael Wilson & Partners Ltd v. Emmott* [2008] EWCA Civ 184, [2008] CP Rep 26.

823 [1941] AC 108 (HL) 137 (Lord Wright).

'business efficacy' to the transaction 'as the parties must have intended'.[824] The court implies terms to give effect to the intention of the parties. By implying terms in fact, courts do not create contractual terms instead of the parties, nor do they refer to policy considerations. Neither do they rely on what is 'reasonable' or 'fair' in the circumstances of the case[825] (by contrast with the implication of terms in law).[826] Thirdly, a court can also imply a term that corresponds to a *custom or trade usage* – rules characteristic to a particular sector of trade and customs – rules proper to a particular location.[827]

A custom or trade usage should fulfil certain criteria in order to be implied. The requirements for an implication based on a custom have been summarized in *Cunliffe-Owen* v. *Teather & Greenwood*. It must be notorious, certain, reasonable and not contrary to law:[828]

> For the practice to amount to such a recognised usage, it must be certain, in the sense that the practice is clearly established; it must be notorious, in the sense that it is so well known, in the market in which it is alleged to exist, that those who conduct business in that market contract with the usage as an implied term; and it must be reasonable.

Furthermore, according to the House of Lords, in order to be implied, the trade usage should be 'universal and acknowledged'.[829] Notably, courts also seek to ascertain that the trade usage to be implied is respected.[830]

824 Ibid.

825 Steyn 1997, at 442.

826 The test of 'business efficacy' and the 'officious bystander' complementing each other are used for this purpose. The '*business efficacy*' test, also called '*The Moorcock* test' assesses whether a contract did not become futile in the circumstances of the case. '*The Moorckock*' case is the main authority on the 'business efficacy' test. The defendant contracted to discharge the claimants' vessel. To do so, the defendant had to moor the vessel along the river. During this process, the vessel was damaged because the jetty of the river was not deep enough for this mooring. The Court of Appeal held that there was an implied term that a company contracted to discharge the vessel should have taken reasonable steps to prevent physical damages to the vessel, if it had to moor it before discharging. Otherwise, the contract for discharging the vessel would not make sense. 'The implication is to give such business efficacy to the transaction as must have been intended at all events by both parties who are businessmen; not to impose on one side all the perils of the transaction, or to emancipate one side from all the chances of failure…'(*The Moorcock* (1889) 14 P.D. 64, CA, at 68 *per* Bowen LJ).
In applying the '*officious bystander*' test, the courts inquire whether parties would have obviously included a term in question in their contract during negotiations. This test has 'a very high threshold' (Andrews 2015, para 13.09) in the sense that the term will not be implied if a party can substantiate that he would not agree on this during the formation of contract (See *Shirlaw* v. *Southern Foundries* [1939] 2 KB 206 (EWCA) and [1940] AC 701 (HL), the leading decision on the 'officious bystander' test).

827 *Liverpool City Council* v. *Irwin* [1977] AC 239 (HL) 253 (Lord Wilberforce); *Baker* v. *Black Sea & Baltic General Insurance Co Ltd* [1998] 1 WLR 974 (HL).

828 [1967] 1 WLR 1421 (EWHC Ch) 1438.

829 *Baker* v. *Black Sea & Baltic General Insurance Co Ltd* [1998] 1 WLR 974 (HL) 983 (Lord Lloyd of Berwick, referring to Lord Millett).

830 *General Reinsurance Corporation and Others* v. *Forsakringsaktiebolaget Fennia Patria* [1983] QB 856 (EWCA).

5.4.4.4. Issues of law and fact

In English law, construction is a mixed issue of law and fact.[831] More specifically, defining the meaning of the parties' acts is regarded as an issue of fact.[832] Once the meaning is defined, the ascertainment of its effects is an issue of law.[833]

5.4.4.5. Parole evidence rule

According to English law, no extrinsic evidence, primarily oral statements, may be used for interpretation of a contract concluded in writing. This is referred to as the 'parole evidence rule'.[834] Interpretation of letter of intent is an exception to this rule. Extrinsic evidence is admitted, in particular if the document was not intended to form the entire agreement between the parties. Furthermore, if a document in question is not intended to be a contract, extrinsic evidence is admitted for defining the intentions of the parties. Finally, in proving customs or mercantile usage, extrinsic evidence may be used.[835]

5.5. Non-contractual doctrines mandatorily applicable to negotiations

The broad scope of freedom of negotiations does not mean that contractual negotiations represent a period of 'no law'. A number of doctrines within non-contractual regulation apply to remedy 'demonstrated unfairness'[836] or 'particular problems of unacceptable conduct occurring in the course of negotiations'[837] in the bargaining process. The regulation includes tort law (5.5.1), duty of confidence developed in equity (5.5.2), and unjust enrichment (5.5.3). The doctrine of estoppel deserves a particular note as well (5.5.4).

5.5.1. Tort law

A simple non-disclosure of information in commercial negotiations is regarded as legally acceptable conduct. Parties have no general obligation to prevent an 'ordinary bargaining mistake'[838] in the process of a transaction. Neither are they subject to a duty to disclose facts relating to their bargaining position, 'however dishonest such undisclosure may be

831 *Chitty on Contracts* 2015, para 13–047.
832 *Simpson* v. *Margitson* (1847) 116 ER 383 (Court of Queen's Bench).
833 *Bowes* v. *Shand* (1877) 2 AC 455 (HL). See also *Chitty on Contracts* 2015, para 13–047.
834 *Goss* v. *Lord Nugent* [1824] All ER Rep 305 (KBD); *Chitty on Contracts* 2015, para 13–099.
835 *Chitty on Contracts* 2015, para 13–110, 13–130.
836 *Interfoto Picture Library Limited* v. *Stiletto Visual Programmes Limited* [1989] QB 433 (EWCA) 439 (Lord Bingham).
837 *Cobbe* v. *Yeoman's Row Management Ltd* [2006] EWCA Civ 1139, [2006] 1 WLR 2964 [4] (Lord Mummery).
838 Andrews 2015, para 9.01.

in particular circumstances'.[839] An exception to this rule is formed by transactions involving a fiduciary relationship between the parties.[840]

The line between the (acceptable) non-disclosure and the unacceptable conduct is drawn on the basis of the doctrine of misrepresentation[841] two torts related to misrepresentation. It is worth noting that English law relies on specific torts rather than on an overarching tort law duty. At the stage of negotiations, the torts of deceit and negligent misstatement are the main tools within tort law that form a part of 'piecemeal solutions'[842] to remedy demonstrated unfairness.

5.5.1.1. Misrepresentation

Misrepresentation is a *false* statement of *fact* made by one party *prior to formation* of a contractually binding obligation[843] that induces *reliance* by the other party and his contractual assent.[844] Misrepresentation made during contractual negotiations can lead to rescission of contract. This is the most frequent way of applying this doctrine. But misrepresentation may also constitute an actionable tort if a contract fails to materialize.[845] To clarify the specific way this is done, the elements of the misrepresentation doctrine may be briefly addressed in some detail.

Misrepresentation is a *statement of fact*. Simple statements of intention or opinion about a fact, about the future or mere 'puffs'[846] do not represent misrepresentation. However, if a statement of intention is made dishonestly, e.g. without a real belief in it, this may amount to misrepresentation (the belief is assessed through the objective test).[847] This test ascertains whether a reasonable person in the same position would believe the statement.[848] Misrepresentation is made 'if, at the time when it was made, the person making the statement did not in fact intend to do what he said or knew that he did not have the ability to put the intention into effect'.[849]

839 *Chitty on Contracts* 2015, para 7–012.

840 These transactions include insurance, contracts for the sale of land, partnership agreements, various relationship of trust and confidence.

841 In this regard, the doctrine of mistake is also mentioned. See Cartwright 2012 on distinction and close relationship between misrepresentation and mistake. See also Cartwright 2010; Chen-Wishart 2009.

842 *Interfoto Picture Library Limited* v. *Stiletto Visual Programmes Limited* [1989] QB 433 (EWCA) 439 (Lord Bingham).

843 *Redgrave* v. *Hurd* (1881) 20 Ch 1 (EWCA); *Baglehole* v. *Walters* 170 ER 1338 (Assizes); *Cottee* v. *Seaton (Douglas) (Used Cars)* [1972] 3 All ER 750 (DC).

844 English law relating to misrepresentation is complex. It includes rules in common law, equity and provisions of Misrepresentation Act 1967. *Chitty on Contracts* 2015, para 7–001 ff.; Feltham/Hochberg/Leech 2004; Andrews 2015, Chapter 9. See also Cartwright 2012.

845 *Chitty on Contracts* 2015, para 2–216; see also Giliker 2002, at 105 ff.

846 *Chitty on Contracts* 2015, para 7–007.

847 See Section 5.4.4.1.

848 *Connolly Limited* v. *Bellway Homes Limited* [2007] EWHC 895 (Ch), 2007 WL 1157898; *Smith* v. *Land and House Property Corporation* (1884) 28 Ch 7 (EWCA).

849 *Chitty on Contracts* 2015, para 7–012.

Misrepresentation is a *false* statement. The falsity is tested through a common law test laid down in *Avon Insurance plc* v. *Swire Fraser Ltd.*[850] If a statement was 'substantially correct' and if a change of fact (contained in a statement) would not induce a reasonable person in the position of the other party to enter into contract, the statement is considered true. By contrast, if a change to a fact made by a statement would induce a reasonable person in the position of the other party to enter into a contract, the statement is false.[851]

Finally, application of the doctrine of misrepresentation requires *reliance* on a statement. The statement should effectively induce the other party to take specific actions,[852] e.g. to accept a particular set of obligations that are less advantageous than the party could negotiate without misrepresentation.[853] Contractual assent or other conduct should be induced by reliance on this precise statement, but not on other statements or facts.

A causal link must be established between the statement and conduct, whereby the statement had a 'decisive influence' on the conduct in question.[854] By contrast, in the absence of reliance, the statement does not amount to misrepresentation.[855] The representee bears the burden of proof to show that he relied on the statement.[856] If the representee proves that the reliance is 'material' upon an objective analysis, that is, if a reasonable person in the same position would rely on this statement, this constitutes a sufficient proof of reliance.[857]

5.5.1.2. Deceit

The tort of deceit is one of the ways to protect reliance in the course of negotiations in English law. It enables recovery for a *fraudulent misrepresentation.*[858] The availability of recovery under the tort of deceit in the context of failed negotiations has been pointed out in *Walford* v. *Miles.*[859] The damages were granted on appeal (before the Court of Appeal), but not discussed subsequently by the House of Lords.

A misrepresentation (a statement with the characteristics mentioned above) is considered fraudulent if it is made without honest belief in its accuracy or truthfulness. In

850 [2000] 1 All ER (Comm) 573 (QBD).

851 *Avon Insurance plc* v. *Swire Fraser Ltd* [2000] 1 All ER (Comm) 573 (QBD) especially [199]-[205].

852 *Strover* v. *Harrington* [1988] Ch 390 (EWHC).

853 *Clef Aquitaine Sarl* v. *Laporte Materials (Barrow) Ltd* [2001] QB 488 (EWCA); *Huyton SA* v. *Distribuidora Internacional de Productos Agricolas SA* [2003] EWCA Civ 1104, [2004] 1 All ER (Comm) 402.

854 Andrews 2015, para 9.04; Assicurazioni Generali SpA v. Arab Insurance Group (BSC) [2002] EWCA Civ 1642 [2003], 1 All ER (Comm); *Clef Aquitaine Sarl* v. *Laporte Materials (Barrow) Ltd* [2001] QB 488 (EWCA).

855 *Peekay Intermark Ltd* v. *Australia & New Zealand Banking Group Ltd* [2006] EWCA Civ 386, [2006] 2 Lloyd's Rep 511.

856 Andrews 2015, para 9.04.

857 *Spice Girls Ltd* v. *Aprilia World Service BV* [2002] EWCA Civ 15, [2002] EMLR 27.

858 The tort of deceit has been established in *Pasley* v. *Freeman* (1789) 100 ER 450 (KBD), developed by the House of Lords in *Derry* v. *Peek* (1889) 14 AC 337 (HL). See also Markesinis/Deakin 2013, Ch. 14.

859 [1992] 2 AC 128 (HL).

establishing fraud, the subjective state of mind of the party making a statement has primary relevance. As noted in *Derry* v. *Peek*, a party making a statement must either know that the statement is false, or be indifferent to its falsity:[860]

> First, in order to sustain an action of deceit, there must be proof of fraud, and nothing short of that will suffice. Secondly, fraud is proved when it is shewn that a false representation has been made (1) knowingly, or (2) without belief in its truth, or (3) recklessly, careless whether it be true or false. ... [I]f fraud be proved, the motive of the person guilty of it is immaterial. It matters not that there was no intention to cheat or injure the person to whom the statement was made.

Reliance on a fraudulent statement is presumed;[861] the presumption is rebuttable. Furthermore, importantly, the liability arising in the tort of deceit may not be contractually disclaimed or limited. Therefore, liability for deceit may be engaged irrespectively of any contractual organization of negotiations.

5.5.1.3. Negligent misrepresentation

The tort of negligent misrepresentation is another means of recovery at the stage of contractual negotiations. However, this tort covers only specific cases where parties are in a fiduciary relationship – the relationship of trust. Parties in negotiations do not have a general duty of care as to the truthfulness of information provided during negotiations.[862]

Liability for negligent misstatement (for misrepresentation negligent at common law) may arise *only* when a *special relationship* exists between parties and implies a duty of care. The duty of care required for the legal protection of reliance on a misrepresentation made negligently (at common law) has been established by the House of Lords in *Hedley Byrne & Co Ltd* v. *Heller & Partners Ltd.*[863] In this case, a bank provided the claimant with information confirming the good financial state of a claimant's client. It turned out, however, that this information did not reflect its real financial state. The House of Lords held that the defendant was liable in tort for negligent misstatement (a new type of liability at this time) and should reimburse pure economic loss sustained by the claimant. A 'reasonable reliance' on the statement was held to be primarily relevant. This reliance was said to be based on the duty of care arising when 'a person takes it upon himself to give information or advice to, or allows his information or advice to be passed on to, another person who, as he knows or should know, will place reliance upon it'.[864] The

860 (1889) 14 AC 337 (HL) 374 (Lord Herschell).

861 *Barton* v. *County Natwest Ltd* [2002] 4 All ER 494 (Note), [1999] Lloyd's Rep Bank 408 (EWCA) [54]-[56]; *Pan Atlantic Insurance Co. Ltd* v. *Pine Top Insurance Ltd* [1995] 1 AC 501 (HL) 542.

862 See *Glen-Mor Fashions Limited* v. The Jaeger Company Shops Limited 1991 WL 11780044 (EWCA); Markesinis/Deakin 2013, at 146.

863 [1964] AC 465 (HL).

864 *Hedley Byrne & Co Ltd* v. *Heller & Partners Ltd* [1964] AC 465 (HL) 509 (Lord Morris). See also Markesinis/Deakin 2013, at 144 ff.

duty of care arises only in a 'special relationship'. The House of Lords named two steps to ascertain whether the duty of care relevant for the tort of negligent misstatement arises:[865]

> First one has to ask whether, as between the alleged wrongdoer and the person who has suffered damage there is a sufficient relationship of proximity or neighbourhood such that, in the reasonable contemplation of the former, carelessness on his part may be likely to cause damage to the latter – in which case a prima facie duty of care arises. Secondly, if the first question is answered affirmatively, it is necessary to consider whether there are any considerations which ought to negative, or to reduce or limit the scope of the duty or the class of person to whom it is owed or the damages to which a breach of it may give rise...

The logical steps for establishing the breach of the duty of care were explained by the House of Lords in *Customs and Excise Commissioners* v. *Barclays Bank Plc*. Lord Bingham reviewed authorities on three sets of factors to be taken into consideration. The first factor is the question 'whether the defendant assumed responsibility for what he said and did *vis-à-vis* the claimant, or is to be treated by the law as having done so'.[866] The second one is the 'policy' test:[867]

> commonly known as the threefold test: whether loss to the claimant was a reasonably foreseeable consequence of what the defendant did or failed to do; whether the relationship between the parties was one of sufficient proximity; and whether in all the circumstances it is fair, just and reasonable to impose a duty of care on the defendant towards the claimant...

The third test prevents a wide expansion of the implication of the duty:[868]

> Third is the incremental test, based on the observation of Brennan J in *Sutherland Shire Council* v *Heyman* (1985) 157 CLR 424, 481, approved by Lord Bridge of Harwich in *Caparo Industries plc* v *Dickman* [1990] 2 AC 605, 618, that:
> "It is preferable, in my view, that the law should develop novel categories of negligence incrementally and by analogy with established categories, rather than by a massive extension of a prima facie duty of care restrained only by indefinable 'considerations which ought to negative, or to reduce or limit the scope of the duty or the class of person to whom it is owed'."

Practically, the duty of care in tort has been identified in various contracts involving some level of trust between the parties. English scholarship refers to such contracts as contracts *uberrimae fidei*. These include insurance, sale of land, partnership, various relationships of trust and confidence, e.g. relations between a bank and its customers, between a lawyer and its clients.

865 *Anns* v. *Merton LBC* [1978] AC 728 (HL) 751–752.
866 [2006] UKHL 28, [2007] 1 AC 181 [4] (Lord Bingham).
867 Ibid.
868 Ibid.

The case *BSkyB Ltd* v. *HP Enterprise Services UK Ltd*[869] illustrates the application of the rules on misrepresentation to letter of intent issued in negotiations. In this case, a company was found liable in the tort of deceit for having provided an incorrect estimate of the time required for performing services under a project. The misrepresentation was made by the employee of the defendant. The employee was aware of the falsity of the information provided. The claimant was a satellite broadcaster. He entered into negotiations with a company providing information technology used in customer relationship management. In the course of negotiations several documents with different titles were signed. The parties signed a 'letter of intent' and thereafter a contract (the 'Prime contract'). The execution of this contract turned out to be longer and more expensive than expected and agreed. The Prime contract was renegotiated and modified by another document called the 'letter of agreement'. However, the parties had further disagreements and the claimant took over the contractual performance from the defendant. A 'memorandum of understanding' was signed to fix this. When a dispute arose, the satellite broadcaster submitted a claim for misrepresentation made during negotiations of the first letter of intent. It alleged that the signing of the 'letter of Intent', the Prime contract and the 'letter of agreement' was induced by a misrepresentation as to the time and costs of the project. He claimed in the alternative damages for negligent misrepresentation made before signing of the 'letter of agreement'. The High Court found no grounds for recovery for negligent misrepresentation, because no duty of care arose the between parties, according to the court. The claim for deceit was honoured.

5.5.2. *Duty of confidence in relations involving trust*

The exchange of information in the course of negotiations may be subject to the duty of confidence. This duty has been developed in equity and implies that information acquired in confidence may not be used in an unauthorized a manner, that is, with the goals other than those pursued during the disclosure.[870] This duty is relevant for the period of negotiations generally, irrespectively of the existence of a contractually binding confidentiality obligation.[871] In the words of Lord Denning MR in *Seager* v. *Copydex Ltd*: the broad principle of equity that he who has received information in confidence shall not take unfair advantage of it. He must not make use of it to the prejudice of him who gave it without obtaining his consent'.[872]

The case of *Seager* v. *Copydex Ltd* concerned negotiations between an owner of a patent of a carpet grip and a company that would market this grip. The negotiations lasted for more than a year, but ultimately failed. Instead of marketing this grip, the company has created its own grip. While the new product did not infringe the other party's patent

[869] [2010] EWHC 86 (TCC), [2010] BLR 267.

[870] *Seager* v. *Copydex* Ltd (No.1) [1967] 1 WLR 923 (EWCA).

[871] Cartwright mentions that the 'proper categorisation of the basis of a claim for breach of confidence is unclear although well-established in English law'. See Cartwright/Hesselink 2008, at 338.

[872] *Seager* v. *Copydex* Ltd (No.1) [1967] 1 WLR 923 (EWCA) 931 (Lord Denning).

rights, its features were based on the information disclosed by the patent's owner during negotiations. The Court of Appeal held that the company had 'unconsciously made use of confidential information given to them by the plaintiff as a spring-board for activities detrimental to him, thereby infringing a duty of confidence'.[873]

The duty of confidence has also been found in a negotiation of a contract for a joint commercial venture for manufacturing a product.[874] For instance, in *James Industries Ltd.'s Patent*, the parties described themselves as 'partners in a joint commercial venture…in negotiations towards a written contract',[875] at the time of negotiations. Some of parties' understandings reached in negotiations were fixed in letters. The court found that the way the parties negotiated this commercial deal led to the duty of confidence being established.

It is unlikely that the duty (or its implications) may be disclaimed by the parties' agreements. The reason for this is the historical roots of the duty which has developed as equitable relief. A relief in equity has been granted in situations where no other cause of action provided an adequate remedy. Therefore, equitable relief is by nature within the discretion of the court, not of the parties.

5.5.3. *Unjust enrichment*

In English law, performance commenced in anticipation that the final contract would be concluded can be recovered under the law of restitution and unjust enrichment. This relatively new branch of law, had developed in the last sixty years and is referred to in some contemporary sources as 'unjust enrichment', whereas earlier sources use the title 'restitution'.[876]

The possibility to recover the reasonable price for goods supplied before the formation of the final contract has been established by *British Steel Corp* v. *Cleveland Bridge & Engineering Co Ltd*.[877] The main authority on the possibility to recover anticipated services is *William Lacey (Hounslow) Ltd* v. *Davis*.[878]

Recovery under the law of unjust enrichment includes the assessment of the following factors. Courts assess firstly, whether the receiving party has been enriched by the

873 Ibid 924.

874 *James Industries Ltd.'s Patent* [1987] RPC 235 (PO); *Coco* v. *A.N. Clark (Engineers) Limited* [1968] FSR 415 (EWHC Ch).

875 [1987] RPC 235 (PO) 235.

876 The first seminal works by Goff and Jones were entitled 'The law of Restitution'. The latest edition of this book uses the term unjust enrichment. See Goff/Jones 2011. As explained by Mitchell with reference to Birks, '[t]he difference between unjust enrichment and restitution is the difference between event and response'. See Mitchell 2015. See also Davies 2010.

877 [1984] 1 All ER 504 (QBD).

878 [1957] 1 WLR 932 (QBD).

anticipated performance of the other party, in other words, whether some benefit has been conferred. Secondly, the unjust factor in this transfer should be in place. Mitchell notes that civil law systems search for absence of legal grounds; by contrast, 'English law approaches the issues differently, by asking if there is a positive reason for restitution or "unjust factor", ie a legally recognized factor making the defendant's enrichment unjust'.[879] The grounds for recovery crystallized in the case law include lack of consent and want of authority (that is deficient intent of the claimant that the defendant enriches at his expense), duress, mistake, undue influence, total failure of consideration.

It is worth noting that to grant recovery, the courts assess whether one has benefitted from the anticipated performance. An important factor in this assessment is the question whether the anticipated performance was *requested* by the defendant. This implies that the works or services would be reimbursed. Though, as has been stressed by Strauss QC, no general principle can be formulated. According to him, it is 'impossible to formulate a clear general principle which satisfactorily governs the different factual situations which have arisen, let alone those which could easily arise in other cases'.[880] He stated furthermore:

> Perhaps, in the absence of any recognition in English law of a general duty of good faith in contractual negotiations, this is not surprising. Much of the difficulty is caused by attempting to categorise as an unjust enrichment of the defendant, for which an action in restitution is available, what is really a loss unfairly sustained by the plaintiff.

Considering the absence of general principles, this Chapter will come back to the cause of action in restitution in the Section that discusses provisions on costs and anticipated performance.[881] There, several possible causes of action will be put next to each other in order to contrast the facts of the case and the reasoning adopted.

5.5.4. *Note on estoppel*

Precontractual reliance can be potentially protected under the doctrine of estoppel. It is worth noting from the outset, that the doctrine of estoppel offers no general protection of precontractual reliance in English law. Furthermore, in cases where it has been invoked in the context of contractual negotiations, this relief has been granted rather infrequently.[882]

879 Mitchell 2015, para 3.10. See also Goff/Jones 2011, Chapter 16.

880 *Countrywide Communications Ltd* v. *ICL Pathway Ltd* [2000] CLC 324 (QBD) 349 (Strauss QC).

881 See Section 5.6.

882 See inter alia *Regalian Properties Plc* v. *London Docklands Development Corp* [1995] 1 WLR 212 (EWHC Ch) promissory estoppel invoked, but not allowed; *Spring Finance Ltd* v, *HS Real Co LLC* [2011] EWHC 57 (Comm), 2011 WL 398119 (following a memorandum of understanding 'subject to contract' signed between parties, estoppel by convention invoked, but not allowed).

English law distinguishes three main types of estoppel: promissory estoppel, proprietary estoppel and estoppel by convention.[883] Promissory estoppel is a defence developed in equity. It prevents a person from acting inconsistently with their own statements or acts: if one is at the point of dramatically changing his conduct, he may be prevented by the court – estopped – from doing so. Promissory estoppel can neither be used as a separate cause of action, nor create new obligations. It is essentially used in disputes arising from an existing contractual relationship.[884] The doctrine is furthermore used limitedly and 'serves as a shield and not a sword' as was metaphorically noted in *Combe* v. *Combe*.[885] This limitation, referred to as the *Combe* v. *Combe* restriction, is consistently maintained in English law.[886] Proprietary estoppel is limited to transactions relating to land. Lord Scott suggested a potentially broader scope for the application of this doctrine in *Cobbe* v. *Yeoman's Row Management Ltd*, namely its possible extension to 'chattels or choses in action'.[887] However, this suggestion has been so far not followed up. Finally, estoppel by convention offers protection arising from a statement of facts on which both parties agree. Once the parties have agreed, they will be estopped (prevented by law) 'as against the other from questioning the truth of the statement of facts so assumed'.[888] This estoppel is not based on a representation, but on a 'pattern of visible conduct which indicates a shared assumption'.[889]

Within the academic debate, the following can be noted. According to English legal academics, a different approach of the Australian High Court might influence the development of English law. For instance, Furmston and Tolhurst[890] discuss an Australian case *Waltons Stores (Interstate) Ltd* v. *Maher*.[891] In that case promissory estoppel was applied to a precontractual relationship. A remedy in damages was awarded as precontractual liability. Parties to the dispute worked in the construction industry and negotiated a project for development of a plot of land. The existing building needed to be demolished and new buildings constructed at a later stage. The negotiations were broken off before finalizing the signing of a contract. When negotiations had stopped, a dispute arose. The draft agreement exchanged by the parties stated that negotiations were 'subject to contract'. However, at the time of breaking off negotiations, one party had already started demolition. The Australian court applied promissory estoppel, reasoning as follows. There was a promise on which one party relied. On the facts of the case, the promissor could not deny the existence of a promise. Therefore, equity applied in favour of the promissor. Another Australian case states that if one party can reasonably

883 Andrews 2015, para 5.45 ff. See *Chitty on Contracts* 2015, para 4–086 ff., 4–139 ff., 4–108 ff.
884 Furmston/Tolhurst 2010, para 3.65.
885 *Combe* v. *Combe* [1951] 1 All E.R. 767.
886 *Chitty on Contracts* 2015, para 4–099; Andrews 2015, para 5.48.
887 [2008] UKHL 55, [2008] 4 All ER 713 [14] (Lord Scott).
888 Spencer Bower 1977, at 157.
889 Andrews 2015, para 5.48, referring to *Bridgewater* v. *Griffiths* [2000] 1 WLR 524, [1999] 2 Costs LR 524 (QBD) 530 (Burton J).
890 Furmston/Tolhurst 2010, at 386 ff.
891 *Waltons Stores (Interstate) Ltd* v. *Maher* (1988) 164 CLR 387.

assume from the conduct of the other party that a contract will be concluded, a defence of promissory estoppel may be granted.[892]

However, despite the fact that the Australian approach has some similarity to the English reasoning,[893] academic commentators note that English law is not likely to literally follow the Australian approach in the future. According to Furmston and Tolhurst, this is precluded by the general differences within the doctrines of promissory estoppel and consideration in English and Australian law. Macfarlane argues that the doctrine of promissory estoppel has not been applied in a coherent way.[894]Cartwright and Hesselink note that the application of the doctrine of estoppel to the precontractual phase 'has not yet fully matured in English law'.[895]

5.6. Dynamics of negotiations addressed in case law

5.6.1. Provisions on costs and anticipated performance: three lines of cases

The English law approach to costs and anticipated performance is demonstrated by three lines of cases. In all of these, the anticipated performance was started before the 'closing' of the transaction. In the first line of cases, the court found that the final contract was formed. Contractual causes of action have been granted to both parties. In the second line of cases, anticipated performance was remedied as unjust enrichment. The third and the last line of cases discussed relates to a situation no less important. In this situation no remedy was granted for anticipated performance that clearly involved risk-taking, inherent to the adversarial position of the parties. The bases of differences drawn between these three approaches will be now discussed in some more detail.

5.6.1.1. Contractual causes of action granted to both parties: RTS Flexible Systems v. Molkerei Alois Müller

In the first line of cases, English courts have upheld the final contract as binding when the transaction has been completed to a large extent on both sides of negotiations. The final contract was upheld as binding in this way in *RTS Flexible Systems Ltd* v. *Molkerei Alois Müller GmbH & Co KG.*[896] The facts of this case are mentioned earlier in Section 5.4.2.3. A letter of intent issued in this case attempted to negate contractual intent. However, as a matter of fact, the transaction proceeded, the equipment was supplied, and a large amount of the price was paid. The Supreme Court emphasized in this decision

892 *Austotel Pty Ltd* v. *Franklins Selfserve Pty Ltd* (1989) 16 NSWLR 582.

893 See Furmston/Tolhurst 2010, para 12.59 (footnote 104) referring to *Amalgamated Investment & Property Co Ltd* v. *Texas Commerce International Bank Ltd* [1982] QB 84; *Taylors Fashions Ltd* v. *Liverpool Trustees Co Ltd* (1979) [1982] QB 133n; *Norwegian American Cruises A/S* v. *Paul Mundy Ltd, The Vistafjord* [1988] 2 Lloyd's Rep 343). See also Bant/Bryan 2015.

894 Macfarlane 2010.

895 Cartwright/Hesselink 2008, at 463.

896 [2010] UKSC 14, [2010] 1 WLR 753.

that the parties had finalized negotiations and had executed a considerable part of the transaction. According to the Supreme Court, this constituted an implied waiver of the 'subject to contract' bar that would otherwise negate any intention to create legal relations. Consequently, contractual causes of action were allowed to both parties. More specifically, one party could claim payment of the contractual price, and the other party was enabled to submit a claim for defects in quality of performance.

By contrast to *RTS Flexible Systems Ltd* v. *Molkerei Alois Müller GmbH & Co KG*, an 'intermediary contract', but not the entire final contract can be recognized as binding. This approach has been applied to letter of intent whereby one party undertook to reimburse preliminary costs necessary for a future eventual contract.[897] A recent example is provided by *Diamond Build Ltd* v. *Clapham Park Homes Ltd*.[898] Parties signed a letter of intent within negotiations of a construction project. The document explicitly mentioned a request to start works. At the same time, it provided that the works would be reimbursed. The letter of intent also contained a limitation of responsibility in case no contract came into existence. The parties formulated this in the following terms:[899]

> We confirm that it is our intention to enter into a Contract with you …[1]
> Clapham Park Homes Ltd wish that you now commit the appropriate resources to permit you to … diligently proceed with the refurbishment works to achieve an overall completion with 36 working weeks from the date of possession. [2]
> …
> Should it not be possible for us to execute a formal Contract with you in place of this letter, we undertake to reimburse your reasonable costs up to and including the date on which you are notified that the Contract will not proceed provided that the Supervising Officer is satisfied that those costs are appropriate and that, in any event, total costs will not exceed the sum of £250,000 … [4]
> Clapham Park Homes Ltd do not undertake to reimburse any anticipated profits for the works as a whole, nor actual costs or actual or theoretically incurred general or specific overheads arising after the date of notification that no further work is to be carried out. [5] …
> It is hereby confirmed that the undertakings given in this letter will be wholly extinguished upon the execution of the formal Contract. [8]

The works were started based on this letter of intent. In a dispute that arose later, the High Court had to assess the meaning and the validity of the letter of intent. It came to the conclusion that the letter of intent 'did give rise to a (relatively) simple form of contract'.[900] The main reason for this conclusion was that the letter of intent expressed

[897] *Diamond Build Ltd* v. *Clapham Park Homes Ltd* [2008] EWHC 1439 (TCC), [2008] CILL 2601; *Jarvis Interiors Ltd* v. *Galliard Homes Ltd* [2000] CLC 411 (EWCA); *Benourad* v. *Compass Group Plc* [2010] EWHC 1882, 2010 WL 2937470 [106] (Beatson J). See also *Smit International Singapore Pte Ltd* v. *Kurnia Dewi Shipping SA (The Kurnia Dewi)* [1997] 1 Lloyd's Rep 552 (QBD).

[898] [2008] EWHC 1439 (TCC), [2008] CILL 2601.

[899] Ibid [7].

[900] Ibid [51].

the intention to enter into a contract. It contained an undertaking to pay reasonable costs, 'albeit up to a specific sum'. Moreover, '[t]he fact in the penultimate paragraph that the undertakings given in the letter are to be "wholly extinguished" upon the execution of the formal contract point very strongly to those undertakings having legal and enforceable effect until the execution of the formal contract'.[901]

A cap on the costs that one of the parties undertakes to reimburse has been also upheld as binding. For example, in *Mowlem Plc (t/a Mowlem Marine)* v. *Stena Line Ports Ltd*, parties signed several letters of intent within a project for the construction of a port terminal. Stena issued a letter of intent stating that the costs will only be paid up to the amount of £10 million:[902]

> Stena's further acceptance of works after the 18 th July 2003 and/or once the value of the Works being carried out exceeded the value of £10 million and/or Stena's further request after these events that the said works be carried through to completion.

Subsequently, a dispute arose. Mowlem claimed in court that it should be implied that Stena should pay a reasonable price for the works, not limited by the provision of letter of intent quoted above. The court decided that each letter of intent was contractually binding. On this basis, the parties' rights to a claim and a counterclaim were granted. The Judge Seymour QC interpreted the letter of intent strictly. He invoked the commercial sense of this document and its literal interpretation:[903]

> Grammatically that is what the letter said, and it would make no commercial sense to have a financial limit on Stena's obligations to make payment which could be avoided by the simple expedient of continuing to carry out work after 18 July 2003. It would be even more bizarre commercially if the financial limitation on Stena's obligations could be avoided simply by Mowlem exceeding that limit.

As a result, the provision limiting the reimbursement of costs was also upheld as binding, and no reasonable price was implied.

5.6.1.2. Only restitution allowed: British Steel Corp v. Cleveland Bridge and Whittle Movers v. Hollywood Express

The second line of cases involves situations where works or services have been requested by one party and executed during the course of negotiations at the stage when no essential conditions of the final contract were agreed. In this type of situation, the existence of a contractual cause of action has been denied. By contrast, an action in restitution for unjust enrichment – a non-contractual cause of action – has been allowed.

901 Ibid.
902 [2004] EWHC 2206 (TCC), 2004 WL 2270265 [8].
903 Ibid [44] (Seymour QC).

The leading case in this line is *British Steel Corp* v. *Cleveland Bridge & Engineering Co Ltd*.[904] In this case, arties entered into negotiations about the fabrication by one party of 'steel nodes' that the other party needed in its construction works. In anticipation of a contract, the goods were requested in a letter of intent. It stated follows:[905]

> We are pleased to advise you that it is the intention of Cleveland Bridge & Engineering Co Ltd to enter into a sub-contract with your Company for the supply and delivery of the steel castings which form the roof nodes… and we request that you proceed immediately with the works pending the preparation and issuing to you of the official form of sub-contract.

The goods were manufactured and a considerable part was supplied, but not paid for. Neither at the time of supply nor later was the contract concluded. The parties never went further than negotiations, because no agreement was reached about the price of goods to be supplied, dates of delivery, or about the liability for consequential loss.[906] The negotiations broke down. The manufacturer of steel nodes sued for payment for the goods supplied on an extra-contractual basis. It sued in restitution on a *quantum meruit* basis.[907] The other party replied by a counterclaim for breach of contract, alleging defects in quality of the delivered goods and a late delivery.

Goff J reasoned as follows. He contended first that the negotiations about the contemplated contract were not finalized substantially. The court had no sufficient guidance in order to decide on its terms:[908]

> not least on the issues of price, delivery dates, and the applicable terms and conditions. In these circumstances, it is very difficult to see how BSC, by starting work, bound themselves to any contractual performance. No doubt it was envisaged by CBE at the time they sent the letter that negotiations had reached an advanced stage, and that a formal contract would soon be signed; but, since the parties were still in a state of negotiation, it is impossible to say with any degree of certainty what the material terms of that contract would be.

Consequently, according to the court, no contractually binding obligations arose out of the letter of intent, while the commenced performance does not automatically imply that a contract was concluded. The claim in restitution was satisfied. The court awarded a sum of restitution deemed to be reasonable, namely the amount of the market price of the 'steel nodes' supplied. By contrast, the contractual counterclaim made by the other party was dismissed. Following *British Steel Corp* v. *Cleveland Bridge & Engineering Co Ltd*,[909] an action in restitution for unjust enrichment on the quantum *meruit basis* is

904 [1984] 1 All ER 504 (QBD).
905 Ibid.
906 Ibid 509–511 (Goff J).
907 See Section 5.5.3 on this cause of action.
908 *British Steel Corp* v. *Cleveland Bridge & Engineering Co Ltd* [1984] 1 All ER 504 (QBD) 510 (Goff J).
909 [1984] 1 All ER 504 (QBD).

available in situations where the court is unable to define conditions of the future contract, but goods have been supplied in the course of negotiations.

A similar cause of action is available for services rendered in contemplation of a contract before finalizing negotiations. Services are reimbursed on a *quantum valebat* basis (on the basis of their reasonable value). This has been established by *Planche* v. *Colbourn*.[910]

A good illustration of an award in *quantum valebat* is provided in *Whittle Movers Ltd* v. *Hollywood Express Ltd*.[911] That case is close in time to *RTS Flexible Systems Ltd* v. *Molkerei Alois Müller GmbH & Co KG*.[912] However, the Court of Appeal came to a different solution. In *Whittle Movers Ltd* v. *Hollywood Express Ltd*,[913] the Court of Appeal applied *British Steel Corp* v. *Cleveland Bridge & Engineering Co Ltd*[914] and allowed a claim on the basis of unjust enrichment, while the existence of a contractual claim was denied. According to the facts of this case, Hollywood announced a tender for distribution of its parent company's food and drink products. The invitation to tender was made 'subject to contract'. This statement was included in clause 2.4 of the tender 'Acceptance of the Tender Response'.[915] Whittle won the tender, and the parties started negotiations in contemplation of a contract. They envisaged that the contract would provide for rights of distributorship for six years. Whittle would undertake to distribute Hollywood's 'blockbuster' products, and during the first year of the contract the distribution would be free of charge. Parties signed a letter of intent cited by the Court of Appeal:[916]

> Letter of intent between Hollywood Express Limited ("HE") and Whittles Movers Limited ("Whittles") regarding provision of distribution services
> Please accept this letter as confirmation of HE's intention to enter into contract with Whittles for the supply of distribution services.
> The implementation of this letter of intent is subject to the negotiation and execution of mutually satisfactory and legally binding documentation. The contract will be on the terms of the draft contract attached to HE's invitation to tender, amended to take into account the commercial details agreed during the tender process. The first draft of the contract will be issued by HE's legal team. For the avoidance of doubt, this letter of intent does not bind either party to enter into a contract for supply of distribution services, and any work undertaken by either party in anticipation of such contract shall be at that party's cost and risk ...

After signing this letter of intent, negotiations continued, but Whittle supplied goods and invoiced for them at the prices mentioned the draft supply agreement. In the

910 (1831) 131 ER 305 (Court of King's Bench). See also *William Lacey (Hounslow) Ltd* v. *Davis* [1957] 1 WLR 932 (QBD).
911 [2009] EWCA Civ 1189, [2009] 2 CLC 771.
912 [2010] UKSC 14, [2010] 1 WLR 753.
913 [2009] EWCA Civ 1189, [2009] 2 CLC 771.
914 [1984] 1 All ER 504 (QBD).
915 *Whittle Movers Ltd* v. *Hollywood Express Ltd* [2009] EWCA Civ 1189, [2009] 2 CLC 771 [5].
916 Ibid.

meantime, Hollywood was acquired by another company. It gave a notice of termination of the relationship with Whittle: either the termination of the agreement with Whittle or of the 'interim agreement' that the parties referred to in negotiations. Whittle claimed that rather than an interim agreement, a long-term contract had been concluded, or, alternatively, that the price to be paid for the goods supplied should be a reasonable price – the amount higher than the lower price stated in the draft long-term agreement. According to Whittle, paying the price stated in the long-term contract would make sense economically only if this was indeed a six-year contract.

The Court of Appeal decided that the parties were not bound by any contractual obligations, because they had not finalized their negotiations. It was held that a payment for goods supplied should be done on the basis of restitution. The amount of the award should equal a reasonable sum for the goods delivered, estimated on the *quantum valebat* basis. The Court of Appeal reasoned as follows. On the facts of this case, negotiations were *not finalized*. According to the Court of Appeal, the first question to answer was whether the relationship could be regarded as contractual, or, by contrast whether it was only an adversarial negotiation. Lord Waller stated:[917]

> There may be little distinction between an "if" contract entitling the provider of services to reasonable remuneration and a restitutionary remedy based on the unjust enrichment of the recipient of the services in many cases but before it is possible to find any contract, whether "if" or executory, it is necessary to analyse precisely the terms so as to test whether the reality is that such terms are still under negotiation and the proper answer is no contract.

Waller LJ also suggested that there is no need to seek to find a contract in cases where relief on the basis of restitution and unjust enrichment is possible.[918]

> In Goff and Jones 7th Edition page 662 there is a reference to an article by Professor McKendrick in which the professor argues that a court should not strain to find a contract because a restitutionary remedy can solve most if not all the problems. [See footnote 7]. That, it seems to me, is the correct approach.

According to the Court of Appeal, the 'subject to contract' statement precluded the formation of a contract[919] and prevented the court from implying an agreement. Therefore a reasonable remuneration on the basis of restitution was granted. It was noted:[920]

> [N]ot only was there no necessity to find some executory contract, there was a difficulty and thus no necessity in finding even what Goff J called an 'if' contract because terms as to

917 *Whittle Movers Ltd* v. *Hollywood Express Ltd* [2009] EWCA Civ 1189, [2009] 2 CLC 771 [15] (Lord Waller).

918 Ibid.

919 Ibid [6], [19], and [90] (Lord Waller).

920 Ibid [19]-[21] (Lord Waller).

> performance were still under negotiation. All negotiations were subject to contract and no binding arrangement was to come into existence until a formal document was signed.

Lord Waller stressed that it 'does not follow that if goods or services were provided before the contract was signed Whittle were not entitled to some remuneration and thus the receipt of remuneration does not of itself dictate that there was a contract'.[921] According to him, the 'question whether he should have directed an inquiry as to whether further remuneration was due depended on whether it was arguable that Hollywood had been unjustly enriched.[922]

As a result, the Court of Appeal awarded a higher price than that intended by the parties (in the letter of intent and other documents exchanged in negotiations). As Andrews notes in analysing this decision, the Court of Appeal had an option to follow the amount of the bargain reflected by the parties in the precontractual documents, rather than a reasonable market price, but did not take up this opportunity. The reference to market price made the approach of the court favourable for the supplier, compared to the party receiving the goods. Edelman notes that an award in restitution for unjust enrichment is always an imposed award, '*imposed* upon the parties irrespective of the price that they might have agreed'.[923]

These two lines of cases illustrate the patterns of remedies available when the works or services are started in contemplation of a contract during the process of contract formation (that is not always finalized). The remedies vary from the full scope of contractual remedies made available by the court to allowing only the claim in restitution. In *Serck Control Ltd* v. *Drake & Scull Engineering Ltd*, Hicks QC stated:[924]

> At the first end of the spectrum ... the measure should clearly be the reasonable remuneration of the claimant; at the other it should be the value to the defendant. In between there is a borderline, the position of which may be debatable.

In *RTS Flexible Systems Ltd* v. *Molkerei Alois Müller GmbH & Co KG*,[925] the contractual causes of action were granted to both parties (not only was the payment for works allowed, but also the other party's counterclaim for alleged defects in performance). As stated by the Supreme Court, '[t]he decision in the *British Steel* case was simply one on the other side of the line'.[926]

921 Ibid.
922 Ibid.
923 Edelman 2010, at 179.
924 (2000) 73 Con LR 100 (QBD) [35].
925 [2010] UKSC 14, [2010] 1 WLR 753.
926 Ibid at [54] (Lord Clarke).

5.6.1.3. No remedy for taking a business risk: Regalian Properties v. London Docklands

The third line of cases relates to the situations where starting works or services in contemplation of a contract is considered as taking a business risk; this does not entail any reimbursement. Starting works or services without being sure that they would be remunerated was considered by English courts as commercial risk taking. A party that takes this risk is not entitled to recover for the costs it incurs, especially if the works have not been requested by the other party.[927]

An illustration is provided in *Regalian Properties Plc* v. *London Docklands Development Corp.*[928] In that case, parties entered into negotiations about a development of land for housing. Regalian was chosen by London Docklands as a potential contractor, but several points had to be agreed. The negotiations started subject to several conditions. These were 'subject to … contract, the district valuer's certificate of market value'. Furthermore, the entire scheme should have achieved 'the desired design quality and the obtaining of detailed planning consent'.[929] In contemplation of the eventual contract Regalian proceeded to prepare the land. It paid almost £3 million to professional firms in respect of the development. However, the parties could not reach agreement on the price, the negotiations broke down, and the project was abandoned. Regalian claimed reimbursement of the costs it incurred, submitting a claim for restitution.

The court refused to grant an award for restitution for the following reasons. Firstly, Rattee J noted that in the course of negotiations, Regalian had requested an assurance that it would be compensated for the preparatory work. London Docklands refused to provide such an assurance. Secondly, the court emphasized that London Docklands did not request Regalian to perform the services in question. He noted that the costs 'had been incurred not by way of accelerated performance of an anticipated contract at the defendant's request but for the purpose of putting themselves in a position to obtain and perform the contract'.[930] According to the court, Regalian 'must be taken to know'[931] that works might not be reimbursed in this situation. The request by the other party constitutes the main difference between this case and the *British Steel Corp* v. *Cleveland Bridge & Engineering Co Ltd*[932] case, where supply of goods was requested by the other party. On this basis, Rattee J has distinguished this case from both *British Steel* and

927 *Brewer Street Investments Ltd* v. *Barclays Woollen Co Ltd* [1954] 1 QB 428 (EWCA); *Jennings and Chapman* v. *Woodman, Matthews & Co* [1952] 2 TLR 409 (EWCA); *Regalian Properties Plc* v. *London Docklands Development Corp* [1995] 1 WLR 212 (EWHC Ch); *Easat Antennas Limited v. Racal Defence Electronics Limited* 2000 WL 1084506 (EWHC); Goff/Jones 2007, para 26–010.

928 [1995] 1 WLR 212 (EWHC Ch).

929 Ibid 212.

930 Ibid 214.

931 Ibid 231.

932 [1984] 1 All ER 504 (QBD).

William Lacey.[933] The High Court added in *Countrywide Communications Ltd* v. *ICL Pathway Ltd*, that the 'the terms in which the request to perform the services was made may be important in establishing the extent of the risk (if any) which the plaintiffs may fairly be said to have taken that such services would in the end be unrecompensed'.[934] Thirdly, London Docklands had not benefited from these works at the expense of Regalian, whereas the fact that one party has benefited at the expense of the other is a necessary element of a claim in unjust enrichment.

5.6.2. *Confidentiality*

A contractual obligation of confidentiality inserted in a letter of intent has been held to be enforceable in English case law.[935] A confidentiality (or non-disclosure) agreement is an 'agreement according to which one or more parties oblige themselves to keep secret the information that was revealed to them during or prior to the conclusion of a contract … as well as not to use such information for another purpose(s) than the one(s) which was (were) foreseen'.[936]

For instance, in *JSD Corporation PTE Ltd* v. *Al Waha Capital PJSC, Second Waha Lease Ltd*,[937] the parties entered into negotiations about the sale of an aircraft. A letter of intent established in the course of negotiations contained a confidentiality clause. Both parties undertook, in particular, not to render the content of negotiations public through a press release, or to disclose the information exchanged in negotiations in any other way. The clause stated as follows:[938]

> 13. Confidentiality
> The terms and conditions set out in this Letter shall remain confidential between the parties and each party acknowledges that this Letter contains commercially sensitive information and agrees not to disclose same except to their respective Boards of Directors, advisers and employees or potential financiers of the Aircraft or as otherwise agreed between the parties or required by applicable law. No press release may be made by either party without the other party's consent to the release and its content.

The potential buyer paid a deposit for the aircraft, but the negotiations broke down. The potential buyer submitted a claim for return of the deposit.

933 *William Lacey (Hounslow) Ltd v. Davis* [1957] 1 WLR 932 (QBD).
934 [2000] CLC 324 (QBD) 349 (Strauss QC).
935 In English law, furthermore if a confidentiality agreement requires the recipient of information to impose a similar restriction on any third party to which it might provide information, and the recipient fails to do so, it can be liable for damages. This principle was introduced by *Dorchester Project Management Ltd* v. *BNP Paribas Real Estate Advisory UK Ltd* [2013] EWCA Civ 176, 2013 WL 617411.
936 Marchandise 2002, at 741.
937 [2009] EWHC 583 (Ch), 2009 WL 648840.
938 Ibid [83].

It is important to note that the provision on the confidentiality obligation as such was not the main issue in this case. The legal issue of the dispute was broader and concerned the meaning and enforceability of the letter of intent. In giving a legal qualification to the provisions of this document, the High Court noted that the parties had expressly mentioned in the letter of intent which obligations should become contractually binding. The confidentiality clause was clearly mentioned as binding in the text of letter of intent. It stated as follows:[939]

> [T]he terms of this Letter do not and are not intended to create binding legal obligations on the parties hereto with the exception of this clause and clauses 5, 11 and 13 [confidentiality]...

The High Court gave effect to the strict meaning of the parties' formulation, and confidentiality was one of the obligations upheld as contractually binding.

A division of the letter of intent into binding and non-binding provisions was also made by the parties in *Charles Shaker* v. *Vistajet Group Holding SA*. There as well the provision on confidentiality was expressly stated to be binding:[940]

> Other than the provisions relating to the application, payment and refund of the Deposit and the confidentiality provisions hereunder, it is specifically understood and agreed that this Letter of Intent does not constitute a binding agreement ...

This division was also upheld as enforceable, indirectly pointing to the legal effect of the obligation of confidentiality.

5.6.3. *Dispute resolution*

5.6.3.1. Choice of law

As noted in the Chapters on Dutch and French law, the law applicable to cross-border contractual relationships is defined according to a uniform instrument: the Rome I Regulation (Rome I).[941] Another uniform instrument – Rome II Regulation (Rome II) – provides the rules on the law applicable to cross-border non-contractual relationships.[942] These instruments are applied by the courts in the EU to disputes with an international element. Rome I expressly excludes obligations related to the mere formation of contract from the scope of this Regulation. Rome II is therefore relevant. According to the main relevant rule of Article 12 Rome II, the law applicable to

[939] *JSD Corporation PTE Ltd* v. *Al Waha Capital PJSC, Second Waha Lease Ltd* [2009] EWHC 583 (Ch), HC, at [83].

[940] [2012] EWHC 1329 (Comm), [2012] 2 All ER (Comm) 1010 [3].

[941] Regulation (EC) No 593/2008 of the European Parliament and of the Council of 17 June 2008 On the Law Applicable to Contractual Obligations (Rome I).

[942] See Section 3.7.9.

precontractual obligations is the law of the contract which would have come about if the negotiations had not failed.[943]

This raises the question of whether English parties may submit negotiations to a chosen law. Reformulating the question, do the courts hold provisions submitting negotiations to a particular law to be an enforceable contractual obligation? This question has not been specifically addressed in the English case law. At the same time, the question may be answered in the positive. In several cases involving a dispute relating to a letter of intent having an international element, the choice of law has been followed. It is fair to note that in all the cases, the parties chose English law as the law applicable to the letter of intent.

For example, in *JSD Corporation PTE Ltd* v. *Al Waha Capital PJSC, Second Waha Lease Ltd*,[944] the High Court gave effect to the choice of law made in a letter of intent. The letter of intent was divided into binding and non-binding provisions, and choice of law was one of the provisions included in the binding part. The parties to the dispute were incorporated in the United Arab Emirates (the defendant) and in Singapore (the claimant). They chose English law in a letter of intent. The High Court accepted jurisdiction. However, it was done in a somewhat nuanced way. In accepting jurisdiction, the court emphasized the link between the nature of the remedy sought and acceptance of jurisdiction by the English court. The dispute related to a sale of an aircraft. The claimant sought to impose a freezing injunction on the aircraft located at the time of the dispute in an airfield in Southend in Essex. The judge noted at the same time that 'even though English law and English jurisdiction were chosen by the parties a judgment obtained in this jurisdiction will not be enforced by the UAE courts'.[945] In this way, 'any judgment would be valueless unless it could be enforced against assets outside the UAE',[946] while 'nothing absent the injunction'[947] would prevent the defendant from removing the aircraft from the English jurisdiction.

In the abovementioned case of *RTS Flexible Systems Limited* v. *Molkerei Alois Müller Gmbh & Company KG*, a dispute arose between an English and a German party (namely a UK branch of a multinational group of companies). The letter of intent stated: 'This Letter of Intent (including any non-contractual obligations arising out of or in connection with the same) shall be governed by the laws of England.[948] The dispute was resolved according to English law. However, the case only indirectly points to the enforceability of the choice of law, because the issue was not extensively discussed at any of the stages of proceedings.

943 Article 12 Rome II provides also rules to define applicable law if the law that would have been applied to the negotiated contract cannot be identified. See also Asser/Kramer & Verhagen 10-III 2015, para 1199–1203.
944 [2009] EWHC 583 (Ch), 2009 WL 648840.
945 Ibid [19].
946 Ibid.
947 Ibid.
948 [2010] UKSC 14, [2010] 1 WLR 753 [6].

5.6.3.2. Choice of court

As noted in Chapters 3 and 4 on Dutch and French law, the choice of court is also regulated in the EU by uniform rules. These are provided by the Brussels I-bis Regulation (Brussels I-bis).[949] Article 25(5) of Brussels I-bis establishes the principle of severability of choice of court agreements. Based on this principle, the validity of the choice of court obligation should be assessed independently of the validity of the document in which such an obligation is contained. This provision separates – severs – the questions of validity of the preliminary document and the validity of a stand-alone choice of court clause. The provision is relatively recent and was introduced in the most recent recast of the Regulation.[950]

This raises the question whether a choice of court made in a preliminary agreement may qualify as a choice of court in contract for the purpose of Article 25(5) of Brussels I-bis. As noted in the previous Chapters, this question should be answered in the affirmative. Touching upon the English case law, in *JSD Corporation PTE Ltd* v. *Al Waha Capital PJSC, Second Waha Lease Ltd*[951] the decision points indirectly to the enforceability of the choice of court provision. In that case, provisions of letter of intent specifically stating that these were binding included the choice of the English court. The choice of court clause was given force. In *RTS Flexible Systems Limited* v. *Molkerei Alois Müller Gmbh & Company KG*, a letter of intent stated that it was 'subject to the exclusive jurisdiction of English courts'.[952] Since the English courts found themselves competent to hear the case (their jurisdiction was not disputed), the case indirectly points to the enforceability of choice of court provision in a letter of intent.

5.6.3.3. Arbitration

A provision in a letter of intent that submits disputes to arbitration can be enforced in English law. To assess its enforceability, the courts address whether this clause fulfils the requirements for a valid arbitration agreement.[953] They scrutinize certainty in the letter of intent, clarity of its formulations, and the commercial purpose of the arbitration agreement. Essentially, courts will assess whether the provision in question fulfils the criteria for a valid arbitration agreement. As Lewison puts it 'Whether a contract incorporates an arbitration clause is a question of construction of the contract[954]... Whether a clause providing for dispute resolution is an arbitration agreement or some

[949] Regulation (EU) No 1215/2012 of the European Parliament and of the Council of 12 December 2012 on Jurisdiction and the Recognition and Enforcement of Judgments in Civil and Commercial Matters (Recast) (Brussels I-bis).

[950] Article 25(5) Brussels I-bis.

[951] [2009] EWHC 583 (Ch), 2009 WL 648840.

[952] [2010] UKSC 14, [2010] 1 WLR 753 [6].

[953] The criteria of validity of arbitration agreements are laid down in the Arbitration Act 1996 (England and Wales) and related leading cases.

[954] Lewison 2011, para 18.01.

other form of dispute resolution is a question of interpretation of the agreement'.[955] The principles of interpretation have been established in *Investors Compensation Scheme Ltd* v. *West Bromwich Building Society (No.1)*[956] and developed thereafter.[957]

Furthermore, the provision will be assessed separately from the document in which it is incorporated (i.e. letter of intent) based on the doctrine of separability or severability of an arbitration agreement. It is established in section 7 of the English Arbitration Act 1996.[958]

The validity of both the arbitration agreement and the main agreement are to be decided by the arbitral tribunal. According to the High Court, this is the way to give effect to the commercial purpose of the arbitration clause. The commercial purpose of arbitration consists therefore in the benefits of resolution of disputes a manner offered by arbitration tribunals. Lord Hoffmann went on to say that based on the commercial purpose, businessmen would not split the disputes regarding the validity of the arbitration agreement and the validity of the main agreement. On the contrary, they would have all disputes solved by arbitration. If 'rational businessmen' would have a 'reasonable expectation' to have the two issues decided separately, they would clearly agree on this.[959]

No case law has yet clarified the application of the 'severability' doctrine to an arbitration clause included into a precontractual agreement. The following statement of Lord Hoffmann may be mentioned in this context:[960]

> Even if the allegation is that there was no concluded agreement (for example, that terms of the main agreement remained to be agreed) that is not necessarily an attack on the arbitration agreement. If the arbitration clause has been agreed, the parties will be presumed to have intended the question of whether there was a concluded main agreement to be decided by arbitration.

This statement might be applicable to an arbitration clause included in a letter of intent. However, two different approaches can be found. According to the first one, an arbitration clause will be upheld in a letter of intent that already contains some enforceable provisions. In *Hackwood Ltd* v. *Areen Design Services Ltd*,[961] the dispute concerned construction works. Parties signed a letter of intent. It contained a request to start the

955 Lewison 2011, para 18.04.
956 [1998] 1 WLR 896 (HL) 912–913 (Lord Hoffmann).
957 Andrews 2015, para 14.01 ff.; Lewison 2011; McMeel 2011.
958 English Arbitration Act 1996. The previous law (based on section 7(1) (e) of the Arbitration Act 1979) applies if a claim was submitted before the entry into force of the Arbitration Act 1996. This has been explained in *Hall & Tawse South Limited* v. *Ivory Gate Limited* 62 Con LR 117 (QBD).
959 *Fiona Trust and Holding Corporation* v. *Privalov* [2007] UKHL 40, [2007] 4 All ER 951 [5]-[6] (Lord Hoffmann).
960 Ibid [7] (Lord Hoffmann).
961 [2005] EWHC 2322 (TCC), (2006) 22 Const LJ 68.

building works on the terms of the letter of intent. This document referred to the JCT Standard Form of Building Contract (JCT). The court first analysed the letter of intent. It found that it constituted a binding 'interim contract'. The court also noted that the JCT standard contract contained an arbitration clause. Drawing the two facts together, the court decided that the letter of intent incorporated, by reference, an arbitration clause in the redaction of the JCT standard contract. This conclusion was reached despite the fact that only the terms of the letter of intent were executed (as opposed to the terms of the JCT contract). Field J reasoned as follows:[962]

> Mr. Bowsher submitted that the parties cannot have intended to incorporate the terms of the JCT Contract when they were still negotiating the terms of the final contract. I reject this submission. The object of the 4th June letter was to establish the terms of an interim contract that the parties appreciated could govern the whole of the project. For the purposes of the interim contract, the scope of the work, the price and the construction programme were all agreed. Against this background, the fact that the parties were negotiating a contract intended to replace the interim contract is not inconsistent with an intention that the JCT Contract's standard terms should be incorporated into the interim contract.

By contrast, in *Merit Process Engineering Ltd* v. *Balfour Beatty Engineering Services (HY) Limited*,[963] an alleged implication of an arbitration clause into a letter of intent was not upheld as valid. Parties negotiated three contracts for the installation of pipe-work and works. A letter of intent that they signed did not contain any arbitration clause. An arbitration clause was only contained in a project of a final contract that was sent by one party to another. Furthermore, the parties mentioned that the letter of intent was 'subject to contract'. The court found no incorporation of an arbitration clause into a letter of intent by reference. Nor was it prepared to imply it.

5.6.3.4. Mediation

Mediation[964] is related to negotiations, though the two are not entirely similar. According to Spencer and Brogan, 'negotiation is a substance, while mediation is a form'.[965] Mediation is an assisted negotiation, with the help of an intermediary and the assistance of a specially trained mediator.[966] A provision in a letter of intent that obliges parties to mediate a dispute can therefore be seen in the light of 'agreements to agree' and treated by law in a similar way. Agreements to negotiate are generally void under

962 Ibid [20] (Field J).

963 [2012] EWHC 1376 (TCC), [2012] CILL 3193.

964 For definitions of mediation see, Brown/Marriott 2011, Joseph 2010, Redfern/Hunter 2009, Spencer/Brogan 2006; Andrews 2013. Within the EU, mediation is defined in Article 3(a) of the Directive 2008/52/EC of the European Parliament and of the Council of 21 May 2008 on Certain Aspects of Mediation in Civil and Commercial Matters OJ L 136.

965 Spencer/Brogan 2006, at 22.

966 See for a discussion regarding definition of mediation Spencer/Brogan 2006, at 4–21 and at 22 for the link between mediation and negotiations.

English law, following the leading decision *Walford* v. *Miles*.[967] However, English case law has drawn a distinction between the two. As a result of this distinction, a mediation clause included in a letter of intent may have sufficient certainty to be given contractual effect. In order to distinguish whether a mediation clause is void as an 'agreement to agree' (following *Walford* v. *Miles*[968]) or a valid and legally binding mediation agreement, English courts assess whether the clause fulfils the requirements of an enforceable mediation agreement.

The requirements of an enforceable mediation agreement have been developed in English law during the last decade. The first requirement is certainty. In *Cable & Wireless* v. *IBM United Kingdom Ltd*,[969] the High Court had to decide whether a purported mediation clause was a mere 'agreement to agree' (agreement to negotiate) or a mediation clause. The High Court emphasized that the parties had not only mentioned that disputes should first be solved by mediation, but had also designated the rules to be applied thereto (the rules of the Centre for Dispute Resolution). These rules were precise and certain, because these laid down the procedure to nominate a mediator and the way mediation can be properly ended. Furthermore, the rules on mediation of the Centre for Dispute resolution were known to both parties to the agreement and third parties, this institution being one of the best known in the UK. In this way, Colman J made a distinction between an agreement to negotiate (in this case, agreement to negotiate in good faith) and a mediation agreement, reiterating the requirement of certainty and the judicial protection of the parties' choice of dispute resolution.[970]

The scope of the requirement of certainty formulated in *Cable & Wireless* v. *IBM United Kingdom Ltd*,[971] has been narrowed in subsequent case law. The following conditions were identified later as requirements.[972] Firstly, it should be certain that negotiations regarding the parties' willingness to mediate are over and there is no need to negotiate further on the subject of whether parties wish to mediate a dispute. In this way a distinction is made between 'matters to be negotiated' and a proper dispute. Secondly, there should be clarity on the mediator and the conditions of his appointment, and thirdly, the rules of mediation should be defined or pointed out by the parties. Lord Ramsey enumerated these requirements[973] in *Holloway* v. *Chancery Mead Limited*.[974]

967 [1992] 2 AC 128 (HL).

968 Ibid.

969 [2002] EWHC 2059 (Comm), [2002] 2 All ER (Comm) 1041.

970 Ibid.

971 Ibid.

972 Andrews 2013a.

973 See Andrews 2013a. According to Andrews, the second and the third requirement named by Ramsey LJ are too restrictive and courts should be able to imply these. Andrews draws an analogy with such a possibility for the courts in relation to arbitration agreements. An agreement to arbitrate in London was upheld in *Naviera Amazonica Peruana* SA v. *Compania Internacional de Seguros de Peru* [1988] 1 Lloyd's Rep 116 (EWCA). Andrews suggests furthermore that agreements to mediate should be upheld in English law by analogy with arbitration. See Arbitration Act 1996, sections 18(2), (3)(d).

974 [2008] 1 All ER (Comm) 653 [81].

Following these requirements, an intention or a mere aspiration to have recourse to mediation do not amount to sufficient certainty for a valid agreement to mediate. This was held in *Balfour Beatty Construction Northern Limited* v. *Modus Corovest (Blackpool) Ltd.*[975] A similar conclusion was reached in *Sulamérica Cia Nacional de Seguros SA* v. *Enesa Engenharia SA*,[976] referred to as one of the leading cases on mediation agreements.[977]

A mediation clause that lacks certainty does not constitute a necessary condition precedent for starting arbitration. This has been held in *Wah* v. *Grant Thornton International Ltd.*[978] These requirements for validity of mediation clauses can be applied to the provisions of a letter of intent (either embedded in a clause requiring an internal escalation procedure or a dispute resolution clause).

Finally, it is worth noting that a mediation agreement is assessed separately from the document in which it is incorporated. This approach was mentioned in *Cable & Wireless* v. *IBM United Kingdom Ltd.*[979] This mode of assessment equates to that applied to arbitration agreements, following the separability or severability doctrine.

5.7. Remedies and liability

5.7.1. Contract law

In English contract law, breach of a bare agreement to agree 'in any of the guises they may take'[980] does not lead to liability. This approach covers agreements to negotiate in good faith and obligations to use 'best efforts' or 'best endeavours' to negotiate a term of a contract in good faith.

By contrast, contractual liability may be engaged following a breach of two types of obligations that form the exception to the unenforceability of bare agreements to agree, if the provisions fulfil the conditions of enforceability. These exceptions are temporary 'lock-out' agreements and obligations to obtain a planning permission or export licence. Furthermore, contractual liability may be engaged for breach of an enforceable agreement on the confidentiality of negotiations, an arbitration agreement and a mediation agreement.

Contract law protects two types of interest – expectation interest and reliance interest. An expectation interest is protected by putting the aggrieved party in the same position

975 [2008] EWHC 3029 (TCC), [2009] CILL 2660 [15]-[17].
976 [2012] EWCA Civ 638, [2013] 1 WLR 102.
977 Ibid. See for analysis Andrews 2013a.
978 [2012] EWHC 3198 (Ch), [2013] 1 All ER (Comm) 1226.
979 [2002] EWHC 2059 (Comm), [2002] 2 All ER (Comm) 1041. Colman J stated: 'The reference to ADR is analogous to an agreement to arbitrate. As such, it represents a free-standing agreement ancillary to the main contract and capable of being enforced by a stay of the proceedings or by injunction absent any pending proceeding'.
980 Peel 2010, at 59.

as if the contract had been performed.[981] A reliance interest consists in placing the aggrieved party in the same position as if the contract was never made. Furthermore, contractual liability is based on breach of contract; no proof of damage is needed. As a consequence, every breach entitles a party to recover 'nominal damages'.[982]

Within academic discussion on the development of English law, commentators have submitted that if agreements to negotiate in good faith were recognized as valid agreements (with limited standards of behaviour similar to the standards of exercising a discretionary power in performance of a contract), a recovery of expenditure wasted in conducting negotiations might be available. This has been submitted by Peel;[983] Mills and Loveridge have argued for the same. Their opinion was substantiated by examples of courts decisions where courts have decreased the amount of the damage awarded by the amount of expenditure (costs) wasted in an 'unreasonable' failure to mediate.[984]

English case law has developed an elaborated approach to the remedies for breach of arbitration agreements. These include firstly, stay of proceedings;[985] the court has a duty to stay proceedings (not a discretionary power as in case of a mediation agreement). It may refuse to grant a stay of proceedings only if the arbitration agreement in question is 'null and void, inoperative or incapable of being performed'.[986] Secondly, the English 'anti-suit injunction' can be granted.[987] Thirdly, damages may be also granted for a breach of an arbitration agreement. Thirdly, damages may also be granted for breach of an arbitration agreement. As Andrews notes, '[i]n England an arbitration agreement is regarded as a species of contract. Breach can expose the guilty party to the usual array of remedies for breach of contract'.[988]

As to the remedies for a failure to comply with a mediation clause, *Cable & Wireless* v. *IBM United Kingdom Ltd*[989] is the leading decision on the remedies that may be granted by English courts. Firstly, the court may stay proceedings, that is, to not start proceedings or to not continue proceedings that have been already started. This remedy, granted in *Cable & Wireless* v. *IBM United Kingdom Ltd*,[990] is currently settled law,[991] since the decision in

981 *Robinson* v. *Harman* [1843–60] All ER 383 (Ex).

982 *Chitty on Contracts* 2015, para 26–009; Andrews 2015, para 17.01.

983 Peel 2010, at 57–59. Peel also discusses 'loss of chance'. He contends that the claim for loss of chance is not entirely appropriate for the purpose, because this type of liability requires a comparison to be made between the parties' conduct and a conduct of a third party.

984 Mills/Loveridge 2011.

985 Section 9 Arbitration Act 1996.

986 Section 9 (4) Arbitration Act 1996.

987 See for an explanation *Turner* v. *Grovit* [2001] UKHL 65, especially at [22]. In the EU context see however C-185/07 Allianz SpA and Generali Assicurazioni Generali SpA v West Tankers Inc. [2009] ECR I-00663.

988 Andrews 2013b, volume 2, para 10.70.

989 [2002] EWHC 2059 (Comm), [2002] 2 All ER (Comm) 1041.

990 [2002] EWHC 2059 (Comm), [2002] 2 All ER (Comm) 1041.

991 *Balfour Beatty Construction Northern Limited* v. *Modus Corovest (Blackpool) Ltd* [2008] EWHC 3029 (TCC), [2009] CILL 2660 [15]-[17].

Channel Tunnel Group Ltd v. *Balfour Beatty Construction Ltd*.[992] The court can lift the stay of proceedings if it is provided with proof that mediation was tried, but failed. Furthermore, the stay of court proceedings is granted at the discretion of the court.[993] It should not stay proceedings if it finds that mediation would not lead to a result.[994] The court would not force parties to mediate if it finds that a claim has obviously no prospects of success.[995] The stay of proceedings may also be granted by an arbitral tribunal, at its own discretion. An injunction to mediate is generally not likely to be granted.[996]

5.7.2. *Tort law*

5.7.2.1. Deceit

The tort of deceit with 'its overtones of wickedness is drawn from the moral world'.[997] Its main aim consists in discouraging fraud, as 'in the battle against fraud civil remedies can play a useful and beneficial role'.[998] Another aim is compensatory. It is worth noting that a clause which purports to exclude claims for deceit is ineffective at common law.[999] It is also worth noting that the recovery in tort of deceit may not be the subject of the parties' agreement, nor can the application of this tort be waived by the parties' agreement. A clause which purports to exclude claims for deceit is ineffective.[1000] Damages for the tort of deceit consist in reimbursement of loss sustained as a result of a fraudulent misrepresentation. The conditions to be fulfilled for recovery in the tort of deceit were addressed in Section 5.5.1.2 earlier in this Chapter. The authorities on the assessment of loss were summarized in *Smith New Court Securities Ltd* v. *Citibank NA* by Lord Browne-Wilkinson:[1001]

> In sum, in my judgment the following principles apply in assessing the damages payable where the plaintiff has been induced by a fraudulent misrepresentation …
> (1) the defendant is bound to make reparation for all the damage directly flowing from the transaction; (2) although such damage need not have been foreseeable, it must have been directly caused by the transaction; (3) is assessing such damage, the plaintiff is entitled to recover by way of damages the full price paid by him, but he must give credit for any benefits which he has received as a result of the transaction; (4) as a general rule, the benefits received

992 [1993] AC 334 (HL).
993 *Cable & Wireless* v. *IBM United Kingdom Ltd* [2002] EWHC 2059 (Comm), [2002] 2 All ER (Comm) 1041.
994 Ibid.
995 *Balfour Beatty Construction Northern Limited* v. *Modus Corovest (Blackpool) Ltd* [2008] EWHC 3029 (TCC), [2009] CILL 2660 [19].
996 Andrews 2015, at 31.
997 *Smith New Court Securities Ltd* v. *Citibank NA* [1997] AC 254 (HL) 280 (Lord Steyn referring to Oliver Wendell Holmes).
998 Ibid.
999 *HIH Casualty and General Insurance Ltd* v. *Chase Manhattan Bank* [2003] UKHL 6, [2003] 1 All ER (Comm) 349 [16] (Lord Bingham), [76] (Lord Hoffmann), [122] (Lord Scott).
1000 Ibid.
1001 *Smith New Court Securities Ltd* v. *Citibank NA* [1997] AC 254 (HL) 266–267 (Lord Browne-Wilkinson).

> by him include the market value of the property acquired as at the date of acquisition; but such general rule is not to be inflexibly applied where to do so would prevent him obtaining full compensation for the wrong suffered; (5) although the circumstances in which the general rule should not apply cannot be comprehensively stated, it will normally not apply where either (a) the misrepresentation has continued to operate after the date of the acquisition of the asset so as to induce the plaintiff to retain the asset or (b) the circumstances of the case are such that the plaintiff is, by reason of the fraud, locked into the property. (6) In addition, the plaintiff is entitled to recover consequential losses caused by the transaction; (7) the plaintiff must take all reasonable steps to mitigate his loss once he has discovered the fraud.

Notably, the defence of contributory negligence[1002] is not applicable against a claim in the tort of deceit.[1003] Liability is construed as a strict liability.[1004]

5.7.2.2. Negligent misrepresentation

The measure of damages under the tort of negligent misstatement is the recovery of the sustained economic loss.[1005] The damages for lost expectations (expectation interest) and loss of bargain are not recoverable.[1006] The elements of the tort of negligent misstatement have been addressed earlier in Section 5.5.1 above.

5.7.3. *Unjust enrichment*

The claim for unjust enrichment is a claim for debt, not for damages. The aggrieved party may recover the reasonable value of works (*quantum valebat*) following *British Steel Corp* v. *Cleveland Bridge & Engineering Co Ltd*[1007] or the reasonable value of services rendered (*quantum meruit*) following *Planche* v. *Colbourn*.[1008] The elements of the doctrine that lay down the conditions for recovery have been discussed in Section 5.5.3 above.

5.7.4. *Breach of duty of confidence*

Breach of the duty of confidence may give rise to damages calculated 'on the basis of reasonable compensation for the use of the confidential information which had been given'.[1009] As Lord Denning MR stated, this remedy is based on 'the broad principle of equity that he who has received information in confidence shall not take unfair advantage

1002 The defence of contributory negligence is a 'partial defence to the claim in tort in case where the claimant's own carelessness was a material cause of his loss'. See Markesinins/Deakin 2013, at 749. See also Contributory Negligence Act 1945; Markesinis/Deakin 2013, at 749–762.

1003 *Standard Chartered Bank* v. *Pakistan National Shipping Corp* [2002] UKHL 43, [2003] 1 AC 959.

1004 Markesinis/Deakin 2013, at 470.

1005 *Hedley Byrne & Co Ltd* v. *Heller & Partners Ltd* [1964] AC 465 (HL).

1006 Ibid; see also Andrews 2015, para 9.18.

1007 [1984] 1 All ER 504 (QBD).

1008 (1831) 131 ER 305 (Court of King's Bench).

1009 *Seager* v. *Copydex* Ltd (No.1) [1967] 1 WLR 923 (EWCA) 924.

of it'.[1010] For instance, in *Seager* v. *Copydex Ltd (No.1)*[1011] it was analysed as an equitable remedy. The damages were ascertained on the basis of restitution.[1012]

Furthermore, an injunction may be granted to restrain the use of confidential information.[1013] If the information is shared in a commercial context with a view to acquiring future gain, courts are willing to grant money damages, rather than an injunction.[1014] Finally, breach of confidence may provide the right to a gain-based recovery: account of profits (made as a result of breach of confidence).[1015]

5.7.5. *Note on exemplary damages*

English private law is not concerned with punishment of civil wrongs.[1016] Nevertheless, an exceptional remedy, also referred to as punitive damages, deserves a note. This remedy may be granted to punish a tort[1017] committed with the aim of profiting from the consequences.[1018] In the context of precontractual negotiations, this points to the tort of deceit. According to some English commentators, exemplary damages may potentially be available in an action for deceit.[1019] However, this is subject to further developments of case law. On a general note, it is worth noting that exemplary damages are currently not available for breach of contract. Furthermore, the court may still refuse to grant punitive damages if it considers that compensatory damages already offer an adequate remedy. If exemplary damages are awarded, they should still be moderate.[1020]

5.7.6. *Concurrence of actions*

Due to the fact that both contractual and non-contractual regulation is applicable to negotiations, one set of facts may give rise to several causes of actions.[1021] For example, a claim in tort, contract, or restitution may be, in principle, available for a payment of works done based only on a letter of intent. In such situations, English law admits the concurrence of actions. This means the aggrieved party has the right to choose a cause of action from those available. The claimant may also plead two alternative causes of action. This allows the claimant to take advantage of this choice. He is able to opt for different regimes of liability available under different causes of action (or combine these) in order

1010 [1967] 1 WLR 923 (EWCA) 931 (Lord Denning).
1011 Ibid 924.
1012 *Seager* v. *Copydex Ltd (No 2)* [1969] 1 WLR 809 (EWCA).
1013 *Coco* v. *A.N. Clark (Engineers) Limited* [1968] FSR 415 (EWHC).
1014 Ibid 423 (Megarry J).
1015 *Attorney General* v. *Observer Ltd* [1990] 1 AC 109 (HL).
1016 Burrows 2015, para 4.163; *Chitty on Contracts* 2015, para 26–043 ff.
1017 *Rookes* v. *Barnard* [1964] AC 1129 (HL).
1018 *Broome* v. *Cassell & Co Ltd* [1972] AC 1027 (HL). See also Burrows 2015, para 4.163 ff.
1019 *Chitty on Contracts* 2015, para 7–070.
1020 Burrows 2015, para 1.164.
1021 *Chitty on Contracts* 2015, para 1–145 - 1–146.

to remedy his claim the most adequately, including the possible advantage relating to the difference in limitation periods, in particular the difference in the moment of accrual of the cause of action.[1022]

In the context of letter of intent, it is worth noting that the choice of action may be limited in the presence of a written document that may contain contractually binding obligations. In such cases, the choice is possible to the extent a claim in tort does not contradict any express or implied terms of enforceable contractual obligations.[1023] The House of Lords adopted such approach in *Henderson* v. *Merrett Syndicates Ltd*[1024] in relation to the 'concurrence' between the duty of care in tort and the duty of care required for the execution of a contractual obligation.

5.8. Conclusion

This Chapter began by emphasizing the piecemeal character of English law applicable to contractual negotiations. Along with the straightforward approach to the unenforceability of a 'bare agreement to agree' and their equivalents (most importantly the agreement to negotiate in good faith), the contract law framework includes elaborate solutions to several questions raised by the practice of issuing letters of intent. More specifically, English law has developed a detailed approach to two types of provisions: exclusivity of negotiations – temporary 'lock-out' agreement; and best endeavours to obtain an export licence or planning permission. Furthermore, English law establishes a clear link between negotiation and mediation which is an assisted form of negotiations. The enforceability of mediation and arbitration clauses in letter of intent has been the subject of attention and considerable elaboration.

It is worth noting that English contract law offers the possibility to imply contractual terms based on trade usage and commercial customs. However, letter of intent or contractual organization of negotiations have not been invoked as a trade usage.

Along with the contract law framework, other solutions include remedies in tort for fraudulent and negligent misrepresentation and breach of the equitable duty of confidence. However the application of these doctrines to misconduct in negotiations is not the subject of extensive elaboration in case law. The doctrine of estoppel is also a possible potential solution rather than an elaborated field of application in this area. The domains of contract law and tort law can be only linked in a limited way by the contractual organization of negotiations by letters of intent, because the rules provided by these non-contractual tools cannot be modified by the parties' agreement.

1022 Andrews 2015, para 1.23.

1023 *Chitty on Contracts* 2015, para 1–161.

1024 [1995] 2 AC 145 (HL). This case clarifies previous case relevant for English law *Tai Hing Cotton Mill Ltd Appellant* v. *Liu Chong Hing Bank Ltd* [1986] AC 80 (Privy Council Hong Kong) that excluded claims in tort if parties are bound by a contractual obligation.

An important role in the regulation of negotiations, including contractually organized negotiations, is played by the law of restitution and unjust enrichment. The relevance of this field of law correlates with the high threshold set by contract law on the enforceability of promises regarding the process of negotiations.

The review of the multifaceted regulation of negotiations as well as of the modern academic debate on *bona fides* in negotiations signals three tendencies. Firstly, it shows that English law has developed since the House of Lords' approach to negotiations of contract formulated in *Walford* v. *Miles*.[1025] Firstly, English law has in fact not been receptive to the trend of accepting a general overarching duty of *bona fides* reflected in international soft law instruments. The development of the regime of regulation of negotiations has relied instead on doctrines that make reference to *bona fides* unnecessary in interpretation. English courts have relied on various classical doctrines of contract formation and extra-contractual tools.

Secondly, on another note, English courts demonstrate particular sensitivity to the need for legal certainty in commercial transactions. It is in disputes between businesses that the texts of letter of intent have been given strict meaning. A good illustration is enforcing the provisions in accordance with a division of the document into binding and non-binding parts made by the parties.

Thirdly, and most generally, the increasing detail in the English approach to negotiations does not increase the protection of any reliance that may arise during negotiations of a contract. The English approach rather specifies under which specific conditions private organization of negotiations may be enforced. It is worth noting that the promises that may be enforceable under English law are assessed by the English courts as stand-alone obligations. These are severed from the final contract and from the other content of a document created in the course of negotiations. The fundamental requirement for their enforceability – that of consideration – is also required for each concrete promise, not for the final contract in its entirety. Furthermore, in no circumstances is a party required to act contrary to his own commercial interest in the course of negotiations. Neither does English law protect parties from an ordinary bargaining mistake. In sum, reliance during negotiations of a contract is protected only from fraud and tortious conduct.

1025 [1992] 2 AC 128 (HL).

Chapter 6

US LAW

6.1. Introduction

The period of contractual negotiations is the time of *alea* – hazard, venture, and risk, with little or no role for contract law.[1026] This view is rooted in the English law[1027] and is fundamental to the US legal system. The so-called 'all or nothing' approach[1028] underpinned by this view completely dominated US contract law until the last decades of the twentieth century. Either all the elements of the formed contract were found, or nothing was binding on the parties. As a result, precontractual documents could be regarded as a fully formed contract, with the risk of trapping 'parties in surprise contractual obligations that they never intended'.[1029] Alternatively, any attempts by the parties to frame their negotiations with preliminary documents were held to be unenforceable. The main reason for this unenforceability was the failure of these documents to fulfil all the conditions of enforceability for a fully formed contract.

While the aleatory view of negotiations is still fundamental, the 'all or nothing' approach has been progressively nuanced since the 1970s.[1030] The US courts have 'relaxed the knife-edge character of the common law by which parties are either fully bound or not bound at all'.[1031] This new trend has admitted that at the stage of negotiations, parties may not yet have the intent to form the final contract, but have an intent to make some of their preliminary commitments binding for different reasons. In a 'major shift in doctrine,'[1032] the 'core theory of a cause of action for breach of contract to negotiate has been more and more readily accepted by courts'.[1033] In particular the courts have begun to distinguish between the final negotiated contract and the preliminary agreements

1026 Holmes 1978, at 384–385; Farnsworth 1987, at 221.

1027 This comes back to the English case *William Lacey (Hounslow) Ltd* v. *Davis* [1957] 1 W.L.R. 932 (QB).

1028 Lake/Draetta 1994, at 172.

1029 *Teachers Ins. and Annuity Ass'n of America* v. *Tribune Co.*, 670 F.Supp. 491, 497 (S.D.N.Y. 1987).

1030 Knapp 1969; Farnsworth 1987; Jeffries 2012; Klass 2009; Schwarz/ Scott 2007; Lake/Draetta 1994; Klein/Bachechi 1994; Kostritsky 1993; Shell 1991; Barnett/Becker 1987; Kessler/Fine 1964.

1031 Schwarz/Scott 2007, at 675.

1032 Ibid.

1033 *Butler* v. *Balolia* 736 F.3d 609, 618 (C.A.1 2013).

preparing it. Scholarship has distinguished 'agreements with open terms' and 'agreements to negotiate'.[1034]

These regimes are intermediary between the non-binding negotiations and the final contract. Courts in some states have held that a preliminary regime entails an enforceable contractual obligation to negotiate the final contract in good faith. They have started to develop the content of *bona fides* in negotiations. This is not to say that the US law imposes a duty of good faith in negotiations. The very possibility of the existence of *bona fides* at the precontractual stage is debated. Its eventual content is also the subject of discussions. State law sharply diverges on this; for instance, federal courts applying New York law have been the most reluctant to recognize precontractual good faith.[1035]

The approach to intermediary regimes has developed towards a further differentiation. Next to good faith, other obligations inserted in precontractual documents have sometimes been enforced. The main indicator guiding the courts' reasoning is the intent of the parties. This objectively assessed intent determines whether parties have concluded a preliminary agreement and if so, guides in defining its content.

This shift from an 'all or nothing' approach towards more differentiation has been also reflected in the US uniform contract law. The Uniform Commercial Code 'rejects… the formula that "an agreement to agree is unenforceable"'.[1036] Instead, the parties' intention to go forward with the deal is regarded as the most important criterion to address whether they are bound immediately from the start of negotiations or may keep their negotiations free from any contractual obligations.[1037]

At the same time, US courts and scholars have become familiar with a more general concept of 'precontractual liability'[1038] – previously highly unusual for this legal system. This concept embraces not only contract law, but also extra-contractual doctrines applicable to the precontractual period. These are the doctrine of promissory estoppel, tort, and the law of restitution and unjust enrichment. The rules contained in these fields of regulation limit the enforceable content of the parties' preliminary agreements.

Precontractual liability has been discussed in the academic literature within two debates. The first related to the protection of precontractual reliance. The second related to the economic efficiency of the choice between enforcement and non-enforcement of preliminary agreements. It is worth noting in this regard that reliance on economic and

1034 Farnsworth 1987, at 243. A landmark case is *Teachers Ins. and Annuity Ass'n of America* v. *Tribune Co.*, 670 F.Supp. 491 (S.D.N.Y. 1987).

1035 See for example *Reprosystem, B.V.* v. *SCM Corp.*, 727 F.2d 257, 264 (C.A.2 1984). For a recent example, see *CAC Group Inc.* v. *Maxim Group LLC*, 523 F.Appx. 802 (C.A.2 2013).

1036 UCC, §2–305 Official Comment 1.

1037 Ibid.

1038 See for example Ayres 2012, at 369 ff.: part entitled 'Precontractual liability'.

policy arguments is a general peculiarity of US law. Law is viewed as a 'means to social end'[1039] and a tool to promote social welfare.[1040] As a consequence, the economic analysis of law or 'law and economics' – the analysis of incentives created by law and their effect on behaviour – has considerable prominence.[1041] For instance, Schwarz and Scott[1042] have analysed whether enforcement confers value on the transaction. They have based their analysis on balancing the economic efficiency of bargaining and the degree of the parties' reliance in negotiations. Schwarz and Scott have also summarized the arguments courts take into account in a large number of cases when they find an enforceable preliminary agreement. Klass has advanced 'law and economics' arguments in favour of non-enforcement of preliminary agreements as the main rule, with a possibility for the parties to deviate from it. Other 'law and economics' debates include the analysis of the distribution of risk in negotiations,[1043] the balancing of *ex ante* costs of negotiating and drafting the agreement and the *ex post* costs of litigation.[1044]

In addition to economic analysis of law, considerable authority has been gained by the 'relational contract' theorists.[1045] Their critique of the static character of the offer and acceptance doctrine has been perhaps the strongest in the Western world. Despite these debates, US case law and the restatements have remained far more conservative than any changes which have been suggested by scholars. The relevant modern law is not completely settled. The possibility of intermediary regimes exists, but their precise scope is still in development, as are the criteria of enforceability of obligations within these regimes.

This Chapter will address to what extent US law enables parties to frame negotiations contractually and what remedies are available. The Chapter will start with a brief overview of the US legal system and explain the approach of this Chapter. The US law is relatively complex because of the multitude of approaches that may be found in the case law. This complexity requires a brief note on the US legal system, addressing the role and the authority of court cases, unified and harmonized law, and scholarship (Section 6.2). Thereafter, the Chapter will take the perspective of contract law and focus on the evolution from the aleatory view of negotiations to a more differentiated approach, discuss the factors taken into account to define the parties' intent and the approach to the validity of preliminary agreements and separate obligations within these documents (Section 6.3). Thereafter, the Chapter will turn to the non-contractual doctrines relevant at the precontractual stage (Section 6.4). Finally, it will address the approach that can be

1039 Ayres 2012, at 54.

1040 American legal thought has evolved from the eighteenth century legal formalism towards legal realism. This perceives law primarily as a 'means to social end', as opposed to a 'goal in itself'. See Ayres 2012, at 54; Speziale 1980; Kimball 2004.

1041 Ayres 2012, at 55. See inter alia Posner 1977; Shell 1991; Katz 1996; Schwarz/Scott 2007; Cohen 2009.

1042 Schwarz/Scott 2007.

1043 See Cohen 2009 with further references.

1044 Katz 1996; Shell 1991; Eisenberg 2000; Cohen 2009; Ben-Shahar 2010.

1045 See Section 2.3.2.

distilled from modern US law to certain obligations framing the dynamics of negotiations (Section 6.5), liability for breach of contractual obligations and under non-contractual doctrines (Section 6.6), and provide concluding remarks (Section 6.7).

6.2. Approach to the US legal system

The United States is a federation of fifty states. The fields of law relevant to the regulation of negotiations are a matter of state law. Therefore, it is necessary to explain why the use of the term 'US law' is appropriate (6.2.1). It is also helpful to briefly provide an overview of the US legal system (6.2.2), and sketch the approach to the US sources adopted in this Chapter (6.2.3).

6.2.1. The term US law and the approach of this Chapter

This study uses the general term 'US law'. The choice of this term has been made for the following reason. On the one hand, the study is primarily interested in state law, developed essentially by the highest appellate courts of the states. An important body of case law relating to the process of negotiations has also been developed by federal courts applying state law. Federal courts may apply state law to 'predict' or 'divine',[1046] as the judges put it, the states' highest court solution.[1047] Certainly, the primary interest in state law needs to take into consideration that the law differs across the states, sometimes taking radically different approaches. An illustrative example is the implication of the precontractual duty of good faith: some states accept it, while others reject the very idea of precontractual duties in contract law. This Chapter will strive to underline the issues handled with considerably different approaches under state law. To do so it relies on several sources. The study will rely on landmark cases referred to in academic literature and search for cases referring to the relevant academic literature. For example, several cases relevant to this study have referred to the article by Farnsworth.[1048] Furthermore the study relies upon a search by topics and lines of cases in the case law database.[1049]

On the other hand, generally, the differences across states' laws lie not in general terms, but only in detail; and the similarities outweigh the differences.[1050] This is to a large extent due to the harmonization and restatement of law mentioned earlier. Courts often refer to restatements of law, systematized and unified law. They may also look for argumentation and inspiration in the approaches of other states or federal courts, especially when courts of a particular state have not yet dealt with a specific issue.

1046 *Butler* v. *Balolia* 736 F.3d 609, 612 (C.A.1 2013).

1047 Ayres 2012, at 398. By way of example see *Channel Home Centers, Div. of Grace Retail Corp.* v. *Grossman*, 795 F.2d 291 (C.A.3 1986); *Venture Associates Corp.* v. *Zenith Data Systems Corp.*, 96 F.3d 275 (C.A.7 1996); *A/S Apothekernes Laboratorium for Specialpraeparater* v. *I.M.C. Chemical Group, Inc.*, 873 F.2d 155 (C.A.7 1989).

1048 Farnsworth 1987.

1049 Case law is available in the database Westlaw International.

1050 Farnsworth 2014, at 134 and 139.

Sometimes the law of one state provides more precedents on a given issue. For example, New York law has been prominent in developing a test of several factors that may be taken into account to assess the intent of the parties. Legal scholars often address US law generally, referring to the most advanced case law on a given subject. Therefore, this study refers to US law in general.

Furthermore, this Chapter will principally study the sources often called 'primary authority'.[1051] These are rules contained in statutes and case law. To complete and explain these sources, reference will also be made to secondary authority, including the restatements of law, model laws, and scholarship including treatises and other publications.

6.2.2. *Judicial system*

Due to the historical development of US federalism, law in the United States is created at two levels – the state level and the federal level. Federal competence covers only a limited number of matters. All the matters not explicitly enumerated as falling within federal competence are relegated to the level of the. Each state adopts its own rules – state law – within this competence.[1052] Private law is a matter of state law. The competence of states thus generally covers contract law and tort law; the law of restitution and unjust enrichment and the doctrine of promissory estoppel also fall within the competence of the states.[1053]

The division of competences mentioned above is also characteristic of the judicial system. The United States has a dual system of courts: the state courts and the federal courts exist in parallel. At the state level, each state has *trial courts* deciding as courts of first instance. These courts are named superior courts, circuit courts or courts of common pleas. Most states also have *intermediate appellate courts*, and all states have an *appellate court* – the highest judicial authority in the state on matters of state law.[1054] These are often called supreme courts, but not always so. For example, the court at this level in New York is called the New York Court of Appeals and in Massachusetts, the Supreme Judicial Court. At the federal level, there are federal US *district courts* situated in each of 94 districts which decide cases in the first instance. The US *courts of appeal* and the *US Supreme Court* are competent to hear cases on appeal as the highest judicial instance.[1055] There are also federal courts with special competence limited to a particular domain, for example the US Court of International Trade for international trade disputes, or Bankruptcy courts with limited jurisdiction.

1051 Farnsworth 2010, at 93.

1052 Constitution of the United States of 1787 (US Constitution) Tenth Amendment; Farnsworth 2010, at 47.

1053 There are few exceptions where the Congress has explicitly carved out private legislation, for example Federal Tort Claims Act 1946 (enabling private parties to sue in a federal court for torts committed by persons acting on behalf of the United States).

1054 Farnsworth 2010, at 44–45.

1055 The US Court of Appeal must hear appeals in certain cases (mandatory jurisdiction) whereas the US Supreme Court has discretionary jurisdiction. In some cases, the US Supreme Court may me the court of both first and last instance.

While the state and federal courts exist in parallel, their jurisdiction follows the divide of state and federal competence. Federal courts only have jurisdiction over cases falling within the specifically enumerated competence of federal power. All other matters fall by default within the jurisdiction of state courts.[1056] Following the Supremacy Clause in the US Constitution, the federal constitution, federal statutes and treaties take precedence over state law. Therefore, in cases of conflict between federal law and state law, state courts are prescribed to apply federal law.[1057] In some cases, federal courts are competent to interpret and apply state law. This is called the *diversity jurisdiction* and arises namely if the parties reside in two different states or are non US residents and the amount in dispute exceeds 75000 US dollars.[1058]

The jury plays an important role in the US legal system. It is competent to resolve *questions of fact* in *first instance* trials. The US Constitution grants litigants the right of a jury trial as under English common law at the time the US Constitution was adopted. This right is furthermore granted by most federal statutes.[1059] The decision of the jury taken at first instance is binding on courts of higher instance. The latter courts may review only on *questions of law*, as opposed to the jury decided *questions of fact*. Trial by jury is available both in the federal and state courts. The jury consists of a minimum of six jurors not qualified as lawyers. Parties may also waive the right to have questions of fact decided by a jury and voluntarily submit the entire case to the judge(s). This is frequently done in commercial cases, and for this reason, jury trial is less relevant for business to business contracts. Questions of fact are then also resolved by the judge(s) along with the question of law.[1060]

6.2.3. *Sources of law*

Private law in the United States is primarily case law based. The most important source of private law is the case law of the higher courts of the states.[1061] The states' appellate courts are also '[t]he most reliable guide to the interpretation of state law'.[1062] Whereas case law is the main source of private law, the US legal system relies also on other sources of law. The most important include the Constitution of the United States and federal statutes, state constitutions and state statutes, such as, for instance Uniform Commercial Code.[1063] These sources represent primary authority.

1056 Farnsworth 2010, at 47.

1057 US Constitution, Article VI §2.

1058 US Constitution, Article III §2; United States Code Title 28, §1332.

1059 Seventh Amendment to the US Constitution. See also Title IV Rule 38 'Right to a Jury Trial; Demand' of the Federal Rules of Civil Procedure for the United States District Courts.

1060 Farnsworth 2010, at 115.

1061 Farnsworth 2010, at 53 stating that 'case law is found primarily in the decisions of appellate courts'.

1062 *Butler* v. *Balolia* 736 F.3d 609, 611 (C.A.1 2013), referring to *Kathios* v. *Gen. Motors Corp.*, 862 F.2d 944 (C.A.1 1988).

1063 Furthermore, federal executive power, e.g. president and federal administrative bodies are also competent to adopt federal executive orders, administrative rules and regulations. State authorities are also empowered to regulate state matters within the state competence. See Farnsworth 2010, at 70–72.

6.2.3.1. Case law

Case law as a method of finding and developing law is the main method of law-making in the United States, following the English common law tradition.[1064] It is based on the doctrine of precedent or *stare decisis* – from the Latin expression *stare decisis en non quieta movere* 'to stand by the decisions and not disturb settled points'.[1065] Within the system of precedent, a legal solution adopted in a decided case can be used by other courts to resolve similar cases later by courts which are bound by the precedent. The holding is the part of the decision containing the law on a concrete matter. Holdings of the decisions of the higher courts have binding authority for the lower courts of the same state. Any court is also bound by the holdings contained in its own previous decisions. Generally, all cases have some persuasive authority for all the courts. Any part of the decision, including dissenting opinions of one of the judges, may be referred to as persuasive authority if it relies on strong argumentation. The system of precedent is not completely rigid. Courts may take decisions overruling existing precedents. These decisions, usually called landmark cases, adapt the law to new situations. Furthermore, despite the internal methodological coherence, the system of precedent still allows for controversial lines of cases where a similar situation is resolved in a different manner.[1066]

The law relating to the precontractual period is one of the fields where not all controversies are settled. Notably, the approach of a US state court in resolving a case includes not only finding and interpreting the relevant law, e.g. statutes and case law, but also consulting 'analogous opinions of that court, decisions of lower courts in the state, precedents and trends in other jurisdictions, learned treatises, and considerations of sound public policy'.[1067]

6.2.3.2. Systematized and unified of law

The case law method has led to the existence of an important body of case law. Very early in the history of the development of US law, it was felt that some systematization was needed, even if only for scholarly and teaching purposes. The first attempts to summarize the existing case law, distil important precedents, and sketch trends were made by the drafters of treatises in order to teach law using the case law method.[1068] At the end of the nineteenth century, considerable systematization took place in the form of restatements of law, uniform laws and model laws.

In 1923 the American Law Institute (ALI) was founded 'to promote the clarification and simplification of the law and its better administration of justice and to encourage and

[1064] With the exception of the law of the state of Louisiana that has adopted a Civil Code and has generally the imprint of civil law tradition under the influence of French law.
[1065] Farnsworth 2010, at 59.
[1066] Farnsworth 2010, at 59–68.
[1067] *Butler* v. *Balolia* 736 F.3d 609, 613 (C.A.1 2013).
[1068] See seminal Samuel Williston, *The Law of Contracts* (1920) and Arthur Linton Corbin, *Corbin on Contracts* (1950).

carry scholarly and scientific work'.[1069] One of the main achievements of the ALI has been the *Restatements* of law. The ALI has undertaken to harmonize and unify several fields of law by extracting general rules, from the basis of the existing case law and sometimes even departing from the existing precedents. In 1932, the work of the ALI on contract law resulted in the creation of the Restatement (First) of Contracts. Later on, the text was revised to become the Restatement (Second) of Contracts, which was completed in 1897.[1070] Tort law has also been subject to three restatements and a separate set of rules has recently been removed from the restatement on tort and edited under the heading of law of unfair competition. Furthermore, in 2010, the ALI also finalized the third Restatement on the law of restitution and unjust enrichment.

Restatements enjoy no legal authority, nor have they acquired binding force for the courts unless adopted by the states in the form of a statute. The US Restatements have only the authority of being a 'product of men learned in the subject who have studied and deliberated over it'.[1071] However, due to the outstanding quality of the work, the Restatements have acquired highly persuasive authority for all legal practitioners and are often referred to by the courts.

In addition to the restatements, US law has been harmonized through *model* laws and *uniform* laws. These instruments are formulated as draft laws to be partly or entirely used by the states in drafting their laws. The American Bar Association and the National Committee of Commissioners on Uniform States Laws (UCL), established at the end of the nineteenth century, have all played an important role in drafting these instruments. Additionally, during the second half of the twentieth century, the ULC and the ALI embarked on a project to draft a uniform law for commercial transactions – the Uniform Commercial Code (UCC). Its first draft was finalized in 1952. The final, official text, created after several amendments, has been adopted by all the states except Louisiana.[1072] The UCC contains articles stating the law, and the articles are accompanied by comments and illustrations which have strong persuasive authority.[1073]

6.2.3.3. Law and equity

The US legal system draws, in several matters, a distinction between the common law and equity. If the common law (e.g. the rules found in case law)[1074] offers no adequate remedy, an equitable relief may be granted. This distinction is rooted in English civil procedure. Historically, in England and Wales, the King's courts were competent to

[1069] 3 ALI Proceedings 159 (1925).

[1070] Restatement (Second) of Contracts Foreword.

[1071] Clark 1933, at 655.

[1072] Louisiana is an exception to the approach of other US states. In Louisiana, the law is not based on common law, but on French and Spanish law.

[1073] Farnsworth 2004, at 35.

[1074] This is the use of this term within the US legal system. In other Chapters, the term 'common law' is used to designate the US and English legal traditions as opposed to the 'civil law' legal tradition.

decide cases instead of local courts if the office of the Chancellor had prepared the case in a form of a writ. The Chancellor of the King's courts progressively acquired the power to use royal 'grace' and decide cases in equity if no legal remedy was appropriate. From the fifteenth century, the Court of Chancery has been competent to sit as a court of equity. Under the English influence, the distinction was upheld in the United States at the time when the judicial system was formed.

In the modern US legal systems, there are no separate courts of equity.[1075] Instead, the law of equity may be developed by both federal and state judges. The rights originating in equity are still called equitable, but the rules which originated in equity form a part of common law.[1076] Several fields of law relevant to contractual negotiations still have a strong 'equitable conception'.[1077] For instance, equity has become an essential device for the development of the doctrine of promissory estoppel in US law. Promissory estoppel has developed as a separate cause of action in equity to protect reasonable expectations arising prior to contract formation. The law of restitution and unjust enrichment also continues to bear a considerable equitable imprint.

The right to a jury trial covers only the issues of law, but not issues of equity. In cases where 'there are both legal and equitable issues in a jury trial, the legal issues of fact are decided by the jury, while the equitable issues are decided by the judge'.[1078]

6.3. From 'all or nothing' to differentiation

6.3.1. *Negotiations as alea*

US contract law has always regarded negotiations as a period of *alea* – the time of risk, bargain, and hazard.[1079] The use of this concept to characterize negotiations introduced by Farnsworth comes from the Latin *alea* – 'anything uncertain or contingent, an accident, chance, hazard, venture, risk'.[1080] This approach goes back to the English roots of US law.[1081] It flows from the principle of freedom of contract[1082] and is reflected by the Restatement (Second) of Contracts[1083] as the underlying idea of bargain in negotiations remains also fundamental in the development of the modern US law approach to contract formation.

1075 The adoption of the Federal Rules of Civil Procedure in 1938 merged law and equity at the federal level. Most states have also merged law and equity into one system of courts. However, some states have retained the distinction, for example, Delaware.

1076 Farnsworth 2010, at 103–105.

1077 Restatement (Third) of Restitution and Unjust Enrichment, §1 Comment b.

1078 Farnsworth 2010, at 104.

1079 Farnsworth 2004, at 190; Klass 2009, at 1487.

1080 Ch. T. Lewis and Ch. Short, *A Latin Dictionary* (Oxford: Clarendon Press, 1879), at 82.

1081 See the English case *William Lacey (Hounslow) Ltd* v. *Davis* [1957] 1 W.L.R. 932 (QB).

1082 Restatement (Second) of Contracts, §26; *Channel Home Centers, Div. of Grace Retail Corp.* v. *Grossman*, 795 F.2d 291, 298 (C.A.3 1986); Calamari/Perillo 2009, at 5.

1083 Restatement (Second) of Contracts, §26 Preliminary Negotiations.

Contract law relies on a model of 'two alert individuals, mindful of their self-interest, hammering out an agreement by a process of hard bargaining'.[1084] As a starting point, the outcome of negotiations is unknown and each party bears the risks of their failure.

The policy argument behind the aleatory view of negotiations is the unwillingness to discourage trade. In particular, the risk of being held contractually liable before a contract is formed might 'chill'[1085] transactions and discourage parties from entering into negotiations.[1086] 'In a business transaction both sides presumably try to get the best of the deal. That is the essence of bargaining and the free market'.[1087] Limitations on the parties' freedom through contract can, therefore, be only voluntary, made by the parties themselves.

Accordingly, US law imposes no general duties on precontractual conduct. For instance, the authors of harmonized and unified law have found no general positive requirement of good faith and fair dealing to be established for the period of negotiations.[1088] The UCC establishes such duty only for the 'performance or enforcement' of the contract, but not for the period of formation.[1089] Courts have also noted on a number of occasions that 'there is no "free-floating" duty of good faith and fair dealing that is unattached to an existing contract'.[1090]

Based on this approach to negotiations, contract formation is assessed following the analysis that has been called 'all or nothing'. Either a fully formed contract is made, or, alternatively, parties may freely walk away from the transaction at any moment and without contractual liability. The period of negotiations and the time after the contract is formed are sharply distinguished. Within the 'all or nothing' approach, all preparatory documents are qualified as acts of aleatory negotiations if there is no clear intention for exchange. As District Judge Leval has put it, '[i]t is fundamental to contract law that mere participation in negotiations and discussions does not create binding obligations, even if agreement is reached on all disputed terms. More is needed than agreement on each detail, which is overall agreement (or offer and acceptance) to enter into a binding contract'.[1091]

Therefore as a starting point of US legal reasoning, 'preliminary agreements typically do not create binding contracts', because typically not all requirements for the formed contract are fulfilled to apply the 'all or nothing' approach.[1092]

1084 Calamari/Perillo 2009, at 5.
1085 Schwarz/Scott 2007, at 670.
1086 Farnsworth 1987, at 221.
1087 *Rambus Inc.* v. *Hynix Semiconductor Inc.*, 629 F. Supp. 2d 979, 1016 (N.D. Cal. 2009).
1088 Restatement (Second) of Contracts, §205 Comment c. Scholars' opinions regarding a precontractual duty of good faith in the US law diverge. Some scholars suggest that the umbrella of the general duty of good faith in negotiations could embrace most situations where liability can be imposed during the precontractual period. See Summers 1968, at 225; Palmieri 1993, Farnsworth 1987, at 239.
1089 UCC, §1–304. See also UCC, §2–109 (requiring good faith in contract modification).
1090 *Keystone Land & Development* v. *Xerox Corp.*, 94 P.3d 945, 949 (Wash. 2004).
1091 *Teachers Ins. and Annuity Ass'n of America* v. *Tribune Co.*, 670 F.Supp. 491, 497 (S.D.N.Y. 1987).
1092 Schwarz/Scott 2007, at 675 in particular footnote 44.

6.3.2. *Preliminary regimes versus ultimate agreement*

While the 'all or nothing' approach remains fundamental to US law, since 1970, the courts' reasoning has evolved towards admitting more differentiation. As has been formulated in a recent case, the 'case law… is a mixed bag' and 'the trend line appears to be moving steadily in favor of recognizing a cause of action for breach of a contract to negotiate'.[1093] The development of this 'modern trend' remains an ongoing process.[1094]

The patterns of differentiation in the courts' approach were first summarized by Farnsworth. This scholar has described a distinction the courts make between the 'ultimate agreement'[1095] – a fully formed contract ('all'), aleatory negotiations ('nothing'), and preliminary agreements (an intermediary regime between the all and nothing regimes). The term 'preliminary agreements' has been used by this scholar for convenience to refer to all the exchanges between parties, whether or not enforceable. Farnsworth has called the ultimate agreement and the aleatory negotiations 'polar regimes'. The first entails full contractual liability, while the second entails no contractual liability.[1096] Next to the two polar regimes, Farnsworth has described the emergence of the 'intermediary regimes'[1097] in the case law. Two intermediary regimes have been sketched: 'agreements with open terms' and 'agreements to negotiate'.[1098] An agreement with open terms fixes some terms of the ultimate agreement. While parties agree to be bound by these terms, they leave a certain number of other terms for further negotiations. According to Farnsworth parties are often regarded as bound by the original agreement, and the missing terms are fleshed out by the court, if necessary.[1099] In an agreement to negotiate, parties lay down a certain number of terms, but do not bind themselves by these terms. If the negotiations fail, parties will not be bound by any agreement.[1100] However, Farnsworth has noted that many of the parties' preliminary agreements contain elements of both types.

This distinction between the ultimate agreement and the intermediary instruments introduced by Farnsworth has been important for US law. The concepts have been taken up by the courts and subsequently used in case law. For instance, a similar distinction has been made in a landmark case, *Teachers Ins. and Annuity Ass'n of America v. Tribune Co.*[1101] Courts have also referred to agreements with open terms as type I and type II

1093 *Butler* v. *Balolia* 736 F.3d 609, 614 (C.A.1 2013).

1094 *Keystone Land & Development* v. *Xerox Corp.*, 94 P.3d 945, 1097 (Wash. 2004) and with further references to case law; *Butler* v. *Balolia* 736 F.3d 609, 614 (C.A.1 2013); *Burbach Broad. Co. of Del.* v. *Elkins Radio Corp.*, 278 F.3d 401 (C.A.4 2002).

1095 Farnsworth 1987, at 243.

1096 Ibid.

1097 Ibid.

1098 Ibid.

1099 Farnsworth 1987, at 250.

1100 Farnsworth 1987, at 251.

1101 670 F.Supp. 491 (S.D.N.Y. 1987).

preliminary agreements, following the numeration made by Farnsworth.[1102] Other terms have also been used, such as 'preliminary commitment'; others use the term 'binding preliminary commitment'.[1103] Academic literature has also proved to be receptive to the emerging differentiation between preliminary agreements.[1104] Based on the broad acceptance of the terminology, this will be also used in this Chapter.

6.3.3. *The three modes of the courts' approach*

The patterns of differentiation emerging against the fundamental background of the aleatory view of negotiations have led the US courts to have three modes of approach to the documents created in preparation of the ultimate agreement.

6.3.3.1. Search for the ultimate agreement

The courts look first for the ultimate agreement in the parties' exchange. In a number of cases involving parties' attempts to contractualize negotiations, courts do not directly address whether the preliminary documents at hand may have any binding effect on their own. This first logical step remains generally embedded in the 'all or nothing' approach. In search for the ultimate agreement, courts have often found the ultimate agreement on the basis of preliminary agreement even in cases where indices of the formed contract were not evident or not sufficiently persuasive, according to legal scholars. *Texaco, Inc.* v. *Pennzoil, Co.* is perhaps the most criticized and commented upon case where the court took the 'all or nothing' approach.[1105] Alternatively, courts find no ultimate agreement, nor any other obligations. Several decisions have characterized the parties' exchanges as simple negotiations. In a recent case, the court has reiterated the parties' freedom to 'walk away from bargaining table' as 'the proper recourse' for failed negotiations, rather than making a court claim.[1106]

It is to be noted that in several cases where the courts have adopted the 'all or nothing' approach, the claim submitted to the court has focused on enforcement of the ultimate agreement, not of the preliminary regime. As a consequence, the courts' reasoning was to a certain extent channelled towards the 'all or nothing' approach.[1107]

1102 See for example, *Butler* v. *Balolia* 736 F.3d 609, 613 (C.A.1 2013); *Keystone Land & Development* v. *Xerox Corp.*, 94 P.3d 945 (Wash. 2004); *Brown* v. *Cara*, 420 F.3d 148 (C.A.2 2005); *Hannah* v. *Tate*, Not reported, WL 6607489 (W. Va. 2014).

1103 See *Teachers Ins. and Annuity Ass'n of America* v. *Tribune Co.*, 670 F.Supp. 491, 499 (S.D.N.Y. 1987).

1104 The distinction made by Farnsworth is followed by Schwarz/Scott at 664; 693; Klass adopts the same classification – see Klass 2009, at 1448–1449.

1105 Kling/Nugent 2005, para 6.03[1]; Lake/Draetta 1994, at 135 ff. with further references.

1106 *Rambus Inc.* v. *Hynix Semiconductor Inc.*, 629 F. Supp. 2d 979, 1016 (N.D. Cal. 2009).

1107 *Beck* v. *American Health Group International, Inc.*, 260 Cal. Rptr. 237 (C.A.3 1989); *Carter* v. *Milestone*, 338 P.2d 569 (D.C.Cal. 1959); *Smissaert* v. *Chiodo*, 330 P.2d 98 (Cal. App. 1st Dist. 1958); *Forgeron Inc.* v. *Hansen*, 308 P.2d 406 (D.C.Cal 1957); *Columbia Pictures Television* v. *Krypton Broad. of Birmingham, Inc.*, 523 U.S. 340 (C.A.9 1998).

6.3.3.2. Implied good faith: diverging state law

If no ultimate agreement is found, the court may assess whether the preliminary agreement binds the parties 'in some way'.[1108] State law differs considerably as to the question of whether this is, in principle, possible.

Some states are reluctant to recognize the possibility of applying any intermediary regime to precontactual agreements. Courts of these jurisdictions refer to the difference between the ultimate agreement and the precontractual documents, but are reluctant to recognize any binding force of the latter. For instance, federal courts applying New York law have done so in a number of cases involving corporate mergers and acquisitions.[1109]

By contrast, the modern law of some jurisdictions, including Washington,[1110] California,[1111] Delaware,[1112] some New York decisions,[1113] and others[1114] makes a distinction between the ultimate agreement and the intermediary regimes. It admits that parties can be bound in some way by a preliminary agreement. At this point, state law differs as to the concrete implications of a preliminary agreement. Courts in some states have found that a preliminary agreement as such gives rise to an obligation to negotiate the ultimate agreement in good faith. In other words, an obligation of good faith may be *implied* by the court, irrespectively of whether parties have expressly included such an obligation into the preliminary document.[1115] Other courts do not go as far as implying good faith. These would only *enforce an express obligation* to negotiate in good faith, provided the parties have intended that this is binding (even within an otherwise non-binding preliminary document). For example, this is the approach of Illinois law. Whereas some provisions of a preliminary agreement have been upheld as binding, this fact alone did not mean that the duty of good faith was implied for negotiations.[1116] Judge Posner provides an argument in favour of recognizing an obligation to negotiate in good faith. The complexity of a future deal, the investment of time and money may make parties more vulnerable when facing the other party's conduct.[1117]

1108 Schwartz/Scott 2007, at 664.

1109 *Venture Associates Corp.* v. *Zenith Data Systems Corp.*, 96 F.3d 275 (C.A.7 1996).

1110 *Butler* v. *Balolia* 736 F.3d 609 (C.A.1 2013); *Keystone Land & Development* v. *Xerox Corp.*, 94 P.3d 945 (Wash. 2004).

1111 *Vestar Development II, LLC* v. *General Dynamics Corp.* 249 F.3d 958 C.A.9 (Cal.), 2001, at 961.

1112 *SIGA Technologies, Inc.* v. *PharmAthene, Inc.*, 67 A.3d 330 (Del. 2013).

1113 *Teachers Ins. and Annuity Ass'n of America* v. *Tribune Co.*, 670 F.Supp. 491 (S.D.N.Y. 1987); *Adjustrite Sys., Inc.* v. *GAB Bus. Servs., Inc.*, 145 F.3d 543, 548 (2d Cir.1998) and a more recent case *Fairbrook Leasing, Inc.* v. *Mesaba Aviation, Inc.*, 519 F.3d 421, 426 ff. (C.A.8 2008) (recognising type I and type II preliminary agreements).

1114 A recent overview of state law approaches is provided in *Butler* v. *Balolia* 736 F.3d 609, 613 (C.A.1 2013).

1115 *Channel Home Centers, Div. of Grace Retail Corp.* v. *Grossman*, 795 F.2d 291 (C.A.3 1986); *Copeland* v. *Baskin Robbins USA.*, 117 Cal. Rptr.2d 875 (Cal.App. 2002).

1116 *Feldman* v. *Allegheny Intern., Inc.*, 850 F.2d 1217 [10]-[11] (C.A.7 1988).

1117 *Venture Associates Corp.* v. *Zenith Data Systems Corp.*, 96 F.3d 275, [2] (C.A.7 1996).

In this way, if an obligation of good faith is implied or enforced, parties may abandon negotiations as long as they have made an effort to come to an ultimate agreement, but failed to reach it. However, parties are not bound by the ultimate agreement, nor may the parties be ordered to reach agreement. The simple fact that parties fail to reach agreement does not amount to breach of the good faith obligation.

This rule has been formulated in *Teachers Ins. and Annuity Ass'n of America* v. *Tribune Co.*[1118] As contended by Schwarz and Scott, the framework adopted in that case is followed in at least thirteen states, sixteen federal district courts, and seven federal circuits.[1119] The court in *Butler* v. *Balolia* has stated generally that 'many more jurisdictions have recognized the enforceability of contracts to negotiate than have repudiated that doctrine'.[1120]

The possibility of implying an obligation of good faith or to recognize this as binding has led to the question of the content of the good faith obligation. For the moment, the discussion of this topic will be postponed. More attention will be paid to this in Section 6.5.3 examining contractualized good faith. As will be explained in Section 6.5.3, the full picture of good faith in US law inevitably needs to take into account non-contractual doctrines relevant to the process of negotiations.

6.3.3.3. Further differentiation

If no ultimate agreement is found, and the court finds that parties may be 'bound in some way' by a preliminary regime, the courts may take a step further in the differentiation of the binding force of preliminary agreements (thus developing the intermediary regime). They may address more closely the validity of various obligations included in the preliminary documents. As has been stated by one of the courts, '[t]he underlying axiom is that parties may contract about their own negotiations'.[1121] This seems to be the latest development; the courts and scholarship have not yet addressed this in a straightforward way. The courts seem to agree that the framework established in *Teachers Ins. & Annuity Ass'n of Am.* v. *Tribune Co*[1122] enables them to regard some concrete obligations as binding in an otherwise non-binding document. The approach to a number of obligations framing the dynamics of negotiations has been clarified in case law (including the provisions on exclusivity, confidentiality and other matters). Courts have also touched upon the specificity, if there is any, of the requirements for enforceability for a provision to be binding within otherwise non-binding negotiations. More detail on this will be provided in Section 6.5.1. Prior to doing so, it is important to clarify the criteria and guidance in the choice between 'all or nothing', intermediary regimes, and further differentiation.

[1118] 670 F.Supp. 491 (S.D.N.Y. 1987).
[1119] Schwarz/Scott 2007, at 664 footnote 7.
[1120] 736 F.3d 609, 614 (C.A.1 2013) with an overview of state laws.
[1121] *Feldman* v. *Allegheny Intern., Inc.*, 850 F.2d 1217, 1222 (C.A.7 1988).
[1122] 670 F.Supp. 491 (S.D.N.Y. 1987).

6.3.3.4. Intent as a criterion for applying a preliminary regime

The main guidance for the courts in qualifying the preliminary agreement and defining its regime is the intent of the parties. Case law invokes the intent of the negotiating parties as a reason to refuse to apply a preliminary regime and to regard the parties' exchanges as non-binding negotiations. Courts refer to the parties' intent in order to distinguish between the ultimate agreement and preliminary agreement. Intent is also used as a guideline to delimit the enforceable content of a preliminary agreement.[1123] Though courts have relied on other indices as well, intent has been seen as the most important for contractually organized negotiations. As one court has put it, preliminary agreements are 'enforced only when parties manifestly so intended'.[1124] Or as formulated by another, '[t]he core theory of a cause of action for breach of contract to negotiate ... inevitably hinges on whether the parties intended to enter a binding contract to negotiate and whether they objectively manifested that intention'.[1125]

6.3.4. *Assessment of intent: factors*

To assess the intent of the parties, the US courts look at a set of factors. The Restatement (Second) of Contracts suggests that several circumstances 'may show that the agreements are preliminary negotiations' and entail no contractual obligations.[1126] These point primarily to the intent to be bound by the ultimate agreement, but the same circumstances are used to assess whether an intermediary regime applies.[1127] These circumstances are:[1128]

- the extent of agreement on the terms of the final agreement;
- the question as to whether the contract at hand is usually made in writing;
- the question as to whether a standard form is often used for this kind of contract;
- the complexity of the final contract ('few or many details' and whether the contract is 'common or unusual');
- the amount at stake;
- the question as to whether performance has already started during negotiations.

1123 *A/S Apothekernes Laboratorium for Specialpraeparater* v. *I.M.C. Chemical Group, Inc.*, 873 F.2d 155 (C.A.7 1989); *Butler* v. *Balolia* 736 F.3d 609, 618 (C.A.1 2013); *Empro Mfg. Co.* v. *Ball-Co Mfg., Inc.*, 870 F.2d 423 (C.A.7 1989); Ayes 2012, at 390.

1124 Klass 2009, at 1449. See also Jeffries 2012, at 20: 'Ultimately...whether or not a preliminary agreement will be enforceable comes down to a question of the intent of the parties'.

1125 *Butler* v. *Balolia* 736 F.3d 609, 616 (C.A.1 2013).

1126 Restatement (Second) of Contracts, §27: 'Manifestations of assent that are in themselves sufficient to conclude a contract will not be prevented from so operating by the fact that the parties also manifest an intention to prepare and adopt a written memorial thereof; but the circumstances may show that the agreements are preliminary negotiations'.

1127 *Teachers Ins. and Annuity Ass'n of America* v. *Tribune Co.*, 670 F.Supp. 491 (S.D.N.Y. 1987).

1128 Restatement (Second) of Contracts, §27 Comment c.

The Restatement notes furthermore that '[s]uch circumstances may be shown by oral testimony or by correspondence or other preliminary or partially complete writings'.[1129]

These guidelines are followed in the courts of most states. The most articulate sequence of reasoning based on the Restatement[1130] has been formulated by the New York courts. New York state law provides a four-factor test to assess the parties' intent. The following factors are assessed:[1131]

1) the language used by the parties;
2) the presence or absence of performance during negotiations (anticipatory performance);
3) the presence or absence of open issues that need to be agreed upon;
4) the question of whether the kind of contract is usually concluded in writing.

Next to this, consideration of the entire context of negotiations is sometimes added as the fifth factor. On the whole, none of these factors is decisive, 'but each provides significant guidance'.[1132]

The New York law factors test is also applied in other states, while states that do not follow any particular settled flow of reasoning interpret all the circumstances of negotiations. It has been noted in the literature that their reasoning essentially comes down to the circumstances as mentioned by the Restatement and New York law.[1133]

It is helpful to examine the application of each of the four factors in more detail in order to understand the reasons for the US court to find obligations in a letter of intent and for refusing to do so.

6.3.4.1. Language

The first factor within the New York law factors test is the language used by the parties in the preliminary document.

Assessment of language as such is underpinned by the theory of literal interpretation. That is, the meaning of the parties is attributed to the direct content of the words they use. The courts look primarily for indications of the parties' intent made in a clear

1129 Ibid. See also Section 6.3.5.3.

1130 Jeffries 2012, at 23 ff. analysing the assessment of intent in various jurisdictions. See earlier Klein/Bachechi 1994.

1131 Jeffries 2012, footnote 127. See also Farnsworth 2004, at 260 referring to a similar list used by the Supreme Judicial Court of Maine *Mississippi & Dominion S.S. Co.* v. *Swift*, 29 A. 1063 (Me. 1894); Kling/Nugent 2005 para 6.03; *Channel Home Centers, Div. of Grace Retail Corp.* v. *Grossman*, 795 F.2d 291 (C.A.3 1986).

1132 *R.G. Group, Inc.* v. *Horn & Hardart Co.*, 751 F.2d 69, 75 (C.A.2 1984).

1133 Jeffries 2012.

language. Clarity of language refers to the formulations having only one distinguishable meaning. By contrast, if the term or a sentence may have two or more meanings or if the reference content cannot be defined (is vague), these terms or sentences are regarded as ambiguous.[1134] In cases involving preliminary agreements, if the language is clear, the court can characterize it either as non-binding language or binding language.[1135] The court then draws conclusions as to the regime applicable to the document.

It is to be noted that classifying and interpreting case law regarding the parties' negotiations is complicated by the fact that ambiguous interpretation is often invoked in litigation. As noted by Burton, '[f]rom an advocacy standpoint, advancing an unlikely interpretation is not a bad strategy when the stakes are high; one wants to and might get to a jury; one is litigating the case anyhow on formation or remedies issues; as an obfuscating tactic; or when non-legal considerations might be weighty. But, from a more neutral standpoint, these are not reasonable interpretive disputes'.[1136]

The following formulations have been regarded by the courts as clearly non-binding language. As noted by Judge Posner, the words 'in principle' to characterize the terms of a preliminary agreement clearly signals the absence of any intent to be bound until the ultimate agreement is formed.[1137] In the same way, a preliminary document does not create any obligations if it states clearly that negotiations are not binding until the ultimate agreement is fully negotiated and formed or a final contract is made in a special form.[1138] Such a provision is often called in practice and literature a *'subject to contract'* clause. Literal interpretation of this provision has often been regarded as pointing to an absence of the parties' intent to be bound by the ultimate agreement. In the same way, references to the possibility that *negotiations might fail* and the *reference to the ultimate agreement* to be completed have suggested that the parties did not intend to be bound.[1139] The same consequence has resulted from a repeated emphasis on the *difference between the stage of negotiations* reflected in the preliminary agreement, on the one hand, and the *future contemplated transaction*.[1140] In *Rennick* v. *O.P.T.I.O.N. Care, Inc.*, the following formulations were regarded as 'unequivocal non-binding language': 'acknowledge *the respective intentions* ... directed toward the creation of a binding interim agreement and other contracts designed to implement various proposed relationships among the parties ... continue good faith discussions directed toward the creation of formal written

1134 Burton 2009, at 8.

1135 *Teachers Ins. and Annuity Ass'n of America* v. *Tribune Co.*, 670 F.Supp. 491, 499 (S.D.N.Y. 1987); *Arcadian Phosphates, Inc.* v. *Arcadian Corp.*, 884 F.2d 69 (C.A.2 1989); *Adjustrite Systems, Inc.* v. *GAB Business Services, Inc.*, 145 F.3d 543, 549 (C.A.2 1998); *Elvin Associates* v. *Franklin*, 735 F.Supp. 1177 (S.D.N.Y. 1990).

1136 Burton 2009, at 12.

1137 *Venture Associates Corp.* v. *Zenith Data Systems Corp.*, 96 F.3d 275, [2] (C.A.7 1996), referring to respective case law.

1138 *Teachers Ins. and Annuity Ass'n of America* v. *Tribune Co.*, 670 F.Supp. 491, 499 (S.D.N.Y. 1987); Jeffries 2012, at 26.

1139 *Arcadian Phosphates, Inc.* v. *Arcadian Corp.*, 884 F.2d 69, 72 (C.A.2 1989).

1140 *Barnes & Robinson Co., Inc.* v. *OneSource Facility Services, Inc.*, 195 S.W.3d 637, 642 (Tenn. App. 2006).

contracts that, upon approval by the board of Directors of each party, will be executed ... with the understanding that this letter of intent is of no binding effect on any party hereto'.[1141] Furthermore, in some cases the negotiators may split preliminary documents, pointing to which terms are binding, and which ones are not. This has guided courts in determining the extent to which the parties have actually intended to be bound.[1142]

The main consequence flowing from relying on clear non-binding language is the qualification of the parties' relations as aleatory negotiations. Each party may resume these without contractual liability.[1143] According to the Restatement (Second) of Contracts: '[I]t is quite plain that if either of the parties manifests its intent not to be bound until a written contract is executed then the parties are not bound until that event occurs'.[1144]

In the absence of any clear statement as to the non-binding nature of the preliminary agreement, courts have often found an intent to form the ultimate agreement. This is the case especially if the preliminary agreement does not (or does not only) frame negotiations, but also sets the terms of the ultimate agreement or enables their construction by the court.[1145]

In addition to this literal interpretation of language, another approach has been also taken by the courts. When interpreting the language, the context of negotiations is also taken into account. The approach where interpretation of the language used is not confined to its literal meaning is underpinned by the objective theory of interpretation. As was formulated in *V'Soske* v. *Barwick*: 'Two rules on this subject are well established: First, if the parties intend not to be bound until they have executed a formal document embodying their agreement, they will not be bound until then; and second, the mere fact that the parties contemplate memorializing their agreement in a formal document does not prevent their informal agreement from taking effect prior to that event'.[1146] In some

1141 77 F.3d 309 77 F.3d 309, 317 and 312 (C.A.9 1996).

1142 *Venture Associates Corp.* v. *Zenith Data Systems Corp.*, 96 F.3d 275 (C.A.7 1996).

1143 *Principal Life Ins. Co.* v. *Revalen Development, LLC.*, 358 S.W.3d 451 (Tex.App. 2012); *Columbia Pictures Corp.* v. *De Toth*, 161 P.2d 217 (Cal. 1945); *Universal Products Co.* v. *Emerson*, 179 A. 387 (Del. 1935); *Rork* v. *Las Olas Co.*, 23 So. 2d 839 (Fla. 1945); *General Realty Corp. v. Douglas Lowell, Inc.*, 354 P.2d 306 (Or. 1960); *Nolan* v. *J. & M. Doyle Co.*, 13 A.2d 59 (Pa. 1940); *Bowling* v. *Palmetto State Life Ins. Co.*, 99 S.E.2d 407 (S.C. 1957); *Rosebud Oil & Cotton Co.* v. *Merchants' & Planters' Oil Co.*, 248 S.W. 116 (Tex. Civ. App. 1922); *Atlantic Coast Realty Co.* v. *Robertson's Ex'r*, 116 S.E. 476 (Va. 1923); *Building Service Employees Intern. Union, Lodge No. 6* v. *Seattle Hosp. Council*, 138 P.2d 891 (Wash. 1943); *Brunette* v. *Vulcan Materials Co.*, 256 N.E.2d 44 (Ill.App. 1970); *Terracom Development Group* v. *Coleman Cable and Wire Co.*, 365 N.E.2d 1028 (Ill.App. 1977).

1144 Restatement (Second) of Contracts, §27 Comment b.

1145 See for a recent example, *Bed Bath & Beyond Inc.* v. *IBEX Const. LLC*, 860 N.Y.S.2d 107 (N.Y.A.D. 2008). Farnsworth calls these agreeemnts 'stop-gap agreement' whereby parties in fact have the entire ultimate agreement with no more terms left for negotiation, but anticipate that the ultimate agreement will be made later. Farnsworth contends that these agreements are subject to the regime of the ultimate agreement. See Farnsworth 1987, at 251.

1146 404 F.2d 495, 499 (C.A.2 1968).

cases, the court has found that the parties had initially expressly reserved the formation of contract (qualifying their exchanges as aleatory negotiations), but thereafter had *waived* this reservation, also in clear language.[1147]

Furthermore, courts may find that parties had intended to establish the ultimate agreement, but regarded this as a mere formality. In this case, the courts have often searched for the ultimate agreement in the parties' relations.[1148] For instance, the court may find that parties have entered into a binding final contract simply by way of oral exchange before they signed any preliminary document (unless the statute of frauds establishes the written form as a requirement of validity of a particular type of contract).[1149]

6.3.4.2. Anticipated performance

Another factor addressed by the courts is the question of whether *any performance has been started* in anticipation of the future contract. This kind of performance, often partial performance, is defined as conferring 'something of value' on the other party which that other party accepts.[1150] For the courts, an accepted partial performance is an indication of the parties' will to be immediately bound either by some obligations or by the entire ultimate agreement. This is regarded as 'an unmistakable signal that one party believes there is a contract; and the party who accepts performance signals, by that act, that it also understands a contract to be in effect'.[1151]

At the same time, the courts distinguish between a merely preparatory performance and the actual start of performance of the final contract. Actions that merely prepare for the future eventual contract do not point towards a binding commitment.[1152] By contrast, if both parties act as if the future contract was concluded (or in accordance with the terms of the future agreement as outlined in the preliminary agreement), this is an argument for holding that the ultimate agreement is formed. For example, in *V'Soske* v. *Barwick*,[1153] the parties negotiated the sale of a business and exchanged letters relating to the future

1147 *Southern Colorado MRI, Ltd.* v. *Med-Alliance, Inc.*, 166 F.3d 1094 (C.A.10 1999) (parties first signed a letter of intent and thereafter exchanged offer and acceptance); *Lamle* v. *Mattel, Inc.*, 394 F.3d 1355, 1360 (Fed. Cir. 2005).

1148 *Teachers Ins. and Annuity Ass'n of America* v. *Tribune Co.*, 670 F.Supp. 491, 500 (S.D.N.Y. 1987); *V'Soske* v. *Barwick*, 404 F.2d 495 (C.A.2 1968); *Gorodensky* v. *Mitsubishi Pulp Sales (MC), Inc.*, 92 F. Supp. 2d 249 (S.D.N.Y. 2000).

1149 The Statue of Frauds establishes that writing is a formal requirement of validity of certain types of contracts. The court will not inquire further into the existence of any agreement, in the absence of writing to indicate that a contract has been made. The Statute of Frauds is the translation into US law (at the level of states) of the English Statute of Frauds 1677 with certain modifications.The rule covers domestic (US) sale of goods between merchants.

1150 *Spencer Trask Software and Information Services LLC* v. *RPost Intern. Ltd.*, 383 F. Supp. 2d 428, 443 (S.D.N.Y. 2003).

1151 *R.G. Group, Inc.* v. *Horn & Hardart Co.*, 751 F.2d 69, 75–76 (C.A.2 1984).

1152 *Blanton Enterprises, Inc.* v. *Burger King Corp.*, 680 F.Supp. 753,773 (D.C.S.C. 1988).

1153 *V'Soske* v. *Barwick*, 404 F.2d 495 (C.A.2 1968).

contract. Their exchange mentioned the date from which the business would be run on the potential buyer's account. Following the exchange of this letter of intent, all transactions outside of the ordinary course of business were made only with the potential buyer's approval. For the court, this was a strong indication that the ultimate, rather than a preliminary, agreement was formed.[1154]

However, a request to start works does not necessarily point to the existence of the final contract. A statement that the work is to be reimbursed if the parties do not form the final agreement is an indication that the parties have no intent to be bound by the ultimate agreement at this stage of negotiations. They are only bound by this obligation to reimburse the cost of works started. This was the reasoning in *Citadel Group Ltd.* v. *Washington Regional Medical Center* (federal court applying Illinois law). The parties negotiated for the development and construction of a building. One party had included in a preliminary document an 'authorization to proceed' with the execution of the future eventual contract. However, the authorization clearly regarded the work as preliminary, because it detailed the work's reimbursement '*whether or not the project is ultimately developed*'.[1155]

6.3.4.3. Open issues

The third factor the courts take into account is the *number of terms in a preliminary agreement that the parties leave open* for further negotiations. Generally, the less definitive and elaborate the conditions of the ultimate agreement, the lower the probability that the court will find the final contract in the precontractual exchange.[1156] At the same time, not all terms left open are equally relevant. The courts look primarily for an agreement on the 'usual' or 'important economic terms' of a particular type of contract.[1157] To establish these, trade usages and customs of a particular sector of trade are taken into account.

However, the fact that terms are left open is not decisive. In some cases, courts have found that the final contract has been formed on the basis of other factors and thereafter has implied the missing terms in construing the ultimate agreement. This has happened primarily in disputes involving relatively simple and common types of contracts, for example, loan agreements.[1158] By contrast, the higher the *complexity and importance of the negotiated deal*, the more reluctant the courts are to find the final binding contract in the preliminary exchanges.[1159] For example in *Songbird Jet Ltd., Inc.* v. *Amax Inc.*, the

[1154] 404 F.2d 495, 500 (C.A.2 1968).

[1155] 692 F.3d 580, 584 (C.A.7 2012).

[1156] *Delicatessen* v. *Schumacher*, 436 N.Y.S.2d 247 (N.Y. 1981).

[1157] *Teachers Ins. and Annuity Ass'n of America* v. *Tribune Co.*, 670 F.Supp. 491, 501 (S.D.N.Y. 1987).

[1158] Ibid; Farnsworth 1987, at 260.

[1159] Farnsworth 1987, at 260–261; *Teachers Ins. and Annuity Ass'n of America* v. *Tribune Co.*, 670 F.Supp. 491, 501–503 (S.D.N.Y. 1987); *Winston* v. *Mediafare Entertainment Corp.*, 777 F.2d 78 (C.A.2 1985); *Skycom Corp.* v. *Telstar Corp.*, 813 F.2d 810 (C.A.7 1987); *Reprosystem, B.V.* v. *SCM Corp.*, 727 F.2d 257 (C.A.2 1984).

judge characterized a purchase of a jet as follows. It was 'no run-of-the-mill, over-the-counter transaction where terms and conditions of a sales contract are fairly well established and, in effect, are recognized as a custom of the trade. It was a structured, multi-faceted deal of magnitude'.[1160] The complexity of the deal was the main reason against accepting that the parties had entered into the final oral agreement.

6.3.4.4. Writing usually used

New York courts also take into account *whether a given type of contract is usually made in writing*. If the final contract contemplated in a preliminary agreement is *usually* concluded in written form, the courts are more willing to find that no intent to be bound by the ultimate agreement is in place. This weighs against the conclusion that the ultimate agreement is formed. It has been generally accepted under New York law that transactions in the business world are usually made in writing and this is especially the case for complex deals.[1161] Furthermore, under New York law, the written form is regarded as customary for complex transactions and transactions involving a large sum.[1162]

6.3.4.5. Entire context of negotiations

Next to these four factors, *the entire context of negotiations* is sometimes also taken into account as the fifth factor. The assessment of the context of negotiations includes analysis of the facts, the parties' conduct and statements.[1163]

In contrast with the states following the Restatements and the New York law factors test, some US states do not apply this, but address 'all of the circumstances surrounding the negotiations, including the actions of the principals both during and after, to determine what the parties intended'.[1164] The courts '... look at the circumstances surrounding the negotiations and the actions of the principals at the time and subsequently. From all of these, the intention of the parties to be bound or not to be bound must be ascertained'.[1165]

The factors test developed in New York law has been criticized in the literature for providing little normative guidance, leading to too wide a discretion for the court and

1160 605 F. Supp. 1097, 1102 (S.D.N.Y. 1985).

1161 *International Telemeter Corp.* v. *Teleprompter Corp.*, 592 F.2d 49 (C.A.2 1979), Friendly, Circuit Judge, concurring.

1162 *Reprosystem, B.V.* v. *SCM Corp.*, 727 F.2d 257, 263 (C.A.2 1984); *Adjustrite Systems, Inc.* v. *GAB Business Services, Inc.*, 145 F.3d 543, 551 (C.A.2 1998).

1163 *Teachers Ins. and Annuity Ass'n of America* v. *Tribune Co.*, 670 F.Supp. 491, 500–501 (S.D.N.Y. 1987); Jeffries 2012, at 32–33.

1164 *Weigel Broadcasting Co.* v. *TV-49, Inc.*, 466 F.Supp.2d 1011 (N.D. Ill. 2006). For states not applying the four factors test, see for example District of Columbia: *Steven R. Perles, P.C.* v. *Kagy*, 473 F.3d 1244, 1251–1252 (D.C. Cir. 2007); Iowa: *Schaller Telephone Co.* v. *Golden Sky Systems, Inc.*, 298 F.3d 736, 744 (C.A.8 2002); Illinois: *Feldman* v. *Allegheny Intern., Inc.*, 850 F.2d 1217, 1222–1223 (C.A.7 1988).

1165 *Itek Corp.* v. *Chicago Aerial Indus., Inc.*, 248 A.2d 625, 629 (Del. 1968).

unpredictable results.[1166] Schwarz and Schott have also pointed to inconsistency in the application of the test by the courts. According to these scholars, the 'baseline for finding an actionable commitment is independent of many of the factors that have been made doctrinally salient, such as the number of open terms and the extent of part performance'.[1167]

Case law has also not always been positive regarding the application of the factors. Discussing the application of the factors test in *Texaco, Inc.* v. *Pennzoil, Co.*,[1168] the judge noted in *Garnes* v. *Fleming Landfill, Inc.* that the court had stated the law, namely the factors test, and had thereafter 'perversely fit into that principle a set of facts to which the principle obviously does not apply… The court then finds that the parties did intend to be bound by the preliminary agreement despite: (1) press releases which stated that "the transaction is subject to execution of a definitive merger agreement;" (2) wording in the preliminary agreement which stated that the parties' obligations would become binding only "after the execution and delivery of this agreement;" and, (3) references in press releases to the preliminary agreement as an "agreement in principle."'[1169] Therefore, the assessment of the factors discussed above serves mainly as guidance for the court, whereas the decisions remain highly fact specific. As a consequence, it is not always easily predictable.[1170]

6.3.5. *The most relevant issues of interpretation*

It is worth noting that the assessment of the parties' intent at the moment they form a contract is primarily an issue of interpretation.[1171] This calls for some precision regarding interpretation of contract terms by the US courts.

6.3.5.1. Subjective and objective intent

US law relies on the objective theory of contract formation. This means that only an objectively assessed manifestation of intent counts in law. The primary relevance of objective intent falls more generally into the objective theory of contract formation adopted by US law. As formulated by Holmes, 'the making of a contract depends … on the agreement of two sets of external signs, – not on the parties having *meant* the same thing but on their having *said* the same thing'.[1172]

1166 Schwarz/Scott 2007, at 675–676 with references to case law.

1167 Ibid.

1168 729 S.W.2d 768 (Tex. App. 1987).

1169 *Garnes* v. *Fleming Landfill, Inc.*, 413 S.E.2d 897, 906 (W. Va. 1991).

1170 Kling/Nugent 2005, para 6.03[1]; Lake/Draetta 1994, at 135 ff. with further references.

1171 Burton 2008, at 2.

1172 Holmes 1897, at 464. See also inter alia *Empro Mfg. Co.* v. *Ball-Co Mfg., Inc.*, 870 F.2d 423 (C.A.7 1989); *Citadel Group Ltd.* v. *Washington Regional Medical Center*, 692 F.3d 580, 588 (C.A.7 2012): the intent to be bound is 'measured objectively, by the parties' words and conduct,' but not by the parties' stated

The antagonism between subjective and objective intent has been the subject of debate between two prominent US scholars and drafters of Restatements of the law of contract. Williston has argued in favour of the search for objective intent in contract law. Another prominent US scholar, Corbin, has suggested that the complex role of subjective intent should not be disregarded.

The Restatements of Contract carry the imprint of both scholars' work,[1173] and the assessment of the parties' intent echoes both theories. In particular, the emphasis on the literal meaning of the terms and formulations used in a preliminary agreement follows from the relevance of the subjective theory. At the same time, modern US courts are not limited to the literal meaning of the parties' formulation in the interpretation of the parties' intent. When the court examines the entire document, the objective circumstances, and other contexts, the objective theory of contract formation is applied.[1174]

This theoretical background is useful for characterizing lines of cases that may seem irreconcilable at first sight. More specifically, one line of cases attaches greater importance to the literal interpretation of the parties' documents. Within this line of cases, language is referred to as the most important criterion to determine the parties' intent. There is a high probability that clear and unambiguous non-binding language will be upheld as pointing to the absence any intent to form the ultimate agreement. Clear and unambiguous statements that some obligations bind parties immediately from the start of negotiations would also be upheld. The other line of cases is underpinned by the objective assessment of the parties' intent. Within this line of cases, courts adopt a more holistic approach. Circumstances other than simply the parties' statements (even if clear and unambiguous at first sight) are taken into account. This approach can lead the courts to disregard the formulations of preliminary agreements, for example, disregarding the so-called 'subject to contract' clauses, as noted earlier.[1175]

6.3.5.2. Questions of fact and questions of law

The assessment of the parties' intent is usually regarded as a question of fact.[1176] Questions of fact are decided by the jury, unless the parties voluntarily submit the questions of fact

subjective intent as to the meaning of the document. *Block* v. *Magura*, 949 N.E.2d 1261 (Ind. Ct. App. 2011); *Keystone Land & Development* v. *Xerox Corp.*, 94 P.3d 945, 949 (Wash. 2004).

1173 Ayres 2012, at 176; Calamari/Perillo 2009, at 23.

1174 Burton 2008, at 9.

1175 See Section 6.3.4.

1176 *Keystone Land & Development* v. *Xerox Corp.*, 94 P.3d 945 (Wash. 2004); *Sea-Van Invs. Assocs.* v. *Hamilton*, 881 P.2d 1035 (Wash. 1994); *Video Central, Inc.* v. *Data Translation, Inc.*, 925 F. Supp. 867 (D. Mass. 1996) (whether a letter of intent was binding is a question for the jury); *Arnold Palmer Golf Co.* v. *Fuqua Industries, Inc.*, 541 F.2d 584 (C.A.6 1976) (whether parties were bound by a preliminary agreement found to be a genuine issue of fact); *I.M.A., Inc.* v. *Rocky Mountain Airways, Inc.*, 713 P.2d 882 (Colo. 1986) (whether a letter of intent on acquisition of an air taxi service represented a formed contract).

to the competence of the court.[1177] The jury is, therefore, often involved in resolving disputes on negotiations of a contract. However, the question of intent may also be resolved as a matter of law. This is possible in situations 'where reasonable minds could reach but one conclusion'.[1178] The case is then decided by the court.

US scholars have noted that the distinction between questions of law and fact within the assessment of contract formation is not straightforward.[1179] It involves two interrelated issues – assessment of the meaning of language and the interpretation of writing. Assessment of the meaning is a question of fact, whereas the interpretation of writing is a question of law[1180] and the line between the two is not always obvious. Jeffries has recently suggested that the question should be treated as a matter of law in each case where the language of the preliminary document is clear and unambiguous and this factor can be regarded as conclusive.[1181]

6.3.5.3. Parol evidence rule

Another peculiarity of the US law is the inapplicability of the parol evidence rule to preliminary agreements.

The parol evidence rule is a substantive rule of US contract law.[1182] The rule prescribes giving preference to written statements above oral ones. It is applicable in particular to attempts to 'influence legal effect of a written document by offering extrinsic evidence to supplement… or interpret its stated terms'.[1183]

Whereas the rule applies to the fully formed ultimate agreement,[1184] it 'does not apply to the question of the enforceability of "binding preliminary commitments"'.[1185] To assess this, the court needs extrinsic evidence, as has been noted in several cases.[1186] In this way, when assessing intent, the parties' agreements and conduct prior to the drafting of a preliminary agreement and also the terms of the document are taken into consideration. Intent is analysed on the basis of all the facts at hand.

1177 See Section 6.2.2 on the role of jury.

1178 See *Keystone Land & Development* v. *Xerox Corp.*, 94 P.3d 945 (Wash. 2004); *Van Invs. Assocs.* v. *Hamilton*, 125 Wash.2d 120, 126, 881 P.2d 1035 (1994); *Ruff* v. *King County*, 887 P.2d 886 (Wash. 1995).

1179 Jeffries 2012, at 51.

1180 Calamari/Perillo 2009, at 141.

1181 Jeffries 2012, at 51.

1182 Rohwer/Skrocki 2010, at 229.

1183 Ibid. See also Restatement (Second) of Contracts, §209–218; UCC §2–202.

1184 *Mastrangelo* v. *Kidder, Peabody & Co., Inc*, 722 F. Supp. 1126 (S.D.N.Y. 1989).

1185 *Pan Am Corp.* v. *Delta Air Lines, Inc.* 175 B.R. 438, [22]-[24] (S.D.N.Y. 1994); *Teachers Ins. and Annuity Ass'n of America* v. *Tribune Co.*, 670 F.Supp. 491, 498–502 (S.D.N.Y. 1987); *Four Seasons Hotels Ltd.* v. *Vinnik*, 127 A.D.2d 310 (N.Y.A.D. 1987).

1186 See for example, *Evergreen Investments, LLC* v. *FCL Graphics, Inc.*, 334 F.3d 750 (C.A.8 2003) (extrinsic evidence needed to assess a letter of intent about acquisition of assets).

6.4. Non-contractual doctrines mandatorily applicable to negotiations

Under US law, it is not only contract law that is relevant to the period of negotiations. The link between contract law and extra-contractual doctrines is established by the Restatement (Second) of Contracts. It states: 'moreover, remedies for bad faith in the absence of agreement are found in the law of torts or restitution'.[1187] Modern textbooks mention these doctrines as part of the concept of precontractual liability,[1188] a term that has long been unusual for US law. This Section will address the relevant extra-contractual doctrines.

6.4.1. *Promissory estoppel: protection of precontractual reliance*

Under the US doctrine of *promissory estoppel*, a party may be held liable for breaking a promise made during negotiations if the other party has detrimentally relied on this promise.[1189] The US courts have developed promissory estoppel as a *separate cause of action in equity*[1190] based on the English doctrine of estoppel. To prevent injustice, a remedy in equity has been granted because no adequate or sufficient recovery was possible under the common law or statutes.

Promissory estoppel forms part of the mandatory extra-contractual rules applicable to all negotiations.[1191] However, remedies on this basis are not often granted, mainly because of the high threshold to overcome in order to establish the kind of reliance required to qualify for recovery.

In the precontractual context, recovery under the doctrine of promissory estoppel was first granted in the landmark case of *Hoffman* v. *Red Owl Stores Inc.*[1192] Hoffman was running a bakery. He entered into negotiations with Red Owl Stores in order to obtain a franchise to run one of the stores. Red Owl assured Hoffman that an investment of 18000 dollars was sufficient to become a franchisee. Red Owl encouraged Hoffman to sell his bakery and to gain more experience in the grocery business in the location where Red Owl's potential store would be. Hoffman did so and moved to the location. Subsequently, Red Owl declared that it would require a substantially higher investment from Hoffman in order for him to become its franchisee. As Hoffman could not afford this investment, negotiations broke down and no franchising contract was concluded. The Supreme Court of Wisconsin balanced the parties' arguments and decided that equity required

1187 Restatement (Second) of Contracts, §205 Comment c.

1188 See for example Ayres 2012, at 369 ff.

1189 Restatement (Second) of Contracts, §90 Comment a: 'Estoppel prevents a person from showing the truth contrary to a representation of fact made by him after another has relied on the representation'.

1190 See Section 6.2.3.3 on equity in the US law.

1191 On the relevance of promissory estoppel to the formation of contract see Katz 1996 (law and economic analysis of *Hoffman* v. *Red Owl Stores, Inc.*, 133 N.W.2d 267 (Wis. 1965) subscribing to the debate about what interests should be protected at the precontractual stage and the way these should be protected; Duhl 2003; Farnsworth 1987 and Farnsworth 2004, at 196.

1192 133 N.W.2d 267 (Wis. 1965).

that Hoffman was entitled to recovery based on Red Owl's precontractual encouragements. The means for recovery was the doctrine of promissory estoppel. The Restatement (Second) of Contracts has taken this development into account. It states:[1193]

> §90 Promise Reasonably Inducing Action or Forbearance
> (1) A promise which the promisor should reasonably expect to induce action or forbearance on the part of the promisee or a third person and which does induce such action or forbearance is binding if injustice can be avoided only by enforcement of the promise. The remedy granted for breach may be limited as justice requires.

Four elements should be in place for the doctrine of promissory estoppel to apply. There should be (1) a promise; (2) reliance on the promise; (3) damage caused by the reliance; and (4) the fact that the promise is not enforced should lead to injustice.[1194]

The *promise* should be clear, unambiguous,[1195] and sufficient to induce reliance by the other party. For instance, a simple statement of opinion is not sufficient.[1196] There should be something more. However, the promise can be less than an offer: 'the promise necessary to sustain a cause of action for promissory estoppel'... may not 'embrace all essential details of a proposed transaction... so as to be the equivalent of an offer'.[1197] Within the context of a preliminary agreement, the primary criterion to establish the promise is the clarity of language of the 'promises and assurances' made in a preliminary agreement.[1198] Generally, the questions as to whether the promise suffices to induce reliance and whether it has effectively induced such reliance are questions of fact (to be decided by the jury).

The *reliance* should be reasonable, foreseeable and detrimental.[1199] To define reasonable reliance, case law makes reference to tort law. Reasonable reliance is namely understood as a 'justifiable' reliance when a party is 'not reckless, in other words not willfully embracing a substantial risk'.[1200] For example, in *Barnes & Robinson Co., Inc.* v. *OneSource Facility Services, Inc.* it was stated that: '[n]o injustice results in refusal to enforce a gratuitous promise where the... promisee's action in reliance was unreasonable or unjustified by the promise'.[1201]

1193 Restatement (Second) of Contracts, §90 Comment d.

1194 *De Pace* v. *Matsushita Elec. Corp. of America*, 257 F. Supp. 2d 543 (E.D.N.Y. 2003).

1195 *Cohen & Co., CPAs* v. *Messina, CPA*, 492 N.E.2d 867 (Ohio App. 1985).

1196 Williston 2014, §8:7.

1197 *Hoffman* v. *Red Owl Stores, Inc.*, 133 N.W.2d 267, 274 (Wis. 1965).

1198 *Corbit* v. *J. I. Case Co*, 424 P.2d 290 [15] (Wash. 1967) refers to an 'action or forbearance of a definite and substantial character' based on language of a 'memorandum of agreement'.

1199 *Hoffman* v. *Red Owl Stores, Inc.*, 133 N.W.2d 267 (Wis. 1965); *Quake Construction, Inc.* v. *American Airlines, Inc.*, 565 N.E.2d 990, 1005 (Ill. 1990); *Bethany Pharmacal Co.* v. *QVC, Inc.*, 241 F.3d 854 (C.A.7 2001); *Colosi* v. *Electri-Flex Co.*, 965 F.2d 500 (C.A.7 1992). See also Restatement (Second) of Contracts, §90 Comment b; Farnsworth 2004, at 176.

1200 *BPI Energy Holdings, Inc.* v. *IEC (Montgomery), LLC* 664 F.3d 131 C.A.7 (Ill.), 2011 referring to Restatement (Second) of Torts, §537(b).

1201 195 S.W.3d 637, 644 (Tenn. App. 2006).

Lack of such reliance is often established if the parties expressly state in a precontractual document that this is not binding. In *Rennick* v. *O.P.T.I.O.N. Care, Inc.*, the court held that '[i]n light of the unequivocal non-binding language in the letter of intent, reliance on the existence of a contract was unreasonable as a matter of law'.[1202]

Furthermore, *damage* should be caused by the reliance, and a causal link between the promise and damage must be demonstrated. As has been noted in *Hoffman* v. *Red Owl Stores Inc.*, 'the wrong is not primarily in depriving the plaintiff of the promised reward but in causing the plaintiff to change position to his detriment'.[1203]

Finally, the fact that the promise is not honoured should cause *injustice*. This is the specificity of the cause of action in equity where the main aim is to remedy injustice. At the same time, in *Hoffman* v. *Red Owl Stores Inc.*, the court warned against the application of promissory estoppel as a 'mechanical or rule of thumb'. The doctrine is applicable to precontractual misconduct and remedies are granted *only if and insofar* as this is necessary to prevent *injustice*.[1204] The assessment of injustice is left to the discretion of the court.

The court in *Hoffman* v. *Red Owl Stores Inc.* also discussed the scope of promissory estoppel *ratio personae*. The right to claim is in principle limited to the promisee, whereas third parties are not entitled to claim against the promissor. An exception applies in a situation where the promissor actually foresees, or has reason to foresee, reliance by a third person on the promise, so that the claim may be established by the third party.[1205]

Whereas these examples illustrate the application of promissory estoppel to the precontractual period, this application is rather exceptional in modern US law. As a matter of fact, the history of the precedent created by *Hoffman* v. *Red Owl Stores Inc.* has shown the US courts to be highly reluctant to grant remedies in disputes involving precontractual negotiations. Despite the fact that *Hoffman* v. *Red Owl Stores Inc.* was welcomed by US legal scholars in the 1980s as a useful sanction for precontractual misconduct and a tool to ensure legal certainty,[1206] the courts maintained a high threshold for the requirements for reliance protected by promissory estoppel.[1207] Modern US scholars writing on the precontractual period still debate the need to protect

1202 77 F.3d 309, 644–645 (C.A.9 1996).

1203 133 N.W.2d 267, 277 (Wis. 1965).

1204 133 N.W.2d 267, 275–277 (Wis. 1965).

1205 Ibid (negotiations have been conducted by a husband and the question was as to the rights of his wife). See also Restatement (Second) of Contracts, §90 Comment c: 'Enforcement of the promise in such cases rests on the same basis and depends on the same factors as in cases of reliance by the promissee. Justifiable reliance by third persons who are not beneficiaries is less likely, but may sometimes reinforce the claim of the promise or beneficiary'.

1206 Farsnworth 1987, at 236–237.

1207 See *Owasso Development Co.* v. *Associated Wholesale Grocers, Inc.*, 873 P.2d 212 (Kan. App. 1994); *Prenger* v. *Baumhoer*, 939 S.W.2d 23 (Mo. App. W. Dist. 1997); *Pertzsch Design, Inc.* v. *Gundersen Lutheran Health System, Inc.*, 647 F. Supp. 2d 1064 (W.D. Wis. 2009).

precontractual reliance, as well as the appropriate extent of the protection. One opinion in the scholarship suggests that the way courts actually protect precontractual reliance comes under the umbrella of a precontractual duty of good faith.[1208] Another opinion has been advanced by Schwarz and Scott based on an analysis of the courts' motivation for allowing recovery where negotiations have broken down. Schwarz and Scott argue that no extension of the duty of good faith to the precontractual period is needed if precontractual reliance is protected by promissory estoppel. Ayres et al come to the same conclusions.[1209]

At the same time, as noted by English scholar Furmston, 'the main difficulty in using reliance as the protecting principle in this context is establishing that the reliance actually occurred'.[1210] This difficulty appears to be the main reason for the courts' reluctance to follow *Hoffman* v. *Red Owl Stores Inc.* For instance, in *BPI Energy Holdings, Inc.* v. *IEC (Montgomery), LLC* reliance on a 'letter of intent' was regarded as 'reckless' and therefore remained at the risk of the relying party.[1211] In *Barnes & Robinson Co., Inc.* v. *OneSource Facility Services, Inc.*, reliance was regarded as unreasonable or unjustified by the promise;[1212] in *FutureFuel Chemical Co.* v. *Lonza, Inc.*, the promise made in a letter of intent was not sufficiently firm to induce the reliance required to sustain a claim in promissory estoppel;[1213] in *St. Joseph Hosp., Augusta, Georgia, Inc.* v. *Health Management Associates, Inc.* no reliance could be established because the party used a 'Pre-Closing Checklist' which indicated that the Asset Sale Agreement still needed to be executed and delivered.[1214] In *Andersen Investments, LLC* v. *Factory Card Outlet of America, Ltd* no reliance was found because the language of the letter of intent was 'decidedly conditional'.[1215]

More generally, the precedent in *Hoffman* v. *Red Owl Stores Inc.* and the US doctrine of promissory estoppel subscribes to the wider debate about the borderline between contract and tort in US scholarship, namely relating to the interests which the fields of contract and tort law should protect during the process of contract formation. The US promissory estoppel solution is much like tort, because it protects objectively assessed reliance, paying little attention to the contractual arrangements between the parties. The protection is in fact granted independently of the parties' acts or preliminary documents. However, the sanctions are formulated as contractual, protecting promises – the obligations parties undertake voluntarily. The development of the law in *Hoffman* v. *Red*

1208 Farnsworth 1987, at 269. Farnsworth finds the term 'fair dealing' more appropriate.
1209 Ayres 2012, at 346.
1210 Furmston 2010, at 56.
1211 664 F.3d 131 (C.A.7 2011) (under Illinois law, the language of letter of intent and subsequent memorandum of understanding pointed to the absence of binding commitments until due diligence was conducted and a formal final contract made. In this context, all the actions of the claimant were considered as 'reckless reliance').
1212 195 S.W.3d 637 (Tenn. App. 2006).
1213 756 F.3d 641 (C.A.8 2014).
1214 705 F.3d 1289, 1297 (C.A.11 2013).
1215 630 F.Supp.2d 1030, 1043 (S.D. Iowa 2009).

Owl Stores Inc. has been echoed by the US 'contract as tort' scholarship, namely Gilmore who is perhaps its most prominent scholar. These scholars have argued that contract has been merged with tort.[1216] However, this scholarship was already in decline in the 1990s.[1217] Time has indeed shown that the precedent in *Hoffman* v. *Red Owl Stores Inc.* has been applied rather exceptionally.

6.4.2. *Tort law*

Some decades ago, the US academic literature acknowledged the concept of precontractual liability, but with a reservation that no such overarching concept can be found in US law. Modern treatises include a separate part on precontractual liability.[1218] This includes not only the distinction addressed earlier between the preliminary regimes and ultimate agreement and promissory estoppel. Under the umbrella of precontractual liability, the literature also addresses specific rules in tort law that apply to (mis)conduct in the course of negotiations.

6.4.2.1. Misrepresentation of intent to reach agreement

Under US law, fraudulently misrepresenting the intent to reach agreement is an actionable tort. This gives rise namely to the common law action of deceit, one of the specific torts involving misrepresentation.[1219] According to the Restatement (Second) of Torts, '[a]] representation of the maker's own intention to do or not to do a particular thing is fraudulent if he does not have that intention'.[1220] The first type of conduct that is regarded as fraudulent misrepresentation is 'entering into negotiations without serious intent to reach agreement'.[1221]The second is continuing negotiations after having lost intent to enter into a contract (for example, after having concluded a contract with another party).[1222] The tort of deceit is referred to in the literature as a part of the concept of 'precontractual liability'. Generally, the tort of deceit is 'colored to a considerable extent by the ethics of bargaining between distrustful adversaries', because[1223] most of the torts involving misrepresentation – the legal term for the 'method of accomplishing various types of tortious conduct'[1224] – have been developed in case law related to bargaining in

1216 Gilmore 1974.
1217 See with further references and scholarly debate in Yorio/Thel 1991.
1218 See inter alia Ayres 2012.
1219 Prosser 1971, at 864.
1220 Restatement (Second) of Torts, §530(1). The draft of the Restatement (Third) of Torts establishes: 'A statement of a speaker's intention to perform a promise is a fraudulent misrepresentation if the intention does not exist at the time the statement is made'. (Tentative Draft No. 2 (April 7, 2014) of Restatement (Third) of Torts, §15 Promissory Fraud).
1221 Farnsworth 2004, at 195; *Markov* v. *ABC Transfer & Storage Co.* 457 P.2d 535 (Wash. 1969).
1222 According to Farnsworth any misrepresentation made in negotiations that has led negotiations to fail may also be actionable in tort on the same grounds.
1223 Keeton 1984, at 726.
1224 Prosser 1971, at 683.

transactions.[1225] Moreover, the previous use of this doctrine was in remedying cases that are now regarded as breach of contractual warranties and regulated in contract law.[1226]

Despite its relevance to contract formation, the tort of deceit has given rise to little case law involving preliminary agreements and failed negotiations.[1227] One of the main reasons for this is the difficulty of establishing fraudulent intent. Fraudulent intent is 'the basis of deceit'[1228] and one of the elements of the tort's cause of action in deceit. Fraudulent intent covers the aim to 'convey false impression',[1229] without belief in its truth or a party being reckless as to its truth.[1230] This is an *intent to induce* the other party 'to act or to refrain from action in reliance upon' the representation (thus, the intent to enter into a contract should be aimed at reaching some result, as the literature invokes, for example, to refrain from negotiations with a competitor). Deceit is an intentional tort, and therefore simple negligence does not amount to fraudulent intent.[1231]

Alongside intent, other elements of an action in the tort of deceit are a false *representation* made by one of the parties (in the precontractual context – false intent to enter in contract); the *knowledge* or *belief* of the party making the representation that the representation is false.[1232] Furthermore, there should be *reliance* upon the representation, *resulting in damage*.[1233] The reliance must play a substantial role in the conduct of the party, namely the relying party would not have acted in the same way, absent the misrepresentation. In the assessment of reliance, reference is usually made to the concept of justifiable reliance. That refers to the 'standard of precaution, or of minimum knowledge, or of intelligent judgment of the hypothetical reasonable man' and to objective assessment.[1234] The aleatory view of negotiations is echoed in the law of tort. This assumes namely, that parties bargain at arm's length and beware of each other and exercise their own judgment.[1235] For instance, under US law 'statements of value, in general, as well as predictions as to profits to be made from the thing sold, fall into the same class of statements not to be relied on'.[1236] Reliance is also a question of fact, usually

1225 Restatement (Second) of Torts, Scope Note to Chapter 22.

1226 Prosser 1971, at 685.

1227 Misrepresentation is often invoked in cases where the ultimate agreement was formed, but a representation had vitiated the parties' consent. By contrast, this Chapter is limited to situations involving misrepresentation where a contract has not been formed.

1228 Prosser 1971, at 702.

1229 Prosser 1971, at 700.

1230 Prosser 1971, at 701.

1231 The US courts have followed the English case *Derry* v. *Peek* (1889) 14 AC 337 (HL). See Prosser 1971, at 701.

1232 In some states this includes negligence. See Prosser 1971, at 693.

1233 Restatement (Second) of Torts, Topic 1 Titles A-E; Prosser 1971, at 685–686; Keeton 1984, Chapter 18. See for a recent example *Mastaba, Inc.* v. *Lamb Weston Sales, Inc.*, 23 F. Supp. 3d 1283, 1292 (E.D. Wash. 2014).

1234 Prosser 1971, at 714, 719, 722.

1235 Prosser 1971, at 721.

1236 Prosser 1971, at 722.

to be decided by the jury. The difficulty in establishing reliance has also been one of the reasons for sustaining a claim for promissory fraud.[1237]

The damages should be established with sufficient certainty and should not be speculative.[1238] Most of the claims for deceit in the context of failed negotiations have been dismissed due to the difficulty of establishing fraudulent intent.[1239] This requires a particularly difficult assessment of fact – assessment of the state of mind of the party making a misrepresentation.[1240] And this is particularly difficult in the context of failed negotiations. The 'mere breach of promise is never enough in itself to establish the fraudulent intent'.[1241] A promise amounts to fraud only if it is made at least without care or concern whether it will be kept.[1242] For example, in *20 Atlantic Ave. Corp.* v. *Allied Waste Industries, Inc.*, no evidence could be provided that a party did not intend to consummate a corporate acquisition at the time it entered into a letter of intent during negotiations. Nor was it possible to establish the absence of its intention to negotiate the final acquisition documents in good faith.[1243]

Furthermore, if an intent to come to an agreement existed initially, but no longer subsists, this does not amount to fraudulent intent.[1244] If the claims under promissory estoppel and deceit are compared, the intent to come to agreement may exist initially in the conduct relevant for promissory estoppel. By contrast, in case of deceit, no such intent is present from the beginning of negotiations.

The case *Markov* v. *ABC Transfer & Storage Co.*[1245] represents an exception and illustrates the situation where fraudulent intent was established. In this case, the landlord assured the tenant that the contract for the lease of a warehouse would be renewed and had communicated its intent to the tenant. However, as it appeared from the circumstances of the case, the landlord was at the same time negotiating the sale of the warehouse to third parties. Ultimately, the contract was not renewed. According to the court, the real intent of the landlord was to keep the warehouse occupied, and to keep an option open

1237 *BPI Energy Holdings, Inc.* v. *IEC (Montgomery), LLC*, 664 F.3d 131 (C.A.7 2011) (reliance not established); *Goldstein* v. *Miles*, 859 A.2d 313 (Md. Spec. App. 2004) (reliance not established).

1238 Prosser 1971, at 730.

1239 See for example *Space Imaging Europe, Ltd.* v. *Space Imaging L.P.*, 38 F. Supp. 2d 326, 338 (S.D.N.Y. 1999).

1240 Prosser 1971, at 728.

1241 Keeton 1984, at 764.

1242 *Zeman* v. *Lufthansa German Airlines*, 699 P.2d 1274 (Alaska 1985) (the claimant could not prove 'reckless indifference' as to the outcome of negotiations).

1243 482 F.Supp.2d 60, 78 (D. Mass, 2007).

1244 Restatement (Second) of Torts, §530 Comment d; see also *Ford* v. *C.E. Wilson & Co.*, 129 F.2d 614 (C.A.2 1942); *Union Pacific R. Co.* v. *Barnes*, 64 F. 80 (C.C.A.8 1894); *Harriage* v. *Daley*, 180 S.W. 333 (Ark. 1915); *Hills Transp. Co.* v. *Southwest Forest Industries*, 72 Cal. Rptr. 441 (Cal. App. 1968); *Beach* v. *Fleming*, 104 S.E.2d 427 (Ga. 1958); *Long* v. *Woodman*, 58 Me. 49 (Me. 1870); *McComb* v. *C.R. Brewer Lumber Co.*, 68 N.E. 222 (Mass. 1903); *Kirk* v. *Vaccaro*, 73 N.W.2d 871 (Mich. 1955).

1245 457 P.2d 535 (Wash. 1969).

that the current tenant would still rent if the contract was renewed. Taking into account that the tenant relied on the landlord's representations, the tenant could recover for fraud. The tenant could recover reliance damages, which included loss of opportunity to provide the usual service to the tenant's main client.[1246]

Another case illustrates the role a provision on exclusivity of negotiations can play in establishing fraudulent intent. In *American Family Service Corp.* v. *Michelfelder*,[1247] the prospective buyer could recover both reliance interest and the benefit of the bargain. In this case, AFSC negotiated with the Michelfelders for the sale of the Michelfelders' childcare business. After some time, AFSC realized that Michelfelders were negotiating with another potential buyer. AFSC demanded, and the parties drafted, a letter of intent, which contained a 'no-shop' provision on exclusivity of the parties' negotiations.[1248] Despite this, Michelfelders continued negotiations with a third party and finally sold the business to third party.

6.4.2.2. Appropriation of a trade secret

Liability in tort may be also imposed for another type of precontractual conduct – conduct relating to the exchange of information during negotiations, which may be relevant in particular if negotiations involve disclosure by one party of its trade secret, negotiations are broken off, and the other party uses this trade secret.

Appropriation of the other's trade value may represent an actionable tort. This head of liability was initially restated as part of tort law.[1249] The tort of misappropriation of a competitor's intangible trade values was first recognized by the United States Supreme Court in *International News Service* v. *Associated Press*.[1250] Two different theories supported the imposition of liability for misappropriation of ideas. One theory regarded trade and commercial information as property and considered the breach as a breach of proprietary rights. The other regarded breach as a breach of the duty of good faith. During the drafting of the Restatement (Second) of Torts, it was decided to treat it

1246 *Markov* v. *ABC Transfer & Storage Co.* 457 P.2d 535 (Wash. 1969).

1247 968 F.2d 667 (C.A.8 1992). In this case, the liable party was represented by a law firm. Whereas agents are usually not held liable if they are strictly following instructions of the principal (under Iowa law), the court found in this case that the law firm on its own was also making misrepresentations regarding its principal's intent to reach agreement. This conclusion was drawn primarily based on awareness of the law firm of the parallel negotiations with a third party (namely an agreement in principle with a third party to sell the business signed despite an exclusivity provision in a letter of intent with another party).

1248 *American Family Service Corp.* v. *Michelfelder*, 968 F.2d 667, 699 (C.A.8 1992) quoting the 'no-shop clause':[N]either the Companies nor any shareholder, officer, director, agent or representative or any of them shall, directly or indirectly, solicit any proposal to acquire any or all of the Business Assets, any or all of the stock of the Companies, or negotiate or enter into any discussions with any person concerning such matters'.

1249 Restatement (First) of Torts, Division 9 'Interference with business relations', §757 'Liability for Disclosure or use of Another's trade secret'.

1250 248 U.S. 215 (1918).

separately as the law of unfair competition. Therefore, currently, appropriation of one's trade secret is restated as part of the law on unfair competition. The reason was the 'development of the law, as well as of the technology and techniques of business competition'.[1251] However, conceptually, it remains to be construed as a tort,[1252] because the US legal system has no specific separate set of rules regulating unfair competition (following in this the English law approach).[1253]

US law favours competition. Therefore sanctions in tort aim only at the *means* of competition if these are considered to be *improper*.[1254] One of the means regarded as improper is the use of another's trade secret.

The Restatement (Third) of Unfair Competition defines the concept of a trade secret broadly. It covers 'any information that can be used in the operation of a business or other enterprise and that is sufficiently valuable and secret to afford an actual or potential economic advantage over others'.[1255] The Restatement notes that 'an agreement between parties that characterizes specific information as "trade secret" can be an important although not necessarily conclusive factor' for the application of this tort.[1256] Furthermore, the Restatement defines the concept of 'improper acquisition'. This comes down to the means by which the information is acquired and excludes information that is publicly available. 'Improper means... include theft, fraud, unauthorized interception of communications, inducement of or knowing participation in a breach of confidence, and other means either wrongful in themselves or wrongful under the circumstances of the case'.[1257]

In addition, a tort law duty of confidence is established for the disclosure of trade secrets. This duty comes down to two types of situation. Firstly, it concerns the situation where the receiving party promises to keep the received information confidential. Secondly, it applies where at the time of disclosure 'under circumstances in which the relationship between the parties or the other facts surrounding the disclosure justify conclusions that... the person knew or had reason to know that the disclosure was intended to be in confidence and... the other party was reasonable in inferring' its consent to confidentiality.[1258]

An example of the application of the rules on the appropriation of a trade secret disclosed in negotiations is provided in *X-It Products, LLC* v. *Walter Kidde Portable Equipment*.[1259]

1251 Restatement (Third) of Unfair Competition, Foreword.
1252 Keeton 1984, at 1002.
1253 De Very 2006, at 203; see also Van Bochove 2013, at 296.
1254 Keeton 1984, at 1012.
1255 Restatement (Third) of Unfair Competition, §39. See also Comment d providing a list of examples of trade secrets – 'formula, pattern, compilation of data' etc.
1256 Restatement (Third) of Unfair Competition, §39 Comment d.
1257 Restatement (Third) of Unfair Competition, §43.
1258 Restatement (Third) of Unfair Competition, §41.
1259 227 F. Supp. 2d 494 (E.D. Va. 2002).

The court found that acquiring information about an innovative product in negotiations and a party then using this for its own purpose (while negotiations were not taking place) amounted to misappropriation of trade secret. Kidde was a large manufacturer and seller of fire protection equipment. It entered into negotiations with a small start-up company – the owners and inventors of an emergency escape ladder called 'X-It'. The parties negotiated a possible collaboration allowing Kidde to use X-It as part of its own product. While negotiations were progressing Kidde made different attempts to copy X-It, procuring information about the X-It patents, and exhibited a similar escape ladder as its own at a technology show. The court decided that 'Kidde's actions operated to deprive X–It of its commercial advantage'.[1260] Both compensatory and punitive damages were awarded.[1261]

6.4.3. *Law of restitution and unjust enrichment*

Another element of regulation applicable to the negotiation process is the law of unjust enrichment. In anticipation of a contract, a negotiating party may confer to the other party some benefit. For example, a negotiating party can disclose sensitive information and the other one use this information. If negotiations fail, the conferring party may recover under the US law of unjust enrichment.[1262] The general underlying principle of recovery under the law of restitution states as follows. 'A person who is unjustly enriched at the expense of another is subject to liability in restitution'.[1263] The law of restitution developed in the United States during the course of the nineteenth century based mainly on the English doctrines[1264] and is still in development.[1265] As Keeton contends, the law of restitution has come to further complicate the interrelation of tort and contract.[1266]

1260 227 F. Supp. 2d 494, 538 (E.D. Va. 2002).

1261 For another example, see *BlueEarth Biofuels, LLC* v. *Hawaiian Elec. Co., Inc.*, 235 P.3d 310 (Hawaii 2010).

1262 Throughout the development of the law of restitution, several terms are often used interchangeably by the courts and scholars. These are 'restitution', 'unjustified enrichment', and 'unjust enrichments' as well as 'quasi-contract' and contract implied in law. Restatement (Third) of Restitution and Unjust Enrichment, §1. Comment b. The latter suggests the following distinction. The term restitution is the broadest. It may, for instance, refer also to a measure of liability in contract. The term 'unjustified enrichment' has a moral connotation, i.e. it explains enrichment as morally inadmissible. Finally, 'unjust enrichment' refers to the cases where enrichment has occurred without legal grounds.
Further complication in the terminology arises due to the fact that the term 'restitution' is also frequently used to designate one of the contractual remedies. Restatement (Third) of Restitution and Unjust Enrichment, §31 Comment e explains that a term claim in quantum meruit is often used interchangeably with the term claim in restitution. However, notes the comment, quantum meruit embraces not only a claim under the law of restitution, but also a claim in contract for reimbursement of its partial performance. On the guidance in the inconsistent use of the term quantum meruit see Dobbs 1993, section 4.2(3).

1263 Restatement (Third) of Restitution and Unjust Enrichment, §1. This is consistent with Restatement (Second) of Contracts, §375.

1264 The treatises of Keener on quasi-contracts (Keener 1893) and Palmer on the law of restitution (Palmer 1978) were seminal. In 1930, the American Law Institute created the Restatement (First) of Restitution. The current redaction of this instrument is the Restatement (Third) of Restitution and Unjust Enrichment.

1265 Restatement (Third) of Restitution and Unjust Enrichment has been published in 2011.

1266 Keeton 1984, at 672.

Recovery under the law of restitution is based on liability without contract. Sometimes reference is made to an older doctrine of quasi-contract. This is a fiction rooted in Roman law, referring to receiving benefits without legal basis, including an ineffective and non-consensual transaction.[1267] The modern US law of restitution deals inter alia with a situation where a contract is unenforceable and unformed for different reasons.[1268] According to the literature, this covers situations where negotiations have not led to formation of a contract.[1269]

The liability is construed as liability in tort but leads to a different remedy. In case 'the commission of tort results in the unjust enrichment of the defendant at the plaintiff's expense, the plaintiff may disregard, or "waive" the tort action, and sue instead on a theoretical and fictitious contract of restitution'.[1270] The plaintiff may choose the remedy, opting either for a remedy in restitution (recovering the amount of the other party's benefit) or in tort (seeking recovery of loss). Double recovery is not possible.[1271]

Though the law of restitution is relevant for the process of contract negotiation and formation, its relevance is limited in two ways. The first limitation is due to the aleatory view of negotiations. As a starting point, parties bear the risk of failure of negotiations. Expenses incurred during negotiations are deemed to benefit that party's own interests in the bargain without being necessarily beneficial for the other party. Expenses incurred in negotiations and other eventual detriment, represent the parties' business risks.[1272] The Restatement (Third) of Restitution and Unjust Enrichment notes: 'A transaction resulting in an indefinite contract must not be confused with a failed negotiation producing no contract at all. There is no claim under this section for a performance for which defendant did not – at least implicitly – agree to pay...'[1273]

Second, the claim in restitution is secondary to a contractual claim. Restitution comes into play only if either the meeting of wills or the mere recovery in contract is not possible for any reason. According to the Restatement, 'any inquiry into unjust enrichment' is displaced to the extent that there is a possibility to make a contractual claim.[1274] It has been contended in the literature regarding the period of negotiations that '[e]ven an

1267 See Restatement (Third) of Restitution and Unjust Enrichment, §31.

1268 Restatement (Third) of Restitution and Unjust Enrichment, §31; see also §31 Comment a; on unenforceable contracts see Dobbs 1993, §13.2.

1269 Farnsworth 1987, at 229.

1270 Keeton 1984, at 672.

1271 Ibid. On the difference in recovery see Farnsworth 2004, at 192.

1272 *Diamond Elec. Inc.* v. *Pace Pacific Corp.*, 346 Fed.Appx. 186 (C.A.9 2009) (unjustified enrichment not sustained because the services rendered were 'part of the competitive bidding process and not performed with an expectation of payment'); in *Shuffle Tech Intern. LLC* v. *Wolff Gaming, Inc.*, 950 F. Supp. 2d 977, 948 (N.D. Ill. 2013) (costs made by a potential distributor were 'nothing more than the investments parties routinely incur in the course of working towards a deal they expect to be mutually beneficial').

1273 Restatement (Third) of Restitution and Unjust Enrichment, §31 Comment d.

1274 Restatement (Thrid) of Restitution and Unjust Enrichment, §2(2).

opportunity to contract can defeat claim for restitution'.[1275] In this way, a precontractual document may be decisive for the applicability of the law of restitution. Such a document can in particular contribute to sustaining a claim in restitution (for example, show that a performance was not solicited or requested or shed light on the main subject of negotiations). '[T]he terms of the unenforceable contract will influence and may even determine the measure of recovery in restitution. The critical fact in this context is that the claimant's performance was requested'.[1276] It contributes then to sustaining a claim in unjust enrichment. Alternatively, a precontractual document can contribute to defeating such claim, that is, the existence of a preliminary agreement can point to the possibility of a contractual claim, thus excluding the claim for unjustified enrichment. The Restatement (Third) of Restitution and Unjust Enrichment provides an illustration.[1277]

> A prepares preliminary designs and cost estimates for the construction of a bridge contemplated by City. The parties agree that A will be compensated for its services only if City decides to construct the bridge and to award the contract to A. The project is abandoned. Five years later City revives the project, using A's earlier studies for planning purposes but awarding the contract to B. A sues City for breach of contract and unjust enrichment, pointing out (correctly) that City has enjoyed the benefit of work for which A was never paid. Yet City's use of A's plans without compensation is in accordance with the terms of the parties' valid agreement. That being so, there is no unjust enrichment of City and no liability in restitution.

The limitations of the law of restitution for the precontractual period are also expressed by the requirements to be met in order to succeed in a claim in restitution. The claimant must show that (1) there was enrichment (2) at its expense, and (3) that it is against equity and good conscience to permit the defendant to retain what is sought to be recovered.[1278]

The Restatement (Third) notes that the fact of enrichment does not in itself enable recovery. It is necessary that the receiving party *benefits* from this, and that the benefit is *unjust*. 'Restitution by the rule of this section [31] is measured by the value of the claimant's performance to the recipient, but by what was promised in exchange, not by what the claimant's performance cost the claimant'.[1279] A benefit for purposes of an unjust enrichment claim is any form of advantage that has a measurable value, including the advantage of being saved from an expense or loss.[1280] As to the fact of enrichment, the courts decide on a case-by-case basis whether the party has received a benefit. In the precontractual context, the conclusion has been that no benefit was in place. This has

1275 Ayres 2012, at 403.

1276 Restatement (Third) of Restitution and Unjust Enrichment, §31 Comment i.

1277 Restatement (Third) of Restitution and Unjust Enrichment, §2 Illustration 4, based on *Chandler* v. *Washington Toll Bridge Authority*, 137 P.2d 97 (Wash. 1943).

1278 For recent cases see *Massachusetts Eye and Ear Infirmary* v. *QLT Phototherapeutics, Inc.* 552 F.3d 47 (C.A.1 2009); *Clark* v. *Daby*, 300 A.D.2d 732 (N.Y.A.D. 2002).

1279 Restatement (Third) of Restitution and Unjust Enrichment, §31 Comment i.

1280 *Anisgard* v. *Bray*, 419 N.E.2d 315 (Mass.App. 1981).

barred the possibility of recovery, because precontractual services often have 'no end product'.[1281] As to the notion of unjust, the authors of the Restatement (Third) note the difficulty of identifying when the enrichment is unjust. As has been contended, the law of restitution is dominated by 'considerations of equity and morality'.[1282] Answers to the following questions may be taken into consideration as factors to assess this. Could remuneration be reasonably expected in a given situation? Was there an opportunity to obtain consent to perform before starting performance? A performance voluntarily conferred does not lead to liability in restitution.[1283] If consent is obtained, the claim should be based on contract as it possibly falls under the illustration mentioned above.[1284]

In the precontractual context, the US courts have dealt with recovery in unjustified enrichment in two main types of situations: misappropriation of benefits from an idea disclosed in negotiations, and benefitting from works done or services rendered in anticipation of a contract. The case *Massachusetts Eye and Ear Infirmary* v. *QLT Phototherapeutics*[1285] provides an example of the application of the law of restitution to the failed negotiations of a contract. In this case recovery was granted. In the case, an eye clinic received positive results from a potential treatment for age-related macular degeneration, a leading cause of adult blindness. QLT Phototherapeutics was interested in the development of a drug treating age-related macular degeneration. The two companies entered into negotiations regarding this development. During the negotiations, the eye clinic disclosed several data underpinning the research. QLT promised to provide licence payments for future use, but failed to do so. At the same time as negotiating with the eye clinic, QLT negotiated a partnership agreement with a pharmaceutical company. As a result of its receipt of the timely sensitive information from the eye clinic, the partnership was concluded and QLT patented the drug Visudyne. As the drug became a successful and highly profitable treatment, and QLT could not have patented the drug without the information provided by the clinic, the eye clinic filed a claim that QLT had been unjustly enriched at its expense. The court upheld the claim in unjust enrichment. It awarded the remedy of a continuing royalty on the sales of Visudyne. The court noted that the 'fair market value' of the benefit was a commonly accepted measure of damage for unjust enrichment.

This case is an example of the way the law of restitution frames the parties' conduct during the contract negotiations. It demonstrates the possibility of recovering an unjustified benefit resulting from conducting negotiations. At the same time, this case is rather exceptional, because of the high threshold set for sustaining the claim in restitution. This is coupled with the fundamental role of the aleatory view of negotiations, which is relevant, as can be seen, also in the tort law setting.

1281 Furmston/Tolhurst 2010, at 391; See also *Earhart* v. *William Low Co.*, 158 Cal.Rptr. 887 (Cal. 1979); *Certified Fire Prot. Inc.* v. *Precision Constr.*, 283 P.3d 250, 257 (Nev. 2012) (failure to establish the benefit).

1282 *Salamon* v. *Terra*, 477 N.E.2d 1029 (Mass. 1985).

1283 Restatement (Third) of Restitution and Unjust Enrichment, §1 Comment a.

1284 Restatement (Third) of Restitution and Unjust Enrichment, §2 Illustration 4, emphasis added.

1285 552 F.3d 47 (C.A.1 2009).

6.5. Dynamics of negotiations addressed in case law

6.5.1. *Development of the enforceability requirements*

The previous Section sketched the development of a differentiated approach to preliminary agreements. Under this approach, separate obligations of a preliminary agreement have been regarded as binding, whereas the rest of the document was regarded as not binding. The possibility of this differentiated approach leads to the following questions. What are the conditions of enforceability of precontractual obligations? Are the usual conditions of validity of the ultimate agreement applicable?

6.5.1.1. Intent as a condition of enforceability

The intention of the parties to form a contract (or to be bound by a preliminary regime) plays a crucial role in the assessment of the extent to which they are bound by a preliminary agreement. Strictly speaking, intent is not a requirement for a formation of contract.[1286] According to the Restatement (Second) of Contracts,[1287] the ultimate agreement may be formed even if the parties do not intend that their actions lead to a formed binding contract, or fail to understand this. But the Restatement contains an important nuance. It states: 'neither is it fatal that the parties are mistaken as to the legal effect of their agreement, *unless it is their intention not to be legally bound*'.[1288] In this way, intent is relevant at the precontractual stage, and especially when parties may not aim to be bound by the ultimate agreement (but eventually, be bound 'in some way'.)[1289] Modern scholarship seems to agree that intent *is* a requirement for the validity of any preliminary obligation.[1290] Case law points to the same conclusion.[1291]

6.5.1.2. Other conditions of enforceability

Besides intent, no clear line of cases defines further requirements for the enforceability of a precontractual obligation. Landmark cases have referred to the requirements of definiteness, consideration, and mutual assent (thus, intent of both parties to form the contract). For instance, the reasoning in *Channel Home Centers, Div. of Grace Retail Corp.* v. *Grossman* identified three requirements of enforceability: *intent* to be bound by the terms of the preliminary agreement, *definiteness* sufficient for enforcement of the

[1286] Restatement (Second) of Contracts, §21; Klass 2009, at 1443; Farnsworth 2004, at 117 ff.; Ayres 2012, at 79.

[1287] Restatement (Second) of Contracts, §21.

[1288] Restatement (Second) of Contracts, §21 Comment a, italics added.

[1289] Schwartz/Scott 2007, at 664.

[1290] Jeffries 2012, at 22; Klass 2009, at 1449: 'It is generally accepted that preliminary agreements should be enforced only when parties manifestly so intended'.

[1291] See inter alia *Teachers Ins. and Annuity Ass'n of America* v. *Tribune Co.*, 670 F.Supp. 491 (S.D.N.Y. 1987); *Empro Mfg. Co.* v. *Ball-Co Mfg., Inc.*, 870 F.2d 423, 425 (C.A.7 1989).

preliminary obligations, and *consideration* on both sides.[1292] In *Butler* v. *Balolia*, the court first identified the parties' *intent* to be bound before the formation of the ultimate agreement. Thereafter, the court noted that in order to be enforceable, an agreement to negotiate should be 'sufficiently *definite* to allow courts to fix liability and the exchange of promises must be supported by *consideration*'.[1293] In *Logan* v. *D.W. Sivers Co.*, the court came to the conclusion that the preliminary document (a letter of intent) was sufficiently *definite*. Furthermore one party's promise to negotiate in good faith represented *consideration* for the other party's promise of 60 days' exclusivity of negotiations.[1294]

Definiteness requires clarity of obligation and sufficient content to be enforced. Indefiniteness is regarded as a sign of intent not to contract.[1295] Therefore, the requirement of definiteness is regarded as important for two reasons. Firstly, the court needs a reference or a standard in order to measure the party's conduct. Secondly, a court can fashion an appropriate remedy only on the basis of an obligation with a clearly defined content. The second reason 'goes to the practicality of the remedy, not the principle of it'.[1296]

Consideration represents essentially something that 'confers a benefit upon the promissor or causes a detriment to the promisee and must be an act, forbearance or return promise bargained for and given in exchange for the original promise'.[1297] The requirement is rooted historically in the common law view of negotiations as a period during which parties bargain.[1298] As stated in a modern contract law treatise: 'The early conception of consideration as either a benefit to the promissor or a detriment to the promisee has today been largely supplanted by what is known as the "bargain" conception of consideration'.[1299]

A reference to the requirement of mutual assent echoes the 'all or nothing' approach.[1300] This points once more to the absence of a settled opinion on the requirement of enforceability in the US case law. The following Sub-sections discuss the courts' approach to particular obligations relating to the dynamics of negotiations, within the intermediary regime.

1292 795 F.2d 291, 298 (C.A.3 1986) with further references to case law for each requirement of validity.

1293 736 F.3d 609, 614 (C.A.1 2013) italics added, referring to *Keystone Land & Development* v. *Xerox Corp.*, 94 P.3d 945 (Wash. 2004).

1294 169 P.3d 1255 (Or. 2007). See also *Frazier Industries, L.L.C.* v. *General Fasteners Co.*, 137 Fed. Appx. 723 (C.A.6 2005) (requirements of definiteness and consideration for the validity of a letter of intent).

1295 *Owen* v. *Owen*, 427 A.2d 933 (D.C. App. 1981); Calamari/Perillo 2009, at 43.

1296 *Venture Associates Corp.* v. *Zenith Data Systems Corp.*, 96 F.3d 275, [3] (C.A.7 1996).

1297 *Curry* v. *Estate of Thompson*, 481 A.2d 658, 661 (Pa.Super 1984).

1298 Restatement (Second) of Contracts Chapter 4. For a discussion of the requirement of consideration in the context of preliminary agreements, see Eisenberg 2000, 1762 ff.

1299 Ayres 2012, at 61, 62.

1300 Schwarz/Scott 2007, at 674.

However some cases have referred to further requirements. In *Keystone Land & Development Co.* v. *Xerox Corp.* a contract to negotiate was regarded as any other contract that needs to be formed. It lists, therefore the following requirements of validity: 'manifestations of *mutual assent* to *definite* terms supported by *consideration*'.[1301]

Alternatively, courts and scholars have referred only to *intent* and *definiteness*. This was the case in *Advent Systems Ltd.* v. *Unisys Corp.* referring to the treatise on contract by Murray:[1302]

> Rather than focusing upon what parties failed to say, the Code and Restatement 2d focus upon the overriding question of whether the parties manifestly intended to make a binding arrangement. If that manifestation is present, the only remaining concern is whether the terms are definite enough to permit courts to afford an appropriate remedy. The second requirement assists courts to determine the degree of permissible indefiniteness.

Finally, some decisions simply state that a precontractual document creates no binding obligations, but thereafter, note in passing that some clauses are exceptions. These include thus obligations that *are* binding. In these cases, courts do not provide reasoning on the requirements of validity of these obligations, presumably being guided by the parties' intent to make these exceptions binding.[1303]

6.5.2. *Agreement to agree*

An agreement to agree – a document whereby parties simply confirm that they are in negotiations – is not enforceable under US law. The regime governing such documents corresponds to the aleatory view of negotiations. This regime is applied if the document drafted by the parties goes no further than simply confirming the existence of negotiations between the parties.[1304] Each party bears the risks inherent to bargaining during contract formation.[1305] The intent of the parties clearly points to the fact that they are only in negotiations. Furthermore, these documents fail to fulfil the requirements of validity – they are not sufficiently definite to be enforced, and lack consideration.

At the same time, as explained in Section 6.3 above, US case law has moved towards a differentiated approach to the enforceability of obligations in a precontractual document since the decision in *Teachers Ins. & Annuity Ass'n of Am.* v. *Tribune Co.*[1306] As one court puts it, '[t]here is a dearth of case law on the issue of whether one provision of an otherwise

1301 94 P.3d 945 (Wash. 2004).
1302 925 F.2d 670, 679 (C.A.3 1991).
1303 *BPI Energy Holdings, Inc.* v. *IEC (Montgomery), LLC*, 664 F.3d 131, 133 (C.A.7 2011).
1304 *Teachers Ins. and Annuity Ass'n of America* v. *Tribune Co.*, 670 F.Supp. 491 (S.D.N.Y. 1987); *Channel Home Centers, Div. of Grace Retail Corp.* v. *Grossman*, 795 F.2d 291 (C.A.3 1986); Farnsworth 1987, at 243; Ayres 2012, at 385 and 387ff.
1305 Restatement (Second) of Contracts, §26.
1306 670 F.Supp. 491 (S.D.N.Y. 1987).

nonbinding preliminary agreement can be enforceable'.[1307] This section will address the approach that can be distilled from the modern US law to certain obligations framing the dynamics of negotiations.

6.5.3. Contractualized good faith

Within the divergent approaches of state law to the obligation of good faith,[1308] an agreement to negotiate the ultimate agreement in good faith can be validly made only under the law of those states that recognize the possibility of the existence of precontractual good faith.[1309] Such phrases as using 'best efforts to negotiate and attempt to agree' have been upheld as amounting to good faith.[1310] The content of the precontractual duty of good faith has been the subject of discussion in case law and has been debated in US scholarship.

Courts are 'cryptic' as to the meaning of good faith, 'though emphatic about its existence'.[1311] A straightforward way of defining good faith in a precontractual document has been provided in the case *A/S Apothekernes Laboratorium for Specialpraeparater* v. *I.M.C. Chemical Group, Inc.* It stated that the scope of this duty is to be determined only from the terms of the letter of intent itself.[1312] In the search for content of the duty of 'best efforts' and good faith, the courts have used the common law view of good faith as exclusionary.[1313] That means that good faith excludes bad faith conduct.[1314] In this way, the courts have stated that good faith consists in an absence of bad faith, e.g. an absence of deliberate misconduct.[1315] However, excluding bad faith does not require a party to accede to one-sided modifications of the deal.[1316] It 'does not prohibit a party from bargaining to its own economic advantage'.[1317] Nor does it create a fiduciary relationship between the parties. Each party remains free to bargain on the future transaction. Within this view, a 'practical, commonsense construction' of good faith is the absence of bad faith or bad intent. For example, the following situation has been characterized as bad intent. 'The defendant spuriously identified deficiencies with the Whirlwind technology [content of the invention to be sold under the contract] and used those

1307 *Space Imaging Europe, Ltd.* v. *Space Imaging L.P.*, 38 F. Supp. 2d 326 (S.D.N.Y. 1999) (by applying the New York law factors test, the court came to the conclusion that a right of first refusal in an otherwise non-binding letter of intent was not binding). See also Eisenberg 2000, especially at 1797 ff.; Lake/Draetta 1994, at 124–125.

1308 The divergence of approaches is discussed in Section 6.3.2.

1309 *Feldman* v. *Allegheny Intern., Inc.*, 850 F.2d 1217, 1223 (C.A.7 1988); *A/S Apothekernes Laboratorium for Specialpraeparater* v. *I.M.C. Chemical Group, Inc.*, 873 F.2d 155, 159 (C.A.7 1989).

1310 Rohwer/Scrocki 2010, at 254.

1311 *Market Street Associates Ltd. Partnership* v. *Frey*, 941 F.2d 588, 593 (Judge Posner) (C.A.7 1991).

1312 873 F.2d 155, 158 (C.A.7 1989).

1313 Summers 1968, at 196.

1314 *Dotson* v. *Former Shareholders of Abraham Lincoln Land & Cattle Co.*, 773 N.E.2d 792 (Ill.App. 2002).

1315 *Venture Associates Corp.* v. *Zenith Data Systems Corp.*, 96 F.3d 275 [3] (C.A.7 1996).

1316 *Auerbach* v. *Great Western Bank*, 88 Cal. Rptr. 2d 718 (C.A.2 1999).

1317 *Phoenix Mut. Life Ins. Co.* v. *Shady Grove Plaza Ltd. Partnership*, 734 F. Supp. 1181 (D. Md. 1990).

canards as a pretext to renegotiate the price'.[1318] Furthermore, a breach of an exclusivity provision in a letter of intent by concluding a contract with third party has been also regarded as bad faith.[1319]

Another way of looking at good faith in case law consists in imposing positive obligations on the parties during negotiations. In *Teachers Ins. and Annuity Ass'n of America* v. *Tribune* the court stated that the obligation of good faith 'does...bar a party from renouncing the deal, abandoning the negotiations, or insisting on conditions that do not conform to the preliminary agreement'.[1320]

Along with the courts, scholars have also disagreed on the content that might be attributed to the precontractual duty of good faith. Modern debate focuses on finding efficiency in the choice between enforcement and non-enforcement of preliminary agreements for the benefits of trade, rather than on doctrinal questions regarding good faith. Within the classical legal analysis, Farnsworth has noted that 'scholars have been more concerned with the imposition of the duty than with its content'.[1321] This scholar has suggested the following components of the content of the obligation of good faith: refusal to negotiate, when parties did clearly agree to negotiate the transaction, including imposing improper conditions that would amount to failure to negotiate fairly. Farnsworth also names 'improper tactics' (namely fraud and duress), returning anew to the issues that have been already negotiated in a complex transaction, and negotiations with others when an exclusivity provision is binding on the parties. Farnsworth suggests that in the presence of an exclusivity provision, the other party should be kept informed about offers made by third parties (i.e. competitors). Furthermore, absence of good faith includes, according to Farnsworth, continuing to negotiate in the absence of an intent to reach agreement. Finally, good faith supposes that a party does not break off negotiations unless the parties have reached a complete disagreement – an impasse). This, Farnsworth notes, is an issue of fact.[1322] The content of the duty of good faith suggested by Farnsworth is based not only on contract law. It is also inspired by extra-contractual doctrines analysed by this scholar as part of the legal regulation of formation of a contract. In particular, improper tactics have a broader application than contract law regulation. Palmieri has advanced an opinion that the general umbrella of good faith in US law embraces the duty of disclosure of information based on various, mainly extra-contractual doctrines.[1323] Generally, contract law regards the assessment of good faith in a party's conduct as an issue of fact.

1318 *Butler* v. *Balolia* 736 F.3d 609, 617 (C.A.1 2013).
1319 *JamSports and Entertainment, LLC* v. *Paradama Productions, Inc.*, 336 F. Supp. 2d 824, 848 (N.D. Ill. 2004).
1320 670 F.Supp. 491, 498 (S.D.N.Y. 1987).
1321 Farnsworth 1987, at 269.
1322 Farnsworth 1987, at 274 ff.
1323 Palmieri 1993.

6.5.4. *Negotiations subject to future contract*

A provision in a preliminary agreement stating that the parties' relations will only become enforceable when a written contract is concluded in the future is assessed primarily from the perspective of finding the parties' intent and the assessment of language (this has been discussed in Section 6.4). The validity of such provision comes down to the intent of the parties and the application of the factors discussed earlier in section 6.4.

6.5.5. *Exclusivity*

Provisions on exclusivity of negotiations are also known in US case law as 'no-shop', 'no-talk', 'non-solicitation' clauses. These clauses are often regarded as valid.[1324] These provisions have been upheld as valid, in particular, as a part of the binding content of an obligation to negotiate in good faith. State law admitting an intermediary regime for preliminary agreements regards exclusivity of negotiations as a valid manner to frame contract formation. As stated in *Logan* v. *D.W. Sivers Co.*, the 'defendant's nonsolicitation promise was directed to the *manner* of the negotiations and not to their *outcome*, and the damages that may be deemed to have arisen from defendant's breach of that promise are similarly limited'.[1325]

In *Butler* v. *Balolia*,[1326] an exclusivity provision in a letter of intent was held to be valid together with two other provisions framing the negotiations. *Logan* v. *D.W. Sivers Co* offers an example of a more concretized approach. In this case, a clear provision of exclusivity had also been regarded as valid. However, the court emphasized that exclusivity itself had not implied a more broad duty to negotiate in good faith. 'We repeat the important distinction here: Defendant's obligation not to solicit or sell to others for 60 days did not include any promise to negotiate in good faith – or at all – during that 60-day period'.[1327]

Generally, the duty of good faith does not necessarily imply that a party may not be engaged in parallel negotiations for the same deal with third parties.[1328] On the contrary, this provision pointed to the parties' intent not to be bound by the ultimate agreement negotiated. For example, in *Evergreen Investments, LLC* v. *FCL Graphics, Inc.*, the court noted that '[t]here would seem to be little need for an exclusivity period "to consummate" the deal if the parties intended to be bound to a sale at the time the letter was signed'.[1329]

1324 *A/S Apothekernes Laboratorium for Specialpraeparater* v. *I.M.C. Chemical Group, Inc.*, 873 F.2d 155 (C.A.7 1989); see also *SuperValu Inc.* v. *Associated Grocers, Inc.*, 428 F. Supp. 2d 985 (D. Minn. 2006); for a recent example see *FCS Advisors, Inc.* v. *Fair Finance Co., Inc.*, 378 F. Appx 65 (C.A.2 2010).

1325 169 P.3d 1255 (Or. 2007).

1326 *Butler* v. *Balolia* 736 F.3d 609, 617 (C.A.1 2013).

1327 169 P.3d 1255, 1262 (Or. 2007).

1328 Knapp has argued that parallel negotiations should be characterized as bad faith. See Knapp 1969, at 721.

1329 334 F.3d 750 (C.A.8 2003); *St. Joseph Hosp., Augusta, Georgia, Inc.* v. *Health Management Associates, Inc.*, 705 F.3d 1289 (C.A.11 2013) (binding exclusivity provision; according to the court this obligation also pointed to an absence of intent to be bound by the final contract).

Notably, in cases where an exclusivity provision has been found binding, courts have paid attention to the limitation of the exclusivity period in time.[1330] In the absence of a clearly stated period of exclusive negotiations, the court suggested that a reasonable period should be implied.[1331] Another approach was taken in *Feldman* v. *Allegheny Intern., Inc.* The exclusivity provision in a letter of intent provided that parties would negotiate exclusively 'while the proposed acquisition is being pursued'.[1332] It was decided that the parties were free to walk away from the transaction at any time, and at that moment the obligation of exclusivity would end.

It is also worth noting that the answer to the question as to whether the duty to negotiate in good faith allows the parties the possibility of negotiating the same contract with third parties may play a role in establishing a claim for tortious interference with prospective contractual relations or economic advantage.[1333] Under US law, a contract in formation, but not yet formed, can represent what tort law calls 'prospective advantage'.[1334] This may be relevant for another type of tort, whereby a third party may be held liable, rather than a party to negotiations – the tort of interference with an existing or prospective contractual relationship. In this way, an unsuccessful party to failed negotiations may hold a successful third party (with which the contract was finally concluded) liable, provided that the conditions of tort liability are in place. This is the tort of interference with prospective advantage, construed along the lines of the tort of interference with a contract.[1335]

6.5.6. *Confidentiality*

Confidentiality provisions in a letter of intent have been held enforceable on a number of occasions. For instance, a confidentiality provision was upheld as a separate enforceable part of an otherwise non-enforceable preliminary agreement in *JamSports and Entertainment, LLC* v. *Paradama Productions, Inc.* The dispute in this case concerned a breach of a letter of intent's exclusivity and confidentiality provisions. The confidentiality clause 'prohibited both parties from divulging the letter of intent's terms to anyone other than its attorneys, accountants, and financial consultants'.[1336] The court has noted that this was an issue of the parties' intent. It found under the circumstances of the case that '[a]s to these provisions, the letter of intent was indisputably a binding contract'.[1337] In *BPI Energy Holdings, Inc.* v. *IEC (Montgomery)*, the Court of Appeal held that a letter of intent was not binding, but noted in passing the binding effect of the confidentiality provision: 'The memorandum of understanding is

1330 See, for example, *Logan* v. *D.W. Sivers Co.*, 169 P.3d 1255 (Or. 2007).
1331 *Channel Home Centers, Div. of Grace Retail Corp.* v. *Grossman*, 795 F.2d 291, 301 (C.A.3 1986).
1332 850 F.2d 1217 (C.A.7 1988).
1333 Restatement (Second) of Torts, §766B and generally Chapter 37.
1334 Keeton 1984, at 1005.
1335 Restatement (Second) of Torts, §766; Keeton 1984, at 1005. See also Van Bochove 2013, chapter 7.
1336 336 F. Supp. 2d 824, 846 (N.D. Ill. 2004).
1337 Ibid.

brief and recites that it is merely "intended to form the basis for negotiation of a final agreement" and that "the parties acknowledge that [it] does not constitute a binding agreement upon the parties" with an immaterial exception regarding confidentiality'.[1338] In *Butler* v. *Balolia*, a letter of intent contained a provision on confidentiality which was upheld.[1339]

Similarly to the exclusivity provision of the letter of intent in question, a binding confidentiality obligation did not imply the existence of any general obligation to negotiate in good faith. Similarly to the approach to exclusivity, US case law has not created a general precontractual duty of confidentiality. Nor does confidentiality unquestionably flow from an obligation to negotiate in good faith.

6.5.7. *Division into binding and non-binding provisions*

US courts have addressed a distinction made in a precontractual document between its binding and non-binding provisions primarily from the point of view of an assessment of the parties' intent. More specifically, such a distinction has been regarded as a sign of intent not to be bound by the ultimate agreement, but to be bound by the terms of the preliminary agreement.

It is to be noted that at least in one case the parties' division of binding and non-binding provisions was not strictly followed by the court. In *Lexington Inv. Co.* v. *Southwest Stainless, Inc.*,[1340] the court simply interpreted the text agreed between the parties in order to hold a forum choice clause binding, despite the fact it was not included in the list of binding provisions.

6.5.8. *Dispute resolution*

Another matter that may become relevant in the course of negotiations is dispute resolution. This issue has been discussed in US academic literature and case law, and the following Section will discuss the approach to the enforceability of choice of law, choice of court, arbitration and mediation clauses inserted in the documents organizing negotiations contractually.

6.5.8.1. Choice of law

Under US law parties may choose the law applicable to a contract.[1341] The Restatement (Second) of Conflict of Laws uses a broad concept of contract, including any 'legally enforceable promises and to other agreements or promises which are claimed to be

1338 664 F.3d 131, 133 (C.A.7 2011).
1339 736 F.3d 609 (C.A.1 2013).
1340 697 F. Supp. 139 (S.D.N.Y. 1988). See recently in the same sense *In re Orange, S.A.*, 818 F.3d 956 (C.A.9 2016).
1341 Restatement (Second) of Conflict of Laws, §187.

enforceable but are not legally so'.[1342] At the same time, case law on choice of law made in a preliminary agreement is not extensive.

Butler v. *Balolia* presents one of the few cases dealing with this question, and the validity of the choice of law clause was followed to apply an intermediary regime to a preliminary agreement. In this case, a letter of intent contained a provision on choice of law in favour of Washington law. A breach of the letter of intent during negotiations led to a dispute and a federal court was seized. The Court of Appeal of the first circuit, predicting state law under the diversity jurisdiction, decided that the Washington Supreme Court would most probably recognize the letter of intent as a binding contract to negotiate. Consequently, according to the court, Washington law was applicable following the choice of law provision in the letter of intent.[1343] In *Giuliano* v. *Anchorage Advisors LLC*,[1344] the court upheld a choice of law clause included in a letter of intent with regard to the substantive law applicable to a dispute which may arise from the letter of intent. By contrast, in *SunLight General Capital LLC* v. *CJS Investments Inc*[1345] a New York court applied New York law stating that a memorandum of understanding represented negotiations and no more (thus no binding preliminary agreement) and disregarded the choice of law clause in the memorandum of understanding (where parties had stated that disputes would be resolved under the law of the state of New Jersey).

6.5.8.2. Choice of forum including arbitration

As with the choice of law, parties may choose a competent court.[1346] At the same time, there is little case law dealing with the enforceability of a choice of forum in an international letter of intent. At least one case points to the validity of the choice of court clause in the precontractual context. This case involved a domestic (not international) case. In *Lexington Inv. Co.* v. *Southwest Stainless, Inc.*,[1347] the parties negotiated the sale of a corporation. In contemplation of a future agreement, they signed a letter of intent. One of its provisions indicated that any dispute arising under the letter of intent would be resolved in Texas, Fort Bend County. Another provision provided a distinction between the binding and non-binding clauses of the letter of intent. Notably, the choice of court clause was not included in the list of binding provisions. Negotiations broke down and no corporate acquisition took place. A dispute arose between the parties and a claim was brought before the United States District Court in New York (under the diversity jurisdiction).[1348] The defendants argued that the choice of court clause was

1342 Restatement (Second) of Conflict of Laws, Introductory Note to Chapter 8. See also a submission that the choice of law clauses in letter of intent could be enforceable in Lake/Draetta 1994, at 231.

1343 736 F.3d 609, 612 (C.A.1 2013). The approach taken in *Butler* v. *Balolia* has been discussed with approval in *Dinan* v. *Alpha Networks, Inc.*, 764 F.3d 64 (C.A.1 2014).

1344 19 F. Supp. 3d 1087 (D. Or. 2014).

1345 *SunLight General Capital LLC* v. *CJS Investments Inc.*, 981 N.Y.S.2d 390 (N.Y. 2014).

1346 See generally Hartley 2015, at 208 ff.

1347 697 F. Supp. 139 (S.D.N.Y. 1988).

1348 697 F. Supp. 139, 188 (S.D.N.Y. 1988).

unenforceable, because it was not included in the list of non-binding provisions in the letter of intent. However, the District Court noted that it is not for that court to decide whether a binding ultimate agreement was formed by the letter of intent (as the claimant invoked the precedent in *Texaco, Inc.* v. *Pennzoil, Co.*[1349] where an ultimate agreement was found). This was regarded as an issue of fact to be resolved by the competent court. Instead, the court limited its findings to the question '*where* the dispute is to be heard'.[1350] The court then applied New York conflict of law rules resulting in the substantive law of Texas being the law under which the contract was made. Under Texas law, the intent of the parties is primarily relevant for the interpretation of documents in writing. Having assessed the parties' intent, the court disregarded the fact that the choice of court clause was not included in the list of binding provisions. According to the court, the parties' intent clearly indicated their will to have disputes litigated in the manner described by the letter of intent.

In addition to the courts, parties may, in principle, choose to have their dispute resolved by arbitration. Contemporary US law favours the parties' choice of arbitration, especially if international parties are involved.[1351] The United States is a contracting State to the New York Convention and follows this instrument in favouring international arbitration.[1352] This generally extends to arbitration clauses in a precontractual document.

Furthermore, US law also adheres to the doctrine of severability of an arbitration agreement,[1353] whereby the validity of the parties' choice for arbitration should be established independently of the question of validity of the document in which it is incorporated. In *Anderra Energy Corp. and Petro Anderra, S.A.* v. *SAPET Development Corporation*[1354] the court clearly stated that a letter of intent contained a valid arbitration clause. The dispute in this case involved a letter of intent between a US and a Peruvian party. It related to the parties' future gas and oil projects in Peru. The letter of intent stated: 'in case of discrepancies between the partners, it is agreed to request arbitration according to international laws of arbitration'.[1355] When a dispute arose, it was not

1349 729 S.W.2d 768 (Tex. App. 1987).

1350 *Lexington Inv. Co.* v. *Southwest Stainless, Inc.*, 697 F. Supp. 139, 144 (S.D.N.Y. 1988).

1351 *Mitsubishi Motors Corp.* v. *Soler Chrysler-Plymouth, Inc.*, 473 U.S. 614 (1985). For the historical development from hostility in the eighteenth and nineteenth centuries to favouring arbitration since the early twentieth century see Born 2014, at 40–43. See also *Mar-L en of La., Inc.* v. *Parsons-Gilbane*, 773 F.2d 633 (C.A.5 1985); *Commerce Park at DFW Freeport* v. *Mardian Construction Co.*, 729 F.2d 334 (C.A.5 1984).

1352 The Convention on the Recognition and Enforcement of Foreign Arbitral Awards (New York, on 10 June 1958, entered into force on 7 June 1959). See also Federal Arbitration Act 1925 and similar state arbitration legislation.

1353 *Virginia Carolina Tools, Inc.* v. *International Tool Supply, Inc.*, 984 F.2d 113 (C.A.4 1993). For discussion of the doctrine of severability in the United States see de Lotbinière McDougall/Ioannou 2006, Samuel 2006. For the definition of severability see Redfern/Hunter 2012, at 116; Born 2014, Chapter 3.

1354 US No. P3, *Anderra Energy Corp. and Petro Anderra, S.A.* v. *SAPET Development Corporation, Chanse Petroleum Corporation and Kai Chang*, United States District Court, 3:94-CV-2683-P, 29 September 1995 10 International Arbitration Report (1995) no 11 pp. E-1 – E-7.

1355 Ibid.

brought to arbitration, because allegedly there was no arbitration agreement binding the parties. The court concluded that the letter of intent contained a valid arbitration agreement. In reaching this conclusion the court relied on the formulation of the arbitration clause, namely its broad scope. The court noted that 'arbitration should not be denied unless it can be said with positive assurance that an arbitration clause is not susceptible of an interpretation which would cover the dispute at issue'.[1356] It noted that 'the parties obviously had the expectation to work together in the future, and to encounter disputes and discrepancies in connection with these projects'.[1357] Another peculiarity of this decision is that the court found that the scope of the arbitration clause also covered the joint ventures created for the realization of the projects contemplated by the letter of intent. This was decided despite the fact that one of the parties was the parent company of the party to the dispute. According to the court, the broad formulation of the arbitration clause implied its broad scope. Therefore, any dispute relating to the parties' projects was deemed to be solved by arbitration. The court granted a motion to compel arbitration and the parties were ordered to arbitrate their dispute.[1358]

Sandvik AB v. *Advent* confirms the validity of including the choice of arbitration to solve disputes arising under a letter of intent. In this case the parties' letter of intent contained no arbitration clause, and a district court was competent to hear the dispute. However, the district court noted as follows: 'our ruling today does not foreclose future negotiating parties from electing to enter pre-agreements to arbitrate disputes arising out of efforts to negotiate future contracts'.[1359]

6.5.8.3. Mediation

One form of dispute resolution is mediation. The question of enforceability of a mediation clause in a precontractual agreement comes back to the concept of agreement to agree. The relevant question is, in particular, whether a mediation clause goes beyond an agreement to agree, which is non-binding under US law and subject simply to the regime applicable to negotiations.[1360] The courts have enforced mediation clauses, provided the intent of the parties (as the main criterion of distinction between different preliminary arrangements) and other requirements of validity enabled the court to characterize the mediation clause as a contract to negotiate, subject to an intermediary regime.[1361]

The US courts have also invoked the Federal Arbitration Act (FAA) to decide on enforcement of mediation clauses. As a matter of fact, US case law has extended the

1356 Ibid.

1357 Ibid.

1358 The place of arbitration, the appointment of arbitrators and other issues have to be solved by §303 of the Federal Arbitration Act 1925.

1359 *Sandvik AB* v. *Advent Intern. Corp.*, 220 F.3d 99, 112 (C.A.3 2000). Cf *Virginia Carolina Tools, Inc.* v. *International Tool Supply, Inc.*, 984 F.2d 113 (C.A.4 1993).

1360 Tochtermann 2008, at 706.

1361 Tochtermann 2008, at 711.

applicability of the FAA to any methods of alternative dispute resolution including mediation clauses, as the FAA itself does not provide a definition of the term 'arbitration'.[1362] The US Supreme Court has guided the courts towards enforceability of alternative dispute resolution clauses. It has stated, namely, that '[t]he Arbitration Act establishes that, as a matter of federal law, any doubts concerning the scope of arbitrable issues should be resolved in favor of arbitration, whether the problem at hand is the construction of the contract language itself or an allegation of waiver, delay, or a like defense to arbitrability'.[1363]

However, US case law has not yet attained uniform results. The main problem for the courts has been the content of a mediation clause regarding the way it should be enforced, whether a specific performance should be ordered or the court should stay proceedings. Commentators have noted these mixed results in enforcement of mediation clauses.[1364]

6.6. Remedies and liability

In the majority of cases, liability for misconduct during negotiations is limited to the costs wasted in negotiations. This limitation appears in all cases of liability, be it liability for breach of contractual obligation, under the doctrine of promissory estoppel, in tort or in the law of restitution. In exceptional cases, loss of future eventual profits resulting from a failed contract could be recovered or an injunction available (for example, to prevent tortious appropriation of a trade secret). Furthermore, exceptionally, punitive damages may be imposed in US law under liability in tort. This Sub-section will address the conditions and measure of liability in contract law (6.6.1), under promissory estoppel (6.6.2), in tort law (6.6.3) and in law of restitution and unjust enrichment (6.6.4) and address the interaction of the causes of action (6.6.5).

6.6.1. *Contract law*

US contract law offers several types of remedies for breach of contractual obligations, recovery of damages being the main remedy. The conditions for imposing contractual liability are breach of a contractual obligation, damage and a causal link between these two. Foreseeable[1365] and certain[1366] damages may be recovered. The standard of proof for damages is a matter of state law. Essentially, the tests allow recovery of damage that is not 'too speculative, vague or contingent upon some unknown factor'.[1367]

1362 *Cecala* v. *Moore*, 982 F. Supp. 609 (N.D. Ill. 1997); Tochtermann 2008, at 700 ff.

1363 *Moses H. Cone Memorial Hosp.* v. *Mercury Const. Corp.*, 460 U.S. 1, 24 (1983). See also Tochtermann 2008, at 699.

1364 Drafting Committee UMA, 22–30 July 1999 Annual Meeting Draft, Annotation to section 5(i).

1365 *Hadley* v. *Baxendale* 156 ER 145 (Ex); Restatement (Second) of Contracts, §351. On the doctrine of foreseeability, see Calamari/Perillo, at 492 ff.

1366 Restatement (Second) of Contracts, §352; Calamari/Perillo, at 497 ff.

1367 *Spang & Co.* v. *US Steel Corp.*, 545 A.2d 861 (Pa. 1988); Restatement (Second) of Contracts, §352.

The main measure of liability for breach of contractual obligation is recovery of damage.[1368] Contract law protects two main interests of the parties:[1369] their expectation and reliance.[1370] The reliance interest is an 'interest in being reimbursed for loss caused by reliance on the contract by being put in as good a position as he would have been in had the contract not been made'.[1371] In a precontractual context, this covers the situation where no precontractual obligation has been taken. The expectation interest consists 'in having the benefit of his bargain by being put in as good a position as he would have been in had the contract been performed'.[1372]

In much of the case law, recovery for breach of a preliminary agreement has been limited to reliance interest.[1373] This is primarily motivated by the courts facing uncertainty as to the outcome of negotiations. As a consequence, the expectation related to the failed ultimate agreement is difficult to assess and measure.[1374] Furthermore, as one court has noted regarding an exclusivity provision in a preliminary agreement, 'it deals primarily with the manner of negotiations, not with their outcome, the damages that may be deemed to have arisen from defendant's breach of that promise are similarly limited'.[1375]

Even within the limitation to reliance interest, defining the measure of liability has been highly problematic for the courts. As has been noted, where the courts have accepted that a precontractual obligation may be created by a preliminary agreement, this has often been the obligation to negotiate the ultimate agreement in good faith. However, the content of the obligation of good faith is uncertain and disputed both by courts and legal scholars. Recovery for breach of obligation to negotiate in good faith has included the costs of the time spent and the 'out-of-pocket' expenses incurred during the negotiations. For example in *Copeland* v. *Baskin Robbins USA.*,[1376] the court noted the enforceability of an obligation to negotiate the ultimate agreement in good faith. It also noted that the

1368 Along with other remedial rights Restatement (Second) of Contracts, Introductory Note to Chapter 16 and §345. Due to the fact US law embraces the theory of 'efficient breach', specific performance is generally regarded as a rather exceptional remedy.

1369 The Restatement (Second) of Contracts names also the third interest – the restitution interest ('interest in having restored to him any benefit that he has conferred on the other parties.) However, it notes that in modern law the law of restitution provides the rules on this third interest. See Restatement (Second) of Contracts, §344 (c) and Restatement (Third) of Restitution and Unjust Enrichment, §38–39.

1370 Restatement (Second) of Contracts points to the interests protected by the non-exhaustive (ref Restatement (Second) of Contacts, Introductory Note to Chapter 16.

1371 Restatement (Second) of Contracts, §344 (b).

1372 Restatement (Second) of Contracts, §344 (a).

1373 *Copeland* v. *Baskin Robbins USA.*, 117 Cal. Rptr. 2d 875 (Cal.App. 2002). See *Fairbrook Leasing, Inc.* v. *Mesaba Aviation, Inc.*, 519 F.3d 421, 430 (C.A.8 2008); *Westerbeke Corp.* v. *Daihatsu Motor Co.*, 304 F.3d 200 (C.A.2 2002); *Gorodensky* v. *Mitsubishi Pulp Sales (MC), Inc.*, 92 F. Supp. 2d 249 (S.D.N.Y. 2000); *Goodstein Const. Corp.* v. *City of New York*, 604 N.E.2d 1356 (N.Y. 1992) (New York law limits recovery to reliance damages for breach of an agreement to negotiate, without distinguishing between Type I and Type II agreements).

1374 Restatement (Second) of Contracts, §349 Comment a.

1375 *Logan* v. *D.W. Sivers Co.*, 169 P.3d 1255, 1263 (Or. 2007).

1376 117 Cal. Rptr. 2d 875 (Cal.App. 2002).

'uncertain concept' of good faith and bad faith should not lead a party to benefit from a transaction that has never been made. According to the court 'the appropriate remedy for breach of a contract to negotiate is not damages for the injured party's lost expectations under the prospective contract but damages caused by the injured party's reliance on the agreement to negotiate'.[1377]

Similarly, recovery for a specific obligation of exclusivity (upheld as binding in an otherwise non-binding preliminary agreement) has been limited to reliance interest. As the court formulates, 'the nonsolicitation promise was directed to the *manner* of negotiations and not to their *outcome*'.[1378]

Another issue raised by the concept of reliance in the precontractual context is the question of whether it includes loss of opportunities. As one court has put it, damage in negotiations might include 'time spent, expenses incurred, opportunities foregone, or perhaps harm to... reputation'.[1379] It has been contended in the literature that in this case recovery of reliance damage would be equivalent to recovery of expectation damage.[1380]

Opinions as to whether recovery in the precontractual context should include an expectation interest are divided. Some scholars have submitted that this remedy is theoretically available, whereas the practical implementation, e.g. granting damages, is problematic. The reason is the difficulty in assessing, measuring and proving the expectation in a precontractual situation within the uncertainty of the content of the precontractual obligations, if these are not sufficiently specified by the parties. This has prevented the courts from granting expectation damages.[1381] Another opinion has been advanced that measuring expectation damage is difficult, but not impossible.[1382] In this way, expectation damage could be proved in *Evans, Inc.* v. *Tiffany & Co.*[1383] The court found that the damages were certain, because the parties would have come to the ultimate agreement, if the defendant had not breached its duty to negotiate in good faith. Similarly, in *Milex Products* v. *Alra Laboratories*,[1384] the court awarded the plaintiff expectation damages for breach of a duty to negotiate in good faith. The damages included loss of

1377 Ibid. See also *Fairbrook Leasing, Inc.* v. *Mesaba Aviation, Inc.*, 519 F.3d 421 (C.A.8 2008); *Westerbeke Corp.* v. *Daihatsu Motor Co.*, 304 F.3d 200 (C.A.2 2002); *Gorodensky* v. *Mitsubishi Pulp Sales (MC), Inc.*, 92 F. Supp. 2d 249 (S.D.N.Y. 2000); *Goodstein Const. Corp.* v. *City of New York*, 604 N.E.2d 1356 (N.Y. 1992).

1378 *Logan* v. *D.W. Sivers Co.*, 169 P.3d 1255, 1263 (Or. 2007) emphasis in original (breach of 'nonsollicitation provision' in a letter of intent).

1379 *Vestar Development II, LLC* v. *General Dynamics Corp.* 249 F.3d 958 C.A.9 (Cal.), 2001, at 262. See also *Copeland* v. *Baskin Robbins USA.*, 117 Cal. Rptr. 2d 875 (Cal.App. 2002) (court noted that the reliance damages may or may not include costs relating to loss of opportunity).

1380 Farnsworth 1987, at 225; Fuller/Perdue 1936.

1381 Farnsworth 2004, at 199. See also the cases where only reliance damages have been admitted, most of the cases discuss and reject the possibility of granting expectation damages.

1382 *Logan* v. *D.W. Sivers Co.*, 169 P.3d 1255, 1265 ff. (Or. 2007); Burton/Andersen1995, at 365; Knapp 1969, at 723.

1383 416 F. Supp. 224 (N.D. Ill. 1976).

1384 603 N.E.2d 1226 (Ill. App 1992).

profits. One commentator has concluded that to avoid liability measured by expectation damages, the breaching party has to offer evidence that the deal would have broken down even absent the breach.[1385]

6.6.2. Promissory estoppel

The doctrine of promissory estoppel gives rise to a remedy in equity. The conditions to be fulfilled in order to engage liability under the doctrine of promissory estoppel have already been addressed in Section 6.4.1 on promissory estoppel, because these conditions form the very essence of the working of this doctrine.

The court has a broad discretion in the choice of remedy under promissory estoppel. As follows from the current case law that the measure of liability for this action has been confined to recovery of damages. No specific enforcement of a precontractual promise has been granted; the courts have not ordered a party to honour its promise or conclude the final contract, the negotiations for which failed.

The amount of the damages recoverable 'should only be such as in the opinion of the court are necessary to prevent injustice'. Generally, recovery under the doctrine of promissory estoppel is not aimed at putting the promissee in a better position than the one in which it would have been if the promise had been kept. The amount of damage recoverable correlates with the extent of reliance that can be ascertained by the court.[1386]

In the same way, only reliance interest was awarded in *Elvin Associates* v. *Franklin*.[1387] Elvin Associates (a musical producer company) negotiated a role in a new musical with singer, Aretha Franklin. During negotiations, the singer was positive about her participation and had discussed several details of her role. The producer went proceeded to hire staff, booking locations for rehearsals and other preparations in New York. However, during negotiations (or shortly before) the singer developed a fear of flying. Franklin's representatives kept on insisting throughout negotiations on rehearsals in Detroit, and Franklin was positive about her role in the show in her personal communication with the producer. The rehearsals started in Detroit, but Franklin never came. Elvin Associates had to cancel the musical and sued Franklin to recover the costs of the preparations for the cancelled musical. After having examined the exchanges between the singer and the producer, the court analysed the intent of the parties, referring to the language of exchanges as the main relevant factor. The court concluded that no contract had come into existence, but found it appropriate to allow recovery on the basis of promissory estoppel. It granted recovery of reliance interest, namely payment of Elvin Associates' out of pocket expenses 'related to the failed production'.[1388]

1385 Eisenberg 2000, at 1809.
1386 *Hoffman* v. *Red Owl Stores, Inc.*, 133 N.W.2d 267 (Wis. 1965).
1387 735 F.Supp. 1177 (S.D.N.Y. 1990).
1388 735 F.Supp. 1177, 1777 (S.D.N.Y. 1990).

By contrast, the court allowed recovery of expectation interest (loss of potential profits) in *Walters* v. *Marathon Oil Co.*[1389] Marathon Oil Company started negotiations with Walters regarding the sale of a petrol station. Marathon Oil assured Walters that it would supply petrol to this station. Based on this assurance, Walters purchased the petrol station. Subsequently, negotiations about further petrol supply proceeded and Walters made improvements to the station. In the meantime instabilities in the oil market increased considerably due to a revolution in Iran. In these circumstances, Marathon Oil decided not to conclude the agreement on the supply of petrol. Walters sued Marathon Oil with a claim in promissory estoppel, asking for recovery of loss of profits. The court found the recovery of lost profits an appropriate measure to avoid injustice. An important argument in favour of allowing recovery of the loss of profit was the possibility of ascertaining the amount of loss from the evidence submitted to the court.[1390]

6.6.3. *Tort law*

Two tort actions are relevant for the precontractual period – the tort of deceit and the tort of appropriation of a trade secret. The elements of these torts have been addressed in Section 6.4, because their operation is best explained in this way. The measure of liability for the tort of deceit consists in recovery of 'pecuniary loss caused … by … justifiable reliance upon the misrepresentation'.[1391] The tort of deceit entitles the claimant to recovery of damages which are certain and not speculative, so damages that would certainly occur in the future may be recovered.[1392] In principle, case law limits recovery to damages that may be 'foreseeably expected to follow from the character of the misrepresentation'.[1393] In the context of misrepresenting intent to come to an agreement, the courts have limited the damages to reliance interest (granting the expenses incurred in negotiations). The abovementioned case of *Markov* v. *ABC Transfer & Storage Co.*[1394] represents rather an exception. There both the reliance interest (expenses caused by the move into another warehouse) and also loss of potential profits (caused by the impossibility of working with the principal customer who left) were allowed.

More generally, due to the fact that deceit is an intentional tort, further damages in tort are in principle available. These are consequential damages consisting of personal injuries, damages to property or expenses related to this property. To be recovered these damages should follow as a 'proximate' result of misrepresentation.[1395] This recovery is,

1389 *Walters* v. *Marathon Oil Co.*, 642 F.2d 1098 (C.A.2 1981).

1390 Compare with *Arcadian Phosphates, Inc.* v. *Arcadian Corp.*, 884 F.2d 69, 73 (C.A.2 1989): 'Out-of-pocket damages are particularly appropriate where, as may be the case here, the plaintiff cannot rationally calculate the benefit of the bargain'.

1391 Restatement (Second) of Torts, §525, see also §549.

1392 Prosser 1971, at 730.

1393 Prosser 1971, at 733.

1394 457 P.2d 535 (Wash. 1969).

1395 Prosser 1971, at 735.

however, unusual at least in the existing case law on fraudulent misrepresentation of an intent to reach agreement in the context of failed negotiations.

Liability for the tort of misappropriation of trade secret consists in reimbursement of 'loss caused by the appropriation or gain resulting from appropriation, whichever is greater'.[1396] This echoes the law of restitution (providing a remedy in the amount of the benefit from misappropriated ideas). Keeton explains such interaction as a choice between remedies to be made by the claimant, as liability in tort and the law of restitution are construed in a similar way.[1397] Furthermore, a specific remedy in the form of injunction is available in order to prevent a continuing or threatened misappropriation of a trade secret.[1398] Both preliminary injunctions and injunctions as final relief may be granted for this purpose.[1399] Finally, under US law, both of these torts may lead to punitive damages.

6.6.4. *Law of restitution and unjust enrichment*

As has been noted, liability in the law of restitution and unjust enrichment is construed as liability in tort. The elements of a claim in restitution have been addressed in Section 6.4. The law of restitution enables recovery of the benefit which the liable party received.[1400] The determination of the amount of benefit conferred to the other party is a question of fact (and thus to be decided by the jury). It has been broadly accepted that the benefit to be recoverable is measured by its market value.[1401] In the case *Massachusetts Eye and Ear Infirmary* v. *QLT Phototherapeutics, Inc.*, discussed earlier, the remedy was of continuing royalties on the sales of a medicine when a manufacturer benefited from an idea disclosed by the clinic in negotiations. As has been noted, this case is rather an exceptional one where recovery under the law of restitution was granted in the context of failed negotiations.

6.6.5. *Interaction of causes of action*

Under US law, contractual organization of negotiations can play a role in the interaction between contract and non-contractual causes of action. Historically, in the United States, the borderline between contract and tort has never been completely distinct. Private law evolved initially as a single body of rules, while the distinction between contract and extra-contractual doctrines was drawn only in the nineteenth century. In the context of contractually organized negotiations, a contractual claim

1396 Restatement (Third) of Unfair Competition, §45(1).

1397 Keeton 1984, at 672.

1398 Restatement (Third) of Unfair Competition, §44.

1399 Restatement (Third) of Unfair Competition, §44 Comment g.

1400 Restatement (Third) of Restitution and Unjust Enrichment, §31 and Comments.

1401 *Massachusetts Eye and Ear Infirmary* v. *QLT Phototherapeutics, Inc.* 552 F.3d 47 (C.A.1 2009); *Dines* v. *Liberty Mut. Ins. Co.*, 548 N.E.2d 1268 (Mass.App. 1990); *Hill* v. *Waxberg*, 237 F.2d 936 (C.A.9 1956); Restatement (Third) of Restitution and Unjust Enrichment, §31 Comment h.

would prevail if the damage is caused by a breach of a contractual obligation, for example, a breach of an agreed temporary exclusivity of negotiations. However, this does not mean that a claim for damage in tort cannot be established. Due to its historical roots in English law, the US legal system allows the claimant to choose the cause of action if one set of facts may lead to recovery under different fields of law. A combination of causes of action is also possible. For example, a claim can include a contract law claim for damages for breach of an obligation of good faith, and a tortious claim for misappropriation of information.[1402] The combination of claims most likely to be allowed is a claim for breach of contract and fraud (related to the breach of contract).

In this way, contractual organization of negotiations adds a possibility of recovery based on contract law instead of recovery on an extra-contractual basis or in addition to an extra-contractual claim. At the same time, pragmatically, a claim in contract is not always an attractive option for the claimant in the US system. The reason for this is that a claim in tort may enable a higher recovery: a breach of a contract entitles only to recovery of the amount bargained for, whereas breach of a duty entitles, by contrast, recovery of all harm caused by such a breach. As a result, claimants frequently 'strive to persuade courts that borderline cases should be classified as tort in order to avoid the contract limitation of damages'.[1403] Therefore, in a case at the borderline between contract and tort, it may be unattractive to establish a claim grounded in contractual organization of negotiations if an extra-contractual duty is breached. However, as noted earlier, the US approach to negotiations establishes no duties related to contractual negotiations, except for those related to exchange of confidential information and fraud. As a consequence, in a number situations, contractual organization of negotiations may provide the only basis for recovery.

6.6.6. *Note on punitive damages*

One peculiarity of US law is the possibility to impose punitive damages. Generally, US law draws a distinction between compensatory and non-compensatory damages. Non-compensatory damages include nominal damages – usually in the amount of six cents or one dollar awarded to symbolize the wrong – and punitive damages.[1404] These damages sanction malicious conduct which is intentional and deliberate. The aim of punitive damages is to provide a deterrent for the general public to prevent the conduct sanctioned in a particular decision. Punitive damages are usually awarded in tort claims, but may also accompany a claim for breach of contract, if the breach of the contractual obligation 'is accompanied by an independent malicious or wanton tort'.[1405] From this function flows the amount of punitive damages – these are usually high and can reach millions of

[1402] Sorensen/Davidson/White 2012.
[1403] McDowell 1985, at 287; *Young* v. *Abalene Pest Control Servs., Inc.*, 444 A.2d 514 (N.H. 1982).
[1404] Calamari/Perillo 2009, at 487.
[1405] Prosser 1971, at 9; Calamari/Perillo 2009, at 488; Sebok 2012.

dollars. Punitive damages are discretionary. They are only awarded at the discretion of the judge or the jury.[1406]

The reason for mentioning punitive damage is that the application of the all or nothing model to the parties' negotiations has indeed led to the imposition of punitive damages.[1407] However, no punitive damages have yet been awarded within the intermediary regime of preliminary agreements.

6.7. Conclusion

Under US law, as a general starting point, one may break off negotiations any time without liability and bargain freely. This is not so if one enters into a preliminary agreement imposing a duty to negotiate in good faith (to the extent state law admits this) or imposing other, more concrete obligations, which are binding prior to the formation of the ultimate agreement. A preliminary regime applies if the agreement in question fulfils the following conditions, progressively developed in the case law. The main condition of validity is the party's intent to be bound by the conditions of the preliminary agreement (by contrast with intent not to be bound by the ultimate agreement). The development of the other conditions for the validity of an obligation in a preliminary agreement is on-going, where the requirements of definiteness of terms and consideration also appear to be relevant.

Whilst a precontractual agreement may lead to liability, it may also limit potential exposure. As a matter of fact, a limited number of binding obligations in an otherwise clearly non-binding document confines contractual liability to recovery for breach of these concrete obligations. It should be noted, at the same time, that the application of a preliminary regime is not the mainstream approach. The main approach of the courts is to search in the first place for a formed ultimate agreement.[1408]

Furthermore, the possibility to contractualize the process of negotiations is limited by a number of non-contractual rules. The doctrine of promissory estoppel, tort, and restitution restrict precontractual behaviour by sanctioning a number of types of conduct that may occur in contractual negotiations. The main types of sanctioned behaviour are creating a precontractual reliance to the detriment of the other party, fraudulently misrepresenting an intention to reach agreement, fraudulently benefiting from information disclosed in negotiations or unjust enrichment from performance rendered in anticipation of a contract.

There is also another, more subtle role for non-contractual doctrines which is relevant for negotiations. Concepts that have no developed or stable content in contract law are

1406 Meurkens 2012, at 10 ff.

1407 *Texaco, Inc.* v. *Pennzoil*, Co., 729 S.W.2d 768 (Tex. App. 1987).

1408 See Section 6.3.3.

developed under the influence of non-contractual doctrines. Two illustrations may be used: firstly, the US doctrine of promissory estoppel, the elements of which are closer to tort law than to contract law; secondly, while it cannot be said that the duty of good faith and fair dealing at the precontractual stage has acquired any general or overarching content, it echoes the tort law requirement to avoid deliberate misconduct. The latter development has been noted by scholars who have summarized the possible content of a duty of good faith at the precontractual stage.[1409]

1409 See inter alia Farnsworth 1987, at 269; Klein/Bachechi 1994; Kessler/Fine 1964; Eisenberg 2000.

Chapter 7

COMPARATIVE OBSERVATIONS

7.1. Introduction

The previous Chapters have addressed the approaches to letter of intent in the Netherlands, France, England and Wales, and the United States. This Chapter will identify commonalities and differences in the national approaches and explain the main converging and diverging tendencies. The comparison will be structured around the main provisions of letter of intent – obligations that contractually organize the dynamics of negotiations. Each obligation will be illustrated and analysed in a comparative perspective. The structure of the Chapter aims to reflect the content of letter of intent used in practice. For this reason, a note on the selection of the provisions will be made prior to the analysis.

Comparative observations will address the following questions. What is the approach of each provision framing the dynamics of negotiations in a comparative perspective? What similarities and differences can be observed? Is each obligation treated as severable and stand-alone, as hypothesized in Chapter 2? Can converging tendencies be revealed in the liability that may be incurred for the breach of the obligations? How can the similarities and differences identified be explained?

After a note on the provenance and selection of the provisions discussed (Section 7.2), the following clauses of letter of intent will be addressed in this Chapter. Firstly, the provisions whereby the parties endorse an obligation to negotiate (Section 7.3) or conduct negotiations in a specific way, for example require *bona fides*, best efforts and similar, with or without specifying the content of the duty (Section 7.4). Secondly, clauses whereby the parties purport to keep negotiations non-binding and free from any regulation, contractual and non-contractual (Section 7.5) or make an explicit division between the binding and non-binding provisions of letter of intent (Section 7.6). Thirdly, the formulations purporting to create stand-alone obligations confined to the process of negotiations and limited in time to contract formation. This is the case with an obligation of confidentiality. Parties may agree on non-disclosure of any information disclosed in the course of negotiations, for example in the domain of innovation. Parties may also aim to keep secret the *mere fact* of negotiations, because it may represent a value in itself, while public disclosure of the fact of negotiations may be used as a bargaining tactic, as noted earlier[1410] (Section 7.7). In the same way, parties establish exclusivity of negotiations. Exclusivity provisions frame and limit the strategies and tactics of bargaining. It may be recalled, for example, that a reference to better conditions offered in parallel negotiations may be used as a bargaining tactic[1411] (Section 7.8). Fourthly, the provisions on the distribution of costs. Parties deal with costs in two main ways: the clause either defines the distribution of costs in the course of negotiations and in the case of their failure or combines the questions of costs and liability by detailing or explicitly limiting liability (both contractual and non-contractual). Such obligations aim to contain and limit potential exposure in case of failure of negotiations and distribute risks (Section 7.9). Fifthly, the dispute resolution clauses: choice of applicable law and competent forum, including arbitration and mediation. These provisions relate primarily to the management of the transaction and legal certainty in case of a dispute (Section 7.10). Thereafter, the Chapter will compare the remedies (Section 7.11) and provide explanations for the similarities and differences in the national approaches (Section 7.12).

7.2. Note on the selection of the provisions addressed

Published case law contains numerous quotes of the texts of letters of intent used in practice. These quotes have been collected during this research in the study of the national approaches. To find and collect these texts, a search by keywords was undertaken in the national case law databases.[1412] The keywords included all the multiple titles given to precontractual documents in practice.[1413] In addition, the selected cases included case law reported as significant in the academic literature of the selected jurisdictions. Thereafter, the criterion formulated in Chapter 2 for identifying the dynamic constituent of negotiations has been applied to the collected texts. Their provisions were divided into two types: those relating to the substance of the final contract, on the one hand, and those framing the dynamics of negotiations, on the other hand. The former were disregarded, while the latter have been taken into consideration for further analysis. As a result of this selection, the main types of provisions found in the texts of letter of intent were extracted. These have been used to structure the comparative observations in this Chapter.

Furthermore, the selection seeks to illustrate those provisions drafted in practice; the results are qualitative. These means no statistically relevant conclusions are drawn from the analysis, but the examples are still representative of the modern drafting practice.

Most of the texts of letter of intent have been found in English and US case law. This is due to the general style of reasoning found in case law of the common law traditions. The

[1410] Section 2.2.1.
[1411] Ibid.
[1412] On the method see inter alia with further references Seale/Tonkiss 2011, at 458 (on keyword analysis).
[1413] Section 1.2.1.

judges state the facts that give rise to the dispute in considerable detail and frequently quote the case materials. By contrast, French and Dutch case law generally refrains from citing original documents or only includes very short quotes. This is why fewer examples are found in French and Dutch case law, but these will be quoted where available. Finally, priority in the selection of illustrations has been given to case law involving international transactions.

One may raise an objection to this approach. For instance, it may be argued that examples of letter of intent quoted in case law are poorly drafted. As a consequence they cause litigation, but are not representative of contracting practice. To this objection the following can be answered. Firstly, as noted in Section 1.2.3, this study has been from the outset narrowed down to documents that do not easily qualify under the existing legal categories and doctrines, as follows from an authoritative analysis based, in its turn, on a collection of letters of intent used in practice.[1414] Secondly, and perhaps more importantly, this research finds that problems posed by issuing letters of intent are not due to inaccurate drafting. Undoubtedly, unclear drafting occurs. But contract law is normally sufficiently well equiped to resolve uncertainties. The problems caused by letter of intent reside, on the contrary, in the difficulty in applying the existing legal doctrines, essentially offer and acceptance, to the process of negotiations. For these reasons, even if a 'perfect sample' of a letter of intent existed,[1415] it would still raise the questions identified at the beginning of this study.

7.3. Obligation to negotiate or agreement to agree

A: Illustration

An obligation to negotiate aims to bind the negotiating parties to continue the negotiations commenced. For instance, in the example that follows, parties undertake to use 'every reasonable effort to agree' on the ultimate agreement. The text also states that should these efforts fail, no further obligations arise.

> Itek and CAI shall make every reasonable effort to agree upon and have prepared as quickly as possible a contract providing for the foregoing purchase by Itek and sale by CAI, subject to the approval of CAI stockholders, embodying the above terms and such other terms and conditions as the parties shall agree upon. If the parties fail to agree upon and execute such a contract they shall be under no further obligation to one another.[1416]

1414 See Fontaine/De Ly 2009, at 4.

1415 Literature proposes some models for drafting. See Lake/Draetta 1994 at 269 ff.; Wessels 2010 (model letters of intent in Annexes); Snijders 2015; Lettre d'Intention Type, Association Française des Investisseurs en Capital, Capital-Risque: Guide des Bonnes Pratiques AFIC 2010, p. 90, www.afic.asso.fr/dl.php?table=etude_publication&chemin=uploads/_afic&nom_file=capital-risque-guide-des-bonnes-pratiques-version-2010_1.pdf and numerous examples on different professional and semi-professional websites.

1416 *Itek Corp.* v. *Chicago Aerial Indus., Inc.*, 248 A.2d 625, 627 (Del. 1968).

B: Analysis

An obligation to negotiate or an agreement to agree aims to limit freedom of negotiations by private regulation. Its enforceability interacts closely with the scope of freedom of negotiations and the mandatory restrictions of this freedom.

The starting point of the English law approach to such clauses marks the distinction between this legal system and all the other approaches addressed. Such a clause creates no legally enforceable obligations because of its indefiniteness, uncertainty, and lack of consideration (clear counterpart).[1417] A party may at any time refuse to negotiate or reach agreement on the grounds of his commercial interest. This is the starting point of the English approach to the enforceability of agreements to negotiate or agreements to agree. It applies as well to other formulations that aim to create an obligation to commence or continue negotiations, and use best efforts, best endeavours or reasonable endeavours in negotiating a transaction.

By contrast to the English approach, in both Dutch and French law, an obligation to negotiate may become contractually binding within the frameworks governing preliminary agreements (*voorovereenkomst*, *avant-contrat*). In this regard, it may be recalled that both legal systems establish a broad requirement of *bona fides* in negotiations. This raises the question of the actual effect of rehearsing the requirement by a contractual obligations. In both legal systems, the possible impact is the following. This provision may supply the detail and concretize the duties established by the national interpretation of *bona fides*. Furthermore, in both France and the Netherlands, an obligation to negotiate transforms the duties implied by *bona fides* into a contractual obligation. This may lead to a change in the nature of liability (from non-contractual liability to liability for breach of a preliminary agreement). Case law demonstrates that such provisions have guided French and Dutch courts in the interpretation of the content of *bona fides*. Courts have been generally sensitive to the description of the parties' actual commitments and expectations, especially in complex transactions.

Notably, a party's commercial self-interest in breaking off negotiations has been upheld as a valid impediment to respecting an obligation to negotiate. More specifically, French courts have referred to commercial interests as good economic reasons and have taken into account only those that could be objectively observed by the court.[1418] Dutch courts have referred, for instance, to a change in economic circumstances enabling negotiations to be broken off without liability (e.g. compliant with the duty of reasonableness and fairness).[1419] In both countries, illustrative examples include walking away from the negotiated deal due to the results of preliminary feasibility studies, verification of the financial information provided by the other party, and changes on the relevant market. However, in neither the Netherlands nor in France, were changes in the internal policy of a company regarded as a valid reason to stop negotiations.

[1417] Section 5.3.2.1.
[1418] Section 4.3.3.1.
[1419] Section 3.3.2.3.

In Dutch and French law, the scope of such a contractual obligation is limited to an obligation to use all available means (*obligation de moyens*; *inspanningsverplichting*) and is confined to the process of negotiations. Parties should not 'sabotage' the process of negotiations, but they are not required to conclude the final contract. Dutch scholars have advanced an opinion that such provision implies an obligation to inform the counterpart about parallel negotiations. According to them it may also imply a right of being given a 'last chance'.[1420] This means that before negotiations are broken off, an offer should be made to the party to the letter of intent on the same conditions as those offered to a third party. In addition, under the Dutch approach, the court may order parties to negotiate by issuing an injunction, but failure to agree does not prevent a subsequent claim in damages.[1421]

The US legal system occupies a middle position. In the United States, contract law is a matter of state law and the approach differs across the states. Some states, for example notably in New York law, adopt a reasoning identical to the English one: an agreement to agree creates no legally binding obligations, because it is not sufficiently certain to be enforced and has no counterpart (consideration). By contrast, in other states, in the presence of an obligation to negotiate, courts have been prepared to imply the requirement of *bona fides*.[1422] US law has developed no overarching duty of good faith, but has been to some extent receptive to the European continental influence. The content of implied *bona fides* resembles the content of an obligation of means known to civil law traditions. Parties should reply in a timely manner and not 'sabotage' negotiations, but are not obliged to conclude the final contract.

Along with the marked divergence addressed above, one converging tendency regarding the obligation to negotiate may be observed. English courts have been ready to enforce a limited number of obligations resembling the obligation to negotiate, but which specify 'some machinery'[1423] of negotiations. In particular, English courts have enforced and obligation to use best endeavours or reasonable endeavours to obtain an export licence or a planning permission. Even when created at the stage of negotiations, this kind of obligation was considered to be sufficiently certain to be enforced.[1424] As to its content, '[t]hese words (best endeavours) oblige the purchaser to take all those reasonable steps which a prudent and determined man acting in his own interests and anxious to obtain planning permission would have taken'.[1425] Obligations on exclusivity and confidentiality of negotiations (to be addressed separately below) are also regarded as clauses containing a 'machinery' which can be enforceable under English law. In sum, in all the legal systems selected, in complex transactions, the higher the level of details in a provision establishing such obligation, the more it has *de facto* influenced the courts in the assessment of its breach.

1420 De Kluiver 1992, at 117–124.

1421 See also Section 7.11.4.

1422 Section 6.3.3.2.

1423 Peel 2010, at 42.

1424 *Little* v. *Courage Ltd* [1995] CLC 164 (EWCA) 476.

1425 *IBM United Kingdom Ltd.* v. *Rockware Glass Ltd.* [1980] FSR 335 (EWCA) 336 (Lord Geoffrey Lane) (obtaining planning permission in a contract for sale of land).

The difference in the approaches discussed above reflects the contrast in assumptions about negotiations. English law perceives negotiations as a genuinely adversarial process. Even if in practice, as Lord Steyn has stated extra-judicially, 'businessmen ... understand very well what bad faith means',[1426] English law on negotiations is based on a moral foundation to a lesser degree than all the other legal systems addressed. This approach of contract law is a matter of policy.[1427] The US legal system adopts a similar starting point, but has a different focus. It perceives negotiations primarily as *alea* – a process of risks and unexpected outcomes where the parties are also in an adversarial position. In this way, the focus is on risk rather than each party's own interest. By contrast, French and Dutch law regard negotiations as a process where *some* cooperation between the parties is in place. A certain level of contractual cooperation or *solidarisme contractuel*,[1428] loyalty, and a taking into account, or at least awareness, of the other party's interests are already assumed at the stage of negotiations before the ultimate agreement is formed. More specifically, French case law has developed rules covering the entire process of negotiations – the 'ethics of negotiations'.[1429] The focal point of Dutch law is the breaking off of negotiations. The main question is whether breaking off of negotiations in a given case is contrary to reasonableness and fairness. The functioning of the duty of reasonableness and fairness has even been compared to an *invisible magnetic field*[1430] between the parties, not allowing them to break off negotiations without liability.

Referring to the concepts from negotiation studies discussed in Chapter 2, it is possible to say that the English and US legal systems address negotiations as a distributive process, while French and Dutch law assume that negotiations represent a cooperative process. It can be said generally that the use of a distributive tactic in negotiations entails a considerably higher risk of being regarded as contrary to the obligation to negotiate in French and Dutch law than it does in English and US law.

7.4. Obligation to negotiate in good faith

A: Illustration

An obligation to negotiate in good faith recalls the duty of *bona fides* that exist in Dutch and French law and aims to create contractually such a duty in the US and English approaches. Parties may namely provide a general requirement of good faith:

> Parties agree[d] to hereby discuss and negotiate in good faith to reach an Agreement.[1431]

[1426] Steyn 1997, at 438.
[1427] Cartwright/Hesselink 2006, at 466.
[1428] See inter alia with further references Boismain 2005; Courdier-Cuisinier 2006.
[1429] Section 4.3.
[1430] Nieuwenhuis 2010, at 289.
[1431] *Sun Pharmaceutical Industries, Inc.* v. *Core Tech Solutions, Inc.*, Not Reported, 2013 WL 1942619, 3 (N.J.Super.A.D. 2013).

Alternatively, the provision may include more details on the content of good faith specific to a particular deal, as illustrated by the following two examples.

> The Seller and Purchaser each agree to negotiate in good faith towards the prompt execution of such documentation.[1432]
> [T]he signatories to this letter confirm their intent to continue good faith discussions directed toward the creation of formal written contracts that, upon approval by the board of Directors of each party, will be executed to establish the following arrangements, and to do such other things as may be required in connection therewith.[1433]

B: Analysis

The enforceability and content of an obligation to negotiate in good faith are ascertained in the same way as the previously discussed agreement to agree. As discussed earlier, English and US law do not recognize that a party has a duty to consider its counterpart's bargaining interests. By contrast, a more cooperative approach underpins French and Dutch law. This approach may require compromising one's negotiating position if negotiations are advanced. In this way, a reference to *bona fides* besides the obligation to negotiate has rather a symbolic character. At the same time, recalling *bona fides* in a contractual obligation might facilitate an argument establishing liability for breaking off negotiations (in the legal systems which admit such liability) or fault in negotiations. Furthermore, in French and Dutch law, this may lead to a change of the nature of liability, making the liability contractual. Finally, the more detailed the provision is, the higher the chance an enforceable obligation will be found.

Some further remarks should be made on the threshold of *bona fides*. Generally, the requirements of *bona fides* can be set at various levels. 'In some systems good faith means no more than subjective honesty in fact, while in others it extends to objective fair dealing and in yet others is considered breached by conduct which does not involve dishonesty or sharp practice but is simply a failure to act reasonably'.[1434] US state law that allows good faith and fair dealing to be implied into negotiations sets subjective standards: honesty in fact is required. French law requires subjective *bona fides*. The judges assess the subjective attitude of the negotiating parties. However, as a matter of fact, French courts often pragmatically refer to objective manifestations of conduct identified and relate these to possible reasonable conduct as a reference. Dutch law requires objective *bona fides*.[1435]

1432 *JSD Corporation PTE Ltd* v. *Al Waha Capital PJSC, Second Waha Lease Ltd* [2009] EWHC 583 (Ch), 2009 WL 648840 [83].
1433 *Rennick* v. *O.P.T.I.O.N. Care, Inc.*, 77 F.3d 309 77 F.3d 309, 316 (C.A.9 1996).
1434 Goode 2012, at 33.
1435 Section 3.3.2.1.

7.5. Keeping negotiations non-binding

A: Illustration

Parties may aim to keep negotiations non-binding or, to be precise, qualify documents created in the course of negotiations as non-binding. For instance, the provisions in the examples below expressly characterize letter of intent as non-binding.

> We will proceed to make arrangements with counsel for each of the parties for the completion of the Interim Agreement ... with the understanding that this letter of intent is of no binding effect on any party hereto.[1436]
>
> This non-binding Letter of Intent represents the fundamental terms and conditions upon which I am prepared to enter into a Stock Purchase Agreement.[1437]

B: Analysis

To what extent is it possible to waive by private regulation the rules applicable to negotiations? In answering this question, it may be noted generally that in all the legal systems discussed, contract law duties and liability are generally easier to waive than a non-contractual framework. At the same time, negotiations are regulated to a large extent by non-contractual rules. As a consequence, even in the legal systems where such a provision is likely to keep negotiations non-binding under contract law (i.e. create no contractual obligations), it may still fail to exclude the application of any non-contractual protection of reliance and limitation on freedom of negotiations.

More specifically, English law acknowledges the possibility to expressly keep agreements binding only in honour, but not in law (honourable pledge).[1438] Such a provision creates no obligations which can be enforced by a court. An obligation binding only in honour is one of the possible qualifications of the provision under discussion purporting to keep negotiations non-binding. By contrast, the non-contractual doctrine of unjust enrichment – one of the important causes of actions at the precontractual stage – would still apply; it may not be waived by such a provision. French law has developed a concept of *engagement d'honneur* and Dutch law that of gentleman's agreement. In both of these civil law traditions, by contrast with English law, an obligation in honour does not place the relationship outside legal regulation. Therefore, this qualification of a letter of intent is unlikely to keep negotiations non-binding in these legal systems.

Furthermore, in English law, an express statement that negotiations are non-binding relates to another doctrine – that of intention to create legal relations. No final contract can be found in the absence of intention to create legal relations. Considerable English case law addresses such provisions, frequently referred to as negotiations 'subject to contract'. In principle, a negation of contractual intent has led in many cases to

1436 *Rennick* v. *O.P.T.I.O.N. Care, Inc.*, 77 F.3d 309 77 F.3d 309, 316 (C.A.9 1996).

1437 *Weigel Broadcasting Co.* v. *TV-49, Inc.*, 466 F.Supp.2d 1011, 1012 (N.D. Ill. 2006).

1438 Section 5.4.1.

negotiations being confirmed as non-binding. As negotiations are generally non-binding from the point of view of English contract law, the question asked in case law was rather whether the final contract was formed). However, the related case law has been increasingly nuanced.[1439] In the cases, where the conclusion of the final contract in a precise form was described as a formality, the provision attempting to keep negotiations non-binding was disregarded by English courts.[1440] In some situations where parties negotiated 'subject to contract', but performed a large part of the final contract, English courts have granted a contractual cause of action to both parties.[1441] More frequently, however, courts granted restitution of the performance made in anticipation of a contract[1442] or no recovery.[1443]

US law acknowledges the concept of gentleman's agreement. However, US courts have assessed such provisions primarily with a detailed inquiry into the intent of the parties. With this aim, a set of factors has been developed and most prominently applied under New York law.[1444] These include the language of the document, anticipated performance, open issues that remain to be negotiated, usual execution of a particular type of transaction in written form, and the general context of the case. It has been noted in US literature that the outcome of disputes involving negotiations is highly influenced by the technique of interpretation applied by the court. It has been argued, for instance, that the textual – literal – interpretation of the language of documents leads to more predictable results than the contextual interpretation, i.e. an interpretation giving greater importance to the context of the case rather than to the written documents accompanying negotiations.[1445] In this way, if more weight is given to factors other than the language of the clause, the clause may fail to prevent the application of mandatory rules applicable to negotiations. US case law includes numerous situations where the courts have disregarded the parties' attempts to keep negotiations non-binding or accorded more weight to other factors in the assessment of intent. This has been most criticized in cases where the court has not applied a preliminary regime, but found the final contract to have been concluded.[1446]

French case law provides fewer insights into the approach to such clauses than the common law. In French law, on the one hand, an important part of regulation may not be waived by the parties' agreement. The negotiation process is primarily regulated by extra-contractual doctrines and the duty of good faith, which may not be waived. On the other hand, the French framework of preliminary regimes includes the concept of project of contract.[1447] This preliminary regime implies only one obligation – the obligation to

[1439] Section 5.4.2.
[1440] Section 5.4.2.2.
[1441] Section 5.6.1.1.
[1442] Section 5.6.1.2.
[1443] Section 5.6.1.3.
[1444] Section 6.3.4.
[1445] Ibid.
[1446] Jeffries 2012; Schwartz/Scott 2007. On the landmark case mentioned in Section 1.1 of this study see inter alia Draetta 1988.
[1447] Section 4.4.1.1.

negotiate, while project of contract is regarded as a final contract in which only the parties' will to form the contract is absent. To a certain extent, this resembles the correlation established in the English law between the reservation about the non-binding character of negotiations and the intent to create legal relations.

Dutch courts have addressed such clauses within an assessment of lawfulness of breaking off negotiations. On the one hand, similarly to the French approach, the overarching duty of *bona fides* may not be waived by the parties' agreement. Dutch literature emphasizes that the parties' attempts to keep negotiations non-binding may be disregarded if they lead to results unacceptable from the point of view of reasonableness and fairness.[1448] On the other hand, Dutch courts have been more willing to regard breaking off negotiation as legitimate if a preliminary document stressed the non-binding character of negotiations. This has been taken into account in an assessment of the circumstances of the case – one of the factors considered to establish the lawfulness of breaking off negotiations.[1449]

More generally, the upholding of the non-binding character of negotiations by the court is strongly related, in all jurisdictions discussed, to two main factors. First, the manner of interpretation adopted by the court (literal or contextual) of the document at hand. Second, the balance between the relevance of the intent to create legal relations, anticipated performance, and risk taking.

7.6. Dividing negotiations into binding and non-binding parts

A: Illustration

Negotiating parties may aim to be bound by one or more contractual obligations starting from the commencement of negotiations, but keep the remaining content of negotiations non-binding. The following three examples illustrate this formulation. There, letter of intent is said to be non-binding, and the provisions that seek to create contractual obligations are mentioned as an exception to the general non-binding character of the letter of intent. The first example refers to concrete obligations. The second and the third illustration point to the number of the relevant clauses in the document.

> This letter of intent does not, except for the provisions of Sec. [8] with respect to the "Lock-Out-Period" and except for the vendor's waiver to increase the purchase price in Sec. 2.1, constitute legally binding and enforceable obligations...[1450]
>
> The terms of this Letter do not and are not intended to create binding legal obligations upon the parties hereto with the exception of this Clause and Clauses 5, 11 and 13 ...[1451]

1448 Section 3.7.3.

1449 Section 3.3.2.

1450 Hof Amsterdam 26 April 2011, ECLI:NL:GHAMS:2011:BQ5836, LJN BQ5836 (Dutch case involving a letter of intent drafted in English).

1451 *JSD Corporation PTE Ltd* v. *Al Waha Capital PJSC, Second Waha Lease Ltd* [2009] EWHC 583 (Ch), 2009 WL 648840 [83]. See also *Barnes & Robinson Co., Inc.* v. *OneSource Facility Services, Inc.*, 195 S.W.3d 637, 640 (Tenn. App. 2006).

In another example, only the seller's undertaking to provide the due diligence documents constitutes an obligation.

> Seller and Purchaser acknowledge that this Letter of Intent proposal is not a binding agreement and that it is intended solely to establish the principal terms of the purchase and as a basis for the preparation of a binding Purchase and Sale Agreement... provided, however, that in consideration of Purchaser's good faith efforts to review the due diligence material provided by Seller, Seller agrees to be bound to provide the required due diligence documents to Purchaser within the time required and to comply with the Non-Solicitation provision set forth above.[1452]
>
> This Letter of Intent is intended as an expression of mutual intent only and does not constitute an obligation binding in any way on the parties, except for the provisions of the third, fourth and fifth paragraphs hereof.[1453]

A similar approach is adopted in the following French example.

> Cette lettre d'intention ne constitue en aucun cas à ce stade, pour aucune des parties, un engagement ferme de réaliser l'Investissement, chacune restant libre de mettre fin à tout moment au projet d'Investissement. Toutefois, les sections [14 à 18 (Exclusivité, Frais, Confidentialité et information, Droit applicable et tribunal compétent, Absence d'effet obligatoire)] de cette lettre d'intention instaurent à la charge de certaines des parties certaines obligations, que les parties concernées s'engagent à exécuter et qui ne peuvent être résiliées ou modifiées qu'avec l'accord de toutes les parties.[1454]

B: Analysis

Three remarks can be made on the provisions dividing negotiations into binding and non-binding parts. First, these provisions should be considered in the light of the earlier observations on the clauses that aim to keep negotiations non-binding.[1455] These observations apply to the presently discussed provisions, because the impact of the non-contractual regime of negotiations may be only excluded in a limited way by private regulation.

Second, English law offers the most explicit approach to dividing negotiations into binding and non-binding parts. English courts have been willing to treat the obligations of exclusivity ('lock-out') and confidentiality as severable from the rest of the documents' content. This was done in cases where the rest of the documents' content was qualified as a non-binding agreement to agree. Notably, according to English courts, unenforceability

1452 *Logan* v. *D.W. Sivers Co.*, 169 P.3d 1255 (Or. 2007).

1453 *St. Joseph Hosp., Augusta, Georgia, Inc.* v. *Health Management Associates, Inc.*, 705 F.3d 1289, 1294 (C.A.11 2013).

1454 Lettre d'Intention Type, Association Française des Investisseurs en Capital, Capital-Risque: Guide des BonnesPratiquesAFIC2010,p.90,www.afic.asso.fr/dl.php?table=etude_publication&chemin=uploads/_afic&nom_file=capital-risque-guide-des-bonnes-pratiques-version-2010_1.pdf.

1455 Section 7.5.

of an agreement to agree included in a document does not lead to unenforceability of the rest of the document. In such a situation, English courts may still enforce the content of the letter. For instance, a provision on such a division has been upheld in a case where a letter of intent was signed between two independent commercial parties and clearly covered only negotiations of a complex transaction. The High Court suggested that the document had to be given a 'strict meaning' that is, the provisions were given the effect suggested by the literal interpretation of their language.[1456] In Dutch law, in the same way, the higher the sophistication of the deal, the higher priority may be given to literal interpretation and less relevance is accorded to the general guidelines for ascertaining the parties' intentions (the *Haviltex* criteria).[1457] The approach of the other legal systems in question is less explicit. In at least one US case, the court has simply disregarded such provision and made a general assessment of the parties' intent.[1458] A Dutch court has also disregarded such provision in a dispute involving an international transaction. However, invoking this Dutch case is problematic, because the court was applying German law on the basis of the choice of law made in the letter of intent and following Article 3 of Rome I Regulation.[1459]

Third, the division of letter of intent into binding and non-binding parts aims to establish contractually the severability of the provisions within the document, whereby each clause is analysed separately and independently from the other provisions of the letter of intent and from the final contract. At the same time, case law of all the jurisdictions discussed demonstrates that not all the provisions are readily treated as severable by the courts. The least doubt arises in relation to the severability of the provisions on dispute resolution, including choice of law and forum, mediation, and arbitration clauses. In the case law of all the jurisdictions analysed, these obligations have been severed from the final contract and, in particular, from the question of the fact of formation and enforceability of the final contract. The doctrine of severability of dispute resolution agreements is also a settled principle at the international level and flows from the New York Convention,[1460] the EU Regulation Brussels I-bis,[1461] and the Hague Convention on Choice of Court Agreements.[1462]

1456 Section 5.4.3.

1457 Section 3.4.3. The priority may be given at the discretion of the court, based on all circumstances of the case.

1458 *Lexington Inv. Co. v. Southwest Stainless, Inc.*, 697 F. Supp. 139 (S.D.N.Y. 1988).

1459 Hof Amsterdam 26 April 2011, ECLI:NL:GHAMS:2011:BQ5836, LJN BQ5836. The court has stated that German law should be applicable on the basis of choice of law made in the letter of intent and Article 3 Rome I Regulation, but no precise reference to German law is made in the reasoning about this provision.

1460 Articles II and V(1)(a) Convention on the Recognition and Enforcement of Foreign Arbitral Awards (New York, 1958). While the New York Convention does not directly establish severability of arbitration agreement, it indirectly assumes it. See Born 2014, at 354 ff.

1461 Article 25(5) Regulation (EU) No 1215/2012 of the European Parliament and of the Council of 12 December 2012 on Jurisdiction and the Recognition and Enforcement of Judgments in Civil and Commercial Matters (Recast) (Brussels I-bis).

1462 Article 3(d) Convention on Choice of Court Agreements (The Hague, 2005).

Furthermore, obligations on exclusivity and confidentiality of negotiations have also often been severed, i.e. analysed and enforced independently from the final contract and from the other obligations within the letter of intent.

As to the other obligations discussed, their severable treatment in case law has a mixed record. The trend appears to be that the higher the complexity of the transaction, the more thorough the analysis of negotiations undertaken by the court. It will then eventually extract the provisions creating obligations binding on their own within the negotiation process and address their legal effect. For example, French law clearly regards preliminary agreements as a regime distinct from the final contract. However, in only a few French cases have provisions of a preliminary agreement been addressed as stand-alone (except for the provisions on dispute resolution, exclusivity and confidentiality). Similarly, Dutch scholarship acknowledges a possibility to create a stand-alone obligation confined to negotiations within the framework of preliminary agreement (*voorovereenkomst*), yet Dutch case law confirming this position is not extensive.

7.7. Confidentiality

A: Illustration

Parties may aim to keep secret the *mere fact* of negotiations, agree on non-disclosure of the *information* disclosed in the course of negotiations or, on the contrary, *emphasize the non-confidential* character of the information exchanged. In the first example, parties make it clear that no privileged information should be exchanged in the course of negotiations.

> Pending the completion of the contract CAI will permit Itek and its representatives to examine CAI's finances, contracts and business and interview its officers and customers, all as designated by CAI, it being understood that CAI shall not be obligated to divulge trade secrets or confidential matters.[1463]

Another part of the same document guides the parties on the public disclosure of the fact of negotiations.

> A joint announcement to the press in the form attached shall be made by both companies on the afternoon of January 19, 1965, for publication in the morning papers January 20.[1464]

In the next illustration, parties establish confidentiality of the content of the letter of intent and the exceptions thereto. Furthermore, a press release can be made only with the consent of the counterpart in negotiations.

> The terms and conditions set out in this Letter shall remain confidential between the parties and each party acknowledges that this Letter contains commercially sensitive information

1463 *Itek Corp. v. Chicago Aerial Indus., Inc.*, 248 A.2d 625, 627 (Del. 1968).
1464 Ibid.

> and agrees not to disclose same except to their respective Boards of Directors, advisers and employees or potential financiers of the Aircraft or as otherwise agreed between the parties or required by applicable law. No press release may be made by either party without the other party's consent to the release and its content.[1465]

In the following illustration, both the existence of the letter of intent and its content are secret. Furthermore, the formulation establishes the way in which information should be disclosed, if this is required in the course of negotiations.

> L'existence et les termes de cette lettre d'intention sont strictement confidentiels. Les destinataires de la lettre d'intention s'engagent à ne pas les divulguer pendant [2 ans] à compter de la date de la lettre, sauf (a) aux tiers (actionnaires de la Société, employés, consultants, avocats et autres conseils) dans la mesure où ceux-ci auront à en prendre connaissance en vue de la réalisation de l'Investissement et dans la mesure où ces tiers seront eux mêmes liés par une obligation de confidentialité, (b) dans les cas requis par la loi et les règlements ou (c) en cas de litige pour les seuls besoins de la procédure.[1466]

The formulation of the final example aims to prevent unauthorized public disclosure.

> No announcements may be made about the Mirror's possible involvement in the de Krant project without the Mirror's prior approval.[1467]

B: Analysis

In all the legal systems discussed, courts have been willing to enforce non-disclosure provisions included in a letter of intent.[1468] This type of clause is one of the most frequently severed provisions, that is to say, clauses which are treated separately from the final contract and from the other content of a letter of intent.[1469] Case law frequently refers to a provision on confidentiality in a letter of intent as a binding agreement on its own. More specifically, English courts do not associate provisions on confidentiality with unenforceable agreements to agree. The same holds true for the United States. As one US court has stated regarding a confidentiality obligation: '[a]s to these provisions,

1465 *JSD Corporation PTE Ltd* v. *Al Waha Capital PJSC*, Second Waha Lease Ltd [2009] EWHC 583 (Ch), 2009 WL 648840 [83].

1466 Lettre d'Intention Type, Association Française des Investisseurs en Capital, Capital-Risque: Guide des BonnesPratiquesAFIC2010,p.90,www.afic.asso.fr/dl.php?table=etude_publication&chemin=uploads/_afic&nom_file=capital-risque-guide-des-bonnes-pratiques-version-2010_1.pdf.

1467 HR 24 November 1995, ECLI:NL:HR:1995:ZC1890, NJ 1996, 162 Van Engen/Mirror Group.

1468 The relevance of confidentiality in commercial transactions is broader than negotiations of contract. There is much to be said about the issues raised by confidentiality clauses (such as the question as to what information may be kept confidential, the questions of balance between public interest in anti-trust regulation and freedom of contract). These broader issues have been discussed in literature, and their detailed assessment is not possible or necessary within this study. This section is focused on the sphere of negotiations and limited to the validity of an obligation of confidentiality (or non-disclosure) in a letter of intent.

1469 See observations on severability in Section 7.6.

the letter of intent was indisputably a binding contract'.[1470] French case law adopts the same approach,[1471] and Dutch courts follow similar reasoning.[1472] Courts have also imposed contractual liability for breach of such an obligation.

The formulations quoted above deal with different aspects of confidentiality in negotiations. Firstly, the secrecy of the mere fact of negotiations appears to aim primarily at preventing the use of the tactic of public disclosure. As noted in Chapter 2, public disclosure of the fact that negotiations are taking place has been identified as a exerting powerful pressure on a party. This may play a role if, for example, the news about the deal may influence the value of the company's shares. The secrecy of the fact of negotiations loses all relevance if the negotiations fail.

Secondly, the obligation establishing confidentiality of information exchanged in negotiations aims to prevent another tactic used in negotiations. Non-confidential information may not be disclosed to third parties in order to induce a third party 'to propose more favourable conditions'.[1473] In the absence of a confidentiality provision, this use of information is authorized for instance in England and Wales and in the United States. According to French law using information obtained in negotiations with an aim other than the one for which it was disclosed is a breach of the ethics of loyalty in negotiations (*concurrence déloyale*). In the Netherlands, such use of information may be limited by the general duty of *bona fides* (to the extent that such disclosure is a detriment to the disclosing party).

Furthermore, in all the legal systems discussed, non-disclosure provisions may be relevant for non-contractual regulation. Provisions on confidentiality may serve as evidence of the parties' awareness of the privileged character of information. It may also confirm the contrary: the non-confidential character of the information received. Furthermore, the provision may streamline the assessment of the actual detriment.

The main categories of non-contractual regulation which may be relevant to confidentiality clauses are the following. In all of the jurisdictions discussed, obtaining profit from the use of information for a purpose other than the one for which it was provided in negotiations can lead to liability. English law is the most restrictive as to the threshold for obtaining recovery, though the possibility of recovery is not excluded. In the United States, this amounts to liability for misappropriation of a competitor's intangible trade values and leads to liability in tort.[1474] In French law, use of information obtained in negotiations to the detriment of the disclosing party may constitute a fault in tort.[1475]

[1470] *JamSports and Entertainment, LLC* v. *Paradama Productions, Inc.*, 336 F. Supp. 2d 824, 846 (N.D. Ill. 2004).

[1471] Section 4.6.4.

[1472] Section 3.7.6.

[1473] Official Comment 1 to Article 2.1.16 UPICC.

[1474] Section 6.4.2.2.

[1475] Section 4.3.2.5.

According to French case law, starting negotiations with the sole purpose of obtaining information is also a fault in tort.[1476] Dutch tort law adopts a similar approach.[1477]

7.8. Exclusivity

A: Illustration

Parties to negotiations may aim to prevent the same deal being negotiated with third parties. They establish exclusivity in negotiations and preclude parallel negotiations. Such clauses are referred to as 'lock-out' provisions in English case law; while in the US they are called 'no-shop', 'no-talk', and 'non-solicitation' provisions.

In the first example, the seller undertakes not to seek contacts with any third parties for 60 days.

> Seller and/or its representatives agree that it will not seek nor enter into a letter of intent or purchase agreement for sale of the Property with any third party for a period of sixty (60) days from the date this Letter of Intent is signed by both parties and becomes effective.[1478]

The following example also illustrates the temporary exclusivity of negotiations.

> Seller agrees to negotiate with Purchaser exclusively during the next ninety (90) day period to complete a mutually agreeable Purchase & Sale Agreement. If the parties are unable to reach final agreement on the formal Purchase & Sale Agreement during such period, neither party shall have any further obligation to the other.[1479]

In another illustration, during the period of exclusivity, parties shall not initiate discussions with third parties or make any commitment without a written agreement of the other party to letter of intent.

> Compte tenu des efforts entrepris par les Investisseurs en vue de la réalisation de l'Investissement, pendant la période courant jusqu'au [– – – –] (la "Période d'Exclusivité"), la Société et ses actionnaires signataires de la présente lettre d'intention donnent l'exclusivité à la présente proposition. Ils s'engagent à ne pas initier ou poursuivre toutes discussions ou à prendre tout engagement à l'égard de tiers en vue d'un investissement dans la Société ou de toute opération pouvant remettre en cause la réalisation de l'Investissement ou du Business Plan, sans l'accord préalable écrit des Investisseurs.[1480]

1476 Section 4.3.3.2.
1477 Section 3.5.
1478 *Logan* v. *D.W. Sivers Co.*, 169 P.3d 1255, 1257 (Or. 2007).
1479 *Vestar Development II, LLC* v. *General Dynamics Corp.*, 249 F.3d 958, 959 (C.A.9 2001).
1480 Lettre d'Intention Type, Association Française des Investisseurs en Capital, Capital-Risque: Guide des BonnesPratiquesAFIC2010,p.90,www.afic.asso.fr/dl.php?table=etude_publication&chemin=uploads/_afic&nom_file=capital-risque-guide-des-bonnes-pratiques-version-2010_1.pdf.

B: Analysis

By agreeing on exclusivity of negotiations, parties contractually limit their freedom of negotiations. It may be recalled that in all the legal systems analysed, freedom of negotiations allows parallel negotiations to be conducted. One transaction may be simultaneously negotiated with several potential partners, only one of which will become party to the final contract.

In all the legal systems in question, courts are favourable to enforcing an obligation of exclusivity of negotiations. Furthermore, provisions on exclusivity are treated as severable from the final contract and from other provisions of a letter of intent. For example, in one English case, exclusivity was 'something that was capable of subsisting as a binding contract independently of the continuing negotiations for the sale'.[1481] At the same time, the conditions for enforceability of such a provision differ. One condition shared by all the jurisdictions is the requirement to define the period of exclusivity, although, this period may also be implied by the court. English law has produced two requirements for the enforceability of a 'lock-out' agreement. Firstly, the period of exclusivity must be specified. This confers on a 'lock-out' agreement the certainty which is lacking in an agreement to agree or agreement to negotiate (the latter two create no binding obligations in English law).[1482] While English courts generally refrain from making an agreement in the place of the parties, courts may also imply the period of exclusivity. Secondly, exclusivity should be granted for consideration. This means some counterpart must be given in exchange for refraining from parallel negotiations. This requirement is specific to English law.

US case law emphasizes that an exclusivity provision in a letter of intent deals with the manner of negotiations as opposed to their outcome. US courts also look at the necessity to limit exclusivity in time. In cases where no time was specified, the period of exclusivity has been implied by the court. US courts have not been unanimous on further requirements; in some cases consideration was required.[1483]

In French law, exclusivity of negotiations may be established by any time of preliminary agreement (*avant-contrat*).[1484] One of these – the pre-emption agreement[1485] – comes close to the exclusivity provision. Pre-emption agreement is not aimed at preventing parallel negotiations, but establishes a priority in the choice of party to the final contract. This priority resembles what an English court has called the 'right of first negotiation'.[1486]

1481 *Pitt* v. *PHH Asset Management Ltd* [1994] 1 WLR 327 (EWCA) 328.
1482 Section 5.3.3.
1483 Section 6.5.1.2.
1484 Section 4.4.
1485 Pre-emption agreement is not only acknowledged in French case law, but is also included in the 2016 *Ordonnance* reforming the *Code civil*. See Section 4.4.2.1.
1486 Section 5.3.3.4.

In Dutch law, a provision on exclusivity in a letter of intent may, in principle, be created as a stand-alone obligation covering the period of negotiations. Courts also have regard to the need to limit the period of exclusivity. For instance, in one case,[1487] a Dutch court considered an exclusivity obligation to be irrelevant, because after a four-month negotiation, the parties had not made any progress in coming to an agreement. In another case,[1488] the court decided that the period of exclusivity ended when all options for further negotiations had been exhausted.

7.9. Provisions on costs incurred in negotiations

Complex negotiations may result in incurring costs. These include costs of due diligence, preliminary research or other preparation of the final contract. If the transaction develops successfully, clarity on cost allocation in the course of negotiations may still be appropriate for the smooth conclusion of the final contract (7.9.1). If the negotiations fail, these costs may represent a wasted expenditure. Their discussion is closely connected to the question of liability (7.9.2).

7.9.1. Cost allocation

A: Illustration

The following examples illustrate various ways in which parties *allocate costs* incurred in negotiations. The provision in the first example provides that *each party bears the costs* incurred in the course of negotiations, for instance consultants' fees, including lawyers and accountants.

> 6.1. Each Party shall pay the fees of the consultants each one of them retains in regard to the Transaction, including legal and accounting fees, and those of any other adviser.
> 6.2. Fees attributable to services provided to both Parties, if any, shall be paid by each of them in the respective proportions as may be agreed upon, provided that in the absence of such agreement the pertaining fees shall be paid equally by both Parties.[1489]

The next example establishes another principle. Each party bears his own costs in negotiations, but costs are allocated in an alternative way if the outcome of a planned audit contradicts the information initially provided in the course of negotiations.

> Si l'Augmentation de Capital ne se réalise pas, chacune des parties supportera les frais exposés par elle, et les Investisseurs supporteront les frais d'audit et relatifs aux conseils... [Toutefois, il est entendu que ces frais seront remboursés par la Société [si les audits révèlent que la

[1487] HR 15 May 1981, ECLI:NL:HR:1981:AG4190 *NJ* 1982, 85 Stuyvers/Eugster.

[1488] HR 27 May 2011, ECLI:NL:HR:2011:BP8707, *RvdW* 2011/686 Hemubo Betontechniek B.V./VVE Flatgebouw Strandhotel Zandvoort.

[1489] Exhibit 10 to Form 8-K filed by Gulf United Energy, Inc. on April 5, 2006 available in the open access database of the US Securities and Exchange Commission. See www.sec.gov/edgar.shtml.

situation de la Société est substantiellement différente de celle présentée dans les informations communiquées aux Investisseurs à la date de signature de cette lettre d'intention...[1490]

In the next illustration, if a party decides to break off negotiations, he undertakes to reimburse the 'reasonable and proper costs' of the anticipated performance.

If for whatever reason we at any time give notice to cease work (in which event you shall as soon as practicable cease all work) we shall reimburse all reasonable and proper costs incurred by you in accordance with the terms of this letter.[1491]

Cost allocation may also be accompanied by an *instruction, request or approval* to proceed with the expenses. The first formulation draws a distinction between the costs involved in the preliminary works, on the one hand, and the commencement of the performance of the final contract, on the other hand.

... this letter would authorise expenditure on preliminaries and specialist design works up to a value of £50,000, but that this letter of intent does not cover construction works which will be the subject of a separate instruction.[1492]

The three subsequent formulations instruct a party to the start performance of the final contract.

This letter constitutes an instruction to you to commence work but only as necessary for you to ensure that the agreed construction programme is met.[1493]
It was agreed that an early start to the works is required and Eugena is to arrange for site operations to commence on 21 February 2003.[1494]
RTS is now to commence all work required in order to meet Müller's deadlines set out in the Offer to allow commencement of full production by Müller on the Repack Lines by 30 September 2005.[1495]

In the following formulation, a request for performance is accompanied by a limitation of the amount that will be reimbursed.

Subject to the terms of this letter, ACC is authorised to proceed with the works up to a total value of £250,000 or any other sum which may subsequently be notified to you in writing by the BBC.[1496]

1490 Lettre d'Intention Type, Association Française des Investisseurs en Capital, Capital-Risque: Guide des BonnesPratiquesAFIC2010,p.90,www.afic.asso.fr/dl.php?table=etude_publication&chemin=uploads/_afic&nom_file=capital-risque-guide-des-bonnes-pratiques-version-2010_1.pdf.
1491 *Hackwood Ltd* v. *Areen Design Services Ltd* [2005] EWHC 2322 (TCC), (2006) 22 Const LJ 68 [14].
1492 *Eugena Ltd* v. *Gelande Corp Ltd* [2004] EWHC 3273 (QB), 2004 WL 2387190 [29].
1493 *ERDC Group Ltd* v. *Brunel University* [2006] EWHC 687 (TCC), [2006] BLR 255 [15].
1494 *Eugena Ltd* v. *Gelande Corp Ltd* [2004] EWHC 3273 (QB), 2004 WL 2387190 [29].
1495 *RTS Flexible Systems Ltd* v. *Molkerei Alois Müller GmbH & Co KG* [2010] UKSC 14, [2010] 1 WLR 753 [6].
1496 *AC Controls Limited* v. *British Broadcasting Corporation* [2002] EWHC 3132 (TCC), 89 Con LR 52 [21].

B: Analysis

A provision on the allocation of costs seeks to re-distribute the risks borne by the parties within the general regime of negotiations. Negotiations are regarded as a business risk in all of the selected legal systems. Each party equally bears the risks involved. These include primarily the risk that negotiations will fail and the investments of time and money will turn out to have been wasted expenditure.

A provision stating that each party bears his own costs in negotiations repeats the general framework of regulation. US courts have expressly noted that an express allocation of costs incurred in the course of negotiations points to the fact that the parties remain at the negotiations stage.[1497] Under the French approach, no damages can be recovered if parties agree by a preliminary agreement that each of them bears their own costs. The French approach thus gives priority to the re-allocation of risks by private regulation over that provided by the general regime of negotiations.[1498] The Dutch approach to some extent differs. Due to the role played by the overarching concept of *bona fides*, Dutch courts have a broad margin of appreciation over the parties' contractual agreements made in letter of intent. In case of dispute, the recoverable costs are subject to judicial approval, and the recoverable amount may be changed by the court, though the judicial discretion is limited.[1499] It is worth noting that in all the legal systems discussed, the courts' approach to the specific allocation of costs, for example, cost allocation that varies depending on the result of preliminary studies (as in the illustration in French above) is highly fact-specific.

Furthermore, a provision allocating costs can play a role in establishing the measure of liability. It is especially true for provisions with an instruction or request to proceed with performance. To explain this relevance, it is worth recalling that in all the discussed legal systems discussed, risks in negotiations are distributed differently if one party creates detrimental reliance by the other party that a contract will be formed. However, this protection of precontractual reliance is exceptional. In reality, it is granted infrequently. The most detailed approach is formulated by the US doctrine of promissory estoppel. French law protects the expectation that negotiations will result in the formation of a contract which increases with the advancement of negotiations – either a prolonged negotiation or simply very intensive negotiations.[1500] Case law includes several examples where inducing reliance or failure to prevent increasing reliance was regarded as a fault in tort. In Dutch law, the relevance of the inducement of reliance has been pointed to by the *Hoge Raad* within its assessment of the lawfulness of breaking off negotiations. To establish whether negotiations may be broken off

1497 *St. Joseph Hosp., Augusta, Georgia, Inc.* v. *Health Management Associates, Inc.*, 705 F.3d 1289 (C.A.11 2013).

1498 See however, on the application of the unjustified enrichment doctrine in exceptional cases of improvement of another's property in anticipation of a contract: Cass 1 civ 13 July 2004 N° 01-03608 Bulletin 2004 nº 208. See Section 4.5.

1499 Articles 6:248 para 2 and 6:94 are formulated restrictively.

1500 Section 4.3.

without breaching the duty of reasonableness and fairness, Dutch courts ascertain to what extent the party withdrawing from negotiations has contributed to raising the legitimate expectation that the negotiated contract will imminently be formed. The higher the extent to which the withdrawing party encourages or induces such reliance, the higher the extent to which the other party's reliance is protected by the law. This criterion in the qualification of the parties' conduct comes close to the English law assessment of inducement of reliance. Within the English approach, the primary relief in case of anticipated performance is the law of unjust enrichment. The English law of unjust enrichment enables recovery of costs made in anticipation of a contract. Within the application of this doctrine, the fact that costs were induced is an important indication in favour of allowing recovery. Requesting, approving or in any other way inducing a party to incur costs in the course of negotiations constitutes an important premise for recovery in unjust enrichment.[1501] Therefore, for the purposes of non-contractual regulation, a provision on cost allocation helps to assess to what extent a party acted at its own risk in incurring expenses, or acted in reliance on the other party's encouragements.

Finally, courts of all the jurisdictions discussed analyse provisions authorizing or requesting expenses in close connection with in close connection with the assessment of the coming about of final contract. These provisions illustrate the delicate boundary between the dynamics of negotiations and the substance of the final contract. In drafting practice, the distinction between preliminary works and final contract in the first example stresses the role of the provision primarily for negotiations.

7.9.2. Anticipating recovery and liability

A: Illustration

Provisions anticipating recovery aim to limit the parties' financial exposure in case negotiations fail. Such clauses establish in advance what reparation would be made and what liability they may incur if negotiations do not result in the final contract. The following example establishes the consequences of breach of the obligations in the letter of intent, but caps the amount to be reimbursed and states that no further claims may be established.

> If DB breaches any of its obligations in this paragraph or if during the Lock-Out Period DB withdraws from negotiations with NBM for the sale of the Property, NBM shall be entitled to recover all of its costs and expenses relating to the investigation and negotiation of the proposed acquisition by it of the Property, however in no case more than EUR 300,000.00 in total, without the possibility of any further claims of any kind of NBM.[1502]

1501 *British Steel Corp* v. *Cleveland Bridge & Engineering Co Ltd* [1984] 1 All ER 504 (QBD).

1502 Hof Amsterdam 26 April 2011, ECLI:NL:GHAMS:2011:BQ5836, LJN BQ5836.

In the next example, if the negotiations fail, liability is limited. Parties expressly exclude recovery for breach of contract, loss of profit, loss of contract, and loss of expectation.

> In the event that a Secondary Sub contract is not concluded we shall reimburse only your reasonable and substantiated direct costs of complying with this instruction until it is revoked. We will not reimburse any other expenditure cost or loss whatsoever. This limitation includes without derogating from the generality of the foregoing any claim for breach of contract, loss of profit, loss of contract, loss of expectation or otherwise.[1503]

Another formulation limits the possible recovery in case of failure of negotiations to reimbursement of reasonable expenditure.

> If, for any unforeseen reason, the contract should fail to proceed and be formalised, then any reasonable expenditure incurred by you in connection with the above will be reimbursed on a quantum meruit basis. Any such payment would strictly form the limit of our client's commitment and our client would not be subject any further payment of compensation for damages for breach of contract.[1504]

The following provision states that a party may notify the other that the transaction will not proceed; costs incurred after that notification will be reimbursed.

> Clapham Park Homes Ltd do not undertake to reimburse any anticipated profits for the works as a whole, nor actual costs or actual or theoretically incurred general or specific overheads arising after the date of notification that no further work is to be carried out.[1505]

B: Analysis

In all the legal systems discussed, the question of recoverable costs is addressed as part of the discussion of liability. The exact question this provision raises is to what extent may the parties agree in advance on recovery in case negotiations fail? In all the legal systems in question, contractual organization of negotiations may change the nature of the parties' relationship. It can render negotiations fully or partially subject to contract law. It is also possible that the same set of facts falls simultaneously under both contractual and non-contractual regulation.

In English law, a limited number of contractual obligations can be enforceable and may be created at the stage of negotiations. These include 'lock-out' agreements, an obligation to obtain an export licence or planning permission, and frequently a non-disclosure provision. Their breach incurs contractual liability. The rules of the latter may be privatized to a large extent. It is worth noting that a provision stipulating in

1503 *Bennett (Electrical) Services Limited* v. *Inviron Limited* [2007] EWHC 49 (TCC), 2007 WL 1518029.
1504 *Harvey Shopfitters Limited* v. *A.D.I. Limited* [2003] EWCA Civ 1757, [2004] 2 All ER 982 [3].
1505 *Diamond Build Ltd* v. *Clapham Park Homes Ltd* [2008] EWHC 1439 (TCC), [2008] CILL 2601 [5].

advance the damages recoverable may be qualified in English law either as a penalty or as liquidated damages. Under English law, penalty clauses are not enforceable (these are the clauses that require such a high amount that it functions as a penalty). By contrast, liquidated damages provisions – clauses that provide an estimation of the damage that may be caused by a specific breach are enforceable. English courts have developed elaborate requirements for such clauses.[1506] In principle, English law allows contractual modification of liability in tort. The main limitation to this possibility is that liability for fraud may not be waived contractually. This is established by the Unfair Contract Terms Act 1977, applicable to both contractual and tortious liability.[1507]

In French law, creation of a preliminary agreement (*avant-contrat*) transforms the nature of the relationship into a contractual one. Parties may to a large extent limit or exclude contractual liability. According to the *Code civil*, the court may reduce the agreed amount of damages if it is manifestly excessive or derisory.[1508] At the same time, in French law, liability for an intentional fault in breaching of a contractual obligation (*faute intentionnelle*) may not be waived or modified by the parties.[1509] Even in the presence of *avant-contrat*, part of the relationship can still remain under regulation by tort law. In fact, only conduct directly in breach of a contractual obligation (in a preliminary documents) gives rise to a contractual claim. The rules on tort still regulate other conduct, for example, a fault in negotiations not covered in the preliminary agreement. Other duties and liability within general tort law may not be excluded by the parties' agreement.[1510] This is due to the fact that the provisions of the *Code civil* on tort are regarded as a part of rules belonging to *ordre public*. These are mandatory and may not be modified or waived by private regulation.[1511]

Within the structure of the Dutch Civil code, the conditions for tortious and contractual liability are different, but the same set of provision applies to the obligation to pay damages. Most of these provisions on the obligation to compensate loss contain rules from which parties may consensually derogate.[1512] In addition, Article 3:40 Dutch Civil code forbids the creation of contractual obligations contradicting public order and good morals. In this way, liability for intentional harm cannot be limited or excluded. Furthermore, a party may be deprived of the right to rely on an obligation that is contrary to reasonableness and fairness.[1513]

1506 *Chitty on Contracts* 2015, para 26–178 ff.
1507 Unfair Contract Terms Act 1977 section 1(1).
1508 Section 4.7.3.
1509 Ibid.
1510 Von Bar/Drobnig 2004, at 161.
1511 For a recent example, see Cass 1 civ 15 May 2015 N° 14–14517 n.p. in Bulletin; for a synthetic note see Von Bar/Drobnig 2004, at 155.
1512 Section 3.7.7.
1513 Lindenbergh 2014, at 35. See also Castermans 2012.

The US case law does not offer a straightforward approach to this question in disputes relating to letter of intent. The reasoning in these cases is primarily embedded in the search for a final contract which has been called in scholarship the 'all or nothing approach'.[1514] As a consequence, provisions on liability have been primarily addressed as contractual clauses when a final contract was found to be concluded, as opposed to the regime applicable to negotiations or preliminary agreements.

7.10. Dispute resolution

This Section will address the choice of law (7.10.1) and choice of court (7.10.2) provisions, as well as the submission of a precontractual dispute to arbitration (7.10.3). Furthermore, a note on mediation will be made (7.10.4).

7.10.1. Choice of law

A: Illustration

Parties may submit their negotiations to a particular national law. The clauses below contain a choice of law applicable to the binding part of the letter of intent. In the first illustration, parties chose English law.

> The terms of this Letter do not and are not intended to create binding legal obligations upon the parties hereto with the exception of this Clause and Clauses 5, 11 and 13 which clauses shall be governed by English law...[1515]

In the second illustration, the law of Georgia (United States) is chosen.

> This Letter of Intent is intended as an expression of mutual intent only and does not constitute an obligation binding in any way on the parties, except for the provisions of the third, fourth and fifth paragraphs hereof. This Letter of Intent will be governed by and construed in accordance with the laws of the State of Georgia.[1516]

Another formulation submits the entire letter of intent to French law.

> 17 DROIT APPLICABLE ET TRIBUNAL COMPÉTENT
> Droit français...[1517]

[1514] Section 6.3.

[1515] *JSD Corporation PTE Ltd* v. *Al Waha Capital PJSC, Second Waha Lease Ltd* [2009] EWHC 583 (Ch), 2009 WL 648840 [83].

[1516] *St. Joseph Hosp., Augusta, Georgia, Inc.* v. *Health Management Associates, Inc.*, 705 F.3d 1289, 1294–1295 (C.A.11 2013).

[1517] Lettre d'Intention Type, Association Française des Investisseurs en Capital, Capital-Risque: Guide des BonnesPratiquesAFIC2010,p.90,www.afic.asso.fr/dl.php?table=etude_publication&chemin=uploads/_afic&nom_file=capital-risque-guide-des-bonnes-pratiques-version-2010_1.pdf.

In the last illustration, English law is chosen not only for contractual claims, but also for non-contractual relations.

> This Letter of Intent (including any non-contractual obligations arising out of or in connection with the same) shall be governed by the laws of England...[1518]

B: Analysis

It should be noted that choice of law has been subject to an important harmonization at international level, especially in the EU. In the EU, the law applicable to cross-border *contractual* relationship is regulated by a uniform instrument: the Rome I Regulation (Rome I).[1519] Another uniform instrument – Rome II Regulation (Rome II)[1520] – provides the rules on the law applicable to cross-border *non-contractual* relationships. Article 1(2) (i) Rome I excludes the obligations related to the mere formation of contract from the scope of this Regulation. Therefore, Rome II is relevant for the general regime of negotiations. According to Article 12 Rome II, the law applicable to precontractual obligations is, in principle, the law governing the contract which would come about if the negotiations had not failed.[1521]

Against this background, the question arises as to whether an obligation submitting negotiations to a chosen law created by a preliminary agreement is a contractual obligation in itself. Although the application of Rome I and Rome II would perhaps often lead to the same applicable law, the question relates to the mere possibility to submit negotiations to one law, while the ultimate agreement would be submitted to another law.

This was asked in in the Dutch case Van Engen/Mirror Group,[1522] where an English and a Dutch publishing houses negotiated the production of a quality newspaper in the Netherlands. They regarded their negotiations as falling under English law, because the letter of intent was drafted in English and used the formulations typical for contracting under English law. However, the final contract between these two parties would not necessarily be submitted to English law. The Dutch court has answered this question in the affirmative.[1523] In the same way, English courts have recognized that English law was applicable when parties submitted their negotiations, i.e. letter of intent to English law.[1524] US case law does not provide extensive analysis of such clauses.[1525]

1518 *Shaker* v. *Vistajet Group Holding SA* [2012] EWHC 1329 (Comm), [2012] 2 All ER (Comm) 1010 [3].

1519 Regulation (EC) No 593/2008 of the European Parliament and of the Council of 17 June 2008 On the Law Applicable to Contractual Obligations (Rome I).

1520 Regulation (EC) No 864/2007 of the European Parliament and of the Council of 11 July 2007 On the Law Applicable to Non-contractual Obligations (Rome II).

1521 Article 12 Rome II also provides the rule for defining the applicable law if the law that would have been applied to the final contract cannot be identified. See also Asser/Kramer and Verhagen 10-III 2015, para 1199–1203.

1522 HR 24 November 1995, ECLI:NL:HR:1995:ZC1890, *NJ* 1996, 162 Van Engen/Mirror Group.

1523 On this question see also Wessels 2009a. Asser/Kramer and Verhagen 10-III 2015, para 952.

1524 Section 5.6.3.1.

1525 Section 6.5.8.1.

7.10.2. *Choice of court*

A: Illustration

Along with submitting contractual negotiations to a particular national law, parties may purport to choose the forum that will be competent to hear their dispute. The clause provided in the first example submits the disputes to English courts.

> The terms of this Letter do not and are not intended to create binding legal obligations upon the parties hereto with the exception of this Clause and Clauses 5, 11 and 13 which clauses … are subject to the jurisdiction of the English courts.[1526]

The second example illustrates the choice of court made not only for disputes related to contract, but also for non-contractual claims.

> This Letter of Intent (including any non-contractual obligations arising out of or in connection with the same) … and the parties hereto submit to the exclusive jurisdiction of the courts of England.[1527]

B: Analysis

Choice of court in international contracting has also been subject to international unification. In the EU, it is regulated by uniform rules provided by Brussels I-bis Regulation (Brussels I-bis).[1528] Article 25(5) Brussels I-bis establishes the principle of severability of the choice of court agreements. Based on this principle, the validity of the choice of court obligation should be assessed independently of the validity of the document in which such an obligation is contained. This provision separates – severs – the questions of validity of the preliminary document and the validity of a stand-alone choice of court clause. The provision is relatively recent, it has been introduced in the last recast of the Regulation. Article 25(5) Brussels I-bis states as follows:[1529]

> An agreement conferring jurisdiction which forms part of a contract shall be treated as an agreement independent of the other terms of the contract. The validity of the agreement conferring jurisdiction cannot be contested solely on the ground that the contract is not valid.

This provision raises the question of whether a choice of court made in a preliminary agreement may qualify as a choice in contract in the sense of Article 25(5) of Brussels I-bis. This question should be answered affirmatively in the light of the existing scholarship[1530] of

1526 *JSD Corporation PTE Ltd* v. *Al Waha Capital PJSC, Second Waha Lease Ltd* [2009] EWHC 583 (Ch), 2009 WL 648840 [83].

1527 *Shaker* v. *Vistajet Group Holding SA* [2012] EWHC 1329 (Comm), [2012] 2 All ER (Comm) 1010 [3].

1528 Regulation (EU) No 1215/2012 of the European Parliament and of the Council of 12 December 2012 On Jurisdiction and the Recognition and Enforcement of Judgments in Civil and Commercial Matters (Recast) (Brussels I-bis).

1529 Article 25(5) Brussels I-bis.

1530 See inter alia Wessels 2009a, at 255.

all the jurisdictions examined. Nevertheless, case law confirming this answer is not extensive.[1531] In the United States, little case law deals with the enforceability of a choice of forum in a letter of intent. At least one case points to the validity of the choice of court clause in the precontractual context. This case involved a domestic (not international) dispute.[1532] Another uniform instrument relevant for this purpose is the Hague Convention on Choice of Court Agreements.[1533] The Convention also establishes the principle of severability of a choice of court clause in Article 3(d). Therefore, clearly, under this Convention, a choice of court provision included in a letter of intent may be regarded as enforceable.

7.10.3. Arbitration

A: Illustration
Arbitration is one form of dispute resolution. The following illustration is an arbitration agreement included in a letter of intent. It submits disputes that may arise during negotiations to the competence of an arbitral tribunal.

> 14.2. Any dispute, controversy or claim arising out of, or in relation to, or in connection with, this LOI shall be resolved by an arbitration tribunal, which arbitration tribunal shall act in accordance with the rules of Conciliation and Arbitration of the International Chamber of Commerce...[1534]

B: Analysis
In all of the jurisdictions examined, an arbitration clause included into a letter of intent is enforceable, provided it fulfils the requirement for a valid and enforceable arbitration agreement. In this way, parties may submit disputes arising in the course of negotiations (thus before the formation of the final contract) to arbitration.

The enforceability of the clause is addressed following the doctrine of severability of arbitration agreements. For international arbitration, this principle flows from the New York Convention[1535] – the international instrument laying down uniform rules for international arbitration. Whereas the instrument does not directly establish the principle, it is widely accepted that the Convention assumes severability of the arbitration agreement. National approaches follow the same principle. It is worth noting that all the discussed jurisdictions favour arbitration. Courts and arbitral tribunals enforce party autonomy in choosing arbitration, especially if an international dispute is involved.[1536]

[1531] See Sections 3.7.9.2; 4.6.5; 5.6.3.2; 6.5.8.2.

[1532] *Lexington Inv. Co.* v. *Southwest Stainless, Inc.*, 697 F. Supp. 139 (S.D.N.Y. 1988).

[1533] Convention on Choice of Court Agreements (The Hague, 2005).

[1534] Exhibit 10 to Form 8-K filed by Gulf United Energy, Inc. on April 5, 2006, available in the open access database of the US Securities and Exchange Commission. See www.sec.gov/edgar.shtml.

[1535] Convention on the Recognition and Enforcement of Foreign Arbitral Awards (New York, 1958). Articles II and V(1)(a) New York Convention indirectly assume severability. See Born 2014, at 354 ff.

[1536] For the historical development from hostility in the eighteenth and nineteenth centuries to favouring arbitration since early twentieth century see Born 2014, at 40–43.

English courts draw attention to an important distinction between a dispute and a failure to agree. An arbitration agreement relating to a dispute is enforceable (if it fulfils the requirement of an enforceable arbitration clause developed by English courts in considerable detail).[1537] However, an obligation to arbitrate a simple failure to agree about the conditions of the negotiated contract falls outside the concept of an arbitration agreement. Instead, it is most likely to be qualified as an unenforceable agreement to agree.

Not many published arbitral awards could be found to confirm the above statements. Some examples can be mentioned. In one published arbitral award of the Netherlands Arbitration Institute (NAI), a clause of the 'Heads of Agreement' submitted precontractual disputes to arbitration by the NAI. The NAI confirmed its competence based on this clause.[1538] The ICC Paris arbitral award discussed in Section 2.4.2 of this study is another case that may be recalled as example.[1539]

7.10.4. Note on Mediation

Mediation is another form of dispute resolution. It represents negotiations assisted by a mediator acting as intermediary.[1540] The involvement of mediator at the stage of contract formation does not appear to be a frequent practice. It if were so, disputes following mediation would still be passed on to courts from time to time. However, no letter of intent containing a mediation clause has been identified in the texts quoted in case law collected for this study. Negotiating complex deals appears to be, in fact, primarily the task of an operational department, not of mediators.

Amongst the jurisdictions addressed, it is only in English scholarship that attention has been drawn to mediation clauses in letter of intent. Within discussions about the non-enforceability of agreements to agree, English scholars have noted the resemblance between an unenforceable agreement to agree and an agreement to mediate. The difference is that mediation agreements may have sufficient certainty to be valid and judicially protected under English law. This is due to the fact that the principle of unenforceability of agreements to agree[1541] was formulated 'before an important development in the law concerning judicial protection of the process of mediation'.[1542] Currently, in order to distinguish whether a mediation clause is an unenforceable 'agreement to agree' or a valid and legally binding mediation agreement, English courts assess whether the clause fulfils the requirements for a valid mediation agreement. These

[1537] Section 5.6.3.3.

[1538] NAI Arbitral Award 5 September 2000 nr. 22, 2000 *Tijdschift voor Arbitrage* 107.

[1539] ICC Paris International Court of Arbitration Award No. 8331 (1996) 10 *Bulletin de la Cour Internationale d'Arbitrage de la CCI* (1999).

[1540] See for a discussion regarding the definition of mediation Spencer/Brogan 2006, at 4–21 and at 22 for the link between mediation and negotiations.

[1541] *Walford* v. *Miles* [1992] 2 AC 128 (HL).

[1542] Mills/Loveridge 2011, at 529.

requirements have crystallized relatively recently and with considerable level of detail.[1543] A notable requirement is this of certainty: not only should a reference to mediation be made, but also the concrete rules, for example, of a specific mediation institution should be mentioned.

7.11. Remedies

Sections 7.8 and 7.9 discussed the approach to provisions on distribution and recovery of costs in letter of intent. This Section provides more detail on the remedies available for breach of obligations within contractually organized negotiations. The main remedy is the recovery of damages (7.11.1). Other types of available recovery include precluding reliance on a right or defence (7.11.2), specific performance, and injunction (7.11.3); finally, punitive damages typical of the US system and exemplary damages typical to English law are worth noting (7.11.4).

7.11.1. Damages

Breach of an obligation contractually organizing negotiations may lead to the payment of various types of damage, the main heads of which include:

- the loss of costs wasted in negotiations and preparation of the final contract;
- the loss of costs of works or services started in anticipation of conclusion of the final contract;
- the loss of profits expected from the final contract;
- the loss of opportunity to conclude a contract with a third party;
- harm to the reputation.

7.11.1.1. Costs wasted in negotiations

The most common remedy in all the legal systems examined is the recovery of costs wasted in negotiations. This is referred to as recovery of reliance interest (in England and Wales and in the United States), material loss recoverable as part of sustained loss (*perte subie* in France), and negative contractual interest (*negatief contractsbelang* in the Netherlands).

Costs wasted in negotiations may include expenses on preliminary studies, for example, feasibility studies, marketing research, fees paid to various external consultants, law firms, travel expenses, and costs of obtaining authorization from public authorities.

In French law, recovery of costs wasted in negotiations represents the main recovery for fault in negotiations. It is also the most frequent measure of contractual liability for a

[1543] Section 5.6.3.4.

breach of a preliminary agreement. Similarly to the French approach, in Dutch law, costs wasted in negotiations are recoverable both as liability for breaking off negotiations and as contractual liability for violation of a preliminary agreement. Notably, Dutch law allows recovery only of such costs wasted in negotiations that would have been discounted in the non-concluded final contract. In the United States, recovery of costs wasted in negotiations is the main recovery in contractual liability for breach of obligation created by a preliminary agreement. Liability in tort in cases of misrepresenting an intention to enter into an agreement is also usually confined to recovery of costs wasted in negotiations. Furthermore, the recovery of costs wasted in negotiations is available as recovery in tort for the appropriation of trade secrets. The latter enables the recovery of either the actual loss or of the amount of the gain, whichever is greater.[1544] In England and Wales, costs wasted in negotiations may be recovered as liability for breach of the limited number of obligations that are recognized as those which parties may create to organize negotiations.

It is worth noting, finally, that in all the legal systems discussed, negotiating parties are expected to be cautious when investing in negotiations, especially when faced with encouragements to invest, at the risk of the reduction of the recoverable amount.

7.11.1.2. Costs incurred in anticipation of a contract

All the legal systems examined provide for recovery of costs made in anticipation that the final contract will be formed. These include firstly, costs related to preparation of the final contract (e.g. preliminary studies, due diligence and similar) and, secondly, costs of starting the actual performance of the final contract while it is established that the parties remained at the stage of negotiations.

Though the result is relatively similar in all the jurisdictions, it is reached via different legal techniques. As a consequence, recovery is subject to diverging conditions. English law enables such recovery under the law of restitution and unjust enrichment. English courts have been especially willing to grant such relief if the start of performance was induced, required, authorized or approved by the party who benefitted from that performance.[1545] The fact of one party's benefit to the detriment of the other also plays an important role in granting recovery. Under US law, such recovery may be granted under the doctrine of promissory estoppel, but in practice is granted very infrequently. In French law, such costs are recoverable primarily for liability in tort. For instance, French courts have granted the recovery of the costs of adapting immovable property for its use under the final contract, provided the party breaking off negotiations could profit from the results of this adaptation. Furthermore, according to the *Cour de Cassation*, restitution of such costs is possible under the French doctrine of unjust enrichment if no cause of action in contract or tort is available (the cause of action in unjust enrichment has a subsidiary character in the French legal system). However, the application of this

1544 Restatement (Second) of Torts, 5256, see also §549.
1545 See observations in Section 7.9.1 above.

doctrine in practice is infrequent. In Dutch law, such a remedy is available under liability for breaking off negotiations and as contractual liability for breach of a preliminary agreement. According to the *Hoge Raad*, the doctrine of unjust enrichment is not applicable to the period of negotiations, whereas most Dutch scholars argue in favour of its applicability.[1546]

7.11.1.3. Loss of opportunity to conclude the negotiated final contract

None of the legal systems examined excludes the possibility to recover the loss of opportunity to conclude the negotiated contract. However, such recovery is exceptional and infrequently granted. For instance, in England and Wales, remedies under the tort of deceit include recovery for any loss directly flowing from the tortious conduct, whether or not it was reasonably foreseeable. However, English courts are generally guarded in granting recovery for a bargain related to the prospects of a deal before the final contract is formed.[1547]

In the United States, recovery of a potential bargain from the non-concluded contract, called the *expectation interest*, has been refused in a considerable number of cases. Cases where such recovery was granted are exceptional. US case law and scholarship contains lively debates on two questions related to the recovery of an expectation interest. First, should a preliminary regime enable such recovery? Second, is the court in principle able to establish the amount of damage? The uncertainty of the outcome of negotiations and the difficulty of proof are the main arguments against such recovery. However, according to the main argument in favour of such recovery, difficulties related to evidence and causality do not amount to the impossibility of proof. This means, should such loss be evident on the facts of the case, recovery for the loss of opportunity to conclude the negotiated contract should be available.[1548] It is worth noting that the US doctrine of promissory estoppel admits recovery of loss of profit, but only to the extent it is necessary to prevent injustice. Furthermore, in the US, remedies in the tort of deceit enable the recovery of 'pecuniary loss caused … by … justifiable reliance upon the misrepresentation'.[1549] De facto, the courts have limited recovery. *Markov* v. *ABC Transfer & Storage Co.* illustrates the exception where a recovery for loss caused by fraudulent misrepresentation of intent to reach agreement was granted.[1550] In France, the possibility to recover profits expected from the non-concluded final contract was also debated for a long time. Following the reform of the French law of obligations, this remedy is explicitly excluded from the remedies available under tortious liability for fault in the course of negotiations. Though, the remedy may still be available for breach of obligation of confidentiality.[1551]

1546 Section 3.6.
1547 Section 5.3.
1548 Sections 6.3.3.2 and 6.6.1.
1549 Restatement (Second) of Torts §525, see also §549.
1550 457 P.2d 535 (Wash. 1969); see also Section 6.4.2.1.
1551 Section 4.7.1.1.

Under Dutch law, profits expected from the non-concluded final contract may be recovered. This remedy is referred to as recovery of the *positive contractual* interest (*positief contractsbelang*). It is available both as liability for breaking off negotiations and for breach of a preliminary agreement. However, similarly to the other legal systems, such recovery is granted in practice fairly infrequently. A case illustrating recovery granted as liability in tort involved the use of confidential information obtained in negotiations.[1552] Notably, according to Dutch case law, even if a contractual limitation is set on the possible amount of recovery, a higher amount may still be granted by the court if the limitation agreed by the parties would lead to results inadmissible from the point of view of reasonableness and fairness. Courts set a high threshold to be fulfilled in finding that the limitation would lead to such results.

7.11.1.4. Loss of opportunity to conclude a contract with a third party

Loss of opportunity to conclude a contract with a third party resembles the loss of opportunity to conclude the negotiated contract, but relates to a contract that could potentially have been concluded with a third party. This loss occurs in the situation where a party starts negotiations with the sole aim of preventing or impeding negotiations with a third party. Recovery of such loss is, in principle, possible in all the legal systems examined. However, the remedy is exceptional and infrequently granted. English law enables the recovery of such loss under the heading of tort of deceit. However, while this tort generally enables recovery of the loss of 'income-generating opportunities',[1553] no case law points to granting such recovery in the context of contractually organized negotiations. In the US legal system, the recovery of loss of opportunity to conclude the contract negotiations of which failed (expectation interest) is possible.[1554] According to the current French case law, the loss of opportunity to conclude a contract with a third party is recoverable both as liability for fault in negotiations and for breach of preliminary agreement. This is the only type of loss of opportunity recoverable in the context of negotiations. The amount of recovery corresponds to the detriment for being 'locked' in the negotiations for a certain period of time, thereby losing the chance to contract with other parties (*perte de chance*). The *Ordonnance* of 2016 specifies that the loss of bargain from the negotiated contract may not be recovered. The question whether the limitation it places on the recovery covers loss of *any* opportunity remains open.[1555] The Dutch approach to this remedy is the least detailed. Dutch case law and literature on precontractual liability have not specifically touched upon recovery for the loss of opoportunity to conclude a contract with a third party. Dutch law offers a theoretical possibility of recovery, because the *Hoge Raad* has explicitly noted that recovery for breaking off negotiations is not limited. But the threshold for recovery would be high,

1552 Hof 's-Gravenhage 28 January 2004, ECLI:NL:GHSGR:2004:AO7536, *PRG* 2004, 6182; see Section 3.5.

1553 Andrews 2015, para 9.18; *Yam Seng Pte Ltd* v. *International Trade Corp Ltd* [2013] EWHC 111 (QB), [2013] 1 All ER (Comm) 1321, especially [119] ff. (Leggatt J).

1554 Section 6.6.1.

1555 Section 4.7.1.

due to the increasingly guarded approach of the Dutch courts to imposing liability in the context of negotiations of a contract.[1556]

7.11.1.5. Harm to the reputation

French case law pays specific attention to the recovery of damage caused by a harm to the reputation. According to French case law harm to the reputation (*atteinte à la réputation*) is recoverable as part of the sustained loss (*perte subie*).[1557] This recovery is available both as a remedy in tort and as remedy for breach of contractual obligation. The other legal systems do not pay particular attention to this type of damage in the context of regulation of negotiations.

7.11.2. Gain-based remedies

Another recovery is worth noting: the gain-based remedy of disgorgement of profits or account of profits. The remedy is illustrated by a situation where a party breaks off negotiations in order to conclude a contract with a third party, and this contract generates profit. The remedy of disgorgement of profits would suppose the transfer of the amount of this profit to the former party to failed negotiations.

This remedy is characteristic primarily to US law, to some extent to England, and to a much lesser extent to France and the Netherlands. In the United States, this remedy is provided under the law of restitution and unjust enrichment. According to the Restatement (Third) of Restitution and Unjust Enrichment, the *benefit* - an advantage with a measureable value – may be recovered.[1558] Case law points to two types of situation where such recovery has been granted in the context of failed negotiations: firstly, receiving profit as a result of misappropriation of an idea disclosed in negotiations and, secondly, receiving profit from works done or services rendered in anticipation of a contract.[1559] In practice, this recovery is admitted infrequently. US courts refuse to grant such recovery mainly because the claimant does not suffer any actual damage. The fact of profit is also difficult to establish, because most precontractual works and services have no 'end product'.[1560]

In English law, account of profits is an equitable remedy; it is also a discretionary remedy granted at the discretion of the court. Such recovery is neither at the centre of the law of restitution, nor of the tort of deceit. The nature of this remedy is not settled in English law. The remedy has been granted for breach of the duty of confidence. As Lord Denning MR stated, this remedy is based on 'the broad principle of equity that he who has received

1556 Sections 3.3.2 and 3.9.

1557 Section 4.7.1.1.

1558 Restatement (Third) of Restitution and Unjust Enrichment §31 Comment i.

1559 Section 6.6.3.

1560 Furmston/Tolhurst 2010, at 391. See Section 6.4.3.

information in confidence shall not take unfair advantage of it'.[1561] However, such duty arises only in negotiations involving a relationship of trust and thus not in every commercial negotiation.[1562]

In French law, the recovery of loss of chance comes close to the disgorgement of profits. French case law has a considerable level of development on this matter. It sets a high threshold for recovery, requiring the existence of a real and serious chance. This is difficult to establish and prove for this reason: it is highly questionable whether the account of profits received from a contract with third party can overcome the threshold set in French law for recovery of loss of chance. As has been noted, the reform of the French law of obligations explicitly limits recovery for fault in negotiations. However, as the provision for misuse of confidential information is placed outside this limitation, it is not entirely clear whether the limitation also precludes the loss of opportunity to conclude the negotiated contract discussed earlier.

Dutch case law does not point to the availability of this remedy in the precontractual context. On the one hand, it may be recalled that no limitation is placed on the damages recoverable. On the other hand, it appears questionable that the Dutch concept of positive contractual interest includes the benefits received by one of the parties of failed negotiations. In this way, Dutch law may potentially offer the possibility to disgorge profits in exceptional cases.

7.11.3. Precluding reliance on a right, remedy or defence

In Dutch law, the breach of the *bona fides* duty precludes a party from relying on a right, remedy or defence that would otherwise be available to this party. In English and US law, a similar function is fulfilled by the principle that a party may not derive a right or remedy based on his own tortious conduct. In French law this function if fulfilled by the concept of abuse of right.

7.11.4. Specific performance and injunction

In the precontractual context, the remedy of specific performance consists in ordering parties to negotiate further or even to conclude the final contract. This may be done by injunction. Furthermore, an injunction may aim to prevent or preclude inappropriate conduct in negotiations, for example, forbid parallel negotiations or prevent disclosure of confidential information.

The approaches to these remedies diverge. In English law, specific performance of preliminary agreements is not available.[1563] By contrast, confidentiality in negotiations

1561 *Seager* v. *Copydex Ltd (No.1)* [1967] 1 WLR 923 (EWCA) 931 (Lord Denning MR).
1562 Section 5.5.2.
1563 Section 5.7.1.

may be protected by an injunction. Injunction in English law is granted at the discretion of the court. In the precontractual context, this remedy is granted exceptionally. English law also draws specific attention to the remedies for failure to mediate. This is another context where English courts may grant an injunction, along with other procedural remedies such as stay of proceedings (if an enforceable arbitration or mediation clause is included into a letter of intent).

Similarly to English law, US law does not admit specific performance of an obligation to negotiate. At the same time, an injunction may be granted to prevent tortious appropriation of trade secret or information disclosed in the course of negotiations. Both a preliminary injunction and an injunction as final relief may be granted.

The French approach is twofold. On the one hand, French law provides no possibility of obtaining an order to negotiate or to conclude the final contract. Such order is regarded as contrary to freedom of contract. More specifically, according to the *Cour de Cassation*, even if a preliminary agreement is violated, the consent on the final contract is still lacking. As a consequence, freedom *not* to contract and the right to break off negotiations preclude specific performance of an obligation to negotiate in French law. On the other hand, one particular remedy developed in French case law amounts de facto to specific performance. This is the remedy provided for breach of a pre-emption agreement.[1564]

Dutch law has another approach to the remedy of specific performance of an obligation to negotiate. Courts do not order parties to conclude the final contract. However, in a situation where breaking off negotiations has led to a dispute, the court may order parties to negotiate further in a 'constructive manner'. The content of this requirement has been elaborated in case law and comes down to the obligation of means.[1565] A court injunction ordering parties to negotiate may be also accompanied by a judicial penalty and even by mandatory involvement of a mediator. Similarly to the three other legal systems, in the Dutch legal system misuse of information may be also prevented by injunction.

7.11.5. Note on punitive and exemplary damages

Punitive damages are peculiar to US law. This measure of liability has no compensatory function. Instead, it discourages intentional malicious conduct and serves as a deterrent for the general public.[1566] On the one hand, punitive damages have a limited relevance if a preliminary regime applies. No case law exists where punitive damages were applied in disputes where the US courts found that the intermediary regime was applicable or that parties remained at the stage of non-binding negotiations. Furthermore, punitive damages are generally not typical in breach of contract, being granted essentially in tort cases.

1564 Section 4.4.2.1.
1565 Section 3.8.1.2.
1566 Section 6.6.6.

On the other hand, it is worth noting that a dispute involving negotiations of a contract in the United States carries the potential for punitive damages to be awarded. The reason is that punitive damages have been granted in cases where the court found an ultimate agreement to have been formed or identified a prospective business relationship. In this situation, a claim against a third party interfering with this relationship has frequently led to punitive damages.

7.12. Main similarities and differences, their explanation

The comparative observations on various provisions of letter of intent made above reveal a number of general similarities and differences (7.12.1). The next, concluding part of this Chapter, will summarize the converging and diverging tendencies and look at the explanation for these (7.12.2 and 7.12.3).

7.12.1. Main similarities and differences

The approaches to letter of intent in the four jurisdictions are characterized by number of similarities. Some similarities exist in the approaches of only two or three of the legal systems discussed, whereas others are present in all of the examined approaches. At the same time, important divergences are in place.

French and Dutch regulation of negotiations generally, and letter of intent in particular, are characterized by two salient commonalities. First, both jurisdictions recognize the regime of precontractual liability. It has been developed under the umbrella of *bona fides*. Second, both legal systems are underpinned by the similar conceptual frameworks of French *avant-contrat* and Dutch *voorovereenkomst* regulated by contract law. Within these frameworks, a distinction is somewhat naturally drawn between the process of negotiations and the final contract. Both frameworks also acknowledge that a contractual obligation may be created at the stage of negotiations and be limited to the process of negotiations. It is worth noting that in both countries, academic literature draws attention to the precontractual and preliminary character of *avant-contrat* and *voorovereenkomst*. Both legal systems make a distinction between preliminary frameworks, on the one hand, and the obligations of the final contract, on the other hand. Courts do not treat the obligations created within these frameworks and the obligations of the final contract in the same way. The most illustrative example of this is perhaps the French pre-emption agreement. It has specific conditions in order to be binding and its breach leads to specific consequences that would not necessarily be entailed by a breach of other types of contract, for example, a sales contract.

These two commonalities in French and Dutch law (on the one hand) contrast with the English and US approaches (on the other hand). Firstly, in England and Wales and in the United States regulation applicable to negotiations does not rely on an overarching concept of precontractual liability. Regulation in these jurisdictions focuses on remedying specific wrongs under the regime of tort and unjust enrichment. Contract law addresses negotiations primarily as an adversarial process, a period of bargaining and risk-taking. In the United States, detrimental precontractual reliance is also protected by the doctrine of promissory estoppel; this protection is absent in English law. Secondly, England and Wales and the United States do not rely on an overarching framework similar to *avant-contrat* and *voorovereenkomst*. This observation requires some nuance. The recent trend in both jurisdictions points to the development of accommodation of separate obligations, the regime of which is comparable to the French and Dutch frameworks of preliminary agreements. However, it is subject to important limitations. In England and Wales it is developed by means that are considerably different from the concept of *bona fides*. In the United States, some state laws rely on the concept of *bona fides* (while other state laws still reject it).

In this way, the emergence of preliminary regimes can be regarded as a similarity between all four jurisdictions. These preliminary regimes are applicable to contractually organized negotiations and are distinct from the final contract. They allow similar results to be reached by private regulation against the background of frequently considerably diverging general regimes of negotiations.

The emerging preliminary regimes are closely connected to another similarity between all the jurisdictions discussed. Obligations within preliminary regimes are increasingly treated as stand-alone and severable (or separable depending on terminological preferences). These obligations are frequently upheld as binding even if the other content of obligations is qualified as non-binding. However, as has been noted, not all types of obligations are treated as severable. Dispute resolution clauses raise the fewest doubts; confidentiality and exclusivity provisions are frequently severed. By contrast, the tendency to sever other types of obligations is more difficult to affirm. In particular, the provisions on costs of negotiations are analysed from the perspective of the rules that would be applicable to liability even in the absence of provisions on cost allocation and details of recovery.

Some degree of similarity between all the legal systems can be observed in the measure of liability and recovery. Liability, where it may be incurred, is predominantly limited in the case law of all legal systems to the recovery of costs wasted in negotiations (or, in some cases, to restitution of the anticipated performance). This is the case in all situations where liability may be incurred: be it for breach of a contractually binding provision of a letter of intent, or within the regime of precontractual liability (in the jurisdictions where it is admitted). Notably, at the same time, exceptional recovery may go as far as disgorgement of profits in all legal systems. However, a high threshold is set for incurring such liability: recovery other than wasted expenditure is subject to the requirement of tort liability and, therefore, most of the time, proof of fraud. It may be recalled that examples include liability for starting negotiations with the sole aim of obtaining business sensitive information (most evidently sanctioned in France) and liability for tortious use of trade secrets disclosed in the course of negotiations (United States).

7.12.2. *Explaining the similarities*

7.12.2.1. Reception and common legal heritage

The first similarity between the French and the Dutch legal systems noted above (the development of a general concept of precontractual liability) is due to the common legal heritage and reception of Roman law. In the early twentieth century, when the Dutch scholar Telders[1567] discussed contractual negotiations, he acknowledged the work of the French lawyer Saleilles,[1568] who introduced the concept of fault in negotiations in French law at approximately the same time. French and Dutch literature refers also to the suggestion of the Italian lawyer Faggella of identifying various stages of the negotiation process[1569] and to the earlier ideas of the German scholar von Ihering on *culpa in contrahendo*.[1570] This cross-fertilization of scholarship might have steered further developments in the same direction.

Notably, all the abovementioned authors place negotiations conceptually within the domain of contract formation, although both in France and the Netherlands, liability has developed mainly as non-contractual. This may explain the second observed similarity. It may be the reason for the relative ease with which the civil law traditions have acknowledged the legal effect of the French *avant-contrat* and the Dutch *voorovereenkomst*. However, direct references to foreign scholarship in the development of these frameworks are not evident. Due to the acknowledgment of these frameworks, French and Dutch courts have also been equally willing to admit the existence of separate and stand-alone obligations before the final contract comes into being.

Liability that may arise in the course of negotiations has developed both in France and in the Netherlands under the umbrella of the duty of *bona fides*. This is perhaps the most salient commonality between the two civil law countries' regulation of negotiations. This resemblance is rooted in the reception of Roman law. Strictly speaking, *bona fides* in the Roman rules on contract did not cover the period of negotiations and formation of contract.[1571] The historical succession and further developments consisted rather in using the concept of *bona fides* as a vehicle for 'adaptation of the codified law to changing social values' and 'realisation of social ideal'.[1572] In both countries, this development subscribes to the general tendency of moralization of law. This is primarily reflected in the assumption that negotiations are primarily a cooperative process.

It is worth noting that the doctrine of unjust enrichment is also rooted in Roman law.[1573] As has been noted, unjust enrichment is one of the fields of law relevant for the regulation

1567 Telders 1937.
1568 Saleilles 1907.
1569 Faggella 1906.
1570 Von Ihering 1861.
1571 Schermaier 2000; see also Zimmermann 1996, chapter 18 Formation of contract.
1572 Schermaier 2000, at 92.
1573 Zimmermann 1996, at 835 ff.

of negotiations. It is especially relevant for England and Wales, where it is the main method of recovery following performance in anticipation of the final contract if this takes place at the stage of negotiations. Unlike many other doctrines relied upon by the civil law traditions via the reception of Roman law, unjust enrichment has reached a much higher level of sophistication in both England and Wales and the US than in France and the Netherlands.

The commonalities mentioned in the English and US approaches are due to the reception of English law in the United States. The legal policy[1574] underpinning both jurisdictions is rooted in the market-centred political economy[1575] and philosophical ideas of individualism.[1576] As a consequence, both English and US law assume that negotiations in practice are primarily a distributive process: each party pursues first and foremost its own economic interest and has a bargaining position which opposes the counterparty's interests.

Another point of historical continuity between the English and US systems is the law of estoppel. The US doctrine of promissory estoppel has English roots. However, English estoppel does not form a separate cause of action in claiming loss caused by detrimental reliance. In England, it is used as a 'shield and not as a sword'.[1577] By contrast, US law has gone further in the development of estoppel to protect precontractual reliance.

7.12.2.2. Judicial endorsement of private regulation

Chapter 1 advanced the idea that letter of intent is a business practice that purports to contractually organize negotiations through private regulation. Chapter 1 also suggested inquiring whether, against the background of considerable differences in the regulation of negotiations, the legal systems in question offer the possibility of reaching similar results via contractual clauses.

As has been noted in the previous Section, the approaches to contractually organized negotiations in the selected jurisdictions demonstrate indeed more similarities than in the general regime of negotiations. These similarities are arguably due to the similar manner in which courts have dealt with complex negotiations and letter of intent created in the course of development of a transaction. Though private regulation may be regarded as an independent level of law-making, it achieves its goals only if it is endorsed *in fine* by public law-making, including courts.[1578]

Business practice must have become a force of convergence in legal solutions, because in all the countries discussed, courts were the first to face changing contracting practices

1574 Van Erp 2011, at 510.
1575 Reitz 2009, at 857.
1576 Siems 2014, at 310; Van Erp 2011, at 510 (referring to the characterization of common law by Finn).
1577 *Combe* v. *Combe* [1951] 2 KB 215 218 (Lord Denning).
1578 Cafaggi 2011b, at 95.

(namely the practice of long and complex negotiations before the final contract is formed). While statutory regulation on this question is scarce, the courts of the civil law tradition and common law have a played similar role in developing the legal approach. Disputes involving letter of intent represent one of the fields where the actual role of the civil law courts has no longer been limited to 'mechanically applying the law'.[1579] Their role in the development of law may have come close to the common law courts – the main law-makers in many domains in the common law tradition. In all four legal systems, the regulation of negotiations has developed under broad principles, but in the situations where 'the practitioner must eventually look at the precedents in order to find out what a court is likely to say'.[1580]

In all four jurisdictions, courts have adopted similar solutions in response to similar practical needs. Such bottom-up convergence is sometimes referred to as 'natural' or 'evolutionary' convergence.[1581] This is primarily the case of development of preliminary regimes (with resembling characteristics in all the four discussed legal systems) and severable treatment of obligations within these regimes. Courts in all the jurisdictions examined have been generally receptive to the concretization of the duties parties have imposed on themselves in the course of negotiations. This receptiveness is relatively independent of the acknowledgment or refusal to impose the general duty of good faith. What appeared to matter for the courts in all the jurisdictions was the 'machinery' of the development of a transaction which may potentially be enforced by the court. Irrespectively of the motivation for the adopted solutions (and the motivation frequently diverges considerably due to the difference in the general regime of negotiations), courts of all the legal systems discussed have adopted a generally pragmatic approach to the relevance of negotiations to modern contracting practice and the lack of a *tertium quid* as a bridge between the absolute 'freedom not to contract' and the binding formed final contract.

Furthermore, as has been noted, preliminary regimes developed most intensively in the second half of the twentieth century. This is the period of transnationalization and regionalization of law – the 'ongoing relations of interdependent laws in an interdependent world'.[1582] As a consequence, documents written for use in one legal tradition began to be used in another legal tradition. Courts had also to consider the effect of formulations initially foreign to their legal systems. For example, courts in civil law countries had to find the meaning and effect of the reservation 'subject to contract', whereas English law was obliged to further its consideration of the requirement to negotiate in good faith. Such transnationalization of drafting practices might have stimulated the evolution of law in solving comparable, if not identical, practical questions.

1579 Markesinis/Fedtke 2009, at 182–183.
1580 Kötz 1987, at 7.
1581 Merryman 1999, at 26–32; De Cruz 2007, at 510.
1582 Glenn 2012, at 72.

7.12.3. *Explaining the differences*

7.12.3.1. Socio-economic development

It is not only similarities that have been observed in the legal systems' approaches. The striking difference between the Dutch and the French approaches, on the one hand, and the English and US approach, on the other hand lies in the assumptions about negotiations. While the former address negotiations as a cooperative process, the latter regard negotiations as an adversarial, distributive process.

This difference can be explained by the divergence in the paths of socio-economic development followed by the countries in question in the nineteenth and twentieth centuries. This has led to two opposing approaches to law: the economic and moralist approaches. More specifically, English policy is said to value mainly individual economic interests. The US approach is also underpinned primarily by valuing the individual interest, with the nuance that the individual interest is enforced because it is regarded as benefitting the market economy and, as a consequence, benefitting society at large.[1583]

By contrast, French law is underpinned by a moralist approach to the law. Value judgment and concepts with moral connotations are apparent in scholarship and the courts' reasoning. The tendency of 'moralization' in French contract law has been noted by Mazeaud in relation to the formulation of a 'rigorous ethics of negotiations'.[1584] It is also explicit in the *Ordonnance* reforming the French law of obligations in 2016. Comparing the common law and civil law approaches to precontractual liability, Van Erp follows up on the characterization of French law made by the French comparative law academic Legrand. He draws attention to the socio-economic development of the French society starting from the 1950s. Since this time, French policy has increasingly reflected social democratic ideas.[1585] These ideas attributed considerable relevance to the interests of society at large. While their main sphere of influence was regulation of consumer contracts, these ideas have also been reflected in the regulation of commercial relations. Policy underpinned by these ideas brought French law away from the Anglo-Saxon approach and later even from the idealist philosophical tradition reflected in the Napoleonic Code.

Dutch legal policy is generally close to the French approach and can be also characterized by moralistic approach.[1586] The cause of action for breaking off negotiations also offers a theoretical possibility of a less limited recovery than in other legal systems. However, on the particular question of liability for breaking off negotiations, Dutch courts appear to follow an increasingly pragmatic reasoning and in practice impose liability very restrictively.

1583 Reitz 2009, at 857.
1584 Mazeaud 2001, at 640.
1585 Van Erp 2011, at 510. See also Valcke 2004, at 731.
1586 Van Kogelenberg 2014, at 153.

7.12.3.2. Historical development

While the English and US law approaches are frequently invoked together, comparative observations made in this Chapter reveal important divergences. Differently to English law, in some US states, the court may imply the requirement of *bona fides* into negotiations of a contract. This often forms then the content of the applicable preliminary regime. US law also went further than English law in its protection of precontractual reliance through the development of the doctrine of promissory estoppel, though this is rarely applied in practice. According to Glenn, the independent evolution of US law in accepting a number of civil law doctrines characterizes the US as a mixed, rather than a common law legal tradition.[1587]

This divergence is due to the contrasting paths in the development of legal policy in the twentieth century. Furthermore, the immigrants who left continental Europe after Second World War brought European continental scholarship to the US. In many respects, the pervasive effects of this intellectual influence have carried US law away from its English roots.[1588] One of the most important illustrations of the civil law influence is the Uniform Commercial Code's requirement of good faith and fair dealing in the execution of contract. In England and Wales, in contrast with the US, the influence of similar post war intellectual immigration on the law has been much less significant.[1589]

1587 Glenn 2014, at 263.
1588 Curran 1998, at 68–69.
1589 Markesinis 2000, at 45. See also Beatson/Zimmermann 2004.

Chapter 8

INTERNATIONAL INSTRUMENTS: CISG AND SOFT LAW

8.1. Introduction

Formation of contract in general, and contractual negotiations in particular, has been a delicate matter for the international uniform law since the beginning of the twentieth century. At the Vienna diplomatic conference for the adoption of the United Nations Convention on Contracts for the International Sale of Goods (CISG),[1590] the question as to whether the Convention should lay down the rules for the precontractual stage generated intense debates. Up to the present time, formation of contract forms one of the issues on which further harmonization and unification of law may be considered.[1591] However, the current political priority of this issue is not high.[1592]

This Chapter will be dedicated to international uniform law. What is the approach to private regulation of negotiations in the uniform international rules? At the level of hard law, the most relevant instrument to be discussed is the CISG. The Convention does not explicitly address contractual negotiations. The question as to whether the Convention's scope covers the precontractual period is a matter of academic discussion. At the level of soft law, the UNIDROIT Principles of International Commercial Contracts (UPICC),[1593] the Principles of European Contract Law (PECL),[1594] and the Draft Common Frame of Reference (DCFR)[1595] contain specific provisions relating to negotiations of contract.[1596] As will be shown below, despite a high level of sophistication of the soft law instruments, their rules provide no straightforward approach to letter of intent.

1590 United Nations Convention on Contracts for the International Sale of Goods (Vienna, 1980).

1591 See United Nations Commission on International Trade Law, Forty-fifth session (2012), A/CN.9/758, 8 May 2012, Possible Future Work in the Area of International Contract Law, at 7.

1592 Veneziano 2013, Loken 2013, Dennis 2014.

1593 UNIDROIT Principles of International Commercial Contracts 2010, www.unilex.info.

1594 Lando/Beale 2000; Lando 2003.

1595 Von Bar/Clive 2010.

1596 Articles 2.1.15, 2.1.16, 1.8 UPICC; Articles 2:301, 2:302 PECL.

The Chapter will provide a brief overview of the genesis and prospects of unification and harmonization of international contract law (Section 8.2).[1597] Thereafter, the debate on the applicability of the CISG to contractual negotiations will be reviewed. Within this broader debate, this study will suggest a nuanced view on the particular question of application of the CISG to letter of intent (Section 8.3). Furthermore, the rules on negotiations included in the UPICC, PECL and DCFR will be addressed. The Chapter will sketch the scope and structure of the soft law instruments (Section 8.4), analyse soft law rules on contractual negotiations (Section 8.5), discuss the remedies (Section 8.6), and provide concluding remarks (Section 8.7).

8.2. Genesis and prospects of uniform and harmonized contract law

The first projects in the field of transnational contract law date back to the beginning of the twentieth century. At that time, the UNIDROIT – International Institute for the Unification of Private Law – started working on uniform instruments in the field of sales law at the initiative of a renowned comparative lawyer Ernst Rabel.[1598] The drafting resulted in two Hague Conventions: the Uniform Law on the International Sale of Goods and the Uniform law on the Formation of Contracts for the International Sale of Goods in 1964. These instruments were ratified only by nine countries and were not a success from a pragmatic perspective. The Conventions represented, nevertheless, a major step towards unification of international sales law. They have inspired the creation of the United Nations Convention on Contracts for the International Sale of Goods (CISG), drafted under the auspices of the United Nations Commission on International Trade Law (UNCITRAL).

The CISG was adopted in 1980 and entered into force in 1988. The Convention has achieved a remarkable success in terms of its ratification: it is currently signed by more than 84 countries.[1599] The success of the Convention from other perspectives remains the subject of debate, but a considerable body of scholarship generated by the CISG considers the Convention to be a notable achievement in harmonizing substantive sales law. Furthermore, CISG is applied in an increasing amount of case law.[1600]

The almost worldwide success of the CISG has been taken up by the UNIDROIT. In the years 1968 to 1971, a group of renowned scholars started working on the UNIDROIT Principles of International Commercial Contracts. Along with the Convention's achievements, the UNIDROIT noted that the Convention might have shortcomings, but

1597 The harmonization and unification of commercial law has generated a vast volume of literature. See inter alia Fletcher/Mistelis/Cremona 2001; Vogenauer/Weatherill 2006; Berger 2010; Boele-Woelki 2010; Hartkamp 2011; Goode/Kronke/McKendrick 2015.

1598 Schlechtriem/Schwenzer 2010, at 1.

1599 See www.uncitral.org. Notable exceptions are the United Kingdom, Ireland, Portugal.

1600 See the PACE database www.cisg.law.pace.edu/ and the database maintained by the University of Basel, www.cisg-online.ch. See also with further references Schlechtriem/Schwenzer 2010; Schwenzer/Atamer/Butler 2014.

to avoid political compromise inherent in the adoption of international conventions, it was decided to create an instrument of soft law, non-binding on states or private parties. Following the US experience in drafting restatements of law, the UNIDROIT working group undertook to restate[1601] the common principles extracted from the case law of different countries. At the same time, the drafters were committed to creating innovative rules which would best serve parties participating in international trade.[1602] The first edition of the UNIDROIT Principles of International Commercial Contracts appeared in 1994. Since this time, this instrument has become an authoritative document of reference for legislators, courts and arbitrators,[1603] academics, and contracting parties in several countries.[1604] The UNIDROIT Principles are conceived as a 'living' document. Its subsequent editions have completed the instrument with new provisions in order to follow evolution of international business practice, and the development of the instrument will be continued. In March 2014, the General Assembly of the UNIDROIT has decided to develop an approach to long-term contracts to be eventually included as a part of the next edition of the Principles.[1605] The current 2010 edition of the UNIDROIT Principles (referred to in this Chapter as UPICC)[1606] provides specific regulation of negotiations; these will be discussed in detail in this Chapter.

Since the years 1970s, initiatives to draw up soft law instruments in the field of international contracts were been undertaken at two main geographical levels: international and regional.[1607] At the international level, the UNIDROIT Principles have remained the main instrument. Next to this, regional harmonization has been developing within the European Union and lately also within the American, African, and Asian countries. Many of these have been inspired by the substance and the underlying method of the UPICC.

At the European level, an important initiative has developed 'in tandem'[1608] with the drafting of the UPICC. Lando and Beale have established the Commission on European Contract Law in view of creating the Principles of European Contract Law (PECL).[1609] The text of the PECL was published in 2000 (parts I and II)[1610] and in 2003 (part III).[1611] Several provisions of PECL have been influenced by the UNIDROIT Principles and *vice*

1601 On this concept see Jansen 2010, at 92 ff.

1602 See 'Introduction to the Third Edition' UPICC; on the UPICC's innovations including the rules on negotiations Bonell 2005, at 48–57.

1603 See an open access database www.unilex.com containing case law referring to the UNIDROIT Principles since 1994.

1604 Lake 2011; Berger 2010, at 202; Bonell 2007, at 259 ff.; Chappuis 2014.

1605 See work programme 2014–2016. UNIDROIT 2013 C.D. (32) 4(b), at 1, UNIDROIT 2014 C.D. (93) 3.

1606 UNIDROIT Principles of International Commercial Contracts 2010, www.unidroit.org/english/principles/contracts/principles2010/ blackletter2010-english.pdf.

1607 For an overview see Basedow 2003.

1608 McKendrick 2006, at 8.

1609 Lando 2006.

1610 See for the historical roots Lando and Beale, 'Preface', in Lando/Beale 2000, at xi.

1611 Lando 2003.

versa. The instruments have many similarities including terminology, structure and the subject matters covered.[1612] Some PECL drafters were members of both working groups on the UNIDROIT Principles and PECL. Similarly to the UNIDROIT Principles, PECL restate soft law based on commonalities in various national laws of the EU countries, but also aim to offer solutions that meet the interests of contracting parties better than national law.[1613] Similarly to the UPICC, the PECL contain provisions dedicated to contractual negotiations. Furthermore, the PECL had a far-reaching goal to make a first step towards a European Civil Code, the idea of which was at that time explored by the European Commission and Parliament.[1614] The European Commission had at that time a strong interest in harmonization of European contract law. This can be dated back to 1999, when the Commission's ideas crystallized in a project to have a 'common frame of reference'.

Subsequently, drawing upon the experience of PECL,[1615] another major project has been started – the Draft Common Frame of Reference (DCFR)[1616] – the text created by the Study Group on a European Civil Code and the Research Group on the Existing EC Private Law.[1617] This was conceived as a systematic academic description of principles, definitions, and model rules. At the same time, the project stemmed not only from academic interest in creating unified and harmonized law. It related as well to the political will to develop a common contract law instrument for all countries of the European Union. The instrument was aimed at drawing upon the commonalities of the EU countries' laws and, perhaps more importantly, to incorporate the existing *acquis communautaire*.[1618] The goal consisted in 'consolidating, codifying and recasting

1612 Lando 2001; Lando 2002; Bonell/Peleggi 2004.

1613 Lando and Beale, 'Introduction', in Lando/Beale 2000, at xxiii ff.

1614 Ibid.

1615 Von Bar/Clive 2010, at 15 (on the follow-up of PECL).

1616 Von Bar/Clive 2010.

1617 The Research Group on the Existing EC Private Law also called Acquis Group was created in 2002 in order to formulate 'Principles of the Existing EC Private Law' or 'Acquis Principles'. Several volumes of this project's outcome have been used in preparation of the DCFR. See Ajani/Schulte-Nölke 2007. Whereas these two research groups were entrusted and funded by the Commission to draft the text of the instrument, several other research groups have been also entrusted with providing comments and support for the DCFR drafters. These were the 'Insurance Group' (Project Group on a Restatement of European Insurance Contract Law), www.uibk.ac.at/zivilrecht/restatement; the *Association Henri Capitant des amis de la culture juridique française*, www.henricapitant.org and the *Société de Législation Comparée*, www.legiscompare.com and the *Conseil Supérieur du Notariat*, www.notaires.fr/notaires/page/conseil-superieur-notariat?page_id = 58; the 'Common Core Group' (The Common Core of European Private Law), www.common-core.org; the 'Economic Impact Group' (Research Group on the Economic Assessment of Contract Law Rules), www.tilburguniversity.nl/tilec; the 'Database Group' http://web.archive.org/web/20100607023519/; http://icd.recherche.jm.u-psud.fr/php/search.php?. All the research groups have formed together the 'Joint Network on European Private Law'. For other outcome of the research, see inter alia Fauvarque-Cosson/Mazeaud 2008.

1618 The concept of *acquis communautaire* refers to the fragmented development of law through number of EU directives, relating to contracts involving consumer, case law of the European Court of Justice and the existing uniform law, for example CISG. See Twigg-Flesner 2009, at 95–96.

existing instruments centred on transparency and clarity'.[1619] This primarily academic text was supposed to provide a 'toolbox' for further reforms of national laws and represent a first step towards a possible political project – the creation of an instrument harmonizing or unifying European private law such as a European Civil Code.[1620]

The first outcome of the project was the 2008 DCFR 'Interim Outline Edition'[1621] submitted for public comments and consultations. In 2010, the drafters published a full and revised version of the DCFR in which the rules were completed with the research group's comments and comparative notes.

The DCFR is a remarkable academic text, but the project of transforming it into a European Civil Code is postponed if not abandoned. This should be seen in the light of two considerations. Firstly, the DCFR has not escaped critiques for failing to provide an appropriate basis for such a uniform text.[1622] At present, conclusions about the authoritative power of this text and the question whether it achieves the goals of providing a toolbox and inspiration for further national legislators, are premature. The extent to which the DCFR has succeeded in achieving these goals will be shown when it becomes possible to assess its impact on national legislative processes and the reasoning of the courts. Secondly, the creation of a European Civil Code was advocated by the Commission with decreasing insistence[1623] even during the DCFR drafting. The Commission has progressively abandoned the idea of creating a unified civil code for Europe,[1624] increasingly focusing on sales law.

In the years 2000 to 2010, the Commission's interest shifted towards creating an optional instrument for sales contracts, including commercial contracts and contracts involving consumers. With this aim, the Commission has set up an expert group[1625] entrusted with assessing the way forward on the basis of DCFR. The assessment involved various

1619 European Commission, Communication to the Council and the European Parliament on European Contract Law COM(2001) 398 OJ 2001 C255/1, para 58.

1620 European Commission, Communication from the Commission to the Council and the European Parliament on European Contract Law COM(2001) 398 OJ 2001 C255/1. The European Parliament has also called for a 'greater harmonization of civil law'. See Resolution A2–157/89 OJ C 205, 25.7.1994, p. 518. The Commission has adopted an Action Plan: A More Coherent European Contract Law; An Action Plan COM(2003) 68. See also a follow-up concretizing the action plan in the Communication from the Commission to the European Parliament and the Council, European Contract Law and the Revision of the Acquis: The Way Forward COM (2004) 651. See also Green Paper on the Review of the Consumer Acquis. COM(2006) 744.

1621 Von Bar/Clive/Schulte-Nölke 2008.

1622 See inter alia Collins 2009; Eidenmüller 2008; Dannemann/Vogenauer 2013.

1623 European Commission, First Annual Progress Report on European Contract Law and the Acquis Review COM(2005) 456, para 3.3.

1624 The change in Commission's approach became explicit already in the 2004 Communication. See Communication from the Commission to the European Parliament and the Council, European Contract Law and the Revision of the Acquis: The Way Forward COM(2004) 651.

1625 European Commission, Commission Decision of 26 April 2010 setting up the Expert Group on a Common Frame of Reference in the area of European contract law OJ L 105, Articles 1, 2.

relevant stakeholders, academics, businesses, consumers, and legal practitioners. The expert group published its findings in the Feasibility Study.[1626] Based on this preparatory work, in 2011, the Commission published the Proposal for a regulation on a Common European Sales Law,[1627] later transformed into a draft Regulation (CESL). The CESL had a narrower scope than the DCFR, and a more limited ambition in unifying law than that of the DCFR.

The CESL received both positive and more guarded reviews in the literature, but the latter opinion has prevailed. In 2014, the CESL project was abandoned in favour of a new draft Regulation focused on online commerce.[1628] This project focuses primarily on the issues involved in contracting online and is strongly underpinned by consumer *acquis*, and is, therefore, not directly relevant for the present study. For this reason, the discussion below will not return to this project for further elaboration.

Coming back to general contract law, the following is worth noting. The current decrease of political will to create a Civil code for Europe does not necessarily imply that the idea is completely abandoned. It is sufficient to recall the two Hague Conventions of the beginning of the twentieth century, which inspired drafting of the CISG, to suggest that the idea of one code for Europe may be revived at any time. A solid background for such revival is provided in the soft law instruments named above and other academic projects mentioned earlier. The UPICC aimed at use by the global audience are regularly updated. By contrast, no projects to update the PECL or DCFR (drafted primarily for EU countries) are in place.

At the global level, a review of the CISG cannot be excluded. However, such review does not seem to lie in the near future. In 2012, the Swiss government suggested a review of the Convention to UNCITRAL.[1629] The proposal identified contract formation as one of the areas where further harmonization and unification of law should be considered. To assess the possibilities and the desirability of the Convention's review, the UNCITRAL organized number of events where various opinions of academics and practitioners were expressed. The general attitude to the review of the Convention was revealed to be guarded. Many commentators suggested exploring the potential of soft law in guiding the application of the CISG instead of reviewing the Convention.[1630] Particular attention

1626 European Commission, A European Contract Law for Consumers and Businesses: Publication of the Results of the Feasibility Study Carried out by the Expert Group on European Contract Law for Stakeholders' and Legal Practitioners' Feedback, 3 May 2011, http://ec.europa.eu/justice/contract/files/feasibility_study_final.pdf.

1627 European Commission, Proposal for a Regulation of the European Parliament and of the Council on a Common European Sales Law, 11 October 2011, COM(2011) 635.

1628 Annex 2, Commission Work Programme 2015, Strasbourg, 16.12.2014 COM(2014) 910, http://ec.europa.eu/atwork/pdf/cwp_2015_withdrawals_en.pdf.

1629 See United Nations Commission on International Trade Law, Forty-fifth Session (2012), A/CN.9/758, 8 May 2012, Possible Future Work in the Area of International Contract Law, at 7.

1630 Veneziano 2013, Loken 2013, Dennis 2014. Compare to more positive opinions in Sorieul/Hatcher/Emery 2014, at 497–498.

was drawn to the UPICC. The general stage of the discussion suggests that no review of the CISG should be expected in the near future, but if this review takes place, close attention will be paid to soft law instruments.

The brief overview of the genesis of unification and harmonization of contract law shows a close interdependence of scholarly views and political implications in drawing up rules for international transactions. While only the CISG currently represents international 'hard law', soft law instruments are also highly relevant. They may become even more relevant as a source of inspiration as to method and content if the political will for further unification of contract law is revived.

8.3. UN Convention on Contracts for the International Sale of Goods (CISG)

The Chapter will now turn to examining the most important instrument in international hard law – the CISG. Whether the Convention's scope (8.3.1) covers the precontractual period is a matter of scholarly debate (8.3.2). Adding further nuance to this debate, this Chapter will submit that letter of intent contractually organizing the dynamics of negotiations falls outside the scope of the CISG. This becomes clear when relating the concepts of the precontractual period, preliminary agreement, and sales contract under the CISG to earlier findings of this study (8.3.2).

8.3.1. Scope and structure of CISG

The CISG contains substantive law rules to be applied by the courts of its Contracting States to the matters within the Convention's scope. Parties to contracts may also expressly 'opt out'[1631] of the Convention and exclude its application to their sales contract.

The CISG regulates only one type of transactions: international sale. It defines 'international contract' as a contract between parties 'whose places of business are in different States'.[1632] The Convention does not define the concept of 'sales contract', but it is widely accepted that a transfer of goods and an obligation to pay for these goods are necessary to qualify a contract as 'sale'.[1633]

The Convention is divided in four Parts, subdivided into Chapters and Articles. It starts with the definition of its field of application (Articles 1 to 6) and general provisions (Articles 7 to 13). These are followed by Articles on the formation of a sales contract, the respective obligations of the seller and buyer, their common obligations, and consequences of breach.

1631 Article 6 CISG; see also with further references Schwenzer/Hachem 2010, at 108 ff.

1632 Article 1 CISG; see also Schwenzer/Hachem 2010, at 37 ff. Place of business is interpreted broadly.

1633 Schwenzer/Hachem 2010, at 31 ff. Distribution contracts, contractual joint ventures are important exceptions to the scope of CISG, unless the obligations relating to sale carry more weight. See Schroeter 2010, at 254.

To understand the debate on the CISG's applicability to precontractual relations and, in particular, to letter of intent, it is important to note that the Convention's provisions are not exhaustive. Some contract law matters fall *outside* its scope. These remain within the field of the national law applicable according to national conflicts of law rules[1634] or a uniform law, if any governs the matter in question.[1635] As to the matters *within* the scope of the CISG, the literature distinguishes the Convention's 'internal' and 'external' gaps. The guidance on the manner of filling these gaps is provided in Article 7 of the Convention. Internal gaps are matters that fall within the Convention's scope, but are not expressly settled by the CISG. These may be regulated by interpretation and application of the CISG's other provisions. External gaps are matters that fall under the Convention's scope, but are neither settled by the CISG nor can be regulated by interpretation of its other rules. External gaps are to be settled by national laws applicable to the contract at hand following conflict of laws rules. Furthermore, external gaps may be filled by applying general principles underpinning the Convention, namely good faith and fair dealing in international trade, the international character of the Convention, and the need to promote uniformity in its application.[1636] Broadly viewed, the search for such principles leads to the inclusion of international soft law instruments and arbitral practice in the sources of inspiration for interpretation. At all times, the international character of the Convention's rules should be taken into account.[1637]

8.3.2. *Applicability to contractual negotiations*

8.3.2.1. Contra

According to the view predominant in the literature, the precontractual stage falls outside the scope of the CISG; in other words, the Convention does not regulate contractual negotiations.[1638]

The first and the main argument of those academics who find that the precontractual stage falls outside the CISG's scope is its legislative history.[1639] The records of the *travaux préparatoires* demonstrate that the question whether the Convention should regulate the precontractual stage was fiercely debated. One of the draft rules imposed, indeed, a duty of good faith in negotiations. However, a consensus could only be reached by deleting the draft rule in question from the Convention's final text.[1640]

1634 Bonell 1987, at 83; Ferrari 2004, at 158, 171; Lookofsky 2006. See also UNCITRAL Digest of case law on the United Nations Convention on the International Sale of Goods, Article 7 (2004) A/CN.9/SER.C/DIGEST/CISG/7,http://daccess-dds-ny.un.org/doc/UNDOC/GEN/V04/547/56/PDF/V0454756.pdf?OpenElement.

1635 Schwenzer/Hachem 2010, at 77.

1636 See Article 7 CISG; Kröll 2005–2006.

1637 Article 7 CISG. See also Bonell 1987, at 78 ff.; Schwenzer/Hachem 2010, at 123.

1638 See for an overview and critical assessment of most of the arguments Spagnolo 2008.

1639 See for relevant excerpts Kritzer undated.

1640 UNCITRAL: Review of 'Formation' Draft; The 1978 Draft Convention, Annex 1 'Summary of Deliberations of the Commission on the Draft Convention on the Formation of Contracts for the International Sale of Goods' Doc. B(3) A/33/17 IX Yearbook 31–45, reprinted in Honnold 1989, at 369.

The second argument relates to the interpretation of the CISG, in particular, the interaction of its norms with national law. This argument places the boundary between the precontractual stage and matters related to the contract. The point of this boundary is the moment of issuing an offer. National law regulates the precontractual stage, but once an offer is made, the Convention applies and excludes the application of national law.[1641] According to this view, remedies available under CISG and under national law (if any) are mutually exclusive.[1642]

The third argument is based on the interpretation of the concept of 'sales contract' in the CISG. The distinctive criterion for the application of CISG is the transfer of goods for which a payment is due. This criterion is said not to be fulfilled by preliminary exchanges that take place during negotiations. According to the scholars taking this view, this approach holds true even if these exchanges are formalized in a preliminary agreement binding parties with some obligations or duties. Even if a 'pre-contractual contract may increase and concretise these duties',[1643] this 'pre-contractual contract' falls outside the scope of the CISG. According to this view, only if the obligations of the preliminary agreement fulfil the criteria of the CISG for a sales contract and might be seen as a full contract within its scope, can the Convention be applicable.[1644]

On a more moderated note, some scholars contend that CISG does not cover precontractual stage, but consider contractual negotiations to be an external gap in the Convention. According to this view, CISG may be supplemented by the existing soft law instruments e.g. the UPICC, PECL and on the basis of its Article 7(2) filling external gaps by recourse to general principles,[1645] while the UPICC, PECL and DCFR contain provisions on negotiations.

8.3.2.2. Pro

The view that the CISG does not cover the precontractual stage is not unanimously held. The most prominent line of arguments defending the applicability of the CISG to the process of negotiations is established by Bonell. According to this commentator, the precontractual stage is an internal gap in the CISG. It applies to contractual negotiations

1641 See with further references Schroeter 2010, at 248 and 247–254.

1642 Honnold 1999, at 54; Schroeter 2010, at 249. See also with further references Lookofsky 2006, at 101 noting that it is unclear whether CISG should pre-empt in any case or can national law prevent. Huber/Mullis 2007, at 28–29 agree that CISG does not cover the precontractual period, but submit that exceptions should be possible under CISG provisions on non-conform goods to ensure the uniform application of the Convention. See also Germany 4 March 1994 Appellate Court Frankfurt, http://cisgw3.law.pace.edu/cases/940304g1.html (national law was applied to the question of precontractual liability within a claim to recognize that a contract was formed).

1643 Schroeter 2010, at 249.

1644 Schroeter 2010, at 253; Torsello 2008, at 233.

1645 Felemegas 2001, at 1–38; Magnus 2007; Gotanda 2008 (stating that UPICC are not a gap filler but may be seen as restating general principles that underpin the CISG).

indirectly via its mention of good faith[1646] and the rule on party autonomy included in the Convention.[1647]

Bonell rejects the argument invoking the Convention's legislative history. He finds that as matter of fact the CISG has established a broad principle of good faith that may entail positive obligations for parties.[1648] For this scholar, who interprets the provision on good faith extensively, Article 7(1) gives rise to obligations at the precontractual stage, because the issues dealt with in negotiations are inseparable from contract formation (the latter being regulated by the CISG). As a consequence, precontractual matters also fall within the scope of the Convention.[1649] Furthermore, according to this view, Article 74 CISG on damages for breach of contract may be extended to give rise to recovery of expectation damages, even if a contract has not been formed.[1650] According to Bonell, liability under the CISG can arise if a negotiated contract is complex, if an advanced stage of negotiations is reached and accompanied by preliminary documents including documents called 'letter of intent' (the degree of elaboration of this document matters as well) and/or if performance has commenced. This scholar also notes the relevance of trade usages relating to contract formation for establishing liability.[1651]

More arguments in the same vein have been advanced by other scholars. Honnold associates precontractual negotiations with the formation of contract. He argues that the issues related to negotiations can fall into the scope of Article 16 CISG if the addressee of an offer has relied on the offer as being irrevocable. More precisely, revoking an offer may entail precontractual liability based on Article 16 CISG.[1652] According to Schroeter, agreements reached in negotiations can be seen in the light of the CISG provision on intention to be bound (Article 8(3) CISG), intention to be bound being a characteristic of offer.[1653] Earlier, Goderre has argued that the CISG potentially enables engaging precontractual liability based on the doctrine of detrimental reliance similar to the one provided in US law. According to this author, the possiblilty of this claim is arises due to the rule on *venire contra factum proprium* of Article 16(2) CISG. She argues that this rule may be applied, in particular, to negotiations accompanied by preliminary agreements.[1654]

Up to the present time, case law and arbitration practice have not provided further arguments or clearer solutions in this debate than those points of view discussed earlier.

1646 Article 7(1) CISG.
1647 Article 6 CISG. See also CISG Explanatory Note B.
1648 Bonell 1990, at 699; see in the same line Klein/Bachechi 1994, at 20 invoking Article 7(1) and 8(3).
1649 Bonell 1990, at 695.
1650 Bonell 1990, at 701.
1651 Bonell 1990, at 697–699.
1652 Honnold 1999, at 168 (using the term *culpa in contrahendo*).
1653 Schroeter 2010, at 271–272 (also referring to the Bonell's analysis of preliminary agreements).
1654 Goderre 1997, para 48–50 (submitting that Article 7 of CISG should be interpreted extensively).

The approach suggested by Goderre has not been confirmed in practice, the assessment of precontractual reliance remaining within national law.[1655]

Notably, all the scholarly opinions examined regarding the (in)applicability of the Convention to the precontractual period have one point in common: commentators regard the process of negotiations of a contract as an issue closely related to contract and to contract law generally. This points to the potential interpretation of the CISG that may be offered by the soft law instruments, because their drafters take the same view.

8.3.2.3. Discussion

Each argument pointed out above focuses on a particular aspect of contractual negotiations, e.g. *bona fides* in negotiations, breaking off negotiations, and creating various documents in the course of negotiations.[1656] Furthermore, scholars define the concepts of precontractual period and precontractual agreement in different manners. An important role in the debate is played by the interpretation of the concept of sales contract in the CISG.

An argument focusing on documents created in the course of negotiations has been recently advanced by Torsello. He discussed whether preliminary agreements fall within the scope of the CISG.[1657] The definition given by Torsello to preliminary agreements is broad. It covers the types of documents issued most frequently in the course of negotiations referred to in literature, but excludes offer and acceptance. The commentator also sketches the obligations frequently contained in such documents according to this scholar. These are compared to the existing interpretation of the concept of 'sales contract' in the CISG. Torsello concludes that the usual obligations of preliminary agreements may not qualify as sales contracts under the CISG. According to this commentator, the CISG does not apply to preliminary agreements.

Keeping in mind the definition of preliminary agreement made by Torsello, one may recall one of the opinions in favour of the CISG's application to the parties' relationship once an offer is issued (this is the second argument *pro* in the Section above). This view adopts a broad definition of preliminary agreement. It takes into account that such a document – preliminary at first sight – may be interpreted as containing an offer or acceptance or both. As a consequence, the CISG may apply. According to this view, the

1655 See for example *Geneva Pharmaceuticals Technology Corp.* v. *Barr Laboratories, Inc. et al*, 201 F.Supp.2d 236 (S.D.N.Y., 2002) where the court has distinguished the claim for promissory estoppel under domestic law, on the one hand, and a claim under implied contract on the basis of Article 16(2) CISG, on the other hand. Another way to impose liability, according to Goderre, is restitution. See Goderre 1997, para 53.

1656 Spagnolo distils arguments that appeal to the practicability of the advocated position, policy considerations, and arguments relying essentially on classical legal hermeneutics. See Spagnolo 2008.

1657 Torsello 2008. See also Torsello 2014.

parties' relationship before the moment of issuing an offer is regulated by national law, but once an offer is issued, the parties' relationship falls within the scope of the CISG.

The latter view in combination with the opinion of Torsello comes close to the distinction between the dynamics and the substance of negotiations advanced in Chapter 2. However, both opinions mentioned above tie the concept of precontractual to time (before an offer is issued). By contrast, this study suggests delimiting dynamics on the basis of the content of the documents' provisions. Furthermore, Chapter 2 explained that the dynamics of negotiations deal precisely with issues unrelated to the substance of the final contract.[1658]

In this way, both arguments may be nuanced. A letter of intent whereby parties contractualize the dynamics of negotiations – the main focus of this study – falls outside the scope of the CISG. By contrast, precontractual documents – in the broader sense adopted by some scholars – may be regulated by the CISG, as long as these contain offer, acceptance, or other provisions on the substance of the future contract sufficient to qualify as a sales contract under CISG.[1659] If the dynamics and statics overlap, it is possible that part of the document is regulated by the CISG, while the other part falls outside its scope.

A similar approach has been adopted at least in one US decision applying the CISG.[1660] The court distinguished the claim for promissory estoppel under domestic law (of one of the US states), on the one hand, and a claim under implied contract on the basis of Article 16(2) CISG, on the other hand.

The nuanced view suggested above still does not contradict the submission by Bonell that the CISG may imply a general duty of good faith in negotiations via Article 7 of the Convention. This part of the debate is broader than the Convention's applicability to documents created in the course of negotiations. If one agrees with Bonell's argument in favour of the application of the CISG to the precontractual period, the following question arises. As noted earlier, an obligation to negotiate in good faith is one of the provisions relating to the dynamics of negotiations. Can contractualized good faith be qualified in the same way as the duty of good faith implied indirectly through Article 7 CISG?

This question should be answered in the negative for the following reason. If Article 7 imposes *bona fides* in contractual negotiations, it implies a positive duty. As has been

[1658] Article 8(3) CISG recalls the relevance of trade usage for the interpretation of the intent of the parties to a concluded contract. The discussion of the question of effects of letter of intent for the concluded contract falls outside the scope of this research.

[1659] Article 8(3) CISG lays down the relevance of trade usage for the interpretation of the intent of the parties to a contract.

[1660] See *Geneva Pharmaceuticals Technology Corp.* v. *Barr Laboratories, Inc. et al*, 201 F.Supp.2d 236 (S.D.N.Y., 2002) applying the CISG and New York choice of law rules leading to the application of New Jersey law.

shown in the comparative observations, the enforceability of an obligation to negotiate in good faith, at least in the courts' approach, correlates strongly with the extent to which the parties provided specific content to this duty. Furthermore, courts appear to address such a provision as stand-alone and independent from the question of whether the final contract is concluded (though in most factual situations, negotiations fail and no contract is concluded). Therefore, if it were to be tested whether such a contractual obligation can 'can stand on its own feet' (irrespectively of the success or failure of negotiations) the obligation would most probably fail to fulfil the criteria of the concept of 'sales contract' under the CISG. As a consequence, a contractualized obligation of good faith appears to fall outside the scope of the CISG.

In accordance with this reasoning, the CISG neither offers a mechanism to recover damage for breach of letter of intent, nor does it provide any other way to enforce contractual organization of negotiations. One may agree or disagree with the suggestion of distinguishing the statics and dynamics of negotiations advanced in this study. But irrespectively of this, on a more pragmatic note, the application of the CISG's provisions to recovery for breach of a precontractual document (or precontractual *bona fides*) would require courts and arbitrators to undertake a most ingenious interpretation. They may be required to venture harmonizing views on matters that considerably diverge across national legal systems.[1661] This may impede the uniform interpretation of the Convention required by the CISG. From this perspective, a finding that the CISG applies to negotiations might lead to uncertainty in application of its provisions on damages.

It is hoped that the nuanced view within the debate may be of assistance in interpreting the Convention. The distinction between the statics and the dynamics in contractual negotiations may help identify the precise cases in which the CISG may be, subject to the adopted point of view, applicable to a particular document.

Furthermore, if the CISG is to be modernized (though, as noted earlier, such modernization is not a matter for the near future) any renewed discussions about the regulation of the way a contract comes into being might lead to the same debates as those that existed during the adoption of the Convention. This would not facilitate further unification, because the need for political compromise is mentioned as one of the main shortcomings of the Convention.[1662] Its authors had to formulate provisions acceptable for all the states negotiating the Convention. Next to this, the provisions had to be appealing to the countries that might adopt the Convention at a later stage so that the CISG avoids the fate of the two Hague conventions. In view of this, the decision to modernize CISG provisions on contract formation does not appear to be an easy one.

1661 See in the same sense DiMatteo 2005, at 35.

1662 See inter alia Bonell 1996, at 28.

8.4. Scope and structure of the soft law instruments discussed

8.4.1. UNIDROIT Principles of International Commercial Contracts (UPICC)

The UPICC harmonize commercial contract law at the global level. This instrument may be used universally, whenever a reference to global soft law is deemed appropriate. For instance, the UPICC may be referred to in dispute resolution as a restatement of international *lex mercatoria*.[1663] Furthermore, contracting parties may incorporate the UPICC into a contract or choose the instrument as the law applicable to a contract,[1664] though this is subject to restrictions national law may impose on such a choice. The adoption of this universalist approach is clearly facilitated by the soft law nature of the UPICC. As noted earlier, the instrument was drawn up without the need to seek the political compromise required in the adoption an international binding instrument, for example, a convention.

The substantial scope of the UPICC covers 'international commercial contracts'.[1665] The term 'international' is understood broadly. Only contracts entirely connected with only one country are excluded, while any other contracts related to international trade fall within the instrument's scope.[1666] The term 'commercial' is also used in its broad meaning: the drafters explain that the UPICC do not cover consumer contracts,[1667] but may apply to other types of transactions.

The instrument's structure follows the European continental models of codification. It is divided into Chapters and Articles. The UPICC begin with the definition of its scope and purpose and with the general provisions (Preamble and Chapter 1). These general provisions guide the interpretation and application of the UPICC specific rules, formulated as legal norms. The UPICC cover the issues of contract formation (Chapter 2) and validity (Chapter 3), interpretation (Chapter 4) content of a contract (Chapter 5), regulates performance (Chapter 6) and non-performance of a contract (Chapter 7), as well as set-off (Chapter 8) and assignment of rights (Chapter 9). The last two chapters of the UPICC address limitation periods (Chapter 10) and the plurality of obligors and obligees (Chapter 11). Furthermore, each provision of the UPICC is accompanied by one or several Official Comments and Illustrations forming an 'integral part' of the instrument.[1668] They were drafted at the same time as the UPICC provisions to ensure a

1663 Preamble UPICC, section 5.

1664 See Preamble UPICC and Official Comments 4–8 to Preamble UPICC. One of the follow-up projects of the UNIDROIT consisted in drafting model clauses based on the UPICC that may be used by the parties. The possibility to choose *lex mercatoria* or soft law as the law applicable to a contract is subject to limitations that may be imposed on such a choice by national laws. Arbitration tribunals are more likely to follow such choice in all or most aspects.

1665 Preamble UPICC.

1666 Official Comment 1 to Preamble UPICC.

1667 Official Comment 2 to Preamble UPICC.

1668 See Vogenauer, 'Introduction', in Vogenauer 2015, at 16. Official Comments including Illustrations are available at www.unilex.info.

uniform understanding and application of the UPICC Articles, while avoiding the creation of lenghty provisions.

One of the features of the UPICC approach is the distinction between mandatory[1669] and non-mandatory rules.[1670] Mandatory rules are understood broadly in the UPICC. These include, first of all, international conventions and national law applicable according to the rules of private international law.[1671] These mandatory rules always prevail, as the UPICC contain soft law. But besides this, the UPICC contain mandatory rules of the instrument itself. These may not be waived (disclaimed), limited or modified by the parties if the UPICC are applicable to parties' relationship. Article 1.5 states in relation to non-mandatory rules as follows: 'The parties may exclude the application of these Principles or derogate from or vary the effect of any of their provisions, except as otherwise provided in the Principles'. As recalled by Official Comment to Article 1.5 UPICC, most of the UPICC rules are not mandatory.

8.4.2. Principles of European Contract Law (PECL)

The PECL aim to harmonize contract law of the European Member States, and the geographical scope of the instrument is limited to the EU.[1672]The PECL are designed to apply to domestic contracts (contracts between parties from the same EU country) and cross-border contracts.[1673] PECL do not provide definitions of any of these types of contract. One of the reasons for this is that PECL are to be applied irrespectively of the type contract at hand.[1674] The PECL provide rules of general contract law for both commercial contracts and contracts involving consumers.[1675] This soft law instrument has been used as reference for further harmonization of contract law in the EU[1676] that is, the DCFR. The PECL are also referred to in case law as persuasive authority.[1677]

The instrument is structured in three Parts. Parts I and II are dedicated to the rules and principles of general contract law. These are divided into Chapters, Sections and Articles. The internal structure of the instrument follows the model of European continental codification. The instrument starts with the general provisions provided in Chapter 1; the Chapters that follow contain rules on contract formation, authority of agents, contract validity, interpretation and performance as well as on remedies on non-performance and restitution.

1669 Article 1.4 UPICC.
1670 Article 1.5 UPICC.
1671 Official Comment to Article 1.4 UPICC.
1672 Artice 1:101(1) PECL.
1673 Article 1:101(1) PECL; Lando and Beale, 'Introduction', in Lando/Beale 2000, at xxi, xxv.
1674 See on the concept of contract Comment A to Article 2:101 PECL.
1675 Artice 1:101 PECL.
1676 See for instance Zimmermann 2006.
1677 DiMatteo 2002; Busch 2008; Meyer 2006.

The PECL make a distinction between mandatory and non-mandatory rules within their structure. 'Mandatory' rules may not be derogated by parties' agreement – an agreement on such derogation is deemed unenforceable.[1678] By contrast, parties may disclaim non-mandatory rules or derogate from these provisions. The PECL specify which provisions are regarded as mandatory. These are first, mandatory provisions of the PECL themselves and second, mandatory rules of national, supranational and international law applicable according to the rules of private international law.[1679]

8.4.3. Draft Common Frame of Reference (DCFR)

8.4.3.1. Scope and structure

The DCFR is designed for the European Union. As noted earlier, the project aimed inter alia to create a 'toolbox' for further eventual harmonization of private law in Europe. The geographical scope of the DCFR is limited to the European Union. Its substantial scope includes rules on contract, tort, unjustified enrichment, and transfer of property.[1680] The DCFR provisions on contract are drafted for both domestic and cross-border contracts. The instrument does not differentiate between the two. Furthermore, DCFR covers both commercial contracts and contracts involving consumers. This is due to the DCFR's aim to incorporate the *acquis communautaire*, especially the consumer *acquis*. Generally, the DCFR is oriented towards the protection of 'weaker parties'[1681] and is not particularly focused on business transactions.[1682] Most of the rules do not differentiate between commercial transactions and consumer contracts.

The structure of the instrument follows the continental tradition of codification, perhaps even more so than the UPICC and PECL. It consists of ten books. The Books are divided into Chapters, some of which are subdivided in Parts; specific rules are provided in Articles accompanied by Comments and comparative notes by the drafters' working groups. Comments form an integral part of the text, shedding further light on the meaning of the rules. The text begins by establishing fundamental principles: freedom, security, justice, and efficiency. Thereafter, Book I DCFR defines several concepts used in the rest of the text. The definitions are followed by general provisions which have an overarching character and underpin the interpretation of all the other specific provisions of the DCFR. Book II provides the rules on 'contract as agreement', including precontractual duties and formation. Book III contains the rules on obligations.

1678 Comment H to Article 1:201 PECL.
1679 See Article 103 PECL and Comment to Article 1:102 PECL.
1680 Article I. – 1:101 DCFR; Von Bar/Clive 2010, at 11.
1681 See Von Bar/Clive 2010, at 12.
1682 DCFR defines the concept of business: see Definitions and Article I. – 1:105 DCFR. For critique of the definition, see Eidenmüller 2008, at 704.

One of the specificities of the DCFR is that Book III covers both contractual and non-contractual obligations.[1683] To facilitate this structure, DCFR introduces the term of 'juridical act' defined as 'any statement or agreement, whether express or implied from conduct, which is intended to have legal effect as such'.[1684] According to the DCFR, obligations arise from 'juridical acts', while 'contract' is one of the types of juridical act. The distinction between contract and juridical act has been eventually used for convenience, namely, to avoid repetition in the provisions,[1685] but its practical utility and functionality have been criticized.[1686] The other Books deal with specific contracts (Book IV), benevolent intervention in another's affairs (Book V), non-contractual liability arising out of damage caused to another (Book VI), unjustified enrichment (Book VII), ownership of goods (Book VIII), property (Book IX), and trust (Book X).

The DCFR draws a distinction between mandatory rules and non-mandatory rules,[1687] but does not elaborate on the definition and content of 'mandatory rules'.[1688] Arguably, the concept refers primarily to the DCFR's own mandatory rules,[1689] but includes also 'fundamental values recognized as such in the Member States of the European Union'.[1690] Therefore, the concept of mandatory rules of the DCFR includes the rules of a national or European character.[1691]

8.4.3.2. Regulation of negotiations within the structure of DCFR

The main DCFR provisions on negotiations are included into the rules on contract. For this reason, this Chapter focuses on Book II 'Contracts and other juridical acts' and to a certain extent on Book III applicable to both contractual and non-contractual obligations.

This focus may be objected to due to two considerations. Firstly, as noted earlier, the DCFR covers not only contract law, but also tort (non-contractual liability arising out of damage caused to another) and unjustified enrichment. As a consequence, the DCFR provisions of Book VI can potentially apply to conduct in negotiations and liability that may arise therefrom. This possibility is noted by the DCFR, for example, with regards to

1683 See the distinction between contract as agreement and obligations explained in Von Bar/Clive 2010, at 12–13.

1684 Article II. – 1:101 DCFR.

1685 Juridical act is an autonomous concept in DCFR. It resembles, but does not entirely correspond to the French concept of *acte juridique* or the German doctrine of legal acts. See Dannemann 2012, at 11 ff. Dannemann traces the term back to the concept of juridical act used and defined in the Scottish Law Commission 'Report on Interpretation in Private law' in 1997 for which E. Clive was Law Commissioner.

1686 Collins 2008, at 841–842; Eidenmüller 2008, at 703.

1687 Article II – 1:102 DCFR.

1688 Rutgers 2009, at 117.

1689 Article II. – 7:302; Article II. – 1:102 DCFR.

1690 Article II. – 7:301 DCFR.

1691 This also points to the fact DCFR does not exclude application of national law. However, having in mind DCFR has been created as an academic 'draft' or 'toolbox' for the eventual further legislative process, the role of national law is not entirely clear. Rutgers 2009, at 117.

non-contractual liability for loss caused by reliance on incorrect information. According to the DCFR, such liability may arise within 'a more general duty not to harm others'[1692] of Book IV. Furthermore, the rules on unjustified enrichment provided in Book VII can in principle also apply to some precontractual situations, for example, to anticipated performance of the final contract that fails to materialize. Notably, within the DCFR structure, a claim in unjustified enrichment is not subsidiary to other claims. Unjustified enrichment can therefore be potentially applicable to (mis)conduct in the course of contractual negotiations. Secondly, the DCFR authors call the right to recover loss caused by other party's breach of precontracutal duties 'a self-standing non-contractual right'.[1693] They acknowledge the difficulty of strictly delimiting the domains of contract and tort. Instead of delimiting them, they address private law as an 'organic entity or unit'.[1694]

Despite the possible objections, the choice to focus primarily on rules of contract is appropriate for the following reasons. The DCFR approaches the regulation of the precontractual period as closely related to contract: the provisions on negotiations are included in the set of rules on contract.[1695] No rules in the DCFR's Books VI and VII are expressly designed to be applicable to the process of contract negotiations nor do Comments to Articles point thereto. Furthermore, a general description of the DCFR approach to tort and unjustified enrichment cannot be made in this Chapter for reasons of space. For this reason, this Chapter will be limited to the express regulation of the negotiation process in the DCFR Books I, II and III, whereas the provisions on tort and unjustified enrichment will not be addressed.

8.5. Provisions on negotiations in soft law

The UPICC, PECL, and DCFR contain specific provisions on negotiations.[1696] The soft law approach to negotiations is generally underpinned by the principle of freedom of negotiations (8.5.2). However, the principle is subject to restrictions. The main restrictions include the duty of *bona fides* (8.5.3), in particular, *bona fides* in negotiations (8.5.4), the requirements relating to consistent behaviour and protection of reliance (8.5.5). Furthermore, soft law instruments specifically address confidentiality in negotiations (8.5.6) and mention some ways for precluding formation of the final contract (8.5.7). In case of breach, the aggrieved party is entitled to remedies (8.5.8). The nature and conditions of liability deserve specific attention (8.5.9).

1692 Comment A to Article III. – 3:701 DCFR.

1693 In characterizing liability as non-contractual, Comment A to Article II. – 3:501 DCFR mentions the reasoning of the Court of Justice of the European Union in Case C-334/00 *Fonderie Officine Meccaniche Tacconi SpA* v. *Heinrich Wagner Sinto Maschinenfabrik GmbH (HWS)* [2002] ECR I-07357.

1694 Von Bar and Clive, 'Introduction', in Von Bar/Clive 2010, at 12.

1695 See Clive 2008, at 26.

1696 See Van Houtte 2014; Zuloaga Rios, 'Formation III: Arts 2.1.15–2.1.16 – Negotiations', in Vogenauer 2015, at 342 ff.; Perales Viscasillas 2001; Kornet 2002.

It is worth noting that the soft law instruments' provisions on negotiations are formulated in a remarkably similar way, because of the continuity of the instruments' drafting history.[1697] However, the commonality of formulation does not lead to identical regulation. The nuances distinguishing the approaches result from the diverging scopes of the three instruments, and the particular attention the instruments' authors paid to commercial negotiations in drawing up the relevant provisions.

8.5.1. *Freedom of negotiations*

8.5.1.1. UPICC

Contractual negotiations are primarily underpinned in the UPICC by freedom of contract. The instrument provides that 'the parties are free to enter into a contract and to determine its content'.[1698] For the drafters of the UPICC, this principle is a 'cornerstone of an open, market-oriented and competitive international economic order'.[1699] Within the structure of the UPICC, freedom of contract is one of the general provisions and is designed to guide the application of its other, more specific rules. Freedom of contract implies in the UPICC that parties are free to undertake obligations that fit them best. Furthermore, it implies freedom *from* contract[1700] – the right not to be bound, insuring 'healthy competition'[1701] in international trade.

Article 2.1.16 (1) UPICC concretizes freedom of contract by establishing freedom of negotiations:[1702] 'a party is free to negotiate and is not liable for failure to reach an agreement'.[1703] The first part of this provision deals with the process of negotiations. It defines freedom of negotiations as liberty for the parties to shape the method of conducting negotiations. Parties are free to define 'if, how, and for how long to proceed with their efforts to reach an agreement',[1704] and decide on the 'terms to be negotiated'.[1705] The second part of the provision establishes that parties may not be compelled to come to an agreement. This places a limit on the liability a party may incur in the course of negotiations: liability may not be engaged by the simple fact of being unwilling or unable to come to an agreement.

The scope of freedom of negotiations is broad. The UPICC impose no restrictions on *parallel negotiations,* allowing parties to conduct simultaneous negotiations with several

1697 See Section 8.2.
1698 Article 1.1 UPICC.
1699 Official Comment 1 to Article 1.1 UPICC.
1700 This freedom *from* contract is called by Kleinheisterkamp the 'central – and only – function' of Article 1.1 UPICC. See Kleinheisterkamp in Vogenauer/Kleinheisterkamp 2009, at 118. See also Vogenauer, 'Article 1.1 Freedom of Contract', in Vogenauer 2015, at 155 ff.
1701 Official Comment 1 to Article 2.1.15 UPICC.
1702 The term is used in Official Comment 1 to Article 2.1.15 UPICC.
1703 Article 2.1.16 (1) UPICC.
1704 Official Comment 1 to Article 2.1.15 UPICC.
1705 Ibid.

potential parties to a future final contract.[1706] Nor does this instrument establish a general precontractual duty to *disclose* information:[1707] parties are not obliged to communicate in negotiations any particular information prior to the conclusion of the future contract.[1708] As an exception to this general rule, if one of the parties is obliged to apply for a special permission under mandatory national law, this party has an obligation to inform the other party in negotiation about this need.[1709] Parties are not bound by a general duty of *confidentiality* in negotiations. As will be noted in the Section on confidentiality below in this Chapter, confidentiality may be exceptionally implied into parties' relationship.

8.5.1.2. PECL

Freedom of contract is the starting point of the rules on negotiations in the PECL. The instrument states that 'parties are free to enter into a contract and to determine its contents'.[1710] The Comment to this provision underlines that the principle of freedom of contract is common to all legal systems of the EU countries. Freedom of contract in the PECL implies the freedom to enter into contractual obligations, negotiate and decide on the content of these obligations, and the freedom not to enter into a contract.

Furthermore, freedom of contract is concretized in the PECL by freedom of negotiations. According to Article 2:301: 'A party is free to negotiate and is not liable for failure to reach an agreement'.[1711] This provision, similar to the one in UPICC, places a limit on liability that may arise in the course negotiations: parties may not be ordered or compelled to reach an agreement, nor may they be held liable for failing to agree. Freedom of negotiations is illustrated in the PECL in an example of simple contracts. Comment B to this Article provides two illustrations: consumers looking at the goods in a shop and leaving without buying and the sale of a house. Comments C, D, and E focus on 'professional' parties, but discuss negotiations contrary to good faith, underlying the importance of this duty in PECL.[1712]

8.5.1.3. DCFR

'Freedom' is one of the four overarching principles in the DCFR. 'Contractual freedom'[1713] is concretized in the provision on party autonomy:[1714] It states: 'Parties are free to make

1706 Kleinheisterkamp in Vogenauer/Kleinheisterkamp 2009, at 303–304.

1707 Official Comment 2 to Article 2.1.16.

1708 To the extent that the non-disclosure does not constitute fraudulent vitiation of consent sanctioned by Article 3.2.5 UPICC. Vitiation of consent falls out of the scope of this study.

1709 Official Comment 2 to Article 6.1.14 UPICC; UNIDROIT 1987 P.C. – Misc 11, at 23–24.

1710 Article 1:102(1) PECL.

1711 Article 2:301 PECL.

1712 See Comments C, D, E including Illustrations 1–3 to Article 2:301 PECL.

1713 DCFR Principles. Freedom (Von Bar/Clive 2010, at 38); see also Von Bar/Clive 2010, at 130.

1714 Rutgers remarks that the term party autonomy has been found to be more appropriate than 'freedom of contract', because this provision deals not only with contracts, but with obligations in general. See Rutgers 2009, at 117.

a contract or other juridical act and to determine its contents'.[1715] The DCFR confirms the possibility for the parties to create obligations, to be bound by these obligations, and to choose their content as well as to be free from contract.

The DCFR also expressly establishes freedom of negotiations. Article II. – 3:301 (1) DCFR provides: '[a] person is free to negotiate and is not liable for failure to reach an agreement'. Parties to negotiations may decide to enter or not to enter into a contract and define its content.[1716] This also limits the liability that may arise in negotiations: this does not arise for the simple fact of not reaching agreement.

8.5.2. *Bona fides* generally

8.5.2.1. UPICC: international standard

Freedom of contract is counterbalanced in the UPICC by the duty of 'good faith and fair dealing in international trade', established by Article 1.7 UPICC as follows:

> (1) Each party must act in accordance with good faith and fair dealing in international trade.
> (2) The parties may not exclude or limit this duty.

The choice of the term 'good faith and fair dealing' in the UPICC follows the formulation of the US Restatement (Second) of Contracts.[1717] This has been done to avoid difficulties in translation and, more importantly, to prevent attempts to argue that the expressions 'good faith', 'fair dealing', and 'good faith and fair dealing' have a different meaning under the UPICC.[1718]

Article 1.7 has a mandatory character.[1719] As a consequence, parties may not consensually waive or limit the application of this duty to their relationship.[1720] However, parties may concretize the content of the duty of good faith and fair dealing by explicitly mentioning the conduct expected. They may also undertake to respect 'more stringent' standards of behaviour than an obligation of best efforts.[1721]

The requirement of good faith and fair dealing is formulated as an open norm. The *travaux préparatoires* show that the UNIDROIT Working Group was convinced that *bona fides* was a 'fundamental idea'[1722] of international commercial contracting.[1723] The

1715 Article II. – 1:102(1) DCFR.
1716 Comment B to Article II. – 3:301 (1) DCFR.
1717 US Restatement (Second) of Contracts §241(e); see on this Farnsworth 1998, at 402.
1718 Comment 3 to Article 1.7 UPICC.
1719 Article 1.7(2) UPICC.
1720 See also Article 1.4 UPICC on mandatory rules and Article 1.5 UPICC on non-mandatory rules.
1721 Official Comment 4 to Article 1.7 UPICC. See also UNIDROIT 1992 P.C. – Misc 18, at 78.
1722 Official Comment 1 to Article 1.7 UPICC.
1723 UNIDROIT 1992 P.C. – Misc 18, at 73 ff.

discussions of the working group stress the relevance of this principle both as guidance for the parties and as a means for the judge or arbitrator to reach an equitable result in case of disputes. At the same time, the authors have also acknowledged a disparity across legal systems as to the meaning of this concept. According to them, most legal systems sanction parties' misconduct in order to reach equitable results, albeit through different legal techniques.

Generally, the UPICC establish an objective standard of good faith and fair dealing: neither the text of the Article 1.7 nor the Official Comment refer to the subjective state of mind of the parties. Only conduct that can be objectively assessed is relevant.[1724]

The open norm formulation of this duty raises the question of its precise content. Without pretending to embrace all the opinions on the possible meaning of *bona fides* advanced in considerable existing literature, the question here is limited to this concept's meaning within negotiations of a commercial contract.[1725]

The formulation of Article 1.7 UPICC provides an important guideline for the interpretation of the good faith and fair dealing concept. The UPICC confine the duty of good faith and fair dealings to standards used at the *international level*. This means that different meanings of good faith in national laws cannot be simply followed in its interpretation.[1726] The concept is tied to the context of *trade*, referring to standards appropriate primarily for commercial parties in trade transactions. Furthermore, conduct contrary to good faith and fair dealing also includes conduct aimed solely at causing damage to the other party, acts of malice called in the UPICC Official Comment 'abuse of right' following the use of this term in some legal systems.[1727]

Yet, this remains a guideline. Published case law and arbitral awards referring to the UPICC offer little further information, because the duty is primarily invoked there to interpret a specific rule or to reinforce an argument for its application.[1728] It is not entirely clear whether UPICC practically sanction breach of a positive *overarching* duty to negotiate in good faith. On the one hand, according to the Official Comment, the scope of this duty covers not only the execution of contractual obligations, but is applicable 'throughout the life of the contract, including the negotiation proces'.[1729]

1724 See in the same vein Vogenauer, 'Art. 1.7 Good faith and Fair Dealing', in Vogenauer 2015, at 212.

1725 See with further references Vogenauer, 'Art. 1.7 Good faith and Fair Dealing', in Vogenauer 2015, at 205 ff.

1726 UNIDROIT 1992 P.C. – Misc. 18, at 62–64 and 76–77. See also Article 1.6(1) UPICC referring to the need to consider the international character of the UPICC in their interpretation. See also Bonell 1990, at 169.

1727 Official Comment 2 to Article 1.7 UPICC.

1728 See for instance, case law reported as related to Article 1.7 UPICC in the database Unilex at www.unilex.info.

1729 Official Comment 1 to Article 1.7 UPICC; see also Vogenauer, 'Article 1.1 Freedom of Contract', in Vogenauer 2015, at 155 ff.; Bonell 2005, at 129.

Besides this, the fact of the formulation of the duty as an open norm suggests a possible its wide application. On the other hand, the UPICC approach to good faith and fair dealing in negotiations is further concretized in the Article prohibiting negotiations in bad faith. Kleinheisterkamp submits in this regard that whereas the duty of good faith may not be disclaimed by the parties, it is practically possible to agree on concrete consequences of its violation. In other terms, under UPICC, parties may contractualize the consequences of negotiations in bad faith, for example agree on an absence of compensation or fix a specific compensation should negotiations in bad faith cause loss.[1730] Kleinheisterkamp advances the following argument. Along with Article 1.7 (on good faith), Article 2.1.15 (2),(3) expressly deals with the parties' conduct during negotiations and establishes liability only for breaking off negotiations in bad faith. This may mean that UPICC sanction only bad faith in negotiations, but not the absence of good faith. According to this view, if a general duty to negotiate in good faith was established, Article 2.1.15 (2) UPICC would have been formulated as 'a party who negotiates or breaks off negotiations contrary to good faith and fair dealing is liable…'.[1731] But instead, a more restrictive formulation has been chosen during the *travaux préparatoires.*

So far, the available case law has confirmed a positive requirement of good faith and fair dealing in negotiations only in cases where parties specifically agree to conduct negotiations in good faith. This also flows from the Official Comment 2 to Article 2.1.15 UPICC. It states: 'Only if the parties have expressly agreed on a duty to negotiate in good faith, will all the remedies for breach of contract be available to them, including the remedy of the right to performance'.[1732] This clearly points to the possibility to provide content to the duty of good faith in negotiations by private regulation.

In an arbitral award, the duty was said to imply a positive obligation of best efforts.[1733] The duty of best efforts is defined in Article 5.1.4 (2) UPICC:

> To the extent that an obligation of a party involves a duty of best efforts in the performance of an activity, that party is bound to make such efforts as would be made by a reasonable person of the same kind in the same circumstances.

A party complying with the duty of best efforts is expected to undertake all that is reasonably possible to reach the result. However, achieving the final result (e.g. reaching an agreement) is not required.[1734] An objective standard of reasonableness in a party's conduct should be used in order assess that party's compliance with the duty of best efforts.

1730 Kleinheisterkamp in Vogenauer/Kleinheisterkamp 2009, at 300.

1731 Kleinheisterkamp in Vogenauer/Kleinheisterkamp 2009, at 302.

1732 Official Comment 2 to Article 2.1.15 UPICC.

1733 ICC International Court of Arbitration Award 8331 (1996) 10 *Bulletin de la Cour Internationale d'Arbitrage de la CCI* (1999). On this award see also Fontaine/De Ly 2009, at 38–39.

1734 Points (1) and (2) of Article 5.1.4 UPICC contrasted. See also Article 5.1.5 UPICC providing the way to distinguish the two types of obligation within the UPICC.

It depends as well on the type of obligation in question.[1735] Arguably, due to the primary focus of the UPICC on commercial contracts, even a duty to cooperate established by the UPICC for the execution of contracts does not require a commercial party to act contrary to his own interest in the negotiated deal.[1736] This echoes the national approaches studied.

In another arbitral award,[1737] the arbitration tribunal made a reference to the UPICC provision on good faith and fair dealing (in conjunction with the principle *pacta sunt servanda* of Article 1.3) in order to impose on the parties an obligation to cooperate. At the same time, the award underlined that parties are not under an obligation to reach an agreement.

Although this award referred to the obligation of 'cooperation', it does not refer to the UPICC provision on cooperation.[1738] As a matter of fact, UPICC establish a duty of cooperation for the parties to a contract: 'Each party shall co-operate with the other party when such co-operation may reasonably be expected for the performance of that party's obligations'.[1739] As follows from the Official Comment, this duty aims primarily to regulate performance of a contract. However, arguably, this duty arises if parties undertake contractual obligations regulating negotiations of a final contract. The Official Comment specifies that the limit to the interpretation of this provision is the party's 'reasonable expectation'. Next to this, the general limitations of UPICC in relation to the reference to the objective assessment of conduct, to the international character of the UPICC and the relation to trade appear to be relevant.

8.5.2.2. PECL: general duty

The PECL explicitly limit the exercise of freedom of contract by a requirement to act in accordance with good faith and fair dealing and respect other mandatory provisions of PECL.[1740] The general duty of good faith[1741] is a mandatory duty[1742] that parties 'may not exclude or limit'.[1743]

1735 Official Comment to Article 5.1.4 UPICC.

1736 Vogenauer, 'Article 5.1.3 Co-operation between the parties', in Vogenauer 2015, at 621.

1737 ICC International Court of Arbitration 9753 ICC International Court of Arbitration Bulletin, Vol. 12, No. 2 (Fall 2001), 82–84, www.unilex.info/case.cfm?pid=1&do=case&id=693&step=Abstract.

1738 Article 5.1.3 UPICC.

1739 Article 5.1.3 UPICC.

1740 Article 1:102 PECL.

1741 Scholars are not unanimous as to whether the duty of good faith and fair dealing generally has an overarching character within the PECL. Some scholars, including one of the PECL editors Lando, as well as MacQueen and Storme, contend that good faith is an overreaching duty under the PECL and is in place even if a specific provision does not expressly refer to this duty. See Storme 2003; MacQueen 2006; Lando 2007. Other authors, including the PECL co-editor Beale, argue that good faith is not an overarching duty under the PECL, but is specifically required only in the provisions where it is expressly mentioned. See Beale 2005.

1742 Article 1:201(2) PECL; see also Comment H to Article 1:201 PECL. See also Lando 1997, at 356.

1743 Article 1:201 PECL.

The PECL explicitly require parties to negotiate according to good faith and fair dealing. The instrument notes that that 'good faith and fair dealing are required in the formation, performance and enforcement of the parties' duties under a contract'.[1744] Parties' compliance with this duty is presumed.[1745]

Good faith and fair dealing in the PECL is an open norm. It is not confined to specific rules,[1746] nor is it limited to the international level or commercial transactions. This is due to the PECL's scope: the instrument covers not only international and commercial contracts, but also domestic transactions and transactions involving consumers.[1747]

Furthermore, the duty refers to both objective standards and the subjective attitude of a party.[1748] The choice of formulation – good faith and fair dealing – follows UPICC and the US Restatement (Second) of Contracts.[1749] To avoid translation problems, Comment E specifies that the entire expression 'good faith and fair dealing' corresponds to the French '*bonne foi*' and German '*Treu und Glauben*'.[1750] The PECL draw a distinction between the concepts of 'good faith' and 'fair dealing'. 'Good faith' is defined as 'honesty and fairness in mind' and 'fair dealing' as 'fairness in fact which is an objective test'.[1751] Other explanations in the PECL invoke concepts with moral connotations, for example, 'standards of decency, fairness and reasonableness in commercial transactions'.[1752]

Besides the duty good faith and fair dealing, PECL do not provide express precontractual duties.[1753] To the extent these may not be implied by good faith and fair dealing, PECL do not establish any duties of disclosure; nor are parallel negotiations expressly prohibited. Due to the mandatory character of the duty of good faith and fair dealing, parties may not exclude by agreement the application of this duty to their negotiations.[1754] PECL are not explicit on the possibility for the parties to agree on consequences of breach the duty. Lando has noted in this regard that this possibility exists: 'some of the other articles, where the principle of good faith and fair dealing is applied, may allow the parties to agree on the terms of their contract. Thus, when making the contract, the parties may agree on who shall bear the risk of certain contingencies and in such cases

1744 Comment A to Article 1:201 PECL.
1745 Comment F to Article 1:201 PECL.
1746 Comment B to Article 1:201 PECL.
1747 See Section 8.4.2. See also Bonell/Peleggi 2004, at 323, noting that PECL do not expressly mention their international character; Article 1:106(1) PECL does not explicitly require the need to take into account the international dimension in interpretation of the PECL.
1748 Comment B to Article 1:201 PECL.
1749 US Restatement (Second) of Contracts §241(e).
1750 Comment E to Article 1:201 PECL.
1751 Ibid.
1752 Comment B to Article 1:201 PECL.
1753 See for instance Storme 2003, at 231. Storme submits that the PECL are remedy-oriented and the duties serve as conditions for liability.
1754 Comment H to Article 1:201 PECL.

they will not be covered by the hardship rule in PECL Article 6:111 such an agreement, however, is subject to the rules on validity in PECL'.[1755]

8.5.2.3. DCFR: overarching duty

Freedom of negotiations is limited in the DCFR by the duty of good faith and fair dealing. The instrument deals with this duty at several instances. Firstly, the DCFR authors note that this duty flows from the overarching general principle of justice.[1756] Secondly, the DCFR defines the expression 'good faith and fair dealing':[1757]

> (1) The expression 'good faith and fair dealing' refers to a standard of conduct characterised by honesty, openness and consideration for the interests of the other party to the transaction or relationship in question.
> (2) It is, in particular, contrary to good faith and fair dealing for a party to act inconsistently with that party's prior statements or conduct when the other party has reasonably relied on them to that other party's detriment.

The definition points to the requirement of subjective good faith. According to DCFR, the reference to 'honesty and openness' aims to prevent dishonest conduct, cheating and acting out of 'pure malice'.[1758] However, taking into account other party's interest does not mean preferring other party's interest to one's own.[1759] Despite the fact that the DCFR attempts to define the expression good faith and fair dealing, even according to the DCFR Comment this definition might be of no assistance for commercial contracts because of its 'vague'[1760] character. According to the DCFR drafters, the definition is not very important for commercial contracts, because these are usually sufficiently detailed.[1761]

Thirdly, a general duty of good faith is established as a requirement for the execution of obligations.[1762] The DCFR draws a notable distinction between the terms 'duty' and 'obligation'. Duty is defined in a general way, without distinction between duty in contracts and duty in tort; duty is more general than an obligation and its breach does not necessarily entail sanctions.[1763] Furthermore, 'breach of a duty does not give rise directly to remedies for non-performance of an obligation but may preclude the person in breach from exercising or relying on a right, remedy or defence which that person

1755 Lando 1997, at 356.
1756 Von Bar/Clive 2010, at 53.
1757 Article I. – 1:103(1) DCFR.
1758 Comment A to Article I. – 1:103 DCFR.
1759 Ibid.
1760 Comment A to Article III. – 1:103 DCFR.
1761 Comment A to Article I. – 1:103 DCFR.
1762 Article III. – 1:103 DCFR.
1763 See 'Duty' in Definitions DCFR Von Bar/Clive 2010, at 70; see also Von Bar 2010, at 20, 22.

would otherwise have'.[1764] In addition, a provision (or a set of provisions) establishing a specific duty can also specify a remedy for its breach.[1765]

8.5.3. *Bona fides* in negotiations

8.5.3.1. UPICC: negotiations in bad faith

The content of the duty of good faith and fair dealing in negotiations is concretized by Article 2.1.15 UPICC. It establishes liability for negotiations in bad faith. The Article starts by confirming freedom of negotiation, but goes on as follows:

> (2) However, a party who negotiates or breaks off negotiations in bad faith is liable for the losses caused to the other party.
> (3) It is bad faith, in particular, for a party to enter into or continue negotiations when intending not to reach an agreement with the other party.

Under the UPICC, it is bad faith if a party undertakes negotiations without the intention to form a contract, but for other reasons, for example, in order to impede negotiations of the same contract with a concurrent party.[1766] It is also bad faith if a party misrepresents facts or does not disclose relevant information in order to reach agreement.[1767] As noted by Kleinheisterkamp in an academic analysis of the UPICC, misrepresenting or omitting facts in negotiations *with an intention to reach agreement* should be qualified as misrepresentation and governed by the provision on vitiation of consent.[1768] By contrast, the same acts committed *with a goal other than reaching agreement* falls within the scope of Article 2.1.15.[1769]

Less detail is provided by Article 2.1.15 on the content of bad faith related to breaking off negotiations. The Official Comment refers to breaking off 'lengthy negotiations' 'abruptly and without justification'.[1770] The word 'lengthy' creates a link between the advancement of negotiations and their duration in time. The longer the negotiations last, the higher the probability that they will be regarded as 'advanced' and breaking off will be considered as 'abrupt'. But besides the duration of negotiations, advancement can also be reached in a different way, according to Official Comment 3 to Article 2.1.15.[1771] There, reliance by

1764 Article III. – 1:103(3) DCFR. See also Comment E to Article III. – 1:103 DCFR.
1765 See, for example, Book II Chapter 5 Section 5 DCFR containing remedies for breach of duties established by Book II Chapter 3: 'Marketing and pre-contractual duties'.
1766 Illustration 1 in Official Comment to Article 2.1.15 UPICC.
1767 Illustration 2 in Official Comment to Article 2.1.15 UPICC. See, however, Official Comment to Article 2.1.15 UPICC (from which a contrary conclusion can be made).
1768 See Section 2 UPICC Grounds for avoidance.
1769 See, however, Illustration 2 in Official Comment to Article 2.1.15 UPICC.
1770 See Official Comment 2 to Article 2.1.15 UPICC, namely Illustrations 2, 3. 'Lengthy negotiations' are also referred to in Illustration 1 to Article 1.8 UPICC.
1771 Official Comment 3 to Article 2.1.15, para 3.

one of the parties on the success of negotiations is also taken into account to conclude that negotiations were 'advanced'. Furthermore, the number of issues agreed by the parties at the time of withdrawal regarding the future contract is also relevant. The higher the objectively assessed reliance, and the larger the number of issues agreed, the more likely it is that negotiations will be considered to be 'advanced' and breaking off to be abrupt.[1772]

The abovementioned explanations of the Official Comment might suggest, on the one hand, an extensive interpretation of the 'bad faith' concept, because the terms used connote national concepts (for example, the concepts of an 'abrupt' withdrawal and 'advanced negotiations' that may point to conduct considered as fault in negotiations in French law). Nevertheless, the scope of the UPICC ties this concept to the context of international trade and commercial contracts (similarly to the concept of good faith in relation to which this link is formulated more explicitly).

The UPICC allow parties to waive or limit liability for breaking off negotiations. As has been mentioned, the UPICC provide two types of provisions: mandatory and non-mandatory ones. The latter provisions can be excluded or limited by the parties, and parties may also derogate from these. Provisions (2) and (3) of Article 2.1.15 on liability for negotiating or breaking off negotiation in bad faith are not mandatory and may be waived by the parties. If parties waive provisions (2) and (3) of Article 2.1.15, the circumstances or motivation of breaking off negotiations representing 'bad faith' become irrelevant; both parties are deemed to have accepted the risk of failed negotiations.[1773] It is worth noting that this limitation is only possible to the extent firstly, that the limitation or disclaimer of liability is not 'grossly unfair'[1774] and, secondly, it does not breach the UPICC requirement of consistent behaviour.

8.5.3.2. PECL: negotiations contrary to bona fides

The PECL sanctions 'negotiations contrary to good faith':[1775]

> (2) A party which has negotiated or broken off negotiations contrary to good faith and fair dealing is liable for losses caused to the other party.
> (3) It is contrary to good faith and fair dealing, in particular, for a party to enter into or continue negotiations with no real intention of reaching an agreement with the other party.

[1772] Reliance and the number of issues already agreed are especially relevant for negotiations that cannot be analysed through offer and acceptance. See Official Comment 3 to Article 2.1.15 UPICC.

[1773] See in the same sense Kleinheisterkamp in Vogenauer and Kleinheisterkamp 2009, at 116 and 302.

[1774] See Article 7.1.6 UPICC (Exemption clauses) A clause which limits or excludes one party's liability for non-performance or which permits one party to render performance substantially different from that which the other party reasonably expected may not be invoked if it would be grossly unfair to do so, having regard to the purpose of the contract.

[1775] Article 2:301(2),(3) PECL.

The PECL provide examples of conduct contrary to good faith and fair dealing: *starting* negotiations in order to obtain information from a competitor and *continuing* negotiations after the decision not to conclude a contract.[1776] This echoes the French approach.[1777] The illustration in Comment E provides an example of *breaking off* negotiations in a manner contrary to good faith. It describes a situation where parties negotiated a contract regarding the creation of software. The potential software author and seller made 'drafts, calculations and other written documentation' in preparing to conclude a contract and submitted these to the potential buyer. Subsequently, 'shortly' before the expected conclusion of a contract, the potential client passed these 'drafts, calculations and other written documentation' to a third party. Because of this, the third party offered a lower price, the potential buyer subsequently broken off negotiations and concluded a contract with this third party. According to the PECL, the potential buyer has acted contrary to good faith.

The emphasis in this illustration is firstly on the fact that the negotiations were elaborate, because a party has made preparatory work, secondly, on the fact it enabled a third party to use preparatory work, and thirdly, on the fact this was done 'shortly' before the expected date of conclusion of a contract. This suggests that the PECL consider misconduct related to breaking off negotiations broadly. It includes not only the extent to which negotiations are elaborate and advanced, but also the reason why a party breaks off.

Furthermore, the PECL draw a line between absence of good faith and misrepresentation. The instrument notes that the conduct mentioned in Article 2:301(3) is similar to misrepresentation (i.e. using improper means to reach agreement). If a contract is subsequently concluded, misrepresentation entails consequences for its validity on the basis of Chapter 4 PECL.[1778] However, if a subsequent contract is not concluded, the conduct falls within the scope of the present Article 2:301(3). Article 2:301 PECL deals with situations where improper means are used with *other aims than reaching agreement*. By contrast, misrepresentation and other vitiation of consent used with the *aim to obtain a contract* fall under the scope of Chapter 4 PECL.[1779]

8.5.3.3. DCFR: negotiations contrary to bona fides and the duty to disclose information

The DCFR establishes a broad requirement of *bona fides* in contractual negotiations. Article II. – 3:301 DCFR begins by confirming freedom of negotiations and goes on to restrict this freedom by the duty of good faith and fair dealing.[1780] The Article stresses

[1776] Comment D to Article 2:301 PECL.
[1777] Section 4.3.3.
[1778] Comment F to Article 2:301 PECL Basis of liability. Comment F notes that misrepresentation is qualified as a tort in some legal systems.
[1779] Comment A to Article 2:301 PECL.
[1780] Comment C to Article II. – 3:301 DCFR: 'freedom qualified by duty'.

the mandatory character of this duty and points out some types of conduct regarded as a breach:

> (2) A person who is engaged in negotiations has a duty to negotiate in accordance with good faith and fair dealing and not to break off negotiations contrary to good faith and fair dealing. This duty may not be excluded or limited by contract.
>
> ...
>
> (4) It is contrary to good faith and fair dealing, in particular, for a person to enter into or continue negotiations with no real intention of reaching an agreement with the other party.

The requirement of good faith and fair dealing is established for both the process of negotiations (the start and conduct of negotiations) and withdrawal from negotiations. Comments provide some examples to illustrate this provision. Comment D explains for instance that the rule aims to preclude entering into negotiations or continuing these with an aim other than reaching agreement, 'knowing that they [negotiations] will never result in a contract'.[1781]

Notably, the DCFR admits that parties may contractualize the duty of good faith and fair dealing. According to Comment E to Article III. – 1:103, an obligation to negotiate in good faith undertaken by the parties transforms the duty into a contractual obligation. The breach of this obligation is then considered as a failure to perform an obligation and entitles the aggrieved party to claim contractual remedies.

Furthermore, as an extension of the duty of good faith and fair dealing, the DCFR imposes on parties a duty to disclose during negotiations as much information as should be disclosed following 'good commercial practice'.[1782]

Of the three DCFR provisions on precontractual disclosure,[1783] only one covers commercial contracts. This provision is furthermore limited to contracts of sale and services contracts.[1784]Article II. – 3:101 DCFR states:

> (1) Before the conclusion of a contract for the supply of goods, other assets or services by a business to another person, the business has a duty to disclose to the other person such information concerning the goods, other assets or services to be supplied as the other person can reasonably expect, taking into account the standards of quality and performance which would be normal under the circumstances.

1781 Comment D to Article II. – 3:301 DCFR.

1782 Article II. – 3:101 (2) DCFR. This Article does not deal with the misleading information. See Comment D to Article II. – 3:101(2).

1783 The DCFR provisions on precontractual duties to disclose information are largely influenced by the *acquis communautaire* of several EU directives regulating contracts involving consumers. See Twigg-Flesner 2009, at 102.

1784 Articles II. – 3:102 and II. – 3:103 DCFR deal with consumer contracts.

(2) In assessing what information the other person can reasonably expect to be disclosed, the test to be applied, if the other person is also a business, is whether the failure to provide the information would deviate from good commercial practice.

Comment A to this provision emphasizes the absence of an overarching duty of disclosure in the DCFR. Negotiating parties need not provide 'all the relevant information which the opposite party may need in order to make a fully-informed decision'.[1785] Instead, the DCFR requires disclosure of as much information as required by 'good commercial practice'[1786] and can be 'reasonably expected by the other party'.[1787] Provisions on special contracts, namely, commercial agency, franchise and distributorship agreements, also include precontractual duties of disclosure of information.[1788]

The standard of 'good commercial practice' is not developed further in the DCFR; the DCFR provision on 'reasonableness' (Article I. 1:104 DCFR) is open-textured. It points to the interpretation of the circumstances of the specific case, but fails to offer further guidance, leaving a broad margin of interpretation for judges or arbitrators.[1789]

8.5.4. Protection of reliance

8.5.4.1. UPICC: explicit prohibition of inconsistent behaviour

The UPICC explicitly prohibit inconsistent behaviour in order to protect precontractual reliance. This limitation to freedom of negotiations is found in Article 1.8 UPICC. It states as follows: '[a] party cannot act inconsistently with an understanding it has caused the other party to have and upon which that other party reasonably has acted in reliance to its detriment'. According to the Official Comment, the scope of this provision extends to the parties' conduct in negotiations.[1790]

The drafting history of this provision reveals that during the preparation of the UNIDROIT Principles 2004 edition, the Working Group discussed the existence of the protection of reasonable reliance in most national legal systems. The instrument's drafters also contended that in different countries, this protection is provided through different legal techniques. These are the doctrines of estoppel, good faith, and general prohibition of inconsistent behaviour that goes back to the Roman law doctrine of *venire contra factum proprium*. The UNDROIT Working Group also noted that the extent of

1785 Comment A to Article II. – 3:101 DCFR.
1786 Article II. – 3:101 (2) DCFR.
1787 Comment A to Article II. – 3:101 DCFR.
1788 Article IV.E. – 2:101 DCFR provides duties applicable to precontractual periods of these three types of contract.
1789 The DCFR provisions requiring 'reasonableness' and acting as 'can be reasonably expected' has been criticized for their open textured character. See inter alia Vogenauer 2013, at 94.
1790 See Illustration 1 Official Comment 2 to Article 1.8 UPICC.

the protection and remedies vary across countries.[1791] The first edition of the UPICC did not contain any rule on inconsistent behaviour. This was supposed to flow from the provision on good faith and fair dealing. Subsequently, the discussions led to including a special article prohibiting inconsistent conduct into the 2004 edition of the UNIDROIT Principles.[1792]

The meaning of this rule is twofold. Firstly, it establishes a positive duty for a party: a prohibition from acting inconsistently with his own previous conduct. Secondly, it protects reasonable reliance by party on the other party's conduct.

Several elements should be in place in order to claim the protection of reliance.[1793] First, there should be reliance. The Official Comment provides that reasonable reliance should be assessed by objectively addressing the facts of the case and the 'communications and conduct of the parties'.[1794] Based on this, a decision should be made whether a reasonable reliance could have been created in these circumstances, and whether it has been indeed created. Second, a party should have acted upon this reliance. Illustration 1 explains this with an example of works started by a party in a belief that negotiations are completed and an agreement reached.[1795] Third, the reliance should be caused by the other party's conduct inconsistent with its previous behaviour. The notion of a party's conduct inconsistent with his previous behaviour is understood broadly. This can be 'misrepresentation', 'conduct' or 'silence when the other party would reasonably expect the other to speak'.[1796] Fourth, a detriment should occur following this reliance.[1797] The detriment consists in loss or disadvantage caused by the previous elements.[1798]

However, Article 1.8 makes no mention of liability for inconsistent conduct, nor does it provide for concrete remedies.[1799] The Official Comment offers a pragmatic solution by stating that Article 1.8 aims to prevent detriment caused by reasonable reliance. It goes on to explain that detriment can be avoided not only by *acting consistently* with the previous conduct, but also by *notifying* the other party reasonably in advance before acting inconsistently or, alternatively, by *reimbursing* the loss caused by acting upon reliance.[1800] The explanation of the Official Comment concretizes the positive duty of

1791 See UNIDROIT 2002 – Study L – Misc. 24, para 379 ff.; UNIDROIT 2002 – Study L – Doc. 78, at 10–16.

1792 See UNIDROIT 2002 – Study L – Misc. 24, para 379 ff. However, Official Comment 1 to Article 1.8 UPICC still state that 'this provision is a general application of the principle of good faith and fair dealing'. See also Vogenauer, 'Article 1.8 Inconsistent behaviour', in Vogenauer 2015, at 231.

1793 On the UPICC Working Group's choice of terms to designate these elements – Vogenauer in Vogenauer/Kleinheisterkamp 2009, at 188.

1794 Official Comment 2 to Article 1.8 UPICC.

1795 Illustration 1 in Official Comment 2 to Article 1.8 UPICC.

1796 Official Comment 2 to Article 1.8 UPICC.

1797 UNIDROIT 2002 Study L – Misc. 25, para 496.

1798 UNIDROIT 2002 Study L – Misc. 25, para 496.

1799 See Study L (2002) – Misc 24, para 390, containing a draft of this provision moved later on into the Official Comment to Article 1.8 UPICC.

1800 Official Comment 3 to Article 1.8 UPICC.

consistent behaviour in the UPICC. If a party is planning a sudden change in its attitude or position in negotiations, it appears to be under a duty to notify the other party reasonably in advance. If this duty is honoured, no liability arises. Alternatively, a party may remedy its inconsistent behaviour by reimbursing the other party's loss.

This concretization leads to the question as to whether parties may consensually waive the requirement of consistent behaviour or derogate from it. For example, may parties agree in advance on a possible reimbursement in case one party decides not to contract, distributing risks in advance? Formulated in the context of the UPICC, the question is whether Article 1.8 is a mandatory provision. The Article itself does not indicate its mandatory character. In an authoritative commentary to the UPICC, Vogenauer submits that Article 1.8 UPICC is non-mandatory. According to this author, the opinion of the UNIDROIT Working Group during discussions on this Article 'rather seemed to come down in favour of permitting parties to deviate from Article 1.8'.[1801] Therefore, it may be concluded with some certainty that parties may consensually derogate from the requirement to act consistently in negotiations by agreeing on specific consequences of failure to comply with this requirement. It is submitted, however, that a complete disclaimer of this requirement might be problematic to the extent that it does not comply with the requirement of good faith if this is interpreted as a broad overarching duty.

8.5.4.2. PECL: implicit requirement as part of bona fides

The PECL provide the duty of good faith and fair dealing with substantive content inter alia through the doctrine of *venire contra factum proprium*. This requires parties to act consistently with their own previous behaviour and protects reasonable reliance. This requirement is not provided in a specific provision, but flows from the duty of good faith and fair dealing in negotiations.[1802] As this is a mandatory provision, parties may not derogate from this principle or waive its consequences (for example waiving either party's liability for acting incoherently in negotiations or breaking them off).

8.5.4.3. DCFR: requirement of transparency in conduct

The definition of the expression 'good faith and fair dealing' provided in Article I.-1:103 DCFR prohibits inconsistent behaviour[1803] through the requirement of 'transparency' in conduct.[1804] As the wording of the Article suggests, the following elements should be in place in order to conclude that the standard of good faith is not met: the conduct of one party, the other party's reliance on this conduct, detriment resulting from this reliance, and the causal link between the conduct and detriment.

[1801] Vogenauer, 'Article 1.8 Inconsistent behaviour', in Vogenauer 2015, at 230.

[1802] Comment C to Article 1:201 PECL. See also UNIDROIT 2002 – Study L – Misc. 24 para 379: 'Lando also expressed interest in such a solution but recalled that PECL did not contain such a provision since it had been felt unnecessary given the presence of the general clause on good faith'.

[1803] See in particular Article I. – 1:103 (2) DCFR.

[1804] See Comment A to Article I. – 1:103 DCFR.

Protection of precontractual reliance is also indirectly provided in Article II. – 7:204 DCFR establishing liability for loss caused by reliance on incorrect information. Indirectly, this provision also prohibits providing information on which one party may rely during negotiations to its detriment. The Comment to this provision states: 'this Article reflects the idea that a party to contractual negotiations should not act in an irresponsible way in giving information to the other party on which the other party may rely'.[1805] However, Article II. – 7:204 DCFR applies only if a subsequent contract is concluded. The DCFR states: this Article applies only to incorrect information given by the other party *to the contract*.[1806] If negotiations fail, this Article provides no basis for recovery for the loss eventually caused by the reliance on incorrect information.

8.5.5. *Confidentiality in negotiations*

8.5.5.1. UPICC

As well as establishing the duties discussed above, the UPICC devote special attention to confidentiality in negotiations. Article 2.1.16 states as follows:

> Where information is given as confidential by one party in the course of negotiations, the other party is under a duty not to disclose that information or to use it improperly for its own purposes, whether or not a contract is subsequently concluded. Where appropriate, the remedy for breach of that duty may include compensation based on the benefit received by the other party.

The starting point is that the UPICC establish no general duty of confidentiality.[1807] Only information disclosed with an indication of its confidential (privileged) character should be treated as confidential. The receipt of such information is regarded as an implicit agreement to observe its confidentiality.[1808] The UPICC do not specify whether the provision is applicable to both the non-disclosure of the information exchanged in negotiations and the secrecy of the fact that negotiations are taking place.[1809]

Other information received in negotiations may be freely used, independently of the outcome of negotiations. Free use means that parties may disclose the information to third parties or use it for their own purpose and profit.[1810] The disclosure to third parties is even possible in situations where this may be a tactic of negotiations. The Official

1805 Comment A to Article II. – 7:204 DCFR.

1806 Comment D to Article Article II. – 7:204 DCFR, emphasis added.

1807 Official Comment 1 to Article 2.1.16; Bonell 2006, at 141.

1808 Official Comment 1 to Article 2.1.16 UPICC.

1809 See Section 7.7 of this study, observing that the secrecy of the fact that negotiations take place plays an important role in the contractual organization of negotiations.

1810 Official Comment 1 to Article 2.1.16 UPICC.

Comment provides an example where a disclosure aimed to 'induce [a third party] to propose more favourable conditions'.[1811]

However, as an exception to the absence of general duty of confidentiality, in certain cases, confidentiality can be *implied* even for information disclosed without an indication of its privileged character.[1812] The implication can be called for by the nature of information or the professional activity of the receiving party.

Illustration 3 provides an example. It discusses negotiations of a joint venture agreement between two car manufacturers. In the course of negotiations, one party discloses to the other a design of a new car. The disclosure is made without mention of the privileged character of the design. Despite this, the receiving party should treat this information as confidential: in particular, it may not use the design in its own production or make it known to any third parties. According to the Official Comment, confidentiality is implied into the relations between the two car manufacturers, because the information about a design of a new car goes in the core of the commercial activity of both parties. In this example, both the nature of the disclosed information and the parties' professional activity point to the need to regard this information as business sensitive and consequently confidential. Here again the UPICC make reference to the general duty of good faith and fair dealing, stating that treating such information as non-confidential may be contrary to this duty.[1813]

The possibility of implying a duty of confidentiality in negotiations raises in particular the question to what extent parties may deviate by consensus from the rules established by the UPICC. The Official Comment notes that the UPICC admit the validity of a precontractual agreement on non-disclosure of information received in negotiations and on the (contractual) liability this entails.[1814] However, no further elaboration on this or on a disclaimer of the provisions on confidentiality is made in the UPICC text or comments. Arguably, parties may preclude the possible implication of the duty of confidentiality into their relations, if they wish to do so, because the provision on confidentiality does not indicate that it is a mandatory rule of the UPICC.[1815]

8.5.5.2. PECL

The PECL also specifically deal with the issue of confidentiality in negotiations. Whereas the instrument imposes no general duty of confidentiality in negotiations,[1816] confidentiality can be implied into the parties' relationship due to the 'special character'

1811 Ibid.
1812 Official Comment 2 to Article 2.1.16 UPICC.
1813 Official Comment 2 to Article 2.1.16 UPICC.
1814 See Official Comment 3 to Article 2.1.16 UPICC.
1815 See also Official Comment 3 to Article 3.1.5 UPICC.
1816 Article 2:302 PECL.

of information disclosed in negotiations and due to the parties' 'professional status'.[1817] Article 2:302 states as follows:

> If confidential information is given by one party in the course of negotiations, the other party is under a duty not to disclose that information or use it for its own purposes whether or not a contract is subsequently concluded. The remedy for breach of this duty may include compensation for loss suffered and restitution of the benefit received by the other party.

This provision requires only the information expressly marked as secret (privileged) when it is disclosed in the course of negotiations to be kept confidential.[1818] Other information may be used by the receiving party for its own purpose or disclosed to third parties.

However, it seems that under the PECL the information may not be used as a tactic of negotiations, for example in order to obtain a lower bid from a third party, because this would be contrary to good faith and fair dealing. This conclusion is suggested by reading the provision on confidentiality in conjunction with the Comment E to the provision on negotiations contrary to good faith. Comment E contains the following case as an Illustration. Parties negotiated a contract regarding the creation of software. The potential software author made 'drafts, calculations and other written documentation' in preparing for concluding a contract and submitted these to the potential buyer. Subsequently, the potential buyer passed these 'drafts, calculations and other written documentation' to a third party. As a result of this, the third party could make an offer with a lower price to the potential buyer. The potential buyer subsequently broke off negotiations and concluded a contract with this third party. According to the PECL, the potential buyer has acted contrary to good faith. This Illustration does not mention whether the information has been given as confidential, but supposedly, if this was the case, the potential software buyer would not have disclosed it to a third party asking for a lower price (otherwise, the Illustration would mention not only breaking off contrary to good faith, but also breach of confidentiality).

Next to this, according to Article 2:302 PECL, if the disclosed information has a special character for the parties or the parties' professional status so dictates, the duty of confidentiality can be *implied*.[1819] This provision covers situations of disclosure of highly business sensitive information relating to the core of the parties' business activity (know-how is mentioned in Comment B to Article 2:302 PECL to illustrate such information). According to the PECL, this information has to be treated as confidential even if no note on its confidential (privileged) character is made at the moment disclosure.

The PECL do not expressly mention the possibility to derogate from the provision regarding confidentiality, for example, to disclaim the implied confidentiality. As

1817 Comment B to Article 2:302 PECL.
1818 Comment A to Article 2:302 PECL stresses this.
1819 Comment B to Article 2:302 PECL.

Article 2:302 PECL is not a mandatory provision, derogation appears to be possible (subject to the duty of good faith and fair dealing being a general limitation to freedom of contract in PECL).

8.5.5.3. DCFR

The DCFR also contain a specific provision on confidentiality of information provided in negotiations.[1820] Whereas the DCFR establishes no general duty of confidentiality in negotiations, it focuses on prevention of the anticipated unwanted disclosure. The DCFR stresses a party's right to ask for a court order to prevent disclosure of privileged information.[1821]

Article II. – 3:302 deals with several issues. It defines the duty not to disclose confidential information, specifies which information should be considered as confidential, emphasizes the possibility for a party to prevent unwanted disclosure, and establishes liability for breach of this duty.

Under the DCFR, all information provided in negotiations on a non-confidential basis is not privileged and may be freely used by the receiving party for its own purpose or disclosed to third parties.[1822] At the same time, Comment B states that confidentiality can arise 'from the special character of information, and from the parties' professional status'.[1823] This means confidentiality can be implied into the parties' relationship. An Illustration provides an example of information with a special nature: this is know-how owned by a party, whereas no example of the parties' professional status is given.[1824] The Comment does not provide further information on the parties' professional status. As to the circumstances in which a party could expect information to be confidential, the Illustration refers to information sent by registered email and discussed 'when they [parties] were alone'.[1825] The DCFR does not provide any elaboration on the possibility of disclaiming the implication of confidentiality.

8.5.6. *Tools for precluding formation of the final contract*

Freedom of contract implies that no party may be *compelled* to reach agreement. But parties may *create* an agreements which binds them and which may be enforced by a court. All three instruments aim to enforce and preserve contracts where possible. They rely on the principle sometimes referred to as *favor contractus*.[1826] It implies that '[w]here there is doubt about the meaning of a contract term, an interpretation that makes the

1820 Comment A to Article II. – 3:302 (3) DCFR.
1821 Article II. – 3:302 (3) DCFR.
1822 Comment A to Article II. – 3:302 DCFR.
1823 Comment B to Article II. – 3:302 DCFR.
1824 Illustration in Comment B to Article II. – 3:302 DCFR.
1825 Ibid.
1826 Kornet 2012; Berger 2010, at 200–201; Bonell 2005, at 102; Keller 2008; Schmitthoff 1987.

contract lawful or effective ("*ut res magis valeat quam pereat*", "*effet utile*")'[1827] should be preferred to the interpretation that would render it unenforceable. This approach relies on the assumption that enforcing contracts is more beneficial for the parties to international transactions than rendering deals unenforceable by establishing stringent standards of enforceability. Parties have to find an alternative solution, and this, according to the *favor contractus* approach is not serving the interests of international trade.[1828]

Favor contractus does not imply that contract formation is at all times presumed, but the instruments provided for creation of a contractual obligation have been referred to as 'liberal', because they do not reproduce national, often intricate and complex, doctrines.[1829] Soft law instruments establish no requirement of form: an obligation can, for instance, be created in writing or orally and needs not respect any other formalities.[1830] Soft law instruments also acknowledge the possibility of concluding a contract by conduct (besides the formation by offer and acceptance). Finally, soft law instruments expressly provide that contracts with terms left open are enforceable. The main requirements for enforceability of contractual obligations in the UPICC is acceptance of an offer or 'conduct of the parties that is sufficient to show agreement'.[1831] This makes intention to be bound and sufficient definiteness of the terms on which parties wish to be bound the only conditions of enforceability of a contractual obligation.[1832] The PECL follows the same approach: the parties' intent to be legally bound and reach sufficient agreement.[1833]

To balance *favor contractus*, soft law instruments provide rules to keep the relationships at the negotiations stage and to prevent the enforceability of a contract. These will be addressed further.

8.5.6.1. UPICC: terms to be agreed and form

The UPICC recognize an important tool enabling parties to preclude formation of a contract during the negotiations. A party may insist that the final contract is not formed until the negotiators reach an agreement on one or several specific terms. The term to be agreed becomes essential to the final contract, and the absence of agreement on this term precludes its formation. Similarly, a party may insist that the final contract will only be formed when it is concluded in a particular form.[1834]

1827 Schmitthoff 1987, at 47.
1828 Bonell 2005, at 102.
1829 Anderson, 'Introduction to Arts 2.1.1–2.1.14', in Vogenauer 2015, at 253 ff. See also Kornet 2010; Kleinheisterkamp in Vogenauer/Kleinheisterkamp 2009, at 118.
1830 Article 1.2 UPICC; Article 2:101 PECL; II. – 1:106 DCFR.
1831 Article 2.1.1 UPICC.
1832 See Nottage, 'Formation I: Arts 2.1.1 – 2.1.5 – Offer Article 2.1.1', in Vogenauer 2015.
1833 Article 2:101 PECL.
1834 Article 2.1.13 UPICC.

This enables parties to delimit the period of negotiations and the moment of formation of the final contract. Official Comment notes that in practice, parties often purport to reach this result by stating in precontractual documents that negotiations are 'subject to contract' or 'subject to formal agreement'.[1835]

The application of Article 2.1.13 to practical situations is explained in the Official Comment. This emphasizes that a party should *insist* on the need to agree a term or conclude a contract in particular form. The contrast between the Illustrations included in the Official Comment[1836] shows the relevance of this requirement for precluding formation of the final contract. In both Illustrations, parties agree on a certain number of essential issues regarding the future contract. In Illustration 1, parties do not consider any other issues besides the ones agreed as crucial for the decision about entering into the future contract. A dispute arises thereafter about an issue that was not negotiated. The issue giving raise to the dispute is considered to be a minor issue that can be implied into the contract. In this situation, a contract is regarded as concluded.[1837] By contrast, in Illustration 2, a party underlines and 'repeatedly declares' that an agreement on a certain term is essential to the future contract. According to the Official Comment, this precludes formation of the final contract. The parties' relationship remains at the stage of negotiations.

A similar approach is applied to the parties' agreement and one party's insistence on the need to conclude a contract in a special form.[1838] The parties' exchanges in other forms constitute only negotiations. Whereas the UPICC establish that no particular form is required for contract formation,[1839] Article 2.1.13 provides an exception to this rule. However, the possibility offered to the parties by Article 2.1.13 should be seen in conjunction with the UPICC restrictions on inconsistent behaviour. If a party insists on the requirement to agree a term or on a formal requirement, but acts as if the contract has been concluded, this party may be precluded from invoking the requirement of form to prove that no contract was concluded.

8.5.6.2. UPICC: suspensive condition within the discretion of one party

Another tool to shape negotiations contractually is recognized by the UPICC. They acknowledge the possibility of concluding a contract under condition: the formation of a final contract depends upon a future uncertain event.[1840] The UPICC envisage

1835 See Official Comment 2 to Article 2.1.13 UPICC mentioning 'preliminary agreement', 'memorandum of understanding', and 'letter of intent.'

1836 Official Comment to Article 1.2.13 UPICC Illustrations 1 and 2.

1837 Articles 2.1.2, 4.8 and 5.1.2 UPICC.

1838 Illustrations 3, 4 in Official Comment 2 to Article 2.1.13 UPICC. See also the Dutch decision of the *Hoge Raad* HR 02 February 2001, ECLI:NL:PHR:2001:AA9771, *NJ* 2001, 179 referring to Article 2.13 of the UPICC 2004, similar to the current Article 2.1.13 in the context of a case decided following the common law approach.

1839 Article 1.2 UPICC.

1840 Conditional contracts are outside the scope of the present study.

situations where the completion of this condition is entirely within the discretion of one party.[1841] For example, parties may agree during the negotiations that a contract will 'come into being' when party A decides to sell a certain type of goods and only if party A decides to do so. According to the UPICC, this obligation (condition) is enforceable, despite the fact the coming into being of a contract depends only on party A's will.[1842]

Besides this, the Official Comment notes that the 'fact that A may be under a pre-contractual obligation not to act in bad faith is irrelevant in this case'.[1843] This Comment is not entirely clear. It might point to pre-emption of parties' agreement, albeit precontractual, over the prohibition to negotiate in bad faith. As a result, the duty not to negotiate in bad faith would not oblige A to *sell* the goods, nor would it influence the *time* to sell or imply liability for not doing so.

8.5.6.3. PECL: agreement to negotiate

Article 2:103 PECL admits that parties can create obligations shaping the formation of a future contract. Comment C to this provision notes that 'an agreement to negotiate a contract (a contract to contract) is in itself binding. It entails a duty on both parties to make serious attempts to conclude the planned contract… However parties are not obliged to reach agreement'.[1844]

The PECL appear to treat an obligation to negotiate agreed during the precontractual stage as a contract *sui generis*. However, the consequences of this contract are limited: the only claim that can be made is a request to make 'serious attempts' to come to an agreement about the future contract. It is unclear whether a valid agreement to negotiate entails a duty to cooperate (this duty established by PECL as a requirement for execution of contractual obligations).[1845] The Comments to the provision on the duty of cooperation frame the duty as one aimed at giving full effect to a final contract (not to an 'agreement to agree'). Comparative notes included in the PECL point in the same direction. It is therefore doubtful that an agreement to negotiate, though enforceable under PECL, implies a duty to cooperate.

8.5.6.4. PECL: preclusion of formation of the final contract

Furthermore, Article 2:103 (2) allows parties to preclude formation of a contract until agreement on a specific term is reached. It states:

[1841] Official Comment 4 to Article 5.3.1 UPICC.

[1842] Ibid.

[1843] Ibid.

[1844] Comment C to Article 2:301 PECL.

[1845] Article 1:202 PECL – Duty to Co-operate: Each party owes to the other a duty to co-operate in order to give full effect to the contract.

(2) However, if one of the parties refuses to conclude a contract unless the parties have agreed on some specific matter, there is no contract unless agreement on that matter has been reached.

According to the Comment to this provision, the final contract will not be formed unless a party accepts a commenced performance. If a performance started, the PECL offer two options. If the negotiated contract is a 'usual type of contract' that is, for example, a sales contract or services contract, the agreement on the type of contract and 'crucial terms' will be sufficient to regard the final contract as concluded. If the negotiated contract is not of the 'usual type', its terms will be assessed for clarity, and in the absence of clarity the final contract will not be regarded as formed.[1846]

8.6. Remedies

8.6.1. UPICC

According to the UPICC, the right to recover damages 'may arise not only in the context of non-performance of the contract, but also during the pre-contractual period'.[1847] Recovery is based on the principle of 'full compensation'[1848] of foreseeable damages ('certain harm').[1849] Punitive damages are not admitted.[1850]

The UPICC draw a general distinction between the sustained damage ('harm sustained'[1851] also called 'reliance interest' or 'negative interest')[1852] and potential gain ('any gain to the aggrieved party' also called 'expectation interest' or 'positive interest').[1853]

The main type of damage recoverable for breach of the UPICC rules on negotiations is the damage sustained. It consists in recovery of expenses wasted in negotiations and in loss of chance to conclude the contract, negotiations for which failed, or loss of chance to conclude a contract with a third party. By contrast, recovery of a potential gain is rather an exception. Potential gain consists in profit that a party might have received if a negotiated contract had been concluded, or if a contract with a third party had been concluded. Disgorgement of benefits from a contract concluded by a party to a failed negotiation with a third party may be classified under the UPICC as part of the potential gain.

1846 Comment B to Article 2:301 PECL.
1847 Official Comment 3 to Article 7.4.1 UPICC; see on the right to recover damage Article 7.4.1 UPICC.
1848 Article 7.4.2 UPICC.
1849 See Article 7.4.3 UPICC 'Certainty of harm'.
1850 Official Comment 2 to Article 7.4.2 UPICC.
1851 Article 7.4.2(1) UPICC. As to the character of harm, generally, this is primarily economic loss. However, according to Article 7.4.2(2), 'physical suffering or emotional distress' may be recovered as well. According to the Official Comment 5 to Article 7.4.2 UPICC, the latter provision covers primarily commercial relations involving 'artists, outstanding sportsmen or women and consultants'.
1852 Official Comment 2 to Article 2.1.15 UPICC.
1853 Ibid.

8.6.1.1. Breach of UPICC rules

Remedies for *conducting* negotiations in bad faith are concretized in the Official Comment to Article 2.1.15. The aggrieved party may recover expenses wasted in negotiations ('expenses incurred in the negotiations'),[1854] and, next to this, may claim compensation for loss of opportunity to conclude a contract with a third party. According to the UPICC, in this case, potential gain is not recoverable.[1855]

Breaking off negotiations in bad faith may also give rise to recovery of the expenses wasted in negotiations.[1856] Furthermore, the UPICC provide that liability in case of the other party's reliance on *inconsistent behaviour* in negotiations entitles a party to recovery of loss. However, no further concretization on the types of loss recoverable is provided.

The instrument also mentions remedies for breach of the *duty of confidentiality*. The aggrieved party may recover damage sustained and the potential gain received by the party breaching the duty of confidentiality as a result of using the information for its own purpose or disclosing it to third parties. The instrument notes that potential gain may be recovered even if the aggrieved party has not suffered any loss.[1857] The UPICC also mention that a party may seek a court injunction to prevent unwanted disclosure.[1858]

One more remedy is worth noting. The UPICC do not spell out remedies for breach of the *duty of good faith and fair dealing*.[1859] However, the Official Comment points to the remedy of 'loss' of right obtained with a breach of this duty.[1860] This means that after discovery of bad faith, one may no longer rely on the existence of right obtained with the breach of the duty. Nor may a party base any claims on it.

8.6.1.2. Breach of obligations undertaken by the parties during negotiations

On two occasions, the UPICC mention remedies for breach of obligations created by parties in the course of negotiations. Firstly, the Official Comment on the provision on negotiations in bad faith states: 'Only if the parties have expressly agreed on a duty to negotiate in good faith, will all the remedies for breach of contract be available to them,

1854 Ibid.

1855 Ibid.

1856 Official Comment 3 to Article 2.1.15 UPICC.

1857 Ibid. The benefit may consist, for example, in the amount the other party saved on research and development of information it used.

1858 Official Comment 3 to Article 2.1.16 UPICC.

1859 This is due to the open-norm character of this duty as well as to the compromised manner this is formulated to reconcile the civil and Roman law and the common law approaches. See the Section on good faith and fair dealing above.

1860 Illustration 7 Official Comment to Article 1.7 UPICC.

including the remedy of the right to performance'.[1861] In this way, if parties *agree to negotiate in good faith*, *bona fides* is transformed from a duty to a contractual obligation. Its breach entitles a party to all remedies available under the UPICC for breach of a contract. Arguably, the 'right to performance' implies only the requirement of using best efforts to reach agreement. One of the reasons for this suggestion is the limited role of specific performance within the UPICC that follows to a certain extent the theory of 'efficient breach'.[1862] Specific performance is granted at the discretion of the court and is not to be granted if performance can be reasonably obtained by other means.[1863]

Secondly, the UPICC refer to a contractual obligation of confidentiality in negotiations: an express agreement on *confidentiality* of certain information exchanged during negotiations may influence the amount of the awarded damages.[1864]

8.6.2. PECL

Breach of the PECL's rules on negotiations leads to liability. The main measure of this liability is recovery of damages. Generally, the PECL enable full compensation[1865] of the foreseeable damage[1866] (however, the rule of foreseeability is not applicable to the cases where the non-performance was 'intentionally grossly negligent').[1867] Within PECL's system, punitive damages are not admitted. The right to recover damages is established in Article 9:501 PECL. The PECL distinguish between damage sustained (protecting the 'negative interest' or 'reliance interest' and potential gain ('positive interest' or 'expectation interest').[1868]

The main type of damage recoverable for breach of the PECL's rules on negotiations is the damage sustained, namely expenses wasted in negotiations and loss of chance to conclude the contract, negotiations for which failed, or a contract with a third party.

8.6.2.1. Breach of PECL rules

The PECL concretize liability for damages for *negotiations contrary to good faith*. The aggrieved party may recover costs wasted in negotiations, including travel costs,[1869]

1861 Official Comment 2 to Article 2.1.15 UPICC.
1862 According to Article 7.2.2(c) UPICC, a party is precluded from claiming specific performance if 'the party entitled to performance may reasonably obtain performance from another source'. See also Schelhaas 'Article 7.2.2 Performance of non-monetary obligations', in Vogenauer 2015, at 887 ff.
1863 Schelhaas, 'Article 7.2.2 Performance of non-monetary obligations', in Vogenauer 2015, at 887 ff.
1864 Official Comment 3 to Article 2.1.16 UPICC.
1865 Article 9:502 PECL.
1866 Article 9:503 PECL.
1867 Ibid.
1868 According to the PECL, loss that may be recovered includes also 'non pecuniary loss' (Article 9:501(2)(a)) and 'future loss which is reasonably likely to occur' and the future loss includes loss of chance (Article 9:501(2)(b).
1869 Comments C and D to Article 2:301 PECL.

costs of work done in anticipation of contract,[1870] and 'loss on transactions made in reliance of the expected contract' may also be compensated.[1871]

Furthermore, the PECL note that in certain cases the loss of opportunities can be compensated, but no further detail is provided.[1872] It is worth mentioning in this regard that the PECL note that liability for breach of *bona fides* does not aim to bring the aggrieved party into the same position as he would have been if the contract was concluded and performed.[1873] It flows from this note that potential gain may not be recovered.

In case of breach of the duty of *confidentiality*, the aggrieved party is entitled to recovery of damage caused by the disclosure. Furthermore, the amount of benefit that the disclosing party has received due to the disclosure may be compensated. The right to recover benefit arises even if the aggrieved party has not suffered any loss.[1874] The PECL also note that injunctions may be granted if a party anticipates a breach of the duty of confidentiality. This would preclude the use of the privileged information.[1875]

Two general remedies for breach of a duty should be also mentioned. The PECL provision on *good faith and fair dealing* does not spell out remedies for breach of this duty. However, according to the existing scholarship, two general remedies are available in the PECL for breach of a duty. The first is loss of the right a party would have had if the duty had been fulfilled.[1876] The second remedy is mentioned in relation to protection of detrimental reliance in negotiations: a party is bound by his previous conduct or information provided. The remedy precludes acting in a way which contradicts this information.[1877]

8.6.2.2. Breach of obligations undertaken by the parties during negotiations

The PECL make no mention of remedies for breach of obligations undertaken by the parties at the precontractual stage. As Article 2:301 recognizes the possibility to enter into an 'agreement to negotiate', the obligations included in this agreement might be regarded by the PECL simply as a contractual obligation. However, the PECL place a limitation on the effects of an 'agreement to negotiate', and this limitation may play a role in determining what remedies are available. The PECL state namely that 'an agreement to agree' entails the duty to make serious efforts to reach agreement, but a party may not be compelled to reach agreement. This may suggest that the effects of a breach of an

1870 Illustration 3 in Comment D to Article 2: 301 PECL.
1871 Comments G and F to Article 2:301 PECL.
1872 Comment G to Article 2:301 PECL.
1873 See Comment G to Article 2:301 PECL, noting that Article 9:502 does not apply.
1874 Comment C to Article 2:302 PECL.
1875 Ibid.
1876 Storme 2003.
1877 Illustration 4 in Comment C to Article 1:201 PECL. See also Muir-Watt 2003, at 57.

'agreement to negotiate' in the PECL are limited to the consequences of the breach of this duty (perhaps even irrespectively of other obligations contained in this 'agreement to negotiate'). As a consequence, specific performance of an obligation to negotiate is unavailable.

8.6.3. DCFR

The DCFR establishes liability that may arise in the course of negotiations in a separate Chapter[1878] and underlines the special character of this liability. While generally, the DCFR provides for recovery of loss suffered and gain of which the injured party was deprived,[1879] the regulation of damages caused by breach of precontractual duties falls outside the scope of the rules on the general measure of damage.[1880] The requirement for foreseeability of damage does not apply.[1881] The remedies of withholding performance or termination of reciprocal obligations are not available.[1882] Instead, the measure of liability is specified by the provision establishing the duties.

Under the DCFR, conducting or breaking off negotiations contrary to *good faith and fair dealing* allows recovery of 'any loss caused to the other party by the breach'[1883] of this duty. Recovery for breach of *bona fides* includes, in the first place, damages.[1884] According to the DCFR, the damages recoverable include loss in the amount of expenditure wasted in negotiations: 'expenses incurred... work done... and loss on transactions made in reliance of the expected contract'.[1885]

By contrast, specific performance is not available. This is due to the fact that according to the DCFR, specific performance of a duty is not possible, while *bona fides* is a duty within the DCFR system.[1886]

The DCFR is not clear on the type of loss that may be recovered. The open formulations point to the possibility of unlimited recovery. The expression 'any loss' opens the way for recovery of potential gain expected from the non-concluded contract. The DCFR Comments neither mention this possibility, nor point to a limitation of liability. Furthermore, the DCFR general rules allow recovery of loss of chance as part of 'future loss'.[1887] However, the DCFR does not elaborate on the possibility to claim damages for

1878 Book II Chapter 3.
1879 Article III. – 3:702 DCFR.
1880 Ibid.
1881 Ibid. See on non-applicability of these provisions Comment B to Article II. – 3:501 DCFR. The provision on foreseeability is applicable only to obligations taken on voluntarily (not to breach of duties).
1882 Comment C to Article II. – 3:301 DCFR.
1883 Article II. – 3:301 (3) DCFR.
1884 Comment C to Article II. – 3:301 DCFR.
1885 Comment H to Article II. – 3:301 DCFR, in particular, the Illustrations it includes.
1886 Comment C to Article II. – 3:301 DCFR.
1887 See Comment G to Article III. – 3:701 DCFR.

the *loss of chance* to conclude a contract, negotiations for which failed, or to conclude a contract with a third party. According to the DCFR, 'in some cases loss of opportunities may also be compensated'.[1888] However, the illustration of this possibility provided by the DCFR[1889] is more complex than a simple failure of negotiations between two parties. The Illustration depicts parallel negotiations conducted by one party with two other parties. A third party induces the breaking off of negotiations[1890] and the conclusion of a contract with this third party. Subsequently, the aggrieved party holds this third party liable 'for lost opportunity and wasted expenses', because the *third party* acted contrary to *bona fides*.[1891] In fact, this Illustration appears to be misplaced. It offers no clarification on the recovery of loss of opportunity in negotiations in a claim for breaking off negotiations. Instead, it touches upon a separate type of recovery – recovery as a result of claim against third party for tortious interference with the prospects of a transaction. At the same time, the Illustration does not offer sufficient grounds to conclude that the DCFR endorses the possibility of holding a third party liable for interfering in negotiations in bad faith. Therefore, the recovery available in the DCFR for breach of *bona fides* in negotiations requires further interpretation.[1892]

One further note can be made on this Illustration. A third party starts negotiations with the first party and provides false information on its copyright ownership relevant to the contract. The Illustration states that the third party conducts negotiations contrary to good faith and fair dealing, but it fails to mention the goal of the third party. It seems that within the DCFR system, such conduct with the aim of obtaining a contract should have consequences for the validity of the contract, whereas only the aim of preventing negotiations between the first and the second party would be covered by the provisions of Article II. – 3:301 DCFR on negotiations contrary to good faith.

As to the breach of the *duty of confidentiality*, the DCFR appreciates the importance of the prevention of disclosure. It states that 'in relation to breach of confidentiality prevention is often more important than the recovery of damages'.[1893] The DCFR emphasizes a possibility for a party to ask for a court order to prevent disclosure of information by the other party.[1894] Another remedy for breach of confidentiality is the recovery of the amount of loss caused by the disclosure of the privileged information and the benefit obtained as a result of this disclosure.[1895]

1888 Comment H to Article II. – 3:301 DCFR.
1889 Illustration 5 to Article II. – 3:301 DCFR.
1890 As a matter of fact, the Illustration in question only states the first party is 'about to order material', without reference to negotiations.
1891 Illustration 5 to Article II. – 3:301 DCFR.
1892 See Chapter 9.
1893 Comment C to Article II. – 3:302 DCFR.
1894 Article II. – 3:302(3) DCFR.
1895 Article II. – 3:302(4) DCFR.

The measure of liability for *breach of the duty to disclose information* provided in Book II, Chapter 3 is the recovery of loss caused by the breach of the duty.[1896] The DCFR offers no further detail on the recovery. As noted earlier, this duty is limited to service contracts. Within the DCFR structure, provisions on special contracts (commercial agency, franchise and distributorship) are included in different books. These provisions also establish a duty of information; comments to these provisions mention remedies. However, these refer only to remedies available where a contract is concluded. Therefore, it is unclear whether the 'recovery of loss' available under Book II Chapter 3 is available also for breach of duty of disclosure in special contracts. It can be supposed that these are available, because of the interaction between the DCFR's general and specific provisions. The rules on specific contracts aim to 'expand and make more specific the general provisions (in Books I-III)'.[1897] Rules on special contracts 'deviate from them where the context so requires or address matters not covered by them'.[1898]

Finally, one general remedy for breach of any duty is relevant to misconduct in negotiations. According to the DCFR, breach of a duty precludes relying on a right arising from conduct contrary to the duty.[1899] Generally, the DCFR makes no mention of punitive damages. It furthermore provides that remedies that are not incompatible may be combined.[1900]

8.6.4. *Nature and conditions of liability*

8.6.4.1. UPICC: contractual liability

UPICC shape liability that may arise during negotiations as contractual liability governed by the rules of Chapter 7 UPICC on non-performance of contract. The following conditions should be fulfilled in order to engage liability under UPICC: the fact of non-performance of an existing obligation, loss suffered by a party, and a causal link between the non-performance and the loss. In the UPICC, liability is not based on fault: no fault is required for establishing the right to remedies. As a consequence, the intention of a non-performing party to cause damage is irrelevant (in other words, it is irrelevant whether damage is caused intentionally or by negligence).[1901]

According to the UPICC, Section 7.4 'may be applied by analogy'[1902] to liability for breach of the rules on negotiations. However, Chapter 7 UPICC is formulated primarily

[1896] Article II. - 3:109 DCFR.

[1897] Von Bar and Clive, 'Introduction', in Von Bar/Clive 2010, at 30.

[1898] Ibid.

[1899] See also Von Bar/Clive 2010, at 54: 'A breach of this duty does not in itself give rise to a liability to pay damages but may prevent a party from exercising or relying on a right, remedy or defence'.

[1900] Article III. - 3:10 2DCFR.

[1901] See in particular Article 7.4.1 UPICC. On damages under UPICC see McKendrick, 'Introduction to Section 7.4 of the PICC' in Vogenauer 2015, at 935 ff. and commentary to the following articles in the section; Eberhard 2005; Gotanda 2008; Gotanda 2004; Mersch/Philippe 2001.

[1902] Official Comment 3 to Article 7.1.4 UPICC.

for non-performance of the final contract. As a consequence, not all of Section 7.4 rules are readily applicable to liability that may arise in the course of negotiations. Some guidance on this analogical application provided by the text of the UPICC has been addressed earlier. This guidance relates primarily to remedies. Nevertheless, the guidance is not extensive and ultimately requires further interpretation of the UPICC.[1903]

8.6.4.2. PECL: contractual liability

The nature of liability for breach of rules on negotiations laid down by the PECL is the subject of scholarly discussion. Some scholars regard this liability as contractual.[1904] According to another view, this is a liability *sui generis* based on breach of duty of precontractual *bona fides*.[1905] It has been also argued that the legal basis for liability in the course of negotiations is left by the provisions of PECL to be decided by the national legal system concerned.[1906] Von Bar and Clive remark on a nuanced note that the PECL 'went well beyond the law on contract as such',[1907] but have no 'dogmatic preliminary determination that these rules are contractual in nature'.[1908] In the Introduction to Parts I and II of PECL, Lando and Beale state indeed as follows. 'The Principles embrace rules which in some legal systems are considered to form part of the law of torts or the law of restitution when the rules in question are closely linked to issues in contract covered by the Principles'.[1909] The authors go on to associate the rules on negotiations with contract formation.[1910]

Practically, the PECL offer no rules on liability other than those shaped as contractual. As a consequence, the conditions of liability for misconduct in negotiations should follow the pattern of contractual liability. The following conditions must be fulfilled to engage liability. Firstly, *non-performance* of an obligation agreed by the parties (or, with a respective adaptation, breach of a duty), secondly, *loss* suffered by the other party and thirdly, the *causal* link between the non-performance and the loss.[1911] In the same way as the UPICC, the PECL provide some detail (addressed above) that facilitates the application of general rules on liability to misconduct in negotiations, including contractually organized negotiations. This guidance is also limited and further interpretation is required.

1903 See on this McKendrick, 'Introduction to Section 7.4 of the PICC', in Vogenauer 2015, at 974. See also Zuloaga Rios, 'Article 2.1.16 Duty of Confidentiality', in Vogenauer 2015, at 370 (on the need of further interpretation of rules on damages for breach of confidentiality).

1904 De Vries 2001, at 110.

1905 Hesselink 1999, at 81.

1906 Nieper 2000, at 436.

1907 Von Bar/Clive 2010, at 11.

1908 Von Bar/Swann 2010, at 172.

1909 Lando and Beale, 'Introduction', in Lando/Beale 2000, at xxv.

1910 Ibid. See also Comment E to Article 1:101 PECL: '[t]he principles arise out of the contract, even if under some national systems the claim might be qualified as delictual rather than contractual'.

1911 Article 9:501 PECL and Comment D to Article 9:501 PECL.

8.6.4.3. DCFR: self-standing non-contractual right to recovery

According to the DCFR, the right to recover loss caused by breach of precontracutal duties is 'a self-standing non-contractual right'.[1912] Liability is to be established based on two sets of provisions: the general rules on liability in Book III and specific rules on negotiations in Book II, Chapter 3.

General rules on liability are laid down in Book II DCFR. Book II applies to breach of contractual as well as non-contractual obligations.[1913] Liability is based on the following elements. Firstly, a *failure to perform* an obligation (not based on fault).[1914] Secondly, the non-performance should entail a *loss*; no damages may be recovered under the DCFR if a party has not suffered any loss.[1915] The DCFR emphasizes that it does not provide for *nominal* damages. Thirdly, there should be a link of causality between breach of obligation (or, arguably, non-compliance with a duty) and the loss.[1916]

However, the general rules on liability in Book III are not 'automatically applicable' to breach of precontractual duties.[1917] General rules on liability are applicable in combination with the specific rules in Book II, Chapter 3. The general rules on liability are to be applied with necessary adaptations. The DCFR provides the following guidance:[1918]

> (1) Where any rule in this Chapter makes a person liable for loss caused to another person by a breach of a duty, the other person has a right to damages for that loss.
> (2) The rules on III. – 3:704 (Loss attributable to creditor) and III. – 3:705 (Reduction of loss) apply with the adaptation that the reference to non-performance of the obligation is to be taken as a reference to breach of the duty.

According to the guidance, two general rules on liability in Book III apply with 'adaptation' to breach of precontractual duties. The following adaptation is pointed out by the DCFR. If the creditor (the injured party/the party suffering loss) has contributed to the non-performance of an obligation, the recovery of loss is reduced 'to the extent

[1912] Comment A to Article II. – 3:501 DCFR. In characterizing liability as non-contractual, Comment A to Article II. – 3:501 DCFR mentions the reasoning of the Court of Justice of the European Union in Case C-334/00 *Fonderie Officine Meccaniche Tacconi SpA* v. *Heinrich Wagner Sinto Maschinenfabrik GmbH (HWS)* [2002] ECR I-07357.

[1913] The DCFR uses the term 'non-contractual liability' as more neutral than 'tort' or 'delict', according to the DCFR authors. See Von Bar/Clive 2010, at 12; Schulze 2012, at 222–223. At the same time, the DCFR avoids a net split into contractual and tortious obligations and liability, because of the difficulty of this split and the aim of approaching 'the whole of the law of obligations' See Von Bar/Clive 2010, at 12 and also for practical reasons to avoid repetition. See Von Bar/Clive 2010, at 12–14. Book III deals therefore with liability for breach of an obligation, irrespectively of the basis of the obligation.

[1914] Comment C to Article III. – 3:701 DCFR.

[1915] Comment B to Article III. – 3:701 DCFR.

[1916] Comment E to Article III. – 3:701 DCFR.

[1917] Comment B to Article II. – 3:701 DCFR.

[1918] Article II. – 3:501 DCFR.

that the creditor caused the debtor's non performance'.[1919] The Illustration refers to a situation where the debtor broke off negotiations contrary to good faith, but the aggrieved party's behaviour towards the debtor was also insulting.[1920] Furthermore, a party breaking off negotiations is not liable for the loss caused if the aggrieved party could have prevented or reduced the loss.[1921]

Further guidance on the interaction between the two sets of rules is given in Comment A to Article II. 3:501 DCFR. It states namely that in the absence of a contractual obligation, the 'test of a sufficient causal link' applies. This refers to the general test of causality in Article VI. – 4:101 to be applied 'by analogy' to breach of precontractual duties. This is, in fact, a general rule for establishing causation in tort under DCFR.

8.7. Conclusion

This Chapter has addressed the rules on negotiations formulated in international hard law and soft law.[1922] These are relevant to the aim of this study, namely the formulation of a harmonized approach to letter of intent in international transactions. This Chapter has discussed, in the first place, the difficulty in advancing the idea that the Convention in question may apply to letter of intent. In the part dedicated to CISG, it was submitted that the distinction between the 'statics' and 'dynamics' of negotiations advanced in Chapter 2 may be relevant for delimiting the Convention's scope. More specifically, the 'statics' of negotiations fall within the Convention's scope, while the 'dynamics', e.g. obligations contractually organizing negotiations, fall outside the scope of the CISG. For this reason, it appears inappropriate to attempt to interpret the Convention in a way that would make it applicable to letter of intent, because the obligations relating to the 'dynamics' of negotiations fail to fulfil the criteria of a sales contract under the CISG. Undoubtedly, the discussion of the Convention's scope in light of the two different dimensions of negotiations may feed the discussions about further modernization of the Convention. However, as noted above, a review of the CISG is not likely in the near future.

It appears appropriate to frame a harmonized approach to letter of intent within the interpretation of the existing soft law: the non-legislative tool of harmonization. Soft law instruments themselves reflect many frequent practices, customs, usages, and principles that are not always spelled out in national law. Usages of international commerce, primarily relevant to commercial transactions discussed in this study, are primarily reflected in the UPICC. The PECL and the DCFR have no particular focus on commercial contracts. However, their approach to negotiations is formulated along the same lines. Therefore, all three instruments may be discussed together.

1919 Comment A to Article III. – 3:301 DCFR.
1920 Illustration 1 Comment A to Article III. – 3:301 DCFR.
1921 Illustration 2 Comment A to Article III. – 3:301 DCFR.
1922 See Section 1.3 for the distinguished levels of rule-making.

This Chapter has contended that the UPICC, PECL, and DCFR provide no straightforward approach to letter of intent. However, the instruments contain specific provisions on negotiations. They also clearly take into account the possibility of contractual organization of negotiations. For instance, the liberal approach to contract formation, sometimes referred to as *favor contractus*,[1923] appears to provide premises for enforceability of a contractual obligation undertaken in the course of negotiations, provided that the intent to be bound by this obligation is demonstrated and the content of the obligation may be defined with sufficient certainty.[1924] The comments and illustrations accompanying rules in soft law instruments point to an acknowledgment of the practice of sophisticated negotiations. As a result, the instruments provide a solid background for their application to contractually organized negotiations. Generally, soft law rules on negotiations are formulated primarily for negotiations that are not organized contractually. The rules on liability are even less tailored to such situations. Therefore, the application of soft law rules to letter of intent requires further interpretation. The reflection on letter of intent undertaken in this study can be used for further interpretation of soft law rules.

Some guidelines for this may be drawn from national approaches discussed in the previous Chapters 3, 4, 5, and 6.[1925] National approaches are echoed in several provisions of the soft law instruments. In particular, the requirement of *bona fides* in negotiations reproduces the approach of the civil law traditions. The general protection of reliance, in particular, the prohibition of inconsistent behaviour (the requirement that one does not contradict one's own earlier conduct)[1926] appears to be formulated along the lines of the common law tradition, in particular, the doctrine of promissory estoppel as it has developed outside the jurisdiction of England and Wales.[1927] At the same time, it resembles the French duty of consistent behaviour.[1928] Furthermore, the approach to confidentiality in negotiations echoes in part the civil law traditions' approach to misconduct in negotiations (for example, the French duty not to use information obtained or generated during negotiations for one's own profit unrelated to the negotiated contract). At the same time, the possibility of implying the duty of confidentiality comes close to the rationale of the US tort of appropriation of a trade secret.[1929] To a certain extent, it recalls the manner in which a duty of confidence may be implied in equity in English law (implied to a limited extent in relationships of trust, for example, a lawyer and its client).[1930] The tools to prevent contract formation, for example, those relating to the requirement of form, echo national solutions on 'subject to contract' clauses in letter of intent.[1931]

1923 Section 8.5.6.
1924 This is further discussed in Section 9.3.
1925 See Section 1.6.4 for a possible critique of using national approaches in interpretation of international soft law instruments and counter-arguments.
1926 Section 8.5.4.
1927 Sections 6.4.1, 6.6.2, 5.5.4. As noted in Section 8.5.4, the UNIDROIT *travaux préparatoires* point to the discussion of these doctrines in different legal systems.
1928 Section 4.3.2.3.
1929 Section 6.4.2.2.
1930 Section 5.5.2.
1931 See for instance the elaborate English approach discussed in Chapter 5; see also Section 7.5.

The main rules of soft law that require interpretation in order to apply to letter of intent include the content of the contractual obligation of *bona fides* created at the stage of negotiations and, in particular, the possibility of defining the consequences of breach, and the remedies for breach of obligations undertaken at the stage of formation of contract. Furthermore, some reflection is required on the possibility to enforce other obligations that parties may attempt to create at the stage of negotiations. Recommendations on this interpretation will be suggested further in the concluding Chapter 9.

Chapter 9

CONCLUSION

The threads running through the previous parts of the study may now be drawn together. This research has focused on the contractual organization of commercial negotiations by letter of intent. The following main research question has been addressed. To what extent can the law, particularly international regulation, accommodate the practice of contractually organizing or 'privatizing' negotiations made through a letter of intent? The research was divided in three sub-questions:

- First, what is the nature of a letter of intent?
- Second, what are the similarities in and the differences between the national approaches of the selected jurisdictions to the legal effect and remedial consequences of the contractual organization of negotiations? How can the converging and diverging tendencies be explained?
- Third, how can the existing international approach to contract negotiations formulated in international instruments (e.g., the UPICC, PECL, and DCFR) be interpreted and developed in light of the answers to the previous questions?

The nature of letters of intent and the related remedies were explored from interdisciplinary and comparative perspectives, with the aim at formulating a harmonized approach to letter of intent in international transactions. Chapter 2 was dedicated to the content of the letter of intent. After drawing attention to the practice of negotiations, the study was narrowed to exploration of the 'dynamics' of negotiations. These were defined as a specific dimension of contract formation: the management of a transaction. It was argued that the provisions relating to the 'dynamics' of negotiations form the content of the letter of intent.[1932] This approach underpinned the subsequent parts of the research. Chapters 3, 4, 5, and 6 discussed the general regime of negotiations and the limits of private organization of the 'dynamics' of negotiations in the national rules of the selected jurisdictions: the Netherlands, France, England and Wales, and the United States. National approaches were addressed in seeking to identify the converging and diverging tendencies relating to the contractual organization of negotiations by letter of intent. Chapter 7 compared the national approaches and proposed explanations for the

[1932] See Chapter 2, in particular Sections 2.4 and 2.5.

similarities and differences observed. Chapter 8 addressed the international uniform hard and soft law. First, it advanced a nuanced view within the debate on the applicability of the United Nations Convention on Contracts for the International Sale of Goods (CISG, also referred to herein as 'the Convention') to letters of intent. Second, Chapter 8 discussed the provisions on negotiations in the instruments of non-legislative harmonization: the UNIDROIT Principles of International Commercial Contracts 2010 (UPICC), the Principles of European Contract Law (PECL), and the Draft Common Frame of Reference (DCFR).

This concluding Chapter submits, in answering the first sub-question, that the letter of intent represents a trade usage. The essence of this usage is the private regulation of negotiations, namely, the organization of various aspects of negotiations through contractually binding obligations. Furthermore, in answering the second sub-question, the study submits that there are sufficient grounds for formulating a harmonized approach to letters of intent. Despite the divergence in the national regulations of precontractual liability, a harmonized legal approach to letters of intent may be formulated within the framework of international soft law instruments, taking into account the relevance of trade usage for the harmonization of law (Section 9.1). To answer sub-question three, the study formulates a twofold recommendation. First it formulates amended soft law rules on negotiations; second, four practical steps to analyse letters of intent are suggested (Section 9.2). The motivation of these recommendations calls for three themes to be discussed. The first is contract formation: in what way can the trade usage of letters of intent be placed into the contract formation mechanism (Section 9.3)? The second theme is the concept of *bona fides*: how can the normative standard of (international commercial) *bona fides* reflect the possible use of strategies and tactics of negotiations (Section 9.4)? The third relevant matter is liability and remedies: where should the threshold for liability and remedies be set given this study's comparative observations and which factors can be taken into consideration for establishing liability (Section 9.5)? The discussion of these points will be concluded with the final remarks (Section 9.6).

9.1. Letter of intent as an international trade usage

The letter of intent can be considered as an international trade usage. The nature of this usage is the regulation of complex negotiations through contractual obligations confined to the process of negotiations. At the outset of this study, the hypothesis[1933] was advanced that the letter of intent is an emerging unwritten trade usage that is, 'a pattern of repetitive behaviour among merchants',[1934] 'observed as a legally binding obligation, not for mere courtesy, convenience or expediency'.[1935] The hypothesis contains two main elements. It supposes, first, the existence of patterns of repetitive behaviour during negotiations

1933 Section 1.3.3.
1934 Goode 1997, at 8. See also Goode/Kronke/McKendrick 2015, para 1.67.
1935 Goode 1997, at 8.

(9.1.1) and, second, that these patterns have acquired normative force among merchants, in essence, they are regarded as legally binding (9.1.2). These two parts of the hypothesis will now be discussed in the light of this study's findings.

9.1.1. *Patterns of repetitive behaviour*

The first supposition of the hypothesis in Chapter 1 is the existence of a distinct pattern of repetitive behaviour among merchants. Chapter 2 addressed negotiations from two intertwined perspectives: the approach to negotiations in business practice and the legal theoretical analysis. It was contended in Chapter 2 that contractual negotiations are not a chaotic process. On the contrary, they represent a structured activity, characterized by distinct patterns of conduct. These patterns may be conceptualized in terms of strategies and tactics of negotiations. It was advanced, therefore, that contractual negotiations between merchants are characterized by some degree of repetitive behaviour.

Within this repetitive behaviour, the provisions of letters of intent are directly related to various strategies and tactics of negotiations, in addition to the negotiation styles: cooperative and distributive ways of negotiating a transaction.[1936] The provisions of letters of intent represent attempts to preclude (by private regulation) the use of different strategies and tactics of negotiations, set concrete limits upon their use, or, on the contrary, allow their use and emphasise the freedom of their exercise. In essence, the letter of intent reflects the 'privatization' of the negotiation process in the way that fits the parties' practical needs. This has been illustrated by the texts of letters of intent available in the published case law, discussed in Chapter 7. Structuring and managing the negotiation process by letter of intent represents a step away from informal relations towards rule-making. It may be concluded that the letter of intent reflects these relatively distinct patterns within the repetitive behaviour of merchants. For example, a clause on exclusivity of negotiations mirrors the practice of conducting parallel negotiations with several parties, only one of which will become party to a future contract. Parallel negotiations are usual in a market economy and foster competition. In principle, none of the analysed legal systems prohibits parallel negotiations. Against this background, an attempt to contractually establish exclusivity aims to place a limit on parallel negotiations. This is a necessary characteristic to qualify a pattern of behaviour as a trade usage. However, this characteristic is not, in itself, sufficient. To qualify as a trade usage, the pattern of repetitive behaviour should also have acquired normative force among merchants. These leads to the second supposition of the hypothesis discussed below.

9.1.2. *Some normative force among merchants*

The second supposition of the hypothesis in Chapter 1 is that the identified pattern of behaviour (contractual organization of negotiations) has acquired binding force among

[1936] See Section 2.2.

merchants and is observed not only due to courtesy, convenience, and/or expediency. While this this pattern of behaviour is observed as a legally binding set of rules that regulates the negotiation process, it emanates not from the state, but from private rule-making.[1937]

This part of the hypothesis was addressed from the perspective of comparative law.[1938] Within this perspective, some light is shed upon merchants' observance of letters of intent by disputes resolved in national courts. Section 7.12.2.1, observed that in all the national legal systems discussed, observing that the courts rather than each country's legislature have confronted these developments (namely, the practice of long and complex negotiations prior to the actual conclusion of the final contract). While statutory regulation on this question is scarce, national courts, along with arbitrators, were the first to develop an approach to the effects of the letter of intent. Since the 1970s, when the courts first faced letters of intent, their approach has evolved. In all the analysed jurisdictions, courts have paid close attention to the texts, meaning, relevance, and the practice of issuing a letter of intent. The developments in case law have been motivated primarily by arguments invoking the significance of letters of intent in modern transactions.

National regimes concerning negotiations admit the possibility of private regulation of negotiations. However, this possibility is limited. In both English and US law, this limitation is primarily related to the assumption that negotiations are an adversarial process. Consequently, a high threshold is set for enforcing the private regulation of the 'dynamics' of negotiations. In both Dutch and French law, negotiations are regarded as a cooperative process. This results in a high threshold being set for the possibility of disclaiming the application of mandatory regulations applicable to negotiations. Conversely, national case law has progressively acknowledged the practice of private regulation of negotiations. It is within this acknowledgment that convergence in national approaches has been identified.[1939]

The evolution points principally in the direction of greater sophistication and, arguably, towards confirmation of party autonomy. This is especially the case for disputes between merchants over deals with a sophisticated structure. In the context of such claims, courts were prepared to give to documents created in the course of negotiations 'strict meaning': in essence, the precise effect described by the parties. As noted in Chapter 7, the approaches to contractually organized negotiations in the selected jurisdictions demonstrate more similarities than in the general legal regime of negotiations. As contended in Section 7.12.2.2, these similarities are arguably due to the similar manner in which the courts have dealt with complex negotiations and letters of intent created in the course of development of a transaction.

1937 See Section 1.3.1.
1938 The methods used were elaborated in Section 1.6.
1939 See the last paragraph of Section 1.6.3.

Further light on the normative character acquired by letters of intent among merchants is shed by the texts of letters of intent quoted in published case law. To assess the degree of normative force that the contractual organization of negotiation 'dynamics' has acquired for merchants, this study has also focused close attention on the texts of letters of intent. It observed, in particular, the texts of letters of intent included in published case law. The content of the quoted texts shows some convergence in drafting practice (as compared to the clearly diverging approaches to the general regime of negotiations in national legal systems). Letters of intent revealed in the published case law deal with notably similar issues.[1940] It may be said, therefore, that the observed drafting practice confirms the second part of the hypothesis.

Whether the observed degree of normative force is sufficient for the letter of intent to qualify as a trade usage can be debated. Clearly, not all the letters of intent quoted in published case law are identical. However, trade usages are always characterized by instability of patterns. This instability makes it difficult to establish and describe the content of a usage, but this does not mean it is impossible to do so.[1941] The divergence and variety of the provisions whereby parties organize negotiations contractually does not prevent the letter of intent from qualifying as a trade usage. One common characteristic of the provisions observed is that they reflect the issues identified in Chapter 2 as relatively stable patterns of negotiation 'dynamics'. For this reason, it may be argued that the private regulation of negotiations has acquired some degree of normative force among merchants and is observed not only from courtesy, convenience or expediency.[1942]

9.1.3. Relevance of the identified trade usage for the harmonization of law

Has the letter of intent's potential qualification as a trade usage any relevance to the reflection on a harmonized approach to this document type? It is worth recalling, in this regard, that this study relies on a broad concept of harmonization, which includes not only the unification of law through international conventions, but also the guidelines contained in non-binding principles: international soft law. Furthermore, harmonization arguably includes the convergence of business practices, because international contract drafting practice can provide a force of bottom-up harmonization of rules observed as legally binding.[1943] This returns the reasoning to the three main levels of rule-making outlined in Chapter 1: national hard law, international hard law, and international soft law, the latter including private rule-making by the business community, often termed *lex mercatoria*.[1944] This helps to define at which level of rule-making and in what ways it

[1940] The findings of the research are qualitative, representative examples illustrate letters of intent used in practice, but the study does not aim to be statistically accurate. See Section 7.2.

[1941] Goode 1997, at 8.

[1942] On the normative or binding force of private rule-making and *lex mercatoria* see Section 1.6.4.

[1943] See Section 1.6.4.

[1944] See Section 1.3.3.

is possible and desirable to formulate a framework for analysis of the contractual organization of negotiations by letter of intent.

At least three ways to formulate a harmonized approach to letters of intent can be identified. First, it can be formulated at the level of national hard law of one or several of the legal systems analysed, independent from the existing international instruments. However, this first possibility does not do justice to the existing body of soft law. The innovative approach to contractual negotiations adopted in soft law provides a good point of departure for further harmonization. Furthermore, following the first option would lead to advocating changes to the liability system of national rules. However, advocating changes to national systems of liability cannot be sustained based only on this study's comparative conclusions. In fact, no convergence in the general regime of regulating contractual negotiations is observed at a more general level. The absence of a common denominator for harmonising rules on 'precontractual liability' has also been recognized by earlier studies.[1945] Besides this issue, changes in national hard law are, to a high extent, a question of political will. For these reasons, this possibility is not further pursued.

The second option for formulating a harmonized approach to letter of intent is the interpretation of the CISG as applicable to the contractual organization of negotiations. This option relates to the existing academic debate on the CISG. The precise question of whether the CISG applies to the precontractual period has generated intense discussions and disagreement.[1946] One opinion within this debate suggests that advancing the Convention's application to letters of intent faces one principal difficulty: the distinction between the 'statics' and 'dynamics' of negotiations advanced in Chapter 2 may delimit the Convention's scope. More specifically, while the 'statics' of negotiations fall within its scope, the 'dynamics', e.g. obligations contractually organizing negotiations, fall outside. For this reason, it appears inappropriate to attempt to interpret the Convention in a manner applicable to letters of intent, because obligations relating to negotiation 'dynamics' fail to fulfil the criteria of a sales contract under the CISG. Undoubtedly, the discussion of the Convention's scope in light of these two different dimensions of negotiations may feed discussions about the further modernization of the Convention. However, a substantive revision of the CISG is not contemplated for the near future. Therefore, the second option is rejected.

By contrast, the third option – to frame the analysis of letters of intent at the level of soft law instruments – is appropriate for the following reasons. As shown in Chapter 8, the existing international instruments establish the premises for a harmonized approach to contractual negotiations. Furthermore, the hypothesis of this study is confirmed: the letter of intent, whereby parties organize negotiations contractually, is an international trade usage. Trade usages, including those related to frequently followed drafting

1945 See Cartwright/Hesselink 2008, at 488.
1946 See Section 8.3.

practices are, in principle, vehicles of harmonization.[1947] An identified trade usage represents, in itself, a pattern of harmonized rules. As stated by Goode, Kronke and McKendrick:[1948]

> International trade usages are vehicles for the harmonisation of commercial law. Courts should, but often do not, take into account decisions and related analysis from other jurisdictions when faced with questions relating to such international trade usages. There are countless examples of fact patterns in which doing so would be justified, prudent, and serve the objectives of unifying the law applicable to commercial transactions.

One of the main goals of soft law instruments is to reflect frequent practices, customs, usages, and principles that are not always expressly addressed in national law.[1949] Usages of international commerce are primarily reflected in the UPICC. While the PECL and the DCFR have no particular focus on international commercial contracts, their approaches to negotiations are formulated similarly. Therefore, all three instruments may be discussed together.

9.2. Recommendations

The recommendations are twofold. The first is addressed to national legislators that may follow the approach of soft law instruments in changing domestic law. It might become relevant in view of the recent renewal of reforming private law in France and the initiated discussions on reforming the Belgian law of obligations. The recommendation of amendment is formulated in terms of the UPICC, because this is the only soft law instrument that is regularly updated. Thus, the UNIDROIT working group may find this study and its recommendations useful for their work on the next edition of the UPICC (9.2.1).

The second recommendation is for legal practitioners who apply soft law instruments to international letters of intent. These practitioners include the arbitrators who may apply soft law instruments without relying on any specific national law. They may also be national judges basing decisions on international trade usage or drawing arguments from the solutions formulated at the level of soft law. This recommendation does not deny that the suggested approach may face the limitations of national laws (for which the extensive analysis of the diverging regulation of negotiations in four selected jurisdictions conducted in Chapters 3, 4, 5, and 6 may be useful). Finally, but not least important, the targeted practitioners include parties to international contractual negotiations: transactional lawyers who may be involved in conducting deals. The recommendations aim to contribute to a clear assessment of the risks and legal arguments based on the identified trade usage (9.2.2).

[1947] Goode/Kronke/McKendrick 2015, para 4.48; De Ly 2012.

[1948] Goode/Kronke/McKendrick 2015, para 4.48.

[1949] See Section 8.2.

9.2.1. *Amended soft law rules on negotiations*

To reflect the conclusions of this study, the provisions of the UPICC may be amended as follows (the suggested changes are marked in italics).

> 2.1.15 Negotiations in bad faith
>
> (1) A party is free to negotiate and is not liable for failure to reach an agreement *nor for breaking off negotiations in pursuing commercial self-interest.*
> (2) However, a party who negotiates or breaks off negotiations in bad faith is liable for the losses caused to the other party.
> (3) It is bad faith, in particular, for a party to enter into or continue negotiations when intending not to reach an agreement with the other party *but to deceive the other party or obtain profit unrelated to the negotiated contract.*
> *(4) Parties may organize the process of negotiations by stand-alone contractual obligations, severable from the final negotiated contract. Liability is then limited to the loss caused by breach of such obligation, except for bad faith mentioned in (3) above and except for breach of confidentiality regulated in Article 2.1.16.*

The text in italics introduces, in point 1, the crucial relevance of commercial self-interest; the addition in point 3 reflects the tort law roots of the liability for breaking off negotiations and restricts the provisions' scope. The added point 4 introduces the distinction between the final contract and the obligations customary in contractually organized negotiations: the latter form the content of the trade usage of letter of intent.

The suggestion holds true for the provisions of the PECL and the DCFR formulated similarly. But the equivalent revised provisions are not detailed here for a practical reason: of the instruments addressed, only the UPICC are updated to new editions, in which the suggested modifications above may be taken into account.

9.2.2. *Four steps for analysing the legal effects of a letter of intent*

From a practical perspective, the following steps may be suggested to ascertain the legal effects of a letter of intent.

9.2.2.1. First step: identification of the provisions on 'dynamics' and 'statics' of negotiations

The first step in the analysis of a letter of intent is to divide the clauses of the document into provisions relating to the negotiations process and provisions relating to the substance of the eventual final contract. The former describe *how* the future possible agreement would be negotiated (the management of a transaction): the 'dynamics' of negotiations. The latter describes *what* is negotiated (the substance of the future contract): the 'statics' of negotiations. Is an intention to be bound by the *final contract* established?

Alternatively, is an intention established to be bound by an obligation from the beginning of negotiations?

9.2.2.2. Second step: defining the relevance and effects of the 'statics' of negotiations

The 'statics' of negotiations represent the provisions on the substance of the final contract. These will be further assessed by the doctrine of offer and acceptance. Consequently, either the final contract may be found or no contract would come into existence. The application of this doctrine has not been discussed by this study. The steps of analysis indicated below should be pursued if the doctrine of offer and acceptance is not easily applicable to the letter of intent.

Here, it should be recognized that a precontractual document can contain clauses relating to both the dynamic and the static constituents of negotiations. It appears that if the final contract is easily found in the documents, the provisions on negotiations are to be considered as part of this final contract. However, if the provisions on the dynamics are preponderant, and no offer and acceptance can be identified in the parties' exchanges, another approach is suggested. Parties should be considered as being only at the stage of negotiations or, in cases where the trade usage of letters of intent is established, at the stage of contractually organized negotiations. The divide suggested in Chapter 2 contributes to remedying the shortcomings of the analysis in terms of the offer and acceptance doctrine criticised in the literature for its static character. Instead of the 'all or nothing' model of offer and acceptance (either 'contract' or 'no contract'), this study suggests an *intermediary* approach. It is intermediary in the sense that it enables parties to create binding obligations of a contractual nature for the earlier issues of management of a transaction, which are, in essence, different from the final negotiated, frequently complex, deal.

9.2.2.3. Third step: ascertaining each obligation relating to negotiation 'dynamics' as stand-alone and severable

The third step in the analysis involves ascertaining the effects of each provision relating to the management of the transaction. For this purpose, each of these obligations should be treated as stand-alone and severable. In essence, the legal effects of each specific provision should be assessed independently from both the other contents of the document at hand and the question of whether the final contract came into being.

The usual issues related to negotiation dynamics are the parties' attempts to keep negotiations non-binding, or, on the contrary, create specific requirements for the parties' conduct during negotiations. The latter may be termed a general requirement to 'negotiate in good faith', with or without providing the specific content of this requirement. They also include the issues of confidentiality during negotiations, exclusive negotiations, and eventual re-distribution of costs incurred in negotiations and liability.

9.2.2.4. Fourth step: assessment of liability

Liability will be discussed in Section 9.5 below. It is suggested to give highest weight to contractual arrangements relating to liability, including the possibility to disclaim liability for negotiations in bad faith, except for cases where one party deliberately deceives the other(s) in negotiations. Further factors to consider in a hierarchical order are the parties' commercial self-interests, the reliance created in negotiations, the fact of inducement to invest or commence performance (which can, for instance, be contained in a letter of intent), and the advancement of negotiations. The recommendation to amend the soft law rule and the suggested steps in analysing the legal effects of a letter of intent are based on this study's findings and reasoning are elaborated below.

9.3. Letter of intent and the contract formation mechanism

How can the letter of intent be placed into the approach of soft law instruments on contract formation? As discussed in Chapter 8, the soft law instruments analysed in this study acknowledge the possibility of organizing negotiations contractually (9.3.1). However, the question of how this possibility fits the mechanism of contract formation remains unanswered. The comparative and theoretical findings of this study suggest that the obligations of letters of intent may be assessed and enforced as stand-alone, severable contractual obligations within the 'liberal' approach to contract formation adopted by the UPICC, PECL, and DCFR (9.3.2). Nevertheless, an obligation contractually organizing negotiations is a special type of obligation – a contractual obligation with two caveats (9.3.3).

9.3.1. Possibility to organize negotiations contractually

The general scope of freedom of negotiations – as reflected in the UPICC, PECL, and DCFR – enables parties to shape negotiations as they consider appropriate. The internal Comments and several provisions of the instruments indicate the possibility of creating a contractual obligation before the negotiated contract is formed. The texts of soft law instruments refer, in particular, to the practice of creating obligations confined to negotiations. More specifically, the UPICC, PECL, and DCFR distinguish between the process of negotiations and the final contract. First, the instruments acknowledge that pre-contractual relations may qualify as an extra-contractual matter. Second, soft law instruments contain specific provisions on negotiations. Third, all the instruments explicitly note that a contractual undertaking of confidentiality may already be made at the stage of negotiations. A strong link between confidentiality in negotiations and the tactics of bargain has been noted in comparative observations[1950] and Chapter 2.

Soft law instruments are clearer on the distinction between the process of negotiations and the final contract than are the national approaches. As observed in Chapter 7, and

[1950] Section 7.7.

particularly in Section 7.12.1, national case law increasingly draws such a distinction, especially in the assessment of complex negotiations. Nevertheless, this is still not the mainstream approach in national case law. The UPICC and PECL are explicit on the possibility to contractualize different aspects of negotiations, whereas the DCFR articles and internal Comments provide scarce information on this. Furthermore, the UPICC and PECL explicitly establish a possibility to create obligations relating primarily to the process of negotiations. More specifically, under both the UPICC and PECL, an 'agreement to agree' (precontractual obligation to negotiate) is enforceable. This provides the duty of good faith and fair dealing in negotiations with substantive content and a limited scope. In both the UPICC and PECL, the content of the obligation requires 'best efforts' or 'serious attempts' to reach agreement. However, neither the UPICC nor the PECL clearly state whether such an agreement also entails a duty of co-operation (established by a separate provision in each instrument).[1951]

Additionally, the UPICC provide two tools for parties to shape their negotiations.[1952] First, the instrument allows the parties to preclude the formation of the final contract until a particular term is agreed or until agreement is made in a concrete form. This may be achieved either consensually or if one party insists on the necessity to reach agreement on a specific term or in a concrete form. Second, the UPICC allow parties to agree to place the formation of contract under a suspensive condition, the performance of which may be within the discretion of only one party. In this way, the formation of the final contract is 'in the hands of one party'. In essence, under the UPICC, a situation is possible in which the final contract is formed only if and when one of the parties decides to form it. The PECL and DCFR do not explicitly provide a similar tool.

9.3.2. *Contractual intention and stand-alone obligations*

Having noted that soft law instruments enable parties to create obligations which are already contractually binding at the stage of negotiations, the following questions arise:

- Is an obligation contractually organizing negotiations a special type of obligation?
- In particular, do the conditions of enforceability established by soft law for contract formation apply to such an obligation without any adaptation?

This study concludes that though an obligation contractually organizing negotiations can be ascertained by applying the conditions for creation of a contractual obligation, it is a special type of obligation. The reasons for this conclusion are provided below.

Soft law instruments can accommodate the obligations whereby parties organize negotiations contractually. In fact, in the national approaches discussed, the conditions of enforceability are still in development. In essence, enforceability is ascertained by

1951 See this study's submission in 9.4.2.
1952 See Section 8.5.6.

applying the conditions for creation of a contractual obligation. National approaches appear to converge on the temporary nature of obligations limited to negotiations. However, other conditions of enforceability diverge. In contrast to national systems, as noted in Chapter 7, soft law instruments establish conditions of enforceability of a contractual obligation which have been characterized as modern, liberal, flexible, and innovative. International instruments favour finding a contract in all situations where the intention to be bound can be established and the terms on which one intends to be bound can be ascertained with certainty. The policy consideration underpinning this approach is that, for participants in international trade, the *effet utile* of an enforceable contractual obligation is higher than the impossibility of enforcing it (which may be due to the stringent requirements for formation of a contract: for example, the requirement of form). Since the intention to be bound is a crucial condition of the enforceability of a contractual obligation,[1953] the following comparative observation may be recalled. Chapter 7 identified a converging tendency to distinguish between the final contract and the preliminary regimes.[1954] The *final contract* is the negotiated deal and the end result of the entire transaction, whereas various *preliminary regimes* apply to obligations that parties aim to make binding in the course of negotiations. As noted in Section 7.12.1, the emergence of preliminary regimes is a clear similarity between all of the four jurisdictions discussed. Preliminary regimes apply to contractually organized negotiations and are distinct from the final contract. The application of preliminary regimes leads to similar results to those reached by private regulation against the background of frequently considerably diverging general negotiations regimes (in essence, the diverging approaches to precontractual liability).

In light of this observation, the ascertainment of intent under soft law instruments may apply to a letter of intent if it is nuanced in the following way. To ascertain the effects of contractually organized negotiations, the following appears to be crucial: is the intention to be bound by the *final contract* established? Alternatively, is an intention established to be bound by an obligation from the beginning of negotiations? This may be the case for an intention to be bound only by exclusivity in negotiations, or only by an obligation of confidentiality, but by no further obligation, or an intention to accept that costs of preliminary studies will be shared by the negotiating parties.[1955] If the intention is assessed in this way, the provisions of a letter of intent may enforceable by applying the soft law instruments' approach to the enforceability of contractual obligations.

However, the assessment of enforceability should be applied not to the document in its entirety, but to each provision separately. Each provision should be assessed as a stand-alone provision, severable (or separable) from both the final contract and from the other provisions of letter of intent. It should be recalled, in this regard, that precontractual

1953 See, in the same vein, Kornet 2010.
1954 See, in particular, Section 7.12.1.
1955 On these provisions, see Chapter 7.

documents do not always contain obligations that will form the future contract. A precontractual documen may be confined to provisions on the management of negotiations. According to this study, dynamics of negotiations relate to question of *how* the parties negotiate a transaction, as opposed to the statics, relating to the question as to *what* is negotiated. Chapter 2 and the subsequent analysis in Chapter 7 contended that the concrete provisions of letters of intent correlate with the frequent 'dynamics' of negotiations. For example, a provision on exclusivity is triggered by the usual practice of conducting negotiations with several potential partners, or a provision on confidentiality is created to preclude a public announcement being used as a means of exerting pressure in negotiations. Consequently, it is submitted that each provision included in a written document whereby parties attempt to contractualy organize negotiations should be addressed as stand-alone, or, depending on the applicable terminology, severable or separable. This means it should be decided whether the provision at hand 'can stand on its own feet' irrespective of, first, other provisions of the same document and, second, the question of whether the final contract is concluded.

Such severable treatment can be traced back to the national approaches. As observed in Chapter 7, obligations within preliminary regimes are increasingly treated as stand-alone and severable (or separable, depending on terminological preferences). These obligations are frequently upheld as binding even if other obligations are non-binding. However, as has been noted, not all the types of obligations are treated as severable. Dispute resolution clauses raise the fewest doubts as to their assessment as severable; confidentiality and exclusivity provisions are frequently severed. By contrast, the tendency to treat as severable other types of obligations is more difficult to affirm. In particular, provisions on the costs of negotiations are analysed by applying the rules that would be applicable to liability even in the absence of a provision on cost allocation and which detail the recovery.[1956]

9.3.3. *Contractual obligation with two caveats*

Is an obligation framing negotiations contractually a special type of obligation? Even if it is subject to the same conditions of validity as those applicable to contract, does it become a contractual obligation in the sense that the duty of cooperation would be required in its performance, thereby leading to more far-reaching consequences, for example, the possibility to assign it or claim all the remedies for contractual liability? National approaches offer little guidance on this. It may be concluded, based on comparative findings, that these obligations have at least two caveats. These are related, first, to the balancing of *bona fides* against freedom of contract, or, more precisely, freedom *from* contract, and, second, to a caveat related to liability. These points will be elaborated in the next two Sections 9.4 and 9.5.

[1956] See Section 7.12.1.

9.4. Strategies and tactics of negotiations and transnational *bona fides*

How can the possibility of using strategies and tactics of negotiations be reflected in the concept of *bona fides*? As submitted in Chapter 2 and reflected in the provisions of letters of intent discussed in Chapter 7, parties do not only address negotiations in practice as a cooperative process. Rather, negotiations are viewed through the lens of strategies and tactics of integrative and distributive negotiations and bargain. Against this background, the private organization of negotiations is used as a tool to limit the exercise of bargaining tactics or to establish the field for their deployment. This may be, for example, a contractual waiver of liability that may open the way to more 'aggressive' negotiation tactics.

It is submitted that the approach to negotiations requires taking into account not only cooperation, but also risk-taking, competition, and bargain, because all of these are inherent to contractual negotiations and acknowledged to varying extents by the national conceptions of freedom of negotiations. In view of this, *bona fides* in negotiations of an international transaction should be interpreted as allowing parties to disclaim liability for breaking off negotiations in all cases where no conduct with an intention to deceive is established. It also appears also that *bona fides* should allow parties to limit the use of strategies and tactics by contractual obligations. Parties may, therefore, be allowed to establish concrete tailor-made standards of conduct in negotiations: for example, to establish exclusivity or confidentiality in negotiations or concretize the remedies for their breach, set limits to their conduct, or establish private regulation standards that are less stringent than the general regime applicable to negotiations.

9.4.1. Standards of bona fides

In suggesting the accommodation of the strategies and tactics of negotiations within the concept of *bona fides*, the following is noteworthy: all of the instruments discussed refer to the requirement of good faith and fair dealing in negotiations. The legal technique chosen to limit freedom of negotiations is in all the instruments are clearly close to the civil law traditions. However, the standards there set at different levels.

Generally, the content of *bona fides* can be limited to ascertaining a party's subjective attitude. This threshold is considered as low, because a judge or an arbitrator has almost no ascertainable criteria to conclude that a party acts subjectively in good faith. Alternatively, the requirement of good faith and fair dealing can refer to conduct that a similar party would employ in similar circumstances. This is a higher threshold, because this standard of conduct should be ascertained through an objective test, i.e. by reference to conduct of a similar party in similar circumstances.

The UPICC associate the requirement of *bona fides* with the party's conduct as it can be understood (tested) objectively, whereas the PECL refer to both the subjective attitude and objective test, and the DCFR refers to the subjective good faith requirement. Nevertheless, it may be said that the UPICC requirement of *bona fides* is narrower than those of the PECL and DCFR. More specifically, the UPICC require an autonomous interpretation of the concepts of good faith and fair dealing. It should be interpreted independently of national concepts and linked to international trade transactions. By contrast, neither the PECL nor DCFR emphasise the international character of the content of the *bona fides* requirement: in the application of the PECL and DCFR, reference to national understanding of these concepts remains possible.[1957] Accordingly, it remains 'not possible to say anything on the "content" of European good faith without knowing the system that it will be operating in'.[1958] Arguably, the UPICC restrict the requirements of good faith and fair dealing in negotiations to the absence of bad faith. By contrast, both the PECL and DCFR establish a positive requirement of good faith in negotiations. The PECL consider the concept of misconduct in negotiations broadly: this includes not only the elaboration and advancement of negotiations, but also the reason why a party breaks off negotiations.

Furthermore, all of the instruments establish liability for negotiations conducted without compliance with the duty of good faith and fair dealing; moreover, their provisions are formulated almost in parallel. However, while the UPICC opt for a restrictive formulation of 'negotiations in bad faith', the PECL and the DCFR formulations are broader and cover 'negotiations contrary to good faith'. All the instruments provide a non-exhaustive list, or rather examples, of conduct that may be considered as a failure to comply with this duty.

In addition, the UPICC explicitly prohibit inconsistent behaviour: each party to negotiations must act consistently with his earlier conduct to prevent detriment that may be caused by reliance on a counterpart's conduct in negotiations. This rule follows the pattern of the Roman law prohibition of *venire contra factum proprium* (to act in contradiction with own previous conduct). It also echoes the protection of reasonable reliance in national systems.[1959] The UPICC define the methods of compliance with this requirement: either timely notification about the change in conduct or reimbursement of loss caused by such detriment. The PECL and DCFR require consistent behaviour under the general duty of good faith and fair dealing.[1960]

According to the DCFR's authors, it does not need to concretize the content of good faith for its application in commercial transactions.[1961] This view is not shared by this study, because the letter of intent provisions discussed in Chapter 7 illustrate that parties may simply agree to negotiate in good faith without specifying the conduct expected. In cases where this content is specified, it is not entirely clear whether such specification may be enforced in accordance with the clause. The reflections below elaborate on the limits for contractual concretisation of the duty of *bona fides* and the role that the letter of intent may play in this.

1957 See Sections 8.5.2 and 8.5.3.
1958 Hesselink 2011, at 649; Zimmermann/Whittaker 2000, at 690 ff.
1959 See Sections 8.5.4 and 8.7.
1960 Section 8.5.4.
1961 Comment A to Article I. – 1:103 DCFR.

9.4.2. *No requirement to sacrifice commercial self-interest*

Despite the differences in the threshold of good faith in each of the three instruments, it is submitted that *bona fides* in international transactions should be interpreted as not requiring parties to sacrifice their own commercial interests. This suggestion is made for the following reason: soft law instruments qualify several types of conduct either as bad faith or as non-compliance with good faith.[1962] In essence, soft law instruments define as bad faith the starting of negotiations without intention to reach agreement and breaking off advanced negotiations. Furthermore, misuse of information disclosed in confidence may be regarded as bad faith, taking into account the rules on confidentiality in negotiations.

Within the national approaches, a number of cases where parties were held liable for misconduct in negotiations demonstrate the possibility of the following concretisation: *bona fides* does not require sacrificing one's own commercial interest. This is clearly the position in English law,[1963] while French law frequently (albeit not always) regards a party's own commercial interests as 'legitimate reasons to break off negotiations'.[1964] In the US approach, this flows from the view of negotiations as risk-taking,[1965] albeit the application of an 'all-or-nothing' approach in finding the final contract may restrict the possibility to withdraw from negotiations, because the final contract may be considered formed. In Dutch law, the justified interest of the party withdrawing from negotiations is an important factor to balance in establishing liability: this is often (albeit not always) his commercial self-interest.[1966] Based on this, it is suggested that even if a letter of intent provision requires parties to negotiate in good faith, and this is held enforceable by applying the instruments' 'liberal' approach to the creation of a contractually binding obligation, such a provision does not require parties to sacrifice their commercial self-interests. A more concrete example of this general statement is that negotiations may be broken off to accept a lower price or conditions that are otherwise better from the perspective of the party withdrawing from negotiations. If such an approach had been adopted in the example of *Texaco, Inc.* v. *Pennzoil, Co*[1967] referred to in this study's Introduction, the negotiations framed by the 'memorandum of agreement' could be broken off because the commercial self-interest of the party accepting a higher bid so dictated. Other examples of the relevance of a party's commercial interest include breaking off negotiations as a result of a feasibility study or audit, or if the other party fails or refuses to prove its sound financial status.

In light of this submission, it is suggested that agreements to agree (the enforceability of which is acknowledged by soft law instruments) do not imply the duty of co-operation,

[1962] Sections 8.5.2 and 8.5.3.
[1963] Section 5.3.
[1964] Section 4.3.3.1.
[1965] Section 6.3.1.
[1966] Section 3.3.2.3.
[1967] *Texaco, Inc.* v. *Pennzoil, Co* 729 S.W.2d 768 (Tex.App 1987), cert. denied 485 U.S. 994 (1988) applying New York law.

because this may preclude the use of any strategies or tactics in negotiations. Furthermore, it is submitted that parties may conduct parallel negotiations. While this is clearly the position of the UPICC, the same cannot be said with the same level of certainty about the PECL and DCFR. The broad requirement of good faith in these instruments may, for example, lead to parallel negotiation being regarded as conduct leading to liability. The PECL and DCFR may follow the interpretation suggested for the UPICC, though this suggestion is limited to their application to international commercial contracts, as consumer contracts are excluded from this study's scope. This study argues for a restrictive interpretation of the international commercial *bona fides*. It is suggested, therefore, that the standard of *bona fides* does not, in any way, preclude parallel negotiations: each party may negotiate with several potential partners to future eventual contracts and make choices based on its commercial self-interest. The only means to preclude parallel negotiations would be an obligation on exclusivity of negotiations created within the contractual organization of negotiations.

9.4.3. *Contractualized* bona fides

9.4.3.1. Interpretation of bona fides as enabling parties to set their own conduct standards

It is suggested that in negotiations organized by letter of intent, the parties should be able to themselves determine the content of the duty of *bona fides*. This suggestion is derived from the comparative observations of Chapter 7. It is, furthermore, grounded in the general manner in which courts have dealt with the cases where parties specified conduct requirements in negotiations. In this regard, the main provisions relating to the dynamics of negotiations discussed from a comparative perspective may be recalled. First, parties should be allowed to keep negotiations non-binding, i.e. to 'contract out' of the legal regime applicable to negotiations. In the same way, *bona fides* should enable parties to keep part of their negotiations outside the contractual regime, but create some obligations binding immediately at the negotiations stage.

Second, exclusivity of negotiations – i.e. clauses 'locking out' the parties from conducting parallel negotiations – is a dynamic that may constitute an enforceable, more stringent standard within the interpretation of *bona fides*. It is noteworthy that national courts pay attention to the temporary character of exclusivity in assessing the enforceability of the provision. English law regards temporariness as a requirement for the enforceability of such an obligation, rendering the English approach the most restrictive. In this way, if soft law is interpreted restrictively (consistent with English law), exclusivity may be upheld as binding only if it is limited in time. In a less restrictive interpretation, any kind of exclusivity can be upheld as binding and enforceable. The provision on exclusivity of negotiations should be upheld as binding but at all times interpreted as having temporary character. If the time of the 'lock-out' is not stated, it should be implied. The time of the implied period of exclusivity may correspond to the time for which the letter of intent is concluded, if it contains the indication thereof. Alternatively, the complexity of the transaction that would require exclusivity, for example, the time required for due diligence can provide a guideline; the level of competition in the given market may also help identifying the time customarily admissible to be locked out from negotiating with third parties.

Third, an issue that may become crucial during negotiations is confidentiality. This relates to confidentiality ranging from the secrecy of the very fact that negotiations are taking place to that attached to the information generated in negotiations (by both parties). It is submitted that the confidentiality provision created at the precontractual stage should be given force. The possibility to enforce the provision on confidentiality of negotiations is acknowledged in soft law instruments. However, the texts address only the confidentiality of information exchanged in the course of negotiations.

Fourth, observations on the choices of law and forum, including arbitration and mediation, these are less relevant for the purpose of interpretation of *bona fides* in soft law instruments. Nevertheless, they may still be important for the application of the UPICC, PECL, and DCFR. The possibilities and caveats related to choice of a soft law instrument as the law applicable to the substance of the dispute is a separate debate. The observations in this study are, therefore, limited to noting the possible enforceability of such clauses as part of the 'dynamics' of negotiations.

Fifth, provisions distributing the risks for expenses incurred in the course of negotiations should be given binding contractual force. Negotiations may be accompanied by the commencement of performance: one or more parties may either start performing the final contract or undertake preparatory work. The possibility of recovery and its legal basis constitute one of the main risks if the negotiations fail. This is also one of the main difficulties faced by national systems in addressing the letter of intent. This highlights that clarity on distribution of costs and risks by contractual provisions is crucial for transaction planning and legal certainty. Therefore, it is submitted that provisions on costs of negotiations should be given force in the following way. Clauses that re-distribute the costs incurred by the parties in the course of negotiations should be upheld as binding and severable from the question of whether negotiations were broken off and the manner in which this occurred. Provisions that deal with the distribution of costs in case negotiations are broken off should be, in principle, given effect following the literal interpretation of the clause. Nevertheless, these are strictly related to the question of liability. It is suggested, in this regard, that no derogation by contractual clause can be made from the rule on liability for deliberate misconduct. This exception will be developed in this section below. Furthermore, in answering the question whether a party may recover the costs of performance already commenced, it is important to define to what extent this performance has been induced by the other party. The situations in practice range from one party requesting the start of performance to pure risk taking in negotiations (as illustrated by national case law).

One further, general remark should be made relating to the interpretation of provisions that establish contractual standards of good faith. The literal, linguistic interpretation – the search for 'strict meaning' of the used words – appears to provide more legal certainty and the highest effect to party autonomy in sophisticated business to business transactions compared to the contextual interpretation. For this reason, in the interpretation of letters of intent, it is suggested that preference should be given to the strict linguistic interpretation in preference to the contextual interpretation.

9.4.3.2. Possibility to disclaim consequences of breach

The duty of *bona fides* in negotiations should be interpreted as allowing parties to disclaim liability for non-compliance with this duty. In line with the previous note on the parties' commercial self-interests in negotiating a transaction, it is submitted that parties should be offered a possibility to tailor their approach to negotiation 'dynamics' in the manner that allows them to pursue their commercial interests.

This may require disclaiming liability for non-compliance with the duty of *bona fides*, which is a mandatory provision in all the soft law instruments. Parties may not disclaim its application or derogate therefrom. It is arguable that under the UPICC, parties may validly agree on the possibility that negotiations may fail without liability, irrespective of their compliance with the requirement of good faith. This means, not that the duty is disclaimed, but that the consequences of its breach are contractually defined. The PECL and DCFR do not expressly recognize the possibility to derogate from the provision prohibiting negotiations contrary to *bona fides*. When applied to the letter of intent, the PECL and DCFR should be interpreted in the same way as the UPICC.

Furthermore, the legislative history of the UPICC identifies the possibility of disclaiming the requirement of consistent behaviour. The UPICC appear to allow parties to derogate from the provision that establishes liability for negotiations in bad faith, whereas the PECL and DCFR establish this requirement implicitly as a part of *bona fides*.[1968] Since *bona fides* is a mandatory provision of these instruments, disclaiming liability for breach of this prohibition does not directly flow from their text. It is suggested that, for the purpose of commercial negotiations, parties should, in principle, be able to disclaim liability for inconsistent behaviour or remedy the prohibition by timely notification (in the same way as under the UPICC).

In sum, the interpretation of *bona fides* that may be suggested supposes that a disclaimer of liability for breach of the duty should be upheld as enforceable. The reason for this suggestion lies in the balance between freedom *from* contract – as part of freedom of negotiations – recognized both at the national level and by soft law instruments and the requirement to negotiate in good faith. Within the framework of assessment of contractual negotiations suggested by this study, the *bona fides* requirement is part of the 'dynamics' of negotiations. It relates primarily to the manner, machinery, and management of a complex transaction. This side of the contract formation process should be left to the parties' discretion and the management which they agree should be given force.

[1968] See Section 8.5.4.

This suggestion fits easily into the UPICC approach. However, *prima facie*, it clashes with the frameworks of the PECL and DCFR. In fact, the instruments differ in the levels to which they restrict freedom of negotiations. This restriction is highest under the UPICC, generally transcended by broad concepts of party autonomy and freedom of contract. Reliance on these broad concepts is facilitated by the UPICC's focus on commercial contracts, because the restrictions to freedom of contract are often rooted in the aim of decreasing the effect of the imbalances in the parties' bargaining power, and the most obvious imbalance is present in contracts involving consumers. The PECL seem to restrict freedom of negotiation more than the UPICC: the PECL provision on freedom of contract explicitly refers to the caveats of its exercise. These caveats equate to the general requirement of good faith and fair dealing inspired by the European continental approach. Freedom of negotiation in the DCFR appears to be limited to a further degree than in the UPICC and PECL. One of the main reasons for this is that the DCFR has extended the incorporation of the consumer *acquis* to certain provisions applicable to business transactions.[1969] Consequently, the PECL and DCFR would necessarily be interpreted in a different way if serving as a reference or inspiration to resolve an international commercial case, as opposed to, for example, a consumer dispute. Hence, this manner of interpretation may be suitable for the PECL and DCFR.

At the same time, liability for deliberate misconduct in negotiations in which a party aims to deceive its counterpart appears to form the exception. This exception is suggested due to the tort law roots of the duty of *bona fides* in negotiations, as elaborated below.

9.4.3.3. Exceptions to this possibility: conduct with intention to deceive or obtain profit unrelated to the negotiated contract

It appears that deliberate conduct with an intention to deceive or obtaining profit not related to the negotiated contract are exceptions to the possibility to limit or disclaim liability for breach of duties established for negotiations, including duties contractualised in a letter of intent. These exceptions are appropriate to translate the non-contractual roots of liability in the national approaches.

The UPICC,[1970] PECL,[1971] and DCFR[1972] provide that the commencement of negotiations without intending to reach agreement represents a breach of *bona fides* and, therefore, leads to liability. Arguably, this formulation is excessively broad in its application to practical situations. Nieuwenhuis illustrated this difficulty in the following example. One party starts negotiations with a seller of boats about buying a vessel. However, this potential buyer simply wants to ensure he neither wants nor needs this item, despite the boat being regarded as a 'must have' by the potential buyer's colleagues. Nieuwenhuis

[1969] See Section 8.2.
[1970] Article 2.1.15(3) UPICC.
[1971] Article 2:301(3) PECL.
[1972] Article II. – 3:301 DCFR.

then questions why one should always start negotiations with the aim of reaching agreement.[1973]

The findings of this study suggest that to effectively apply this provision to practical situations, a restrictive interpretation is appropriate. More specifically, only conduct with an intention to deceive the counterpart in negotiations or to obtain commercial profit not related to the conclusion of the contract should be considered as bad faith or breach of good faith and fair dealing. This suggestion is supported by the following arguments.

First, it may be recalled the national approaches discussed earlier converge at a high threshold of liability, meaning that a simple breach of a duty (if any relevant duty exists for a concrete type of conduct) does not automatically lead to liability. Comparative observations suggest that even in jurisdictions that recognize the possibility of engaging liability for breach of precontractual *bona fides*, more than a breach of a duty is required. To engage liability, further conditions should be fulfilled: these are, essentially, the conditions of tortious liability. For example, US law establishes liability in tort for misrepresentation of intent to reach agreement.[1974] Generally, recovery within the national approaches appears to be granted with regard to using strategies and tactics in negotiations to the extent that they are *intended to deceive* the other party. An illustrative example is entering into negotiations with the sole aim of preventing or impeding parallel negotiations with a competitor. National approaches converge in imposing liability for such use of strategies and tactics, in which a party disregards any possible detriment to the counterpart to negotiations. One of the remedies provided by the soft law instruments for breach of *bona fides* pursues a similar objective. This is the remedy according to which one may not rely on a right or defence resulting from a breach of duty.[1975] For example, A starts negotiations with B and agrees with B on exclusivity of negotiations. A negotiates with the sole aim of precluding parallel negotiations. B nevertheless starts parallel negotiations with C and breaks off negotiations with A. In this case, A would not be able to hold B liable for breaking off or breach of exclusivity of negotiations. Another corresponding example is starting negotiations only to obtain confidential or business sensitive information and using this information thereafter for one's own profit. In all these cases, the breach of the duty of *bona fides* is accompanied by either intention to harm or negligence, characterized primarily as liability in tort in the national approaches.

Second, the situation in which negotiations are always started with an intention to form a contract corresponds to the assumption that negotiations are at all times cooperative. However, as argued in Chapter 2, this is not always the case. From a comparative

[1973] Nieuwenhuis 2010, at 289. The reflections of this scholar are further limited to Dutch law. He advocates formulating factors to be taken into account to hold a party liable for breaking off negotiations, and Dutch law has evolved since the quoted publication.

[1974] Section 6.4.2.1.

[1975] See Section 8.6.

perspective, this assumption underpins the regime of regulation of negotiations in the civil law systems, while common law systems assume that negotiations are adversarial, i.e. in essence, distributive.

The restrictive interpretation of the duty of *bona fides* reflects the threshold of liability set in national approaches. This interpretation also limits contractual disclaimers of liability, following the principal approaches of the national systems. Therefore, it is to be agreed with Kleinheisterkamp who contends that a 'manifestly dishonest and vexatious' act is needed to qualify conduct as bad faith under the UPICC.[1976] The concept of *bona fides* is perhaps also the most appropriate vehicle for reflecting the tort law roots of liability for the contractual organization of negotiations. As noted in Chapter 8, the UPICC and PECL provide contractual liability for breach of their rules on negotiations. Neither the UPICC nor the PECL base liability on fault: only breach of an obligation is required or, with a necessary adaptation, breach of a duty established for the conduct of negotiations, i.e. primarily the breach of the duty of *bona fides* or, with further adaptation, breach of a contractual obligation to negotiate a contract in good faith. In this way, an intention to harm or negligence on the part of the party breaching an obligation (or duty) is not a condition of liability. As noted by the drafters of the PECL, 'precontractual liability' is one of the areas where the instrument went beyond the 'classical' domain of contract into the field considered by many national legal systems as tort. In the same vein, Storme has noted that in the PECL, the duty of good faith and fair dealing does not serve as a positive requirement, but primarily as a condition for liability. This means that a duty can be enforced only if a breach of duty leads to a detriment.[1977] The same also holds true for the DCFR, despite its adoption of a more complex approach. The right to recover for a breach of the provisions on negotiations is a self-standing non-contractual right, and specific provisions on this recovery interact with the DCFR's general rules on liability in contract and tort. The DCFR refers to its provisions on tort only in relation to causality. Arguably, the DCFR perceives the relevant liability as belonging to the domain of contract and relies primarily on contract law in the relevant regulation.[1978]

9.5. Effects of private regulation of negotiations on liability and remedies

9.5.1. Special character of liability and limits on recovery

It flows from all three soft law instruments addressed in Chapter 8 that a precontractual duty concretized in an agreement (i.e. an agreement confined to the period of negotiations) transforms it into a contractual obligation. Its breach leads to remedies available for breach of a contract. With a different degree of detail, the UPICC, PECL, and DCFR specify that their rules on breach of contract apply to liability in the course of negotiations

1976 Kleinheisterkamp in Vogenauer/Kleinheisterkamp 2009, at 302 (suggesting this with reference to French and US law).

1977 Storme 2003, at 231.

1978 Section 8.4.3.2.

in a limited way, by analogy, and with necessary adaptations. This indicates the special nature of liability that may arise in negotiations. Imposing such liability in the same manner as liability for breach of contract would be, indeed, contrary to the principle of freedom of contract. The special nature of liability is translated primarily through the limits placed by the soft law instruments on the recovery available for breach of their provisions on negotiations.

Soft law instruments limit the court's or arbitrator's interference with the parties' negotiations: parties may not be ordered to conclude a contract if they remain in negotiations and still have disagreements over the final contract. The remedy of specific performance of an obligation to negotiate is not available. In all the instruments, a breach of the duty of good faith and fair dealing precludes a party from relying on a right, remedy, or defence that would otherwise be available to this party. Furthermore, soft law instruments do not admit punitive damages.

The main type of damages recoverable is material damage sustained. It consists primarily in costs wasted in negotiations, and the costs of work done or services executed in anticipation of a contract. It also includes damage caused by loss of a chance to conclude a contract: either the contract for which the negotiations failed, or a contract with a third party (the UPICC clearly reference both, the PECL refer to loss of opportunities, while the DCFR is not clear on whether the recoverable loss of chance relates to the contract for which negotiations failed or to a contract with a third party).[1979]

To specify the approach to remedies for breach of contractually organized negotiations, it is submitted that recovery for breach of obligations which organize negotiations contractually should be limited to remedying breach of concrete obligation(s) created to manage the negotiation process. This approach corresponds also to the principle of addressing each obligation as stand-alone, as suggested in Section 9.3.2 above.

9.5.2. Factors to balance in establishing liability

Soft law instruments establish liability for breaking off advanced negotiations. The instruments refer, for instance, to breaking off lengthy negotiations abruptly and without justification. The word 'lengthy' creates a link between the advancement of negotiations and their duration in time: the longer the negotiations last, the higher the probability that they qualify as 'advanced' and that breaking off from them will be considered 'abrupt'.[1980] Despite these references echoing civil law approaches, this reflects only a part of the rationale of imposing liability.

It is submitted that the concept of advancement of negotiations should be associated primarily with the substance of the final contract. By contrast, the management (or

1979 See Section 8.6.3.
1980 Section 8.5.3.

machinery) of the transaction – in essence, the mere negotiations or their 'dynamics' – do not necessarily imply the advancement of negotiations. Accordingly, issuing a letter of intent whereby parties create obligations confined to the process of negotiations would not mean that negotiations are advanced. Negotiations would be advanced only when agreements are reached on the substance of the final contract.

Furthermore, the study suggests that factors other than advancement of negotiations may be balanced in establishing liability for breach of *bona fides* in negotiations (contractualized or not contractualized) and stand-alone obligations created by the contractual organization of negotiations. These factors may be arranged in a hierarchical order, whereby deliberate misconduct (as discussed earlier) has the highest weight, and even advanced negotiations (in the national interpretations of this concept) may be broken off without liability, even such breaking off that French law may qualify as rude and abrupt, if the economic and commercial interests of a party withdrawing from negotiations so dictate.

9.5.2.1. Deliberate misconduct

As noted in Section 9.4.3 above, deliberate misconduct in negotiations may lead to liability, and the consequences of such misconduct may not be waived or limited by contractual organization of negotiations.

9.5.2.2. Commercial self-interest

As noted in Section 9.4.2 above, *bona fides* in negotiations should not be interpreted as requiring a party to sacrifice its commercial interests. Accordingly, negotiations may at all times be broken off (without liability) if this is required by the commercial self-interest of the party breaking off negotiations or of both parties. This approach appears to flow from the regime of regulating negotiations in all the analysed national approaches, though commercial self-interest does not always outweigh other factors therein. Even in the French and Dutch approaches (which establish a positive requirement to conduct negotiations in accordance with *bona fides*), the commercial interests of the party withdrawing from negotiations are highly weighed in the assessment of liability.[1981]

9.5.2.3. Reliance

International instruments protect precontractual reliance. As noted in Chapter 8, the soft law approach does not only echo the civil law traditions (e.g. the relevance of reliance on the conclusion of the final contract). It also reminds the protection of reliance under the doctrines of estoppel in US law and unjust enrichment in English law and US law. It may be suggested therefore that to apply the instruments' provisions on protection of reliance, it must be ascertained whether a promise is made, to what extent there is effective reliance on the promise, and whether the reliance has caused damage.

[1981] Sections 3.3.2.3; 4.3.3; 5.3.2; 6.3.1.

Furthermore, the fact that the promise is not enforced should lead to injustice. Assessment of reliance is relevant for both contractualised good faith and for other obligations created by letter of intent.

9.5.2.4. Inducement to invest or commence performance

Inducement, encouragement, authorisation, and a request to invest at the stage of negotiations provide strong arguments in favour of recovery in unjust enrichment under the national approaches. Therefore, provisions of this kind made in a letter of intent may be taken into account to establish liability. However, a note of caution should also be introduced here. It is submitted in this regard that at least the following provisions of the UPICC are readily applicable to negotiations. The UPICC provides rules on reduction of damages if the aggrieved party has contributed to the loss he suffered[1982] and a provision requiring a party to be cautious and mitigate harm.[1983] The PECL and DCFR contain similar provisions.[1984] As applied to liability in negotiations, these balance freedom of contract and its limitations, to the extent that involvement in negotiations may represent a business risk.

9.5.2.5. Advancement of negotiations and other factors

According to the soft law rules, the advancement of negotiations should be taken into account in determining liability. The approach to this has been suggested in Section 9.4.4.1 above. Other factors that may be considered include refusal to negotiate ('sabotage' of negotiations) and late notification about the breaking off of negotiations: in essence, continuing negotiations after taking the decision not to proceed with the underlying transaction. It is suggested that liability for losses caused by these factors may be contractually limited, waived, or concretized (including more stringent standards).

9.5.3. Remedies

As noted in the previous section, recovery for a breach of the rules on negotiations is subject to limitations both in soft law and in national approaches. National approaches either place explicit limits (e.g. French law),[1985] or translate the guarded approach to recovery by setting a high threshold to liability (as seen in Dutch,[1986] English,[1987] and US[1988] law). These limitations cover the main types of remedies that were discussed in

[1982] Article 7.4.7 UPICC.
[1983] Article 7.4.8 UPICC.
[1984] See Articles 9:504 and 9:505 PECL; Articles III – 3:704 and III – 3:705 DCFR.
[1985] Section 4.7.1.
[1986] Sections 3.3.1 and 3.8.1.1.
[1987] Sections 5.3.1 and 5.7.
[1988] Sections 6.3.1 and 6.6.

Chapter 8.[1989] The following remedies may be considered under the interpretation of the soft law instruments:

9.5.3.1. The loss of costs wasted in negotiations and preparation of the final contract

This is the main form of recovery and is identified by the texts of the soft law instruments.[1990]

9.5.3.2. The loss of costs of works or services started in anticipation of conclusion of the final contract

This remedy echoes the national doctrines of unjust enrichment. The availability of this remedy is closely related to the extent to which such performance is induced by the party benefitting from the performance, the extent of the actual benefit, and the aggrieved party's risk-taking, as noted in Section 9.4.2 above.

9.5.3.3. The loss of opportunity to conclude a contract with a third party

This remedy is not excluded by soft law. In accordance with the previous submissions, this remedy may be available when a deliberate misconduct in the course of negotiations aimed at impeding or preventing negotiations with a third party occurs. The availability of this remedy is subject to the high threshold of liability suggested.

9.5.3.4. The harm to the reputation

Recovery for harm to reputation is not excluded by the soft law instruments. However, the existing case law and academic literature do not offer extensive guidance on this remedy in the context of contractual negotiations. It may be concluded that the remedy is exceptional in the context of contractual negotiations. This exceptional character might not be due to specific conditions of liability, but rather to the eventual difficulty of establishing the evidence and causality.

9.5.3.5. The loss of bargain

Loss of bargain is mentioned in the soft law in relation to breach of confidentiality (either breach of the duty of confidentiality that may be implied or breach of an enforceable obligation on confidentiality of negotiations). This remedy is perhaps the least elaborated in soft law instruments.[1991] According to all the instruments addressed, non-compliance

[1989] Section 8.6.
[1990] Ibid.
[1991] See Zuloaga Rios, 'Article 2.1.16 Duty of confidentiality', in Vogenauer 2015, at 370 (noting the necessity of further interpretation of the UPICC on this matter).

with the provisions on confidentiality (and with implied confidentiality) may lead not only to losses caused by the disclosure, but also to the recovery for the loss of bargain. It consists in the recovery of the profit received by the other party as a result of using the confidential information. From the analysis of the national approaches, the US law offers an elaborate reasoning on this remedy. The soft law approach on the implication of this duty also echoes US law: in the US approach to misappropriation of information, recovery consists in 'reimbursement of loss caused by the appropriation or gain resulting from appropriation, whichever is greater'.[1992] Granting this remedy is subject to the condition that the information in question 'can be used in the operation of a business or other enterprise and that is sufficiently valuable and secret to afford an actual or potential economic advantage over others'.[1993] It need not be information which is protected by intellectual property rights. It is noteworthy however, that the remedy is highly exceptional in the US. English law allows, in principle, an award of gain-based damages; however, these are not typical at the stage of contract formation. This remedy would also be exceptional within the framework of the soft law instruments.

9.5.3.6. Injunction and protective measures

This remedy is particularly relevant for breach of agreed confidentiality and exclusivity in negotiations. Looking at the national case law, this remedy is not granted frequently. In case of breach of confidentiality, all instruments recognize the possibility of asking a court for protective measures. The PECL and DCFR also emphasise the prevention of unwanted disclosure. An injunction aimed at preventing parallel negotiations appears to be available under the soft law rules, but only in the presence of an enforceable obligation of exclusivity. Injunctions and other protective measure appear to be, indeed, a useful means to ensure the respect of confidentiality and 'lock-out' provisions of the letter of intent. However, its practical implementation in an international transaction – in essence, as a cross-border protective measure – may face obstacles not addressed by the soft law instruments on contract law.

9.6. Final remarks

This study has attempted to add a new dimension to the understanding of private regulation of negotiations by letter of intent. Contractual negotiations are a complex and multidimensional process with its own 'statics' and 'dynamics'. These have been taken into account in formulating a harmonized approach to the privatization of negotiations within the framework of the soft law rules: restatements that may be taken into account by private parties, judges, arbitrators, academics, and policymakers. It is hoped that the findings offer a clearer view on the negotiations and formation of an international contract. The aspiration is that the findings will enhance the flexibility of legal frameworks

[1992] Restatement (Third) of Unfair Competition §45(1).

[1993] Restatement (Third) of Unfair Competition, §39. See also Comment d providing a list of examples of trade secrets: 'formula, pattern, compilation of data', etc.

by furthering the development of new commercial instruments and practices and contributing to the financial security and legal certainty of parties involved in international commerce.

SAMENVATTING

Inleiding

In de meeste rechtstelsels wordt de totstandkoming van een overeenkomst in de eerste plaats bepaald aan de hand van aanbod en aanvaarding. Het model van aanbod en aanvaarding is ontwikkeld voor eenvoudige transacties. Moderne overeenkomsten worden echter steeds complexer. Om alle details van de beoogde definitieve overeenkomst te formuleren, moet intensief worden onderhandeld. Deze manier van het tot stand komen van een overeenkomst laat zich niet altijd vatten in het model van aanbod en aanvaarding. In de meeste rechtstelsels worden onderhandelingen behalve door het model van aanbod en aanvaarding ook beheerst door niet-contractuele beginselen. Zo schept in *civil law* landen het ruime beginsel van precontractuele aansprakelijkheid een positieve verplichting ten aanzien van de manier waarop partijen zich tijdens de onderhandelingen moeten gedragen. Onrechtmatig gedrag wordt primair gesanctioneerd door het onrechtmatige daadsrecht. In de rechtstelsels van de *common law* worden daarentegen veel minder eisen gesteld aan het gedrag gedurende de onderhandelingen.

Om de verplichtingen en aansprakelijkheid al aan het begin van de onderhandelingen te kunnen bepalen, of juist het niet-bindende karakter van de onderhandelingen te benadrukken, wordt in de praktijk van het internationaal contracteren vaak gebruik gemaakt van verschillende precontractuele documenten zoals de intentieverklaring, '*letter of intent*', '*memorandum of understanding*' en '*heads of agreement*'.

De *letter of intent* heeft sinds de jaren zeventig van de vorige eeuw op veel aandacht vanuit de literatuur kunnen rekenen. Volgens de heersende leer zijn de rechtsgevolgen van de *letter of intent* in elke specifieke geval voornamelijk afhankelijk van de interpretatie van de tekst van het document. Vooral één type document blijkt echter moeilijk te beoordelen aan de hand van de bestaande leerstukken: de *letter of intent* waarbij partijen het onderhandelingsproces contractueel vormgeven.

Onderzoeksvraag, onderzoeksmethode en doelstelling

De onderzoeksvraag is in hoeverre het recht – met name internationale regelingen – zou kunnen inspelen op de bestaande praktijk om het onderhandelingsproces contractueel vorm te geven middels een *letter of intent*.

Om de onderzoeksvraag te beantwoorden wordt gebruikgemaakt van de functionele rechtsvergelijkende methode. Het onderzoek beschrijft de benaderingen ten aanzien van het contractueel vormgeven van onderhandelingen in vier rechtstelsels: Nederland, Frankrijk, Engeland en Wales en de Verenigde Staten. Deze rechtstelsels zijn gekozen omdat zij de meest uiteenlopende benaderingen voor de regulering van de onderhandelingen weergeven. De keuze om zowel het Engelse als het Amerikaanse recht te bespreken, is ingegeven door het feit dat deze rechtsstelsels laten zien dat ook binnen de *common law*-traditie verschillende benaderingen worden gehanteerd. Om de parameters voor het vergelijken te formuleren worden teksten van de *letter of intent*, zoals aangehaald in de rechtspraak en de 'klassieke' juridische analyse, onder de loep genomen. Dit onderzoek maakt ook gebruik van interdisciplinaire inzichten uit de praktijk van onderhandelingen.

De resultaten van de rechtsvergelijking worden vervolgens gebruikt in de beschouwing over een mogelijke geharmoniseerde benadering van *letter of intent* op internationaal niveau. Het onderzoek bespreekt in dit kader het Weens Koopverdrag en de *soft law*-instrumenten *UNIDROIT Principles of International Commercial Contracts* (UPICC), *Principles of European Contract Law* (PECL) en *Draft Common Frame of Reference* (DCFR). Ook *hard law*-instrumenten die conflictenregels unificeren – in het bijzonder de EU-Verordeningen Rome I en Rome II – worden kort besproken.

Het doel van dit onderzoek is een nieuw perspectief te ontwikkelen over de rol van *letter of intent* bij de totstandkoming van een internationale overeenkomst. Dit onderzoek streeft ernaar de kennis op het gebied van internationale handelsgebruiken te vergroten, waardoor de rechtszekerheid en financiële zekerheid van partijen in de beginfase van een internationale handelsbetrekking kunnen worden verbeterd.

Statische en dynamische aspecten van onderhandelingen

Hoofdstuk 2 gaat in op de inhoud van de *letter of intent* door de aandacht te vestigen op de praktijk van de onderhandelingen. De onderhandelingen worden in de praktijk vaak aangepakt door middel van strategieën en tactieken. In dit hoofdstuk wordt betoogd dat deze benadering kan worden uitgedrukt in juridische termen. Het onderzoek onderstreept het belang van het onderscheid tussen de verplichtingen uit het definitieve contract (de statica van de onderhandelingen) en de verplichtingen die beperkt blijven tot het proces van de onderhandelingen (de dynamiek van de onderhandelingen). Daarnaast geeft het hoofdstuk een handvat om deze twee dimensies te scheiden.

Door middel van de bepalingen in een *letter of intent* stellen de onderhandelende partijen de grenzen vast met betrekking tot de eventuele uitoefening van onderhandelingstactieken, verduidelijken ze de kwesties die primair van belang zijn voor het onderhandelingsproces en minimaliseren ze de risico's die betrokken bij zijn het beheer van complexe transacties.

Resultaten van de rechtsvergelijking

De hoofdstukken 3, 4, 5 en 6 zijn gewijd aan de nationale aanpak van de *letter of intent* in het Nederlandse, Franse, Engelse en Amerikaanse recht. In hoofdstuk 7 worden de convergerende en divergerende tendensen samengetrokken en uitgelegd. Dit hoofdstuk bevat een analyse van de belangrijkste clausules die worden opgenomen in de teksten van de *letter of intent*, zoals aangehaald in de gepubliceerde rechtsspraak. Elke bepaling wordt geïllustreerd en daarna besproken in vergelijkend perspectief.

De rechtsvergelijkende analyse laat zien dat tussen de onderzochte rechtsstelsels een aantal algemene overeenkomsten bestaat. Zo vertonen de status en de gevolgen van een *letter of intent* in het Nederlandse, Franse, Engelse en Amerikaanse recht op een aantal punten gelijkenissen. Het Franse en Nederlandse recht komen op twee belangrijke punten overeen. Ten eerste erkennen beide rechtstelsels het regime van precontractuele aansprakelijkheid. Ten tweede worden beide rechtssystemen ondersteund door de gelijkende conceptuele kaders van de Franse *avant-contrat* en de Nederlandse voorovereenkomst, beide gereguleerd door het contractenrecht. Binnen deze kaders wordt een duidelijk onderscheid gemaakt tussen het onderhandelingsproces en de beoogde overeenkomst. In de Engelse en de Amerikaanse benadering worden specifieke problemen daarentegen veelal aangepakt via de onrechtmatige daad en ongerechtvaardigde verrijking. Het contractenrecht van deze rechtsstelsels beschouwt onderhandelingen voornamelijk als *bargain* en het nemen van risico. Engeland en Wales en de Verenigde Staten kennen geen overkoepelend begrip dat vergelijkbaar is met de *avant-contrat* en voorovereenkomst. Echter, een recente tendens in beide rechtsstelsels wijst op de ontwikkeling van een regime vergelijkbaar met de Franse en Nederlandse kaders van de *avant-contrat* en voorovereenkomst. Het Engelse en Amerikaanse regime is echter onderworpen aan belangrijke beperkingen. In Engeland en Wales wordt een preliminaire regime ontwikkeld door middelen die aanzienlijk verschillen van het concept van de goede trouw. In de Verenigde Staten gaan sommige deelstaten (zoals Illinois, Pennsylvania, Mississippi, Kentucky) uit van het concept van *bona fides*, terwijl dit concept in andere deelstaten, bijvoorbeeld in New York, nog altijd wordt verworpen. Het ontstaan van voorafgaande preliminaire regimes is een gelijkenis tussen alle vier besproken rechtstelsels. Deze preliminaire regimes zijn van toepassing op contractueel vormgegeven onderhandelingen. De regimes zijn ook te onderscheiden van het definitieve contract. Hoewel de benaderingen van precontractuele aansprakelijkheid in de onderzochte rechtsstelsels veelal sterk uiteenlopen, kunnen door het feit dat de onderhandelende partijen de mogelijkheid hebben de onderhandelingen grotendeels zelf te reguleren toch vergelijkbare resultaten worden bereikt.

Een andere belangrijke gelijkenis tussen de Nederlandse, Franse, Engelse en Amerikaanse benadering wordt vertoont vanuit het perspectief van de clausules die worden opgenomen in de teksten van de *letter of intent*. De verplichtingen binnen preliminaire regimes worden in toenemende mate afzonderlijk behandeld (beginsel van separabiliteit). Dit betekent dat de verbintenissen onafhankelijk van de inhoud van de beoogde overeenkomst worden beoordeeld en vaak als bindend worden gekwalificeerd, zelfs wanneer de rest van het document als niet-bindend wordt aangemerkt. Echter, het separabiliteitsbeginsel geldt niet voor alle soorten verplichtingen. Het lijdt weinig twijfel dat het kan worden toegepast op geschillenbeslechtingsclausules. Ook vertrouwelijkheids- en exclusiviteitsbepalingen worden in de rechtspraak veelal als scheidbaar beschouwd. Daarentegen is het aanzienlijk moeilijker om een separate behandeling van andere soorten verplichtingen in de rechtspraak te traceren.

De onderzochte rechtsstelsels vertonen eveneens een zekere gelijkenis met betrekking tot de mate van aansprakelijkheid en vergoeding. Indien aansprakelijkheid wordt aangenomen, wordt deze in alle rechtsstelsels voornamelijk beperkt tot het vergoeden van de kosten die zijn gemaakt tijdens de onderhandelingen (of, in sommige gevallen, tot teruggave van de prestatie die is verricht). Dit geldt voor alle situaties waarin aansprakelijkheid kan worden aangenomen: dus zowel voor de schending van een contractueel bindende bepaling van een *letter of intent* als binnen het regime van precontractuele aansprakelijkheid (in de rechtsstelsels waarin dit wordt toegelaten). Opmerkelijk is verder dat alle rechtsstelsels erkennen dat een partij in uitzonderlijke gevallen kan worden veroordeeld tot winstafdracht.

Voor de waargenomen gelijkenissen kunnen de volgende verklaringen worden aangedragen. De overeenkomst tussen het Franse en het Nederlandse recht met betrekking tot de ontwikkeling van een algemeen concept van de precontractuele aansprakelijkheid kan worden teruggevoerd op het gemeenschappelijke juridische erfgoed en de receptie van het Romeinse recht. De geïdentificeerde gelijkenissen tussen de vier jurisdicties wat betreft de aanpak van de contractueel vormgegeven onderhandelingen zijn waarschijnlijk te verklaren door twee omstandigheden. Ten eerste zijn de rechterlijke instanties van de vier rechtsstelsels op een vergelijkbare manier omgegaan met complexe onderhandelingen en de *letter of intent*. Dit zou het gevolg zijn van de manier waarop moderne overeenkomsten worden onderhandeld. Ten tweede hebben de preliminaire regimes zich ontwikkeld als gevolg van de transnationalisering van de handelspraktijken. Dit kan de evolutie van het recht hebben gestimuleerd om vergelijkbare, zo niet identieke, praktische vragen op te lossen.

Een opvallend verschil tussen de Nederlandse en de Franse aanpak enerzijds en de Engelse en de Amerikaanse aanpak anderzijds betreft de aannames over onderhandelingen. Terwijl de eerstgenoemde rechtsstelsels de onderhandelingen zien als een samenwerkingsproces, benaderen de laatstgenoemde de onderhandelingen als confrontatief proces. Dit verschil kan worden verklaard door de verschillende manieren waarop deze landen zich in de negentiende en twintigste eeuw op sociaaleconomisch gebied hebben ontwikkeld. Deze verschillen hebben geleid tot twee tegengestelde benaderingen (Engeland en de VS) van het recht: de economische en de moralistische (Nederland en Frankrijk).

Hoewel beide *common law*, zijn er ook belangrijke verschillen waar te nemen tussen het Engelse en Amerikaanse recht. In sommige Amerikaanse deelstaten kan de rechter, in tegenstelling tot zijn Engelse collega, de eisen van goede trouw betrekken in de onderhandelingen over een contract. Dit vormt dan vaak de inhoud van het toepasselijke preliminaire regime. Het Amerikaanse recht gaat ook verder dan het Engels recht in de bescherming van het precontractuele vertrouwen door de ontwikkeling van de leer van de *promissory estoppel*, hoewel deze zelden wordt toegepast in de praktijk. Deze verschillen vloeien ongetwijfeld voort uit de contrasterende wijze waarop het juridische beleid zich heeft ontwikkeld in de twintigste eeuw, maar kunnen ook worden verklaard door de intellectuele invloed van de Europese continentale ideeën in de tweede helft van de vorige eeuw. Deze invloed is sterker geweest in de Verenigde Staten dan in Engeland en Wales.

Suggesties voor een geharmoniseerde aanpak van de *letter of intent* bij internationaal contracteren

In hoofdstuk 9 wordt besproken dat de *letter of intent* kan worden gekwalificeerd als een internationaal handelsgebruik. *De letter of intent* wordt aangeduid als de 'privatisering' van de dynamische aspecten van de onderhandelingen door contractueel bindende verplichtingen. Een handelsgebruik is een vorm van harmonisatie – de harmonisatie door het opstellen van contractuele clausules in de praktijk.

Het onderhavige onderzoek beschouwt harmonisatie als een breed begrip dat niet alleen bestaat uit de eenmaking van het recht door middel van internationale verdragen en andere bindende instrumenten, maar ook uit unificatie door niet-bindende beginselen, *restatements* van het recht en de convergentie van handelspraktijken. In dit licht kunnen met betrekking tot de formulering van een geharmoniseerde aanpak ten minste drie alternatieven worden geïdentificeerd.

Ten eerste kan worden gekozen voor een formulering die los staat van de bestaande internationale instrumenten, ten tweede kan harmonisatie plaatsvinden via de interpretatie van het Weens Koopverdrag en ten derde via de interpretatie van de bestaande *soft law*-instrumenten. Deze alternatieven worden in hoofdstuk 8 besproken.

De eerste mogelijkheid wordt afgewezen, omdat zij geen recht doet aan de bestaande *soft law*-instrumenten.

De tweede mogelijkheid hangt samen met de reeds bestaande academische discussie over de vraag of het Weens Koopverdrag ook van toepassing is op de precontractuele fase. De contractuele verplichtingen met betrekking tot de dynamiek van de onderhandelingen komen niet overheen met de definitie van de koopovereenkomst onder het Weens Koopverdrag. Als gevolg daarvan valt de contractuele organisatie van de onderhandelingen buiten het toepassingsgebied van het Weens Koopverdrag. De tweede mogelijkheid wordt om deze reden dan ook afgewezen.

Met betrekking tot de derde mogelijkheid wordt erop gewezen dat de UPICC, PECL en DCFR de onderhandelingen wel specifiek noemen. Zoals vermeld in hoofdstuk 8 leggen de bestaande internationale instrumenten het fundament voor een geharmoniseerde aanpak. Deze fundamenten worden onderzocht in hoofdstuk 8, waarna wordt voorgesteld om de interpretatie van de *soft law*-instrumenten te gebruiken als basis voor een geharmoniseerde aanpak van de *letter of intent*. De formulering kan echter aangepast worden. Deze moet de cruciale relevantie van de commerciële belangen van de partijen expliciet weerspiegelen. De formulering moet het verschil tussen de verbintenissen uit, aan de ene kant, het definitieve contract en, aan de andere kant, de verplichtingen die beperkt blijven tot het proces van de onderhandelingen verduidelijken. De mogelijkheid om aan de laatste type verbintenissen contractueel vorm te geven moet expliciet genoemd worden. Deze mogelijkheid wordt begrensd door opzettelijk gedrag om te bedriegen en het verkrijgen van winst die niet is gerelateerd aan het tot stand gekomen contract. Deze benadering weerspiegelt de niet-contractuele wortels van de relevante aansprakelijkheid in de verschillende nationale benaderingen.

Hoofdstuk 9 beveelt de volgende aanpassingen van het artikel 2.1.15 UPICC aan (de aanpassingen zijn uitgelicht in cursief):

> 2.1.15 Negotiations in bad faith
>
> (1) A party is free to negotiate and is not liable for failure to reach an agreement *nor for breaking off negotiations in pursuing commercial self-interest.*
> (2) However, a party who negotiates or breaks off negotiations in bad faith is liable for the losses caused to the other party.
> (3) It is bad faith, in particular, for a party to enter into or continue negotiations when intending not to reach an agreement with the other party *but to deceive the other party or obtain profit unrelated to the negotiated contract.*
> *(4) Parties may organize the process of negotiations by stand-alone contractual obligations, severable from the final negotiated contract. Liability is then limited to the loss caused by breach of such obligation, except for bad faith mentioned in (3) above and except for breach of confidentiality regulated in Article 2.1.16.*

Daarnaast, worden in hoofdstuk 9 vier stappen aanbevolen om de juridische gevolgen van een *letter of intent* bij internationaal contracteren te bepalen.

Ten eerste, identificatie en scheiding van de clausules in de *letter of intent* die de statische en de dynamische dimensies van onderhandelingen inhouden.

Ten tweede, het bepalen van de effecten van de statische dimensie: indien het aanbod en aanvaarding model aangepast kan worden, zou de definitieve overeenkomst tot stand kunnen komen.

Ten derde, het bepalen van de effecten van elke clausule binnen de dynamische dimensie afzonderlijk – onafhankelijk van de inhoud van de beoogde overeenkomst en van de andere clausules van de *letter of intent*.

Ten vierde, het bepalen van de eventuele aansprakelijkheid en schadevergoeding.

Hoofdstuk 9 sluit het onderzoek af met een aanbeveling met betrekking tot de interpretatie van de *soft law*-instrumenten zodat zij kunnen worden gebruikt voor het beoordelen van de *letter of intent*.

Ten eerste, op welke wijze kan het handelsgebruik van de *letter of intent* in het mechanisme van het tot stand komen van een overeenkomst worden geplaatst? Zoals in hoofdstuk 9 wordt betoogd, bieden de *soft law*-instrumenten de mogelijkheid om bindende verplichtingen te creëren vanaf het begin van de onderhandelingen. Dit wordt mogelijk gemaakt door de moderne, flexibele aanpak die soms wordt aangeduid als *favor contractus*. Deze benadering berust op het *effet utile* van een afdwingbare contractuele verplichting voor de deelnemers van de internationale handel. Toch moet de afdwingbaarheid worden beoordeeld per bepaling, en dus niet van het document als geheel. Elke bepaling dient te worden beschouwd als een *severable* bepaling, die los staat van het definitieve contract en van de overige bepalingen van de *letter of intent*. Daarnaast wordt in hoofdstuk 9 de conclusie getrokken dat een verbintenis waarin onderhandelingen contractueel worden geregeld een speciaal type verbintenis is. Zelfs als deze verbintenis is onderworpen aan dezelfde voorwaarden wat betreft de geldigheid als die gelden voor een contract, rijst de vraag of zij een contractuele verplichting wordt in de zin dat er een verplichting aanwezig is om medewerking te verlenen aan de uitvoering ervan, ingrijpende gevolgen zou hebben, waaronder de mogelijkheid om de verbintenis over te dragen of alle remedies te vorderen die beschikbaar zijn als gevolg van contractuele aansprakelijkheid. De nationale benaderingen bieden op dit punt weinig houvast. Bij deze verplichtingen kunnen belangrijke kanttekeningen worden geplaatst. Deze kanttekeningen hebben betrekking op het in evenwicht brengen van de goede trouw en de vrijheid van contract.

Ten tweede, hoe kan de normatieve standaard van de (internationale) goede trouw het mogelijke gebruik van strategieën en tactieken van de onderhandelingen weerspiegelen? Niet alleen de samenwerking, maar ook het nemen van risico, concurrentie en afdingen moet in beschouwing worden genomen, omdat deze inherent zijn aan contractonderhandelingen en in verschillende mate erkend worden in de nationale opvattingen over de vrijheid van onderhandelingen. Om die reden moeten deze begrippen ook onder gebracht worden in het concept van de internationale goede trouw. Om strategieën en tactieken van de onderhandelingen onder te kunnen brengen in het concept van de goede trouw, wordt betoogd dat de goede trouw bij internationale transacties zo moet worden uitgelegd dat zij niet vereist dat partijen hun eigen commerciële belangen opofferen. In wezen kwalificeren *soft law*-instrumenten kwade trouw als het in onderhandeling treden zonder de bedoeling om tot overeenstemming te komen en het afbreken van vergevorderde onderhandelingen. Daarnaast kan het misbruik maken van vertrouwelijke informatie worden beschouwd als kwade trouw, waarbij rekening wordt gehouden met de regels inzake vertrouwelijkheid in de onderhandelingen. Binnen de nationale benaderingen geeft een aantal zaken waarin partijen aansprakelijk werden gehouden wegens wangedrag tijdens de onderhandelingen de mogelijkheid het begrip goede trouw nader te concretiseren.

Goede trouw vereist geen opoffering van het eigen commercieel belang. Dit is duidelijk de positie die wordt ingenomen in het Engelse recht. In de Franse jurisprudentie worden de eigen commerciële belangen van een partij vaak (maar niet altijd) gezien als een legitieme reden om de onderhandelingen af te breken. In de Amerikaanse benadering vloeit ditzelfde voort uit de visie op onderhandelingen als het nemen van risico (zij het dat de toepassing van de alles-of-niets-benadering de mogelijkheid kan beperken om zich terug te trekken uit de onderhandelingen, omdat het definitieve contract dan al als gevormd kan worden beschouwd). In het Nederlandse recht zijn de gerechtvaardigde belangen van een partij om zich terug te trekken uit onderhandelingen een belangrijke factor in het vaststellen van de aansprakelijkheid. Dat belang bestaat vaak (maar niet altijd) uit zijn commerciële eigenbelang. De *soft law*-instrumenten moeten zo worden uitgelegd dat zij partijen in staat stellen om de vereisten van de goede trouw te concretiseren door middel van private regulering en in beginsel de aansprakelijkheid wegens het niet nakomen van een verplichting contractueel te verhogen, te beperken of af te wijzen.

Niettemin betoogt dit onderzoek dat de bovengenoemde vrijheid van partijen tot zelfregulering begrensd wordt, wat ook lijkt te worden geaccepteerd in de verschillende nationale benaderingen. Opzettelijk gedrag om te bedriegen en het verkrijgen van winst die niet is gerelateerd aan het tot stand gekomen contract vormen uitzonderingen op de mogelijkheid om de aansprakelijkheid wegens een schending van verbintenissen die zijn vastgelegd in een *letter of intent* te beperken. Met deze uitzonderingen worden de buitencontractuele wortels van de nationale benaderingen tot uitdrukking gebracht.

Ten derde, waar dient de drempel voor aansprakelijkheid worden gelegd in het licht van de vergelijkende observaties? Het onderhavige onderzoek betoogt dat wanneer een dergelijke aansprakelijkheid op dezelfde wijze zou worden opgelegd als de aansprakelijkheid voor de schending van een contractuele verbintenis zij in strijd zou komen met het beginsel van de contractsvrijheid. Om deze reden moet de vergoeding worden beperkt tot de vergoeding van schade veroorzaakt door de schending van concrete verplichting(en) die zijn gecreëerd om het onderhandelingsproces te beheren.

Ten slotte worden de gezichtspunten besproken die moeten worden afgewogen om de aansprakelijkheid voor de niet-nakoming van de verplichtingen uit de contractueel vormgegeven onderhandelingen vast te stellen en de omvang ervan te bepalen.

- Voortgang van de onderhandelingen. Gesteld wordt dat het concept van de voortgang van de onderhandelingen in de eerste plaats in verband dient te worden gebracht met de inhoud van het definitieve contract. Het beheer van de transactie, de loutere

onderhandelingen, met andere woorden de 'dynamiek' van de onderhandelingen, wijzen daarentegen niet altijd op de voortgang van de onderhandelingen. De onderhandelingen zouden enkel kunnen worden beschouwd als vergevorderd wanneer afspraken worden gemaakt over de inhoud van het definitieve contract.
- Opzettelijk wangedrag (zoals hierboven blijkt, wordt aan deze factor het grootste gewicht toegekend).
- Commercieel eigenbelang.
- Vertrouwen.
- Aansporingen om investeringen te doen of te beginnen met de nakoming.
- De weigering om te onderhandelen – 'sabotage' van de onderhandelingen, late berichtgeving over het afbreken van de onderhandelingen: de voortzetting van de onderhandelingen na het nemen van het besluit om door te gaan met de transactie. Er wordt gesuggereerd dat de aansprakelijkheid voor schade die veroorzaakt wordt door deze factoren contractueel kan worden beperkt, uitgesloten of geconcretiseerd (met inbegrip van strengere normen).

De volgende remedies kunnen eveneens worden overgewogen, maar dan als uitzonderlijke aansprakelijkheidsmaatregelen.

- Verlies als gevolg van gemaakte kosten tijdens de onderhandelingen en ter voorbereiding op het definitieve overeenkomst.
- Verlies als gevolg van kosten van werk of diensten die reeds zijn verricht in afwachting van de sluiting van het definitieve overeenkomst.
- Verlies van de kans om een overeenkomst met een derde te sluiten.
- Reputatieschade.
- Winstafdracht (in uitzonderingsgevallen).
- Een bevel tot nakoming en beschermende maatregelen.

BIBLIOGRAPHY

A

Ajani/Schulte-Nölke 2007

G. Ajani and H. Schulte-Nölke, 'Preface – The Principles of the Existing EC Contract Law: A Preliminary Output of the Acquis Group', in Research Group on the Existing EC Private Law (Acquis Group), *Principles of the Existing EC Contract Law (Acquis Principles): Contract I* (München: Sellier European Law Publishers, 2007) p. ix

Albarian 2010

A. Albarian, 'De l'Impératif de la Liberté (Pre)Contractuelle dans le Contentieux de la Rupture des Pourparlers Précontractuels' (2010) 2010 *International Business Law Journal* 252–271

Albiges/Dumont-Lefrand 2011

Ch. Albiges and P. Dumont-Lefrand, *Droit des Sûretés* (Paris: Dalloz, 2011)

Allen 2000

D. Allen, 'The Gentleman's Agreement in Legal Theory and in Modern Practice' (2000) 29 *Anglo-American Law Review* 204–227

Andrews 2013a

N.H. Andrews, 'Mediation Agreements: Time for a More Creative Approach by the English Courts' (2013) 18 *Uniform Law Review* 6–16

Andrews 2013b

N.H. Andrews, *Andrews on Civil Processes* (Cambridge: Intersentia, 2013)

Andrews 2015

N.H. Andrews, *Contract Law*, 2nd ed. (Cambridge: Cambridge University Press, 2015)

Andrews 2016

N.H. Andrews, *Contract Rules* (Cambridge: Intersentia, 2016)

Arnaud 1969

A.-J. Arnaud, *Les Origines Doctrinales du Code Civil Français* (Paris: L.G.D.J., 1969)

Arrighetti/Bachmann/Deakin 1997

A. Arrighetti, R. Bachmann and S. Deakin, 'Contract law, Social Norms and Inter-firm Cooperation' (1997) 21 *Cambridge Journal of Economics* 171–195

Atiyah 1979
P.S. Atiyah, *The Rise and Fall of Freedom of Contract* (Oxford: Clarendon, 1979)

Atiyah/Smith 2005
S. Smith (ed.), *Atiyah's Introduction to the Law of Contract*, 6th ed. (Oxford: Clarendon Press, 2006)

Aubert 2005
J.-L. Aubert, 'Quelques Remarques sur la Faute de l'Appauvri dans l'Enrichissement sans Cause', in *Études Offertes à Jacques Dupichot: Liber Amicorum* (Bruxelles, Bruylant, 2004) p. 2

Audit 1990
B. Audit, *La Vente Internationale de Marchandises: Convention des Nations-Unies du 11 avril 1980* (Paris: L.G.D.J, 1990)

Ayres 2012
I. Ayres and G. Klass; with E.J. Murphy and R.E. Speidel (eds.), *Studies in Contract Law*, 8th ed. (New York: Foundation Press, 2012)

B

Asser/Van den Berg 7-VI 2013
M.A.M.C. Van Den Berg, *Mr. C. Assers Handleiding tot de Beoefening van het Nederlands Burgerlijk Recht. 7. Bijzondere Overeenkomsten. Deel VI. Aanneming van Werk* (Deventer: Kluwer, 2013)

Bac 2005
A. Bac, 'La Position de la Fédération Bancaire Française sur le Projet de Réforme des Sûretés' (2005) *Droit et Patrimoine* 98 ff.

Baloch 2009
T.A. Baloch, *Unjust Enrichment and Contract* (Oxford; Portland, OR: Hart, 2009)

Bant/Bryan 2015
E. Bant and M. Bryan, 'Fact, Future and Fiction: Risk and Reasonable Reliance in Estoppel' (2015) 35 *Oxford Journal of Legal Studies* 427–452

Von Bar 2000
Ch. von Bar, 'A new Jus Commune Europaeum and the Importance of the Common Law', in B. Markesinis (ed.), *The Clifford Chance Millenium Lecures: The Coming Together of the Common Law and the Civil Law* (Oxford: Hart, 2000)

Von Bar 2010
Ch. Von Bar [et. al.], 'Introduction' in Ch. von Bar and E. Clive (eds.), *Principles, Definitions and Model Rules of European Private Law: Draft Common Frame of Reference (DCFR)* (Oxford: Oxford University Press, 2010) p. 1

Von Bar/Clive 2010
Ch. von Bar and E. Clive (eds.), *Principles, Definitions and Model Rules of European Private Law: Draft Common Frame of Reference (DCFR)* (Oxford: Oxford University Press, 2010)

Von Bar/Clive/Schulte-Nölke 2008
Ch. von Bar, E. Clive and H. Schulte-Nölke (eds.), *Principles, Definitions and Model Rules of European Private Law Draft Common Frame of Reference (DCFR) Outline Edition* (München: Sellier European Law Publishers, 2008)

Von Bar/Drobnig 2004
Ch. von Bar and U. Drobnig (eds.), *The Interaction of Contract Law and Tort and Property Law in Europe: A Comparative Study* (München: Sellier European Law Publishers, 2004)

Von Bar/Swann 2010
Ch. von Bar and S. Swann, *Unjustified Enrichment (PEL Unj. Enr.)* (München: Sellier European Law Publishers; Brussels: Bruylant; Berne: Stämpfli, 2010)

Barnes 2008
W. Barnes, 'The French Subjective Theory of Contracts: Separating Rhetoric from Reality' (2008) 83 *Tulane Law Review* 359–393

Barnett 2010
R.E. Barnett, *The Oxford Introductions to U.S. Law: Contracts* (Oxford N.Y.: Oxford University Press, 2010)

Barnett/Becker 1987
R.E. Barnett and M.E. Becker, 'Beyond Reliance: Promissory Estoppel, Contract Formalities, and Misrepresentations' (1987) 15 *Hofstra Law Review* 443–497

Barré 1995
X. Barré, *La Lettre d'Intention: Technique Contractuelle et Pratique Bancaire* (Paris: Economica, 1995)

Basedow 2003
J. Basedow, 'Worldwide Harmonisation of Private Law and Regional Economic Integration – General Report' (2003) 8 *Uniform Law Review* 31–49

Basedow 2007
J. Basedow, 'Lex Mercatoria and the Private International Law of Contracts in Economic Perspective' (2007) 12 *Uniform Law Review* 697–714

Beale 2005
H.G. Beale, 'General Clauses and Specific Rules in the Principles of European Contract Law: The "Good Faith" Clause', in S. Grundmann and D. Mazeaud (eds.), *General Clauses and Standards in European Contract Law: Comparative Law, EC Law and Contract Law Codification* (The Hague: Kluwer Law International, 2005) p. 205

Beale 2008
H.G. Beale, 'The Nature and Purposes of the Common Frame of Reference' (2008) 14 *Juridica International* 10–17

Beale 2010
H.G. Beale [et. al.], *Cases, Materials and Text on Contract Law*, 2nd ed. (Oxford; Portland, OR: Hart, 2010)

Beale 2010
H.G. Beale [et. al.], *Cases, Materials and Text on Contract Law*, 2nd ed. (Oxford; Portland, OR: Hart, 2010)

Beale 2013
H.G. Beale, 'Characteristics of Contract Laws and the European Optional Instrument', in H. Eidenmüller (ed.), *Regulatory Competition in Contract Law and Dispute Resolution* (München: Beck, 2013) p. 313

Beale/Dugdale 1975
H.G. Beale and T. Dugdale, 'Contracts between Businessmen: Planning and the Use of Contractual Remedies' (1975) 2 *British Journal of Law and Society* 45–60

Beatson/Friedmann 1995
J. Beatson and D. Friedmann (eds.), *Good Faith and Fault in Contract Law* (Oxford: Clarendon Press, 1995)

Beatson/Zimmermann 2004
J. Beatson and R. Zimmermann (eds.), *Jurists Uprooted: German-speaking Émigré Lawyers in Twentieth-century Britain* (Oxford: Oxford University Press, 2004)

Bebchuk/Ben-Shahar 2001
L.A. Bebchuk and O. Ben-Shahar, 'Precontractual Reliance' (2001) 30 *Journal of Legal Studies* 423

Beever 2009
A. Beever, 'Agreements, Mistakes, and Contract Formation' (2009) 20 *King's Law Journal* 21–51

Beignier 1995
B. Beignier, *L'Honneur et le Droit* (Paris: L.G.D.J, 1995)

Beignier 1998
B. Beignier, 'La Conduite des Négociations' (1998) *Revue Trimestrielle de Droit Commercial* 463–470

Benedict 2013
J. Benedict, 'Die Culpa in Contrahendo im IPR und IZPR', in O. Deinert (ed.), *Internationales Recht im Wandel: Symposium für Peter Winkler von Mohrenfels* (Baden-Baden: Nomos, 2013) p. 19

Ben-Shahar 2010
O. Ben-Shahar, 'Pre-Closing Liability' (2010) *The University of Chicago Law Review* 977–995

Berg 2003
A. Berg, 'Promises to Negotiate in Good Faith' (2003) 119 *Law Quarterly Review* 357–363

Van den Berg 1990
M.A.M.C. van den Berg, *Samenwerkingsvormen in de Bouw* (Deventer: Kluwer 1990)

Berger 2010
K.P. Berger, *The Creeping Codification of the New Lex Mercatoria* 2nd ed. (Austin, TX: Wolters Kluwer, Law & Business, 2010)

Berman/Dasser 1990
H.J. Berman and F.J. Dasser, 'The "New" Law Merchant and the "Old": Sources, Content, and Legitimacy', in T.E. Carbonneau (ed.), *Lex Mercatoria and Arbitratio: A Discussion of the New Law Merchant* (Dobbs Ferry, N.Y.: Transnational Juris Publications, 1990) p. 21

Bernheim-Desvaux 2015
S. Bernheim-Desvaux, 'Les Négociations', in M. Latina and G. Chantepie (eds.) *Supplément au Code civil 2016 Édition Limitée - Livret sur le Projet de Réforme du Droit des Obligations* (Paris: Dalloz, 2015) p. 8

Bernstein/Zekoll 1998
H. Bernstein and J. Zekoll, 'The Gentleman's Agreement in Legal Theory and in Modern Practice: United States' (1998) 46 *American Journal of Comparative Law* 87

Van Beukering-Rosmuller 2004
E.J.M. van Beukering-Rosmuller, 'De Inschakeling van een Mediator bij het Rechterlijk Bevel tot Dooronderhandelen bij Afgebroken Contractonderhandelingen: Een Nieuwe Loot aan de ADR-stam?' (2004) 4 *Tijdschrift voor Mediation* 82–88

De Boer 2011
D. de Boer, 'De Verplichting tot Dooronderhandelen', in W.H. van Boom, J.H. van Dam - Lely and S.D. Lindenbergh (eds.), *Rake Remedies: Opstellen over Handhaving van Rechten, Naleving van Plichten en Sanctionering van Verkeerd Gedrag in het Privaatrecht* (Den Haag: Boom Juridische Uitgevers, 2011) p. 105
http://ec.europa.eu/justice/policies/civil/docs/dcfr_outline_edition_en.pdf

Van Bijnen 2005
R.H.J. van Bijnen, *Aanvullend Contractenrecht*, diss. Tilburg 2005 https://pure.uvt.nl/portal/files/682318/168372.pdf

Birks 2005
P. Birks, *Unjust Enrichment*, 2nd ed. (Oxford: Oxford University Press, 2005)

Bix 2010
B. Bix, 'Consent in Contract Law', in F.G. Miller and A. Wertheimer (eds.), *The Ethics of Consent: Theory and Practice* (Oxford: Oxford University Press, 2010) p. 251

Blanchard 2008
P. Blanchard, 'Offer and Acceptance in International Contract Negotiation: a Comparative Study' (2008) 2008 *International Business Law Journal* 3-27

Blei Weissmann 2013
I.Y.G. Blei Weissmann, 'Precontractuele Fase bij: Burgerlijk Wetboek Boek 6, Artikel 217 [Aanbod en Aanvaarding]', in C.J.H. Brunner and E.H. Hondius (eds.), *Groene Serie Verbintenissenrecht* (Deventer: Kluwer, since 1994, loose-leaf, last update in 2013)

Boele-Woelki 2010
K. Boele-Woelki, *Unifying and Harmonizing Substantive Law and the Role of Conflict of Laws* (Leiden: Nijhoff, 2010)

Van Bochove 2013
L.M. van Bochove, *Betrokkenheid van Derden bij Contractbreuk* (Oisterwijk: Wolf Legal Publishers, 2013)

Boismain 2005
C. Boismain, *Les Contrats Relationnels* (Aix-Marseille: PUAM, 2005)

Bollen 2004
C. Bollen, 'Afbreken van Onderhandelingen: de Drie Mythes van Plas/Valburg. Van Drie Fasen naar Twee Stadia in het Onderhandelingsproces' (2004) 6596 *Weekblad voor Privaatrecht, Notariaat en Registratie* 857–866

Bonell 1987
M.J. Bonell, 'Article 7 Interpretation of the Convention', in C.M. Bianca and M.J. Bonell, *Commentary on the International Sales Law: The 1980 Vienna Sales Convention* (Milano: Giuffrè, 1987) p. 65

Bonell 1990
M.J. Bonell 'Formation of Contracts and Precontractual Liability under the Vienna Convention on International Sale of Goods', in *International Chamber of Commerce. Formation of Contracts and Precontractual Liability* (Paris: ICC Publishing, 1990) p. 157

Bonell 1990
M.J. Bonell, 'Vertragsverhandlungen und *Culpa in Contrahendo* nach dem Wiener Kaufrechtsübereinkommen' (1990) 36 *Recht der Internationalen Wirtschaft* 693–702 *http://tldb.uni-koeln.de/php/pub_show_document.php?pubdocid=119600*

Bonell 1992
M.J. Bonell, 'Unification of Law by Non-Legislative Means: The UNIDROIT Draft Principles for International Commercial Contracts' (1992) 40 *The American Journal of Comparative Law* 617–633

Bonell 1996
M.J. Bonell, 'The UNIDROIT Principles of International Commercial Contracts and CISG – Alternatives or Complementary Instruments?' (1996) 1 *Uniform Law Review* 26–39

Bonell 2005
M.J. Bonell, *An International Restatement of Contract Law*, 3rd ed. (Ardsley, NY: Transnational Publishers, 2005)

Bonell 2006
M.J. Bonell (Ed.), *The UNIDROIT Principles in Practice: Caselaw and Bibliography on the UNIDROIT Principles of Commercial Contracts*, 2nd ed. (Ardsley, New York: Transnational Publishers, 2006)

Bonell 2007
M.J. Bonell, 'The UNIDROIT Principles a Decade After their Appearance: What Have They Achieved and What Are Their Prospects for the Future?', in E. Cashin Ritaine and E. Lein (eds.), *The UNIDROIT Principles 2004: Their Impact on Contractual Practice, Jurisprudence and Codification. Reports of the ISDC Colloquium (8/9 June 2006)* (Zürich: Schulthess, 2007) p. 259

Bonell/Peleggi 2004

M.J. Bonell and R. Peleggi, 'UNIDROIT Principles of International Commercial Contracts and Principles of European Contract Law: A Synoptical Table' (2004) 9 *Uniform Law Review* 315–396

Bonell/Peleggi 2009

M.J. Bonell and R. Peleggi, 'UNIDROIT Principles of International Commercial Contracts and Draft Common Frame of Reference: A Synoptical Table' (2009) 14 *Uniform Law Review* 437–554

Van Boom/Giesen/Verheij 2008

W.H. van Boom, I. Giesen and A.J. Verheij (eds.), *Gedrag en Privaatrecht: Over Gedragspresumpties en Gedragseffecten bij Privaatrechtelijke Leerstukken* (Den Haag: Boom Juridische Uitgevers, 2008)

Van Boom/Giesen/Verheij 2013

W.H. van Boom, I. Giesen and A. J. Verheij (eds.), *Capita Civilologie: Handboek Empirie en Privaatrecht*, 2nd ed. (Den Haag: Boom Juridische Uitgevers, 2013)

Van Boom/Lindenbergh 2009

W.H. van Boom and S.D. Lindenbergh, 'Effectenlease: Dwaling, Zorgplicht en Schadevergoeding' (2010) 2010 *Ars Aequi* 188–196

Van Boom/Van Dam-Lely/Lindenbergh 2011

W.H. Van Boom, J.H. van Dam-Lely and S.D. Lindenbergh (eds.), 'Over Rake Remedies: Handhaving van Rechten, Naleving van Plichten en Sanctionering van Verkeerd Gedrag', in W.H. van Boom, J.H. van Dam - Lely and S.D. Lindenbergh (eds.), *Rake Remedies: Opstellen over Handhaving van Rechten, Naleving van Plichten en Sanctionering van Verkeerd Gedrag in het Privaatrecht* (Den Haag: Boom Juridische Uitgevers, 2011) p. 1

Born 2014

G.B. Born, *International Commercial Arbitration*, 2nd ed. (Alphen aan den Rijn: Kluwer Law International, 2014)

Bortolotti 2014

F. Bortolotti, 'The UNIDROIT Principles as a Basis for Alternative Choice-of-Law Clauses, with Particular Reference to the ICC Model Contracts' (2014) 19 *Uniform Law Review* 542–549

Braucher/Kidwell/Whitford 2013

J. Braucher, J. Kidwell and W.C. Whitford (eds.), *Revisiting the Contracts Scholarship of Stewart Macaulay: On the Empirical and the Lyrical* (Oxford: Hart, 2013)

Bridgeman/Goldberg 2012

C. Bridgeman and J.C.P. Goldberg, 'Do Promises Distinguish Contract from Tort?' (2012) 45 *Suffolk University Law Review* 873–895

Brown/Marriott 2011

H. Brown and A. Marriott, *ADR Principles and Practice*, 3rd ed. (London: Sweet and Maxwell, 2011)

Brownsword 1997
R. Brownsword, 'Contracts, Co-operation, and Good Faith: The Movement from Static to Dynamic Market-Individualism', in S. Deakin and J. Michie (eds.), *Contracts, Co-operation, and Competition: Studies in Economics, Management, and Law* (Oxford: Oxford University Press, 1997) p. 255

Brownsword 2006
R. Brownsword, *Contract Law: Themes for the Twenty-first Century*, 2nd ed. (Oxford: Oxford University Press, 2006)

Brownsword 2013
R. Brownsword, 'Contract in a Networked World', in L.A. DiMatteo [et. al.] (eds.), *Commercial Contract Law: Transatlantic Perspectives* (New York, NY: Cambridge University Press, 2013) p. 116

Brunner 1984
C.J.H. Brunner, *Beginselen van Samenloop*, 2nd ed. (Arnhem: Gouda Quint, 1984)

Burgard 2011
M. Burgard, 'Obligation de se Renseigner' (2011) *Petites Affiches*, 28 septembre 2011 n° 193, p. 7

Burrows 2011
A.S. Burrows, *The Law of Restitution*, 3rd ed. (Oxford: Oxford University Press, 2011)

Burrows 2015
A.S. Burrows (ed.), *Principles of the English Law of Obligations* (Oxford, UK: Oxford University Press, 2015)

Burrows/McKendrick/Edelman 2007
A.S. Burrows, E. McKendrick and J. Edelman, *Cases and Materials on the Law of Restitution*, 2nd ed. (Oxford: Oxford University Press, 2006)

Burrows/Peel 2010
A. Burrows and E. Peel (eds.), *Contract Formation and Parties* (Oxford: Oxford University Press, 2010)

Burton 2009
S.J. Burton, *Elements of Contract Interpretation* (Oxford: Oxford University Press, 2009)

Burton/Andersen 1995
S.J. Burton and E.G. Andersen, *Contractual Good Faith: Formation, Performance, Breach, Enforcement* (Boston: Little, Brown, 1995)

Busch 2008
D. Busch, 'The Principles of European Contract Law before the Supreme Court of the Netherlands: On the Influence of the PECL in Dutch Legal Practice' (2008) 16 *Zeitschrift für Europäisches Privatrecht* 549–562

C

Cafaggi 2011a

F. Cafaggi, 'New Foundations of Transnational Private Regulation', in C. Scott, F. Cafaggi and L. Senden (eds.), 'The Challenge of Transnational Private Regulation: Conceptual and Constitutional Debates' (2011) 38 *Journal of law and society* 20–29

Cafaggi 2011b

F. Cafaggi, 'Private Regulation in European Private Law' in A.S. Hartkamp [et. al.] (eds.), *Towards a European Civil Code*, 4th ed. (Alphen aan den Rijn: Kluwer Law International; Nijmegen: Ars Aequi Libri, 2011) p. 91

Calamari/Perillo 2009

J.M. Perillo (ed.), *Calamari and Perillo on Contracts*, 6th ed. (St. Paul, MN: West, 2009)

Campbell 2001

D. Campbell (ed.), *The Relational Theory of Contract: Selected Works of Ian Macneil* (London: Sweet & Maxwell, 2001)

Campbell 2014

D. Campbell, 'Good Faith and the Ubiquity of the 'Relational' Contract' (2014) 77 *The Modern Law Review* 475–492

Capecchi 2004

G. Capecchi, 'Nature and Enforceability of a Letter of Intent under Italian law' (2004) 2004 *International Business Law Journal* 151–160

Carbonnier 2004

J. Carbonnier 'Le Code Civil', in *Le Code Civil 1804-2004: Livre du Bicentenaire* (Paris: Dalloz LexisNexis Litec, 2004) p. 17

Carducci 2012

G. Carducci, 'The Arbitration Reform in France: Domestic and International Arbitration Law' (2012) 28 *Arbitration International* 125–157

Cartwright 2009a

J. Cartwright, 'Negotiation and Renegotiation: An English perspective', in J. Cartwright and S. Wogenauer, S. Whittaker (eds.), *Reforming the French Law of Obligations. Comparative Reflections on the Avant-projet de Réforme du Droit des Obligations et de la Prescription ('the Avant-projet Catala')* (Oxford: Hart, 2009), p. 51

Cartwright 2009b

J. Cartwright, 'The English Law of Contract, Time for Review?' (2009) 17 *European Review of Private Law* 155–175

Cartwright 2010

J. Cartwright, 'Liability in Tort for Pre-Contractual Non-Disclosure', in A. Burrows and E. Peel (eds.), *Contract Formation and Parties* (Oxford: Oxford University Press, 2010) p. 137

Cartwright 2012
J. Cartwright, *Misrepresentation, Mistake and Non-Disclosure*, 3rd ed. (London: Sweet & Maxwell, 2012)

Cartwright/Hesselink 2008
J. Cartwright and M. Hesselink, *Precontractual Liability in European Private Law* (Cambridge: Cambridge University Press, 2008)

Cashin Ritaine/Lein 2007
E. Cashin Ritaine and E. Lein (eds.), *The UNIDROIT Principles 2004: Their Impact on Contractual Practice, Jurisprudence and Codification. Reports of the ISDC Colloquium (8/9 June 2006)* (Zürich: Schulthess, 2007)

Castelijns/Janssen 2011
D.D. Castelijns and M.A.J.G. Janssen, 'Contractuele Beperking van Aansprakelijkheid bij Afgebroken Onderhandelingen' (2011) 7 *Tijdschrift Overeenkomst in de Rechtspraktijk* 29–32

Castermans 1994
A.G. Castermans, 'Walford v Miles' (1994) 1994 *European Review of Private Law* 290–295

Castermans 2012
A.G. Castermans, 'Partijautonomie Tussen Contract en Onrechtmatige Daad' (2012) 61 *Ars Aequi* 859-868

Catala 2005
P. Catala, '*Avant-Projet de Réforme du Droit des Obligations et de la Prescription* (Paris: Documentation Française, 2006) English translation by J. Cartwright and S. Whittaker available at: www.justice.gouv.fr/art_pix/rapportcatatla0905-anglais.pdf

Chao-Duivis 2012
M.A.B. Chao-Duivis, *Het Bouwteam Model: Een Studie naar de Juridische Vormgeving en het Functioneren in de Praktijk* (Den Haag: IBR, Stichting Instituut voor Bouwrecht, 2012)

Chappuis 2014
C. Chappuis, 'The Significance of the UNIDROIT Principles for International Contract Practice', in M. Fontaine and D. Philippe (eds.), *Contrats Internationaux et Arbitrage = International Contracts and Arbitration* (Bruxelles: Larcier, 2014) p. 29

Chen-Wishart 2009
M. Chen-Wishart, 'Contractual Mistake, Intention in Formation and Vitiation: The Oxymoron in *Smith* v. *Hughes*', in J.W. Neyers, R. Bronaugh and S.G.A. Pitel. (eds.), *Exploring Contract Law* (Oxford; Portland, Or.: Hart Publishing, 2009) p. 341

Chitty on Contracts 2015
H.G. Beale [et. al.] (eds.), *Chitty on Contracts*, Volume I, 32nd ed. (London: Sweet & Maxwell, 2015)

Clark 1933
Ch.E. Clark, 'The Restatement of the Law of Contracts' (1933) 42 *Yale Law Journal* 643–667

Clerk & Lindsell on Torts 2014
M.A. Jones (ed.), J.F. Clerk and W.H.B. Lindsell, *Clerk & Lindsell on Torts*, 21st ed. (London: Sweet & Maxwell, 2014)

Clive 2008
E. Clive, 'European Initiatives (CFR) and Reform of Civil Law in New Member States: Differences between the Draft Common Frame of Reference and the Principles of European Contract Law' (2008) 14 *Juridica International* 18–26

Coetzee 2015
J. Coetzee, 'The Role and Function of Trade Usage in Modern International Sales Law' 20 *Uniform Law Review* 243–270

Cohen 2009
G.M. Cohen, 'The Fault Lies Within our Contract Law' (2009) 107 *Michigan Law Review* 1445–1460

Collins 2008
H. Collins, Book review 'DCFR Interim Outline Edition' (2009) 71 *Modern Law Review* 840–844

De Coninck 2002
B. De Coninck, 'Le Droit Commun de la Rupture des Négociations précontractuelles', in M. Fontaine (ed.), *Le Processus de Formation du Contrat: Contributions Comparatives et Interdisciplinaires à l'Harmonisation du Droit Européen* (Bruxelles:, Paris: Bruylant, L.G.D.J., 2002) p. 17

Cordero Moss 2007a
G. Cordero Moss, 'The Function of Letters of Intent and their Recognition in Modern Legal Systems', in R. Schulze (ed.), *New Features in Contract Law* (München: Sellier European Law Publishers, 2007) p. 139

Cordero Moss 2007b
G. Cordero Moss, 'Harmonized Contract Clauses in Different Business Cultures', in Th. Wilhelmsson, E. Paunio and A. Pohjolainen (eds.), *Private Law and the Many Cultures of Europe* (Alphen aan den Rijn: Kluwer Law International; Biggleswade: Turpin Distribution Services, 2007) p. 221

Cornu 2004
G. Cornu, 'Réflexions en Attendant le Tricentenaire', in *Le Code Civil 1804–2004: Livre du Bicentenaire* (Paris: Dalloz LexisNexis Litec, 2004) p. 709

Courdier-Cuisinier 2006
A.-S. Courdier-Cuisinier, *Le Solidarisme Contractuel* (Paris: LexisNexis-Litec, 2006)

Couret/Dondero 2012
A. Couret and B. Dondero, 'The Breaking Off of Negotiations in M&A Operations: Comparative Approach' (2012) 23 *European Business Law Review* 347–373

Craswell 2006
R. Craswell, 'Taking Information Seriously: Misrepresentation and Nondisclosure in Contract Law and Elsewhere' (2006) 92 *Virginia Law Review* 565–632

Cravetto/Pasa 2011
Ch. Cravetto and B. Pasa, 'The "Non-sense" of Pre-contractual Information Duties in Case of Non-concluded Contracts' (2011) 19 *European Review of Private Law*, 759–785

Cross/Harris 1991
R. Cross and J. Harris, *Precedent in English Law*, 4th ed. (Oxford: Clarendon Press, 1991)

De Cruz 2007
P. de Cruz, *Comparative Law in a Changing World*, 3rd ed. (London: Routledge-Cavendish, 2007)

Cuniberti 2014
G. Cuniberti, 'The International Market for Contracts: The Most Attractive Contract Laws' (2014) 34 *Northwestern Journal of International Law & Business* 455–517

Curran 1998
V.G. Curran, 'Cultural Immersion, Difference and Categories in U. S. Comparative Law' (1998) 46 *The American Journal of Comparative Law* 43–92

D

Dalhuisen 2013
J.H. Dalhuisen, *Dalhuisen on Transnational Comparative, Commercial, Financial and Trade Law. Volume 1: Introduction – The new "Lex Mercatoria" and its sources*, 5th ed. (Oxford: Hart, 2013)

Dannemann 2012
G. Dannemann, 'Contracts and other Juridical Acts in the DCFR', in V. Sagaert, M.E. Storme and E. Terryn, *The Draft Common Frame of Reference: National and Comparative Perspectives* (Cambridge: Intersentia, 2012) p. 9

Dannemann/Vogenauer 2013
G. Dannemann and S. Vogenauer (eds.), *The Common European Sales Law in Context: Interactions with English and German Law* (Oxford: Oxford University Press, 2013)

David 1988
C. Jauffret-Spinosi (ed.), R. David, *Les Grands Systèmes de Droit Contemporains*, 9th ed. (Paris: Dalloz, 1988)

David/Brierley1968
R. David and J.E.C. Brierley, *Major Legal Systems in the World Today: An Introduction to the Comparative Study of Law* (London: Stevens, 1968)

Davies 2010
P.S. Davies, 'Anticipated Contracts: Room for Agreement' (2010) 69 *Cambridge Law Journal* 467–475

Dawson 1981
J.P. Dawson, 'Restitution without Enrichment' (1981) 61 *Boston University Law Review* 563–622

De Ly 1992
F.J.M. De Ly, *International Business Law and Lex Mercatoria* (Amsterdam: North-Holland, 1992)

De Ly 2001
F.J.M. De Ly, 'Lex Mercatoria (New Law Merchant): Globalisation and International Self-regulation', in R.P. Appelbaum, W.L. Festiner and V. Gessner (eds.), *Rules and Networks. The Legal Culture of Global Business Transactions* (Oxford: Hart Publishing, 2001), p. 159

De Ly 2012
F.J.M. De Ly, 'De Facto Harmonization by Means of Party Autonomy and Model Contract Clauses', in M.M. Fogt (ed.), *Unification and Harmonization of International Commercial Law: Interaction or Deharmonization?* (Alphen aan den Rijn: Kluwer Law International, 2012) p. 151

Deelen 1984
J.E.J.Th. Deelen, *I.P.R. en de Afgebroken Onderhandelingen* (Deventer: Kluwer, 1984)

Den Tonkelaar 2009
J.D.A. den Tonkelaar, 'Artikel 213 Boek 6 BW', in C.J.H. Brunner and E.H. Hondius (eds.), *Groene Serie Verbintenissenrecht* (Deventer: Kluwer since 1994, loose-leaf, last update in 2009)

Dennis 2014
M.J. Dennis, 'Modernizing and Harmonizing International Contract law: The CISG and the Unidroit Principles Continue to Provide the Best Way Forward' (2014) 19 *Uniform Law Review* 114–151

Deshayes 2004
O. Deshayes, 'Le Dommage Précontractuel' (2004) *Revue Trimestrielle de Droit Commercial* 187–204

Deshayes 2008
O. Deshayes (ed.), *L'Avant-contrat: Actualité du Processus de Formation des Contrats* (Paris: Presses Universitaires de France, 2008)

Deshayes 2010
O. Deshayes, 'Le Dommage Réparable en cas de Rupture Brutale d'une Relation Commerciale Établie' (2010) 51 *Revue Lamy Droit des Affaires* p. 94

Desideri 1997
J.-P. Desideri, *La Préférence dans les Relations Contractuelles* (Aix-Marseille, PU Aix-Marseille, 1997)

Dickinson 2008
A. Dickinson, *The Rome II Regulation: The Law Applicable to Non-contractual Obligations* (Oxford: Oxford University Press, 2008)

DiMatteo 2002
L.A. DiMatteo, 'Contract Talk: Reviewing the Historical and Practical Significance of the Principles of European Contract Law' (2002) 43 *Harvard International Law Journal* 569–581

DiMatteo 2005
L.A. DiMatteo [et. al.], *International Sales Law: A Critical Analysis of CISG Jurisprudence* (Cambridge, New York, N.Y.: Cambridge University Press, 2005)

Dirix 1986
E. Dirix, 'Gentlemen's Agreements en Andere Afspraken met Onzekere Rechtsgevolgen, preadvies XXXII° Congres Vlaamse Juristenvereniging, Antwerpen' (1986) 86 *Rechtskundig Weekblad* 2119–2146

Dobbs 1993
D.B. Dobbs, *Dobbs Law of Remedies: Damages, Equity, Restitution*, 2nd ed. (St. Paul, Minn.: West Publishing Co., 1993)

Domeniconi 2013
A. Domeniconi, *Letter of Intent* (Zürich; Basel; Genf: Schulthess Verlag, 2013)

Dondero 2011
B. Dondero, 'La Valeur d'une Lettre d'Intention' (2011) *Recueil Dalloz* 2848–2852

Draetta 1988
U. Draetta, 'The Pennzoil Case and the Binding Effect of the Letters of Intent in the International Trade Practice' (1988) 1988 *International Business Law Journal* 155–172

Drago 2008
R. Drago, 'General introduction', in G.A. Bermann and E. Picard (eds.), *Introduction to French Law* (The Hague: Wolters Kluwer, 2008) p. xxix

Drion 1967
H. Drion, 'Precontractuele Verhoudingen naar Nederlands Recht. Preadvies voor de Vereniging voor de Vergelijkende Studie van het Recht van België en Nederland 1967/1968', in A.R. Bloembergen [et. al.] (compilation), *Geschriften van H. Drion* (Deventer: Kluwer, 1982) p. 231

Druckman 2011
D. Druckman, 'Frameworks, Cases, and Risk: Dupont's Legacy', in A. Colson (ed.), *Entrer en Négociation. Mélanges en l'Honneur de Christophe Dupont* (Bruxelles: Larcier, 2011) p. 141

Duffy 2006
A. Duffy, 'La Constitutionnalisation de la Liberté Contractuelle' (2006) 6 *Revue du Droit Public* 1569–1600

Duhl 2003
G.M. Duhl, 'Red Owl's Legacy' (2003) 87 *Marquette Law Review* 297–321

Van Dunné 1972
J.M. van Dunné, *Normatieve Uitleg van Rechtshandelingen: Een Onderzoek naar de Grondslagen van het Geldende Verbintenissenrecht* (Deventer: Kluwer, 1972)

Van Dunné 1990
J.M. van Dunné, 'The Prelude to Contract, the Threshold of Tort. The Law of Precontractual Dealings in the Netherlands', in E.H. Hondius and G.J.W. Steenhoff (eds.), *Netherlands Reports to the Thirteenth International Congress of Comparative Law, Montreal 1990* (The Hague: T.M.C. Asser Instituut, 1990) p. 71

Van Dunné 2004
J.M. van Dunné, *Verbintenissenrecht Deel 1 Contractenrecht*, 5th ed. (Deventer: Kluwer, 2004)

Dupont 1990
C. Dupont, *La Négociation. Conduite, Théorie, Applications*, 3rd ed. (Paris: Dalloz, 1990)

Dupont 2006
C. Dupont, *La Négociation Post-moderne, Bilan des Connaissances, Acquis et Lacunes, Perspectives* (Paris: Éditions Publibook, 2006)

Dupont 2011
C. Dupont, 'Coopérer pour s'Entendre ou s'Affronter', in A. Colson (ed.), *Entrer en Négociation. Mélanges en l'Honneur de Christophe Dupont* (Bruxelles: Larcier, 2011) p. 39

E

Eberhard 2005
S. Eberhard, *Les Sanctions de l'Inexécution du Contrat et les Principes UNIDROIT* (Lausanne: Centre du Droit de l'Entreprise de l'Université de Lausanne, 2005)

Edelman 2010
J. Edelman, 'Liability in Unjust Enrichment where a Contract Fails to Materialise', in A. Burrows and E. Peel (eds.), *Contract Formation and Parties* (Oxford: Oxford University Press, 2010) p. 159

Eidenmüller 2008
H. Eidenmüller [et. al.], 'The Common Frame of Reference for European Private Law - Policy Choices and Codification Problems' (2008) 28 *Oxford Journal of Legal Studies* 659–708

Eisenberg 2000
M.A. Eisenberg, 'The Emergence of Dynamic Contract Law' (2000) 88 *California Law Review* 1743–1814

Van Engelen 2010
S.M. van Engelen, 'In Hoeverre zijn Break Fees Toelaatbaar?' (2010) 5 *Tijdschrift voor de Ondernemingsrechtspraktijk* 178–183

Van Erp 2011
J.H.M. van Erp, 'The Pre-contractual Stage', in A.S. Hartkamp [et. al.] (eds.), *Towards a European Civil Code*, 4th ed. (Alphen aan den Rijn: Kluwer Law International; Nijmegen: Ars Aequi Libri, 2011) p. 493

F

Fabre-Magnan 1992
M. Fabre-Magnan, *De l'Obligation d'Information dans les Contrats: Essai d'une Théorie* (Paris: L.G.D.J., 1992)

Fabre-Magnan 2012
M. Fabre-Magnan, 'L'engagement du Promettant - Engagement au Contrat Préparatoire' (2012) 2012 *Revue des Contrats* 633 ff.

Fages 2008
B. Fages, 'De Bonnes Raisons Économiques de Rompre des Pourparlers Avancés' (2008) *Revue Trimestrielle de Droit Civil* 101 ff.

Fages 2008
B. Fages, 'Pre-contractual Duties in the Draft Common Frame of Reference – what Relevance for the Negotiation of Commercial Contracts?' (2008) *European Review of Contract Law* 4(3) 304–316

Fages 2011a
B. Fages, 'Étude 105 L'entrée en Pourparler', in B. Fages (ed.), *Lamy Droit du Contrat* (Paris: Wolters Kluwer France, 2012)

Fages 2011b
B. Fages, 'Étude 115 Les accords de pourparlers', in B. Fages (ed.), *Lamy Droit du Contrat* (Paris: Wolters Kluwer France, 2012)

Fages 2011c
B. Fages, 'Étude 117 La rupture des pourparlers', in B. Fages (ed.), *Lamy Droit du Contrat* (Paris: Wolters Kluwer France, 2012)

Fages 2011d
B. Fages, 'Étude 120 Le Pacte de Préférence', in B. Fages (ed.), *Lamy Droit du Contrat* (Paris: Wolters Kluwer France, 2012)

Fages 2011e
B. Fages, 'Étude 125 Les Promesses Unilatérales de Contrat', in B. Fages (ed.), *Lamy Droit du Contrat* (Paris: Wolters Kluwer France, 2012)

Fages 2011f
B. Fages, 'Étude 130 Les Promesses Synallagmatiques de contrat', in B. Fages (ed.), *Lamy Droit du Contrat* (Paris: Wolters Kluwer France, 2012)

Fages 2012
B. Fages (ed.), *Lamy Droit du Contrat* (Paris: Wolters Kluwer France, 2012)

Fages 2013
B. Fages, 'L'Annulation d'un Pacte de Préférence pour Indétermination du Prix' (2013) *Revue Trimestrielle de Droit Civil* 110 ff.

Fages 2014
B. Fages, 'La Promesse Unilatérale et le Pacte de Préférence dans le Projet d'Ordonnance de Réforme du Droit des Obligations' (2014) 240 *Droit et Patrimoine* 42 ff.

Fages 2015
B. Fages, 'Rapport Français – Le Processus de Formation du Contrat', in R. Schulze, G. Wicker, G. Mäsch and D. Mazeaud (eds.), *La Réforme du Droit des Obligations en France: 5èmes Journées Franco-Allemandes* (Paris: Société de Législation Comparée, 2015) p. 41

Faggella 1906
G. Faggella, 'Dei Periodi Precontrattuali e della loro Vera ed Esatta Costruzione Scientifica', in *Studi Giuridici in Onore di Carlo Fadda pel XXV Anno del Suo Insegnamento* (1906) p. 269

Farnsworth 1987
E.A. Farnsworth, 'Precontractual Liability and Preliminary Agreements: Fair Dealing and Failed Negotiations' (1987) 87*Columbia Law Review* 217–294

Farnsworth 1990a

E.A. Farnsworth, 'Developments in Contract Law During the 1980's: The Top Ten' (1990) 41 *Case Western Reserve Law Review* 203–230

Farnsworth 1990b

E.A. Farnsworth, 'General Report', in *International Chamber of Commerce. Formation of Contracts and Precontractual Liability* (Paris: ICC Publishing, 1990) p. 15

Farnsworth 1995

E.A. Farnsworth, 'Duties of Good Faith and Fair Dealing under the UNIDROIT Principles, Relevant International Conventions, and National Laws' (1995) 3*Tulane Journal of International and Comparative Law* 47–63

Farnsworth 1998

E.A. Farnsworth, 'The American Provenance of the Unidroit Principles' (1998) *Uniform Law Review* (April 1998) 3 (2–3): 397–403

Farnsworth 2004

E.A. Farnsworth, *Contracts*, 4th ed. (New York: Aspen Publishers, 2004)

Farnsworth 2006

E.A. Farnsworth, 'Comparative Contract Law', in M. Reimann and R. Zimmermann, *The Oxford Handbook of Comparative Law* (Oxford: Oxford University Press, 2006) p. 899

Farnsworth/Sheppard 2010

S. Sheppard (ed.), E.A. Farnsworth, *An Introduction to the Legal System of the United States*, 4th ed. (New York; Oxford: Oxford University Press, 2010)

Fauvarque-Cosson 2014

B. Fauvarque-Cosson, 'The French Contract Law Reform in a European Context' (2014) *ELTE Law Journal* 59–71

Fauvarque-Cosson 2015

B. Fauvarque-Cosson, 'Towards an Important Reform of the French Civil Code' (2015) 2015 *Montesquieu Law Review* 2–15

Fauvarque-Cosson/Mazeaud 2008

B. Fauvarque-Cosson and D. Mazeaud (eds.), *European Contract Law: Materials for a Common Frame of Reference: Terminology, Guiding Principles, Model Rules* (München: Sellier European Law Publishers, 2008)

Feinman 1990

J.M. Feinman, 'The Significance of Contract Theory' (1990) 58 *University of Cincinnati Law Review* 1283–1318

Felemegas 2001

J. Felemegas, 'Comparative Editorial Remarks on the Concept of Good Faith in the CISG and the PECL' (2001) 13 *Pace International Law Review* 399–406

Felemegas 2007
J. Felemegas (ed.), *An International Approach to the Interpretation of the United Nations Convention on Contracts for the International Sale of Goods (1980) as Uniform Sales Law* (Cambridge: Cambridge University Press, 2007)

Feltham/Hochberg/Leech 2004
P. Feltham, D. Hochberg and T. Leech (eds.), George Spencer Bower, *The Law Relating to Estoppel by Representation*, 4th ed. (London: Butterworths, 2004)

Ferrari 2004
F. Ferrari 'Interpretation of the Convention and Gap Filling: Article 7', in F. Ferrari, H.M. Flechtner and R.A. Brand, *The Draft UNCITRAL Digest and Beyond: Cases, Analysis and Unresolved Issues in the U.N. Sales Convention: Papers of the Pittsburgh Conference Organized by the Center of International Legal Education (CILE)* (London: Sweet & Maxwell; München: Sellier European Law Publishers, 2004)

Ferrari 2012
F. Ferrari, 'Offer and Acceptance "Inter Absentes"', in J.M. Smits (ed.), *Elgar Encyclopedia of Comparative Law*, 2nd ed. (Cheltenham: Elgar, 2012) p. 625

Fisher/Ury/Patton 2012
R. Fisher and W. Ury with B. Patton (ed.), *Getting to Yes: Negotiating an Agreement without Giving In*, 3rd ed. (London: RandomHouse Business Books, 2012)

Flechtner 1998
H.M. Flechtner, 'The Several Texts of the CISG in a Decentralized System: Observations on Translations, Reservations and Other Challenges to the Uniformity Principle in Article 7(1)' (1997–1998) 17 *Journal of Law and Commerce* 187–218

Fletcher/Mistelis/Cremona 2001
I.F. Fletcher, L. Mistelis and M. Cremona (eds.), *Foundations and Perspectives of International Trade Law* (London: Sweet & Maxwell, 2001)

Fogt 2014
M.M. Fogt, 'Contract Formation under the CISG: the Need for a Reform', in L.A. DiMatteo (ed.), *International Sales Law: A Global Challenge* (New York, NY: Cambridge University Press, 2014) p. 179

Fontaine 1977
M. Fontaine, 'Les Lettres d'Intention dans la Négociation des Contrats Internationaux' (1977) 3 *Droit et Pratique du Commerce International* 73–122

Fontaine 2000
M. Fontaine, 'Offre et Acceptation, Approche Dépassée du Processus de Formation des Contrats', in *Mélanges Offerts à Pierre Van Ommeslaghe* (Bruxelles: Bruylant, 2000) p. 115

Fontaine 2002
M. Fontaine (ed.), *Le Processus de Formation du Contrat: Contributions Comparatives et Interdisciplinaires à l'Harmonisation du Droit Européen* (Bruxelles, Paris: Bruylant, L.G.D.J., 2002)

Fontaine 2013
M. Fontaine, 'La Théorie de la Formation du Contrat et la Pratique du "Closing"', in *Liber Amicorum: Mélanges en l'Honneur de Camille Jauffret-Spinosi* (Paris: Dalloz, 2013) p. 361

Fontaine/De Ly 2009
M. Fontaine and F. De Ly, *Drafting International Contracts, An Analysis of Contract Clauses* (Ardsley, N.Y.: Transnational Publishers, 2009)

Fouchard 2007
P. Fouchard, *Écrits: Droit de l'Arbitrage, Droit du Commerce International* (Paris: Comité Français de l'Arbitrage, 2007)

François 2016
C. François, 'Table de Correspondance (Nouveaux Articles - Anciens Articles)' (2016) *Revue des Contrats Hors-série* 58–98

Fuller/Perdue 1936
L.L. Fuller and W.R. Perdue Jr., 'The Reliance Interest in Contract Damages' (1936) 46 *Yale Law Journal* 52–96 (part 1) and 373–420 (part 2)

Furmston 2010
M. Furmston, 'Letter of Intent', in A. Burrows and E. Peel (eds.), *Contract Formation and Parties* (Oxford: Oxford University Press, 2010) p. 17

Furmston/Norisada/Poole 1998
M. Furmston, T. Norisada and J. Poole, *Contract Formation and Letters of Intent: A Comparative Assessment* (Chichester: Wiley, 1998)

Furmston/Tolhurst 2010
M. Furmston and G.J. Tolhurst, *Contract Formation. Law and Practice* (Oxford, Oxford University Press, 2010)

G

Gaillard 2001
E. Gaillard, 'Transnational Law: A Legal System or a Method of Decision-making?', in K.P. Berger (ed.), *The practice of Transnational Law* (The Hague: Kluwer Law International) p. 53

Gaillard 2005
E. Gaillard, 'Thirty Years of Lex Mercatoria: Towards- the Selective Application of Transnational Rules' (2005) 10 *ICSID Review* 208–231

Gaillard/De Lapasse 2011
E. Gaillard and P. de Lapasse, 'Le Nouveau Droit Français de l'Arbitrage Interne et International' (2011) *Recueil Dalloz* 175–188

Ghestin 2007a
J. Ghestin, 'Les Dommages Réparables à la Suite de la Rupture Abusive des Pourparlers' (2007) *La Semaine Juridique Edition Générale* n° 22, 30 Mai 2007, I 157

Ghestin 2007b
J. Ghestin, 'La Responsabilité Délictuelle pour Rupture Abusive des Pourparlers (2007) *La Semaine Juridique Edition Générale* n° 20, 16 Mai 2007, I 155

Ghestin 2008
J. Ghestin, 'La Responsabilité Contractuelle pour Rupture des Pourparlers', in *Études Offertes à Geneviève Viney* (Paris: L.G.D.J., 2008) p. 455

Ghestin/Viney 2008
J. Ghestin and G. Viney, *Traité de Droit Civil. Introduction à la Responsabilité*, 3rd ed. (Paris: L.G.D.J, 2008)

Giliker 2002
P. Giliker, *Pre-contractual Liability in English and French Law* (The Hague: Kluwer Law International, 2002)

Gilmore/Collins 1995
R.K.L. Collins (ed.), G. Gilmore, *The Death of Contract* (Columbus: Ohio State University Press, 1995)

Gilson 2001
R.J. Gilson, 'Globalizing Corporate Governance: Convergence of Form or Function' (2001) 49 *The American journal of comparative law* 329–357

Ginestet 2006
C. Ginestet, 'Pacte de Préférence et Droit des Sociétés' (2006) 144 *Droit et Patrimoine* 62–67

Glenn 2012
H.P. Glenn, 'The Aims of Comparative Law', in J.M. Smits, *Elgar Encyclopedia of Comparative Law*, 2nd ed. (Cheltenham: Elgar, 2012) p. 65

Glenn 2014
H.P. Glenn, *Legal Traditions of the World: Sustainable Diversity in Law*, 5th ed. (Oxford: Oxford University Press, 2014)

Goderre 1997
D.M. Goderre, 'International Negotiations Gone Sour: Precontractual Liability" under the United Nations Sales Convention' (1997) 66 *University of Cincinnati Law Review* 257–281

Goff/Jones 2011
Ch. Mitchell, P. Mitchell and S. Watterson (eds.), R. Goff and G. Jones, *The Law of Unjust Enrichment*, 8th ed. (London: Sweet & Maxwell, 2007)

Goldman 1964
B. Goldman, 'Frontières du droit et "lex mercatoria"' (1964) IX *Archives de Philosophie du Droit* 177–192

Goldman 1986
B. Goldman, 'The Applicable Law: General Principles of Law – The *Lex Mercatoria*', in J.D.M. Lew (ed.), *Contemporary Problems in International Arbitration* (London: Centre for Commercial Law Studies, 1986) p. 113

Goode 1997
R.M. Goode, 'Usage and its Reception in Transnational Commercial Law' (1997) 46 *International and Comparative Law Quarterly* 1–36

Goode 2012
R.M. Goode [et. al.] (eds.), *Transnational Commercial law: International Instruments and Commentary*, 2nd ed. (Oxford: Oxford University Press, 2012)

Goode/Kronke/McKendrick 2015
R.M. Goode, H. Kronke and E. McKendrick, *Transnational Commercial Law: Text, Cases and Materials*, 2nd ed. (Oxford, UK: Oxford University Press, 2015)

Goode/McKendrick 2010
R.M. Goode, E. McKendrick, *Goode on Commercial Law*, 4th ed. (London: Penguin, 2010)

Gordley/von Mehren 2006
J. Goderley and A.T. von Mehren, *An Introduction to the Comparative Study of Private Law: Readings, Cases, Materials* (Cambridge: Cambridge University Press, 2006)

Gotanda 2004
J.Y. Gotanda, 'Recovering Lost Profits in International Disputes' (2004) 36 *Georgetown Journal of International Law* 61–112

Gotanda 2008
J.Y. Gotanda, 'Using the UNIDROIT Principles to Fill Gaps in the CISG', in D. Saidov and R. Cunnington (eds.), *Contract Damages: Domestic and International Perspectives* (Oxford, Hart Publishing, 2008) p. 107

Goudeket 1906
J. Goudeket, *Afspraken tot het Sluiten van Overeenkomsten: (Pacta de Contrahendo)* (Amsterdam: De Bussy, 1906)

Grosheide 1989
F.W. Grosheide, 'Naar een Juridisch Statuut Voor Internationale Intentieverklaringen? (Variaties op een Bekend Thema)', in B.E. Reinhartz, D. Kokkini-Iatridou and F.W. Grosheide (eds.), *Eenvormig en Vergelijkend Privaatrecht* (Lelystad: Koninklijke Vermande, 1989) p. 119

Grosheide 2004
F.W. Grosheide, 'The Gentleman's Agreement in Legal Theory and in Modern Practice: the Dutch Civil Law Perspective', in K. Boele-Woelki, F.W. Grosheide and E. Hondius (eds), *International Contract Law: 2003: Articles on Various Aspects of Transnational Contract Law* (Antwerp: Intersentia, 2004) p. 41

Guinchard/Debard 2015
S. Guinchard and T. Debard (eds.) *Lexique des Termes Juridiques*, 23th ed. (Paris: Dalloz, 2015)

H

De Hoon 2010
M.W. de Hoon, 'Investeren in Samenwerken: Wie Betaalt de Rekening voor niet Terugverdiende Kosten?', in M.A.B. Chao-Duivis (ed.), *Alleen Samen: Opstellen Aangeboden aan prof. mr.*

M.A.M.C. van den Berg ter Gelegenheid van zijn Afscheid als Hoogleraar aan de Universiteit van Tilburg (Den Haag: Stichting Instituut voor Bouwrecht, 2010)

Hage-Chahine 2012
N. Hage-Chahine, '"Culpa in contrahendo" in European Private International Law: Another Look at Article 12 of the Rome II Regulation' (2012) 32 *Northwestern Journal of International Law & Business* 451–540

Hall/Wright 2008
M.A. Hall and R.F. Wright, 'Systematic Content Analysis of Judicial Opinions' (2008) 95 *California Law Review* 63–122

Halpérin 2004
J.-L. Halpérin, 'Le Regard de l'Historien', in *Le Code Civil 1804–2004: Livre du Bicentenaire* (Paris: Dalloz LexisNexis Litec, 2004) p. 43

Hardenberg 1967
L.L. Hardenberg, 'De Onderhandeling. Enkele Beschouwing over Zgn. Precontractuele Verhouding' (1967) 4971 *Weekblad voor Privaatrecht, Notariaat en Registratie* 470

Hart 2009
D.K. Hart, 'Contract Formation and the Entrenchment of Power' (2009) 41 *Loyola University of Chicago Law Journal*, 175–220

Hartkamp 2005
A.S. Hartkamp, *Compendium van het Vermogensrecht voor de Rechtspraktijk*, 6th ed. (Deventer: Kluwer, 2005)

Hartkamp 2011
A.S. Hartkamp [et.al.], *Contract Law in the Netherlands*, 3rd ed. (Alphen aan den Rijn: Kluwer Law International, 2011)

Asser/Hartkamp and Sieburgh 6-III 2014
A.S. Hartkamp and C.H. Sieburgh, *Mr. C. Assers Handleiding tot de Beoefening van het Nederlands Burgerlijk Recht. 6. Verbintenissenrecht. Deel III. Algemeen Overeenkomstenrecht*, 14th ed. (Deventer: Kluwer, 2014)

Hartley 2015
T.C. Hartley, *International Commercial Litigation*, 2nd ed. (Cambridge: Cambridge University Press, 2015)

Hartlief 2005
T. Hartlief, 'Aansprakelijkheid ter Zake van Afgebroken Onderhandelingen: Terughoudendheid Troef' (2005) 54 *Ars Aequi* 1027–1034

Harvey/Schillig 2010
C. Harvey and M. Schillig, 'Conclusion of Contract', in G. Dannemann and S. Vogenauer (eds.), *The Common European Sales Law in Context: Interactions with English and German Law* (Oxford: Oxford University Press, 2013)

Hesselink 1992
M.W. Hesselink, 'De Schadevergoedingsplicht bij Afgebroken Onderhandelingen in het Licht van het Europese Privaatrecht' (1992) 6248 *Weekblad voor Privaatrecht, Notariaat en Registratie* 879–883, http://dare.uva.nl/record/1/423024

Hesselink 1999
M.W. Hesselink, *De Redelijkheid en Billijkheid in het Europese Privaatrecht* (Deventer: Kluwer, 1999)

Hesselink 2004
M.W. Hesselink, *Contractenrecht in Perspectief* (Den Haag: Boom Juridische uitgevers, 2004)

Hesselink 2011
M.W. Hesselink, 'The Concept of Good Faith', in A.S. Hartkamp [et. al.] (eds.), *Towards a European Civil Code*, 4th ed. (Alphen aan den Rijn: Kluwer Law International; Nijmegen: Ars Aequi Libri, 2011) p. 619

Heuzé 1992
V. Heuzé, *La Vente Internationale de Marchandises* (Paris: GLN Joly, 1992)

Hijma 2013
J. Hijma [et. al.], *Rechtshandeling en Overeenkomst*, 7th ed. (Deventer: Kluwer, 2013)

Hijma/Olthof 2014
J. Hijma and M.M. Olthof, *Compendium van het Nederlands Vermogensrecht*, 12th ed. (Deventer: Kluwer, 2014)

Hillman 1995
R.A. Hillman, 'Applying the United Nations Convention on Contracts for the International Sale of Goods: The Elusive Goal of Uniformity' (1995) *Cornell Review of the Convention on Contracts for the International Sale of Goods* 21–49

Holger 2000
J. Holger, *Der Letter of Intent* (Frankfurt am Main: Lang, 2000)

Holmes 1978
E.M. Holmes, 'Contextual Study of Commercial Good Faith: Good-Faith Disclosure in Contract Formation' (1978) 39 *University of Pittsburgh Law Review* 381–452

Holmes 1987
O.W. Holmes, 'The Path of the Law' (1987) 10 *Harvard Law Review* 457

Hondius 1991
E. Hondius (ed.), *Precontractual Liability: Reports to the XIIIth Congress, International Academy of Comparative Law, Montreal, Canada, 18–24 August 1990* (Deventer: Kluwer Law & Taxation Publishers, 1991)

Hondius 2004
E.H. Hondius, 'Pre-contractual Liability', in K. Boele-Woelki, F.W. Grosheide and E. Hondius (eds), *International Contract Law: 2003: Articles on Various Aspects of Transnational Contract Law* (Antwerp: Intersentia, 2004) p. 5

Hondius 2011

E. Hondius, 'Introduction', in A.S. Hartkamp [et. al.] (eds.), *Towards a European Civil Code*, 4th ed. (Alphen aan den Rijn: Kluwer Law International; Nijmegen: Ars Aequi Libri, 2011) p. 3

Honnold 1989

J.O. Honnold, *Documentary History of the Uniform Law for International Sales: The Studies, Deliberations, and Decisions that Led to the 1980 United Nations Convention with Introductions and Explanations* (Deventer: Kluwer Law and Taxation, 1989)

Honnold 1999

J.O. Honnold, *Uniform law for International Sales Under the 1980 United Nations Convention*, 3rd ed. (The Hague: Kluwer Law International, 1999)

Horn 1972

N. Horn, *Das Recht der Internationalen Anleihen* (Frankfurt/Main: Athenäum, 1972)

Hoskins 2014

H. Hoskins, 'Contractual Obligations to Negotiate in Good Faith: Faithfulness to the Agreed Common Purpose' (2014) 130 *Law Quarterly Review* 131–159

Huber/Mullis 2007

P. Huber and A. Mullis, *The CISG: A New Textbook for Students and Practitioners* (München: Sellier European Law Publishers, 2007)

Van Hooijdonk/Tjittes 2009

M. van Hooijdonk and R.J.P.L. Tjittes, 'Precontractuele Aansprakelijkheid bij Onderhandelen met een Voorbehoud', in B. Wessels and S.Y.Th. Meyer (eds.), *Bedrijfsovername*, 3rd ed. (Deventer: Kluwer, 2009) p. 71

Van Houtte 2014

H. van Houtte, 'Contract Negotiations and the UNIDROIT Principles' (2014) 19 *Uniform Law Review* 550–560

Von Hein 2012

J. von Hein, 'Culpa in Contrahendo', in J. Basedow, K.J. Hopt and R. Zimmermann; with A. Stier (eds.), *The Max Planck Encyclopedia of European Private Law, Volume II* (Oxford: Oxford University Press, 2012) p. 430

I

Von Ihering 1861

R. von Ihering, 'Culpa in Contrahendo oder Schadensersatz bei Nichtigen oder Nicht zur Perfection Gelangten Vertragen' (1861) *Jahrbücher für Dogmatik des Heutigen Römischen und Deutschen Privatrechts*, IV, 1

Illmer 2012

M. Illmer, 'Contract (Formation)', in J. Basedow, K.J. Hopt and R. Zimmermann, with Andreas Stier (eds.) *The Max Planck Encyclopedia of European Private Law* (Oxford: Oxford University Press, 2012) p. 378

J

Jambort 2007

S. Jambort, 'Les Lettres d'Intention Sont-Elles Mortes?' (2007) *Bulletin Joly Sociétés*, 01 juin 2007 n°6, p. 668

Jansen 2009

C.E.C. Jansen, *De Aanbestedingsovereenkoms: Aanbesteden in Verbintenisrechtelijk Perspectief. Preadvies voor de Nederlandse Vereniging voor Aanbestedingsrecht 2009* (Den Haag: Sdu Uitgevers, 2009)

Jansen 2010

N. Jansen, *The Making of Legal Authority: Non-legislative Codifications in Historical and Comparative perspective* (Oxford [etc.]: Oxford University Press, 2010)

Jansen 2012

K.J.O. Jansen, *Informatieplichten: over Kennis en Verantwoordelijkheid in Contractenrecht en Buitencontractueel Aansprakelijkheidsrecht* (Deventer: Kluwer, 2012)

Jansen/Zimmermann 2010

N. Jansen and R. Zimmermann, 'A European Civil Code in All but Name': Discussing the Nature and Purposes of the Draft Common Frame of Reference' (2010) 69 *Cambridge Law Journal* 98–112

Jarrosson 2006

Ch. Jarrosson, 'La Bonne Foi, Instrument de Moralisation des Relations Économiques Internationales', in *L'Éthique dans les Relations Économiques Internationales: En Hommage à Philippe Fouchard* (Paris: Pedone, 2006) p. 185

Jarrosson/Pellerin 2011

Ch. Jarrosson and J. Pellerin, 'Le Droit Français de l'Arbitrage Après le Décret du 13 Janvier 2011' (2011) *Revue de l'Arbitrage* 5–86

Jeffries 2012

B. Jeffries, 'Preliminary Negotiations or Binding Obligations? A Framework for determining the intent of the parties' (2012) 48 *Gonzaga Law Review* 1–60

Jobard-Bachellier 1995

M.-N. Jobard-Bachellier, 'Les Lettres d'Intention en Droit International Privé', in *Travaux du Comité Français de Droit International Privé, 1993–1994, 1994–1995* (Paris: Pedone, 1996) p. 125

Jourdain 1992

P. Jourdain, 'La bonne Foi dans la Formation du Contrat', in *La Bonne Foi: Travaux de l'Association Henri Capitant des Amis de la Culture Juridique Française*, n°43 (Paris: Litec, 1992) p. 121

K

Kahn 1961

P. Kahn, *La Vente Commerciale Internationale* (Paris: Sirey, 1961)

Kaplan 2010

M. Kaplan, *Commercieel Onderhandelen: Een Transdisciplinaire Aanpak*. Doctoral thesis Leiden University (2010) https://openaccess.leidenuniv.nl/handle/1887/16231

Kassis 1984
A. Kassis, *Théorie Générale des Usages du Commerce: Droit Comparé: Contrats et Arbitrage Internationaux: Lex Mercatoria* (Paris: Librairie Générale de Droit et de Jurisprudence, 1984)

Katz 1996
A. Katz 'When Should an Offer Stick? The Economics of Promissory Estoppel in Preliminary Negotiations' (1996) 105 *The Yale Law Journal* pp. 1249–1309

Keener 1893
W.A. Keener, *A Treatise on the Law of Quasi-contracts* (New York: Baker, Voorhis, 1893)

Keeton 1984
W.P. Keeton (ed.), *Prosser and Keeton on the Law of Torts*, 5th ed. (St. Paul, Minn.: West, 1984)

Keily 1999
T. Keily, 'Good Faith and the Vienna Convention on Contracts for the International Sale of Goods (CISG)' 3 *Vindobona Journal of International Commercial Law and Arbitration* (1999) 15.

Keller 2008
B. Keller, 'Reading the CISG in Favor of the Contract: "Favor Contractus"', in C.B. Andersen and U.G. Schroeter (eds.), *Sharing International Commercial Law across National Boundaries: Festschrift for Albert H. Kritzer on the Occasion of His Eightieth Birthday* (London: Wildy, Simmonds & Hill, 2008) p. 247

Kessedjian 2013
C. Kessedjian, *Droit du Commerce International* (Paris: Presses Universitaires de France, 2013)

Kessler/Fine 1964
F. Kessler and E. Fine, 'Culpa in Contrahendo, Bargaining in Good Faith, and Freedom of Contract: A Comparative Study' (1964) 77 *Harvard Law Review* 401–449

Kimball 2004
B.A. Kimball, 'The Langdell Problem: Historicizing the Century of Historiography, 1906–2000s' (2004) *22 Law and History Review* 277–337

Klass 2009
G. Klass, 'Intent to Contract' (2009) 95 *Virginia Law Review* 1437–1503

Klein 1988
A.R. Klein, 'Devil's Advocate: Salvaging the Letter of Intent' (1988) 37 *Emory Law Journal* 139–170

Klein/Bachechi 1994
J. Klein and C. Bachechi, 'Precontractual Liability and the Duty of Good Faith Negotiation in International Transactions' (1994) 17 *Houston Journal of International Law* 1–26

Kling/Nugent 2015
L.R. Kling and E. Nugent, *Negotiated Acquisitions of Companies, Subsidiaries and Divisions (Corporate Securities*, 24th ed. (New York: Law Journal Press 2015)

Van Klink/Taekema 2011
B. van Klink and S. Taekema, *Law and Method: Interdisciplinary Research into Law* (Tübingen: Mohr Siebeck, 2011)

De Kluiver 1992
H.-J. de Kluiver, *Onderhandelen en Privaatrecht* (Deventer: Kluwer, 1992)

De Kluiver 2003
H.-J. de Kluiver, 'Overnamecontracten, Letters of Intent en Garanties' (2003) 58 *Onderneming en Financiering* 36–45

De Kluiver/Schwarz 1998
H.-J. de Kluiver and C.A. Schwarz, 'Onderhandelen onder Voorbehoud in het Bijzonder met Rechtspersonen', in L.G. Eykman [et. al.], *Onderhandelen, Bemiddelen en Schikken*, 2nd ed. (Deventer: Kluwer, 1998) p. 101

Knapp 1969
Ch.L. Knapp, 'Enforcing the Contract to Bargain' (1969) 44 *New York University Law Review* 673–728

Knigge 2012
M. W. Knigge, *De Procesovereenkomst. Over de Vrijheid van Partijen het Civiele Proces Vorm te Geven* (Deventer: Kluwer, 2012)

Van Kogelenberg 2014
M. van Kogelenberg, 'Deliberate Breach of Contract and Consequences for Remedies: Exploration of a Neglected Area in the Law of Contract' (2014) 21 *Maastricht Journal of European and Comparative Law* 141–161

Kornet 2002
N. Kornet, 'Contract Formation in England, the Netherlands and the Principles of European Contract Law', in J.M. Smits and S. Stijns (eds.), *Totstandkoming van de Overeenkomst naar Belgisch en Nederlands Recht* (Antwerp: Intersentia, 2002) p. 33

Kornet 2010
N. Kornet, 'Evolving General Principles of (International) Commercial Contracts: the Unidroit Principles and "Favor contractus"', in I. Samoy (eds.), *Evolutie van de Basisbeginselen van het Contractenrecht* (Antwerp: Intersentia, 2010) p. 179

Korobkin 2002
R.B. Korobkin, 'Empirical Scholarship in Contract Law: Possibilities and Pitfalls' (2002) 2002 *University of Illinois Law Review* 1033–1066

Korobkin/Moffitt/Welsh 2004
R.B. Korobkin, M.L. Moffitt and N. Welsh 'The Law of Bargaining' (2004) 87 *Marquette Law Review* 839–845

Kostritsky 1993
J.P. Kostritsky, 'Bargaining with Uncertainty, Moral Hazard, and Sunk Costs: A Default Rule for Precontractual Negotiations' 44 *Hastings Law Journal* 621–705

Kötz 1987
H. Kötz, 'Taking Civil Codes Less Seriously' (1987) 50 *The Modern Law Review* 1–15

Kovacic-Fleischer 2007
C.S. Kovacic-Fleischer, 'Quantum Meruit and the Restatement (Third) of Restitution and Unjust Enrichment' (2007) 27 *Review of Litigation* 127–139

Kramer 2001
X.E. Kramer, *Het Kort Geding in Internationaal Perspectief: Een Rechtsvergelijkende Studie naar de Voorlopige Voorziening in het Internationaal Privaatrecht* (Deventer: Kluwer, 2001)

Kramer 2014
X.E. Kramer, 'Competitie in de Europese Civiele Rechtsruimte. Een Spanningsveld in de Grensoverschrijdende Geschillenbeslechting?' (2014) 51 *Tijdschrift voor Privaatrecht* 1745–1806

Asser/Kramer and Verhagen 10-III 2015
X.E. Kramer and H.L.E. Verhagen (with S. van Dongen, A.P.M.J. Vonken), *Mr. C. Assers Handleiding tot de Beoefening van het Nederlands Burgerlijk recht. 10. Internationaal Privaatrecht. Deel III. Internationaal Vermogensrecht* (Deventer: Kluwer, 2015)

Kritzer undated
A.H. Kritzer, *Editorial Remark: Pre-Contract Formation* (undated), www.cisg.law.pace.edu/cisg/biblio/kritzer1.html

Kröll 2005–2006
S. Kröll, 'Selected Problems Concerning the CISG's Scope of Application' (2005–2006) 25 *Journal of Law and Commerce* 39–57

L

De Lotbinière McDougall/Ioannou 2006
A. de Lotbinière, McDougall and L. Ioannou, 'Separability Saved: U.S. Supreme Court Eliminates Threat to International Arbitration' (2006) 21 *Mealey's International Arbitration Report* 65

Laithier 2010
Y.-M. Laithier, 'La Rupture des Pourparlers' (2010) 51 *Revue Lamy Droit des Affaires* 117 ff.

Laithier/Mazeaud 2012
Y.-M. Laithier and D. Mazeaud, 'La Nature de la Sanction: Satisfaction du Bénéficiaire par des Dommages-Intérêts ou Primauté de l'Exécution Forcée en Nature?' (2012) 2 *Revue des Contrats* 681 ff.

Lake 2011
S. Lake, 'An Empirical Study of the UNIDROIT Principles – International and British Responses' (2011) 16 *Uniform Law Review* 669–703

Lake/Draetta 1994
R.B. Lake and U. Draetta, *Letters of Intent and Other Precontractual Documents: Comparative Analysis and Forms*, 2nd ed. (Salem, NH: Butterworths Legal Publishers, 1994)

Lalive 1983
J.-F. Lalive, *Contrats Entre États ou Entreprises Étatiques et Personnes Privées: Développements Récents. Collected Courses of the Hague Academy of International Law, Volume 181* (Leiden, Boston: Brill Nijhoff, 1983)

Lando 2000
O. Lando, 'Some Features of The Law of Contract in the Third Millennium' (2000) *Scandinavian Studies in Law* 343 www.scandinavianlaw.se/pdf/40-13.pdf

Lando 2001
O. Lando, 'Salient Features of the Principles of European Contract Law: A Comparison with the UCC' (2001) 13 *Pace International Law Review* 339–369

Lando 2002
O. Lando, *Principles of European Contract Law and Unidroit Principles: Similarities, Differences and Perspectives* (Rome: Centro di Studi e Ricerche di Diritto Comparato e Straniero, 2002)

Lando 2003 = PECL Part III
O. Lando [et. al.] 2003, *The Principles of European Contract law, Part III. Prepared by the Commission on European Contract Law* (The Hague: Kluwer Law International, 2003)

Lando 2006
O. Lando, 'How the Principles of European Contract Law (PECL) Were Prepared' (2006) 8 *European Journal of Law Reform* 477 1875–8274

Lando 2007
O. Lando 'Is Good faith an Overarching General Clause in the Principles of European Contract Law?', in M. Andenas (ed.) *Liber Amicorum Guido Alpa: Private Law Beyond the National Systems* (London: British Institute of International and Comparative Law) p. 601

Lando/Beale 2000 = PECL Parts I and II
O. Lando and H.G. Beale (eds.), *The Principles of European Contract law, Parts I and II. Prepared by the Commission on European Contract Law* (The Hague: Kluwer Law International, 2000)

Larroumet 1998
Ch. Larroumet, *Les Obligations, Le Contrat*, 4th ed. (Paris: Economica, 1998)

Latina/Chantepie 2015
M. Latina and G. Chantepie (eds.), *Supplément au Code Civil 2016 Édition Limitée - Livret sur le Projet de Réforme du Droit des Obligations* (Paris: Dalloz, 2015)

Laude 1992
A. Laude, *La Reconnaissance par le Juge de l'Existence d'un Contrat* (Aix-en-Provence: Presses universitaires d'Aix-Marseille, 1994)

Lax/Sebenius 2006
D.A. Lax and J.K. Sebenius, *3-D Negotiation: Powerful Tools to Change the Game in Your Most Important Deals* (Boston: Harvard Business Review Press, 2006)

Le Tourneau 2014
Ph. Le Tourneau (ed.), *Droit de la Responsabilité et des Contrats*, 10th ed. (Paris: Dalloz, 2014)

Legrand 1999
P. Legrand, *Le Droit Comparé* (Paris: Presses Universitaires de France, 1999)

Lempereur/Colson 2010
A. Lempereur and A. Colson, *Méthode de Négociation*, 2nd ed. (Paris: Dunod, 2010)

Lequette 2013
S. Lequette, 'Réflexions sur la Durée du Pacte de Préférence' (2013) *Revue Trimestrielle de Droit Civil* 491–517

Lewicki/Barry/Saunders 2015
R. Lewicki, B. Barry and D. Saunders, *Negotiation*, 7th ed. (New York, NY: McGraw-Hill Education, 2015)

Lewis 1982
R. Lewis, 'Contracts between Businessmen: Reform of the Law of Firm Offers and an Empirical Study of Tendering Practices in the Building Industry' (1982) 9 *Journal of Law and Society* 153–175

Lindenbergh 2014
S.D. Lindenbergh, *Schadevergoeding*, 4th ed. (Deventer: Kluwer, 2014)

Lipstein1981
K. Lipstein, *Principles of the Conflict of Laws, National and International* (The Hague: Martinus Nijhoff, 1981)

Loken 2013
K. Loken, 'A New Global Initiative on Contract Law in UNCITRAL: Right Project, Right Forum?' (2013) 58 *Villanova Law Review* 509–520

Lookofsky 2006
J. Lookofsky, 'Walking the Article 7(2) Tightrope Between CISG and Domestic Law' (2005–2006) 25 *Journal of Law and Commerce* 87–105

Loncle/Trochon 1997
J.-M. Loncle and J.-Y. Trochon, 'The Negotiating Phase of International Contracts' (1997) 1997 *International Business Law Journal* 3–35

Loquin 2013
E. Loquin, 'Retour sur les Sources Premières de la "Lex Mercatoria": Les Usages du Commerce International', in M. Kohen and D. Bentolila (eds.), *Mélanges en l'Honneur du Professeur Jean-Michel Jacquet: le Droit des Rapports Internationaux Économiques et Privés* (Paris: LexisNexis, 2013) p. 215

Lutter 1998
M. Lutter, *Der Letter of Intent: Zur Rechtlichen Bedeutung von Absichtserklärungen*, 3rd ed. (Köln: Heymann, 1998)

M

Macaulay 1963
S. Macaulay, 'Non-Contractual Relations in Business: A Preliminary Study' (1963) 28 *American Sociological Review* 55–67

Macaulay 1985.
S. Macaulay, 'An Empirical View of Contract' (1985) 1985 *Wisconsin Law Review* 465–482

Macfarlane 2010
B. Macfarlane, 'Promissory Estoppel and Debts', in A. Burrows and E. Peel (eds.), *Contract Formation and Parties* (Oxford: Oxford University Press, 2010) p. 115

Macneil 2001
I. Macneil 'Relational Contract Theory: Challenges and Queries', in D. Campbell (ed.), *The Relational Theory of Contract: Selected Works of Ian Macneil* (London: Sweet & Maxwell, 2001) p. 365

MacQueen 2006
H. MacQueen 'Good Faith' in H. MacQueen and R. Zimmermann (eds.*), European Contract Law: Scots and South African Perspectives* (Edinburgh: Edinburgh University Press, 2006) p. 43

Magnus 1995
U. Magnus, 'General Principes of UN-Sales Law' (1995) 59 *Rabels Zeitschrift für Ausländisches und Internationales Privatrecht* 469–494 http://cisgw3.law.pace.edu/cisg/text/magnus.html

Magnus 2007
U. Magnus, 'Comparative Editorial Remarks on the Provisions Regarding Good Faith in CISG Article 7(1) and the UNIDROIT Principles Article 1.7', in J. Felemegas (ed.) *An International Approach to the Interpretation of the United Nations Convention on Contracts for the International Sale of Goods (1980) as Uniform Sales Law* (Cambridge: Cambridge University Press, 2007) p. 45

Mainguy 2011
D. Mainguy, 'L'Efficacité de la Rétractation de la Promesse Unilatérale de Contracter' (2011) *Recueil Dalloz* 1460 ff.

Mainguy 2014
D. Mainguy, 'Promesse Unilatérale et Pacte de Préférence: Des Définitions Inopérantes' (2014) 240 *Droit et Patrimoine* 44 ff.

Mak 2002
Ch. Mak, 'Aansprakelijkheid voor Afgebroken Onderhandelingen' (2002) 51 *Ars Aequi* 62-70

Malaurie/Aynès/Stoffel-Munck 2015
Ph. Malaurie, L. Aynès and Ph. Stoffel-Munck, *Les Obligations*, 7th ed. (Paris: L.G.D.J., 2015)

Marchandise 2002
Ph. Marchandise, 'Confidentiality Agreement, a Real Commitment!' (2002) 2002 *International Business Law Journal* 741–748

Markesinis 2000
B.S. Markesinis, 'Our Debt to Europe: Past, Present and Future', in B.S. Markesinis (ed.), *The Clifford Chance Millennium Lectures: The Coming Together of the Common Law and the Civil Law* (Oxford, Hart Publishing, 2000) p. 37

Markesinis/Fedtke 2009
B.S. Markesinis and J. Fedtke, *Engaging with Foreign Law* (Oxford: Hart Publishing, 2009)

Maude 2014
B. Maude, *International Business Negotiation: Principles and Practice* (Houndmills, Basingstoke, Hampshire: Palgrave Macmillan, 2014)

Mazeaud 2001
D. Mazeaud, 'Mystères et Paradoxes de la Période Précontractuelle', in *Le Contrat au Début du XXIe Siècle: Études Offertes à Jacques Ghestin* (Paris: L.G.D.J., 2001) p. 637

Mazeaud 2006
D. Mazeaud, 'Réparation des Préjudices Précontractuels: Toujours Moins…?' (2006) *Recueil Dalloz* 2963 ff.

Mazeaud 2008
D. Mazeaud, 'La Période Précontractuelle en Droits Positif et Prospectif Français, Européen et International: Comparaisons', in O. Deshayes (ed.), *L'avant-contrat: Actualité du Processus de Formation des Contrats* (Paris: Presses Universitaires de France, 2008) p. 13

Mazeaud 2009
D. Mazeaud 'La Réforme du Droit Français des Contrats: Trois Projets en Concurrence', in S. Bros and B. Mallet-Bricout (eds.), *Liber Amicorum Christian Larroumet* (Paris: Economica, 2009) p. 329

Mazeaud 2011
D. Mazeaud, 'Promesse Unilatérale de Vente: La Cour de Cassation a ses Raisons' (2011) *Recueil Dalloz* 1457 ff.

Mazeaud/Mazeaud/Mazeaud/Chabas 1991
H. Mazeaud, L. Mazeaud, J. Mazeaud, F. Chabas (contributor), *Leçons de Droit Civil. Tome 2. Premier Volume. Obligations: Théorie Générale*, 9th ed. (Paris: Montchrestien, 1998)

McDowell 1985
B. McDowell, 'Foreseeability in Contract and Tort: The Problems of Responsibility and Remoteness' (1985) 36 *Case Western Reserve Law Review* 286–325

McKendrick 2006
E. McKendrick, 'Harmonisation of European Contract Law: the State We Are in', in S. Vogenauer and S. Weatherill (eds.), *The Harmonisation of European Contract Law: Implications for European Private Laws, Business and Legal Practice* (Oxford; Portland, OR: Hart Publishing, 2006) p. 5

McMeel 2011
G. McMeel, *The Construction of Contracts: Interpretation, Implication, and Rectification*, 2nd ed. (Oxford New York: Oxford University Press, 2011)

Von Mehren 1991
A.T. von Mehren, 'The Comparative Study of Law' (1991) 6 *Tulane Civil Law Forum* 43–60

Von Mehren 2008
A.T. von Mehren, 'The Formation of Contracts', in A.T. von Mehren (ed.), *International Encycolpedia of Comparative Law, Volume VII: Contracts in General* (2008) Chapter 9

Von Mehren/Murray 2007
A.T. von Mehren and P.L. Murray, *Law in the United States*, 2nd ed. (Cambridge: Cambridge University Press, 2007)

Mercadal 2016
B. Mercadal, *Réforme du Droit des Contrats. Ordonnance du 10 février 2016* (Paris: Francis Lefebvre, 2016)

Merryman 1999
J.H. Merryman, *The Loneliness of the Comparative Lawyer: And Other Essays in Foreign and Comparative Law* (The Hague: Kluwer Law International, 1999)

Van der Mersch/Philippe 2001
M. Van der Mersch and D. Philippe, 'L'Inexécution dans les Contrats du Commerce International', in M. Fontaine and G. Viney (eds.), *Les sanctions de l'Inexécution des Obligations Contractuelles: Études de Droit Comparé* (Bruxelles: Bruylant, 2001) p. 701

Mestre 1993
J. Mestre, 'De la Violation d'un Pacte de Préférence' (1993) *Revue Trimestrielle de Droit Civil* 346 ff.

Mestre 1998
J. Mestre, 'La Prudence Est Toujours de Rigueur… Pour la Cour de Cassation dans la Sanction des Pactes de Préférence' (1998) *Revue Trimestrielle de Droit Civil* 98 ff.

Mestre/Fages 2005
J. Mestre and B. Fages, 'L'Après-pourparlers Peut Provoquer un Enrichissement sans Cause' (2005) *Revue Trimestrielle de Droit Civil* 120 ff.

Meurkens 2012
R. Ch. Meurkens, 'The Punitive Damages Debate in Continental Europe: Food for Thought', in R. Ch. Meurkens and E. Nordin (eds.), *The Power of Punitive Damages – Is Europe Missing Out?* (Cambridge: Intersentia, 2012) p. 3

Meurling 2009
E. Meurling, 'La Lettre d'Intention dans les Droits Scandinaves', in J. Mestre, A. Bonomi and A. Albarian (eds.), *Regards Comparatistes sur le Phénomène Contractuel* (Aix-en-Provence: Presses Universitaires d'Aix Marseille, 2009) p. 59

Meyer 2006
L. Meyer, 'Soft Law For Solid Contracts?: A Comparative Analysis of the Value of the Unidroit Principles of International Commercial Contracts and the Principles of European Contract Law to the Process of Contract Law Harmonization' (2006) 34 *Denver Journal of International Law and Policy* 119–143

Michaels 2006
R. Michaels, 'The Functional Method of Comparative Law', in M. Reimann and R. Zimmermann (eds.), *The Oxford Handbook of Comparative Law* (Oxford: Oxford University Press, 2006) p. 339

Micklitz 2007
H.-W. Micklitz, 'Review of Academic Approaches to the European Contract Law Codification Project', in *Liber Amicorum Guido Alpa: Private Law Beyond the National Systems* (London: British Institute of International and Comparative Law, 2007) p. 699

Mills/Loveridge 2011
A. Mills and R. Loveridge, 'The Uncertain Future of Walford v. Miles' (2011) 4 *Lloyd's Maritime and Commercial Law Quarterly* 528–545

Mitchell 2009
C. Mitchell, 'Narrativising Contract Law' (2009) 29 *Legal Studies* 19–46

Mitchell 2015
C. Mitchell, 'Unjust enrichment', in A.S. Burrows (ed.), *Principles of the English Law of Obligations* (Oxford, UK: Oxford University Press, 2015) p. 239

Mnookin 2010
R. Mnookin, *Bargaining with the Devil: When to Negotiate and when to Fight* (New York: Simon & Schuster, 2010)

Morgan 2013
J. Morgan, *Contract Law Minimalism: A formalist Restatement of Commercial Contract Law* (Cambridge: Cambridge University Press, 2013)

Mousseron 1998
J.-M. Mousseron, 'Rapport de Synthèse' (1998) *Revue Trimestrielle de Droit Commercial* 559 ff.

Mousseron/Guibal/Mainguy 2001
J.-M. Mousseron, M. Guibal and D. Mainguy, *L'Avant-contrat* (Paris: Éditions Francis Levebvre, 2001)

Muir-Watt 2003
H. Muir-Watt, 'Les Pourparlers: De la Confiance Trompée à la Relation de Confiance', in P. Rémy-Corlay and D. Fenouillet (eds.), *Les Concepts Contractuels Français à l'Heure des Principes du Droit Européen des Contrats* (Paris: Dalloz, 2003) p. 53–64

Muller/Riske 2013
C. Muller and O. Riske, 'La Convention d'Arbitrage par Lettre d'Intention en Droits Suisse et Français' (2013) 2013 *Revue de Droit des Affaires Internationales* 191–215

Mustill 1988
M.J. Mustill, 'The New *Lex Mercatoria*: The First Twenty-five Years' (1988) 4 *Arbitration International: The Journal of LCIA Worldwide Arbitration* 86–119

N

Nieper 2000
E. Nieper, 'Aansprakelijkheid voor Onderhandelingen. Onderhandelingen in Strijd met de Goede Trouw (Art. 2:301 PECL)' (2000) 2000 *Nederlands Tijdschrift voor Burgerlijk Recht* 433–437

Nieuwenhuis 2010
J.H. Nieuwenhuis, 'Het Dieptepunt: Plas/Valburg' (2010) 2010 *Ars Aequi* 288–290

Nolan 2010
D. Nolan, 'Offer and Acceptance in the Electronic Age', in A. Burrows and E. Peel (eds.), *Contract Formation and Parties* (Oxford: Oxford University Press, 2010) p. 61

Nottage 2012
L. Nottage, 'Commercial Regulation', in J.M. Smits (ed.), *Elgar Encyclopedia of Comparative Law*, 2nd ed. (Cheltenham: Elgar, 2012) p. 157

O

Ofner 2005
W. Ofner, 'Break-up Fees en Openbare Biedingen' (2003) 2003 *Vennootschap & Onderneming* 78–81

Oppetit 1979
B. Oppetit, 'L'engagement d'Honneur' (1979) *Dalloz* p. 107

Örücü 2012
A.E. Örücü, 'Methodology of Comparative Law', in J.M. Smits (ed.), *Elgar Encyclopedia of Comparative Law*, 2nd ed. (Cheltenham: Elgar, 2012) p. 560

P

Du Perron 1999
C.E. du Perron, *Overeenkomst en Derden: Een Analyse van de Relativiteit van de Contractswerking* (Deventer: Kluwer, 1999)

Palmer 1978
G.E. Palmer, *The Law of Restitution* (Boston: Little, Brown & Co., 1978)

Palmieri 1993
N.W. Palmieri, 'Good Faith Disclosures Required During Precontractual Negotiations' (1993) 24 *Seton Hall Law Review* 70–213

Pannebakker 2013
E. Pannebakker, 'Offer and Acceptance and the Dynamics of Negotiations: Arguments for Contract Theory from Negotiation Studies' (2013) 6 *Erasmus Law Review* 131–141

Pannebakker 2016
E. Pannebakker, 'Pre-contractual Phase: Reflections on the Attractiveness of the New French rules for the Parties to International Commercial Transactions', in S. Stijns and S. Jansen (eds.), *The French Contract Law Reform: Source of Inspiration?* (Cambridge: Intersentia, 2016) p. 29–47

Peel 2010
E. Peel, 'Agreements to Negotiate in Good Faith', in A. Burrows and E. Peel (eds.), *Contract Formation and Parties* (Oxford: Oxford University Press, 2010) p. 37

Péloquin/Assié 2006
L. Péloquin and Ch. Assié, 'La Lettre d'Intention' (2006) 40 *Revue Juridique Thémis* 175–204

Perales Viscasillas 2001
M. del P. Perales Viscasillas, 'The Formation of Contracts and the Principles of European Contract Law' (2001) 13 *Pace International Law Review* 371–397

Perfumi 2011
C. Perfumi, 'La Vigueur Restaurée du Pacte de Préférence dans l'Ordre Juridique Français: Points de Vue Comparatistes' (2011) *Revue des Contrats*, 01 January 2011 n°1, p. 267

Perillo 1994
J.M. Perillo, 'Unidroit Principles of International Commercial Contracts: The Black Letter Text and a Review' (1994) 63 *Fordham Law Review* 281–317

Pevtchin 1979
G. Pevtchin, 'La lettre d'intention' (1979) 1 *Droit et Pratique du Commerce International* 50–69

Piazzon 2009
Th. Piazzon, 'Retour sur la Violation des Pactes de Préférence' (2009) *Revue Trimestrielle de Droit Civil* 433 ff.

Pin/Devin 2011
X. Pin and L. Devin, *JurisClasseur Code civil Art. 1370 et 1371 Fascicule Unique: Quasi-Contrats. Théorie Générale* 13 Mai 2011

Pomart 2008
C. Pomart, 'La Lettre d'Intention après l'Ordonnance du 23 Mars 2006 Relative aux Sûretés' (2008) *Les Petites Affiches* 27 mars 2008, p. 19

Posner 1977
R.A. Posner, *Economic Analysis of Law* (Boston: Little, Brown and Company, 1977)

Pothier 1806
R.J. Pothier, *A Treatise on the Law of Obligations, or Contracts*, Translated from the French, with an introduction, appendix, and notes, illustrative of the English law on the subject by William David Evans (London: printed by A. Strahan. For Joseph Butterworth; and J. Cooke, Dublin, 1806)

Prosser 1971
W.L. Prosser, *Handbook of the Law of Torts*, 4th ed., 3rd repr. (St. Paul, Minn.: West, 1971)

Py/Garinot 2015
E. Py and J.-M. Garinot, *La Protection des Secrets d'Affaires: Enjeux et Perspectives* (Paris: Lexisnexis, 2015)

R

Rachlinski 2006
J.J. Rachlinski, 'Bottom-Up versus Top-Down Lawmaking' (2006) 37 *The University of Chicago Law Review* 933–964

Radley-Gardner 2003
O. Radley-Gardner (ed.), *Fundamental Texts on European Private Law* (Oxford: Hart, 2003)

Reehuis/Slob 1991
W.H.M. Reehuis and E.E. Slob, *Parlementaire Geschiedenis van het Nieuwe Burgerlijk Wetboek: Parlementaire Stukken Systematisch Gerangschikt en van Noten Voorzien. Invoering Boeken 3, 5 en 6* (Deventer: Kluwer, 1991)

Reinhart 1984
G. Reinhart, 'Development of a Law for the International Sale of Goods' (1984) 14 *Cumberland Law Review*, 89–102

Reitz 1998
J.C. Reitz, 'How to Do Comparative Law' (1998) 46 *The American Journal of Comparative Law* 617–636

Reitz 2009
J.C. Reitz, 'Legal Origins, Comparative Law, and Political Economy' (2009) 57 *The American Journal of Comparative Law* 847–862

Rigaux 1990
F. Rigaux, 'Détermination du Droit Applicable aux Relations Précontractuelles', in *International Chamber of Commerce. Formation of Contracts and Precontractual Liability* (Paris: ICC Publishing, 1990) p. 12

Riles 2001
A. Riles (ed.) *Rethinking the Masters of Comparative law* (Oxford: Hart, 2001)

Rinkes 2003
J.G.J. Rinkes, 'Letters of Intent en het Afbreken van Onderhandelingen: Contact is Contract? (2003) *Praktisch Procederen* 66–71

Rodière 1976
R. Rodière (ed.), *La Formation du Contrat* (Paris: Pedone, 1979)

Rohwer/Skrocki 2010
C.D. Rohwer and A.M. Skrocki, *Contracts in a Nutshell*, 7th ed.(St. Paul, MN: Thomson Reuters, 2010)

Romano 2002
S. Romano, *L'Ordre Juridique* / trad. française [de l'italien] de *Ordinamento Giuridico* (Firenze: [s.n.] 1945) par L. François and P. Gothot, 2nd ed. (Pars: Dalloz, 2002)

Van Rossum 2011
M.M. van Rossum, *De Redelijkheid en Billijkheid bij Commerciële Contracten. In het Bijzonder in het Kader van Precontractuele Onderhandelingen* (Deventer: Kluwer, 2011)

Roumélian 2010
O. Roumélian, 'Rupture de Pourparlers: Évolutions Jurisprudentielles Récentes' (2010) *Petites Affiches*, 22 juillet 2010 n° 145, p. 5

Rozès 1996
L. Rozès, 'Le Projet de Contrat', in *Mélanges Dédiés à Louis Boyer* (Toulouse: Presses de l'Université des Sciences Sociales de Toulouse, 1996)

Rozès 1998
L. Rozès, 'Projets et Accords de Principe' (1998) 1998 *Revue Trimestrielle de Droit Commercial* 501–510

Rudden 1999
B. Rudden, 'The Gentleman's Agreement in Legal Theory and in Modern Practice' (1999) 7 *European Review of Private Law* 199–220

Ruygvoorn 2009
M.R. Ruygvoorn, *Afgebroken Onderhandelingen en het Gebruik van Voorbehouden* (Deventer: Kluwer, 2009)

S

Sacco 2000–2001
R. Sacco, 'One Hundred Years of Comparative Law' (2000–2001) 75 *Tulane Law Review* 1159–1176

Sagaert 2012
V. Sagaert, M. Storme and E. Terryn (eds.), *The Draft Common Frame of Reference: National and Comparative Perspectives* (Cambridge: Intersentia, 2012).

Saleilles 1907
R. Saleilles, 'De la Responsabilité Contractuelle: A Propos d'une Étude Nouvelle sur la Matière' (1907) 6 *Revue Trimestrielle de Droit Civil* 697–751

Samuel 2006
A. Samuel, 'Separability and the US Supreme Court Decision in Buckeye v. Cardegna' (2006) 22 *Arbitration International* 477–494

Savaux 2012
E. Savaux, 'Les Conditions de l'Opposabilité de l'Engagement aux Tiers' (2012) *Revue des Contrats* 663

Schelhaas 2004
H.N. Schelhaas, *Het Boetebeding in het Europese Contractenrecht* (Deventer: Kluwer, 2004)

Schelling 2006
T.C. Schelling, *Strategies of Commitment and Other Essays* (Cambridge, MA: Harvard University Press, 2006)

Schermaier 2000
M.J. Schermaier, '*Bona fides* in Roman Contract Law', in R. Zimmermann and S. Whittaker (eds.), *Good Faith in European Contract Law* (Cambridge: Cambridge University Press, 2000) p. 63

Van Schilfgaarde 1983
P. van Schilfgaarde, 'Precontractuele Goede Trouw. Afgebroken Onderhandelingen' (1983) 1983 *Ars Aequi* 758–763

Schlechtriem/Schwenzer 2010
P. Schlechtriem and I. Schwenzer, 'Introduction', in I. Schwenzer (ed.), *Commentary on the UN Convention on the International Sale of Goods (CISG)* 3rd ed. (Oxford: Oxford University Press, 2010) p. 1

Schlesinger 1968
R.B. Schlesinger (ed.), *Formation of Contracts, A study of the Common Core of Legal Systems* (Dobbs Ferry, N.Y.: Oceana, 1968)

Schlesinger 1968a
R.B. Schlesinger 'General Introduction', in R.B. Schlesinger (ed.), *Formation of Contracts: A Study of the Common Core of Legal Systems* (Dobbs Ferry, N.Y.: Oceana, 1968) p. 1

Schmidt 2002
J. Schmidt, 'Letters of Intent' (2002) 2002 *International Business Law Journal* 257–270

Schmidt-Szalewski 2000
J. Schmidt-Szalewski, 'La Force Obligatoire à l'Épreuve des Avant-contrats' (2000) 2000 *Revue Trimestrielle de Droit Civil* 25–46

Schmitthoff 1968
C.M. Schmitthoff, 'The Unifcation or Harmonisation of Law by Means of Standard Contracts and General Conditions' (1968) 17 *International and Comparative Law Quarterly* 551–570

Schmitthoff 1987
C.M. Schmitthoff, *International Trade Usages, Institute of International Business Law And Practice. Newsletter, Special Issue* (Paris: ICC Publishing, 1987)

Schnyder/Straub 1999
A.K. Schnyder and R.M. Straub, 'The Conclusion of a Contract in Accordance with UNIDROIT Principles' (1999) 1 *European Journal of Law Reform* 243–268

Scholten 1969
G.J. Scholten, note to HR 18 April 1969, ECLI:NL:HR:1969:AC4925, *NJ* 1969, 336 Katwijk/Westdijk (1969) *Nederlands Juristenblad* 336 ff.

Schoordijk 1984
H.C.F. Schoordijk, *Onderhandelen te Goeder Trouw* (Deventer: Kluwer, 1984)

Schoordijk 1999
H.C.F. Schoordijk, 'Vergoeding van Werk Verricht Vooruitlopend op een Contract dat Tenslotte niet Totstandkomt', in H.C.F. Schoordijk [et. al.], *Rond de Tafel: De Juridische Kaders van het Onderhandelen* (Deventer: Kluwer, 1999) p. 1

Schroeter 2010
U.G. Schroeter, 'Introduction to Articles 14–24', in I. Schwenzer (ed.), *Commentary on the UN Convention on the International Sale of Goods (CISG)*, 3rd ed. (Oxford: Oxford University Press, 2010) p. 221

Schulze 2012
R. Schulze, 'Non-contractual Liability Arising out of Damage Caused to Another in the DCFR' in V. Sagaert, M. Storme and E. Terryn (eds.), *The Draft Common Frame of Reference: National and Comparative Perspectives* (Cambridge: Intersentia, 2012)

Schulze/Schulte-Nölke 2011
R. Schulze and H. Schulte-Nölke (eds), *European Private Law – Current Status and Perspectives* (Munich: Sellier European Law Publishers, 2011)

Schulze/Wicker/Mäsch/Mazeaud 2015
R. Schulze, G. Wicker, G. Mäsch and D. Mazeaud (eds.), *La Réforme du Droit des Obligations en France: 5èmes Journées Franco-Allemandes* (Paris: Société de Législation Comparée, 2015)

Schut 1986
W.S.M. Schut, *Letters of Intent* (Zwolle: W.E.J. Tjeenk Willink, 1986)

Schwartz/Scott 2007
A. Schwartz and R.E. Scott, 'Precontractual Liability and Preliminary Agreements' (2007) 120 *Harvard Law Review* 661–707

Schwenzer 2010
I. Schwenzer (ed.), *Commentary on the UN Convention on the International Sale of Goods (CISG)*, 3rd ed. (Oxford: Oxford University Press, 2010)

Schwenzer/Atamer/Butler 2014
I.H. Schwenzer, Y.M. Atamer and P. Butler (eds.), *Current Issues in the CISG and Arbitration* (The Hague: Eleven International Publishing, 2014)

Schwenzer/Hachem 2010
I. Schwenzer and P. Hachem, 'Articles 1–6', in I. Schwenzer (ed.), Schlechtriem and Schwenzer: Commentary on the UN Convention on the International Sale of Goods (CISG) 3rd ed. (Oxford: Oxford University Press, 2010) p. 28

Schwenzer/Mohs 2006
I. Schwenzer and F. Mohs, 'Old Habits Die Hard: Traditional Contract Formation in a Modern World' (2006) 6 *Internationales Handelsrecht* 239–246

Seale/Tonkiss 2011
C. Seale and F. Tonkiss, 'Content and Comparative Keyword Analysis', in C. Seale (ed.) *Researching Society and Culture*, 3rd ed. (London: SAGE Publications Ltd, 2011) p. 458

Seavey 1951
W.A. Seavey, 'Reliance upon Gratuitous Promises or Other Conduct' (1951) 64 *Harvard Law Review* 913–927

Sebok 2009
A.J. Sebok, 'Punitive Damages in the United States', in H. Koziol and V. Wilcox (eds.), *Punitive Damages: Common Law and Civil Law Perspectives* (Wien: Springer, 2009)

Sebok 2012
A.J. Sebok, 'The U.S. Supreme Court's Theory of Common Law Punitive Damages: An Inauspicious Start', in R. Ch. Meurkens and E. Nordin (eds.), *The Power of Punitive Damages - Is Europe Missing Out?* (Cambridge: Intersentia, 2012) p. 133

Sefton-Green 2009
R. Sefton-Green, 'The DCFR: a Technical or Political Toolbox?', in A. Somma (ed.) *The Politics of the Draft Common Frame of Reference* (Alphen aan den Rijn: Kluwer Law International, 2009) p. 39

Shapiro/Posner 2006
B.P. Shapiro and R.S. Posner, 'Making the Major Sale' (2006) 84 *Harvard Business Review* 140–149

Shell 1991
G.R. Shell, 'Opportunism and Trust in the Negotiation of Commercial Contracts: Toward a New Cause of Action' (1991) 44 *Vanderbilt Law Review* 221–282

Siems 2004
M.M. Siems, '"Unevenly Formed Contracts": Ignoring the "Mirror of Offer and Acceptance"' (2004) 12 *European Review of Private Law* 771–788

Siems 2014
M.M. Siems, *Comparative Law* (Cambridge, UK: Cambridge University Press, 2014)

Simler 2008
Ph. Simler, *JurisClasseur Code Civil Art. 2322 Fascicule Unique: Lettres d'Intention* 12 Février 2008

Smeehuijzen/van Oosten 2015
J.L. Smeehuijzen and M.L. van Oosten, 'Plas/Valburg: Veel Rechtsonzekerheid en Ondermaats Resultaat in de Feitenrechtspraak' (2015) 2015 *Ars Aequi* 72–77

Smith 2004
S.A. Smith, *Contract Theory* (Oxford: Oxford University Press, 2004)

Smits 2003
J.M. Smits, *Bronnen van Verbintenissen* (Deventer: Kluwer, 2003)

Smits 2008
J.M. Smits, 'A European Law on Unjustified Enrichment?: A Critical View of the Law of Restitution in the Draft Common Frame of Reference', in A. Vaquer Aloy (ed.), *European Private Law Beyond the Common Frame of Reference: Essays in Honour of R. Zimmermann* (Groningen: Europa Law Publishing, 2008) p. 151

Smits/Stijns 2002
J.M. Smits and S. Stijns (eds.), *Totstandkoming van de Overeenkomst naar Belgisch en Nederlands Recht* (Antwerp: Intersentia, 2002)

Snijders 2015
H. Snijders, 'I.6.5.10 Intentieovereenkomst', in H. Snijders (ed.), *Modellen voor de Rechtspraktijk* (Kluwer loose-leaf, updated in 2015)

Sorensen/Davidson/White 2012
T. Sorensen, M. Davidson and M. White, 'When Can a Breach of Contract Be a Tort and What Difference Does It Make?' Written materials to ABA Section of Litigation 2012 Corporate Counsel CLE Seminar, www.americanbar.org/content/dam/aba/administrative/litigation/materials/2012_cccle_materials/12_tort.authcheckdam.pdf

Sorieul/Hatcher/Emery 2014
R. Sorieul, E. Hatcher and C. Emery, 'Possible Future Work by Uncitral in the Field of Contract Law: Preliminary Thoughts from the Secretariat' (2014) 58 *Villanova Law Review* 491–508

Spagnolo 2008
L. Spagnolo, 'Opening Pandora's Box: Good Faith and Precontractual Liability in the CISG' (2008) 21 *Temple International and Comparative Law Journal* 261–310

Spencer/Brogan 2006
D. Spencer and M. Brogan, *Mediation Law and Practice* (Cambridge: Cambridge University Press, 2006)

Speziale 1980
M. Speziale, 'Langdell's Concept of Law as Science: the Beginning of Anti-formalism in American Legal Theory' (1980) 5 *Vermont Law Review* 1–37

Steensgaard/Twigg-Flesner 2013
K. Steensgaard and Ch. Twigg-Flesner, 'Pre-Contractual Duties', in G. Dannemann and S. Vogenauer (eds.), *The Common European Sales Law in Context: Interactions with English and German Law* (Oxford: Oxford University Press, 2013) p. 216

Steiner 2010
E. Steiner, *French Law: A Comparative Approach* (Oxford: Oxford University Press, 2010)

Steyn 1997
J. Steyn, 'Contract Law: Fulfilling the Reasonable Expectations of Honest Men' (1997) 113 *Law Quarterly* 433–441

Stijns/Jansen 2016
S. Stijns and S. Jansen (eds.), *The French Contract Law Reform: Source of Inspiration?* (Antwerp: Intersentia, 2016)

Stoffel-Munck 2015
Ph. Stoffel-Munck, *Réforme du Droit des Contrats et Pratique des Affaires* (Paris: Dalloz, 2015)

Stone/Adams 2012
B. Stone and K.D. Adams, *Uniform Commercial Code in a Nutshell*, 8th ed. (St. Paul, MN: Thomson West, 2012)

Storme 2003
M.E. Storme 'Information Requirements and Remedies in the Principles of European Contract Law', lezing congres "Information requirements and remedies in European contract law", Europäische Rechtsakademie Trier 24 Januari 2003, in R. Schulze, M. Ebers and H.C. Grigoleit (eds.), *Informationspflichten und Vertragsschluss im Acquis communautaire* (Tübingen: Mohr Siebeck, 2003) p. 231, www.storme.be/PECLinformationTrier.pdf

Storme 2006
M.E. Storme, 'Freedom of Contract: Mandatory and Non-mandatory Rules in European Contract Law' (2006) 14 *Juridica International* 34–44

Summers 1968
R.S. Summers, '"Good Faith" in General Contract Law and the Sales Provisions of the Uniform Commercial Code' (1968) 54 *Virginia Law Review* 195–267

T

Tamanaha 2000
B.Z. Tamanaha, 'A Non-Essentialist Version of Legal Pluralism' (2000) 27 *Journal of Law and Society* 296–321

Telders 1937
B.M. Telders, 'Praecontractueele verhoudingen' (1937) 3536 *Weekblad voor Privaatrecht, Notariaat en Registratie* 453–455 continued in 3537 *Weekblad voor Privaatrecht, Notariaat en Registratie* 461–463

Terré 2009
F. Terré (ed.), *Pour une Réforme du Droit des Contrats: Réflexions et Propositions d'un Groupe de Travail* (Paris: Dalloz, 2009)

Terré/Lequette 1994
F. Terré and Y. Lequette (eds.), *Les Grands Arrêts de la Jurisprudence Civile*, 10th ed. (Paris: Dalloz, 1994)

Terré/Simler/Lequette 2013
F. Terré, Ph. Simler and Y. Lequette, *Droit Civil: Les Obligations*, 11th ed. (Paris: Dalloz, 2009)

Tettenborn 1990
A. Tettenborn, 'Book Review Letters of Intent and Other Precontractual Documents: Comparative Analysis and Forms. By Ralph B. Lake and Ugo Draetta. [London: Butterworth Legal Publishers 1990' (1990) 49 *The Cambridge Law Journal* 543–544

Teubner 1997
G. Teubner, '"Global Bukowina': Legal Pluralism in the World Society", in G. Teubner (ed.), *Global Law Without a State* (Aldershot: Dartmouth, 1997) p. 3

Teubner 1998
G. Teubner, 'Legal Irritants: Good Faith in British Law or How Unifying Law Ends up in New Divergences' (1998) 61(1) *The Modern Law Review* 11–32

Tjittes 2006
R.P.J.L. Tjittes, 'De Afbraak van de Aansprakelijkheid voor Afgebroken Onderhandelingen', in H.J. van Kooten [et. al.] (eds.) *Hartkampvariaties: Opstellen Aangeboden aan Prof. Mr A.S. Hartkamp op 20 Januari 2006, ter Gelegenheid van zijn Afscheid als Procureur-generaal bij de Hoge Raad der Nederlanden* (Deventer: Kluwer, 2006) p. 139

Tochtermann 2008
P. Tochtermann, 'Agreements to Negotiate in the Transnational Context – Issues of Contract Law and Effective Dispute Resolution' (2008) 13 *Uniform Law Review* 685–712

Torsello 2008
M. Torsello, 'Preliminary Agreements and CISG Contracts', in H.M. Flechtner, R.A. Brand and M.S. Walter (eds.), *Drafting Contracts under the CISG* (New York, NY: Oxford University Press, 2008) p. 191

Torsello 2014
M. Torsello, 'Precontractual Liability and Preliminary Agreements', in L.A. DiMatteo (ed.), *International Sales Law: A Global Challenge* (New York, NY: Cambridge University Press, 2014) p. 630

Trakman/Sharma 2014
L.E. Trakman and K. Sharma, 'The Binding Force of Agreements to Negotiate in Good Faith' (2014) 73 *The Cambridge Law Journal* 598–628

Twigg-Flesner 2009
C. Twigg-Flesner, 'Pre-contractual Duties – From the *Acquis* to the Common Frame of Reference', in R Schulze (ed.), *CFR and Existing EC Contract Law*, 2nd ed. (Munich: Sellier European Law Publishers, 2009) p. 99

V

De Very 2006
R.W. de Very, *Towards a European Unfair Competition Law: A Clash between Legal Families: A Comparative Study of English, German and Dutch law in Light of Existing European and International Legal Instruments* (Leiden: Nijhoff, 2006)

De Vries 2001
G.J.P. de Vries, 'Are The Principles Of European Contract Law Better Than Dutch Contract Law?' in M.W. Hesselink and G.J.P. de Vries, *Principles of European Contract law Preadvies Uitgebracht voor de Vereniging voor Burgerlijk Recht* (Deventer: Kluwer, 2001) p. 107
www.verenigingvoorburgerlijkrecht.nl/pdf_files/preadviezen/2001%20Preadvies%20 2001%20Hesselink%20en%20De%20Vries.PDF

Valcke 2004
C. Valcke, 'Comparative Law as Comparative Jurisprudence: the Comparability of Legal Systems' (2004) 52 *The American Journal of Comparative Law* 713

Veneziano 2013
A. Veneziano, 'The Soft Law Approach to Unification of International Commercial Contract Law: Future Perspective in Light of UNIDROIT's Experience' (2013) 58 *Villanova Law Review* 521–528

Verhagen 1997
H.L.E. Verhagen, 'La Responsabilité Civile pour la Rupture des Négociations', in *Les métamorphoses de la responsabilité (Sixièmes Journées René Savatier)* (Paris: P.U.F., 1997) p. 81

Vincent-Jones 2001
P.C. Vincent-Jones, 'The Reception of Ian Macneil's Work on Contract in the UK', in D. Campbell (ed.), *The Relational Theory of Contract: Selected Works of Ian Macneil* (London: Sweet & Maxwell, 2001) p.67

Vogenauer 2012
S. Vogenauer, 'Pre-contractual Duties', in G. Dannemann and S. Vogenauer (eds.), *The Common European Sales Law in Context: Interactions with English and German Law* (Oxford: Oxford University Press, 2012) p. 217

Vogenauer 2014
S. Vogenauer, 'UNIDROIT Principles of International Commercial Contracts at Twenty: Experiences to Date, the 2010 Edition, and Future Prospects' (2014) 19 *Uniform Law Review* 480–518

Vogenauer 2015
S. Vogenauer (ed.), *Commentary on the UNIDROIT Principles of International Commercial Contracts (PICC)* 2nd ed. (Oxford: Oxford University Press, 2015)

Vogenauer/Kleinheisterkamp 2009
S. Vogenauer and J. Kleinheisterkamp (eds.), *Commentary on the UNIDROIT Principles of International Commercial Contracts (PICC)* (Oxford: Oxford University Press, 2009)

Vogenauer/Weatherill 2006
S. Vogenauer and S. Weatherill (eds.), *The Harmonisation of European Contract Law: Implications for European Private Laws, Business And Legal Practice* (Oxford: Hart, 2006)

Volders 2008
B. Volders, *Afgebroken Contractonderhandelingen in het Internationaal Privaatrecht* (Gent: Larcier, 2008)

Van De Wynckele-Bazela 2004
A. Van De Wynckele-Bazela, 'Pacte de Préférence et Contrat de Franchise' (2004) *Recueil Dalloz* 2487–2491

W

Wakkie 2000
P.N. Wakkie, 'Afgebroken Overnameonderhandelingen', in J.B. Huizink [et. al.] (eds.), *A-T-D: Opstellen Aangeboden aan Prof. Mr. P. van Schilfgaarde* (Deventer: Kluwer, 2000) p. 443

Walton/McKersie 1991
R.E. Walton and R.B. McKersie, *A Behavioral Theory of Labor Negotiations. An Analysis of Social Interaction System*, 2nd ed. (Ithaca, N.Y.: ILR Press, 1991)

Warendorf/Thomas/Curry-Sumner 2013
H. Warendorf, R. Thomas and I. Curry-Sumner, *The Civil Code of the Netherlands / [transl. from the Dutch]*, 2nd ed. (Alphen aan den Rijn: Kluwer Law International, 2013)

Weiss 2006
S.E. Weiss, 'International Business Negotiation in a Globalizing World: Reflections on the Contributions and Future of a (Sub)Field' (2006) 11 *International Negotiation* 287

Wessels 1984
B. Wessels, 'Gentlemen's Agreements Regulating Business Relations Under Dutch Civil Law' (1984) 31 *Netherlands International Law Review* 214–254

Wessels 2009a
B. Wessels, 'Letters of Intent', in B. Wessels and S.Y.Th. Meyer (eds.), *Bedrijfsovername*, 3rd ed. (Deventer: Kluwer, 2009) p. 249

Wessels 2009b
B. Wessels, 'Pre-contractuele Aspecten van een Bedrijfsovername', in B. Wessels and S.Y.Th. Meyer (eds.) *Bedrijfsovername*, 3rd ed. (Deventer: Kluwer, 2009) p. 263

Wessels 2010
B. Wessels, *Letters of Intent* (Nijmegen: Ars Aequi Libri, 2010)

Wessels/Van Wechem 2003
B. Wessels and T.H.M. van Wechem, *Grensoverschrijdende Contractonderhandelingen* (Deventer: Kluwer, 2003)

Wessels/Van Wechem 2011
B. Wessels and T.H.M. van Wechem, *Contracteren in de Internationale Praktijk*, 3rd ed. (Deventer: Kluwer, 2011)

Wicker 2012
G. Wicker, 'L'engagement du Promettant: Engagement au Contrat Définitif'(2012) 2 *Revue des Contrats*, 649 ff.

Wijffels 2003
A. Wijffels, 'Book Review: Ph. Bihr (ed.) Dalloz: Paris 2000, Code Civil Français: Évolution des Textes depuis 1804' (2003) 71 *The Legal History Review* 245–247

Williston on Contracts 2014
R.A. Lord (ed.), S. Williston, *A Treatise on the Taw of Contracts*, 4th ed. (Rochester, N.Y.: Lawyers Cooperative Publishing, 1990 with annually cumulative supplement)

Y

Yorio/Thel 1991
E. Yorio and S. Thel, 'The Promissory Basis of Section 90' (1991) 101 *The Yale Law Journal* 111–167

Z

Zimmermann 1996
R. Zimmermann, *The Law of Obligations: Roman Foundations of the Civilian Tradition* (Oxford: Oxford University Press, 1996)

Zimmermann 2006
R. Zimmermann, 'The Principles of European Contract Law: Contemporary Manifestation of the Old, and Possible Foundation for a New, European Scholarship of Private Law', in F. Faust and G. Thüsing (eds.), *Beyond Borders: Perspectives on International and Comparative Law: Symposium in Honour of Hein Kötz* (Köln: Heymann, 2006) p. 111

Zimmermann/Whittaker 2000
R. Zimmermann and S. Whittaker (eds.), *Good Faith in European Contract Law* (Cambridge: Cambridge University Press, 2000)

Zweigert/Kötz 1998
K. Zweigert and H. Kötz, *Introduction to Comparative Law*, translated from the German by Tony Weir, 3rd ed. (Oxford: Clarendon Press), 1998

Collective

ICC 1990
International Chamber of Commerce. Formation of Contracts and Precontractual Liability (Paris: ICC Publishing, 1990)

Lettre d'Intention Type, Association Française des Investisseurs en Capital, Capital-Risque: Guide des Bonnes Pratiques AFIC 2010, p. 90,
www.afic.asso.fr/dl.php?table=etude_publication&chemin=uploads/_afic&nom_file=capital-risque-guide-des-bonnes-pratiques-version-2010_1.pdf

Congrès des Notaires de France 1964
La Formation du Contrat: l'Avant-contrat – Congrès des Notaires de France (Lyon: Imprimerie A. Rey, 1964)

Institutional Documents

Uncitral

UNCITRAL 2012
United Nations Commission on International Trade Law, Forty-fifth Session (2012), A/CN.9/758, 8 May 2012, Possible Future Work in the Area of International Contract Law

UNCITRAL Digest of case law on the United Nations Convention on the International Sale of Goods, Article 7 (2004) A/CN.9/SER.C/DIGEST/CISG/7
http://daccess-dds-ny.un.org/doc/UNDOC/GEN/V04/547/56/PDF/V0454756.pdf?OpenElement

UNIDROIT

UNIDROIT 2013 C.D. (32) 4(b)
www.unidroit.org/english/governments/councildocuments/2013session/cd92-04b-e.pdf
UNIDROIT 2014 C.D. (93) 3
www.unidroit.org/english/governments/councildocuments/2014session/cd-93-03-e.pdf

UNIDROIT *Travaux préparatoires* to the UPICC (UNIDROIT Archives, Rome)
Study L (1979) – Doc 16
Study L (1989) – Doc 40.2
Study L (2003) – Misc 25
UNIDROIT 2002 Study L – Misc. 25
UNIDROIT 2002 Study L – Misc. 24
UNIDROIT 2002 Study L – Doc. 78
UNIDROIT 1992 P.C. – Misc. 18

European Commission

Communication to the Council and the European Parliament on European Contract Law COM(2001) 398 OJ 2001 C255/1

Communication from the Commission to the European Parliament and the Council – A more coherent European contract law – An action plan COM(2003) OJ C 63

Communication from the Commission to the European Parliament and the Council, European Contract Law and the Revision of the Acquis: The Way Forward COM(2004) 651

Communication from the Commission to the European Parliament and the Council, European Contract Law and the Revision of the Acquis: The Way Forward COM(2004) 651

First Annual Progress Report on European Contract Law and the Acquis Review COM(2005) 456

Green Paper on the Review of the Consumer Acquis. COM(2006) 744

Commission Decision of 26 April 2010 setting up the Expert Group on a Common Frame of Reference in the area of European contract law OJ L 105

A European Contract Law for Consumers and Businesses: Publication of the Results of the Feasibility Study Carried out by the Expert Group on European Contract Law for Stakeholders' and Legal Practitioners' Feedback, 3 May 2011, http://ec.europa.eu/justice/contract/files/feasibility_study_final.pdf

Proposal for a Regulation of the European Parliament and of the Council on a Common European Sales Law, 11 October 2011, COM(2011) 635, Annex 2, Commission Work Programme 2015, Strasbourg, 16.12.2014 COM(2014) 910, http://ec.europa.eu/atwork/pdf/cwp_2015_withdrawals_en.pdf

European Parliament

Resolution A2–157/89 OJ C 205, 25.7.1994

TABLE OF CASES BY COUNTRY

The Netherlands (in chronological order)

Hoge Raad der Nederlanden

Lower courts

France (in chronological order)

Cour de cassation

Lower courts

England and Wales (in alphabetical order)

United States (in alphabetical order)

Germany

Court of Justice of the European Union (CJEU)

Arbitral awards

CURRICULUM VITAE

Ekaterina Pannebakker was born in 1981 in Moscow, Russia. She graduated in French law (*Maîtrise* in 2004, *Universtiés Panthéon Assas* and *Aix Marseille*), Russian law (Master *cum laude*, 2009, Moscow State Law Academy), and obtained an LL.M. in Business, Corporate and Maritime Law (2011, Erasmus University Rotterdam).

After obtaining her first law degree, Ekaterina Pannebakker worked as a lawyer in a French consulting company, since 2006 as legal counsel at Danone Dairy (a multinational dairy producer) in Moscow, Russia, and from 2009 to 2011, as legal counsel for Danone Baby and Medical nutrition Headquarters in the Netherlands. From September 2011 to August 2016 she worked as a doctoral researcher at Erasmus University Rotterdam on her thesis on letter of intent in international contracting. During her doctoral trajectory, Ekaterina Pannebakker was a visiting scholar at the University of Cambridge (UK), Clare College and at the UNIDROIT – International Institute for the Unification of Private law in Rome (Italy), holding a scholarship from the UK Foundation for International Uniform Law. Since September 2011, Ekaterina Pannebakker has also been the Secretary of the *Groupe de Travail Contrats Internationaux* (GTCI) chaired by Prof. Dr. Filip De Ly. GTCI is an international think tank formed by in-house counsel, barristers, and academics to analyse the main provisions of international contracts in order to improve contract drafting.

Ekaterina Pannebakker is fluent in four languages and has extensive cross-cultural experience. Since September 2016, Ekaterina Pannebakker teaches Private International Law at Leiden University (the Netherlands). She publishes on various aspects in the field of international contracting.

IUS COMMUNE EUROPAEUM

A peer-reviewed book series in which the common foundations of the legal systems of the Member States of the European Union are the central focus.

The *Ius Commune Europaeum* series includes horizontal comparative legal studies as well as studies on the effect of treaties within the national legal systems. All the classic fields of law are covered. The books are published in various European languages under the auspices of METRO, the Institute for Transnational Legal Research at Maastricht University.

Recently published:
Volume 143: *A European Legal Framework for Nuclear Liability. Rethinking Current Approaches*, T. Heldt
Volume 144: *The Development of European Private Law in a Multilevel Legal Order*, E.A.G. Van Schagen
Volume 145: *Property Law Perspectives IV*, D. Gruyaert, E. Ramaekers and L. Rostill (eds.)
Volume 146: *The Citizen in European Private Law: Norm-setting, Enforcement and Choice*, C. Cauffman and J. Smits (eds.)
Volume 147: *Legal Certainty in Real Estate Transactions: A Comparison of England and France*, B. Du Marais and D. Marrani (eds.)
Volume 148: *Scarcity and the State I. The Allocation of Limited Rights by the Administration*, P. Adriaanse, F. Van Ommeren, W. Den Ouden and J. Wolswinkel (eds.)
Volume 149: *Optional Instruments of the European Union. A Definitional, Normative and Explanatory Study*, W.A. Bull
Volume 150: *The European Union and National Civil Procedure. A Smooth Process or a Rocky Road for Member States?*, A. Nylund and B.H. Krans (eds.)
Volume 151: *Different Paths Towards Sustainable Biofuels? A Comparative Study of the International, EU, and Chinese Regulation of the Sustainability of Biofuels*, T. Yue
Volume 152: *Regulation of Cross-Border Establishment in China and the EU. A Comparative Law and Economics Approach*, G. Shen
Volume 153: *The French Contract Law Reform: a Source of Inspiration?*, S. Stijns and S. Jansen (eds.)
Volume 154: *Convergence in European Consumer Sales Law. A Comparative and Numerical Approach*, C. Goanță
Volume 155: *Quality and Speed in Administrative Decision-Making: Tension or Balance?*, C. Backes, M. Eliantonio and S. Jansen (eds.)

www.ingramcontent.com/pod-product-compliance
Ingram Content Group UK Ltd.
Pitfield, Milton Keynes, MK11 3LW, UK
UKHW051925100926
8556IPUK00022B/1372

9 781780 684499